SOCIAL INTERACTION

IN

EDUCATIONAL

SETTINGS

Edited by

ALBERT H. YEE
UNIVERSITY OF WISCONSIN

Prentice-Hall, Inc., Englewood Cliffs, New Jersey

TO BEN AND NATE

13–815720–0

Library of Congress Catalog Card Number: 70–135401

Current printing (last digit):
10 9 8 7 6 5 4 3 2 1

Printed in the United States of America

PRENTICE-HALL INTERNATIONAL, INC., *London*
PRENTICE-HALL OF AUSTRALIA, PTY. LTD., *Sydney*
PRENTICE-HALL OF CANADA, LTD., *Toronto*
PRENTICE-HALL OF INDIA PRIVATE LIMITED, *New Delhi*
PRENTICE-HALL OF JAPAN, INC., *Tokyo*

Contents

iii

4

Social Interaction Involving Learners, Teachers, and Administrators, 251

Preface

Social psychology continues to mature and extend its influence. More and more social scientists apply and identify themselves with social-psychological approaches and theories. These developments can be seen in the increasing literature in the area of social psychology; many books in the area have emerged, journals have been expanded, and new ones initiated to accommodate the proliferating conceptual and research output. Textbooks, such as those by Brown[1]; Newcomb, Turner, and Converse[2]; Krech, Crutchfield, and Ballachey[3]; Shibutani[4]; and Jones and Gerard[5] become familiar readings to an ever greater audience of undergraduate and graduate students each year.

Primarily focused upon interpersonal behavior events, the theory and research of social psychologists have contributed significantly to the description and interpretation of social phenomena. More and more psychologists and sociologists are finding that the relevance of their investigations into human behavior increase when they focus upon the individual in social settings rather than the individual and the group as separate objects of concern. Social psychologists also see their field as truly interdisciplinary and

1 Brown, R. *Social psychology*. New York: The Free Press, 1965.

2 Newcomb, T. M., Turner, R. H., & Converse, P. E. *Social psychology: The study of human interaction*. New York: Holt, Rinehart, & Winston, 1965.

3 Krech, D., Crutchfield, R. S., & Ballachey, E. L. *Individual in society*. New York: McGraw-Hill, 1962.

4 Shibutani, T. *Society and personality*. Englewood Cliffs, N. J.: Prentice-Hall, 1961.

5 Jones, E. E., & Gerard, H. B. *Foundations of social psychology*. New York: Wiley, 1967.

relevant to an era of social change and concern for vital issues. For example, Weick[6] wrote:

> To the social psychologist everything is relevant; it is relevant because it is relevant to the people that he studies. He knows full well that the only way he can understand complexity in his subject matter is to register that complexity by means of tools and concepts that are equally complex; having registered this complexity he then reshuffles his concepts and data to make as economical a summary of his impressions as he possibly can, but this reshuffling is done with a minimum of rejection (p. 990).

For advanced studies, there have been books of readings, such as those by Cartwright and Zander[7]; Maccoby, Newcomb, and Hartley[8]; Proshansky and Seidenberg[9]; Steiner and Fishbein[10]; Charters and Gage[11]; and Charters and Miles[12]. The interdisciplinary interest in social psychology is evidenced by the fact that the last five works were sponsored by the Society for the Psychological Study of Social Issues. Preparation of the second edition of the *Handbook of Social Psychology* in five volumes (versus two for the first edition) by Lindzey and Aronson[13] provides further concrete evidence that social psychology continues to expand in theory and method and involves an increasing number of those concerned with the study of social behavior. A chapter devoted to a social psychology of education appears in the second edition. According to its author, J. W. Getzels,[14] such a chapter denotes increasing recognition of social-psychological studies relevant to education. Getzels found little such attention in the first edition published in 1954, even in the chapter on socialization.

With its interdisciplinary orientation to social behavior, social psychology is a natural foundational approach for students and workers in education. In point of fact, most social-psychological studies have been

---

[6] Weick, K. E. Social psychology in an era of social change. *American Psychologist,* 1969, *24,* 990–98.

[7] Cartwright, D., & Zander, O. (Eds.). *Group dynamics: Research and theory.* New York: Harper & Row, 1960.

[8] Maccoby, E. E., Newcomb, T. M., & Hartley, E. L. (Eds.). *Readings in social psychology* (3rd ed.). New York: Holt, Rinehart, & Winston, 1958.

[9] Proshansky, H., & Seidenberg, B. (Eds.). *Basic studies: Social psychology.* New York: Holt, Rinehart, & Winston, 1965.

[10] Steiner, I. D., & Fishbein, M. (Eds.). *Current studies in social psychology.* New York: Holt, Rinehart, & Winston, 1965.

[11] Charters, W. W., & Gage, N. L. (Eds.). *Readings in the social psychology of education.* Boston: Allyn and Bacon, 1963.

[12] Charters, W. W., & Miles, M. (Eds.). *Learnings in social settings: New readings in the social psychology of education.* Boston: Allyn & Bacon, 1970.

[13] Lindzey, G., & Aronson, E. (Eds.). *The handbook of social psychology* (2nd ed.) Volumes I–V. Reading, Mass.: Addison-Wesley, 1968.

[14] Getzels, J. W. A social psychology of education. In G. Lindzey & E. Aronson (Eds.), *Handbook of social psychology.* Volume 5, *Applied social psychology.* (2nd ed.) Reading, Mass.: Addison-Wesley, 1969. Pp. 459–537.

directly related to educational settings, since so many of them utilized students as subjects and educational situations in their research.

In the design of educational research and evaluation, Gage's[15] critical analysis of paradigms for research on teaching indicates that the most promising research paradigms for teaching are those that focus upon social interaction, which involves complex facets of teachers' and pupils' perceptual, cognitive, and interpersonal behavior. However, the social psychology of education has been slow to develop and has only been adequately defined recently by Getzels' chapter in the *Handbook*. While contemporary textbooks for educational foundations are traditionally directed at psychological or sociological concerns, there should be increased emphasis in the future on combining the two broad foundational areas and more from the social sciences into what may be termed educational social psychology. Hopefully, the number of courses in educational social psychology will increase to meet the growing need for such studies, especially in the area of social interaction.

This book is intended to be the main or supplementary textbook for courses covering the areas of psychological or sociological foundations of education and social psychology of education. It may also become a useful reference book for professors and advanced students who require ready access to its content. Readings selected for the book are articles relevant to the greater understanding and study of social interaction in educational situations. Focus is given social interaction because the interpersonal behavior events involving teacher and learner and others in educational settings, in the opinion of this writer, comprise a significant set of variables influencing the nature and outcomes of education. Thus, this book attempts to delimit its concern to social-psychological concepts, variables, and methods that relate to important interaction settings influencing formal education, whether they be dyadic relationships, e.g., teacher-pupil; triadic, e.g., learner-teacher-administrator; or groups, e.g., classrooms and sororities.

Many fine works are far too lengthy for inclusion in a book of readings, and their abridgement would not do justice to the integrity of their message. Then there is the matter of satisfying one's editorial biases that runs against the editorial desire to represent diverse views, as well as the problem of grouping articles together in meaningful chapters. Contrary to the impressions of some people, editing a book of readings is not "a piece of cake." It is a challenging and worthwhile learning experience, one that can only help the editor become a more humble scholar, as he develops a broader and in-depth view of his area of interest.

Because of the compromises mentioned, many fine works, often equal and sometimes superior in some respects to those chosen, could not be included, even after permission to use them had been obtained from their

---

15 Gage, N. L. Paradigms for research on teaching. In N. L. Gage (Ed.), *Handbook for research on teaching*. Chicago: Rand McNally, 1963. Pp. 94–141.

authors and publishers. Regretfully, many fine articles could not be included; however, to help readers recognize other useful readings, a supplemental reading list will be added at the end of each chapter's introductory statements.

Whatever his own input into a book of readings may be, however, the editor is obligated to the authors who produced the articles selected and must recognize their contribution. This high regard for the authors is expressed through an arrangement whereby profits from this book will be shared equally with the American Educational Research Association. Such an arrangement, however, implies no endorsement or editorial involvement by AERA. I assume full editorial responsibility for the development of the book. Hopeful that its merits will surpass its deficiencies, I take this opportunity to dedicate the book to two teachers and friends, Professors L. B. Bennion and N. L. Gage, with deepest appreciation for their constructive guidance, ever-generous encouragement, and indefatigable patience.

Madison   A.H.Y.

The Relevance

of Social Interaction

to Education

Only a simple bench—Mark Hopkins on one end
and I on the other—and you may have all the buildings,
apparatus and libraries without him.
President James H. Garfield

The three readings in this introductory chapter provide an overall rationale for this book. Although written independently, taken together they form a comprehensive frame of reference for the study of social interaction in educational situations. Their conceptions of educational processes indicate the great potential of social-psychological approaches to increase the understanding, control, and prediction of relevant variables influencing educational settings. Reading these articles for the first time, one may begin to sense why educational theory and research often lack relevance and depth when a social-psychological frame of reference is ignored. For example, the issue of school integration takes on new meaning when viewed from the perspective of social interaction (Yee, 1969a), and the problems inherent in the criterion-of-effectiveness paradigm are largely overcome by social interactional paradigms (Gage, 1963).

Subsequent chapters will show that such approaches help establish priorities among relevant educational variables and help determine how they might be related in hypotheses formulated for testing. The study of social interaction in educational settings should prove its value by helping promote more parsimonious and less segmented instructional theory than available today. The developing study of educational social interaction may very well lead to the greater interrelationship and implementation of general systems theory and design (e.g., Von Bertalanffy, 1967, 1968) with the description and improved structuring of educational systems and processes (e.g., Gage, 1963; Yee, 1969b). With admitted need for greater evidence than this book can provide, it is also inferred that the greater relevance of social interaction to education will be revealed when we reject the superficial assumption that all elements in education are somehow equivalent or are of indeterminate educational weight and concentrate centrally on teaching-learning transactional behavior.

Social interaction may be said to be the mutual modification of behavior by individuals responding each to the other in social settings. Educational situations, by the very nature of their meaning and purpose, involve and are comprised of social interaction processes and systems. Modern schools contain vast and complex elements such as building plants and grounds, library and textbook materials, furniture and facilities for learning, sports and other extra-curricular activities, units of study, and so on, all of which provide uncertain and we might well assume, disproportionate weights in affecting learner achievement or whatever criteria is presented. However, they amount to little educationally without the key elements of interpersonal behaviors involved in teaching-learning and associated activities.

In other words, teaching and learning in schools could function without many things considered essential but could hardly exist without teachers, learners, and administrators interacting with each other and with others actively involved in schools. Perhaps one way to view the significant priority of social interaction is to regard it as being the major common aspect of all educational elements, binding them together and giving them relative purpose and meaning. For this writer, the sense of such a simple but over-looked truth can be seen in a school after hours when the pupils are not present. Sounds of such a school—the hollow ring of footsteps in the hall, the clatter of custodians sweeping and disposing of trash, the clanging and tinging of playground equipment in the breeze—contrast so realistically with the unique sounds of teaching and learning. Also, the relevance of social interaction in education is clear in the misguided teacher who asserts, "I taught them algebra as well as anybody could, but they didn't learn anything."

Since education is so engrossed in modifying behavior, the following statement by Sherif (1970) in his exposition of social psychology's relevance supports and explains our view:

> To an important extent, the locus of change lies in the interaction of people with people. The greatest and most lasting changes in institutions, as well in human relations and attitudes, are products of interaction in social movements (p. 147).

American educational systems are often perceived as operating with all relevant elements in schools contributing equivalently, but they do not and should not be supported as if they did. Most Americans seem to recognize the importance of teacher-pupil relationships, but think of them in extremely simple terms, a situation which will be discussed further in

Chapter IV. Classroom interaction is not a simple matter, as Withall (1956) found in objective measurements of one outstanding teacher's interactions or contacts with his pupils. Withall discovered that the teacher and pupils normally made thousands of interpersonal contacts with each other per hour and that there was great variance in the number of contacts between pupils. The range of contacts was 1.9 to 62.9 per hour when the teacher was unaware of being observed for such contacts and 1.6 to 72.6 when he was aware of the observations being made and was attempting to *equate* teacher-pupil contacts.

Commenting on the interactional complexity of the classroom, Jackson (1968, p. 11) wrote:

> Anyone who has ever taught knows that the classroom is a busy place, even though it may not always appear so to the casual visitor. . . . In one study of elementary classrooms. . .the teacher (engaged) in as many as 1000 interpersonal interchanges each day. An attempt to catalogue the interchanges among students or the physical movement of class members would doubtlessly add to the general impression that most classrooms, though seemingly placid when glimpsed through the window in the hall door, are more like the proverbial beehive of activity.

The articles in this chapter should help stress and clarify interpersonal behaviors and processes that account significantly for the variance in teaching-learning situations.

In 1960, the National Society for the Study of Education published a remarkably far-sighted yearbook on the social-psychological aspects of teaching and learning (Henry, 1960). The Yearbook Committee, Gale E. Jensen (Chairman), Jack R. Gibb, Max R. Goodson, and Willard C. Olson, developed a theoretical volume that continues to be challenging and ahead of social-psychological developments in the field. One of its 13 articles was selected for this book.

The penetrating selection by Getzels and Thelen identifies broad dimensions of phenomena that the authors believe significantly determine classroom processes—classroom goals, participants, leadership, and relationships to other groups and institutions. Out of such descriptions, a "social systems" model is formulated that relates sociological and psychological levels of analysis which speak directly to the relevance of social interaction approaches to classroom concerns. The authors apply their model to two problems illustrative of its wide usefulness and relevance. The broad applicability of their general model can be seen in its use by Getzels (1969) to formulate a framework for a social psychology of education: ". . .a social psychology of education is concerned with the interaction of role and personality in the school or classroom as a social system in the context. . .of the cultural or community values" (p. 463). Unfortunately, Getzels' review appears in print in 1970 "with the perspective of 1965," and therefore, cannot interrelate what has been produced since 1965, which is considerable.

More than any other, the work by Withall and Lewis helped to inspire the formation of this book, which may be viewed as an attempt to extend their *Handbook* chapter. It would be most difficult to surpass the comprehensive case they presented for a concentrated study of social interaction in classrooms. In large part, their historical review of theory and research on social interaction in education and consideration of needs and problems remains fairly up-to-date, partly due to the high quality of their work and partly to the continuing lag in the production of theory for the area.

Snow's article fulfills two major purposes. It presents the seminal views of Brunswick and others not covered by the two preceding selections. Also, it gives Snow's reflection upon them, from which he synthesized a model that deals with the dynamics and micro-analysis of classroom interaction. The intended purpose of the approach Snow described is categorizing and describing the interpersonal behavior of teachers and learners.

However, since we want to understand why something happens beyond knowing just what is happening, we need a complementary theory to help explain what is observed. Consistency theory, a very important basic for understanding human behavior, is reviewed in Zajonc's article in Chapter II.

Social exchange theory is another such possibility. It has been found to be a potentially powerful tool to integrate bits and pieces of interpersonal research as well as help generate new hypotheses. Writings by Blau (1964) and Nord (1969) can help the reader see how analyses of cost-reward exchanges or economic relationships help explain interpersonal behavior in classrooms. Other theoretical points of view will be briefly discussed in most selections and extended discussions will be presented in other chapters, such as Hollander and Julian's article on leadership in Chapter V.

OTHER READINGS

BERTALANFFY, L. VON. *General systems theory*. New York: Braziller, 1968.

BERTALANFFY, L. VON. *Robots, men and minds*. New York: Braziller, 1967.

BLAU, P. M. *Exchange and power in social life*. New York: John Wiley, 1964.

BOYD, R. D. The group as a sociopsychological setting for learning. *Review of Educational Research*, 1965, *35*, 209–217.

GAGE, N. L. Pardigms for research on teaching. In N. L. GAGE (Ed.), *Handbook for research on teaching*. Chicago: Rand McNally, 1963. Pp. 94–141.

GETZELS, J. W. A social psychology of education. In G. LINDZEY & E. ARONSON (Eds.), *Handbook of social psychology*. Vol. 5. *Applied social psychology*. (2nd ed.) Reading, Mass: Addison-Wesley, 1969. Pp. 459–537.

HEIDER, F. *The psychology of interpersonal relations*. New York: John Wiley, 1958.

HENRY, N. B. (Ed.) *The dynamics of instructional groups: Sociopsychological aspects of teaching and learning.* 59th Yearbook—II of the National Society for the Study of Education. Chicago: University of Chicago Press, 1960.

JACKSON, P. W. *Life in Classrooms.* New York: Holt, Rinehart & Winston, 1968.

NORD, N. R. Social exchange theory: An integrative approach to social conformity. *Psychological Bulletin,* 1969, *71,* 174–208.

SHERIF, M. On the relevance of social psychology. *American Psychologist,* 1970, *25,* 144–156.

SMITH, B. O. A concept of teaching. *Teachers College Record,* 1960, *61,* 229–241.

WITHALL, J. An objective measurement of a teacher's classroom interactions. *Journal of Educational Psychology,* 1956, *47,* 203–212.

YEE, A. H. Social interaction in classrooms: Implications for the education of disadvantaged pupils. *Urban Education,* 1969, *4,* 203–219(a).

YEE, A. H. A cybernetic system for WETEP: A model design for the preparation of teachers. In *Wisconsin Elementary Teacher Education Project.* Washington, D. C.: U. S. Government Printing Office, Documents Catalog No. FS 5.258: 58025, 1969. Pp. 47–77(b).

THE CLASSROOM GROUP
AS A
UNIQUE SOCIAL SYSTEM

Jacob W. Getzels / Herbert A. Thelen

INTRODUCTION

All working groups, including, of course, the classroom group, have certain characteristics in common. All groups, for example, have a *goal* they seek to achieve; they have *participants* who are joined together for the purpose of achieving the goal; the activities of the group are founded in some type of control or *leadership*; the group has explicit or implicit *relationships to other groups* or institutions.

These parameters are applicable to all working groups. But in addition to these general qualities, each group, like each individual, has its own unique character. Wherein does the uniqueness of the classroom group lie? It lies not so much in any single differentiating feature, for we know of no single quality of the classroom group that cannot be found in other groups. Rather, the unique character of the classroom group lies in the peculiar

From: N. B. Henry (Ed.), The dynamics of instructional groups: Sociopsychological aspects of teaching and learning. *Chicago: University of Chicago Press, 1960. Pp. 53–82. Copyright © 1960 by the National Society for the Study of Education, and reproduced by permission of the authors and NSSE.*

configuration of the specific characteristics. To communicate this unique configuration, we must describe, first, the separate characteristics and, then, seek to construct from these descriptions the unique overall pattern.

Accordingly, we shall divide our presentation into two sections: (*a*) We shall attempt first to describe in rather broad terms the nature of the goals of the classroom group, the nature of its participants, its leadership, and its relationship to other groups and institutions. (*b*) We shall then attempt to formulate a conceptual framework within which we may systematize and clarify the phenomena we have described and point to the pattern they provide.

ON THE NATURE OF CLASSROOM GOALS, PARTICIPANTS, LEADERSHIP, AND RELATIONSHIPS TO OTHER GROUPS

CLASSROOM GOALS

The classroom group comes together for the purpose of learning. This is not to say that other groups do not also learn, but the classroom is a *planned* learning situation. Learning is held *consciously* as the primary reason for the group's being together at all. The educational activity of the class is seen not so much as preparatory to other activities but as rising above them to provide general wisdom. Education is not only introductory to other virtues, it is a virtue in itself. Like truth or beauty, education is in many ways its own excuse for being, and, in this sense, learning is not merely a means to other goals, it is *the* goal. And this despite the immediate and particular motives of the learners themselves.

Indeed, not only is learning the prescribed objective of the classroom group, but that which is to be learned and the means by which the learning is to be accomplished are also "given." Educational subjects and methods are stipulated in advance by authorities external to the actual group that is to do the learning. In the typical school setting there is an explicit or implicit "curriculum of instruction" specifying desired outcomes and kinds of procedures to which both teachers and pupils in the classroom must adhere.

Within these specified limits there is room for flexibility, and specific short-term goals and methods may be improvised to suit the immediate needs and interests of a particular group. But ultimately substantive and procedural standards must be met. To cite one extreme instance from many, New York State administers Regents examinations which attempt to "quality-control," so to speak, what is taught in all classroom groups with respect to certain subjects. This, then, is one distinctive feature of the classroom group in the typical school setting, namely, that learning is the consciously held goal, and the specific content and method of what is to be learned is in large part given in the situation before the classroom group itself comes into being.

CLASSROOM PARTICIPANTS

There is a second distinctive feature of the classroom group that is not unrelated to the first. Not only is *what* shall be done a "given" but *who* shall do it is also a given. Both the goal and the participants are *mandatory*. The answer obtained from certain parents as to why they send their children to school is that "You can go to jail if you don't." And the answer obtained from certain children as to why they attend class is that "You can get sent up the river if you don't." The school and classroom are perhaps the extreme instances in the United States of group participation required by society entirely apart from any ascertained volition of the participants themselves. Attendance in classroom groups is compulsory, and in this respect, at least, school service is not dissimilar from military service.

Of course, the one may perhaps be looked upon as a benefit and the other as an obligation. But even so, as Harry Kalven points out, "There is usually a great difference between offering a benefit and compelling a man to accept it."[1] Indeed, he suggests, that "the analogies between commitment of the mentally ill for therapy and commitment of the child for education are many and inviting...."[2]

Not only, as we have seen, is participation in classroom groups compulsory but, from the point of view of the individual participant, the composition of the group is pretty much casual and haphazard. The mere accident of time of birth and place of residence determines the association, a circumstance sharply different from nearly all other associations, where membership is determined at least in part by factors over which the individual has some control. When the child walks into

[1] Harry Kalven, Jr., "Law and Education," *School Review,* LXV (1957), 288.
[2] *Ibid.,* p. 289.

the classroom the first day of school in the autumn, he may find with him friends, rivals, strangers comprising an entirely accidental social milieu. And, in most instances, if the child is disturbed by these involuntary associations, he has no recourse. Under these conditions, the would-be learner's major preoccupation in the classroom may center not on the learning task but on the predicament of getting along for the greater part of his waking hours with an accidentally selected group of disturbing associates with whom he is required to work toward a common goal chosen by someone else.

To the extent that the nature of the learning process is affected by the nature of the social interaction, the compulsory and random selection of p· pils will have an effect on what is learned, and the compulsory and random nature of the classroom group can be considered another distinctive feature of the classroom as a working group.

CLASSROOM LEADERSHIP

The third of the characteristics to which we should like to call attention is the distinctive nature of the control or leadership exercised in the classroom. The control and leadership of the classroom group are vested in the teacher. This authority is sanctioned by law and custom and is reinforced by the fact that the teacher is an expert, trained professionally and certified officially, to exercise the authority. In addition, in the usual school setting, he is older, more mature, and presumably wiser than his students. From almost any point of view, teachers form a ruling elite, set apart from the other participants in the classroom group.

This is not to say, of course, that the authority of the teacher must be exercised in an authoritarian manner or that there are not *informal* lines of authority among the pupils themselves. Indeed, even formally, authority can in fact be delegated for certain functions to the pupils, and frequently is. But such delegation cannot occur without the teacher's permission, given explicitly or implicitly. If one thinks of authority, control, and leadership in political terms, it is clear that the classroom group, at least in its formal aspects, is about as far from democracy as one can get. Not only do the students have no control over the selection of their leader, they normally also have no recourse from his leadership, no influence on his method of leadership beyond that granted by him, and no power over the tenure of his leadership. There are very few working groups in our society in which these essentially despotic conditions are legitimately so much the rule.

CLASSROOM RELATIONSHIPS TO OTHER GROUPS AND INSTITUTIONS

In addition to the distinctive nature of the goals, the participants, and the leadership, the classroom group is also distinctive in the nature of its relationships to other groups and institutions. Consider for a moment only the varied points of contact between any given classroom group and other groups within the same school. Any class is only one link in a sequence, and what it may or may not do, indeed what it must and must not do, is defined as much by what other groups have done or can do as by what any particular class *wants* to do. A fourth-grade class, for example, is integrally related to the third-grade class that preceded it and the fifth-grade class that follows it. At least in its objectives, the fourth-grade group is very much a part of the other groups. Moreover, even on any given day, the individual pupil is a member not solely of one classroom group but is simultaneously a participant of several overlapping groups—an

English group, a gymnasium group, a home-economics group, and so on. He must accommodate himself to each group, and each group must be geared in to all other groups.

Nor can we forget the child's associations outside the school, for surely he does not discard these by merely closing the classroom door behind him. His membership in particular gangs, blocks, teams, clubs, and families cuts across his membership in the classroom group and may govern his behavior in the classroom more than the teacher or classroom associates do. Even with the best of intentions, the pupil may find himself in the dilemma that behavior which brings rewards in the school only proves to those outside that he is a "square"; that subscribing to what the teacher likes in algebra may cost him the regard of his best friend.

It is, accordingly, no exceptional occurrence for the child to disrupt school activity in order to prove himself to the gang, and it is surely no exceptional occurrence for children to do less well than they are able within the classroom group in order to conform to the expectations of a competing group. Failure in school may be a badge of achievement elsewhere, as, for example, the Gentlemen's *C* can be more prestigeful than the Greasygrind's *A*.

If we may put it this way, over and above the interacting participants in the classroom, there are numerous "invisible" participants: individuals and groups whose pressure and influence are felt but not seen directly. There are the peer groups, whose effect we have already noted. There are the parents, concerned with the training and progress of their own children; counselors, concerned with the psychological effects of the classroom on individual children; state officials, concerned with whether the demonstrable school achievement meets some a priori standard; a multitude of vested interest groups, each

concerned with the inculcation of what it conceives to be the proper attitudes and knowledge regarding *its* interests; and religious and political groups, concerned with what the children are exposed to in the area of special importance to them.

What we have been saying about the multiple pressures upon the children holds also for the teacher. Indeed, his situation may be even more complex, since the conflicting expectations for him in the school and the community are perhaps less clearly defined than they are for his pupils. Consider in this connection the status of the teacher as a resident in the community. It is probably safe to say that there are more constraints and demands upon him as a private citizen than upon almost any other member of the community. He may, for example, be required to reside only in a certain approved neighborhood. He may be prohibited from using tobacco or liquor. At least, he must not be *seen* using them. His political affiliations may be the subject of public scrutiny. His religious practice, certainly a matter of private conscience for most Americans, may become a public concern. In many ways, the teacher is like the minority group member, who has a high public visibility. And the effects of this equivocal community status are reflected in his relations to the community's children in the classroom.

Not only do teachers seem to occupy a peculiar place on the private level but on the professional level as well. Although the teacher is classified as a professional person—that is, as an expert and specialist in a particular sphere of activity—nearly everyone feels free to exert pressure on how this expert should behave in his own field of specialization. The contrast between the community's attitudes in this respect toward teachers as a professionally trained and certified group and toward other professional groups is marked. Ordinarily, no one would dream of telling a doctor what to do in the hospital, or the lawyer how to address the court, or the pharmacist how to fill a prescription. On the other hand, nearly everyone feels free to tell the teacher what to do or what not to do in the classroom. Yet, these very same people would be shocked at the idea of their community's not employing professionally trained and certified teachers for their children.

It may, of course, be argued that doctors, lawyers, and pharmacists are not on the public payroll and that teachers are. This is not an entirely satisfactory argument, for the teacher is quick to observe that firemen, for example, are also on the public payroll, but that hardly gives every property owner a right to tell the fireman how to deal with a fire, even a fire on the property-owner's own property.

There is no intention in any of this discussion to imply that the parents and public may not be properly critical of educational policies and practices. We are pointing out that the conditions within which the teacher is placed personally and professionally in the community affect both his own behavior and the perceptions children have of him as an individual and group leader. Since the community does not make plain its respect and esteem for the teacher, it is difficult for children to grant him the confidence their parents fail to bestow.

From the point of view of the teacher, he seldom knows with certainty how to assess his work in relation to the community's expectations. He must take a risk that makes him liable to swift retribution every time he departs from the usual way of doing things. On the one hand, the teacher cannot safely act with the autonomy of other professional persons; on the other hand, there is confusion over just how much autonomy a teacher should have. Although the structure of the class-room group nominally gives him as much professional freedom as, say, the structure of the hospital gives the physician, practically the teacher is often a lackey, so to speak, in his own empire. As we have pointed out, although the teacher is hired because of his training and certification as a professional person in a particular field of expertness, many of the crucial decisions with respect to his field of expertness are made by nonprofessional persons and transmitted to him as "orders."

That the classroom group should be the focus of such public concern and turbulent crosscurrents is no accident. From one point of view, the school is an independent institution having a particular structure and function. In this sense, it is no different from other institutions serving the social order. But, from another point of view, it is unique. For, if the educational institution is one among others, as indeed it is, it is uniquely the institution upon which, perhaps more than on any others, the effective functioning of all related institutions depends.

In a recent symposium, we asked a group of social scientists to indicate the relationship of education as an institution to the social institutions with which their particular discipline was most concerned.[3] In each case, education was given a central place in the functioning of the institution represented by the particular discipline. The political scientist, for example, wanted the school to prepare children for the wise exercise of political power; in this sense, the classroom is very much a part of the political scientist's domain. The economist wanted the school to prepare for the wise selection among economic alternatives; in this sense, the classroom is part of *his* domain. The geographer wanted the school to prepare

[3] Herbert A. Thelen and Jacob W. Getzels, "Symposium: Social Science and Education," *School Review,* LXV (1957), 245–355.

for the wise utilization of natural resources; in this sense, the classroom is part of *his* domain. In short, the school and the classroom seem unique in the centrality of their relationships, at least theoretically, to the other institutions within the social order. The school is charged with responsibility for the "socialization," "politicization," and "acculturation" of the child.

The nature of the interaction between the school and other institutions in the community determines the extent to which the school will be an instrument for changing other institutions as distinguished from supporting them as they are. Given certain kinds of interaction, the school can exist only to hand down that which is traditional, while under other conditions it can be at the forefront of that which is emerging. In any event, here is another distinctive and profound characteristic of the classroom group; there is nothing that goes on in the classroom that is not of ultimate consequence for the social order; and there is not much that is of immediate consequence for the social order that is not reflected in some way in the classroom.

CLASSROOM FREEDOM AND ITS PROTECTION

In attempting to sketch the unique characteristics of the classroom group, we have necessarily endeavored to portray the extraordinary complexity of the forces meeting and perhaps clashing in the school situation. We have, for example, emphasized the involuntary nature of the participation. The pupils are in the unique circumstance of being compelled to accept a benefit, as it were. We pointed to the confusing status of the teacher, at once so potentially despotic and oddly vulnerable. Does the legitimacy of his authority and responsibility reside in his status as a professional person or in his status as a civil

servant? Or to put the question somewhat differently in Anselm Strauss's terms: Who ultimately is the teacher's customer, the pupils? the parents? the taxpayers? the immediate community? the larger society?[4] And we pointed, also, to the extraordinary centrality of the school with respect to other aspects of the social order and to the resulting complexity in the relationships of the classroom to other groups and institutions.

The number and kind of complexities, conflicts, and confusions in the classroom group appear to be unique—but unique, also, are the opportunities and, in a sense, the safeguards built into the situation. The situation may be intricate, but it is not therefore bleak.

To be sure, participation in the classroom group is compulsory, but this is not to say that the participants may not be delighted to have the benefit that is thrust upon them. There is no necessary contradiction between the imposed structure of the classroom and the voluntary motivations of the pupils. The pupil may truly want what he is compelled to have. In addition, the students may within limits establish their own standards in the classroom. One can, for example, be graduated from school with *C*'s rather than *A*'s, major in economics rather than English, emphasize vocational training rather than liberal arts.

The potential despotism of the teacher toward his pupils and his peculiar vulnerability to oppression by the parents of school children, as we have seen, are threats to the effective functioning of the classroom group. But just as there are safeguards for the pupil, so there is also protection for the teacher. On the one hand, the teacher's power is subject to at least two controls. It is the objectives of

4 Anselm Strauss, "A Sociological Approach to Educational Organization," *School Review*, LXV (1957), 330–38.

education rather than the teacher's whim which dictates most choices, and, if the teacher wishes to communicate effectively, he must heed the views of his class. On the other hand, his own vulnerability to oppression is subject to powerful control. There is perhaps no more highly regarded principle in American custom and law than that of "academic freedom." This principle not only protects the teacher from the tyranny of the mob but safeguards his autonomy of educational thought and action.

Finally, we should like to say a word about the safeguards against the complexities arising from what we called the "invisible participants" in the classroom, represented by the pressures of vested-interest groups and by other institutions. That there are these pressures and that they affect the classroom is unquestionable. But their impact is not unbridled, for here too there are controls. For one thing, the various groups are often at cross-purposes as to what they want in the classroom, and, in effect, one pressure group balances another pressure group. For another, there is an overwhelming popular regard in America for the value of "an education." In this sense, even if education is not seen as a virtue in itself, the school is clearly appreciated as a vehicle for social and economic mobility. Whatever the philosophical crosscurrents and confusions about learning, there are few Americans who would not subscribe to the general proposition that "education is a fine thing." And supporting all of this at a more fundamental level is our ingrained tradition that the very fabric of democracy depends on our educational institutions.

SOME ISSUES FOR SYSTEMATIC ANALYSIS

The preceding description of the crosscurrents in the classroom suggest a number of issues requiring systematic analysis. For example:

1. Learning in the classroom involves bringing about change through consciously planned experiences. This involves the exercise of conscious choice of alternatives. Question: How can we conceptualize the choices available to the teacher and the class?

2. The goals of learning, the procedures by which the goals will be achieved, and the subject-content to be learned are all more or less specified in advance, that is, they are "givens" in the classroom situation. Question: What are the sources of these givens, and what is the relative stability or modifiability of each?

3. The classroom is an "accidental" collection of persons, having little or no legitimate recourse from participating in a priori goals and procedures of the school. Question: What are the dimensions of the problem generated by this "accidental" and "enforced" nature of the classroom group, and what is the effect of these factors on classroom learning?

4. In addition to the problem of relating one's self to the associations and activities required in the classroom, each individual must also "gear in" his own needs, goals, and attitudes to the way of life that is prescribed in the classroom. Question: What is the relationship of this problem to the preceding one, and again what are the implications of this issue for classroom learning?

5. The teacher is in almost absolute authority in the sense that the only power students may legitimately have over the classroom group is that permitted or delegated by the teacher. Question: With respect to what kind of matters can the teacher delegate authority to students, and how may this transfer of power be accomplished?

6. The "accidental" and compulsory interaction in the classroom may be modified by students who set and enforce their own goals and standards within the classroom. Question: How does this occur, and

what are the factors tending to encourage or discourage such development?

7. Every participant in the classroom group is also a member of numerous groups outside the classroom. Each is subject to various group pressures and loyalties which may be in opposition to each other. Question: What is the nature of the conflicts to which these pressures give rise, what are the differential reactions thereto, and what is the effect of such conflicts on classroom learning?

8. The classroom is part of the school, and the school is a central institution in the community. There is widespread public interest, pressure, and conflict with respect to the school as representative of the community. Question: What is the nature of these community pressures and conflicts, and how do they affect the classroom group?

9. The school as a central social institution is integrally related to the other institutions of the community. It may be an instrument for promoting change or of maintaining the status quo of these institutions and, accordingly, of the social order as a whole. Question: Under what circumstances does the classroom serve in one capacity or the other, and what would be involved in changing the role of the school with respect to the other institutions?

10. Although the teacher is in many ways "trapped" by community pressures on his personal and professional status, there is, on the other hand, the powerful principle of "academic freedom" which protects the teacher's right to make choices for educational purposes. Question: What is the relationship between the type of choice the teacher makes and the kind of classroom learning situation that ensues?

If we are to deal systematically either in research or practice with issues of the sort to which we have been pointing, we must attempt to move from discursive description to conceptual analysis.

For systematic research and practice requires the mediation of related concepts that will give meaning and order to observations already made and will specify areas where observations still need to be made. In short, we must have an explicit framework within which to classify, relate, and clarify the various phenomena under consideration. By this means we would be impelled to deal systematically with what is and to move with greater confidence to what ought to be.

The purpose of the next section is to present such a conceptual framework. We need hardly add that we do not believe it is the only possible framework or for that matter that it is even a "good" one, whatever *good* means in this context. We do venture to believe, however, that the framework may be useful in guiding research and practice, and in stimulating further conceptual effort in this area.

A CONCEPTUAL FRAMEWORK FOR THE STUDY OF THE CLASSROOM GROUP AS A SOCIAL SYSTEM

THE GENERAL MODEL

We may begin a description of our model with a consideration of the most general context of interpersonal or group behavior, i.e., a given social system.[5] The term

---

[5] The same general set of concepts and categories have been applied to other areas of the school, notably administration, and portions of this section are paraphrased or taken verbatim from the following: J. W. Getzels, "A Psycho-Sociological Framework for the Study of Educational Administration," *Harvard Educational Review*, XXII (1952), 235–46; J. W. Getzels and E. G. Guba, "Social Behavior and the Administrative Process," *School Review*, LXV (1957), 423–41; J. W. Getzels, "Administration as a Social Process," in *Administrative Theory in Education* (edited by Andrew W. Halpin, Mid-west Administration Center, University of Chicago, 1958). Our debt to the work of Talcott Parsons will be self-evident.

"social system" is, of course, conceptual rather than descriptive and must not be confused with society or state, or as somehow applicable only to large aggregates of human interaction. So, within this framework, for one purpose a given community may be considered a social system, with the school a particular organization within the more general social system. For another purpose, the school itself or a single class within the school may be considered a social system in its own right. The model proposed here is applicable regardless of the level or size of the unit under consideration.

We initially conceive of the social system as involving two classes of phenomena which are at once conceptually independent and phenomenally interactive. First, there are the institutions with certain roles and expectations that will fulfil the goals of the system. Secondly, there are the individuals with certain personalities and need-dispositions inhabiting the system, whose observed interactions comprise what we call social or group behavior. We shall assert that this behavior can be understood as a function of these major elements: institution, role, and expectation, which together constitute what we call the *nomothetic* or normative dimension of activity in a social system; and individual, personality, and need-disposition, which together constitute the *idiographic* or personal dimension of activity in a social system. In a sense, the one may be thought of as the "sociological" level of analysis, the other the "psychological" level of analysis.

To understand the nature of observed behavior and to be able to predict and control it, one must understand the nature of the relationships of these elements. We shall briefly make four points of definition in this connection:

1. All social systems have certain imperative functions that are to be carried out in certain established ways. Such functions as governing, educating, or policing within a state may be said to have become "institutionalized," and the agencies carrying out these institutionalized functions for the social system may be termed "institutions."

2. The most important analytic unit of the institution is the role. Roles are the "dynamic aspects" of the positions, offices, and statutes within an institution, and they define the behavior of the role incumbents or actors.[6]

3. Roles are defined in terms of role-expectations. A role has certain privileges, obligations, responsibilities, and powers. When the role-incumbent puts these obligations and responsibilities into effect, he is said to be performing his role. The expectations define for the actor what he should or should not do so long as he is the incumbent of the particular role.

4. Roles are complementary. They are interdependent in that each role derives its meaning from the other related roles. In a sense, a role is a prescription not only for the given role-incumbent but also for the incumbents of other roles within the institutions and for related roles outside the institutions. Thus, for example, the role of teacher and the role of pupil cannot be defined or implemented except in relation to each other. It is this quality of complementarity which fuses two or and which makes it possible for us to conceive of an institution (or group) as more roles into a coherent, interactive unit having a characteristic structure.

This dimension of the social system may be represented schematically as follows:

Social System → Institutions → Roles → Expectations → Institutional Goal-behavior

6 Ralph Linton, *The Study of Man.* New York: D. Appleton-Century Co., 1936.

Within this framework then, the class may be conceived as a social system with characteristic institutions, roles, and expectations for behavior. The class as a social system is related to the school as a social system, which in turn is related to the community as a social system, and so on. Ideally, the goal-behaviors of one social system are "geared in" to the goal-behaviors of the other related social systems. Within the class itself, goal-behavior is achieved through the integration of institutions, the definition of roles, and the setting of expectations for the performance of relevant tasks. In performing the role-behaviors expected of him, the teacher "teaches"; in performing the role-behaviors expected of *him,* the pupil "learns."

So far we have examined the elements constituting the nomothetic or normative aspects of group behavior. At this level of analysis, it was sufficient to conceive of the role incumbents as only "actors," devoid of personalistic or other individualizing characteristics, as if all incumbents were exactly alike and as if they implemented a given role in exactly the same way. This is not, by any means, to derogate the power of this level of analysis. Indeed, for certain gross understanding and prediction of behavior, this is exactly the right level of abstraction. For example, if we know the roles in a given educational institution, we can make some rather accurate predictions of what the people in these institutions do without ever observing the actual people involved.

But roles are, of course, occupied by real individuals, and no two individuals are alike. Each individual stamps the particular role he occupies with the unique style of his own characteristic pattern of expressive behavior. Even in the case of the relatively inflexible military roles of sergeant and private, no two individual sergeants and no two individual privates fulfil their roles in exactly the same way. To under-

stand the observed behavior of *specific* sergeants and *specific* privates, or of *specific* teachers and *specific* pupils, it is not enough to know only the nature of the roles and expectations—although, to be sure, their behavior cannot be understood apart from these—but we must also know the nature of the individuals inhabiting the roles and reacting to the expectations. That is, in addition to the nomothetic or normative aspects, we must consider the idiographic or individualizing aspects of group behavior. We must, in addition to the sociological level of analysis, include the psychological level of analysis.

Now, just as we were able to analyze the institutional dimension into the component elements of role and expectation, so we may, in a parallel manner, analyze the individual dimension into the component elements of personality and need-disposition. We may briefly make two points of definition in this connection:

1. The concept of personality, like institution or role, has been given a variety of meanings. But for our purposes, personality may be defined as the dynamic organization within the individual of those need-dispositions that govern his *unique* reactions to the environment and, we might add, in present model, to the expectations in the environment.

2. The central analytic elements of personality are the need-dispositions, which we can define with Parsons and Shils as "individual tendencies to orient and act with respect to objects in certain manners and to expect certain consequences from these actions."[7]

This dimension of the social system may be represented schematically as follows:

[7] Talcott Parsons and Edward A. Shils, *Toward a General Theory of Action,* p. 114. Cambridge, Massachusetts: Harvard University Press, 1951.

Social System → Individuals → Personalities → Need-Dispositions → Individual Goal-behavior

Returning to the example of the sergeant and private, we can now make an essential distinction between two sergeants, one of whom has a high need-disposition for "submission" and the other a high need-disposition for "ascendance"; and a similar distinction between two privates, one with a high need-disposition for "submission" and the other for "ascendance," in the fulfilment of their respective roles, and for the sergeant-private interaction. And we may make similar distinctions in the role-fulfilment and interaction among teachers and pupils of varying personality types.

In short, as we have remarked before, to understand the behavior and interaction of specific role-incumbents in an institution, we must know both the role-expectations and need-dispositions. Indeed, needs and expectations may both be thought of as *motives for behavior,* the one deriving from personalistic sets and propensities, the other from institutional obligations and requirements.

By way of summarizing the argument so far, we may represent the general model pictorially. [See below.]

The nomothetic axis is shown at the top of the diagram and consists of institution, role, and expectation, each term being the analytic unit for the term preceding it. Thus, the social system is defined by its institutions, each institution by its constituent roles, each role by the expectations attaching to it. Similarly, the idiographic axis is shown at the lower portion of the diagram and consists of individual, personality, and need-disposition, each term again serving as the analytic unit for the term preceding it.

A given act is conceived as deriving simultaneously from both the nomothetic and idiographic dimensions. That is to say, social behavior results as the individual attempts to cope with an environment composed of patterns of expectations for his behavior in ways consistent with his own independent pattern of needs. Thus, we may write the general equation: $B = f(R \times P)$, where B is observed behavior, R is a given institutional role defined by the expectations attaching to it, and P is the personality of the particular role incumbent defined by his need-dispositions.

The proportion of role and personality factors determining behavior will, of course, vary with the specific act, the specific role, and the specific personality involved. The nature of the interaction can be understood from another graphic representation. [See next page.]

A given behavioral act may be conceived as occurring at a line cutting through the role and personality possibilities represented by the rectangle. At the left, the proportion of the act dictated by considerations of personality is relatively small. At the right, the proportions are

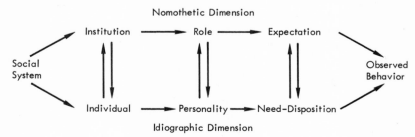

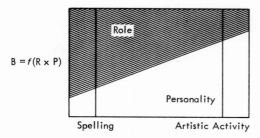

$$B = f(R \times P)$$

reversed, and considerations of personality become greater than considerations of role-expectations. In these terms, the participants in the classroom situation may define their overt activity along a continuum between two modes of operation from primary emphasis on *role-relevant* performance to primary emphasis on *personality-relevant* performance. Thus, some tasks require maximum adherence to role-expectations, e.g., learning to spell; others permit greater freedom of personal spontaneity, e.g., artistic activity. We may presume that each educational objective calls for a characteristic proportion or balance between these two types of performance.

In any case, whether the proportion tends toward one end or the other, behavior in the classroom group remains a function of both role and personality, although in different degree. When role is maximized, behavior still retains some personal aspect because no role is ever so closely defined as to eliminate all individual latitude. When personality is maximized, group behavior still cannot be free of some role prescription. Indeed, the individual who divorces himself from such prescription is said to be autistic, and he ceases to communicate with the group.

The major problem of social or group behavior involves exactly this issue of the dynamics of the interaction between the externally defined role-expectations and the internally defined personality-

dispositions. To put the problem concretely, we may ask: How is it, for example, that some complementary role-incumbents understand and agree at once on their mutual privileges and obligations, while others take a long time in reaching such agreement and, quite frequently, do not come to terms either with their roles or with each other?

The essential relevant concept we should like to propose here is *selective interpersonal perception*. In a sense, we may conceive of the publicly described normative relationship of two complementary role-incumbents—the prescribed means and ends of the interaction as set forth, say, in a table of organization or in a curriculum of instruction—as being enacted in two separate private interactions, one embedded in the other. On the one hand, there is the prescribed relationship as perceived idiosyncratically and organized by the one role-incumbent in terms of his own needs, dispositions, and goals; on the other hand, there is the same prescribed relationship as perceived idiosyncratically and organized by the other role-incumbent in terms of his needs, dispositions, and goals. These private situations are related through those aspects of the existential public objects, symbols, values, and expectations, which have to some extent a counterpart in the perceptions of both individuals.

When we say two role-incumbents (such as a teacher and a pupil or a teacher and several pupils in the classroom group) understand each other, we mean that their perceptions and private organization of the prescribed complementary expectations are congruent; when we say they misunderstand each other, we mean that their perceptions and private organization of the prescribed complementary expectations are incongruent.

Like all theoretical formulations, the present framework is an abstraction and, as such, an oversimplification of "reality" —some factors in the classroom have been brought into the foreground, others put into the background. By focusing on the sociological dimension with the central concept role and on the psychological dimension with the central concept personality, we have omitted other dimensions contributing to classroom behavior. We should like to mention, however briefly, two other relevant dimensions.

There is first the *biological* dimension, for just as we may think of the individual in personalistic terms, we may also think of him in constitutional terms. The individual's personality is embedded, so to speak, in a biological organism with certain constitutional potentialities and abilities. The need-dispositions of the personality are surely related in some way to these constitutional conditions, probably as mediating between constitutional and nomothetic factors. In this sense, we must bear in mind that underlying the psychological dimension is a biological dimension, although the one is not reducible to the other. We may represent this dimension schematically. [See first figure below.]

Secondly, there is the *anthropological* dimension. Just as we may think of institutions in sociological terms, we may also think of them in cultural terms, for the institution is embedded in a culture with certain mores and values. The ex-

pectations of the roles must in some way be related to the ethos or cultural values. The pupil cannot be expected to learn Latin in a culture where knowledge of Latin has little value, nor can he be expected to identify with teachers in a culture where teachers have little value. In this sense, we must bear in mind that interacting with the sociological dimension there is an anthropological dimension, although again that one is not immediately reducible to the other. We may represent this relationship schematically. [See second figure below.]

If we may put all the dimensions together into a single, and we are afraid rather unwieldly, pictorial representation, the relationships would look something like the figure on page 19.

It is our belief that the model can help clarify and systematize the issues we raised in the first section. By way of illustration, we should like to apply the model to two of these issues, notably the issues dealing with the *nature and sources of conflict* and with the *nature of teacher choices in changing classroom behavior*.

APPLICATIONS OF THE MODEL I: CLASSROOM CONFLICT

We may identify for present purposes four major types of conflict, although these do not necessarily exhaust the list:

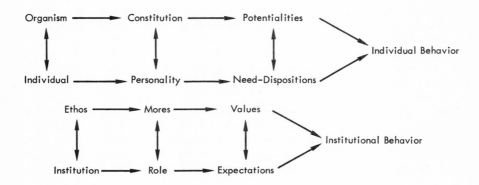

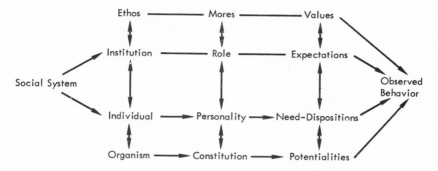

1. Conflict between the cultural values outside the classroom and the institutional expectations within the classroom. Consider the following instance with respect to the motivation for achievement in the classroom, assuming only the substantive data regarding the state of present values to be as people like Riesman and Wheelis have described it.[8] It is expected by the school that the child will work hard in the classroom in order to achieve to the fullest extent of his potentiality. Accordingly, the child must be motivated to strive and sacrifice present ease for future attainment. But recent studies suggest that our cultural values are coming more and more to prize sociability and hedonistic, present-time orientations, rather than achievement, as goals. In this sense, the criteria of worth in the classroom and in society at large are incongruent, and to this extent the child is subject to conflict with respect to his classroom behavior. Or consider the potential conflict of the so-called gifted or creative child or *teacher* in the classroom. If the potentially creative person is to be productive and inventive, the cultural values must encourage, or at least be receptive to, personal independence and autonomy. If these people are to express

their exceptional talents, they must be able to maintain firm commitments to their own standards and to their own beliefs. But again recent studies suggest that our values are coming to prize conformity more than autonomy, moral relativism more than commitment. We are not here arguing the validity of the substantive data—we are illustrating one potential source of conflict in the classroom, i.e., the incongruity between values and expectations.

2. Conflict between role-expectations and personality-dispositions. Conflicts of this type occur as a function of discrepancies between the pattern of expectations attaching to a given role and the pattern of need-dispositions characteristic of the incumbent of the role. Recall again our example of the individual with high need-dispositions for "ascendance" placed in the role of an army private. Or more specifically, consider the issues we raised with respect to the "accidental" and compulsory nature of the classroom group. Particular children have not been chosen for particular roles, or particular roles for particular children. There may be mutual interference between the nomothetic or normative expectations for the "bunch" and the idiographic or differentiated dispositions of each child. In effect, the child is in the classic conflict situation and he must choose whether he will fulfil indi-

---

[8] See David Riesman *et al., The Lonely Crowd* (New Haven: Yale University Press, 1950); Allen Wheelis, *The Quest for Identity* (New York: W. W. Norton & Co., 1958).

vidual needs or institutional requirements. If he chooses the later, he is liable to unsatisfactory *personal integration* in the classroom; he is frustrated and dissatisfied. If he chooses the former, he is liable to unsatisfactory *role adjustment* in the classroom; he is ineffective and inefficient as a pupil. In practice, there are usually compromises and accommodations, but the point we want to make here is that the nature of the classroom group activity is quite different when the expectations and the dispositions are incongruent than when they are congruent.

3. *Role conflict*. There is a whole range of conflicts that occur when a role incumbent is required to conform simultaneously to a number of expectations which are mutually exclusive, contradictory, or inconsistent so that adjustment to one set of requirements makes adjustment to the other set of requirements impossible or at least difficult.[9] It is essentially these types of conflict that are illustrative of the issues we raised in the first section regarding the multiple group and institutional memberships of the participants in the classroom. Role conflicts are evidence of dislocation in the nomothetic dimension of the social system and may arise in several ways.

a) Disagreement within the referent group defining the role. For example, the principal of the school may be expected, by some teachers, to visit them regularly to give constructive help and, by others, to

[9] There are numerous empirical studies in the area of role conflict. See, for example, Samuel A. Stouffer, "An Analysis of Conflicting Social Norms," *American Sociological Review,* XIV (1949), 707–17; Samuel A. Stouffer and Jackson Toby, "Role Conflict and Personality," *American Journal of Sociology,* LVI (1951), 395–406; J. W. Getzels and E. G. Guba, "Role, Role Conflict, and Effectiveness: An Empirical Study," *American Sociological Review,* XIX (1954), 164–75; J. W. Getzels and E. G. Guba, "The Structure of Roles and Role Conflict in the Teaching Situation," *Journal of Educational Sociology,* XXIX (1955), 30–40.

trust them as professional personnel not in need of such supervision. Or, the pupil may be expected by some teachers to emphasize the mechanics of writing, the substance being useful only for the practice of correct form; by other teachers, to emphasize the content and substance, the form being merely an incidental vehicle for the communication. Or perhaps at a more fundamental level, the pupil may be expected by some teachers within the school to conceive of learning as essentially the rote remembrance of information provided by the teacher, and by other teachers as essentially the solution of problems meaningful to the pupil himself.

b) Disagreement among several referent groups, each having a right to define expectations for the same role. To use an example outside our immediate context, the university faculty member may be expected by his department head to emphasize teaching and service to students but by his academic dean to emphasize research and publication. Although these two sets of expectations for the same role do not necessarily conflict, it is clear that the time given to implementing the one set can be seen as taking away time from implementing the other, and to this extent, they *do* conflict.

c) Contradiction in the expectations of two or more roles which an individual is occupying at the same time. It is here that we have all those problems arising from the fact that pupils and teachers are members of numerous different groups in addition to the classroom group. Each group has expectations for its members, and these expectations may be incongruent so that conformity to the expectations of one group may mean nonconformity to the expectations of the other group. Consider here the simple instance of a teacher who is attempting to be, simultaneously, a devoted mother and wife and a successful career woman in her profession. Although the expectations of these roles need not inevitably clash, there is the possibility that attending conferences on teaching may get in the way of keeping up with the progress of her children and husband.

4. Personality conflict. This type of conflict occurs as a function of opposing needs and dispositions within the personality of the role incumbent as a function of unresolved discrepancies between his needs and his potentialities. The effect of such personal disequilibrium is to keep the individual at odds with the institution either because he cannot maintain a stable relationship with a given role or because he habitually misperceives the expectations placed upon him in terms of his autistic reactions. In any case, just as role conflict is a situational given, personality conflict is an individual given and is independent of any particular institutional setting. No matter what the situation, the role is, in a sense, detached from its institutional context and function and is used by him to work out personal and private needs and dispositions, however inappropriate these may be to the goals of the social system as a whole.

APPLICATION OF THE MODEL II:
CLASSROOM LEADERSHIP IN CHANGING
BEHAVIOR

We wish, finally, to apply the terms and categories of our model of the classroom group as a social system to the problem of changing behaivor in the teaching-learning situation. In the terms of our model, changing behavior may involve, at one extreme, adaptation of idiographic personality-dispositions to nomothetic role-expectations. We may call this the *socialization of personality.* At the other extreme, changing behavior may involve the adaptation of nomothetic role-expectations to idiographic personality-dispositions. We may call this the *personalization of roles.*

In attempting to achieve change, i.e., learning in the classroom, the teacher as the formal group leader always works within these extremes, emphasizing the one, the other, or attempting to reach an appropriate balance between the two. The way the possibilities between socialization of personality and personalization of roles is handled in the classroom determines the kind of group that is achieved and the kind of learning that results.

In this context, we may identify three types of group leadership or, more specifically, three teaching styles:

1. The nomothetic style. This orientation emphasizes the nomothetic or normative dimension of behavior and, accordingly, places stress on the requirements of the institution, the role, and the expectation rather than on the requirements of the individual, the personality, and the need-disposition. Education is defined as the handing down of what is known to those who do not yet know. In the equation $B = f(R \times P)$, P is minimized, R is maximized. It is assumed that, given the institutional purpose, appropriate procedures can be discovered through which the role is taken, despite any personal dispositions of the learner to the contrary, so that he will incorporate the expectations. It then follows that if roles are clearly defined and everyone is held equally responsible for doing what he is supposed to do, the required outcomes will naturally ensue regardless of who the particular role-incumbent might be, provided only that he has the necessary technical competence.

2. The idiographic style. The orientation emphasizes the idiographic dimension of behavior and accordingly places stress on the requirements of the individual, the personality, and the need-disposition rather than on the requirements of the institution, the role, and the expectation. Education is defined as helping the person know what he wants to know, as it were.

In the equation $B = f(R \times P)$, R is minimized, P is maximized. This does not mean that the idiographic style is any less goal-oriented than is the nomothetic style; it means that the most expeditious route to the ultimate goal is seen as residing in the people involved rather than in the nature of the institutional structure. The basic assumption is that the greatest accomplishment will occur, not from enforcing adherence to rigorously defined roles, but from making it possible for each person to seek what is most relevant and meaningful to him. This point of view is obviously related to particular individuals who fill the roles at a particular time, and expectations must be kept vague and informal. Normative prescriptions of the sort included in typical role-expectations are seen as unnecessarily restrictive and as a hindrance rather than a guide to productive behavior. The teacher frowns upon a priori class "lesson plans," and is not embarrassed to ask the individual pupil, if we may exaggerate the typical case somewhat, "Well, what would you like to do today?"

In short, the emphasis is on what we have called the personalization of roles rather than on the socialization of personality. In many ways, neither the nomothetic nor the idiographic definitions of the teaching-learning situation make any demands on the classroom group as a group—the nomothetic mode emphasizes uniform adherence to a given role, the idiographic mode emphasizes the discrete expression of individual personalities. The fact that the roles and personalities exist in the classroom within a group context is more or less irrelevant.

3. *The transactional style.* This orientation is intermediate to the other two and is, therefore, less amenable to "pure" or even clear-cut definition. Since the goals of the social system must be carried out, it is obviously necessary to make explicit the roles and expectations required to achieve the goals. And, since the roles and expectations will be implemented by the efforts of people with needs to be met, the personalities and dispositions of these people must be taken into account. But the solution is not so simple as it appears from just saying that one should hew to the middle course between expectations and needs, that is, at some midpoint between the nomothetic and idiographic axes. What we are calling the transactional mode is not just a compromise. Instead, the aim throughout is to acquire a thorough awareness of the limits and resources of both individual and institution within which the teaching-learning process may occur (that is, from the nomothetic and to the idiographic extremes) and to make an intelligent application of the two as a particular problem may demand. In the equation $B = f(R \times P)$, R and P are maximized or minimized as the situation requires. Institutional roles are developed independently of the role-incumbents, but they are adapted to the personalities of the actual individual incumbents. Expectations are defined as sharply as they can be but not so sharply that they prohibit appropriate behavior in terms of need-dispositions. Role conflicts, personality conflicts, and role-personality conflicts are recognized and handled. The standard of behavior is both individual integration and institutional adjustment. In short, both the socialization of personality and the personalization of roles is taken into account, and the processes in the classroom may be seen as a dynamic transaction between roles and personalities.

In this mode, the actual balance of emphasis on the performance of role requirements and the expression of personality needs changes as a function of interaction within the classroom group. Account is taken of the common or deviant perceptions of existential objects and roles, and of explicit or implicit agreements on how to deal with conflicts and deviant perceptions. In this sense, the group *qua* group is of crucial significance. It mediates between the institutional requirements and the individual dispositions. On the one hand, it can support the institution by imposing, if necessary, certain normative role-expectations on the group members; on the other hand, it can support the individual in expressing, if necessary, certain idiosyncratic personality-dispositions. In working out this balance between the institution and the individual, the group develops a "culture" or, perhaps better here, a *climate,* which may be analyzed into the constituent *intentions* of the group, and, in effect, the group climate represents another general dimension of the classroom as a social system:

Social System → Group → Climate → Intentions → Group Behavior

The stability and concomitant flexibility of the group in moving between the nomothetic and idiographic extremes depends on the *belongingness* that the individuals feel within the group. The development of this belongingness is accompanied by increased security for all the members of the group. The greater the belongingness, the greater the ease of significant communication between the teacher and the pupils and among the pupils themselves and the greater the shared pride in the achievement of both institutional *and* individual goals. What was an "accidental" and compulsory group becomes a planful and voluntary group. The rigidity of the *platoon* or the *instability* of the *crowd* is changed into the resourcefulness and flexibility of the *team.* They "know" what to expect, what to give, what to take. They find emotional support for their risk-taking, and the consequent increased individual security encourages "open"

transactions between personality and role. The boundaries between the private world and the public world become permeable, and the overlap in the perception of a given situation within the classroom is enlarged. There is, at once, both greater autonomy and heteronomy for the individual. The depth of the person's involvement in the classroom is increased, and, in this sense, learning becomes more meaningful.

Within this framework, this then might be conceived as the ideal-type model of the classroom as a social system: (*a*) Each individual *identifies* with the goals of the system so that they become part of his own needs. (*b*) Each individual believes that the expectations held for him are *rational* if the goals are to be achieved. (*c*) He feels that he *belongs* to a group with similar emotional identifications and rational beliefs.

By way of summarizing the characteristics of the several dimensions presented, we now offer the final pictorial example selected from the categories of goal behavior. [See page 24.]

In this final picture we have located the classroom as a social system. From this point of view, the most impressive characteristic of the classroom group, despite its apparent uniqueness, is that it can be studied systematically like *any* other group, be it a board of directors, a neighborhood club, or working team. The fundamental dimensions and concepts remain the same, and in studying any given group within a unified model, we both gain from and contribute to the study of all groups. The dimensions and concepts we have used are derived from the social sciences, and we believe one implication of our effort is that the social sciences have a great deal to contribute to the systematic analysis of education. In so far as there is going to be a "science" of education, it will be related to concepts, findings, and

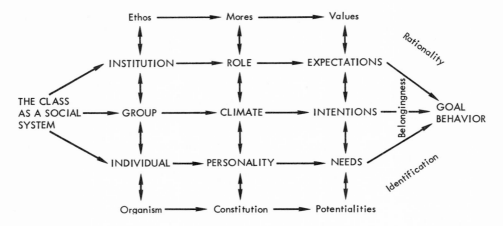

propositions from the whole range of disciplines called social science. It will be an integrative structure of ideas about the ways in which cultural, institutional, group, individual, and organismic factors interact and, in the process of interacting, change and bring about change.

The appropriate application of science to a particular situation is an art. Educational science is translated into educative outcomes through making choices, and this calls for the exercise of judgment. We see the learning group as an emergent reality developing out of the transactions between role and personality in the classroom. The nature of the group is determined ultimately by the way the teacher responds to the specific behavior of the students. But the judgment of the teacher on how to respond depends not merely on his ability to perceive the behavior to which he is responding as an immediate act but to look behind the act and to comprehend the behavior as a transaction within the social system as a whole. For it is within this sort of comprehension that not only the particular group but the particular individual within the group can be most readily understood. And it is through this understanding that the teacher can wisely judge how to respond.

One fundamental concern of teacher and student alike, then, is surely the nature of the group they are establishing. If they are working at cross-purposes, the likelihood of educational achievement is slim, for the chief preoccupation of the individuals will be the problem of dealing with a situation in which they cannot perceive order and consistency—at least not *their* order and consistency. Yet, if the classroom is to be genuinely challenging—and it must be this to be educative—dislocation in goals, expectations, potentialities, needs, and intentions is bound to arise, for the relationships among the various factors in the social system are continually undergoing change, and are, if we may put it this way, always transacting with one another.

It appears to us then that these considerations tell us something about the image of the classroom group that is needed. This is a Utopian ideal. It is not the image of a social system in equilibrium. It is rather the image of a system in motion or, if you will, in dynamic disequilibrium. It is the image of a group continually facing emergent complexity and conflict (if not confusion) and dealing with these realities, not in terms of sentiment but in terms of what the complexity and conflict suggest about the modifications that have to be made in the goals, expectations, needs, and selective perceptions of the teachers and learners. It is through this experience of recognizing and dealing with complexity, conflict, and change in the classroom situation that we can educate children to take their places as creative and autonomous participants in the other social systems that constitute the larger social order.

SOCIAL INTERACTION IN THE CLASSROOM

John Withall / W. W. Lewis

Our concern in this chapter is with the interactions, the behavioral transactions, between the human beings in the school learning situation. We shall focus attention on the cognitive and affective interactions between teachers and learners, and learners and learners, and on the research that has been done to assess and quantify these acts. The phenomena are overt and may be verbal or nonverbal. It is assumed that observation and analysis of these overt behaviors will enable us to make some inferences about the covert dynamics of

From: N. L. Gage, (Ed.), Handbook of research on teaching. *Chicago: Rand McNally, 1963. Pp. 683–714. Copyright © 1963 by the American Educational Research Association, and reproduced by permission of the authors and AERA.*

these interactions. In contrast to the methodological focus of Chapter 6, which deals with some of the same literature, the present chapter gives primary attention to substantive problems and findings.

Social interaction is, of course, a relation between persons such that "the behavior of either one is stimulus to the behavior of the other" (English & English, 1958, p. 270). Sears (1951) defined a related concept, the dyadic unit, as "one that describes the combined actions of two or more persons" (p. 479). It is sometimes important in using the concept of interaction that the referent differ from anything that can be ascribed to the participants in the interaction considered alone. Cronbach explained it as follows:

The term *dyadic* therefore may be applied to any study which compares descriptions of, statements about, or actions by two persons. These studies test hypotheses about interactions between two sets of data; their principal difficulty is that interpretations dealing with interactions can be advanced meaningfully only after the simpler main effects associated with the perceiver or the object of perception [or any two components of an interaction] have been given separate consideration (Cronbach, 1958, p. 355).

Cronbach's proviso has not always been observed in research on social interaction. The literature considered in this chapter has handled the interaction concept less rigorously than such a stipulation would allow. Often the research merely deals with how people behave in relation to other people, e.g., how teachers treat pupils, without distinguishing "simpler main effects" from interactions. It will be useful to the reader to keep in mind, however, the distinction between the loose and rigorous conceptions of interaction.

We shall trace the historical background of current trends and indicate the several stages through which research on social interaction in the classroom has moved. These stages appear to have concentrated in turn on teacher qualities or traits, child development, sociometric relationships, and, currently, socio-psychological phenomena. Attempts at assessment of classroom interaction have moved from the rating and opinionnaire stage, through the observation and analysis of perceptions by pupils and teachers of their interpersonal relations, to analyses of some of the specific variables in the socio-psychological content of the instructional process. We shall cite some of the major research to substantiate our thesis regarding the several stages through which the research seems to have progressed. Finally, we shall offer a summary and prognosis derived from what we have examined.

HISTORICAL PERSPECTIVE

From a historical perspective, three principal streams of influence, arising from educational, clinical, and social psychology, have shaped research on social interaction in the classroom. Although these are three somewhat independent areas of concern, workers in each have been aware of what the others have been doing. In recent years especially, each group has incorporated aspects of the others' work into its own. Each of the three areas of interest has reflected a somewhat different set of assumptions. Further, each has witnessed an upsurge of interest and has had its main impact upon public school practices at different points in time.

The first of these influences, coming naturally enough from within the field of education, reflected a concern with the conditions under which effective classroom learning can take place. Studies of classroom learning can be divided according to their concern with three kinds of conditions: characteristics of teachers which make for effective learning by pupils, characteristics of children which make some kinds of learning experiences more effective than others, and characteristics of the mechanical aspects of the learning act. A second kind of influence came from what has been called the mental hygiene movement, more specifically from clinical psychologists and psychiatrists who elaborated their concepts of mental illness to include concepts of mental health, and who saw the public schools as one institutional vehicle for promulgating mental health. The third and most recent influence has been the effort of social psychologists and sociologists to study the behavior of groups —especially small, relatively permanent, face-to-face groups like those in classrooms.

THE INFLUENCE
FROM WITHIN EDUCATION

In most studies by educators on the effectiveness of learning, it has been assumed that there is probably a straightforward cause-and-effect relationship between the conditions or ingredients present in any learning situation and the quality of learning produced in that situation. Educators are practical people with a job to do, and much of their research reflects this practical turn of mind. Without saying it in so many words, they have seemed to use the "black box" paradigm in classroom learning research; i.e., the processes of teaching and learning in themselves have been left unexamined. Researchers have looked for consistent relationships between what was put into the "black box," the conditions of learning, and what came out of the "black box," the outcomes of learning, without looking into the classroom process itself.

Teacher characteristics. One obvious condition of learning is, of course, the classroom teacher, to whom the major responsibility for devising the learning experiences is given. The researcher assumes here that the "right" combination of personality traits, attitudes, and background characteristics on the part of the teacher will enable her to provide the "right" kinds of learning experiences for her pupils. This approach has an obvious implication for recruitment of new members of the teaching profession: On the one hand, if there are certain permanent human qualities that good teachers must have, then candidates who do not have these qualities must be screened out; on the other hand, if the necessary qualities can be learned, then provision for learning them should be included in teacher education curricula.

As reflected in research on teaching,

interest in discovering these characteristics of the good teacher dates back to the early 1920's and continues to the present. Initially, the teacher characteristics studies dealt with easily obtained demographic variables —type of training, scholarship, and so on. More recently, subtler variables, such as attitudes and personality, have appeared in these studies. But, in spite of more sophisticated measurement and design techniques, the basic assumption has remained unaltered: the teacher is the primary ingredient in the learning process, and the characteristics of good teachers should be identified in order to provide more good teachers and fewer poor ones.

Child development. Another way of viewing the conditions of learning which go into the "black box" is to look at the qualities brought to the situation by the learner. Here the assumption again seems reasonable and practical: Since children obviously differ in the skills they bring to a learning situation, the most effective learning will take place when the material to be learned is most appropriate to whatever skills the child is currently able to muster. One primary outcome of the interest in child-conditions in learning has been the evolving body of research in child development, beginning in the early 1930's and continuing to the present.

These studies have dealt with a variety of kinds of behavior including intellectual, linguistic, social, and motor. But two dominant themes have been relevant to the education of children: (1) the concept of development itself, comprising lawful and predictable stages of growth, emphasizing the similarities between different children at the same stage of development and the dissimilarities between different stages of development of the same child; and (2) the existence of a relationship between the developmental, or maturational stage of the individual and his readiness for certain kinds of learning activities, such that too early or too late introduction of experiences results in inefficient learning. In combination, these concepts led to (1) curricula designed to fit the average abilities and interests of children at different ages and (2) an emphasis on understanding the unique needs of individual children through personal contact. In either case, educators have continued to assume that the most effective learning experiences will result from adapting the curriculum to the developmental level of the individual learner.

Impersonal conditions of learning. Still another way of looking at the conditions of learning in the classroom is to relate outcomes to the method of presentation, the sequence, or the timing of experiences, aside from the teacher and pupils as persons. The assumption in this approach is that, given an "average" teacher and class, the arrangement of the learning experiences would be crucial to obtaining good outcomes.

Many concepts currently taught in educational psychology courses reflect the findings of research on such conditions of learning. The earliest research on learning reflected the educator's practical concern with the most efficient methods of getting information and skills incorporated into the behavioral repertoire of learners—the advantages of distributed practice over massed practice, of whole over part learning, of arranging for transfer of training, and so on.

Most questions raised in this kind of research appeared to have a direct relevance for classroom learning and were incorporated into the subject matter to be learned by prospective teachers during their training. Investigators of the conditions of learning made a concerted attempt to evolve precise relationships among independent and dependent variables in learning; for example, the independent variable of similarity of performance required in

two situations and the dependent variable of transfer of training from one to the other. But the search for increased precision in studying the conditions of learning has led to the investigation of systematic, quasi-mathematical concepts that seem to have decreasing relevance for classroom learning. The most recent formulations of Hull, Guthrie, or Tolman, for example, have few direct implications for the practices of the classroom teacher. Nonetheless, these approaches provided the first systematic attempts, regardless of the directions they eventually pursued, to formulate and test relationships relevant to the learning process.

THE INFLUENCE OF THE MENTAL HYGIENE MOVEMENT

Although most clinical workers in the mental hygiene professions have been interested primarily in the treatment of mental illness, they quickly recognized that a child's school experiences probably have, next to his family experiences, the most influence on his emotional well-being. The clinical workers were also quick to suggest, on the basis of individual cases handled in clinics, that a child's emotional well-being could have a striking effect on his progress in school. The interests of educators and mental hygienists seemed to overlap naturally. Two rather different assumptions seem to be implicit in much of the writing which connects clinical concepts with educational experiences: (1) a child must be in a reasonable state of adjustment to make optimum use of school learning experiences, and (2) a child's state of adjustment is subject to modification as a result of what happens to him in school.

Probably because clinical workers usually deal with single individuals in a one-to-one situation, much of the writing in this field satisfies only a loose definition of research. Studies often report findings and develop concepts based on a single case. But since the findings on each case tend to be rather elaborate and detailed, the arguments for the interdependence of emotional well-being and learning are often quite convincing. To many educators, the concepts dealt with—emotional blocks to learning, transference, unconscious motivation, and the like—have seemed somewhat vague, and at times ridiculous, when applied to the classroom situation. Clinical conceptualizations of human behavior have, however, focused the attention of educators on the continuous, interactive nature of the learning process. However inarticulately the concepts were formulated, learning was taken out of the "black box" and exposed to daylight. Learning was conceived as determined not by a set of prior conditions but by a series of ongoing interactions between two or more human beings with feelings as well as ideas and skills. The influence of mental hygiene workers in helping conceptualize learning as a complicated and continuous interaction served to raise new questions, rather than to answer the older questions previously raised in the research of educators.

THE INFLUENCE FROM STUDIES OF GROUP LIFE

The most recent influence on studies of social interaction in the classroom—namely, studies of group life—has proceeded independently but concurrently with much of the educational research and has only recently become incorporated in the educational literature (e.g., Glidewell, 1959; Henry, 1960). Studies of group life by sociologists and social psychologists, beginning particularly with the Lewinian studies of group climate in the 1930's, have evolved concepts relevant to the ways in which group members in different roles influence each other. The concepts of group influence, problem-solving, and decision-making did not entirely overlap with the educator's concepts of learning in the classroom. Yet both the social psychologist and the educator were concerned with changing behavior elicited in a group situation.

The assumption of mutual interest to educators and students of group life is that interactive influences emanating from the group itself bring about changes in the behavior of individual members of the group. The earliest studies of group life looked for independent variables of an antecedent nature, for example, the autocratic versus the democratic leader. But such studies soon shifted to a concern with the interaction of variables during group process. Like the mental hygiene sources, the group process studies seem to demand that classroom learning be conceptualized as a resultant of mutual influences in a dynamic process.

FRAMEWORK OF EARLY RESEARCH

Most human learning occurs in a social context. The neonate is in contact with, dependent on, and nurtured by the physician, nurse, and mother as soon as it emerges from the uterus. From that moment on, most of the individual's knowledge, ideas, feelings, goals, values, and ways of behaving are developed in interaction with other persons. Most of the knowledge any one of us possesses derives from direct or vicarious interaction with our fellows in the psychological and social context of "objective reality."

In the preschool years, youngsters learn—through social interaction with their parents or parent surrogates, siblings, peers, and other human beings—the meaning of the world around them and ways of behaving toward that world. The meaning is obviously colored by the cultural, socioeconomic, moral, and ethical values or mores of the key persons in the child''s environment (Barker, Kounin, & Wright, 1943; Blair, 1946; Dollard, 1937; Hollingshead, 1949; Murchison, 1933). For example, of the studies included in the book edited by Barker, Kounin, and Wright, six are directly concerned with cultural influences on the development of children. The kinds of influence investigated were social class differences (Skodak, pp. 259–278; Davis, pp. 607–620), longitudinal trends (Macfarlane, pp. 307–328), group leader roles (Anderson, pp. 459–484; Lippitt & White, pp. 485–508), and "primitive" culture (Dennis, pp. 621–636).

The process of socializing and acculturating the individual has been institutionalized in our society by setting up schools. Here, trained workers deliberately utilize social interaction to bring about changes in the knowledge, skill, and attitudes of the youth put into their charge. For many years it was imagined that social interaction was confined merely to traffic in ideas between an adult teacher and younger learners. Closer examination of the process soon revealed that classroom learning inevitably involved traffic in feelings as well as ideas. Also, the traffic was not limited to lines running from teacher to learner but extended to channels among all the individuals in the classroom.

The earlier view of classroom interaction as confined to a learner and the teacher was exemplified best by the efforts of researchers and writers to identify the teacher traits, qualities, and behaviors hypothesized to facilitate learning. Thus, by means of rating scales and questionnaires completed in the early days of such research, by administrators and subsequently completed by pupils as well, attempts were made to identify the specific teacher traits that ultimately spelled success in terms of pupil achievement.

These efforts hardly constituted research on social interaction in the classroom; that is a relatively recent development. The studies focused on the behavioral or professional qualities of teachers deemed to make them "effective." Such a study may be an indirect way of assessing social interaction, but it is hardly a frontal attack on the problem. For instance, if the teacher is not continued in his job, then we might conclude that the teacher-pupil relationship had not been conducive to the intellectual, emotional, social, or physical development of the learners in his charge.

However, the early research did not put the problem in this framework. Rather, the question asked in early investigations was: What contributes to teacher effectiveness? The criterion for judging "effectiveness" was frequently the simple one of ascertaining whether the teacher retained or lost his job. A number of studies (James, 1930; Morrison, 1927; Nanninga, 1924) used this criterion, along with the opinions of teachers, superintendents, school board members, and, eventually, of students, to identify the factors that contributed to the teacher's failure to be reappointed. James (1930) employed what he labeled the "case method." This involved interviewing principals and others and inquiring whether they personally knew of a teacher who had "failed," i.e., had not been reappointed. The interviewees were asked to describe the case they knew of and to tell the salient details, including reasons for dismissal. These descriptions afforded the researcher a list of 10 factors entering into teacher-failure. Freshman students, teachers, and principals were then asked to rate these factors in terms of the contribution each was believed to have made to a teacher's being dismissed. Poor discipline headed the list in all cases.

Another high-ranking problem was too much dating. Intimacy with pupils also ranked high. Lack of knowledge of subject matter was placed midway by all groups of raters.

Morrison (1927) reported that he used "a careful record of forty interviews," without, however, specifying how the record was kept or how the interviews, once "recorded," were analyzed. The interviewees in this study were school superintendents and members of school boards. The results of analyzing these interviews permitted Morrison to indicate the frequency of causes for failure and to offer a composite picture of the teacher who "fails." The resulting composite picture indicated that the teacher who didn't get reappointed was a poor disciplinarian, contributed to school gossip, made an unwise choice of associates, lacked teaching skill, had no desire to grow professionally, left the classroom immediately at dismissal time, and reported late for duty. Morrison's final sentence, both hopeful and highly inferential, stated: "These facts show quite definitely that many of the causes which lead to failure can be controlled" (p. 105).

The careful study by Nanninga (1924) made use of a questionnaire sent to superintendents of schools in cities having a population of 2,500 or more in Oregon, Washington, Kansas, and Nebraska. Of 143 questionnaires sent out, 55 per cent were returned. The questionnaire contained only two items: (1) the number of teachers employed in the high school and their sex; (2) the number of teachers who had been dismissed or resigned and the reason for the "failure." Like the other studies cited, Nanninga's reported that poor discipline, lack of cooperation, and poor instruction were most often mentioned as reasons for "failure." Poor discipline, it appears, headed the list of causes in nearly all studies. Questionnaires

and rating scales, based on traits or qualities which superintendents and supervisors considered necessary and desirable, controlled the field at this stage of the research movement. A refinement was added later as students' opinions of teachers and their desirable qualities were used to assess the teacher's effectiveness.

In this wilderness of ratings and questionnaires appeared Wickman's study (1928). It, too, relied on opinionnaires to assess teachers' attitudes regarding children's behaviors. The instruments Wickman used were no more refined than those used by other researchers at that time. He made some attempt, however, to identify items that were more discriminating by using a more methodical approach and a somewhat larger population of teachers from whom the items were derived. Furthermore, he sought to assess the perceptions of teachers themselves of children's behaviors in the classroom. In addition, some basic statistical tests were used in processing the data. Neither the instruments nor the techniques used in Wickman's study, however, caused it to stand out. It was rather the inferences he drew concerning the kinds of individuals needed in teaching, the importance of the methods they used in dealing with their private emotions and needs, and most significant of all, the kind of teacher education program that would cultivate the qualities, attitudes, and skills needed by teachers for working with children most effectively. This less well-known aspect of Wickman's study is not to be confused with his well-publicized finding that teachers and mental hygienists tend to view children's school behaviors quite differently. The latter difference, as Wickman was at pains to emphasize, was a function, in part, of the kind of question put to each professional group.

Barr (1935) summarized the outlook of the professionally unsophisticated by quoting from the Twenty-Third Yearbook of the National Society of College Teachers of Education, published in 1935:

> all graduate schools and research divisions...should be encouraged to develop a measure or measures of teaching merit.... A hoped-for result from these investigations would be the discovery of one or two tests—simple, short, inexpensive, easily administered, quickly and accurately scored, reliable, and obviously related to teaching—which will measure a teacher's success. With such a measure many troublesome issues could be removed from the controversial group (Barr, 1935, p. 561).

Barr went on to demonstrate the forlornness of this hope. He reported a study on 99 elementary school teachers in Grades 2–7. Nineteen instruments were applied to these teachers and the pupils they taught. These instruments included the Moss-Hunt-Omwake Social Intelligence Test, A.C.E. Psychological Examination for High School Graduates and College Freshmen; the Morris Trait Index; the New Stanford Arithmetic Test; an informal 10-point scale for assessing personality; the Strong Vocational Interest Blank; and the Standard Achievement Test. The criteria of teaching success were (1) a composite of gains in test scores made by pupils on the Stanford; (2) a composite of ratings of teachers by superintendents on seven rating scales used twice; (3) a composite of scores by teachers on nine measures of qualities such as health, intelligence, personality, knowledge of subject matter, and professional interest, and (4) a composite of all the foregoing measures. Barr reported that the "values calculated were exceedingly low...most...in terms of coefficients of correlations, falling between 0 and .35" (p. 565). He concluded that such results are "disappointing." In light of the use of rating scales of questionable validity

and reliability, and in view of the shakiness of personality assessments by pencil-and-paper tests and the highly tenuous nature of the several variables being assessed, it is not astonishing that low coefficients of correlation were derived. Barr explained that the negative results were due to the "minuteness of the contribution made by the different aspects of teaching measured when compared with the whole of teaching ability" (p. 566). He concluded that qualities, such as knowledge of subject and mastery of teaching skills, that are readily measured are overshadowed by the difficult-to-measure and subtler variables of the teacher's philosophy, personality, interpersonal relationships, and the whole area of teacher-pupil relationships. He argued that we "need functional tests measuring the teacher in action" and that the "ultimate criterion of teaching success will have to be found in the changes produced in pupils..." (p. 568).

Melby (1936) set forth a similar view:

> there is greater need than ever for technics of describing the learning activities of children.... If we can devise methods for describing the learning activities of children we can at least know how children live while they are learning even though we cannot measure all that is learned (p. 333).... We can only say that in a given situation certain things were done and here is a picture of what happened. If we have a large number of such cases, certain generalizations will be possible (Melby, 1936, p. 335).

Despite the weight of evidence and despite the eloquence of the pleas for more reliable and valid techniques for measuring one facet of social interaction, i.e., teacher-pupil relationships in the teaching-learning process, the dependence on rating scales, questionnaires, and opinionnaires persists. But some effort is being made today to utilize observational instruments which can quantify relevant observable behaviors and interactions in vivo.

As it became more and more evident that superintendents', principals', supervisors', and board members' ratings of teachers showed very little reliability and little relationship to one another's assessments the researchers on teacher behaviors in the classroom began assiduously to collect student ratings of teachers. A more realistic attitude began to appear, one which held that student ratings might be merely "taken purely as an accumulation of opinion without raising any question of how valid that opinion may be. The views of the students may be prejudiced, mistaken, superficial, immature, but, whatever their validity, they exist and exert a powerful influence on the effectiveness of the course" (Bryan, 1933, p. 296, quoting from Wilson, 1932, p. 79).

Our reservations and skepticism regarding rating scales can be summed up in the following strictures. It appears that ratings encourage inferences and extrapolations beyond the observed behavior, in that large, global, undifferentiated segments of behavior are rated in terms of private, unstated criteria of the rater. Gage and Cronbach (1955) have stressed the importance of considering *"degree of extrapolation* or inference required between Input and Outtake" (p. 412). Requiring much extrapolation of this kind, as is often the case in the kinds of ratings made of teachers, makes ratings lack comparability in that each rater has his own private frame of reference and tends to select those aspects of the global behavior which particularly suit his frame of reference. Sociometric devices, if viewed as rating instruments (as in Chapter 7, especially on pp. 345–360), deliberately exploit this fact of the uniqueness of individual

perceptions and predilections to get a picture of the peculiar perceptions of each of the participants in a group. Ratings of qualities, global behaviors, traits, and skills (frequently not defined specifically), on the other hand, are usually tossed into the hopper on the basic assumption that the same behavioral phenomena were assessed and that the criteria governing each individual's rating were similar and comparable.

SOCIOMETRY AND THE TEACHER'S VERBAL CONTROL OF CHILDREN'S BEHAVIOR

Parallel with the burgeoning interest in students' ratings of their teachers as a means of assessing teacher impact on learners came Moreno's *Who Shall Survive?* (1934) and its exposition of a new device for measuring relationships within groups. The fact that rating scales had been used and found wanting made it inevitable that, when educators became acquainted with the sociometric devices of Moreno, they would see the value of them for their purposes. It took a little while, however, as it often does with a promising and useful device, for Moreno's devices to be discovered and used in schools.

A number of worth-while sociometric studies of social relationships in the classroom appeared in the 1940's (Bonney, 1947; McLelland & Ratliff, 1947; Young, 1947) along the lines laid down by Jennings (1947, 1948). Bonney sought to ascertain how effectively teachers could identify students who have the most and the least friends. He asked 291 students to rate their best friends on a personality scale. He also asked 13 teachers to check in one of four columns (High, Middle, Low, and Unable to Judge) how they thought each student ranked in number of friends. Teachers appeared to overrate students who were active in formal class and student activities, who were amenable to teacher directions, who were socially inhibited, and who had desirable personality traits, but who were looked on as outsiders as far as other students were concerned. Teachers underrated students who were academically inept but who had good interpersonal relationships with their own clique and who were apt to disregard teacher regulations but were well liked by their peers.

To collect data on the social relationships of a group of 41 seventh-graders, Young (1947) used controlled interviews about the school, the Ohio Social Acceptance Scale, and a "guess-who" technique, in addition to a standard sociometric test requesting the subject to pick someone to sit with, play on his team, go on a picnic, and be his best friend. A rank-order correlation of .90 was obtained between the sociometric test and the Ohio Social Acceptance Scale. It appears that the same factors which enter into a child's choice of friends influence his selecting them for his team and as president of his class.

Planned change was initiated through small-group activities in which social relationships would be encouraged and developed in a study by McLelland and Ratliff (1947). They asked 35 ninth-graders to indicate someone (1) with whom they'd like to go to a show; (2) with whom they'd like to study; (3) whom they'd like to have at home as a guest; and (4) with whom they'd rather share a secret. After isolates and rejectees were identified, the experimental treatment was applied. Follow-up sociometric tests indicated that social acceptance was more widespread. These investigations represented attempts to assess the interpersonal relationships of pupils with their peers by collecting data on social relationships directly from the members of the class group under study.

One tack pursued in the interim was that of analyzing the behaviors of teachers in the situation. This marked a considerable advance over attempts to assess a teacher's relationships with her pupils by out-of-class-room ratings. Johnson's study (1935) demonstrated that positive, directive, and approving verbal communication to pupils ensured a greater degree of complying with requests and directions by learners, as compared with directions or requests to learners that were negative, nonspecific, and reproving. She used two groups of 38 children each and asked them one at a time to perform simple tasks, solve problems, and to inhibit certain activities. One type of positive verbal direction was used with the "experimental" group with explicit directions and requests, e.g., "Cut it in the corner to save the paper." Negative and unexplicit directions, such as "Don't waste paper," were given to the "control" group. The "Do" type of directions appeared more effective than the "Don't," in that consistently larger percentages of the experimental group children than of control group children succeeded in performing tasks assigned them (cutting a paper circle). Johnson pointed up the greater number of successes in the one group where "more positive, unhurried, specific and encouraging types of directions" were given, as compared with the situation where "more negative, general, hurried and discouraging verbal directions" were given (p. 204).

Olson and Wilkinson (1938) examined the same question by a time-sampling technique and substantiated Johnson's findings that directive, approving, specific statements are more efficacious in obtaining compliance and cooperation than negative, blanket, and nonspecific statements or requests. They recorded during each five-minute period just one reaction by the student teacher to marked inattention or restlessness on the part of the children. The student teacher's verbal behavior was labeled positive if she suggested "Do this"; it was labeled negative if she said "Don't do that or else you'll suffer"; and finally, "blanket" responses were identified when one child's behavior was reprimanded by such statements as: "We should all be working right now" or "Pupils in my class don't run." In addition, "gestural" responses, i.e., movements of head, hands, and shoulders were noted. The researchers sought an answer to the question, Does the type of language and the control techniques of the teacher indicate his probable teaching efficiency? On the basis of ratings by the principal and critic teacher, it was found that quantity of control was unimportant but that quality of control was important (see Kounin & Gump's recent work, 1958, 1961). Furthermore, it appeared that "blanket" responses were used by the least efficient teachers, while abler teachers used more discriminating and varied control procedures and a larger proportion of directing and approving statements. The percentage of positive language used correlated .59 with the Haggerty-Olson-Wickman rating scale.

The work of Anderson and his collaborators (Anderson & Helen M. Brewer, 1945; Anderson & J. E. Brewer, 1946; Anderson, Brewer, & Reed, 1946), Jersild and others (1939), Thorndike, Loftus, and Goldman (1941), as well as the descriptions, analyses, and summaries of the then current research and its implications by various writers (e.g., Jones, Conrad, & Murphy, 1939; Leonard & Eurich, 1942; Ohio State University, University High School Class, 1938; and Stoddard, 1939), pushed still further the examination of teachers' and children's classroom behavior. This type of research may have become prominent, in part, because of the international political currents then running and because a developing sensitivity to mental hygiene principles encouraged educators and researchers to view the teacher's behaviors in terms of their controlling or facilitating influence.

The work of Anderson and his coworkers was reported fully in a series of *Applied Psychology Monographs.* These researchers worked from the basic postulate that the main direction of influence in the classroom is from teacher to pupil. To measure this, Anderson developed teacher-behavior categories, and Brewer developed child-behavior categories. With these categories they were able to determine the extent to which teacher behavior influenced the behavior of the pupils and the psychological atmosphere of the classroom. Their subjects were teachers and pupils in kindergarten and the primary grades.

Anderson developed 26 categories for the classification of teacher behavior. These categories embraced two main types of teacher behavior vis-à-vis the child: "dominative" and "integrative." The dominative teacher behaviors were further divided into three kinds: (1) dominative with conflict; (2) dominative without conflict; and (3) dominative with evidence of working together. Integrative teacher behaviors were divided into two kinds: (1) integrative contacts without working together; (2) integrative contacts with evidence of working together. Nonverbal as well as verbal behavior of the teacher was sampled by means of the categories. Contacts of the teacher with each pupil individually or with the group as a whole were recorded on a standard observation blank developed by Anderson and Brewer. Some examples of dominative behaviors by teachers included (1) telling a child to move to another part of the room; (2) using warnings, threats, and reminders; (3) punishing by sending out of room; (4) making gratuitous judgment, and (5) calling to attention. Integrative behaviors included (1) questioning to obtain information regarding possible interest of child; (2) helping child to define, redefine, and solve a problem; (3) approving, commending, and accepting the spontaneous self-initiated behavior of the child; and (4) asking questions regarding the child's expressed interests.

The reliability of the observers was determined by computing percentages of agreement between the simultaneous, independent observations of two categorizers. The mean percentages of agreement for two observers were 90 per cent for teacher behavior and 95 per cent for child behavior. It appeared that identifiable teacher behaviors could be categorized so that teachers could be differentiated on the basis of the relative number of their integrative and dominative contacts with children. Furthermore, concomitant differences in pupil behavior were found to be consistent with the classroom personalities of the teachers. Children with more integrative teachers showed significantly lower frequencies of distracted and nonconforming behavior, and significantly higher frequencies of spontaneous, cooperative, and self-directed behavior. In order to assess further the validity of the instruments, a study was made of the same groups of children who had been observed in Grade 2 after they moved into Grade 3. It was found, using Brewer's categories, that the pupils' behavior in Grade 3 was different from what it had been in Grade 2. These behavior differences were consistent with the behaviors of the Grade 3 teachers as identified by Anderson's categories. Another follow-up study, made on the Grade 2 teachers, found that those teachers, although working with new groups of children, maintained virtually the same patterns of behavior that they had exhibited the previous year and that the new second-graders reacted with behaviors that were highly similar to those of their predecessors.

The studies of Anderson and his coworkers tended to demonstrate that the teacher's classroom personality and behaviors influenced the behavior of the children she taught. Teachers who used dominative techniques produced in their pupils aggressive and antagonistic behaviors which were expressed toward both their teachers and their peers. On the other hand, teachers who used socially integrative behaviors appeared to facilitate friendly, cooperative, and self-directive behaviors in the children.

Jersild, Thorndike, Goldman, and Loftus (1939) set out to assess the influence of "activity" programs in selected schools in New York City. They developed procedures for recording pupil behaviors, and measured the learning outcomes with pencil-and-paper tests of work-skills, overall achievement, intelligence, and social beliefs and attitudes. Pupils in eight "activity" schools and eight "control" (traditional) schools comprised the Ss. The youngsters studied were elementary school children (Grades 1–6), most of them in Grades 4, 5, and 6. The behavioral data were collected through coded observations of seven major types of activities: (1) cooperative; (2) critical; (3) experimental; (4) leadership; (5) recitational; (6) self-initiated; and (7) negative work spirit. The quantified data of the coded observations were supplemented by anecdotal observations. Detailed notes of behaviors of particular youngsters were related to the coded observations of the same youngsters. Concurrent but independent observations in the same classroom by two observers yielded median percentages of agreement between observers ranging from 70 to 97 per cent when the coded records were compared item by item. However, the problem of obtaining adequate reliability and agreement when specific behaviors have to be recorded is demonstrated by the median corrected split-half coefficient of .47 obtained in assessing the reliability of coded observation scores of single individuals, where correlations were computed between first and second periods of observation for each of 1,833 pupils in 51 classes. On the other hand, a median coefficient of .97 was obtained between class averages assigned to the same records by two sets of two independent raters of 76 classes when rating the global data of anecdotal observation.

This study demonstrated that behaviors of children in activity programs differed from those of children in traditional classes. The activity children participated more in planning and directing activities, were able to capitalize more on their interests and aptitudes, gave more outward appearance of self-direction, utilized their greater freedom constructively, and engaged in more diverse activities in the classroom. Nonetheless, the pencil-and-paper tests indicated that children under the activity regime did less well on the Comprehensive Achievement Test and lagged behind the control groups in certain tool subjects—mainly arithmetic and spelling. Jersild and his co-workers suggested that the paper-and-pencil instruments used to measure the learning of the activity program youngsters were not adequate to the task of measuring outcomes in the activity classes.

> To determine the immediate values, or the ultimate benefits of the various performances in which the activity children surpassed the controls would require more intensive study. More intensive investigation likewise would be required to determine the extent and nature of other learnings and performances that were not measured by the methods so far employed, and to explore the extent to which such learnings might offset, or outweigh, the somewhat greater degree of competence that the control pupils meanwhile had gained in certain academic subject...(Jersild, et al., 1939, p. 206).

Thorndike, Loftus, and Goldman (1941) reported in more detail the development of the categories used in recording the behaviors of the children studied in the New York City "activity" investigation. The differences in the behaviors of the two groups were spelled out, and the disappointingly low percentages of agreement (around 50 per cent) were highlighted.

CHILD DEVELOPMENT AND GROUP CLIMATE

Two other mainstreams of influence—research on child growth and development (Blos, 1941; Prescott, 1938; Zachry & Lichty, 1940) and the assessment of group life and climate by Lippitt (1940)—began to influence research at about this time. Ojemann and Wilkinson (1939) conducted a study to ascertain whether teachers became more effective when they made a careful study of children's behavior and the bases for it. Their study represents an attempt to assess the value of the child-development point of view in the learning situation. The question asked was: If the teacher is helped to develop a comprehensive understanding of how children grow and develop, will not the children's learning and personal-social development be enhanced? The writings of Dearborn and Rothney (1941), Prescott (1938), Rothney and Roens (1949), and the Division on Child Development and Teacher Personnel (1945) consistently exemplify this orientation. Ojemann and Wilkinson's study can be viewed as the prototype of studies concerned with the teacher's understanding of child development and behavior as a determiner of her ability to facilitate learning and enhance personality development. Their method consisted of selecting experimental and control groups of 33 children each in a ninth grade. The groups were matched on chronological age, intelligence scores (Otis Group Test), school achievement, and home background. The teachers of the experimental group received and discussed the comprehensive data gathered on each child from tests, home interviews, and school records. Suggested procedures were developed from these discussions on the planning of daily classwork and ways of conducting the class. One of the investigators in this study dropped in occasionally to discuss the experimental group's progress with their teachers. The experimental group made a significantly greater gain academically, differed significantly from the control group in its attitudes toward school, and seemed to manifest fewer personality conflicts and psychological disturbances than pupils in the control group. It was concluded that teachers are more effective guides of children's learning when they know about the youngster's abilities, home environment, emotional problems, and attitudes.

In an experiment somewhat resembling that of Ojemann and Wilkinson, Burrell (1951) attempted to test the effectiveness of a deliberate effort on the part of teachers to meet the emotional needs of youngsters who were evincing learning problems and blocks. The researcher's question was: Can learning be facilitated if the teacher makes a concerted effort to meet the child's emotional needs? She selected two schools in Brooklyn, New York, and within School A chose three classes in the intermediate grades as the experimental subjects. School B provided three classes of control subjects. The six teachers (three control and three experimental) were asked to identify five students in each class who were having learning difficulties. The Wishing Well Test, Ohio Social Acceptance Scale, Otis-Pintner, Stanford Achievement Tests, and Wetzel Grid were administered to both the control and experimental pupils. Beyond collecting the data on the control subjects,

nothing else was done with that group. The teachers working with the experimental groups were instructed to try to meet the emotional needs of the five youngsters in each of their classes who were having learning difficulties. Statistical analyses indicated that the experimental subjects manifested improved learning (as judged by results on posttests), improved social relationships, diminished deviate behavior, improved work habits, and reduced truancy; furthermore, the experimental teachers' attitudes toward the youngsters improved.

One question raised by experiments of the kind done by Ojemann-Wilkinson and Burrell is: To what extent can the results be explained by the "Hawthorne effect"? Thus, it may have been the superior motivation, due to the additional attention given to teachers and pupils by the investigators, rather than the teachers' superior understanding of their pupils, that produced the greater gains in the experimental group. More adequately designed experiments (see Chapter 5) are needed to rule out this rival hypothesis.

Brookover's study (1940) on the relationship of measured person-to-person interactions between teachers and pupils and the ratings of pupils and administrators epitomizes the many studies of its kind. To measure the "person-person interaction" of the teacher and her pupils, Brookover carefully developed a nine-item multiple-choice scale. The scale appears to have measured the pupil's impression of the pleasantness of his relationships with his teacher. Teachers with high ratings by their pupils on this instrument were also rated high ($r = .64$) as instructors by pupils using the Purdue Rating Scale for Instructors. This correlation probably reflects the strong operation of social desirability factors in both instruments. In a sense, both get at the degree to which the student likes the teacher, and it is little wonder that they correlate substantially.

Furthermore, the students' mean ratings of their teachers on the Interaction Scale correlated only −.08 with the ratings of the teachers by a single administrator. Finally, the ratings by two groups of principals and administrators of their teachers' effectiveness on the Purdue Rating Scale correlated only .24.

Another study in student-teacher relationships at this time (Bush, 1942) examined the relevance—to the teacher's effectiveness—of such variables as the teacher's social beliefs, the student's opinion of the teacher's fairness, the teacher's personal liking for students, and the teacher's opinion of the student's thinking ability. Bush decided to explore the nature of effective teacher-pupil relationships "by focusing upon the student-teacher relationship rather than upon only the teacher, or the student, or the teaching method" (p. 645). His subjects in the ninth grade and up were drawn from a private boys' school. The relationships between nine social science teachers and the students in their classes were his basic concern. Tests, rating scales, anecdotal records, interviews, questionnaires, and regular school records were all used as sources of the basic data. He found that the more discriminating variables for assessing student-teacher relationships were similarity of social beliefs between teacher and students, mutual personal liking of student and teacher, the teacher's skill in developing harmonious relations with students, the teacher's effectiveness in counseling, and the teacher's belief that he has an effective relationship with a student. Nondiscriminatory variables were the teacher's appearance and possession of more knowledge than the student.

A useful summary of the major research up to this time was made by Tiedeman (1942). He collated materials dealing with pupil-teacher relationships based on child development studies (e.g., Meek,

1940; Prescott, 1938) and students' ratings of teachers (e.g., Jersild & Holmes, 1940; Remmers, 1934).

A study resulting in the development of an inventory to measure the attitudes of teachers relevant to teacher-pupil relationships (Leeds & Cook, 1947) is a good example of research based on psychometric tools and approaches. (This work is also considered in Chapter 11.) Judgments by principals were used in the selection and identification of the two extreme groups on the criterion of rapport with students; against this criterion, about 150 attitude statements were validated and selected. The principals rated a subsequent group of teachers on a six-item scale, Leeds himself used Baxter's rating scale for assessing the same teachers, and a 50-item "My Teacher" scale was used by the pupils to rate their teachers. It is not surprising to learn that "the single validating criterion showing the highest correlation (.486) with the Inventory was the writer's rating of the teacher's classroom behavior" (p. 155). Since the researcher had developed the inventory within a certain orientation and framework for observing the teachers' behaviors, this finding seems to indicate that the same orientation and framework guided him in making on-the-spot classroom observations. The correlations of the inventory with the principal's rating and the pupils' mean rating of the teacher were .43 and .45, respectively. Such variables as the sex, marital status, or parental status of the teacher and such matters as size of school and subjects taught had little or no relationship to the teachers' inventory scores or to ratings by pupils of their teachers.

SOCIAL-EMOTIONAL CLIMATE IN THE CLASSROOM

The Iowa studies. Lewin, Lippitt, and White's work (1939) on interpersonal interactions of children in differing social climates opened up, as did the techniques of sociometry, new horizons for the study of social interaction in learning situations. Recently presented in book form (White & Lippitt, 1960), this work reflected, implicitly at least, the concern with values stemming from the international situation and the expansion of totalitarianism in the 1930's.

The early work on the effect of social climate and of leadership roles on group life and productivity is best represented by Lippitt's Iowa investigation. He organized four clubs of five boys each. The boys were eleven years old and drawn from public school populations. Each club met for six weeks under a leader who implemented a specified style of leadership. Thus, in a consecutive 18-week period the four clubs each had three different leaders who employed either a democratic, autocratic, or laissez-faire leadership style. The leadership styles were rotated among the several leaders so that personality might be partialled out as a biasing factor. Two clubs met concurrently in adjoining rooms and were headed by leaders implementing two different leadership methodologies according to stated criteria. Two sets of observers recorded (1) quantitative running accounts of social interaction between the five boys and the leader; (2) a continuous stenographic record of the conversation of the six persons in each club; (3) activity subgroupings and activity goals of each; (4) a running account of psychologically interesting interactions in each group; and (5) an account of interclub contacts. The mean percentage of agreement between two investigators categorizing the verbal behavior was 80 per cent. Other data included interview material secured from each club member; interview data from the parents of the boys at the end of the experiment; ratings by parents of a boy's cooperativeness, hobbies, and develop-

mental history; information on the boy filled out by his classroom teacher; and, finally, the results of a Rorschach test given to each child. Analyses were made of the verbal behavior of the six individuals in each club. Their social behavior was analyzed in terms of (1) ascendant, (2) fact-minded, (3) submissive, and (4) ignoring categories.

The social climate resulting from different leadership styles produced significant differences among the several groups in amount of expression of discontent, out-of-group-field conversation, and work-centered conversation. At the same time, it was demonstrated that club personnel (as distinguished from leadership style) produced somewhat less significant differences among the groups in amount of expression of discontent, friendliness, group-mindedness, and out-of-group-field conversation.

Lippitt's major conclusions were (1) that different styles of leader behavior produce differing social climates and differing group and individual behaviors; (2) that conversation categories differentiated leader-behavior techniques more adequately than did social-behavior categories; (3) that different leaders playing the same kind of leadershipy roles displayed very similar patterns of behavior and that group members reacted to the same kind of leadership style in strikingly similar and consistent fashion; (4) that group members in a democratic social climate were more friendly to each other, showed more group-mindedness, were more work-minded, showed greater initiative, and had a higher level of frustration tolerance than members in the other groups; (5) that leader-behavior categories represent the important parameters to which the children reacted.

The significance of Lippitt's work lies in the fact that it is the earliest, major, successful attempt to observe and control objectively the climate variable in group life. Subsequent work in the area has been influenced and helped by his concepts and methodology. His clear demonstration of the influence of the leader on group life and productivity had strong implications for teachers and education.

Subsequent to Lippitt's work, the entire complex or network of relationships in learning groups began to be examined. Such concepts as the socio and psyche group (Jennings, 1947) were offered as one way of organizing the data with which the researcher has to be concerned in understanding social interaction in group situations—whether in the classroom or elsewhere. Jennings conceptualized group life and interaction as fulfilling two major groups of needs of individuals, i.e., (1) the friendship, or psyche, needs and (2) the task or work, or socio, needs. Usually, different social groups serve one of these functions much more adequately and efficiently than the other, though all groups tend to serve both sets of needs to a lesser or greater extent (Thelen, 1960b, pp. 114–121). The bridge club, golf foursome, or recreational group where the individual is prized and accepted for himself and not for his role may be seen as the epitome of the psyche group. Work groups, task-oriented organizations such as medical teams including doctors, nurses, and technicians, and task forces of all kinds, where the individual is prized for the roles or functions he can perform to achieve the group's work goals, constitute socio groups. It appears, however, that the psyche needs of man are pre-eminent, regardless of whatever formal or informal group in which he finds himself, since subgroups to meet individual needs come into being even in the most work-centered situations. Where individuals have similar interests and social-emotional needs which they perceive the other can fulfill, they gravitate to each other as they work on the substantive problem and thus sustain and affirm each other's unique, individual worth apart from their role and responsibilities in the task-centered operation.

The Chicago studies. In the late 1940's, Thelen (1951) and others at the University of Chicago began to capitalize on several streams of thought: Lewin's field theory; the work of Prescott, Havighurst, and Tryon in child study and development; Rogers' client-centered therapy; and group dynamics. They sought to develop a theory of instruction which utilized constructs drawn from child development, field theory, and psychotherapy.

The Chicago research was interdisciplinary and both theoretically and empirically oriented. Hypotheses were derived from analysis of time-lapse pictures, recordings, and observations in the classroom by sensitive and trained educators. The earliest of a train of researches that is still continuing (Flanders, 1959; Thelen, 1959a, 1959b) was that of Withall (1949). In his study, social-emotional climate was treated as a group phenomenon determined primarily by the teacher's verbal behavior taken as representative of her total behavior. He developed an instrument, called the Climate Index, for categorizing and quantifying the verbal behavior of the teacher in any class. The procedure involved making an intensive study and analysis of tape recordings of daily classroom sessions of some junior high school classes. Teacher statements within the context of students' questions, responses, and statements were analyzed. The emotional tone and inferred dominant intent of each teacher verbalization were assessed with considerable care. At first, 25 kinds of teacher statements seemed identifiable, but further analysis of the records showed that the types identified were not mutually exclusive. Thirteen types were then identified. These 13 kinds of statements in turn were consolidated into seven categories. The seven categories into which all teacher verbalizations appeared to fall encompassed statements or questions by the teacher which (1) commended or approved the learner (learner-supportive); (2) conveyed understanding or acceptance of the learner (clarifying or acceptant); (3) gave information to or asked questions of fact vis-à-vis the learner (problem-structuring); (4) comprised "chitchat" and routine administrative items (neutral); (5) limited or controlled the learner's behavior (directive); (6) deprecated or disapproved (disapproving or reproving); (7) defended or supported the teacher (teacher-supportive).

It seemed that the first three categories (1, 2, and 3) could be viewed as learner-supportive and the last three (5, 6, and 7) as teacher-supportive. In categorizing a statement, the categorizer was asked at the outset to determine whether the dominant intent of the statement was to sustain the teacher or the learner. Once the dominant intent had been determined, the decision had to be made as to which one of the first three or last three categories was represented by the statement.

The objectivity and reliability studies involved computing correlations (tetrachoric) between the judgments of five categorizers. The median correlations between categorizers on three discrete samples of data were .84, .76, and .93. Contingency coefficients computed on the same data ranged between .76 and .89. The validation of the instrument involved (1) a comparison of the categorizations of the Climate Index with Anderson's (1946) Integrative-Dominance Ratio secured on the same data; (2) pencil-and-paper assessment of their classroom situation by pupils on the basis of seven standardized questions; and (3) the use of an electrical graph mechanism for recording pupils' positive and negative feelings expressed by their pushing one of two buttons while they were exposed to experimentally varied

"learner-centered" and "teacher-centered" social-emotional climates (Thelen & Withall, 1949).

The development of a Climate Index with demonstrable reliability and validity (see Mitzel & Rabinowitz, 1954) spotlighted several issues for further research. One crucial question was how learning and achievement were influenced in the classroom by the nature and quality of the teacher-pupil interaction. Flanders (1949) undertook an investigation of this problem. Psychological and physiological measures (GSR and heartbeat measures) were made of seven high school students exposed to standardized, 25-minute learning experiences under two experimental climates. The student was placed in two different learning situations having reasonably equivalent learning tasks. The social-emotional differences between the two situations were created by the role of the teacher. In a teacher-centered (TC) situation, the behavior of the teacher tended to support himself first, the problem second, and the student third. As a consequence, it was difficult for the student to operate efficiently in the situation, and, as a result, interpersonal anxieties were created. In a learner-centered (LC) situation, the behavior of the teacher tended to support the student first, the problem second, and the teacher third. As a consequence, the student was able to clarify his position in the structure of the interaction, and his interpersonal anxiety remained within tolerable limits. Thus, an experimental sequence of events was organized which permitted the student to participate in the TC and LC learning sessions, then to distribute 121 statements (Q sort) into 11 categories of student feelings about and perceptions of the teacher with reference to the learning periods just experienced and, finally, to participate in a postlearning interview. Pre- and posttesting of mastery of content and principles to be learned was carried out. With the climate treated as an independent variable, measured by Withall's Climate Index, it was demonstrated that student behavior reflecting interpersonal anxiety took precedence over behavior oriented to the objective problem and learning content. It appeared, too, that demanding, directive, and deprecating teacher behavior vis-à-vis pupils resulted in withdrawal, apathy toward the achievement problem, aggressiveness, and hostility on the part of the pupils. On the other hand, teacher behavior which was oriented to the problem, analytical of student procedures according to publicly stated criteria, and generally learner-centered elicited less interpersonal anxiety, more problem-solving behavior, and a degree of emotional integration.

Rehage (1948), with matched eighth-grade social studies classes, investigated the quality of social interaction in pupil-teacher relationships in the planning stages of classroom work. He also investigated the similarities and dissimilarities in problem-solving and knowledge of the two matched classes. The experimental group planned its own program in social studies problems with particular attention to democratic values and institutions in the nearby community. The plans and activities developed by the experimental group were utilized by the social studies teacher as the program for the control group, which was given no opportunity to participate in planning its program or identifying its goals. In group problem-solving and group planning skill, as well as in flexibility of the network of social relations in the classroom, the differences revealed by the investigation favored the experimental group.

Perkins (1949) investigated the influence of social interaction at the adult level, i.e., with in-service teachers. He compared learner-centered and teacher-centered classes as differentiated by Withall's Cli-

mate Index. The study demonstrated that the variable of learner- versus teacher-centeredness of classroom "climate" makes a remarkable difference in problem-orientation, in attitudes toward other persons, in learning of facts, and in human relations skills. The evidence he cited included the following: as compared with leader-centered groups, study groups in which the leader was learner- or group-centered made markedly superior use of evidence to substantiate their ideas and interpretations of child behavior and gave more evidence of useful insights and sound reasoning. Learner-centered study groups revealed greater objectivity and warmth in their attitudes toward children, whereas leader-centered groups were more conventional and cold. Finally, more child development concepts were expressed in group- or learner-centered climates. All of these findings, based on a content analysis of group members' verbalizations in the in-service study groups, favored the learner-centered groups.

The studies of Glidewell (1951), Singletary (1951), and subsequent co-workers with Thelen in the Human Dynamics Laboratory at the University of Chicago represent a trend toward examining the dynamics of social interaction at the overt level of teachers' and learners' observable behaviors and at the same time trying to relate these behaviors, as observed and interpreted by the "actors" themselves, to the inferred covert dynamics. Glidewell raised the question of how effective a teacher's leadership can be when she denies her own feelings. To answer this he set up controlled group situations involving four experienced role-players and the subject (leader). The group situations were arranged so that both acceptable and unacceptable feelings could be engendered in the leader-subject. It appeared obvious from the analysis of the recorded discussions and the statistical relationship between predictions of ratings and actual ratings by six observers, that "denial of feelings by the leader was accompanied by a reduction of leadership effectiveness; acceptance, by an increase of effectiveness" (p. 126). "The most effective teacher can be seen as one who seeks, through her feelings as one medium, the reality of her own needs and those of her students [the psyche aspect] with an eye toward a need-meeting group learning activity" [the socio aspect] (p. 120). This approach is founded on the view that group processes are geared to the resolution of the psyche (emotional) as well as the socio (problem-solving) needs of the individual and of the total group.

Singletary (1951), by means of interviews and questionnaires directed to administrators and teachers in one school, sought to get at teachers' and administrators' perceptions of pupils and of each other with respect to expectations, demands, group relations, and social organization. The data were assessed for their impact on the interactions and roles of pupils, teachers, and administrators. The findings included the fact that a group's social organization depends on its perceptual consistency. Fundamental differences in perception existed between teachers and administrators regarding the basic expectations that the administrators have for pupils. Teachers and administrators were most consistent in perceiving the things that teachers do which administrators like and dislike, and the things that pupils do that teachers like and dislike.

Thelen and his colleagues went beyond the efforts of Moreno and others who examined the dynamics of groups in terms of the observed behaviors and the stated perceptions of the actors. Thelen drew on the theory-based inferences and hypotheses of an external observer to test the validity of the interpretations and perceptions of the participants in the group. Moreno

managed to demonstrate the complexity of lines of communication and interaction in groups at one level. The Chicago group went ahead to relate the observable complex of interactions—and the interactors' interpretations of those interactions—to theory-based inferences. For instance, teachers' behaviors can be hypothesized to determine to a large extent the quality of the teacher-student interaction and the learning that takes place in an instructional situation. Flanders' (1949) study dealt with this inference, which was based on a developing socio-psychological theory of school learning. From the same theoretical foundations, Rehage's (1948) study assessed the effect of having teachers and learners jointly plan the instructional process and identify goals. Finally, the needs of the teacher in the learning situation would appear to be as pertinent to the learning process as those of the learners, and the teacher's ability to recognize and accept these needs may be hypothesized to have considerable significance for her effectiveness in guiding the pupils' learning. This is the issue to which Glidewell (1951) addressed himself.

A widely applicable system of observation of group interaction was developed by Bales (1950). Although his original intention was to provide a method of analyzing the behavior of small work groups, the categories he used seem appropriate to describe the behavior of a teacher or pupils in a classroom. The recording is done "live," that is, by an observer in the actual situation. The observer takes the point of view of the "generalized other," or recipient of the behavior being recorded. He records every discriminable act of the group members in one of 12 categories: (1) shows solidarity, (2) shows tension release, (3) agrees, (4) gives suggestion, (5) gives opinion, (6) gives orientation, (7) asks for orientation,

(8) asks for opinion, (9) asks for suggestions, (10) disagrees, (11) shows tension, and (12) shows antagonism.

RESEARCH ON SOCIAL INTERACTION IN THE CLASSROOM SINCE 1950

About 1950, a number of statements signaled the beginning of heightened activity in research on social interaction in the classroom. In this section we shall review developments of the past decade, beginning with a review of various programmatic and theoretical statements. Then we shall consider, in turn, research on interpersonal perception in school settings, on social climate, and on teaching styles.

PROGRAMMATIC AND THEORETICAL STATEMENTS

The statement by Thelen and Tyler (1950) that "realization of the very great influence of the classroom group upon individual learning follows from a consideration of the implications of much of the recent research in social psychology" (p. 307) can be regarded as a kind of prologue to the period in which educational research began to capitalize on a view of the classroom group as a social milieu in which learning and instruction occurred. They identified four functional interrelationships between the individual and the group in which the classroom group helps the individual to learn, to progress toward self-realization, to test social concepts and conduct, and to adapt to his culture.

Thelen's (1950) impressive monograph elaborated even more pointedly on concepts and principles that could help in understanding, predicting, and controlling teacher-pupil interaction. The major concepts specified by Thelen were "experiencing" (in the sense of the term used by John Dewey), "interdependence," and "conflict." Conflict he dubbed the "most significant social psychological phenomenon." He offered nine principles to guide the study of classroom teaching and learning. These principles asserted that classroom learning experiences (1) serve to meet the psyche (affective, interpersonal) and socio (achievement) needs of the learner; (2) have potency for the learner to the extent they help him meet his needs; (3) deal with the basic problem of learning the experimental method; (4) when structured and planned, provide goals and limits for the learner; (5) are highly susceptible to anxiety pressures arising from interpersonal conflict; (6) are only a fraction of the total life of the learner; (7) can provide reinforcement to the culturally approved sides of student ambivalence; (8) can best be guided through an assessment of group affect and group problems; and (9) will be most effective when governed by the "Principle of Least Group Size" (see Thelen, 1949). These papers emphasized the need to examine and understand the individual learner's frame of reference within the context of the group values and pressures in the classroom situation. This understanding requires the development by the teacher of ability to hypothesize the internal frame of reference of each learner (a kind of "empathy" or interpersonal perception), and to ascertain how she can use group forces and group problem-solving mechanisms to bring about learning.

These kinds of analyses of educational processes from the vantage point of research in social psychology led into a kind of three-dimensional investigation of (1) the teacher's actual behaviors in the classroom and her comprehension of the learners' self and social perceptions, (2) the learners' perceptions of the instructional activities, and (3) the group-life context in which the teacher and learner interacted. This view added up to a much more complex process than had heretofore been spelled out. Classroom processes comprised a much more dynamic interaction of learner and teacher, along with content to be learned and the over-all learning environment, including the material resources (books, films, pictures, and audio-visual aids) and the human resources.

Cunningham and her associates (1951) attempted to tie up a whole series of insights in one neat bundle. The authors related the curriculum—defined as meaningful experiences for the learners—to the group interaction process in the classroom which determines the development of social skills, creativity, democratic skills, and subject-matter mastery. The development of these outcomes is governed in turn by the learner's desire for maximum individual development and for the development of social interaction skills. Cunningham and her associates, viewing all learning as problem-solving, believed the teacher can best fulfill her function in the classroom group as a skilled practitioner of evocative leadership. The teacher would help learners to identify common goals, common values, and roles of members, and also to develop institutionalized methods of problem-solving and evaluating goal achievement.

Jenkins (1951) pointed up the interdependent nature of the pupil-teacher relationship by asserting that learning will be more effective not only when the pupil's emotional needs are met in the classroom, but also when learners are made aware of their part in helping teachers fulfill some of the teachers' legitimate emotional needs in the classroom, e.g., the needs to become more effective in fulfilling their professional responsibilities and to achieve a sense of adequacy and worthwhileness.

Wright, Barker, Nall, and Schoggen (1951) delineated the rationale of a some-

what different research. They urged the value of field observations of teachers and learners in identifying the "psychological habitat" of each person, so that better prediction and control of the learning process might be assured. They indicated that "an adequate psychological ecology of the classroom must describe the psychological habitats that *are* brought about in this setting and the particular behaviors which these habitats engender" (p. 190). As a beginning point for spelling out the psychological ecology of a classroom, they suggested keeping an anecdotal record which would give a naturalistic description of a child's behavior in the learning process. In addition to behavior episodes such as making a May basket, drawing a picture on the chalkboard, and listening to the teacher telling a story, the raw behaviors observed in a classroom would be noted, ordered, and categorized. Furthermore, if behavior categories within these episodes such as direction of action, form of interpersonal activity, and outcome of action are developed, then the task of assessing, analyzing, and predicting classroom behavior will be facilitated. Data on "Raymond" were cited to demonstrate how a description of this child's psychological habitat in the classroom could be used to interpret and predict his overt behaviors in the instructional situation.

Jensen (1955) formulated a rationale for assessing the social structure of the classroom which sums up one aspect of the methods of analyzing classroom interaction. He specified the needs of class members as individuals and as group members. Like Thelen, he emphasized the close interdependence of personal needs and group needs, and the fact that fulfillment of the one kind depends directly on the satisfaction of needs of the other kind. Individuals in the learning situation have to help ensure the satisfaction and resolution of group needs if their private personal needs are to be met optimally.

Furthermore, unless individuals are relating effectively to one another in a class, the achievement, or socio, problems cannot be dealt with.

Jensen identified seven dimensions of interaction (problem-solving, authority-leadership, power, friendship, personal prestige, sex, and privilege) under which the two problems of group productivity and group cohesiveness fall. These "dimensions" are conceptualizations of critical variables which must be taken into consideration in developing an effective learning situation. For example, the authority-leadership dimension focuses attention on the importance of how decisions are arrived at—what the task goals will be, who will carry out different parts of the assignment, and how the work is to be evaluated. An adequate description of any of these activities, however, should take into consideration other dimensions, such as power, for an individual's ideas must be attractive to other members of the group if he is to have a role in group decision-making, and this attractiveness is dependent upon the others' regarding him as having superior resources or ability. Jensen suggested:

> The conceptual framework also indicates to the practitioner that the productivity of a class, the achievement of its members as individuals, and the member-satisfaction with life in the class is a function of the relationships within and between the seven different dimensions. This is "how" a classroom group must be conceived in order to analyze or diagnose effectively the conditions that upset class productivity and class cohesiveness (Jensen, 1955, p. 374).

In evidencing concern with the public, or socio, problems of the classroom group, and the psyche, or interpersonal relationship, problems of the group, Jensen focused the attention of teachers on two dimensions of the situation with which they inevitably have to concern themselves.

Trow (1960a), in the third edition of the *Encyclopedia of Educational Research* and elsewhere (Trow, Zander, Morse, & Jenkins, 1950; Trow, 1960b), set forth the group dynamics rationale for group process in education. He distinguished a group from a mere collection of human beings in one place, in that the latter, although it may have some qualities in common, has no genuine interaction. A group, on the other hand, is characterized by the interaction of its members in such a way that each person is changed by the group and changes as the group changes. A collection of individuals becomes a group as members accept a common purpose, become interdependent in implementation of this purpose, and interact with one another to promote its accomplishment—whether that purpose be to get a car out of a mudhole, or to organize a lobby, or to fulfill individual needs. Trow discussed group climate, autocratic versus democratic control, the questions of group morale and group structure, the importance of position and role, and the nature of various roles in a group. His discussion of leadership goes into the question of power relationships, where the superior-subordinate relationship of teacher to learner is emphasized. In describing the roles teachers are expected to fulfill, Trow mentions "therapist," "controller," "democratic strategist," and "instructor." The controversial nature of the therapeutic role is brought out, while the general acceptance of the appropriateness of the other roles is noted.

INTERPERSONAL PERCEPTIONS OF TEACHERS AND STUDENTS

The postwar *zeitgeist* in social psychology and perception made it seem almost inevitable that research workers would turn to interpersonal perception as a realm of phenomena in which to seek improved understanding of social interaction in the classroom.

The study by Jenkins and Lippitt (1951) of teachers', students', and parents' interpersonal perceptions took a naturalistic, descriptive approach resembling somewhat that of the psychological ecologists. They asked all three groups in one community a series of open-ended questions about "What do (teachers, parents, pupils) do that you (parents, pupils, teachers) like (or dislike)?" Coding and tabulating the replies made it possible to describe how each group saw the school setting through the eyes of the others. There was no attempt in this study to measure "variables" such as accuracy of interpersonal perception, or to relate these to other variables such as effectiveness in interpersonal relations. The Jenkins-Lippitt study was a piece of "action research," in tune with the times, with only limited and modest theoretical pretensions.

In contrast, Gage and Suci (1951) sought to determine the accuracy of the teachers' perceptions of pupils' attitudes as one variable in the intricate dynamic interactions of teachers and learners. They tested the hypothesis that teachers who perceive their pupils' attitudes more accurately will be regarded more favorably by their pupils. They asked 20 teachers to estimate the percentage of 200 pupils in a small high school who would respond affirmatively to a set of opinion items. The items had to do with scholastic, recreational, and student government issues. In addition, they used a preliminary form of the Minnesota Teacher Attitude Inventory. Their conclusion was that a teacher's accuracy of social perception was positively related ($r = .50$) to the pupils' mean favorability toward the teacher.

A study by Bush (1954) was involved with interpersonal "knowledge" as well as many other variables. Working in several schools with a total of over 650 students, he measured the amount of

knowledge about the pupils possessed by the teachers and found no direct linear relationship between such knowledge and satisfactoriness of interpersonal interactions between teachers and pupils. He also assessed teacher-pupil relationships on the dimension of liking for each other by pupil and teacher and found little significant relationship in the mutuality of such liking. The correlation between the teacher's liking for the pupil and the pupil's liking for the teacher was .28 for 150 cases at School A, and .25 for 500 cases of Schools B and C. Yet, it seemed reasonable to Bush to assume that pupils must like teachers if they are to learn most effectively.

Bush's study raised important questions about the dimensions of teacher-learner compatibility that influence the learning process, the kinds of information the teacher ought to possess about individual learners, and the legitimacy of expecting the teacher to be all things to all students. The study also identified some factors that may be relevant to the teacher-pupil relationship: the teacher's and learner's selective knowledge about each other, the manner in which the teacher fulfills her leadership role, the teacher's own appraisal of her effectiveness with the learners, and the student's need for a balance between freedom and limits in the learning situation.

Whether interpersonal perception, and variables derived from it, has implications for teaching is still questionable. Gage's review (1958) of his own varied approaches in the search for such implications yields an impression of unfulfilled promise in this area.

> Our own negative results should cause us to look more closely at what we mean by "understanding of pupils." Such understanding is a basic objective of teacher education curricula.... It is indeed highly plausible as a desideratum for teachers. Yet up to now, in our

own...and in others' research, support for this proposition has been hard to come by (Gage, 1958, pp. 100–101).

SOCIOMETRY IN THE CLASSROOM

The general utility of sociometric assessments by the classroom teacher as a means of enhancing pupil growth is persuasively presented by Gronlund (1959), whose book is primarily intended as a practical manual for classroom teachers. But one major section of the book is devoted to an extended review and interpretation of the literature on the reliability and validity of sociometric choices and the relationship of these choices to personal and social factors. The conception of classroom learning as an interactional process involving the reciprocal interplay of person upon person is reflected in studies of the significance of sociometry and sociodrama for teacher-pupil rapport (Dysart, 1952).

Just how sociometric differentials arise in the classroom has not been as well studied as the differences in status themselves. It is plausible that the teacher helps determine which pupils become over- and under-chosen by their peers. But how does the teacher do this? Withall's study (1956) shed some light on the process. He offered, at a rather specific level, objective evidence, through the use of time-lapse photography, concerning a way of measuring teacher-pupil interaction in terms of the proximity of learners to the teacher, i.e., in terms of whether the learner was within a 36-inch radius and facing toward the teacher. It seemed that within the limits of this approach there were gross variations in the amount of attention bestowed on each learner by the teacher. More interesting still, it was extremely difficult —even after the teacher had been alerted to the discrepancies in attention she gave to differing pupils—for her to redistribute her attention in the light of the inferred needs of each learner.

In a study on a similar phenomenon, Polansky (1954) examined eight classrooms in terms of the group social climate and the teacher's supportiveness of group status systems. Using the Wrightstone "Pupil-Teacher Rapport" scale and the learner-supportive, teacher-supportive, and neutral categories of the Withall Climate Index, she found that teachers in "good climate" classrooms supported the group status system, whereas teachers in "poor climate" classrooms did not.

If the pupil's acceptance by his peers depends in part on the amount and kind of attention he receives from the teacher, and if that attention varies with different pupils, it is reasonable to suppose that the teacher's values should be related to sociometric status. Among other things, what the teacher values, it is safe to assume, is the pupils' achievement of the objectives of schooling. At this point of the argument, a study of relationships between achievement and sociometric status becomes relevant. Buswell (1953) used a population of 300 fifth-grade pupils and a number of standardized tests including the Stanford-Binet, the Iowa Test of Basic Skills, the Ohio Social Acceptance Scale, and a sociometric test of best-liked peers to find out whether there was any relationship between how a learner performs intellectually in class and his relationships with his peers. The highly accepted group, as identified and perceived by their peers, were significantly higher than the rejected group in mean achievement. It appeared that achievement is related to social acceptability and, in fact, that acceptability by peers is founded in many instances on the learner's achievement.

Interpupil relationships are significant not only to a pupil's social adjustment but also to his achievement of skills in working with others. Such skills have long been upheld as important objectives of education for living in a democracy. Until recently, however, no convenient and standardized method was available for measuring the achievement of such objectives by a classroom group. With considerable ingenuity, Damrin (1959) has remedied this lack. Her Russell Sage Social Relations Test, intended to measure the competence of elementary school pupils in group planning and group work, provides three construction-type problems with miniature blocks. The problems are given in turn to the small subgroups that are set up within a classroom. The task involves a Planning Stage, in which the group decides how it is going to construct the figure, and an Operations Stage, in which the figure is constructed. No time limit is set on the planning period; a 15-minute limit is allowed for the implementation session. During both the Planning and Operations Stages and observer keeps a record of behavior, using standardized observation sheets.

Seven types of groups have been identified by Damrin through studying the learners at work during the Planning Stage. These groups have been labeled (1) mature, (2) dependent, (3) immature, (4) semicontrolled, (5) semirestrained, (6) uncontrolled, (7) restrained. Nine types of groups have been identified in the Operations Stage: (1) mature, (2) immature, (3) disinterested, (4) rollicking, (5) excited, (6) rowdy, (7) suppressed, (8) bickering, (9) quarreling. The promise of the instrument lies in the fact that it draws on socio-psychological concepts and focuses on specific, observable learner behaviors in the classroom setting.

Teacher-Centered versus Learner-Centered Instruction

One recurrent theme in much research on social interaction has been the differential effects of conducting classroom work in teacher-centered and learner-centered styles. The teacher-centered style is typically defined as one in which the teacher does most, by far, of the talking, directing, explaining, goal-setting, assignment-making, and evaluation. In the learner-centered style, these activities are all permitted by the teacher to devolve to a far greater extent upon the learners. Although terminology and various details of execution have varied, a number of significant studies in this tradition have enough in common to bear examination as a group. We turn now to such studies, representative of many others.

In a study that sought to point up the value of taking into consideration the emotional and intellectual needs of college students, Wispé (1951) provided either directiveness or permissiveness according to the needs and expectations of the students. He selected eight instructors who utilized one of two styles of teaching, i.e., directive or permissive. The instructors, selected on the basis of "what came naturally" to them, were given training to sharpen up these teaching proclivities. Eight sections of 20 students each were organized, matched in terms of a pretest on content mastery, Scholastic Aptitude Test (SAT) scores, secondary school background, and year in college. The course was an elementary one in social relations. The end-of-semester tests included (1) a TAT-type test using pictures of teaching situations; (2) Stein's Sentence Completion Test; (3) a 25-item questionnaire on attitude toward sections, on interests, and on feelings of students in sections; (4) a three-hour final examination, containing both essay and multiple-choice items. It appeared that the majority of the students preferred the directive sections, and that the teaching styles had no effect on the final examination scores of the brighter (high SAT score) students, whereas the less able students did better in the directive sections. Wispé identified three types of students through analysis of their questionnaire responses: (1) a want-more-direction group, (2) a want-more-permissiveness group, and (3) a satisfied group. He was interested in the intensity of the desires for either directiveness or permissiveness and noted that one-third of those already receiving directive teaching wanted more directiveness, and one-third of those already in the permissive teaching sections indicated a desire for more permissiveness. One of his major conclusions was that students who do less well on the SAT benefit more from directive-type teaching. To Wispé, this indicated that the student's emotional and intellectual needs should be taken into consideration in determining the kind of instruction he is to receive.

In a similar study of the interaction between teaching style and student intelligence, Calvin, Hoffman, and Harden (1957), although modest in their claims, found indications that the mere creation of a permissive climate is not a sufficient, though it may be a necessary, condition of more effective teaching and group problem-solving. Their research, somewhat similar in direction to Wispé's, indicated that permissiveness with individuals of high intelligence yielded better learning than did a traditional teaching-learning situation with bright students or a permissive situation with average students. In fact, the permissive situation tended to handicap subjects with average intelligence.

In a study by Maier and Maier (1957), small groups of college students were placed in "permissive" and "developmental" group problem-solving situations. (In the latter, the leader helped the group break down the problem into subparts.) A significant difference was obtained between the two groups; 40 per cent of the "developmental" discussion

groups reached high-quality decisions as against 19 per cent of the "free" or "permissive" groups.

Haigh and Schmidt (1956) concerned themselves with a similar question, How much subject matter is mastered by learners in so-called teacher-centered and group-centered classes? The students were placed in the teacher-centered and group-centered sections on the basis of stated preferences, and the amount of subject matter learned was assessed. The students in the group-centered class did not derive their grade from a final examination, although they and the control group were both given the Horrocks-Troyer test on knowledge of facts and principles in adolescent development. There was no significant difference between the two classes in knowledge of subject matter.

In an experiment on attitude change as a function of teaching by these two socially different styles, McKeachie (1954) assessed the conformity of individuals to the attitudes and norms of their classroom groups. He set up six sections comprising 25–35 undergraduates each and had each of three instructors teach two sections, each by a different method: leader-centered and group-centered. The hypothesis was that the individual tends to adopt attitudes corresponding to those of the group with which he is currently associated or identified. McKeachie suggested that certain attitudes learned in key primary groups, such as the family, are not easily superseded by attitudes espoused by a classroom group. Congruence of perceptions of group standards and values was *not* consistently higher in liked class groups than in nonliked groups. He explained this by pointing out that, in liked groups, a higher degree of rapport permitted verbalized disagreement to be accepted, encouraged, and sustained more readily than in nonliked groups, where pressure was applied to ensure greater conformity of all members to the same norms and attitudes.

In a report of work altogether non-experimental in any rigorous sense, but rather clinical, anecdotal, and observational, Moustakas (1956) started with the proposition that the most effective learning occurs in the educational situation where threat to the learner's self is minimal. He proceeded to indicate, by descriptions of specific teachers and their methods of relating to children, the kinds of teacher behavior that he judged necessary for learning and growth. To him, the resulting interpersonal relationship was one

> where there was freedom of expression within the limits of the classroom, where each person could state himself in terms of himself without fear of criticism or condemnation, where feelings were expressed and explored, where ideas and creative thinking were treasured, and where growth of self was the most important value (Moustakas, 1956, p. 259).

To make operational this global conception of the conditions of teacher-learner interaction which were most conducive to learning and development, Moustakas narrated the ways in which the teachers he observed implemented these ideas. He described (pp. 110–120) an "experiment" intended to help second-grade youngsters face and express their feelings openly. To introduce them to the procedure, the teacher invited the children in her class to discuss some of their common feelings. The youngsters tended to dwell in this discussion on "anger." "Constructive" ways of expressing angry feelings were identified.

Later he arranged a number of sessions in which both structured and unstructured procedures were used. During the structured periods, directions were given by the teacher and all the children did the same thing. During the unstruc-

tured sessions, the children were told "to do as they pleased" as long as they were fairly quiet and did not bother one another or children in other rooms. On these occasions they tended to talk with the teacher or told about pictures they were encouraged to draw. The teacher showed interest in and complete acceptance of what the children were doing and saying. Of the 26 children involved in the study, 14 followed a definite pattern, such as drawing and talking about fighting and war, and adhered to it throughout. Seven of them said little at first but were quite vocal at the end of the experience and revealed their feelings and attitudes quite clearly. Five children, after drawing their pictures, described them without expressing much feeling. We are told that the angry and unsettled youngsters tended to reflect these qualities in their pictures and stories.

Moustakas emphasized that many of these children were aggressive and unsettled. This program, he felt, provided an acceptable outlet for their hostility, enabled the children to understand that it helps to express one's feelings even in imagination and fantasy, and thus reduced their impulse to act out tensions in everyday life.

At the high school level, Moustakas reported (pp. 202–204) on a program which a teacher carried out with a group of 30 twelfth-grade students. The class met twice a week for one hour over a period of one semester. The teacher told the group that they were free to present any concepts, ideas, and problems for discussion. A number of problems in human relationships including dating, petting, early marriage, child-rearing, parental authority, and independence were discussed. The teacher asked each member of the class to keep a journal of his reactions to the sessions, and explained that the journal need not, but could, be turned in to her.

Toward the end of the semester the

teacher gave the group an opportunity to write a paper exploring personal experience. No one was required to write the paper but every student decided to, and each turned it in to the teacher. The teacher "felt that the explorations showed considerable growth in self-understanding on the part of several members of the group" (p. 204).

THE SOCIAL-INTERACTION VIEW OF CLASSROOM PROCESSES

Until very recently, the approach to the analysis of teacher-pupil and pupil-pupil interaction in the learning situation was that of examining and quantifying certain "monadic" variables, such as the teacher's training and experience, the learners' socioeconomic status and intellectual capacities, the goals of the school and community, and the materials provided to help achieve those goals. The examination of such variables has tended to be unrewarding and sterile. Researchers thus tried to examine social processes and interactions through static means. It was long believed that if we manipulated one or two variables, we would create conditions that would ensure both predictability and control of the quality and type of learning. Much experience has shown that this expectation is unsupported, that variables in the learning situation interact with each other in kaleidoscopic complexity, and that specification of the interactions and outcomes is extremely difficult.

We have known for a long time (but have not accepted the implications of this knowledge) that groups of learners are vehicles for fulfilling the personal goals and needs of the learners—not to mention those of the teachers (Jenkins, 1951)—as well as for ensuring attainment of content-mastery goals. In recent years we have begun to examine the group forces in the instructional situation that mediate fulfill-

ment of both cognitive and affective needs.

Along with this trend has emerged the realization that examination of these phenomena requires a rationale and instrumentation adequate to the "motility" of the data being treated. Getzels and Thelen (1960) describe the image of the classroom that should guide our research:

> It is not the image of a social system in equilibrium. It is rather the image of a system in motion or, if you will, in dynamic disequilibrium. It is the image of a group continually facing emergent complexity and conflict (if not confusion) and dealing with these realities, not in terms of sentiment but in terms of what the complexity and conflict suggest about the modifications that have to be made in the goals, expectations, needs, and selective perceptions of the teachers and learners. It is through this experience of recognizing and dealing with complexity, conflict and change in the classroom situation that we can educate children to take their places as creative and autonomous participants in the other social systems that constitute the larger social order (Getzels & Thelen, 1960, p. 82).

Jensen (1960) has pointed out that the way a group is organized derives from the efforts of members of the group (1) to develop need-meeting relationships with others and (2) to establish working relationships necessary for the attainment of work goals. The result of the interrelationship of the need-meeting and work-doing activities seems to be a gratification-deprivation ratio which makes it possible for the needs of some members to be met and prevents the needs of others from being met. In Jensen's view, this situation has significance for the whole matter of motivation, progress, individual achievement, class morale, and discipline.

Jenkins (1960) delineated areas of conflict that emerge as the individuals in a class work toward achievement of both subject-matter mastery and personal goals. He also offered principles for the resolution of these conflicts including the following: The teacher should (1) accept the full responsibilty that devolves upon him because of the power and authority the school and community vest in him; (2) define, with the class, the authority and behavioral limits that will guide both his and the learners' activities; (3) permit decision-making by the students within predefined limits; (4) be open to influence by the students so as to be amenable, within mutually defined and acceptable limits, to their point of view. If these things are done by the teacher, Jenkins argued, the full potential of group forces in the classroom can be harnessed to enhance both the fulfillment of personal needs and the mastery of subject matter.

It would seem, however, that we need to look beyond this objective of mastery of subject matter to the development of the skills of problem-solving and inquiry. Thelen (1960a) has outlined the general procedures required for modern education, including (1) relating learning activities to the developmental processes of learners and to their current and immediate interests and needs, and (2) utilizing evaluation procedures that support rather than contradict our efforts to develop democratic individuals skilled in cooperative activity, question-raising, and problem-solving.

Much of the early research on classroom learning was set in the stark framework of the given conditions in an educational situation. Given a group of children with standard physical, intellectual, and psychological equipment, and given some subject-matter content, what are the characteristics of the teacher who can effectively arrange a meeting of the two? Research effort was directed toward identifying the traits, skills, and personal qualities needed by teachers, toward iden-

tifying the instructional procedures, motivational techniques, and disciplinary methods to be used, and toward finding correlates of effective instruction in such extra-class variables as marital status, age, and experience. It seems that the researchers of the 1920's and the mid-1930's sought to analyze the process of teaching in terms of the conditions brought to it by the teacher as a professional worker. She was presumed to be devoid of any personal needs, purposes, or idiosyncrasies. The other actors in the classroom, i.e., the learners, were even more taken for granted. The independent variables were the teacher's skills, abilities, and traits; the dependent variables were the pupils' learnings.

At the other end of the channel lay the goals of education. These objectives were relatively fixed and predetermined without regard for differences among individual learners in physiological organization, family background, and community resources. The conditions represented by teacher competencies have been manipulated to see which ones produce specified educational outcomes most efficiently, usually in the language of achievement tests. The identification or construction of satisfactory criteria of teacher effectiveness has been a persistent problem, but it is, of course, primarily a question of values rather than one to be resolved by empirical research. In any event, supervisors' ratings, students' opinions, and psychometric assessments all have, in their own way, shortcomings as serious as those of achievement tests in the evaluation of teaching.

A way out of the single-criterion impasse has been suggested by the combined influence of the mental health and group dynamics viewpoints. In both these points of view, attention is focused on complicated patterns of interaction and molar concepts of influence, rather than single indices of effectiveness, such as the mean reading achievement of children in a classroom. The studies on experimentally induced social climate (Lewin, Lippitt, & Escalona, 1940) provide an example of a more molar approach to the assessment of group-life phenomena. Procedures for analyzing the patterns of interactive process in the classroom have been slowly developed and utilized. The problems indicated here may stem, in part, from the harnessing of educational activity to predetermined educational objectives used to guide classroom instruction at all levels, and from the ambiguity with which such objectives must be surrounded in order to be applicable to millions of children of varying ages and abilities.

Some consistent trends can be discerned in the pattern of research reported in this chapter. With some misgivings, we may project these trends to form expectations as to the directions that future research will take. Some of the most significant of these trends seem to come under the rubric of philosophy of science, the rules for formulating questions and finding answers. Operationism, with its procedures for defining sets of theoretical constructs, has had an impact on educational research, just as it has influenced research in other social sciences. One important ramification of this impact is the slow abandonment of the search for a "philosopher's stone" of teacher effectiveness. Although the research pattern of establishing a single, easily measured criterion of effectiveness has been persistent, it is gradually being replaced by a more complicated construct-making approach to multiple criteria (see Jahoda, 1958). Instead of assuming that some effectiveness criterion would be available if one were only clever enough to discover it, current research tends to lower its sights to less evaluative concepts, such as classroom control, communication patterns

(Withall, 1962), achievement of specified goals, and so on. These concepts most often serve as summaries for several kinds of behaviors, or conversely, several different kinds of behaviors serve as operations defining the concepts. In either event, the concepts in current use are less abstract and are pointed more directly toward behavioral referents; research workers are less likely to ask an observer to make a global judgment about the effectiveness of the teacher. Rather, they now ask him to record physical movement of the teacher in the room or the dominant intent of individual statements of teachers (see Lewis, Newell, & Withall, 1961) and children, and to relate these operations to an organizing concept like classroom control or climate.

Accompanying the change away from the single-criterion study has been a change in conceptualizing the significance of behavior in the classroom. Earlier studies attempted to isolate qualities or traits of a relatively permanent nature in the teacher's personality or conduct that would hold regardless of the group with whom she was working. More recently, what happens in the classroom has been viewed more as a function of a constellation of factors, not all of which reside in the teacher, and as part of some kind of overall change process rather than as a permanent cause-and-effect relationship. A study of classroom control, for example, would probably not be conceived in terms of permissiveness or punitiveness of the teacher, but in terms of some complex pattern of inferences regarding initiation of a sequence of behavior by the teacher, responses by her students to her cues, and so on to the end of the sequence. The inferences made would probably not include generalizations to all of her teaching behavior, e.g., "She is a permissive teacher," but attempt to specify under what circumstances she is permissive and under what circumstances she may be controlling or punitive.

These brief references to current concerns suggest that future research on social interaction in the classroom may give increasing attention to careful development of theories of the classroom interaction as a dynamic process in which the teacher is an important participant but is not the total determiner of the outcomes of learning. The theories, taking the lead from group dynamics studies, may be miniature systems rather than attempts to encompass all behavior, and may contain sets of related concepts referring directly to behavioral events defined in the language of operations performed by participants in or observers of a process. What the content of these theoretical systems will be, we can only guess, but prevailing interest in applying concepts from group dynamics, social psychology, psychotherapy, and information theory to classroom interaction suggests a general direction that may be taken by research on teaching in the immediate future.

REFERENCES

ANDERSON, H. H., & BREWER, HELEN M. Studies of teachers' classroom personalities. I. Dominative and socially integrative behavior of kindergarten teachers. *Appl. Psychol. Monogr.*, 1945. No. 6.

ANDERSON, H. H., & BREWER, J. E. Studies of teachers' classroom personalities. II. Effects of teachers' dominative and integrative contacts on children's classroom behavior. *Appl. Psychol. Monogr.*, 1946, No. 8.

ANDERSON, H. H., BREWER, J. E., & REED, MARY F. Studies of teachers' classroom personalities. III. Follow-up studies of the effects of dominative and integrative contacts on children's behavior. *Appl. Psychol. Monogr.*, 1946, No. 11.

BALES, R. F., *Interaction process analysis.* Cambridge, Mass.: Addison-Wesley, 1950.

BARKER, R. G. KOUNIN, J. S., & WRIGHT, H. R. (Eds.) *Child behavior and development: A course of representative studies.* New York: McGraw-Hill, 1943.

BARR, A. S. The measurement of teaching ability. *J. educ. Res.*, 1935, 28, 561–569.

BLAIR, A. W. Social and personal integration during later childhood. Unpublished doctoral dissertation, Harvard Univer., 1946.

BLOS, P. *The adolescent personality: A study of individual behavior.* New York: Appleton-Century, 1941.

BONNEY, M. E. Sociometric study of agreement between teacher judgments and student choices: In regard to the numbers of friends possessed by high school students, *Sociometry*, 1947, 10, 133–146.

BROOKOVER, W. B. Person-person interaction between teachers and pupils and teaching effectiveness. *J. educ. Res.*, 1940, 34, 272–287.

BRYAN, R. C. A study of student ratings of college and secondary-school teachers. *Educ. Admin. Superv.*, 1933, 19, 290–307.

BURRELL, ANNA P. Facilitating learning through emphasis on meeting children's basic emotional needs. *J. educ. Sociol.*, 1951, 24, 381–393.

BUSH, R. N. A study of student-teacher relationships. *J. educ. Res.*, 1942, 35, 645–656.

BUSH, R. N. *The teacher-pupil relationship.* New York: Prentice-Hall, 1954.

BUSWELL, MARGARET M. The relationship between the social structure of the classroom and the academic success of the pupils. *J. exp. Educ.*, 1953, 22, 37–52.

Calvin, A. D., Hoffman, F. K., & Harden, E. L. The effect of intelligence and social atmosphere on group problem solving behavior. *J. soc. Psychol.*, 1957, 45, 61–74.

Cronbach, L. J. Proposals leading to analytic treatment of social perception scores. In R. Tagiuri & L. Petrullo (Eds.), *Person perception and interpersonal behavior.* Stanford, Calif.: Stanford Univer. Press, 1958. Pp. 353–379.

Cunningham, Ruth, & Associates. *Understanding group behavior of boys and girls.* New York: Bur. of Publs., Teachers Coll., Columbia Univer., 1951.

Damrin, Dora E. The Russell Sage Social Relations Test: A technique for measuring group problem-solving skills in elementary school children. *J. exp. Educ.*, 1959, 28, 85–99.

Dearborn, W. F., & Rothney, J. W. M. *Predicting the child's development.* Cambridge, Mass.: Sci-Art Press, 1941.

Division on Child Development and Teacher Personnel, Commission on Teacher Education. *Helping teachers understand children.* Washington, D.C.: American Council on Education, 1945.

Dollard, J. *Caste and class in a southern town.* New Haven, Conn.: Yale Univer. Press. 1937.

Dysart, J. M. A study of the effect of in-service training in sociometry and sociodrama on teacher-pupil rapport and social climate in the classroom. Unpublished doctoral dissertation, New York Univer., 1952.

English, H. B., & English, Ava C. *A comprehensive dictionary of psychological and psychoanalytical terms.* New York: Longmans, Green, 1958.

Flanders, N. A. Personal-social anxiety as a factor in learning. Unpublished doctoral dissertation, Univer. of Chicago, 1949.

Flanders, N. A. Teacher-pupil contacts and mental hygiene. *J. soc. Issues*, 1959, 15, 30–39.

Gage, N. L. Explorations in teachers' perceptions of pupils. *J. teacher Educ.*, 1958, 9, 97–101.

Gage, N. L., & Cronbach, L. J. Conceptual and methodological problems in interpersonal perception. *Psychol. Rev.*, 1955, 62, 411–422.

Gage, N. L., & Suci, G. J. Social perception and teacher-pupil relationships. *J. educ. Psychol.*, 1951, 42, 144–152.

Getzels, J. W., & Thelen, H. A. The classroom group as a unique social system. In N. B. Henry (Ed.), *Yearb. nat. Soc. Stud. Educ.*, 1960, 59, Part II, 53–82.

Glidewell, J. C. The teacher's feelings as an educational resource. *J. educ. Res.*, 1951, 45, 119–126.

Glidewell, J. C. (Ed.) Mental health in the classroom. *J. soc. Issues*, 1959, 15, No. 1.

Gronlund, N. E. *Sociometry in the classroom,* New York: Harper, 1959.

Haigh, G. V., & Schmidt, W. The learning of subject-matter in teacher-centered and group-centered classes. *J. educ. Psychol.*, 1956, 47, 295–301.

Henry, N. B. (Ed.) The dynamics of instructional groups. *Yearb. nat. Soc. Stud. Educ.*, 1960, 59, Part II.

Hollingshead, A. B. *Elmtown's youth.* New York: Wiley, 1949.

Jahoda, Marie. *Current concepts of positive mental health.* New York: Basic Books, 1958.

James, H. W. Cause of teacher failure in Alabama. *Peabody J. Educ.*, 1930, 7, 269–271.

Jenkins, D. H. Interdependence in the classroom. *J. educ. Res.*, 1951, 45, 137–144.

Jenkins, D. H. Characteristics and functions of leadership in instructional groups. In N. B. Henry (Ed.), *Yearb. nat. Soc. Stud. Educ.*, 1960, 59, Part II, 164–184.

JENKINS, D. H., & LIPPITT, R. *Interpersonal perceptions of teachers, students, and parents.* Washington, D.C.: Division of Adult Education, National Education Association, 1951.

JENNINGS, HELEN H. Leadership and sociometric choice. *Sociometry,* 1947, 10, 32–39.

JENNINGS, HELEN H. Using children's social relations for learning. *J. educ. Sociol.,* 1948, 21, 543–552.

JENSEN, G. E. The social structure of the classroom group: An observational framework. *J. educ. Psychol.,* 1955, 46, 362–374.

JENSEN, G. E. The sociopsychological structure of the instructional group. In N. B. HENRY (Ed.), *Yearb. nat. Soc. Stud. Educ.,* 1960, 59, Part II, 83–114.

JERSILD, A. T., & HOLMES, F. B. Characteristics of teachers who are "liked best" and "disliked most." *J. exp. Educ.,* 1940, 9, 139–151.

JERSILD, A. T., THORNDIKE, R. L., GOLDMAN, B., & LOFTUS, J. J. An evaluation of aspects of the activity program in the New York City public elementary schools. *J. exp. Educ.,* 1939, 8, 166–207.

JOHNSON, MARGUERITE W. The influence of verbal directions on behavior. *Child Devlpm.,* 1935, 6, 196–204.

JONES, H. E., CONRAD, H. S., & MURPHY, LOIS B. Emotional and social development and the educative process. In G. M. WHIPPLE (Ed.), *Yearb. nat. Soc. Stud. Educ.,* 1939, 38, Part I, 361–389.

KOUNIN, J. S., & GUMP, P. V. The ripple effect in discipline. *Elem. sch. J.,* 1958, 59, 158–162.

KOUNIN, J. S., & GUMP, P. V. The comparative influence of punitive and non-punitive teachers upon children's concepts of school misconduct. *J. educ. Psychol.,* 1961, 52, 44–49.

LEEDS, C. H., & COOK, W. W. The construction and differential value of a scale for determining teacher-pupil attitudes. *J. exp. Educ.,* 1947, 16, 149–159.

LEONARD, J. P., & EURICH, A. C. *Evaluation of modern education.* New York: Appleton-Century, 1942.

LEWIN, K., LIPPITT, R., & ESCALONA, SIBYLLE K. Studies in topological and vector psychology. *Univer. Iowa Stud. Child Welf.,* 1940, 16, No. 3.

LEWIN, K., LIPPITT, R., & WHITE, R. K. Patterns of aggressive behavior in experimentally created social climates. *J. soc. Psychol.,* 1939, 10, 271–299.

LEWIS, W. W., NEWELL, J. M., & WITHALL, J. An analysis of classroom patterns of communication. *Psychol. Rep.,* 1961, 9, 211–219.

LIPPITT, R. An experimental study of the effect of democratic and authoritarian group atmospheres. Studies in topological and vector psychology. *Univer. Iowa Stud. Child Welf.,* 1940, 16, No. 3. 43–195.

MAIER, N. R. F., & MAIER, R. A. An experimental test of the effects of "developmental" vs. "free" discussions on the quality of group decisions. *J. appl. Phychol.,* 1957, 41, 320–323.

MCKEACHIE, W. J. Individual conformity to attitudes of classroom groups. *J. abnorm. soc. Psychol.,* 1954, 49, 282–289.

MCLELLAND, F. M., & RATLIFF, J. A. The use of sociometry as an aid in promoting social adjustment in the ninth grade home room. *Sociometry,* 1947, 10, 147–153.

MEEK, LOIS H. *The personal-social development of boys and girls.* Washington, D.C.: Progressive Education Association, 1940.

MELBY, E. O. Supervision. *Rev. educ. Res.,* 1936, 6, 324–336.

MITZEL, H. E., & RABINOWITZ, W. Assessing social-emotional climate in the classroom by Withall's technique. *Psychol. Monogr.*, 1954, 67, No. 18.

MORENO, J. L. *Who shall survive?* Washington, D.C.: Nervous and Mental Disease Publ. Co., 1934.

MORRISON, R. H. Factors causing failure in teaching. *J. educ. Res.*, 1927, 16, 98–105.

MOUSTAKAS, C. E. *The teacher and the child: Personal interaction in the classroom.* New York: McGraw-Hill, 1956.

MURCHISON, C. (Ed.) *Handbook of child psychology.* Worcester, Mass: Clark Univer. Press, 1933.

NANNINGA, S. P. Teacher failures in high school. *Sch. & Soc.*, 1924, 19, 79–82.

Ohio State Univer., Univer. High Sch. Class, 1938. *Were we guinea pigs?* New York: Holt, 1938.

OJEMANN, R. H., & WILKINSON, FRANCES R. The effect on pupil growth of an increase in teacher's understanding of pupil behavior. *J. exp. Educ.*, 1939, 8, 143–147.

OLSON, W. C., & WILKINSON, N. MURIEL. Teacher personality as revealed by the amount and kind of verbal direction used in behavior control. *Educ. Admin. Superv.*, 1938, 24, 81–93.

PERKINS, H. V. The effects of social-emotional climate and curriculum on learning of in-service teachers. Unpublished doctoral dissertation, Univer. of Chicago, 1949.

POLANSKY, LUCY. Group social climate and the teacher's supportiveness of group status systems. *J. educ. Sociol.*, 1954, 28, 115–123.

PRESCOTT, D. A. *Emotion and the educative process.* Washington, D.C.: American Council on Education, 1938.

REHAGE, K. J. A comparison of pupil-teacher planning and teacher-directed procedures in eighth-grade social studies classes. Unpublished doctoral dissertation, Univer. of Chicago, 1948.

REMMERS, H. H. Reliability and halo effect of high school and college students' judgments of their teachers. *J. appl. Psychol.*, 1934, 18, 619–630.

ROTHNEY, J. W. M., & ROENS, B. A. *Counseling the individual student.* New York: Dryden, 1949.

SEARS, R. R. A theoretical framework for personality and social behavior. *Amer. Psychologist*, 1951, 6, 476–483.

SINGLETARY, J. Teacher-administrative leader perceptions of pupils, *J. educ. Res.*, 1951, 45, 126–132.

STODDARD, G. D. Child development: A new approach to education. *Sch. & Soc.*, 1939, 49, 33–38.

THELEN, H. A. Group dynamics in instruction: Principle of Least Group Size. *Sch. Rev.*, 1949, 57, 139–148.

THELEN, H. A. Educational dynamics: Theory and research. *J. soc. Issues*, 1950, 6, 5–95.

THELEN, H. A. (Ed.) Experimental research toward a theory of instruction *J. educ. Res.*, 1951, 45, 89–136.

THELEN, H. A. Classroom grouping of students. *Sch. Rev.*, 1959, 67, 60–78. (a)

THELEN, H. A. Work-emotionality theory of the group as organism. In S. KOCH (Ed.), *Psychology: A study of a science.* Vol. III. *Formulations of the person and the social context.* New York: McGraw-Hill, 1959. Pp. 544–611. (b)

THELEN, H. A. The triumph of "achievement" over inquiry in education. *Elem. sch. J.*, 1960, 60, 190–197. (a)

THELEN, H. A. *Education and the human quest.* New York: Harper, 1960. (b)

THELEN, H. A., & TYLER, R. W. Implications for improving instruction in the high school. In N. B. HENRY (Ed.), *Yearb. nat. Soc. Stud. Educ.*, 1950, 49, Part 1, 304–335.

THELEN, H. A., & WITHALL, J. Three frames

of reference: The description of climate. *Human Relations*, 1949, 2, 159–176.

THORNDIKE, R. L., LOFTUS, J. J., & GOLDMAN, B. Observations of the behavior of children in activity and control schools. *J. exp. Educ.*, 1941, 10, 138–145.

TIEDEMAN, S. C. A study of pupil-teacher relationships. *J. educ. Res.*, 1942, 35, 657–664.

TROW, W. C. Group processes. In C. W. HARRIS (Ed.), *Encyclopedia of educational research*. (3rd ed.) New York: Macmillan, 1960. Pp. 602–612. (a)

TROW, W. C. Role functions of the teacher in the instructional group. In N. B. HENRY (Ed.), *Yearb. nat. Soc. Stud. Educ.*, 1960, 59, Part II, 30–50. (b)

TROW, W. C., ZANDER, A. F., MORSE, W. C., & JENKINS, D. H. Psychology of group behavior: The class as a group. *J. educ. Psychol.*, 1950, 41, 322–338.

WHITE, R. K. & LIPPITT, R. *Autocracy and democracy: An experimental inquiry.* New York: Harper, 1960.

WICKMAN, E. K. *Children's behavior and teacher's attitudes.* New York: Commonwealth Fund, 1928.

WILSON, W. R. Students rating teachers. *J. higher Educ.*, 1932, 3, 75–82.

WISPÉ, L. G. Evaluating section teaching methods in the introductory course. *J. educ. Res.*, 1951, 45, 161–186.

WITHALL, J. The development of a technique for the measurement of social-emotional climate in classrooms. *J. exp. Educ.*, 1949, 17, 347–361.

WITHALL, J. An objective measurement of a teacher's classroom interactions. *J. educ. Psychol.* 1956, 47, 203–212.

WITHALL, J. A symposium on conceptual frameworks for analysis of classroom interaction: Introductory comment. *J. exp. Educ.*, 1962, 30, 307–308.

WRIGHT, H. F., BARKER, R. G., NALL, J., & SCHOGGEN, P. Toward a psychological ecology of the classroom. *J. educ. Res.*, 1951, 45, 187–200.

YOUNG, L. L. Sociometric and related techniques for appraising social status in an elementary school. *Sociometry*, 1947, 10, 168–177.

ZACHRY, CAROLINE B., & LICHTY, Margaret. *Emotion and conduct in adolescence.* New York: Appleton-Century, 1940.

BRUNSWIKIAN APPROACHES TO
RESEARCH ON TEACHING

Richard E. Snow

The ultimate goals of research on teaching are theories of teaching and these, in turn, involve the development of a critical language for the analysis of classroom behavior. A language consists of both syntax and vocabulary. Hence, both a general paradigm and a general taxonomy must be sought. The paradigm provides the syntactic structure upon which theoretical vocabulary can then be built. The position taken here is that the production of vocabulary has too frequently proceeded without adequate models to serve as syntax and has been limited by overconcern for the practical problems of classroom observation. This paper therefore concentrates on the metalanguage and methods needed in developing a critical language rather than on the details of the language itself or of its use.

Over the years, a number of paradigms for research on teaching have been generated (Gage, 1963, 1964). Gage's 1963 summary documented a growing transition from the older and more gen-

From: American Educational Research Journal, *1968, 5, 475–89. Copyright © 1968 by the American Educational Research Association, and reproduced by permission of the author and AERA.*

eral "criteria-of-teacher-effectiveness" terminology to a newer and narrower concern with "micro-criteria" and classroom teaching processes. The principal models in this latter category were shown to be quite similar in terms of the characteristics of classroom behavior they included or ignored. A general paradigm would seek to consolidate these earlier models, particularly the macro- and micro-criterion views, into a suggested common pattern and then to incorporate those additional features considered critical. Four such features can be suggested. First, the paradigm must recognize and allow for the probabilistic, vicarious nature of classroom behavior. Second, it must service idiographic, developmental conceptions of the single classroom as well as nomothetic approaches to classroom behavior. Third, it must treat behavior in the classroom as, and in relation to, behavior in general, not as some kind of island universe. Finally, related to all of the above must be an explicit methodology capable of multivariate representation and analysis. These considerations lead to the suggestion that some aspects of Egon Brunswik's theoretical position, formally called "Probabilistic Functionalism," may be applicable.

The relevance of Brunswikian views for research on teaching has apparently not been considered before, despite the fact that several existing models derive from theoretical positions closely related, both temporally and conceptually, to Brunswik's. Smith's (1960) paradigm adapts the earlier views of Tolman (1952) while Ryans (1960) has applied Lewinian conceptions (Lewin, 1946), in addition to those of Sears (1951). Because Brunswik died prematurely, his ideas were never fully developed or fully explained. The present effort can generalize only imperfectly from directions perceived in Brunswik's original writings (1952, 1955a, 1955b, 1956; see also Tolman and Brunswik, 1935) but has been aided considerably by excellent discussions offered by others, notably, Postman and Tolman (1959) and contributors to a memorial volume edited by Hammond (1966). It cannot be known of course whether Brunswik would consider the present work a legitimate representation or extrapolation of his views.

REGIONAL REFERENCE

A Brunswikian approach begins with a classification of variables in terms of their remoteness from the central processes of

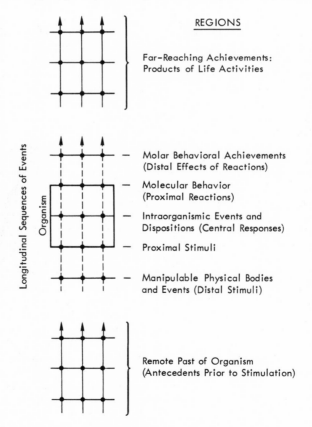

Figure 1. The regional reference of psychological systems: a classification of variables in terms of their distance from the organism.

a behaving organism. Hence, the variables potentially affecting behavior may be seen to lie in regions or layers increasingly and symmetrically peripheral to the organism's central response: each such variable has a regional reference as shown by Figure 1. As the figure might suggest, the focus of analysis may be on variables or events occurring at different distances from the organism. "Central" here refers to events within the organism, "proximal" refers to events at the interface between the organism and the environment, and "distal" suggests events with which the organism is not in direct contact, or over which the organism does not exercise immediate control. A selection of variables representing all layers may be conceived

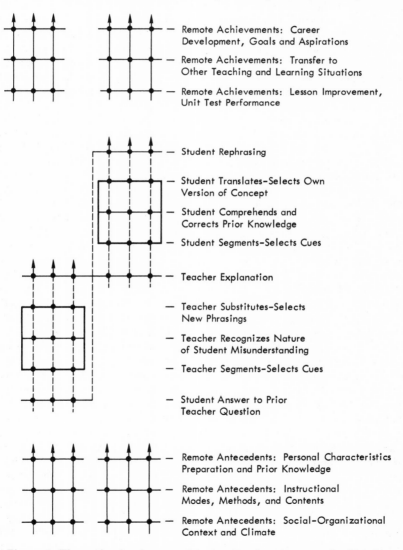

Figure 2. The regional reference of instructional systems: a classification of variables in terms of their distance from the act of teaching.

as forming a causal chain the links of which are *probabilistically,* rather than deterministically, related.

The present development seeks a model for not one organism but several, a teacher and one or more students in interaction within a classroom. In the interests of simplified presentation, Brunswik's regional reference concept is here generalized only to the case of one teacher and one student, as depicted in Figure 2. Later in this paper it will be possible to deal with any number of students for research purposes.

Figure 2 shows the relevant regions for both teacher and student and provides some examples of variables to be found in each region. Remote antecedent and achievement variables would be defined operationally, in most instances, by test, questionnaire, and rating scale responses. Here may be found the macro-criteria of teacher effectiveness mentioned earlier. The inner regions represent micro-criteria of teaching and learning processes typically quantified through classroom observation. The reciprocal sequence shown can be considered formally equivalent to Smith's (1960) teaching cycle, although the earlier model has been elaborated here by inclusion of what in Figure 1 were termed "proximal" regions.

The "central-proximal-distal" terminology of Figure 1 has been dropped from Figure 2 to facilitate the shift from a one-person to a two-person system, since the terms will shortly be used in a different way for the latter case. It should be noted that these terms are general and can be used to characterize the distance between variables regardless of the initial point of focus chosen for central consideration.

THE LENS MODEL

The notions of regional reference and probabilistic relations among events are given clearest expression in Brunswik's basic theoretical tool, the lens model. As shown in Figure 3, it has been adapted by Brunswik and others to characterize various aspects and foci of perceptual and behavioral processes. Figure 3a depicts the nature of human vicarious functioning. Cues relating to some stimulus variable, let us say the size of a distant object, are available from the ecology as an array of projections on the individual's sensorium, represented as a convex lens. These are focussed, that is, used in some combination, to produce a central response, in this case a size judgment. The correlation between these initial and terminal size variables, computed for a single individual over a number of naturalistically varying situations, expresses the functional validity of size judgment for that individual. Correlations computed between the distal variable and each cue separately provide statements of ecological validity for each cue; those computed between individual cues and the judgmental response provide cue utilization coefficients. Multiple correlational and other varieties of multivariate analyses can also be used to represent criterion variables in terms of weighted combinations of cue variables, to interrelate obtained or predicted criterion variables, or to investigate dimensions and patterns among the cue variables. Any of these coefficients may vary systematically from person to person, or for the same person under different conditions, but will always be less than unity due to the probabilistic character of natural behavior. Brunswik's representative sampling of real situations permits, and forces, research on teaching to deal with the full complexity of natural behavior in the classroom. In Figure 3b, Leeper (1966) has expanded the model to form a double lens showing both receptor and motor aspects of an individual's behavior. In Figure 3c, Hammond, Hursch, and Todd (1964) have produced another variety of double lens

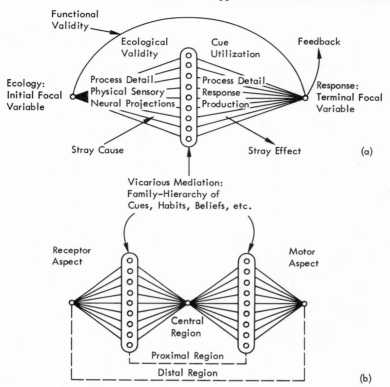

Figure 3. (a) The lens model (from Brunswik, 1952). (b) A double lens model (from Leeper, 1966). (c) A lens model of clinical inference (from Hammond, Hursch, and Todd, 1964). (d) A lens model of interjudge comparison (from Naylor and Schenck, 1966). [See over.]

model for research on the nature of clinical inference. Here for the first time, two individuals are involved but the flow of information is in only one direction, from observed, through various test scores and other cues, to observer. Finally, in Figure 3d, a single lens has been used by Naylor and Schenck (1966) in comparing two judges' responses. This last diagram defines the several kinds of correlational indices that are available from data organized in lens model form. Note that judges A and B could well be any two focal variables or individuals: two observers, a teacher and an observer, a teacher and averaged or individual students, etc.

While the models relating to observer judgments (Figures 3c, 3d) are directly applicable to analyses of the classroom observer, a model for teacher-student interaction requires still further adaptation. Hence, Figure 4 combines the regional representation of Figure 2 with a kind of circuit-lens designed to portray two-way communication between teacher and student. It is now apparent that, for the analysis of classroom behavior, the interpersonal cue variables must be considered centrally important in the analysis of teaching acts. They mediate communication between the teacher and student: the teacher's "proximal" traits in the form of dispositions, intended meanings, etc., are

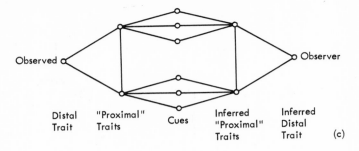

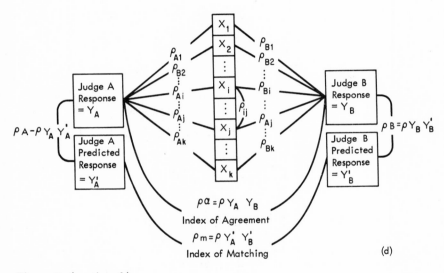

Figure 3. (continued.)

imperfectly represented at the student focal point and, similarly, student internal activity and attention are not fully conveyed to the teacher. It should also be apparent that the model leads most directly to idiographic rather than nomothetic research. That is, the model suggests that the variables involved in teacher-student interaction be studied longitudinally in single teachers as they vary over a number of teaching situations arranged in a time series. For general purpose, the units used to segment such a time series into a number of situations might be minutes, days, weeks or years, or teaching cycles, episodes, lessons, or courses. The important units for the present discussion would probably be the smaller ones—minutes, cycles, episodes, or days. The objective is to study variation in cues across units, to discover natural organizations in such cue variables, and to relate these to more basic behavioral characteristics of the human beings involved. We might, for example, quantify various behaviors of a single teacher—perhaps the use of gestures, voice changes, or emotion-laden words—as these appear in video tape recordings of teaching cycles and relate these to photographic records of student attending behaviors. Or,

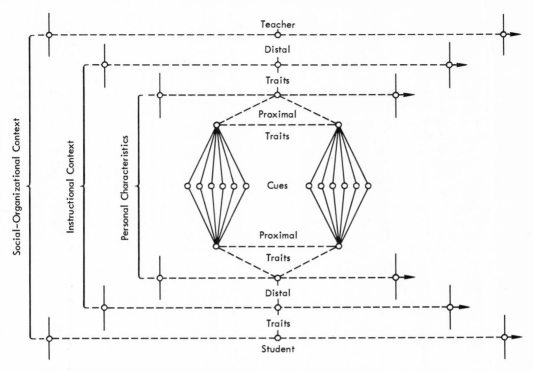

Figure 4. Circuit-lens model of Teacher-student classroom interaction showing central, proximal, and distal levels of longitudinal analysis.

we might measure the teacher's use of reinforcements, probing questions, or certain explaining behaviors, together with the extent to which students participate, translate among alternative statements of a concept, or answer specific questions "spliced" into the instructional sequence. Matrices of such variables may be developed for single teachers and defined to include classes of variables chosen from distinctly different prior investigations, as for example the inclusion of some of McDonald's (1967) technical skills of teaching variables together with some of Bellack and Davitz's (1963) pedagogical move variables. Teacher cue variables can readily be related to individual or grouped student cue variables in this way but it is also possible to obtain clusters, factors, or

other systematic patterns of teacher or student variables and these might well be related to periodically collected physiological data, self ratings of attitudes, or observer ratings of various teacher qualities like warmth, anxiety, preparation, or intrinsic motivation. Such clusters or combinations would be represented as the proximal traits of Figure 4. It should be noted that, historically, research on teaching has sought to move from the more general variables found in the outer, distal regions toward or across the inner central regions of specific classroom behavior. Attempts to construct such relationships have met with limited success perhaps because of a kind of "principle of correlational distance": The farther apart two variables are from one another in terms of regional reference, the more probabilistic connections must be bridged between them and, hence, the lower the correlation. Relations between teacher personal characteristics and student test performance have been particularly difficult to obtain, it is contended, because cue variables and proximal traits have been left out of the probabilistic chain.

The findings of consistencies over time in given teachers or students can be taken as indices of individual differences and, in combination with data from similar analyses on other teachers or students, can be related to other personal characteristics or experimental variables. The arrangement of relevant matrices is shown in Figure 5. While many complicated statistical methods are applicable here, discussion of them cannot be included in the present paper (see Harris, 1963; Cattell, 1966: also, for a discussion of the use of similar matrix arrangements in other areas of instructional research, see Seibert and Snow, 1965). It should be clear however that micro-analyses of teaching acts may be connected with more macro-analyses supporting conceptions of teachers and students as persons engaged in ongoing educational and psychological development outside the classroom. Similarly, differences between individuals in these kinds of analyses may be used to evaluate the effects of antecedent experimental vari-

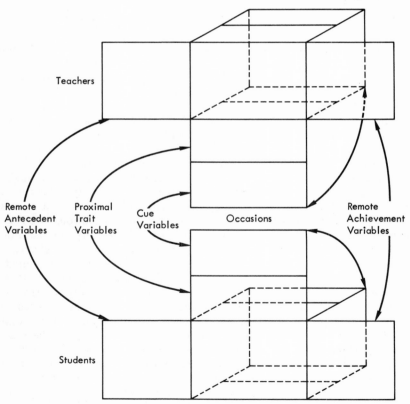

Figure 5. Data matrices relevant to proposed analyses.

ables imposed, for example, in a teacher training program. Thus, while the methodology proposed is essentially correlational, it allows the effects of training treatments on single dependent variables to be traced out into the multivariate context of real classroom behavior. Its idiographic character should make such methodology also compatible with case study approaches to research on teaching.

THE FACET MODEL

The foregoing discussion suggests rather large scale correlational studies of cue and trait variables so that relationships among such variables can be used to identify potentially important features of classroom behavior. These features might be represented as patterns of separate variables or as composites of some sort. In any event, they are the concepts to be labelled and manipulated by our critical language. No implication of blind empirical search is intended here, however. In Brunswik's approach, situations are sampled representatively so that variables are free to vary naturalistically. But the variables themselves are not sampled; they are selected or constructed systematically according to some logical structuring of the domain of inquiry. As an aid in this structuring process, facet design and analysis (Foa 1961, 1962, 1965) is suggested. The formalization of facet theory is due to Guttman but several of the basic ideas involved owe their origin also to Brunswik. Essentially, the approach divides a domain of inquiry into facets each with a set number of elements. In test construction, for example, "test content" is a facet and "figural," symbolic," and "semantic" are elements of that facet. "Item form" might be another facet, with "recall" and "recognition" as two elements. All possible combinations of such elements define the domain of interest. Variables may be selected from individual cells or constructed from combinations of cells. A general recall test, for example, would have all three kinds of content. Because it was constructed using a facet model, its inclusion of all three kinds of content is insured and it displays what Humphreys (1962) has referred to as "controlled heterogeneity."

There have been many attempts in the past to construct category systems for use in classroom observation and analysis (see Medley and Mitzel, 1963; Kliebard, 1966). Among the most recent and comprehensive efforts is the taxonomy produced by Openshaw and Cyphert (1966), which approximates a facet model in several respects but is not explicitly based on one. The proposal offered here is that taxonomic work should proceed from this base using a facet approach and aim not at categories into which observed signs can be classed but rather out of which signs or cue variables can be selected or constructed. Such variables would then be quantified in audio visual recordings of classroom behavior and treated to the kinds of analyses suggested earlier. In other words, rather than produce a vocabulary which is based on and limited to classroom observer use, I would propose the construction of a vocabulary far more extensive than anything a classroom observer could be expected to use. In view of the present state of recording technology, in fact, it is suggested that classroom observers no longer be used as objective recorders for research purposes, as Medley and Mitzel (1963) required, but that they be used instead to make what Hammond Hursch, and Todd (1964) called "clinical inferences about proximal traits." Observers should thus be considered as part of the system for analytical purposes, as Figures 3c and 3d suggest.

The construction of variables from a kind of universal taxonomy of signs to fit various theoretical or practical purposes seems preferable to premature commit-ment to any particular category system or theoretical vocabulary. As some indication of where the approach outlined here would lead, however, it should be noted that both the Brunswik and the Guttman developments are based largely on the terminology of differential psychology which, in turn, most readily supports a cognitive-information processing view of behavior. Information-processing models of classroom behavior are also supported by the work of Smith (1960) and Ryans (1960, 1963).

CONCLUSION

In summary, the point of the argument is that the analysis of classroom behavior should be a kind of quantitative case study, where multiple cue variables are quantified in detail from raw records of behavior and related to inferred behav-ioral traits. The organization of these cues and traits should be studied both cross-sectionally and longitudinally using pro-cedures similar to those employed in the study of intellectual organization. It is suggested that Brunswik's lens model and Guttman's facet model, together with related correlational and nonmetric scaling methodology, provide uniquely useful and compatible approaches to these ends. While this may sound overly ambitious and a bit unrealistic, it does seem clear that available language for identifying and describing the significant events of the classroom does not nearly match the com-plexity of the behavior to be found there. We have hardly begun to exploit the technological, methodological, and infer-ential power available to us.

REFERENCES

BELLACK, ARNO and DAVITZ, J. R. *The Lan-guage of the Classroom.* New York: Teachers College, Columbia University, 1963. 200 pp.

BRUNSWIK, EGON. "The Conceptual Frame-work of Psychology." *International Encyclopedia of Unified Science,* 1952, 1, No. 10.

BRUNSWIK, EGON. "Representative Design and Probabilistic Theory in a Functional Psychology." *Psychological Review* 62: 193–217; May 1955, a.

BRUNSWIK, EGON. "In Defense of Probabi-listic Functionalism: A Reply." *Psy-chological Review* 62: 236–242; May 1955, b.

BRUNSWIK, EGON. *Perception and the Repre-sentative Design of Psychological Ex-periments.* Berkeley, Calif.: University of California Press, 1956. 154 pp.

CATTELL, RAYMOND B. (Ed.) *Handbook of Multivariate Experimental Psychology.* Chicago: Rand McNally, 1966. 959 pp.

FOA, URIEL G. "Convergences in the Analysis of the Structure of Interpersonal Be-havior." *Psychological Review* 68: 341–353; September 1961.

FOA, URIEL G. "The Structure of Interpersonal Behavior in the Dyad." In CRISWELL, JOAN, SOLOMON, H., and SUPPES, P. *Mathematical Methods in Small Group Processes.* Stanford, Calif.: Stanford University Press, 1962, pp. 166–179.

FOA, URIEL G. "New Developments in Facet Design and Analysis." *Psychological Re-view* 72: 262–274; July 1965.

GAGE, N. L. "Paradigms for Research on Teaching." In GAGE, NATHAN L. (ed.) *Handbook of Research on Teaching.* Chicago: Rand McNally, 1963, pp. 94–141.

GAGE, N. L. "Theories of Teaching." In HILGARD, ERNEST R. (ed.) *Theories of Learning and Instruction.* Sixty-Third Yearbook of the National Society for the Study of Education, Part 1, 1964. pp. 268–285.

HAMMOND, KENNETH R., HURSCH, CAROLYN, and TODD, FREDERICK J. "Analyzing the Components of Clinical Inference." *Psy-*

chological Review 71: 438–456; November 1964.

HAMMOND, KENNETH R. (Ed.) *The Psychology of Egon Brunswik.* New York: Holt, Rinehart, and Winston, 1966. 549 pp.

HARRIS, CHESTER W. (Ed.) *Problems in Measuring Change.* Madison, Wisc.: University of Wisconsin Press, 1963. 259 pp.

HUMPHREYS, LLOYD G. "The Organization of Human Abilities." *American Psychologist* 17: 475–483; 1962.

KLIEBARD, H. M. "The Observation of Classroom Behavior—Some Recent Research." *The Way Teaching Is, Report of the Seminar on Teaching.* Wash., D.C.: Assoc. for Supervision and Curriculum Development, National Education Association, 1966, pp. 45–76.

LEEPER, ROBERT W. "A Critical Consideration of Egon Brunswik's Probabilistic Functionalism." In HAMMOND, K. R. (Ed.) *The Psychology of Egon Brunswik.* New York: Holt, Rinehart, and Winston, 1966.

LEWIN, KURT. "Behavior and Development as a Function of the Total Situation." In CARMICHAEL, L. (Ed.) *Manual of Child Psychology.* New York: Wiley, 1946, pp. 791–844.

McDONALD, FREDERICK J. "Applying the Language of Behavioral Models to Teaching Acts." Research Memorandum No. 3, Stanford Center for Research and Development in Teaching, Stanford University, Stanford, California, 1967.

MEDLEY, DONALD M. and MITZEL, HAROLD E. "Measuring Classroom Behavior by Systematic Observation." In GAGE, N. L. (Ed.) *Handbook of Research on Teaching.* Chicago: Rand McNally, 1963, pp. 247–328.

NAYLOR, JAMES and SCHENCK, E. A. "ρm as an 'Error-Free' Index of Rater Agreement." *Educational and Psychological Measurement* 26: 815–824; Winter 1966.

OPENSHAW, M. K. and CYPHERT, F. R. *Development of a Taxonomy for the Classification of Teacher Classroom Behavior.* Columbus, Ohio: Ohio State University Research Foundation, 1966.

POSTMAN, LEO, and TOLMAN, EDWARD C. "Brunswik's Probabilistic Functionalism." In Koch, Sigmund (Ed.) *Psychology: A Study of a Science.* Vol. 1. New York: McGraw-Hill, 1959, pp. 502–564.

RYANS, DAVID G. *An Information-System Approach to Theory of Instruction with Special Reference to the Teacher,* SP-1079. Santa Monica, Calif.: System Development Corporation, 1963.

RYANS, DAVID G. *Characteristics of Teachers.* Washington, D.C.: American Council of Education, 1960. 416 pp.

SEARS, ROBERT R. "A Theoretical Framework for Personality and Social Behavior." *American Psychologist* 6: 476–483; 1951.

SEIBERT, WARREN F. and SNOW, RICHARD E. "OASIS: A Methodology for Instructional and Communications Research." In *Proceedings of the 73rd Annual Convention of the American Psychological Association.* Wash., D.C.: American Psychological Association, 1965, pp. 333–334.

SMITH, B. OTHANIEL. "A Concept of Teaching." *Teachers College Record* 61: 229–241; February 1960.

TOLMAN, EDWARD C. "A Psychological Model." In Parsons, Talcott and Shils, Edward A. (Eds.) *Toward a General Theory of Social Action.* Cambridge: Harvard University Press, 1952, pp. 279–302.

TOLMAN, EDWARD C., and BRUNSWIK, EGON. "The Organism and the Causal Texture of the Environment." *Psychological Review* 42: 43–77; 1935.

2

The Individual

in Social Interaction

*For the critical problem toward which all the behavioral
sciences must be directed is how man can remain
an individual in society. On the outcome of the solution
to this problem rests the possibility of the very existence
of a society as a stable group, and the very existence of
the individual as an "intact" man of dignity within
the society.*
D. Krech, R. S. Crutchfield, and E. L. Ballachey

Man is at once an individual and a social creature. As readings in the first
chapter emphasized, human behavior is a fluctuating and complex blend of
individual (idiographic) and social (nomothetic) characteristics. One can
pretend that they can be separated, but it hardly seems feasible at any time
to consider one without the other. This relationship between the individual
and his society can be seen in Chapter II where we attempt to concentrate
major attention on the individual's socialization and see how it affects his
perceptions and cognitive development.

Responding to and manipulated by his socio-cultural environment,
man is neither a turtle nor a fish, creatures that form appropriate behavior
and characteristics primarily through biological maturation and instincts.
Parents and teachers who are troubled by problem children may wish it
were so, but the broad capacities and potentials of man over and above
his physical powers create tremendous possibilities for individual growth
and social systems. Therein remains the challenge for all mankind (Yee,
1968). Because societies have cultural patterns they want preserved and
transmitted to the young, and because societies function according to social
routines and expectations, they attempt to socialize their young into what
they consider to be tolerable human behavior.

In modern, urbanized, complex societies such as the United States,
however, socialization is never uniform. The significant socializers (family
members, teachers, and peers) can vary considerably in their purposes and
practices and do not always function in concert. The socializing force of a

Kwakiutl village or Amish community, where people relate collectively with each other in familiar, face-to-face terms and work together to fulfill common, well-defined tasks, would be more influential in making youngsters conform to established behavior patterns. In his latest work comparing socialization in Russia with socialization in the United States, Urie Bronfenbrenner (1970) says that the Russian system is more effective, because all social groups of which Russian children are members are purposely organized (i.e., collectivized) and coordinated to promote self-discipline, obedience, morality, dedication to the group, and subordination of the self. Bronfenbrenner certainly feels that the Russian system has limitations, especially in child-rearing goals; but, he believes that the United States needs a reinvolvement of parents, teachers, older children, and peers to help form and reform modes of behavior for the individual's well-being and society's progress.

From the individual's perspective, the characteristics and capacities of the person being socialized must be considered active determinants in modern America. We may wonder why socialization in America does not create greater variance than it does when we look at our country from the perspective of an American youngster, growing up in the world's greatest educational complex with permissive family life, televised pseudo-life, and in an era of affluence and uncertainty. But taking note of significant configurations in societies—especially in social interaction—that do operate with more or less set probabilities, we may not wonder too long. The social development of an individual is formed by social powers invested in and interpreted by his family, teachers, and others, in combination with the responses and choices the individual makes from the alternatives he perceives to be available.

Bronfenbrenner may perceive that the Russians are more "efficient" in their socialization than Americans, but such a highly centralized, authoritarian society as the U.S.S.R. can establish more uniform, purposeful processes for socializing their young. Authoritarian social systems have the dubious advantage of imposing state goals and expectations upon their people and enforcing them with constraints. Socialization in a free society and in a closed one are difficult to compare; unless one is willing to accept the relevant operating principles of the other, borrowing goals and methods for socialization seems questionable. In his critical review of Bronfenbrenner's book, Geiger (1970) wrote: "It is hard to understand how a report on patterns of child-rearing in the United States and the Soviet Union finds absolutely nothing to say...about the political implications of the observed differences. Is it so easy to forget that in the recent past the imposition of 'adult standards of conformity' has in some places crippled the minds of youth with political irrationality and hatred?" (p. 1191).

Cultural anthropologists would find it difficult to recommend that a trait or a process of one culture, especially from the culture's configuration of socialization, be adopted by other cultures. In his provocative work which has helped more people understand anthropology than any other single work, Kluckholn (1944) made it quite clear how complex cultures were and how silly it would be to consider and attempt oversimplifications. He wrote: "It is especially absurd to seize upon a single childhood discipline as the magic key to the whole tone of a culture." (p. 173).

The complexities of culture can be seen in the broad contrasts between the orientations of two cultures' socializations. Examining socialization in American and Chinese cultures, Hsu (1953) saw a basic difference between the two cultures' socialization mechanisms. According to Hsu, American culture causes individuals to internalize self-discipline and emphasize self while traditional Chinese culture focuses upon familial guidance and group control over the individual. As is true of all socio-cultural systems, the American system has its own proper logic; and although it has its contradictions (Dubois, 1955), it generally bases its primary idealistic emphasis upon the individual and upon democratic social values. In a time when attitudes and values are subject to increasing change, new goals and methods for socialization in American society will hopefully materialize without a social shift toward greater authoritarianism.

To achieve any understanding of the American people or any other, one needs to regard socio-cultural settings as complex systems. Focusing upon relevant interpersonal behavior events, one should regard what happens within them as basic keys to the social system. Social scientists have observed the shifting patterns of American family life and its diminishing functions largely through demographic data such as divorce rates, marrying age, size of family, income, mobility, etc. Greater understanding of the American family and its changes might well be found by studying the nature of its social interaction patterns. Concerning ourselves with educational settings, we consider interpersonal behavior events that significantly develop and influence the characteristics of a person, not just in his youth with parents, siblings, teachers, etc. but throughout his life. Therefore, social interaction in educational situations relates quite meaningfully to an individual's total development as a person through a life-time of teaching-learning transactions. Such an approach seems to be more fruitful than static analyses of demographic classifications alone.

As Eric Erikson (1950) so brillantly described the process, a person grows into maturity through the complex interrelatedness of psychic and social development. His "Eight Stages of Man" describes the basic sequence of such a process and the significance of each stage in human development. In the first stage, *trust* vs. *basic mistrust,* the babe first interacts with another person, typically his mother, and through "the experience of a mutual regulation of his increasingly receptive capacities with the maternal techniques of provision," lays the basic foundation for inner and outer confidence, identity, and belongingness (p. 219). About the highest stage of maturity he says, "Ego Integrity, . . . implies an emotional integration which permits participation by followership as well as acceptance of the responsibility of leadership" (p. 233). In the first and so through all of his stages of life, man is one a member of social settings and, two, an individual being influenced from without and determining his behavior from within. Beginning with the simple assertion that "Perception involves an act of categorization," Bruner (1957) discusses the development of a person's perceptual readiness and carefully shows why it is a process of considerable complexity. Such perceptual equipment screens the probability of events a person's environment presents and makes sense of what he perceives in order for him to respond.

In the chapter's first selection, Bruner carefully describes how socio-cultural influences—especially in the education of the young—determine the growth of a person, for "the growth of mind is always growth assisted from the outside." Bruner suggests appropriate teaching strategies for cognitive development and calls upon the entire intellectual community to be concerned with the amplification of the powers of the human mind, i.e., the "growth sciences." This selection, therefore, raises challenging questions, such as, How do socio-cultural patterns determine probabilities for outcomes in human growth? Since Bruner says that teachers play a crucial role in maximizing the cognitive growth of the young and indicates in part how they can, we need to consider the question, What teaching-learning processes are most conducive to the growth of mind, especially for modern societies such as the United States?

The Zajonc selection describes a general theory and its variants which have had a tremendous, lasting impact upon the course of social psychology. The theory helps us understand how people's "natural tendency to seek balance, congruity, and consonance, i.e., consistency, explains their perceptions, beliefs, and behavior." Need for consistency indicates how naïve psycho-logic (i.e., simplex affective-cognitive strategies and resolutions) influences human nature. The theory raises the need to overcome such limitations in the intellectual and socio-emotional development of children, especially in the area of interpersonal relations. Concerned with hypotheses drawn from the general theory Zajonc reviewed, the Priest and Sawyer article in Chapter III and the Daw and Gage article in Chapter IV illustrate the wide application of consistency theory.

How does a young person's family and others he relates to in primary-group relationships influence his basic personality and characteristic behavior patterns? Why has such influence been so powerful? What problems does it present in human development? How can it be improved? Freeberg and Payne's article reviews in detail studies of how parents influence young children's cognitive development through their particular rearing practices, and social-class characteristics. It also describes innovative attempts to enhance cognitive growth with specialized training techniques.

Painstaking research by Sewell and Shah provides clear evidence that the nature of parental encouragement is a very powerful variable in determining high school seniors' college plans and shows how it intervenes between the students' sex, social-class background, and educational aspirations. Demonstrating the importance of parent-student social interactions in respect to educational plans and decisions, such findings indicate the benefits educational counselling can give parents and potential college students. All too often, unfortunately, educational decisions such as academic versus vocational pursuits have been made on the basis of factors that are difficult and slow to influence, such as social-class background and sex.

The work by Mutimer and Rosemier shows how the perceptions of children in different grade levels, boys, girls, or teachers can differ in some respects and yet be similar in others. The authors were concerned specifically with children's behavior problems, but their findings suggest that a wide range of views may exist in respect to almost any other prominent issue. Yee and Runkel's work demonstrates the powerful effect of pupils' social-class background in how they perceive and may be perceived. Their study found differing hierarchical structures in middle- and lower-class pupils' attitudes toward their teachers, and their discussion suggests that teacher-pupil social interaction may differ considerably depending upon the pupil's social-class background.

OTHER READINGS

BARKER, R. G. On the nature of the environment. *Journal of Social Issues,* 1963, *19,* 17–38.

BRONFENBRENNER, U. *Two worlds of childhood.* New York: Russell Sage, 1970.

BRUNER, J. S. On perceptual readiness. *Psychological Review,* 1967, *64,* 123–152.

CARTWRIGHT, D. & HARARY, F. Structural balance: A generalization of Heider's theory. *Psychological Review,* 1956, *63,* 277–293.

DAVIS, F., & OLESEN, V. L. Initiation into a women's profession: Identity problems in the status transition of coed to student nurse. *Sociometry,* 1963, *26,* 89–101.

DUBOIS, C. The dominant value profile of American culture. *American Anthropologist,* 1955, *57,* 1232–1239.

ERIKSON, E. H. *Childhood and society.* New York: Norton, 1950.

FESTINGER, L. *A theory of cognitive dissonance.* Evanston, Ill.: Row, Peterson, 1957.

GEIGER, H. K. Other People's Children. *Science,* 1970, *169,* 1190–1192.

HSU, F. L. K. *Americans and Chinese: Two ways of life.* New York: Henry Schuman, 1953.

JENSEN, A. R. Social class, race, and genetics: Implications for education. *American Educational Research Journal,* 1968, *5,* 1–42.

KLUCKHOLN, C. *Mirror for man: A survey of human behavior and social attitudes.* Greenwich, Conn.: Premier, 1944.

LINDZEY, G., & ARONSON, E. (Eds.) *Handbook of social psychology,* Vol. 3. *The individual in a social context.* Reading, Mass.: Addison-Wesley, 1968.

MASLOW, A. H. A theory of motivation. *Psychological Review,* 1943, *50,* 370–396.

NEWCOMB, T. M. Individual systems of orientation. In S. Koch (Ed.), *Psychology: A study of a science.* Vol. 3, New York: McGraw-Hill. Pp. 348–422.

OLIM, E. G., HESS, R. D., SHIPMAN, V. C. Role of mothers' language styles in mediating their preschool children's cognitive development. *School Review,* 1967, *75,* 414–424.

ROSEN, B. C. Family structure and value transmission. *Merrill-Palmer Quarterly,* 1964, *10,* 59–76.

ROSEN, B. C., & D'ANDRADE, R. The psychological origins of achievement motivation. *Sociometry,* 1959, *22,* 185–218.

SPINDLER, G. D. *Education and culture: Anthropological approaches.* New York: Holt, Rinehart and Winston, 1963.

SPINDLER, G. D. Education in a transforming American culture. *Harvard Educational Review,* 1955, *25,* 145–156.

THOMPSON, O. E. Student values in transition. *California Journal of Educational Research,* 1968, *19,* 77–86.

TOLOR, A., SCARPETTI, W. L., & LANE, P. A. Teachers' attitudes towards children's behavior revisited. *Journal of Educational Psychology,* 1967, *58,* 175–180.

WOOD, J. R., WEINSTEIN, E. A. & PARKER, K. Children's interpersonal tactics. *Sociological Inquiry,* 1967, *37,* 129–138.

YEE, A. H. Preparation for the future. *Social Studies,* 1968, *59,* 18–26.

THE GROWTH OF MIND

Jerome S. Bruner

These past several years, I have had the painful pleasure—and it has been both —of exploring two aspects of the cognitive processes that were new to me. One was cognitive development, the other pedagogy. I knew, as well all know, that the two were closely related, and it was my naive hope that, betimes, the relation would come clear to me. Indeed, 2 years ago when I first knew that in early September 1965 I would be standing here, delivering this lecture, I said to myself that I would use the occasion to set forth to my colleagues what I had been able to find out about this vexed subject, the relation of pedagogy and development. It seemed obvious then that in 2 years one could get to the heart of the matter.

The 2 years have gone by. I have had the privilege of addressing this distinguished audience (Bruner, 1964) on some of our findings concerning the development of cognitive processes in children, and I have similarly set forth what I hope

From: American Psychologist, *1965,* 20, *1007–17. Copyright* © *1965 by the American Psychological Association, and reproduced by permission of the author and APA.*

are not entirely unreasonable ideas about pedagogy (Bruner, in press). I am still in a very deep quandary concerning the relation of these two enterprises. The heart of the matter still eludes me, but I shall stand by my resolve. I begin on this autobiographical note so that you may know in advance why this evening is more an exercise in conjecture than a cataloguing of solid conclusions.

What is most unique about man is that his growth as an individual depends upon the history of his species—not upon a history reflected in genes and chromosomes but, rather, reflected in a culture external to man's tissue and wider in scope than is embodied in any one man's competency. Perforce, then, the growth of mind is always growth assisted from the outside. And since a culture, particularly an advanced one, transcends the bounds of individual competence, the limits for individual growth are by definition greater than what any single person has previously attained. For the limits of growth depend on how a culture assists the individual to use such intellectual potential as he may possess. It seems highly unlikely—either empirically or canonically—that we have any realistic sense of the furthest reach of such assistance to growth.

The evidence today is that the full evolution of intelligence came as a result of bipedalism and tool using. The large human brain gradually evolved as a sequel to the first use of pebble tools by early near-man. To condense the story, a near-man, or hominid, with a slightly superior brain, using a pebble tool, could make out better in the niche provided by nature than a near-man who depended not on tools but on sheer strength and formidable jaws. Natural selection favored the primitive tool user. In time, thanks to his better chance of surviving and breeding, he became more so: The ones who survived had larger brains, smaller jaws, less ferocious teeth. In place of belligerent anatomy, they developed tools and a brain that made it possible to use them. Human evolution thereafter became less a matter of having appropriate fangs or claws and more one of using and later fashioning tools to express the powers of the larger brain that was also emerging. Without tools the brain was of little use, no matter how many hundred cubic centimeters of it there might be. Let it also be said that without the original programmatic capacity for fitting tools into a sequence of acts, early hominids would never have started the epigenetic progress that brought them to their present state. And as human groups stabilized, tools became more complex and "shaped to pattern," so that it was no longer a matter of reinventing tools in order to survive, but rather of mastering the skills necessary for using them. In short, after a certain point in human evolution, the only means whereby man could fill his evolutionary niche was through the cultural transmission of the skills necessary for the use of priorly invented techniques, implements, and devices.

Two crucial parallel developments seem also to have occurred. As hominids became increasingly bipedal, with the freed hands necessary for using spontaneous pebble tools, selection also favored those with a heavier pelvic bony structure that could sustain the impacting strain of bipedal locomotion. The added strength came, of course, from a gradual closing down of the birth canal. There is an obstetrical paradox here: a creature with an increasingly larger brain but with a smaller and smaller birth canal to get through. The resolution seems to have been achieved through the immaturity of the human neonate, particularly cerebral immaturity that assures not only a smaller head, but also a longer period of transmitting the necessary skills required by human culture. During this same period, human language must have emerged, giving man not only a new and powerful way of representing reality but also increasing his power to assist the mental growth of the young to a degree beyond anything before seen in nature.

It is impossible, of course, to reconstruct the evolution in techniques of instruction in the shadow zone between hominids and man. I have tried to compensate by observing contemporary analogues of earlier forms, knowing full well that the pursuit of analogy can be dangerously misleading. I have spent many hours observing uncut films of the behavior of free-ranging baboons, films shot in East Africa by my colleague Irven DeVore with a very generous footage devoted to infants and juveniles. I have also had access to the unedited film archives of a hunting-gathering people living under roughly analogous ecological conditions, the !Kung Bushman of the Kalahari, recorded by Laurance and Lorna Marshall, brilliantly aided by their son John and daughter Elizabeth. I have also worked directly but informally with the Wolof of Senegal, observing children in the bush and in French-style schools. Even more valuable than my own informal observations in Senegal were the systematic experiments carried out later by my colleague, Patricia Marks Greenfield (in press).

Let me describe very briefly some salient differences in the free learning patterns of immature baboons and among !Kung children. Baboons have a highly developed social life in their troops, with well-organized and stable dominance patterns. They live within a territory, protecting themselves from predators by joint action of the strongly built, adult males. It is striking that the behavior of baboon juveniles is shaped principally by play with their peer group, play that provides opportunity for the spontaneous expression and practice of the component acts that, in maturity, will be orchestrated into either the behavior of the dominant male or of the infant-protective female. All this seems to be accomplished with little participation by any mature animals in the play of the juveniles. We know from the important experiments of Harlow and his colleagues (Harlow & Harlow, 1962) how devastating a disruption in development can be produced in subhuman primates by interfering with their opportunity for peer-group play and social interaction.

Among hunting-gathering humans, on the other hand, there is *constant* interaction between adult and child, or adult and adolescent, or adolescent and child. !Kung adults and children play and dance together, sit together, participate in minor-hunting together, join in song and story telling together. At very frequently [*sic*] intervals, moreover, children are party to rituals presided over by adults—minor, as in the first haircutting, or major, as when a boy kills his first Kudu buck and goes through the proud but painful process of scarification. Children, besides are constantly playing imitatively with the rituals, implements, tools, and weapons of the

adult world. Young juvenile baboons, on the other hand, virtually never play with things or imitate directly large and significant sequences of adult behavior.

Note, though, that in tens of thousands of feet of !Kung film, one virtually never sees an instance of "teaching" taking place outside the situation where the behavior to be learned is relevant. Nobody "teaches" in our prepared sense of the word. There is nothing like school, nothing like lessons. Indeed, among the !Kung children there is very little "telling." Most of what we would call instruction is through showing. And there is no "practice" or "drill" as such save in the form of play modeled directly on adult models —play hunting, play bossing, play exchanging, play baby tending, play house making. In the end, every man in the culture knows nearly all there is to know about how to get on with life as a man, and every woman as a woman—the skills, the rituals and myths, the obligations and rights.

The change in the instruction of children in more complex societies is twofold. First of all, there is knowledge and skill in the culture far in excess of what any one individual knows. And so, increasingly, there develops an economical technique of instructing the young based heavily on *telling* out of context rather than *showing* in context. In literate societies, the practice becomes institutionalized in the school or the "teacher." Both promote this necessarily abstract way of instructing the young. The result of "teaching the culture" can, at its worst, lead to the ritual, rote nonsense that has led a generation of critics from Max Wertheimer (1945) to Mary Alice White (undated) of Teachers' College to despair. For in the detached school, what is imparted often has little to do with life as lived in the society except insofar as the demands of school are of a kind that reflect *indirectly* the demands of life in a technical society. But these indirectly imposed demands may be the most important feature of the detached school. For school is a sharp departure from indigenous practice. It takes learning, as we have noted, out of the context of immediate action just by dint of putting it into a school. This very extirpation makes learning become an act in itself, freed from the immediate ends of action, preparing the learner for the chain of reckoning remote from payoff that is needed for the formulation of complex ideas. At the same time, the school (if successful) frees the child from the pace setting of the round of daily activity. If the school succeeds in avoiding a pace-setting round of its own, it may be one of the great agents for promoting reflectiveness. Moreover, in school, one must "follow the lesson" which means one must learn to follow either the abstraction of written speech—abstract in the sense that it is divorced from the concrete situation to which the speech might originally have been related—or the abstraction of language delivered orally but out of the context of an ongoing action. Both of these are highly abstract uses of language.

It is no wonder, then, that many recent studies report large differences between "primitive" children who are in schools and their brothers who are not: differences in perception, abstraction, time perspective, and so on. I need only cite the work of Biesheuvel (1949) in South Africa, Gay and Cole (undated) in Liberia, Greenfield (in press) in Senegal, Maccoby and Modiano (in press) in rural Mexico, Reich (in press) among Alaskan Eskimos.

What a culture does to assist the development of the powers of mind of its members is, in effect, to provide amplification systems to which human beings, equipped with appropriate skills, can link themselves. There are, first, the amplifiers of action—hammers, levers, digging sticks, wheels—but more important, the programs of action into which such implements can be substituted. Second, there are amplifiers of the senses, ways of looking and noticing that can take advantage of devices ranging from smoke signals and hailers to diagrams and pictures that stop the action or microscopes that enlarge it. Finally and most powerfully, there are amplifiers of the thought processes, ways of thinking that employ language and formation of explanation, and later use such languages as mathematics and logic and even find automatic servants to crank out the consequences. A culture is, then, a deviser, a repository, and a transmitter of amplification systems and of the devices that fit into such systems. We know very little in a deep sense about the transmission function, how people are trained to get the most from their potential by use of a culture's resources.

But it is reasonably clear that there is a major difference between the mode of transmission in a technical society, with its schools, and an indigenous one, where cultural transmission is in the context of action. It is not just that an indigenous society, when its action pattern becomes disrupted falls apart—at a most terrifying rate—as in uncontrolled urbanization in some parts of Africa. Rather, it is that the institution of a school serves to convert knowledge and skill into more symbolical, more abstract, more verbal form. It is this process of transmission—admittedly very new in human history—that is so poorly understood and to which, finally, we shall return.

There are certain obvious specifications that can be stated about how a society must proceed in order to equip its young. It must convert what is to be known—whether a skill or a belief system or a connected body of knowledge—into a form capable of being mastered by a beginner. The more we know of the process of growth, the better we shall be at such conversion. The failure of modern man to understand mathematics and science may be less a matter of stunted abilities than our failure to understand how to teach such subjects. Second, given the limited amount of time available for learning, there must be a due regard for saving the learner from needless learning. There must be some emphasis placed on economy and transfer and the learning of general rules. All societies must (and virtually all do) distinguish those who are clever from those who are stupid—though few of them generalize this trait across all activities. Cleverness in a particular activity almost universally connotes strategy, economy, heuristics, highly generalized skills. A society must also place emphasis upon how one derives a course of action from what one has learned. Indeed, in an indigenous society, it is almost impossible to separate what one does from what one knows. More advanced societies often have not found a way of dealing with the separation of knowledge and action—probably a result of the emphasis they place upon "telling" in their instruction. All societies must maintain interest among the young in the learning process, a minor problem when learning is in the context of life and action, but harder when it becomes more abstracted. And finally, and perhaps most obviously, a society must assure that its necessary skills and procedures remain intact from one generation to the next— which does not always happen, as witnessed by Easter Islanders, Incas, Aztecs, and Mayas.[1]

Unfortunately, psychology has not concerned itself much with any of these five requisites of cultural transmission— or at least not much with four of them. We have too easily assumed that learning is learning is learning—that the early version of what was taught did not matter much, one thing being much like another and reducible to a pattern of association, to stimulus-response connections, or to our favorite molecular componentry. We denied there was a problem of development beyond the quantitative one of providing more experience, and with the denial, closed our eyes to the pedagogical problem of how to represent knowledge, how to sequence it, how to embody it in a form appropriate to young learners. We expended more passion on the part-whole controversy than on what whole or what part of it was to be presented first. I should except Piaget (1954), Köhler (1940), and Vygotsky (1962) from these complaints—all until recently unheeded voices.

Our neglect of the economy of learning stems, ironically, from the heritage of Ebbinghaus (1913), who was vastly interested in savings. Our nonsense syllables, our random mazes failed to take into account how we reduce complexity and strangeness to simplicity and the familiar, how we convert what we have learned into rules and procedures, how, to use Bartlett's (1932) term of over 30 years ago, we turn around on our own schemata to reorganize what we have mastered into more manageable form.

---

[1] I have purposely left out of the discussion the problems of impulse regulation and socialization of motives, topics that have received extended treatment in the voluminous literature on culture and personality. The omission is dictated by emphasis rather than evaluation.

Obviously, the shaping of character by culture is of great importance for an understanding of our topic as it bears, for example, upon culture-instilled attitudes toward the uses of mind. Since our emphasis is upon human potential and its amplification by culturally patterned instrumental skills, we mention the problem of character formation in passing and in recognition of its importance in complete treatment of the issues under discussion.

Nor have we taken naturally to the issue of knowledge and action. Its apparent mentalism has repelled us. Tolman (1951), who bravely made the distinction, was accused of leaving his organisms wrapt in thought. But he recognized the problem and if he insisted on the idea that knowledge might be organized in cognitive maps, it was in recognition (as a great functionalist) that organisms go somewhere on the basis of what they have learned. I believe we are getting closer to the problem of how knowledge affects action and vice versa, and offer in testimony of my conviction the provocative book by Miller, Galanter, and Pribram (1960), *Plans and the Structure of Behavior*.

Where the maintenance of the learner's interest is concerned, I remind you of what my colleague Gordon Allport (1946) has long warned. We have been so concerned with the model of driven behavior, with drive reduction and the *vis a tergo* that, again, until recently, we have tended to overlook the question of what keeps learners interested in the activity of learning, in the achievement of competence beyond bare necessity and first payoff. The work of R. W. White (1959) on effectance motivation, of Harlow and his colleagues (Butler, 1954; Harlow, 1953) on curiosity, and of Heider (1958) and Festinger (1962) on consistency begins to redress the balance. But it is only a beginning.

The invention of antidegradation devices, guarantors that skill and knowledge will be maintained intact, is an exception to our oversight. We psychologists have been up to our ears in it. Our special contribution is the achievement test. But the achievement test has, in the main, reflected the timidity of the educational enterprise as a whole. I believe we know how to determine, though we have not yet devised tests to determine, how pupils use what they learn to think with later in life—for there is the real issue.

I have tried to examine briefly what a culture must do in passing on its amplifying skills and knowledge to a new generation and, even more briefly, how we as psychologists have dealt or failed to deal with the problems. I think the situation is fast changing—with a sharp increase in interest in the conversion problem, the problems of economy of learning, the nature of interest, the relation of knowledge and action. We are, I believe, at a major turning point where psychology will once again concern itself with the design of methods of assisting cognitive growth, be it through the invention of a rational technology of toys, of ways of enriching the environment of the crib and nursery, of organizing the activity of a school, or of devising a curriculum whereby we transmit an organized body of knowledge and skill to a new generation to amplify their powers of mind.

I commented earlier that there was strikingly little knowledge available about the "third way" of training the skills of the young: the first being the play practice of component skills in prehuman primates, the second the teaching-in-context of indigenous societies, and the third being the abstracted, detached method of the school.

Let me now become highly specific. Let me consider a particular course of study, one given in a school, one we are ourselves constructing, trying out, and in a highly qualitative way, evaluating. It is for schools of the kind that exist in Western culture. The experience we have had with this effort, now in its third year, may serve to highlight the kinds of problems and conjectures one encounters in studying how to assist the growth of intellect in this "third way."

There is a dilemma in describing a course of study. One begins by setting forth the intellectual substance of what is to be taught. Yet if such a recounting tempts one to "get across" the subject, the ingredient of pedagogy is in jeopardy. For only in a trivial sense is a course designed to "get something across," merely to impart information. There are better means to that end than teaching. Unless the learner develops his skills, disciplines his taste, deepens his view of the world, the "something" that is got across hardly worth the effort of transmission.

The more "elementary" a course and the younger its students, the more serious must be its pedagogical aim of forming the intellectual powers of those whom it serves. It is as important to justify a good mathematics course by the intellectual discipline it provides or the honesty it promotes as by the mathematics it transmits. Indeed, neither can be accomplished without the other. The content of this particular course is man: his nature as a species, the forces that shaped and continue to shape his humanity. Three questions recur throughout:

> What is human about human beings?
> How did they get that way?
> How can they be made more so?

In pursuit of our questions we explore five matters, each closely associated with the evolution of man as a species, each defining at once the distinctiveness of man and his potentiality for further evolution. The five great humanizing forces are, of course, tool making, language, social organization, the management of man's prolonged childhood, and man's urge to explain. It has been our first lesson in teaching that no pupil, however eager, can appreciate the relevance of, say, tool making or language in human evolution without first grasping the fundamental concept of a tool or what a language is. These are not self-evident matters, even to the expert. So we are involved in teaching not only the role of tools or language in the emergence of man,

but, as a necessary precondition for doing so, setting forth the fundamentals of linguistics or the theory of tools. And it is as often the case as not that (as in the case of the "theory of tools") we must solve a formidable intellectual problem ourselves in order to be able to help our pupils do the same. I should have said at the outset that the "we" I employ in this context is no editorial fiction, but rather a group of anthropologists, zoologists, linguists, theoretical engineers, artists, designers, camera crews, teachers, children, and psychologists. The project is being carried out under my direction at Educational Services, Incorporated, with grants from the National Science Foundation and the Ford Foundation.

While one readily singles out five sources of man's humanization, under no circumstances can they be put into airtight compartments. Human kinship is distinctively different from primate mating patterns precisely because it is classificatory and rests on man's ability to use language. Or, if you will, tool use enhances the division of labor in a society which in turn affects kinship. So while each domain can be treated as a separate set of ideas, their teaching must make it possible for the children to have a sense of their interaction. We have leaned heavily on the use of contrast, highly controlled contrast, to help children achieve detachment from the all too familiar matrix of social life: the contrasts of man versus higher primates, man versus prehistoric man, contemporary technological man versus "primitive" man, and man versus child. The primates are principally baboons, the prehistoric materials mostly from the Olduvai Gorge and Les Eyzies, the "primitive" peoples mostly the Netsilik Eskimos of Pelly Bay and the !Kung Bushmen. The materials, collected for our purposes, are on film, in story, in ethnography, in pictures and drawings, and principally in ideas embodied in exercises.

We have high aspirations. We hope to achieve five goals:

1. To give our pupils respect for and confidence in the powers of their own minds

2. To give them respect, moreover, for the powers of thought concerning the human condition, man's plight, and his social life

3. To provide them with a set of workable models that make it simpler to analyze the nature of the social world in which they live and the condition in which man finds himself

4. To impart a sense of respect for the capacities and plight of man as a species, for his origins, for his potential, for his humanity

5. To leave the student with a sense of the unfinished business of man's evolution

One last word about the course of study that has to do with the quality of the ideas, materials, and artistry—a matter that is at once technological and intellectual. We have felt that the making of such a curriculum deserved the best talent and technique available in the world. Whether artist, ethnographer, film maker, poet, teacher—nobody we have asked has refused us. We are obviously going to suffer in testing a Hawthorne effect of some magnitude. But then, perhaps it is as well to live in a permanent state of revolution.

Let me now try to describe some of the major problems one encounters in trying to construct a course of study. I shall not try to translate the problems into refined theoretical form, for they do not as yet merit such translation. They are more difficulties than problems. I choose them, because they are vividly typical of what one encounters in such enterprises. The course is designed for 10-year-olds in the fifth grade of elementary school, but we have been trying it out as well on the fourth and sixth grades better to bracket our difficulties.

One special point about these difficulties. They are born of trying to achieve an objective and are as much policy bound as theory bound. It is like the difference between building an economic theory about monopolistic practices and constructing policies for controlling monopoly. Let me remind you that modern economic theory has been reformulated, refined, and revived by having a season in policy. I am convinced that the psychology of assisted growth, i.e., pedagogy, will have to be forged in the policy crucible of curriculum making before it can reach its full descriptive power as theory. Economics was first through the cycle from theory to policy to theory to policy; it is happening now to psychology, anthropology, and sociology.

Now on to the difficulties. The first is what might be called *the psychology of a subject matter*. A learned discipline can be conceived as a way of thinking about certain phenomena. Mathematics is one way of thinking about order without reference to what is being ordered. The behavioral sciences provide one or perhaps several ways of thinking about man and his society—about regularities, origins, causes, effects. They are probably special (and suspect) because they permit man to look at himself from a perspective that is outside his own skin and beyond his own preferences—at least for awhile.

Underlying a discipline's "way of thought," there is a set of connected, varyingly implicit, generative propositions. In physics and mathematics, most of the underlying generative propositions like the conservation theorems, or the axioms of geometry, or the associative, distributive, and commutative rules of analysis are by now very explicit indeed. In the behavioral sciences we must be content with more implicitness. We traffic in inductive propositions: e.g., the different activities of a society are interconnected such that if you know something about the technological response of a society to an environment, you will be able to make some shrewd guesses about its myths or about the things it values, etc. We use the device of a significant contrast as in linguistics as when we describe the territoriality of a baboon troop in order to help us recognize the system of reciprocal exchange of a human group, the former somehow provoking awareness of the latter.

There is nothing more central to a discipline than its way of thinking. There is nothing more important in its teaching than to provide the child the earliest opportunity to learn that way of thinking—the forms of connection, the attitudes, hopes, jokes, and frustrations that go with it. In a word, the best introduction to a subject is the subject itself. At the very first breath, the young learner should, we think, be given the chance to solve problems, to conjecture, to quarrel as these are done at the heart of the discipline. But, you will ask, how can this be arranged?

Here again the problem of conversion. There exist ways of thinking characteristic of different stages of development. We are acquainted with Inhelder and Piaget's (1958) account of the transition from preoperational, through concrete operational, to propositional thought in the years from preschool through, say, high school. If you have an eventual pedagogical objective in mind, you can translate the way of thought of a discipline into its Piagetian (or other) equivalent appropriate to a given level of development and take the child onward from there. The Cambridge Mathematics Project of Educational Services, Incorporated, argues that if the child is to master the calculus early in his high school years, he should start work early with the idea of limits, the earliest work being manipulative, later going on to images and diagrams, and finally moving on to the more abstract notation needed for delineating the more precise idea of limits.

In "Man: A Course of Study," (Bruner, 1965) there are also versions of the subject appropriate to a particular age that can at a later age be given a more powerful rendering. We have tried to choose topics with this in mind: The analysis of kinship that begins with children using sticks and blocks and colors and whatnot to represent their own families, goes on to the conventional kinship diagrams by a meandering but, as you can imagine, interesting path, and then can move on to more formal and powerful componential analysis. So, too, with myth. We begin with the excitement of a powerful myth (like the Netsilik Nuliajik myth), then have the children construct some myths of their own, then examine what a set of Netsilik myths have in common, which takes us finally to Lévi-Strauss's (1963) analysis of contrastive features in myth construction. A variorum text of a myth or corpus of myths put together by sixth graders can be quite an extraordinary document.

This approach to the psychology of a learned discipline turns out to illuminate another problem raised earlier: the maintenance of interest. There is, in this approach, a reward in understanding that grows from the subject matter itself. It is easier to engineer this satisfaction in mathematics, for understanding is so utter in a formal discipline—a balance beam balances or it does not; therefore there is an equality or there is not. In the behavioral sciences the payoff in understanding cannot be so obviously and startlingly self-revealing. Yet, one can design exercises in the understanding of man, too—as when children figure out the ways in which, given limits of ecology, skills, and materials, Bushmen hunt different animals, and then compare their predictions with the real thing on film.

Consider now a second problem: *how to stimulate thought in the setting of a school.* We know from experimental studies like those of Bloom and Broder (1950), and of Goodnow and Pettigrew (1955), that there is a striking difference in the acts of a person who thinks that the task before him represents a problem to be solved rather than being controlled by random forces. School is a particular subculture where these matters are concerned. By school age, children have come to expect quite arbitrary and, from their point of view, meaningless demands to be made upon them by adults—the result, most likely, of the fact that adults often fail to recognize the task of conversion necessary to make their questions have some intrinsic significance for the child. Children, of course, will try to solve problems if they recognize them as such. But they are not often either predisposed to or skillful in problem finding, in recognizing the hidden conjectural feature in tasks set them. But we know now that children in school can quite quickly be led to such problem finding by encouragement and instruction.

The need for this instruction and encouragement and its relatively swift success relates, I suspect, to what psychoanalysts refer to as the guilt-ridden oversuppression of primary process and its public replacement by secondary process. Children, like adults, need reassurance that it is all right to entertain and express highly subjective ideas, to treat a task as a problem where you *invent* an answer rather than *finding* one out there in the book or on the blackboard. With children in elementary school, there is often a need to devise emotionally vivid special games, story-making episodes, or construction projects to reestablish in the child's mind his right not only to have his own private ideas but to express them in the public setting of a classroom.

But there is another, perhaps more serious difficulty: the interference of intrinsic problem solving by extrinsic. Young children in school expend extraordinary time and effort figuring out what it is that the teacher wants—and usually coming to the conclusion that she or he wants tidiness or remembering or to do things at a certain time in a certain way. This I refer to as extrinsic problem solving. There is a great deal of it in school.

There are several quite straightforward ways of stimulating problem solving. One is to train teachers to want it and that will come in time. But teachers can be encouraged to like it, interestingly enough, by providing them and their children with materials and lessons that *permit* legitimate problem solving and permit the teacher to recognize it. For exercises with such materials create an atmosphere by treating things as instances of what *might* have occurred rather than simply as what did occur. Let me illustrate by a concrete instance. A fifth-grade class was working on the organization of a baboon troop—on this particular day, specifically on how they might protect against predators. They saw a brief sequence of film in which six or seven adult males go forward to intimidate and hold off three cheetahs. The teacher asked what the baboons had done to keep the cheetahs off, and there ensued a lively discussion of how the dominant adult males, by showing their formidable mouthful of teeth and making threatening gestures had turned the trick. A boy raised a tentative hand and asked whether cheetahs always attacked together. Yes, though a single cheetah sometimes followed behind a moving troop and picked off an older, weakened straggler or an unwary, straying juvenile. "Well, what if there were four cheetahs and two of them attacked from behind and two from in front. What would the baboons do then?" The question could have been answered empirically—and the inquiry ended. Cheetahs *do not* attack that way, and so we do not know what baboons *might* do. Fortunately, it was not. For the question opens up the deep issues of what might be and why it is not. Is there a necessary relation between predators and prey that share a common ecological niche? Must their encounters have a "sporting chance" outcome? It is such conjecture, in this case quite unanswerable, that produces rational, self-consciously problem-finding behavior so crucial to the growth of intellectual power. Given the materials, given some background and encouragement, teachers like it as much as the students.

I should like to turn now to the *personalization of knowledge*. A generation ago, the progressive movement urged that knowledge be related to the child's own experience and brought out of the realm of empty abstractions. A good idea was translated into banalities about the home, then the friendly postman and trashman, then the community, and so on. It is a poor way to compete with the child's own dramas and mysteries. A decade ago, my colleague Clyde Kluckholn (1949) wrote a prize-winning popular book on anthropology with the entrancing title *Mirror for Man*. In some deep way, there is extraordinary power in "that mirror which other civilizations still hold up to us to recognize and study...[the] image of ourselves [Lévi-Strauss, 1965]." The psychological bases of the power are not obvious. Is it as in discrimination learning, where increasing the degree of contrast helps in the learning of a discrimination, or as in studies of concept attainment where a negative instance demonstrably defines the domain of a conceptual rule? Or is it some primitive identification? All these miss one thing that seems to come up frequently in our interviews with the children. It is the experience of discovering kinship and likeness in what at first seemed bizarre, exotic, and even a little repellent.

Consider two examples, both involving film of the Netsilik. In the films, a single nuclear family, Zachary, Marta, and their 4-year-old Alexi, is followed through the year—spring sealing, summer fishing at the stone weir, fall caribou hunting, early winter fishing through the ice, winter at the big ceremonial igloo. Children report that at first the three members of the family look weird and uncouth. In time, they look normal, and eventually, as when Marta finds sticks around which to wrap her braids, the girls speak of how pretty she is. That much is superficial—or so it seems. But consider a second episode.

It has to do with Alexi who, with his father's help, devises a snare and catches a gull. There is a scene in which he stones the gull to death. Our children watched, horror struck. One girl, Kathy, blurted out, "He's not even human, doing that to the seagull." The class was silent. Then another girl, Jennine, said quietly: "He's got to grow up to be a hunter. His mother was smiling when he was doing that." And then an extended discussion about how people have to do things to learn and even do things to learn how to feel appropriately. "What would you do if you had to live there? Would you be as smart about getting along as they are with what they've got?" said one boy, going back to the accusation that Alexi was inhuman to stone the bird.

I am sorry it is so difficult to say it clearly. What I am trying to say is that to personalize knowledge one does not simply link it to the familiar. Rather one makes the familiar an instance of a more general case and thereby produces awareness of it. What the children were learning about was not seagulls and Eskimos, but about their own feelings and preconceptions that, up to then, were too implicit to be recognizable to them.

Consider finally the problem of *self-conscious reflectiveness*. It is an epistemological mystery why traditional education has so often emphasized extensiveness and coverage over intensiveness and depth. We have already commented on the fact that memorizing was usually perceived by children as one of the high-priority tasks but rarely did children sense an emphasis upon ratiocination with a view toward redefining what had been encountered, reshaping it, reordering it. The cultivation of reflectiveness, or whatever you choose to call it, is one of the great problems one faces in devising curriculum. How lead children to discover the powers and pleasures that await the exercise of retrospection?

Let me suggest one answer that has grown from what we have done. It is the use of the "organizing conjecture." We have used three such conjectures—what is human about human beings, how they got that way, how they could become more so. They serve two functions, one of them the very obvious though important one of putting perspective back into the particulars. The second is less obvious and considerably more surprising. The questions often seemed to serve as criteria for determining where they were getting, how well they were understanding, whether anything new was emerging. Recall Kathy's cry: "He's not human doing that to the seagull." She was hard at work in her rage on the conjecture what makes human beings human.

There, in brief, are four problems that provide some sense of what a psychologist encounters when he takes a hand in assisting the growth of mind in children in the special setting of a school. The problems look quite different from those we encounter in formulating classical developmental theory with the aid of typical laboratory research. They also look very different from those that one would find in an indigenous society, describing how children picked up skills and knowledge and values in the context of action and daily life. We clearly do not have a theory of the school that is sufficient to the task of running schools—just as we have no adequate theory of toys or of readiness building or whatever the jargon is for preparing children to do a better job the next round. It only obscures the issue to urge that some day our classical theories of learning will fill the gap. They show no sign of doing so.

I hope that we shall not allow ourselves to be embarrassed by our present ignorance. It has been a long time since we have looked at what is involved in imparting knowledge through the vehicle of the school—if ever we did look at it squarely. I urge that we delay no longer.

But I am deeply convinced that the psychologist cannot alone construct a theory of how to assist cognitive development and cannot alone learn how to enrich and amplify the powers of a growing human mind. The task belongs to the whole intellectual community: the behavioral scientists and the artists, scientists, and scholars who are the custodians of skill, taste, and knowledge in our culture. Our special task as psychologists is to convert skills and knowledge to forms and exercises that fit growing minds—and it is a task ranging from how to keep children free from anxiety and how to translate physics for the very young child into a set of playground maneuvers that, later, the child can turn around upon and convert into a sense of inertial regularities.

And this in turn leads me to a final conjecture, one that has to do with the organization of our profession, a matter that has concerned me greatly during this past year during which I have had the privilege of serving as your President.

Psychology is peculiarly prey to parochialism. Left to our own devices, we tend to construct models of a man who is neither a victim of history, a target of economic forces, or even a working member of a society. I am still struck by Roger Barker's (1963) ironic truism that the best way to predict the behavior of a human being is to know where he is: In a post office he behaves post office, at church he behaves church.

Psychology, and you will forgive me if the image seems a trifle frivolous, thrives on polygamy with her neighbors. Our marriage with the biological sciences has produced a cumulation of ever more powerful knowledge. So, too, our joint undertakings with anthropology and sociology. Joined together with a variety of disciplines, we have made lasting contributions to the health sciences and, I judge, will make even greater contributions now that the emphasis is shifting to the problems of alleviating stress and arranging for a community's mental health. What I find lacking is an alignment that might properly be called the growth sciences. The field of pedagogy is one participant in the growth sciences. Any field of inquiry devoted to assisting the growth of effective human beings, fully empowered with zest, with skill, with knowledge, with taste is surely a candidate for this sodality. My friend Philip Morrison once suggested to his colleagues at Cornell that his department of physics grant a doctorate not only for work in theoretical, experimental, or applied physics, but also for work in pedagogical physics. The limits of the growth sciences remain to be drawn. They surely transcend the behavioral sciences cum pediatrics. It is plain that, if we are to achieve the effectiveness of which we as human beings are capable, there will one day have to be such a field. I hope that we psychologists can earn our way as charter members.

REFERENCES

ALLPORT, G. Effect: A secondary principle of learning. *Psychological Review*, 1946, 53, 335–347.

BARKER, R. On the nature of the environment. *Journal of Social Issues,* 1963, 19, 17–38.

BARTLETT, F. *Remembering.* Cambridge, England: Cambridge Univer. Press, 1932.

BIESHEUVEL, S. Psychological tests and their application to non-European peoples. *Yearbook of Education.* London: Evans, 1949. Pp. 87–126.

BLOOM, B., & BRODER, L. Problem solving processes of college students. *Supplementary Educational Monograph, No. 73.* Chicago: Univer. Chicago Press, 1950.

BRUNER, J. The course of cognitive growth. *American Psychologist,* 1964, 19, 1–15.

BRUNER, J. Man: A course of study. *Educational Services Inc. Quarterly Report,* 1965, Spring-Summer, 3–13.

BRUNER, J. *Toward a theory of instruction.* Cambridge: Harvard Univer. Press, in press.

BUTLER, R. A. Incentive conditions which influence visual exploration. *Journal of Experimental Psychology* 1954, 48, 19–23.

EBBINGHAUS, H. *Memory: A contribution to experimental Psychology.* New York: Teachers College, Columbia University, 1913.

FESTINGER, L. A theory of cognitive dissonance. Stanford: Stanford Univer. Press, 1962.

GAY, J., & COLE, M. Outline of general report on Kpelle mathematics project. Stanford: Stanford University, Institute for Mathematical Social Studies, undated. (Mimeo)

GOODNOW, JACQUELINE, & PETTIGREW, T. Effect of prior patterns of experience on strategies and learning sets. *Journal of Experimental Psychology,* 1955, 49, 381–389.

GREENFIELD, PATRICIA M. Culture and conservation. In J. BRUNER, ROSE OLVER, & PATRICIA M. GREENFIELD (Eds.), *Studies in cognitive growth.* New York: Wiley, in press. Ch. 10.

HARLOW, H., & HARLOW, MARGARET. Social deprivation in monkeys. *Scientific American,* 1962, November.

HARLOW, H. F. Mice, monkeys, men, and motives. *Psychological Review,* 1953, 60, 23–32.

HEIDER, F. *The psychology of interpersonal relations.* New York: Wiley, 1958.

INHELDER, BARBEL, & PIAGET, J. *The growth of logical thinking.* New York: Basic Books, 1958.

KLUCKHOLN, C. *Mirror for man.* New York: Whittlesey House, 1949.

KÖHLER, W. *Dynamics in psychology.* New York: Liveright, 1940.

LÉVI-STRAUSS, C. The structural study of myth. *Structural anthropology.* (Trans. by Claire Jacobson & B. Grundfest Scharpf) New York: Basic Books, 1963. Pp. 206–231.

LÉVI-STRAUSS, C. Anthropology: Its achievements and future. Lecture presented at Bicentennial Celebration, Smithsonian Institution, Washington, D. C., September 1965.

MACCOBY, M., & MODIANO, NANCY. On culture and equivalence. In J. BRUNER, ROSE OLVER, & PATRICIA M. GREENFIELD (Eds.), *Studies in cognitive growth.* New York: Wiley, in press. Ch. 12.

MILLER, G., GALANTER, E., & PRIBRAM, K. *Plans and the structure of behavior.* New York: Holt, 1960.

PIAGET, J. *The construction of reality in the child.* New York: Basic Books, 1954.

REICH, LEE. On culture and grouping. In J. BRUNER, ROSE OLVER, & PATRICIA M. GREENFIELD (Eds.), *Studies in cognitive growth.* New York: Wiley, in press. Ch. 13.

TOLMAN, E. Cognitive maps in rats and men. *Collected papers in psychology.* Berkeley & Los Angeles: Univer. California Press, 1951. Pp. 241–264.

VYGOTSKY, L. *Thought and language.* (Ed. & trans. by Eugenia Hanfmann & Gertrude Vakar) New York: Wiley, 1962.

WERTHEIMER, M. *Productive thinking.* New York & London: Harper, 1945.

WHITE, MARY A. The child's world of learning. Teachers College, Columbia University, undated. (Mimeo)

WHITE, R. W. Motivation reconsidered: The concept of competence. *Psychological Review,* 1959, 66, 297–333.

THE CONCEPTS OF BALANCE, CONGRUITY, AND DISSONANCE

Robert B. Zajonc

Common to the concepts of balance, congruity, and dissonance is the notion that thoughts, beliefs, attitudes, and behavior tend to organize themselves in meaningful and sensible ways.[1] Members of the White Citizens Council do not ordinarily contribute to NAACP. Adherents of the New Deal seldom support Republican candidates. Christian Scientists do not enroll in medical schools. And people who live in glass houses apparently do not throw stones. In this respect the concept of consistency underscores and presumes human *rationality*. It holds that

behavior and attitudes are not only consistent to the objective observer, but that individuals try to appear consistent to themselves. It assumes that inconsistency is a noxious state setting up pressures to eliminate it or reduce it. But in the *ways* that consistency in human behavior and attitudes is achieved we see rather often a striking lack of rationality. A heavy smoker cannot readily accept evidence relating cancer to smoking;[2] a socialist, told that Hoover's endorsement of certain political slogans agreed perfectly with his own, calls him a "typical hypocrite and a liar."[3] Allport illustrates this irrationality in the following conversation:

MR. X: The trouble with Jews is that they only take care of their own group.

MR. Y: But the record of the Community Chest shows that they give more generously than non-Jews.

MR. X: That shows that they are always trying to buy favor and intrude in

From: Public Opinion Quarterly, *1960, 24, 280–95. Copyright © 1960 by the Columbia University Press, and reproduced by permission of the author and publisher.*

[1] The concepts of balance, congruity, and dissonance are due to Heider, Osgood and Tannenbaum, and Festinger, respectively. (F. Heider, "Attitudes and Cognitive Organization," *Journal of Psychology,* Vol. 21, 1946, pp. 107–112. C. E. Osgood and P. H. Tannenbaum, "The Principle of Congruity in the Prediction of Attitude Change," *Psychological Review,* Vol. 62, 1955, pp. 42–55. L. Festinger, *A Theory of Cognitive Dissonance,* New York: Harper & Row, 1957.) For purposes of simplicity we will subsume these concepts under the label of consistency.

[2] Festinger, *op. cit.,* pp. 153–156.

[3] H. B. Lewis, "Studies in the Principles of Judgments and Attitudes: IV, The Operation of 'Prestige Suggestion'," *Journal of Social Psychology,* Vol. 14, 1941, pp. 229–256.

Christian affairs. They think of nothing but money; that is why there are so many Jewish bankers.

MR. Y: But a recent study shows that the percent of Jews in banking is proportionally much smaller than the percent of non-Jews.

MR. X: That's just it. They don't go in for respectable business. They would rather run night clubs.[4]

Thus, while the concept of consistency acknowledges man's rationality, observation of the means of its achievement simultaneously unveils his irrationality. The psychoanalytic notion of rationalization is a literal example of a concept which assumes both rationality and irrationality —it holds, namely, that man strives to understand and justify painful experiences and to make them sensible and rational, but he employs completely irrational methods to achieve this end.

The concepts of consistency are not novel. Nor are they indigenous to the study of attitudes, behavior, or personality. These concepts have appeared in various forms in almost all sciences. It has been argued by some that it is the existence of consistencies in the universe that made science possible, and by others that consistencies in the universe are a proof of divine power.[5] There is, of course, a question of whether consistencies are "real" or mere products of ingenious abstraction and conceptualization. For it would be entirely possible to categorize natural phenomena in such a haphazard way that instead of order, unity, and consistency, one would see a picture of utter chaos. If we were to eliminate one of the spatial dimensions from the conception of the physical world, the consistencies we now know and the consistencies which allow

us to make reliable predictions would be vastly depleted.

The concept of consistency in man is, then, a special case of the concept of universal consistency. The fascination with this concept led some psychologists to rather extreme positions. Franke, for instance, wrote, "...the unity of a person can be traced in each instant of his life. There is nothing in character that contradicts itself. If a person who is known to us seems to be incongruous with himself that is only an indication of the inadequacy and superficiality of our previous observations."[6] This sort of hypothesis is, of course, incapable of either verification or disproof and therefore has no significant consequences.

Empirical investigations employing the concepts of consistency have been carried out for many years. Not until recently, however, has there been a programmatic and systematic effort to explore with precision and detail their particular consequences for behavior and attitudes. The greatest impetus to the study of attitudinal consistency was given recently by Festinger and his students. In addition to those already named, other related contributions in this area are those of Newcomb, who introduced the concept of "strain toward symmetry,"[7] and of Cartwright and Harary, who expressed the notions of balance and symmetry in a mathematical form.[8] These notions all assume inconsistency to be a painful or at least psychologically uncomfortable state, but they differ in the generality of application. The most restrictive and spe-

[4] G. W. Allport, *The Nature of Prejudice*, Cambridge, Mass., Addison-Wesley, 1954.

[5] W. P. Montague, *Belief Unbound*, New Haven, Conn., Yale University Press, 1930, pp. 70–73.

[6] R. Franke, "Gang und Character," *Beihefte, Zeitschrift für angewandte Psychologie*, No. 58, 1931, p. 45.

[7] T. M. Newcomb, "An Approach to the Study of Communicative Acts," *Psychological Review*, Vol. 60, 1953, pp. 393–404.

[8] D. Cartwright and F. Harary, "Structural Balance: A Generalization of Heider's Theory," *Psychological Review*, Vol. 63, 1956, pp. 277–293.

cific is the principle of congruity, since it restricts itself to the problems of the effects of information about objects and events on the attitudes toward the source of information. The most general is the notion of cognitive dissonance, since it considers consistency among any cognitions. In between are the notions of balance and symmetry, which consider attitudes toward people and objects in relation to one another, either within one person's cognitive structure, as in the case of Heider's theory of balance, or among a given group of individuals, as in the case of Newcomb's strain toward symmetry. It is the purpose of this paper to survey these concepts and to consider their implications for theory and research on attitudes.

THE CONCEPTS OF BALANCE AND STRAIN TOWARD SYMMETRY

The earliest formalization of consistency is attributed to Heider,[9] who was concerned with the way relations among persons involving some impersonal entity are cognitively experienced by the individual. The consistencies in which Heider was interested were those to be found in the ways people view their relations with

[9] Heider, *op. cit.*

other people and with the environment. The analysis was limited to two persons, labeled P and O, with P as the focus of the analysis and with O representing some other person, and to one impersonal entity, which could be a physical object, an idea, an event, or the like, labeled X. The object of Heider's inquiry was to discover how relations among P, O, and X are organized in P's cognitive structure, and whether there exist recurrent and systematic tendencies in the way these relations are experienced. Two types of relation, linking (L) and so-called U, or unit, relations (such as possession, cause, similarity, and the like) were distinguished. On the basis of incidental observations and intuitive judgment, probably, Heider proposed that the person's (P's) cognitive structure representing relations among P, O, and X are either what he termed "balanced" or "unbalanced." In particular, he proposed, "In the case of three entities, a balanced state exists if all three relations are positive in all respects or if two are negative and one positive." Thus a balanced state is obtained when, for instance, P likes O, P likes X, and O likes X; or when P likes O, P dislikes X, and O dislikes X; or when P dislikes O, P likes X, and O dislikes X (see Figure 1). It should be noted that within Heider's conception a relation

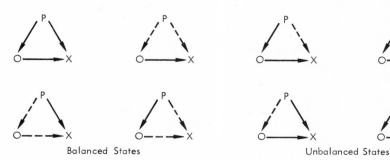

Balanced States   Unbalanced States

Figure 1. Examples of balanced and unbalanced states according to Heider's definition of balance. Solid lines represent positive, and broken lines negative, relations.

may be either positive or negative; degrees of liking cannot be represented. The fundamental assumption of balance theory is that an unbalanced state produces tension and generates forces to restore balance. This hypothesis was tested by Jordan.[10] He presented subjects with hypothetical situations involving two persons and an impersonal entity to rate for "pleasantness." Half the situations were by Heider's definition balanced and half unbalanced. Jordan's data showed somewhat higher unpleasantness ratings for the unbalanced than the balanced situations.

Cartwright and Harary[11] have cast Heider's formulation in graph-theoretical terms and derived some interesting consequences beyond those stated by Heider. Heider's concept allows either a balanced or an unbalanced state. Cartwright and Harary have constructed a more general definition of balance, with balance treated as a matter of degree, ranging from 0 to 1. Furthermore, their formulation of balance theory extended the notion to any number of entities, and an experiment by Morrissette[12] similar in design to that of Jordan obtained evidence for Cartwright and Harary's derivations.

A notion very similar to balance was advanced by Newcomb in 1953.[13] In addition to substituting A for P, and B for O, Newcomb took Heider's notion of balance out of one person's head and applied it to communication among people. Newcomb postulates a "strain toward symmetry" which leads to a communality of attitudes of two people (A and B) oriented toward an object (X). The strain toward symmetry influences communication between A and B so as to bring their attitudes toward X into congruence. Newcomb cites a study in which a questionnaire was administered to college students in 1951 following the dismissal of General MacArthur by President Truman. Data were obtained on students' attitudes toward Truman's decision and their perception of the attitudes of their closest friends. Of the pro-Truman subjects 48 said that their closest friends favored Truman and none that their closest friends were opposed to his decision. Of the anti-Truman subjects only 2 said that their friends were generally pro-Truman and 34 that they were anti-Truman. In a longitudinal study, considerably more convincing evidence was obtained in support of the strain-toward-symmetry hypothesis. In 1954 Newcomb set up a house at the University of Michigan which offered free rent for one semester for seventeen students who would serve as subjects. The residents of the house were observed, questioned, and rated for four to five hours a week during the entire semester. The study was then repeated with another set of seventeen students. The findings revealed a tendency for those who were attracted to one another to agree on many matters, including the way they perceived their own selves and their ideal selves, and their attractions for other group members. Moreover, in line with the prediction, these similarities, real as well as perceived, seemed to increase over time.[14]

Newcomb also cites the work of Festinger and his associates on social communication[15] in support of his hypoth-

[10] N. Jordan, "Behavioral Forces That Are a Function of Attitudes and of Cognitive Organization," *Human Relations,* Vol. 6, 1953, pp. 273–287.

[11] Cartwright and Harary, *op. cit.*

[12] J. Morrissette, "An Experimental Study of the Theory of Structural Balance," *Human Relations,* Vol. 11, 1958, pp. 239–254.

[13] Newcomb, *op. cit.*

[14] T. M. Newcomb, "The Prediction of Interpersonal Attraction," *American Psychologist,* Vol. 11, 1956, pp. 575–586.

[15] L. Festinger, K. Back, S. Schachter, H. H. Kelley, and J. Thibaut, *Theory and Experiment in Social Communication,* Ann Arbor, Mich., University of Michigan, Institute for Social Research, 1950.

esis. Festinger's studies on communication have clearly shown that the tendency to influence other group members toward one's own opinion increases with the degree of attraction. More recently Burdick and Burnes reported two experiments in which measures of skin resistance (GSR) were obtained as an index emotional reaction in the presence of balanced and unbalanced situations.[16] They observed significant differences in skin resistance depending on whether the subjects agreed or disagreed with a "well-liked experimenter." In the second experiment Burdick and Burnes found that subjects who liked the experimenter tended to change their opinions toward greater agreement with his, and those who disliked him, toward greater disagreement. There are, of course, many other studies to show that the attitude toward the communicator determines his persuasive effectiveness. Hovland and his co-workers have demonstrated these effects in several studies.[17] They have also shown, however, that these effects are fleeting; that is, the attitude change produced by the communication seems to dissipate over time. Their interpretation is that over time subjects tend to dissociate the source from the message and are therefore subsequently less influenced by the prestige of the communicator. This proposition was substantiated by Kelman and Hovland,[18] who produced attitude changes with a prestigeful communicator and re-

tested subjects after a four-week interval with and without reminding the subjects about the communicator. The results showed that the permanence of the attitude change depended on the association with the source.

In general, the consequences of balance theories have up to now been rather limited. Except for Newcomb's longitudinal study, the experimental situations dealt mostly with subjects who responded to hypothetical situations, and direct evidence is scarce. The Burdick and Burnes experiment is the only one bearing more directly on the assumption that imbalance or asymmetry produces tension. Cartwright and Harary's mathematization of the concept of balance should, however, lead to important empirical and theoretical developments. One difficulty is that there really has not been a serious experimental attempt to *disprove* the theory. It is conceivable that some situations defined by the theory as unbalanced may in fact remain stable and produce no significant pressures toward balance. Festinger once inquired in a jocular mood if it followed from balance theory that since he likes chicken, and since chickens like chicken feed, he must also like chicken feed or else experience the tension of imbalance. While this counterexample is, of course, not to be taken seriously, it does point to some difficulties in the concepts of balance. It is not clear from Heider's theory of balance and Newcomb's theory of symmetry what predictions are to be made when attraction of both P and O toward X exists but when the origin and nature of these attractions are different. In other words, suppose both P and O like X but for different reasons and in entirely different ways, as was the case with Festinger and the chickens. Are the consequences of balance theory the same then as in the case where P and O like X for the same reasons and in the same way? It is also

[16] H. A. Burdick and A. J. Burnes, "A Test of 'Strain toward Symmetry' Theories," *Journal of Abnormal and Social Psychology,* Vol. 57, 1958, pp. 367–369.

[17] C. I. Hovland, I. L. Janis, and H. H. Kelley, *Communication and Persuasion: Psychological Studies of Opinion Change,* New Haven, Conn., Yale University Press, 1953.

[18] H. C. Kelman and C. I. Hovland, " 'Reinstatement' of the Communicator in Delayed Measurement of Opinion Change," *Journal of Abnormal and Social Psychology,* Vol. 48, 1953, pp. 327–335.

not clear, incidentally, what the consequences are when the relation between P and O is cooperative and when it is competitive. Two men vying for the hand of the same fair maiden might experience tension whether they are close friends or deadly enemies.

In a yet unpublished study conducted by Harburg and Price at the University of Michigan, students were asked to name two of their best friends. When those named were of opposite sexes, subjects reported they would feel uneasy if the two friends liked one another. In a subsequent experiment subjects were asked whether they desired their good friend to like, be neutral to, or dislike one of their strongly disliked acquaintances, and whether they desired the disliked acquaintance to like or dislike the friend. It will be recalled that in either case a balanced state obtains only if the two persons are negatively related to one another. However, Harburg and Price found that 39 percent desired their friend to be liked by the disliked acquaintance, and only 24 percent to be disliked. Moreover, faced with the alternative that the disliked acquaintance dislikes their friend, 55 percent as opposed to 25 percent expressed uneasiness. These results are quite inconsistent with balance theory. Although one may want one's friends to dislike one's enemies, one may not want the enemies to dislike one's friends. The reason for the latter may be simply a concern for the friends' welfare.

OSGOOD AND TANNENBAUM'S PRINCIPLE OF CONGRUITY

The principle of congruity, which is in fact a special case of balance, was advanced by Osgood and Tannenbaum in 1955.[19] It deals specifically with the prob-

[19] Osgood and Tannenbaum, *op. cit.*

lem of *direction* of attitude change. The authors assume that "judgmental frames of reference tend toward maximal simplicity." Thus, since extreme "black-and-white," "all-or-nothing," judgments are simpler than refined ones, valuations tend to move toward extremes or, in the words of the authors, there is "a continuing pressure toward polarization." Together with the notion of maximization of simplicity is the assumption of identity as being less complex than the discrimination of fine differences. Therefore, related "concepts" will tend to be evaluated in a similar manner. Given these assumptions, the principle of congruity holds that when change in evaluation or attitude occurs it always occurs in the direction of increased congruity with the prevailing frame of reference. The paradigm of congruity is that of an individual who is confronted with an assertion regarding a particular matter about which he believes and feels in a certain way, made by a person toward whom he also has some attitude. Given that Eisenhower is evaluated positively and freedom of the press also positively, and given that Eisenhower $(+)$ comes out in favor of freedom of the press $(+)$, congruity is said to exist. But given that the *Daily Worker* is evaluated negatively, and given that the *Daily Worker* $(-)$ comes out in favor of freedom of the press $(+)$, incongruity is said to exist. Examples of congruity and incongruity are shown in Figure 2. The diagram shows the attitudes of a given individual toward the source and the object of the assertion. The assertions represented by heavy lines imply either positive or negative attitudes of the source toward the object. It is clear from a comparison of Figures 1 and 2 that in terms of their formal properties, the definitions of balance and congruity are identical. Thus, incongruity is said to exist when the attitudes toward the source and the object are similar and the asser-

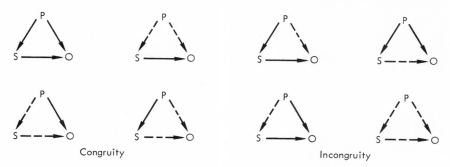

Figure 2. Examples of congruity and incongruity. Heavy lines represent assertions, light lines attitudes. Solid heavy lines represent assertions which imply a positive attitude on the part of the source, and broken heavy lines negative attitudes. Solid light lines represent positive, and broken lines, negative, attitudes.

tion is negative, or when they are dissimilar and the assertion is positive. In comparison, unbalanced states are defined as having either one or all negative relations, which is of course equivalent to the above. To the extent that the person's attitudes are congruent with those implied in the assertion, a stable state exists. When the attitudes toward the person and the assertion are incongruent, there will be a tendency to change the attitudes toward the person and the object of the assertion in the direction of increased congruity. Tannenbaum obtained measures on 405 college students regarding their attitudes toward labor leaders, the *Chicago Tribune,* and Senator Robert Taft as sources, and toward legalized gambling, abstract art, and accelerated college programs as objects. Some time after the attitude scores were obtained, the subjects were presented with "highly realistic" newspaper clippings involving assertions made by the various sources regarding the concepts. In general, when the original attitudes toward the source and the concept were both positive and the assertion presented in the newspaper clippings was also positive, no significant attitude changes were observed in the results. When the original attitudes

toward the source and the concept were negative and the assertion was positive, again no changes were obtained. As predicted, however, when a positively valued source was seen as making a positive assertion about a negatively valued concept, the attitude toward the source became less favorable, and toward the concept more favorable. Conversely, when a negatively valued source was seen as making a positive assertion about a positively valued concept, attitudes toward the source became more favorable and toward the concept less favorable. The entire gamut of predicted changes was confirmed in Tannenbaum's data; it is summarized in the accompanying table, in which the direction of change is represented by either a plus or a minus sign, and the extent of change by either one or two such signs.

A further derivation of the congruity principle is that incongruity does not invariably produce attitude change, but that it may at times lead to incredulity on the part of the individual. When confronted by an assertion which stands in an incongruous relation to the person who made it, there will be a tendency not to believe that the person made the assertion, thus reducing incongruity.

TABLE 1

CHANGE OF ATTITUDE TOWARD THE SOURCE AND THE
OBJECT WHEN POSITIVE AND NEGATIVE ASSERTIONS
ARE MADE BY THE SOURCE

Original Attitude Toward the Source	Positive Assertion About an Object Toward Which the Attitude Is		Negative Assertion About an Object Toward Which the Attitude Is	
	Positive	Negative	Positive	Negative
CHANGE OF ATTITUDE TOWARD THE SOURCE				
Positive	+	− −	− −	+
Negative	+ +	−	−	+ +
CHANGE OF ATTITUDE TOWARD THE OBJECT				
Positive	+	+ +	− −	−
Negative	− −	−	+	+ +

There is a good deal of evidence supporting Osgood and Tannenbaum's principle of congruity. As early as 1921, H. T. Moore had subjects judge statements for their grammar, ethical infringements for their seriousness, and resolutions of the dominant seventh chord for their dissonance.[20] After two and one-half months the subjects returned and were presented with judgments of "experts." This experimental manipulation resulted in 62 percent reversals of judgments on grammar, 50 percent of ethical judgments, and 43 percent of musical judgments. And in 1935 in a study on a similar problem of prestige suggestion, Sherif let subjects rank sixteen authors for their literary merit.[21] Subsequently, the subjects were given sixteen passages presumably written by the various authors previously ranked. The subjects were asked to rank-order the passages for literary merit. Although in actuality *all* the passages were written by Robert Louis Stevenson, the subjects were able to rank the passages. Moreover, the correlations between the merit of the author and the merit of the passage ranged from between .33 to .53. These correlations are not very dramatic, yet they do represent some impact of attitude toward the source on attitude toward the passage.

With respect to incredulity, an interesting experiment was conducted recently by Jones and Kohler in which subjects learned statements which either supported their attitudes or were in disagreement with them.[22] Some of the statements were plausible and some implausible. The results were rather striking. Subjects whose attitudes favored segregation learned plausible prosegregation statements and implausible antisegregation statements much more rapidly than plausible antisegregation and implausible prosegregation statements. The reverse was of course true for subjects whose attitudes favored desegregation.

While the principle of congruity presents no new ideas, it has a great advantage over the earlier attempts in its precision. Osgood and Tannenbaum have formulated the principle of congruity in quantitative terms allowing for precise

[20] H. T. Moore, "The Comparative Influence of Majority and Expert Opinion," *American Journal of Psychology,* Vol. 32, 1921, pp. 16–20.

[21] M. Sherif, "An Experimental Study of Stereotypes," *Journal of Abnormal and Social Psychology,* Vol. 29, 1935, pp. 371–375.

[22] E. E. Jones and R. Kohler, "The Effects of Plausibility on the Learning of Controversial Statements," *Journal of Abnormal and Social Psychology,* Vol. 57, 1958, pp. 315–320.

predictions regarding the extent and direction of attitude change—predictions which in their studies were fairly well confirmed. While balance theory allows merely a dichotomy of attitudes, either positive or negative, the principle of congruity allows refined measurements using Osgood's method of the semantic differential.[23] Moreover, while it is not clear from Heider's statement of balance in just what direction changes will occur when an unbalanced state exists, such predictions can be made on the basis of the congruity principle.

FESTINGER'S THEORY OF COGNITIVE DISSONANCE

Perhaps the largest systematic body of data is that collected in the realm of Festinger's dissonance theory. The statement of the dissonance principle is simple. It holds that two elements of knowledge "... are in dissonant relation if, considering these two alone, the obverse of one element would follow from the other."[24] It further holds that dissonance "... being psychologically uncomfortable, will motivate the person to try to reduce dissonance and achieve consonance" and "... in addition to trying to reduce it, the person will actively avoid situations and information which would likely increase the dissonance."[25] A number of rather interesting and provocative consequences follow from Festinger's dissonance hypothesis.

First, it is predicted that all decisions or choices result in dissonance to the extent that the alternative not chosen contains positive features which make it attractive also, and the alternative chosen contains features which might have resulted in rejecting it. Hence after making

a choice people seek evidence to confirm their decision and so reduce dissonance. In the Ehrlich experiment cited by Cohen in this issue the finding was that new car owners noticed and read ads about the cars they had recently purchased more than ads about other cars.[26]

Post-decision dissonance was also shown to result in a change of attractiveness of the alternative involved in a decision. Brehm had female subjects rate eight appliances for desirability.[27] Subsequently, the subjects were given a choice between two of the eight products, given the chosen product, and after some interpolated activity (consisting of reading research reports about four of the appliances) were asked to rate the products again. Half the subjects were given a choice between products which they rated in a similar manner, and half between products on which the ratings differed. Thus in the first case higher dissonance was to be expected than in the second. The prediction from dissonance theory that there should be an increase in the attractiveness of the chosen alternative and decrease in the attractiveness of the rejected alternative was on the whole confirmed. Moreover, the further implication was also confirmed that the pressure to reduce dissonance (which was accomplished in the above experiment by changes in attractiveness of the alternatives) varies directly with the extent of dissonance.

Another body of data accounted for by the dissonance hypothesis deals with situations in which the person is forced (either by reward or punishment) to express an opinion publicly or make a public judgment or statement which is

23 C. E. Osgood, "The Nature and Measurement of Meaning," *Psychological Bulletin,* Vol. 49, 1952, pp. 197–237.

24 Festinger, *op. cit.,* p. 13.

25 *Ibid.,* p. 3.

26 D. Ehrlich, I. Guttman, P. Schönbach, and J. Mills, "Post-decision Exposure to Relevant Information," *Journal of Abnormal and Social Psychology,* Vol. 54, 1957, pp. 98–102.

27 J. Brehm, "Post-decision Changes in the Desirability of Alternatives," *Journal of Abnormal and Social Psychology,* Vol. 52, 1956, pp. 384–389.

contrary to his own opinions and beliefs. In cases where the person actually makes such a judgment or expresses an opinion contrary to his own as a result of a promised reward or threat, dissonance exists between the knowledge of the overt behavior of the person and his privately held beliefs. Festinger also argues that in the case of noncompliance dissonance will exist between the knowledge of overt behavior and the anticipation of reward and punishment.

An example of how dissonance theory accounts for forced-compliance data is given by Brehm.[28] Brehm offered prizes to eighth-graders for eating disliked vegetables and obtained measures of how well the children liked the vegetables. Children who ate the vegetables increased their liking for them. Of course, one might argue that a simpler explanation of the results is that the attractiveness of the prize generalized to the vegetable, or that, even more simply, the vegetables increased in utility because a reward came with them. However, this argument would also lead one to predict that the increment in attraction under such conditions is a *direct* function of the magnitude of the reward. Dissonance theory makes the opposite prediction, and therefore a test of the validity of the two explanations is possible. Data collected by Festinger and Carlsmith[29] and by Aronson and Mills[30] support the dissonance point of view. In Festinger and Carlsmith's experiment sub-

jects were offered either 20 dollars or 1 dollar for telling someone that an experience which had actually been quite boring had been rather enjoyable and interesting. When measures of the subjects' private opinions about their actual enjoyment of the task were taken, those who were to be paid only 1 dollar for the false testimony showed considerably higher scores than those who were to be paid 20 dollars. Aronson and Mills, on the other hand, tested the effects of negative incentive. They invited college women to join a group requiring them to go through a process of initiation. For some women the initiation was quite severe, for others it was mild. The prediction from dissonance theory that those who had to undergo severe initiation would increase their attraction for the group more than those having no initiation or mild initiation was borne out.

A third set of consequences of the theory of dissonance deals with exposure to information. Since dissonance occurs between cognitive elements, and since information may lead to change in these elements, the principle of dissonance should have a close bearing on the individual's commerce with information. In particular, the assumption that dissonance is a psychologically uncomfortable state leads to the prediction that individuals will seek out information reducing dissonance and avoid information increasing it. The study on automobile-advertising readership described above is a demonstration of this hypothesis.[31] In another study Mills, Aronson, and Robinson gave college students a choice between an objective and an essay examination.[32] Following the decision, the subjects were given arti-

[28] J. Brehm, "Increasing Cognitive Dissonance by a *Fait Accompli*," *Journal of Abnormal and Social Psychology,* Vol. 58, 1959, pp. 379–382.

[29] L. Festinger and J. M. Carlsmith, "Cognitive Consequences of Forced Compliance," *Journal of Abnormal and Social Psychology,* Vol. 58, 1959, pp. 203–210.

[30] E. Aronson and J. Mills, "The Effect of Severity of Initiation on Liking for a Group," *Journal of Abnormal and Social Psychology,* Vol. 59, 1959, pp. 177–181.

[31] Ehrlich *et al., op. cit.*

[32] J. Mills, E. Aronson, and H. Robinson, "Selectivity in Exposure to Information," *Journal of Abnormal and Social Psychology,* Vol. 59, 1959, pp. 250–253.

cles about examinations presumably written by experts, and they were asked if they would like to read them. In addition, in order to vary the intensity of dissonance, half the subjects were told that the examination counted 70 percent toward the final grade, and half that it counted only 5 percent. The data were obtained in the form of rankings of the articles for preference. While there was a clear preference for reading articles containing positive information about the alternative chosen, no significant selective effects were found when the articles presented arguments against the given type of examination. Also, the authors failed to demonstrate effects relating selectivity in exposure to information to the magnitude of dissonance, in that no significant differences were found between subjects for whom the examination was quite important (70 percent of the final grade) and those for whom it was relatively unimportant (5 percent of the final grade).

Festinger was able to account for many other results by means of the dissonance principle, and in general his theory is rather successful in organizing a diverse body of empirical knowledge by means of a limited number of fairly reasonable assumptions. Moreover, from these reasonable assumptions dissonance theory generated several nontrivial and nonobvious consequences. The negative relationship between the magnitude of incentive and attraction of the object of false testimony is not at all obvious. Also not obvious is the prediction of an increase in proselytizing for a mystical belief following an event that clearly contradicts it. Festinger, Riecken, and Schachter studied a group of "Seekers"—people who presumably received a message from outer space informing them of an incipient major flood.[33]

When the flood failed to materialize on the critical date, instead of quietly withdrawing from the public scene, as one would expect, the "Seekers" summoned press representatives, gave extended interviews, and invited the public to visit them and be informed of the details of the whole affair. In a very recent study by Brehm, a "nonobvious" derivation from dissonance theory was tested.[34] Brehm predicted that when forced to engage in an unpleasant activity, an individual's liking for this activity will increase more when he receives information essentially berating the activity than when he receives information promoting it. The results tended to support Brehm's prediction. Since negative information is said to increase dissonance, and since increased dissonance leads to an increased tendency to reduce it, and since the only means of dissonance reduction was increasing the attractiveness of the activity, such an increase would in fact be expected.

CONCLUSIONS

The theories and empirical work dealing with consistencies are mainly concerned with intra-individual phenomena, be it with relationships between one attitude and another, between attitudes and values, or information, or perception, or behavior, or the like. One exception is Newcomb's concept of "strain toward symmetry." Here the concern is primarily with the interplay of forces among individuals which results in uniformities or consistencies among them. There is no question that the concepts of consistency, and especially the theory of cognitive dissonance, account for many varied atti-

[33] L. Festinger, J. Riecken, and S. Schachter, *When Prophecy Fails*, Minneapolis, University of Minnesota Press, 1956.

[34] J. W. Brehm, "Attitudinal Consequences of Commitment to Unpleasant Behavior," *Journal of Abnormal and Social Psychology*, Vol. 60, 1960, pp. 379–383.

tudinal phenomena. Of course, the various formulations of consistency do not pretend, nor are they able, to account completely for the phenomena they examine. Principles of consistency, like all other principles, are prefaced by the *ceteris paribus* preamble. Thus, when other factors are held constant, then the principles of consistency should be able to explain behavior and attitudes completely. But the question to be raised here is just what factors must be held constant and how important and significant, relative to consistency, are they.

Suppose a man feels hostile toward the British and also dislikes cricket. One might be tempted to conclude that if one of his attitudes were different he would experience the discomfort of incongruity. But there are probably many people whose attitudes toward the British and cricket are incongruent, although the exact proportions are not known and are hardly worth serious inquiry. But if such an inquiry were undertaken it would probably disclose that attitudes depend largely on the conditions under which they have been acquired. For one thing, it would show that the attitudes depend at least to some extent on the relationship of the attitude object to the individual's needs and fears, and that these may be stronger than forces toward balance. There are in this world things to be avoided and feared. A child bitten by a dog will not develop favorable attitudes toward dogs. And no matter how much he likes Popeye you can't make him like spinach, although according to balance theory he should.

The relationship between attitudes and values or needs has been explored, for instance, in *The Authoritarian Personality*, which appeared in 1950.[35] The authors of this work hypothesized a close relationship between attitudes and values on the one hand and personality on the other. They assumed that the "... convictions of an individual often form a broad and coherent pattern, as if bound together by a mentality or spirit." They further assumed that "... opinions, attitudes, and values depend on human needs and since personality is essentially an organization of needs, then personality may be regarded as a determinant of ideological preference." Thus the *Authoritarian Personality* approach also stresses consistency, but while the concepts of congruity, balance, and dissonance are satisfied with assuming a general tendency toward consistency, the *Authoritarian Personality* theory goes further in that it holds that the dynamic of consistency is to be found in personality, and it is personality which gives consistency meaning and direction. Attitudes and values are thus seen to be consistent among themselves and with one another because they are both consistent with the basic personality needs, and they are consistent with needs because they are determined by them.

The very ambitious research deriving from the *Authoritarian Personality* formulation encountered many difficulties and, mainly because of serious methodological and theoretical shortcomings, has gradually lost its popularity. However, some aspects of this general approach have been salvaged by others. Rosenberg, for instance, has shown that attitudes are intimately related to the capacity of the attitude objects to be instrumental to the attainment of the individual's values.[36] Carlson went a step further and has shown that, if the perceived instrumentality of the object with respect to a person's values

[35] T. W. Adorno, E. Frenkel-Brunswik, D. J. Levinson, and R. N. Sanford, *The Authoritarian Personality*, New York, Harper & Row, 1950.

[36] M. J. Rosenberg, "Cognitive Structure and Attitudinal Affect," *Journal of Abnormal and Social Psychology*, Vol. 53, 1956, pp. 367–372.

and needs is changed, the attitude itself may be modified.[37] These studies, while not assuming a general consistency principle, illustrate a special instance of consistency, namely that between attitudes and utility, or instrumentality of attitude objects, with respect to the person's values and needs.

The concepts of consistency bear a striking historical similarity to the concept of vacuum. According to an excellent account by Conant,[38] for centuries the principle that nature abhors a vacuum served to account for various phenomena, such as the action of pumps, behavior of liquids in joined vessels, suction, and the like. The strength of everyday evidence was so overwhelming that the principle was seldom questioned. However, it was known that one cannot draw water to a height of more than 34 feet. The simplest solution of this problem was to reformulate the principle to read that "nature abhors a vacuum below 34 feet." This modified version of *horror vacui* again was satisfactory for the phenomena it dealt with, until it was discovered that "nature abhors a vacuum below 34 feet only when we deal with water." As Torricelli has shown, when it comes to mercury "nature abhors a vacuum below 30 inches." Displeased with the crudity of a principle which must accommodate numerous exceptions, Torricelli formulated the notion that it was the pressure of air acting upon the surface of the liquid which was responsible for the height to which one could draw liquid by the action of pumps. The 34-foot limit represented the weight of water which the air pressure on the surface of earth could

maintain, and the 30-inch limit represented the weight of mercury that air pressure could maintain. This was an entirely different and revolutionary concept, and its consequences had drastic impact on physics. Human nature, on the other hand, is said to abhor inconsistency. For the time being the principle is quite adequate, since it accounts systematically for many phenomena, some of which have never been explained and all of which have never been explained by one principle. But already today there are exceptions to consistency and balance. Some people who spend a good portion of their earnings on insurance also gamble. The first action presumably is intended to protect them from risks, the other to expose them to risks. Almost everybody enjoys a magician. And the magician only creates dissonance —you see before you an event which you know to be impossible on the basis of previous knowledge—the obverse of what you see follows from what you know. If the art of magic is essentially the art of producing dissonance, and if human nature abhors dissonance, why is the art of magic still flourishing? If decisions are necessarily followed by dissonance, and if nature abhors dissonance, why are decisions ever made? Although it is true that those decisions which would ordinarily lead to great dissonance take a very long time to make, they are made anyway. And it is also true that human nature does not abhor dissonance absolutely, as nature abhors a vacuum. Human nature merely avoids dissonance, and it would follow from dissonance theory that decisions whose instrumental consequences would not be worth the dissonance to follow would never be made. There are thus far no data to support this hypothesis, nor data to disprove it.

According to Conant, *horror vacui* served an important purpose besides explaining and organizing some aspects of

[37] E. R. Carlson, "Attitude Change through Modification of Attitude Structure," *Journal of Abnormal and Social Psychology,* Vol. 52, 1956, pp. 256–261.

[38] James B. Conant, *On Understanding Science,* New Haven, Conn., Yale University Press, 1947.

physical knowledge. Without it the discomfort of "exceptions to the rule" would never have been felt, and the important developments in theory might have been delayed considerably. If a formulation has then a virtue in being wrong, the theories of consistency do have this virtue. They do organize a large body of knowledge. Also, they point out exceptions, and thereby they demand a new fomulation. It will not suffice simply to reformulate them so as to accommodate the exceptions. I doubt if Festinger would be satisfied with a modification of his dissonance principle which would read that dissonance, being psychologically uncomfortable, leads a person to actively avoid situations and information which would be likely to increase the dis-

sonance, except when there is an opportunity to watch a magician. Also, simply to disprove the theories by counterexamples would not in itself constitute an important contribution. We would merely lose explanations of phenomena which had been explained. And it is doubtful that the theories of consistency could be rejected simply *because* of counterexamples. Only a theory which accounts for all the data that the consistency principles now account for, for all the exceptions to those principles, and for all the phenomena which these principles should now but do not consider, is capable of replacing them. It is only a matter of time until such a development takes place.

PARENTAL INFLUENCE ON COGNITIVE DEVELOPMENT IN EARLY CHILDHOOD: A REVIEW

Norman E. Freeberg / Donald T. Payne

Despite the extent of child development research on intellectual skills and learning, the answer to a parent who asks specifically "What can I do during my

From: Child Development, *1967, 38, 65–87. Copyright © 1967 by the Society for Research in Child Development, and reproduced by permission of the authors and publisher.*

child's preschool years to improve his learning ability or intelligence?" would have to be couched in fairly broad and guarded generalizations. If the question were pressed further by our hypothetical parent and an optimum sequence of training techniques was requested, the child specialist might feel that his recommendations were even further removed from a body of relevant literature. Perhaps little more than a generalization to provide "maximum environmental enrichment" could, at present, be supported with confidence. But it appears that evidence for an outline of more substantial proportions is beginning to emerge. The present review will attempt to deal with the extent and applicability of available literature to the question posed and those aspects of the research effort that remain to be undertaken if a more satisfactory answer is to be given.

SIGNIFICANCE OF EARLY LEARNING

It has been no small task to arrive at a point where one could speak with assurance of even as general a concept as the enhancing of human cognitive development through an early environment "rich in experience." To do so has required marshaling evidence for the effects of experience upon intellectual growth and against the two long-entrenched assumptions of fixed intelligence, and a maturational hypothesis that prescribes the unfolding of cognitive abilities in a predetermined relation to anatomic development. Hunt (1961) has dealt with the task incisively. With Hebb's (1949) work on the neurophysiological basis of intellectual growth as one theoretical cornerstone, Hunt builds his conception of learning and intelligence as a form of dynamic information processing dependent upon infantile experience.

In effect, Hebb (1949) concluded that experience is an essential mediator of neural connections and a requirement for the formation of so-called cell assemblies. These neural assemblies become relatively fixed functional units ("autonomous central processes") whose sequence and phasing in the associative cortex can only be

formed by receptor inputs (i.e., sensory experience). Thus, it is the earliest experience or "primary" learning which forms much of the pattern for later information-processing capability in the system and serves as the "programmer of the human brain-computer" (Hunt, 1964, p. 242).

Evidence from animal studies of the effects of infantile experience on later learning lends substantial support to the above concepts and tends to negate consideration of a central nervous system that functions as a "passive switchboard" (Newell, Shaw, & Simon, 1958). Beach and Jaynes (1954) as well as Hunt (1961, chap. iv) review much of the work dealing with the enhancement of later learning by rich environmental stimulation in early life. Rats reared in darkness take longer to learn pattern discrimination than normals, and chimps reared in a darkened room for the first 16 months of life fail, initially, to show normal responses to moving objects in the visual field. Pets (cats and dogs) reared in the home perform better in learning situations than laboratory-reared animals. In addition, animals provided with the early experience of living with a variety of objects in their cages perform better in later learning situations and with less emotional interference than animals not exposed to such variations in the stimulus environment. The degree and permanence of this retardation depend largely upon the extent of deprivation. In the case of chimps reared in darkness, there is an eventual recovery of normal visual functioning if the deprivation does not go beyond an assumed critical point where physiological deterioration begins to occur (Riesen, 1958). Similarly, in human development, the ability to recover from the handicap of various forms of perceptual-motor deprivation (given sufficient time and opportunity to practice the requisite skills) indicates that, despite the importance of the early environment, maturational components cannot be ignored (Dennis & Najarian, 1957; Senden, 1932).

Although the behavioral evidence for the role of early learning has been impressive, the more recent works of Krech, Rosenzweig, and Bennett (1962) and Bennett, Diamond, Krech, and Rosenzweig (1964) have served to anchor this evidence in neural correlates. Behavioral measurement as well as chemical and neuroanatomical changes in the cortex of rats raised in enriched and impoverished environments (with and without designs and objects in the cage; variations in number of litter mates) have revealed significant differences in favor of the animals raised under conditions of greater environmental complexity. This improvement is evidenced by (*a*) superior learning ability on a variety of tasks, (*b*) neurochemical changes known to facilitate learning, and (*c*) increased quantity (weight) of cortical tissue in brain areas *specific* to those aspects of sensory stimulation provided by the environmental variables (e.g., greater development of the occipital cortex was related to greater environmental visual stimulation).

Evidence for early learning effects in children and "cumulative deficit" (decline in IQ scores) resulting from deprived environments have been reviewed extensively by Bloom (1964) and others (Anastasi, 1958; Bayley, 1955; Klineberg, 1963; Yarrow, 1964). Largely through studies of intellectual growth in twins reared apart, children separated from parents early in life by adoption, and effects of environmental deprivation in childhood, there has been mounting evidence for the potency of early environment in shaping later cognitive abilities. The extent to which such adverse environmental effects are reversible for retardation of higher-level cognitive skills in man remains poorly defined. But there appear to be extremes of social and cultural deprivation beyond which compensatory training provides only limited benefit (Zingg, 1940).

Bloom (1964) re-evaluates the data from longitudinal studies of the past four decades in an attempt to support a hypothesis of differential growth rate for human intellectual ability. He concludes that, in terms of intelligence measured at age 17, approximately 50 per cent of the variance can be accounted for by age 4 so that as much intellectual growth is achieved between birth and 4 years of age as is achieved for the remaining 13 years. (Assumptions of behavior overlap, absolute scaling, and a unidimensionality of measured intelligence, which are required for such a conclusion, remain open to contention.) Unfortunately, most of the evidence available has not dealt with specific mechanisms to explain conclusions regarding early environmental effects upon the child, and Bloom (1964) feels that it is now necessary to bridge the inferential gap with more detailed and meaningful measures of the environment in order to relate these to cognitive performance.

This brief discussion of an extensive and complex topic is intended only to serve as background for the assumption upon which the balance of this review is predicated, that is, that the formation of cognitive and intellectual skills can reasonably be conceived of as developmental in nature and modifiable by variation in the environment. If this is granted, then how might changes be effected in early intellectual development through the use of appropriate child-rearing and educational practices? Hunt touches upon the need for such knowledge when he states: "Various bits of the evidence reviewed hint that if the manner in which encounters with the environment foster the development of intellectual interest and capacity were more fully understood, it might be possible to increase the average level of intelligence within the population substatially" (Hunt, 1961, p. 346). Similarly, Bloom feels that we are at a level where one can "specify some of the major characteristics of an environment which will positively or negatively affect the development of general intelligence or school achievement" (Bloom, 1964, p. 196). If cultural effects on intellectual functioning are, in some measure, "from the outside in" (Bruner, 1964), then the techniques by which this process can be influenced through parental practices are certainly an area of legitimate concern.

Three major aspects of the literature can be utilized to deal with the problem. The first is of primary concern for this review and deals with those studies that attempt to relate parental influences directly to some aspect of the child's cognitive performance. Second are the studies of child-rearing behavior in various social classes as linked with the evidence of intellectual achievements of children from these classes, and third is the experimental and descriptive literature dealing with educational techniques that have been used for developing cognitive skills in the very young child.

DIRECT MEASURES OF PARENTAL INFLUENCE

Research concerned with direct relations between parental practices and child development has tended to focus upon dependent variables concerned with physical development, personality formation, and behavior adjustment. Attempts to incorporate measures of cognitive skill and intelligence are relatively recent by comparison. Where such studies have been undertaken, they generally deal with children of elementary school levels, and they rely heavily upon retrospective reports by the mother regarding parental practices in early childhood. If there is a willingness to accept a relative continuity of home environment for the period of years from early childhood to the later grades and/or some measure of accuracy for mothers' retrospective reporting, then a number of pertinent studies to be considered in this review can provide insight into the nature of those family influences that might affect intellectual achievement.

One such study by Bing (1963) used sixty mothers of fifth-grade children. All of these children had similar total IQ scores and were divided by sex into "high" and "low" verbal groups. This grouping was based upon the contrast of verbal scores with spatial and numerical scores. For example, a "high verbal" subject was one whose verbal scores were high in relation to his numerical and spatial scores. Data were obtained from questionnaires and from interviews with the mother as well as from observation of an "interaction situation" during which the mother engaged in various problem-solving activities with the child. Responses on the retrospective questionnaire and interview indicated that mothers of "high verbal" children provided more verbal stimulation in early childhood (highly significant for boys but not for girls). These mothers also remembered more of the child's early accomplishments (significant for boys but not for girls), were more critical of poor academic achievement, provided the child with more storybooks, and let him take a greater part in mealtime conversations. Time spent reading to the child by the father was associated with high verbal scores for girls only, although no comparable association was found for reading time spent by the mothers with the child of either sex. The various sex differences that characterized these results were often difficult to reconcile on the basis of any previously stated hypotheses. In the observational situation, mothers of children with high verbal ability generally provided more assistance voluntarily, provided it sooner when requested by the child, and pressured the child more for improvement.

This influence of the mother's pattern of interaction and communication with the child appears to play a pivotal role in cognitive skill level, as is also evident in the work by Hess (1965). Utilizing the observational situation, Hess is presently conducting a series of studies with preschool children that require mother-child interaction in a problem-solving situation. His focus is on the way in which the mother assists the child in solving problems and the nature of the "cognitive environment" which she provides. Results indicate that, when mothers provide "restrictive language codes" (i.e., language that provides a smaller number of alternatives for action, fewer choices to be made, and fewer possibilities for thought), the child's problem-solving ability is diminished.

Maternal behavior toward the preschool child, which includes emphasis on verbal skill acquisition along with other phases of achievement, has also been shown to be related to measured IQ scores. Data obtained from parents of middle-class children from the Fels Longitudinal Study (Moss & Kagan, 1958) were used to develop a "maternal acceleration" score derived from ratings of "pressure" for the child's achievement, as evidenced by the mother in interviews. A significant relation between the child's IQ and maternal acceleration was found only for boys at the 3-year level but not for either sex in the 6-year age group. The study was essentially repeated in a second phase using another sample of children. The child's IQ scores at the 3- and 6-year levels were positively correlated with the mother's IQ and educational level, but the maternal acceleration score was, again, found to be related only to the boy's IQ at the 3-year

level. The authors note that one possible explanation lies in the fact that four of six items on the $2\frac{1}{2}$-year scale of the Stanford-Binet test are of the type that mothers who had high maternal acceleration scores emphasized (i.e., identifying objects by use, naming objects and body parts, and picture vocabulary).

There is evidence that early childhood achievement behaviors, as well as parental practices, are age- and sex-dependent in their predictive ability for later adult achievement behavior (Sontag & Kagan, 1963). Indications of sex differences were not only apparent in the Moss and Kagan study (1958), but Bing (1963) also reported that variables derived from the retrospective interview, which distinguished between high and low verbal groups, did so mainly for boys, while those from the contemporaneous observation situation indicated such differences primarily for girls. This finding of sex differences, based upon parental recall of earlier practices as contrasted with present behavior of the parent (observational data), represents a result that merits further verification. It is hardly surprising that mothers would respond differently to broad classes of behavior displayed by the male than they would for the female child (Sears, Maccoby, & Levin, 1957). Such differences for intellectual and achievement behaviors might also be culturally determined to some extent and could stem from differences in parental expectation for later intellectual and vocational achievement (Freeberg & Payne, 1965).

Age dependence has also become a variable of recent concern. Variations in the consequences of a parental practice, as a function of the child's age level at the time the practice is introduced, have been termed the "sleeper effect" by Kagan and Moss (1962). Evidence presented by these authors indicates that there may be critical periods in the child's development when a particular parental practice may be more effective in shaping later development than if it is introduced at other than the "optimum" age or developmental level. Obvious difficulties in evaluating research and defining suitable criteria of cognitive development are introduced by the need to identify such complex and incompletely understood effects of age and sex.

Another approach to uncovering pertinent aspects of parental influences is through the child's responses to questions about the home environment, an approach used by Milner (1951). First-grade children were classed as "high" and "low" scorers on the Haggerty Reading Examination and the Language Factors subtest of the California Test of Mental Maturity. The findings support the general pattern of subsequent studies, with the "high scores" showing significantly more responses for such parental behavior-related items as: expressed appreciation for the time the mother spent taking them places and reading to them, possession of several or a great many storybooks, and the fact that the parents regularly read to them.

One of the most comprehensive, and apparently successful, attempts to relate parental influence to intelligence test performance of the child used data obtained from sixty fifth-grade students and from interviews with their mothers (Wolf, 1964). Those aspects of the home which were considered as most relevant to the development of general intelligence were incorporated as items in an interview schedule of 63 questions. The items were then used as a basis for ratings on 13 scales designated as "Environmental Process Characteristics." The correlation of the total score (which was a summation of the 13 scale scores) and the child's IQ score was a striking .69. Of particular interest for our purposes are the individual correlations of the 13 scales with the intelligence test score. The best relations were found for those scales dealing with the parents' intellectual expectations for the child, the amount of information that the mother had about the child's intellectual development, the opportunities provided for enlarging the child's vocabulary, the extent to which the parents created situations for learning in the home, and the extent of assistance given in learning situations related to school and non-school activities. Dave (1963), using the same 63-item interview schedule as Wolf (1964) and apparently the same data, categorized the scales into five "Environmental Process Variables" that could be grouped to form an "Index of Educational Environment." The correlation of this overall "Index" with an "Educational Achievement Score" (composed of such areas as word knowledge,, spelling, reading, and arithmetic computation) was found to be .80.

The findings from these two studies are indeed impressive as indications of parental influence on intellectual development. However, a number of the reported correlations between the intelligence measure and variables of social class are at odds with previous studies and require clarification. For example, the index of social class and parental education level were found to be unrelated to the child's intelligence test scores, whereas measures of this sort are customarily found to possess a moderate but significant degree of relation with intelligence. In any event, the general pattern of results from the several studies considered here is fairly consistent. Children of superior intellectual ability come from homes where parental interest in their intellectual development is evidenced by pressures to succeed and assistance in doing so, particularly in the development of the child's verbal skills.

ACHIEVEMENT

The concept of achievement has frequently been used as a criterion of performance for cognitive and intellectual development. As is the case for many of the criterion and predictor variables utilized in parent-child studies, the concept is not a unitary one. In this case it has been used to refer to "need," or motivation for achievement, measured proficiency, and opinions about achievement. Crandall lends some clarification to this widely used criterion variable. He distinguishes achievement variables from other behavior variables such as dependency, aggression, etc., on the basis of "positive reinforcement for demonstrated competence" and achievement situations from other social situations on the basis of the provision of "cues pertaining to some 'standard of excellence'" (Crandall, 1963, p. 418). Contrasted with these is the concept of achievement motivation or "need (*n*) achievement."

Several studies have attempted to relate specific parental child-rearing practices or attitudes to the development of either achievement behavior or achievement motives in the child. Ratings were obtained for: (*a*) achievement behavior in a nursery school free-play situation, (*b*) *child*-mother interaction in the home, and (*c*) mother reactions to child behavior (Crandall, Preston, & Rabson, 1960). The results depict a high-achieving child as one who is less dependent upon the mother for emotional support and whose mother frequently rewarded achievement efforts.

A series of studies conducted at the Fels Institute dealt with the relation of parents' attitudes concerning their own achievement to the achievement behaviors of their child (Crandall, Dewey, Katkovsky, & Preston, 1964; Katkovsky, Preston, & Crandall, 1964a; 1964b). The general findings of interest for this review include a similarity between intellectual achievement values that parents hold for themselves and those they expect for their child, as well as a relation between intellectual expectations and their participation with the child in intellectual activities. Academic achievement of children in the early grades and "general" parental behaviors (largely descriptive of "social climate") were found to be significantly related, but primarily with regard to mothers and daughters—such that mothers of academically competent girls were less affectionate and less nurturant toward their daughters than were mothers of less proficient girls. The essential distinction for fathers was a tendency for those who had academically proficient daughters to use praise more often and to criticize less. More "specific" variables, such as parents' expressed values for intellectual performance and satisfaction with the child's performance, were related to the child's achievement regardless of sex.

These findings of the Fels group are supported in general by the results of Callard's (1964) study with nursery school children and, in addition, by Rosen and D'Andrade (1959), who found that boys with high-need achievement scores had parents with higher aspirations for them and a higher regard for their competence and were fairly quick to disapprove if the child performed poorly. Biglin (1964), on the other hand, had little success in attempting to relate parents' attitudes (as measured by the Nebraska Parent Attitude Scale) to academic achievement when intellectual ability and socioeconomic status were controlled. The explanation for such differences would probably be found in the nature of the attitude scales utilized or in differences between interview results and those of attitude questionnaires. Moving from preschool and early elementary school to the high school level, some consistency of results can be demonstrated by reported relations of academic achievement with parental encouragement, approval, and sharing of activities (Mannino, 1962; Morrow & Wilson, 1961).

In the measurement of achievement, as for intellectual performance, the pattern of parental influence that emerges from these studies would appear to be sex-dependent as well as the result of overt parental pressures for achievement along with expressed attitudes indicating a high level of aspiration for the child.

SOCIAL ENVIRONMENT

One area of controversy that still requires clarification has centered about the social environment in the home and its effects upon the intellectual performance of the child. An early article by Baldwin, Kalhorn, and Breese (1945) reported that children reared in families characterized as Acceptant-Democratic-Indulgent showed higher IQ scores and more favorable changes in IQ, over several years, than children from authoritarian and rejecting homes. A controversy was sparked by Drews and Teahan (1957) who found that high achievers tend to have been reared in families where adult standards were not questioned and where mothers were more "authoritarian and restrictive." Hurley (1959) attempted to serve as mediator and re-evaluated the Drews and Teahan data (1957) to show that although mothers of high academic achievers tended to be more dominant and ignoring toward their children, mothers of "gifted" (high Binet IQ) children tended to be less so. Watson (1957) presented results that tend to favor the "permissive" home as one that stimulated intellectual activity of better quality. The controversy remains unresolved, and results have been difficult to reconcile simply on the basis of the techniques employed and the variables chosen.

To complicate the matter further, a similar and parallel controversy has arisen for what probably represents a related constellation of variables concerned with fostering dependence and independence in early childhood. It has been reported by Winterbottom (1958) that boys with high-need achievement had mothers who prompted earlier self-reliance and independence, while indulgent and overprotective mothers in Stewart's (1950) study had children who tended to be inferior in reading achievement. In support of this pattern, emotional dependence upon the mother by the preschool child was shown to be related to lower-need achievement and declining IQ scores, in a study by Sontag, Baker, and Nelson (1958). Shaw (1964) adds further positive evidence for early independence as a factor favoring academic achievement.

The trend toward agreement was upset, however, by Chance (1961) who found that first-grade children (particularly girls) whose mothers favored earlier demands for independence made less adequate school progress. Crandall et al. (1960) found that "neither maternal affection nor independence training was predictive of the children's achievement behavior." The results do indeed indicate, as Hurley (1959) has suggested, the "complex nature of relationships between maternal child rearing attitudes and children's behavior." Resolution of such a controversy can only be achieved by better understanding of the relations between those child-rearing variables that underlie the authoritarian-democratic, dependence-independence, and permissive-restrictive dimensions, along with greater precision of behavioral definitions for these concepts than has been shown in a number of the studies cited. Differences in criterion measures of achievement (i.e., academic performance, need achievement, measured intelligence) also require reconciliation in future attempts to deal with the controversy.

COGNITIVE STYLE

It has long been recognized that cognitive skill development and achievement are somehow related to personality characteristics. Linking of the causal sequence has been vague, however, until recent studies of cognitive style have attempted to deal with the relation of conceptual strategies in problem solving to personality correlates. Emotional dependence on parents, aggressiveness, self-initiation, and competitiveness in the preschool years were found to be predictive of intellectual growth, from an analysis of the Fels Longitudinal Study data (Sontag et al., 1958). The problem remains one of defining consistent, specific differences in the individual's approach to the environment. Kagan, Moss, and Sigel (1963) have established measures of distinctive cognitive (conceptual) styles in grade-school children that indicate "analytic" and "relational" (nonanalytic) approaches which differentiate between males and females. These resemble the "field-dependent," "field-independent" dimension found by Witkin, Dyk, Faterson, Good-enough, and Karp (1962) who, in addition, attempted to relate the perceptual differences in cognitive styles to maternal influence in early childhood. "Field-independent" boys tended to be more resistant to social group pressure, showed greater consistency of behavior, used intellectualization as a defense mechanism rather than repression, and had mothers who encouraged greater autonomy and curiosity in early childhood. Hess and Shipman (1965) have argued that the child's style of response to problem-solving situations can be associated with the mother's ability to utilize verbal concepts in her interaction with him. Measures of cognitive style were obtained from a sorting task by Sigel (reported in Hess & Shipman, 1965) that defines the level and mode of abstraction displayed by the individual. One version of this instrument was used to obtain scores for the mothers' cognitive style and another was used for their children. Levels of conceptualization displayed by the mother were associated with the cognitive style and conceptual "maturity" of the child as well as with the child's performance on several problem-solving tasks. Cognitive style and levels of conceptual maturity were also found to be differentiated by the social status of the mothers and children.

Although the importance of maternal language style as a mediating factor may lead to stressing of environmental and situational variables in the shaping of cognitive patterns, the possibility of genetic influences has also been suggested, based upon two lines of evidence. First is the persistent finding of sex differences along the cognitive style dimensions reported by Kagan et al. (1963) and by Witkin et al. (1962). Second is a rather interesting discovery of unusual cognitive patterns among girls with Turner's syndrome, a genetic abnormality in the complement of x chromosomes (Witkin, Faterson, Goodenough, & Birnbaum, 1965). Intelligence test performance of twenty girls exhibiting Turner's syndrome was analyzed by these investigators using data from a study by Shafer (reported in Witkin et al., 1965). Significant discrepancies were found between verbal intelligence and ability on "analytical" tasks (i.e., perceptual organization skills characterized by such Wechsler Adult Intelligence Scale subtests as Block Design, Picture Completion, and Object Assembly). Having previously found strong relations between such discrepancies and scores on the perceptual field-dependence, field-independence dimension, Witkin et al. (1965) hypothesize strong field dependency for girls with the Turner syndrome.

ACCURACY OF PARENTAL EVALUATION AND REPORT

A number of the studies that have been cited depend heavily upon the parents' (most frequently the mother's) evaluation of the child. It is, therefore, pertinent to consider this source of data in terms of its error contribution to any study.

Crandall and Preston (1955) compared mother's self-ratings of their behavior with psychologists' ratings of this same behavior based upon observations, and found that the simpler maternal self-rating scales were not correlated highly enough with the more time-consuming observational ratings to be considered as a substitute. Significant agreement between scales, where it existed, depended upon the particular area of maternal behavior evaluated. Similar use of the observational situation by Zunich (1962) resulted in negligible agreement when questionnaire results were compared with observational ratings.

Other studies have demonstrated either a selective accuracy or general distortion of mothers' reports on developmental data and child-rearing practices (Mednick & Shaffer, 1963; Pyles, Stolz, & MacFarlane, 1935). This has been found even in situations where parents participated in a longitudinal study and were virtually "practiced" respondents (Robbins, 1963). Among such respondents, it was found that mothers displayed greater accuracy in recall of the child's early behavior than fathers when their responses were compared with prior reports obtained during the course of the longitudinal study. Hefner (1963) found overall agreement to be poor between mothers' reports $2\frac{1}{2}$

years apart, with wide variation for different aspects of child development. Somewhat superior reliability was found for mothers' on first-born children and for those mothers whose husbands were of higher occupational level.

Sources of bias and questionable validity were also reported for selected areas of parent-child behavior with the interview technique (McCord & McCord, 1961). Attitude scale biases based on social desirability effects have been shown to influence responses on a number of widely used scales (Taylor, 1961). Yarrow (1963) discusses some of these problems in parent-child research and reviews a number of studies that indicate low agreement between parent-child data contemporaneously obtained and retrospective interview reports. Only Walters (1960) defends the questionnaire as preferable to the more time-consuming interview method for measurement of family behavior, but this is based exclusively upon criteria of economy and reliability.

Since the questionnaire or interview are often the only practical sources of information for studies of parent-child relationships, knowledge of the extent of the deficiencies of these instruments is critical. A review by Bell (1958) lends some perspective to the methodological considerations and to the means of improving the research design for the retrospective parent-child study. It seems evident that there is a need to combine parental report with observational data or with other sources of verification where possible.

SOCIAL CLASS AND INTELLECTUAL GROWTH

One major area of the research literature that bears a largely circumstantial relation to parental practices and intellectual characteristics of the child is concerned with performance of children from families of different social classes. Considerable detail exists regarding the behavior of parents of different social classes during various stages of child rearing, but rarely has there been any effort to relate specific practices to specific cognitive skills. For example, only brief mention of intellectual concomitants of achievement behavior is given in the Sears et al. (1957) widely quoted study of child-rearing practices. Others have been concerned largely with measures of personality and behavior adjustment that derive from practices which might logically be related to such measures (Havighurst & Davis, 1955; Kohn, 1959; Minturn & Lambert, 1964; White, 1957). The middle-class values that stress consideration, self-control, and higher educational expectation have been contrasted with lower- or working-class values of neatness, cleanliness, and obedience. These differences have tended to hold up from study to study, although Havighurst and Davis' (1955) evidence leads them to caution against generalizing too broadly from samples taken in geographically restricted areas to an entire social class.

Differences in intellectual achievement among children of different social classes have long been known to exist (Anastasi, 1958; Eells, Davis, Havighurst, Herrick, & Tyler, 1951), but any inference that these differences stem from particular parental behaviors has been tenuous at best. Attempts to explain variations in intellectual skill among social strata (Eells et al., 1951) have been based on the argument that intelligence tests, in general, favor children from middle and upper social classes. Efforts to devise "culture-free" tests have been made in order to overcome this supposed unfair advantage. However, even if adequate tests of this sort could be devised, they do not solve the problems resulting from poor early learning environments, since chil-dren of lower social class are, in fact, less likely to succeed in an academic setting. Questions remain regarding specific parental practices requiring revision if changes are to be effected. Jensen (1964) addresses himself to the evidence that supports the relation of the child's social class membership to verbal learning and reviews the literature in the areas of early experience, perceptual development, environmental deprivation, and laboratory studies of verbal learning in an attempt to show that it is the verbal deficit to which much of the lower-class cognitive disadvantage can be attributed.

SOCIAL CLASS AND DEPRIVATION

Declines in IQ during early childhood have been shown to occur repeatedly under environmental conditions of extreme cultural deprivation (Stoddard, 1943; Wheeler, 1932). Similar trends in measured intellectual ability have been used to support a "cumulative deficit" hypothesis for children of the lower socioeconomic classes (Deutsch, 1965; Deutsch & Brown, 1964; Wiener, Rider, & Oppel, 1963) and a conception of their retarded intellectual development as being the result of "cultural deprivation." Support for the deprivation pattern comes from work by Milner (1951), in which differences in reading ability could be attributed to differences in verbal interaction with the child by parents of high and low social class, and from similar findings by Deutsch (1965) that associate poorer language functioning with lower-class groups. Bernstein (1960) explains these differences on the basis of verbal styles in the use of language by different classes, along a "convergent" ("restrictive")-"divergent" ("elaborative") dimension. His concepts have served as a framework for examination of maternal verbal styles in relation to the child's cognitive behavior by Olim, Hess, and Shipman (1965). Language scales have been developed by these investigators which served to differentiate among mothers on the basis of social class—primarily middle- from lower-class mothers—with the middle-class mother exhibiting a more elaborate language style that includes a greater degree of complexity and a higher level of abstraction. Their evidence points to the mother's language usage as the mediating factor in the child's conceptual development, rather than to the child's IQ or the verbal IQ of the mothers. Class differences in maternal verbal style are credited with the superior problem-solving performance for middle-class mothers working with their children than is found for mothers and children of lower social status. In the view of Hess and Shipman (1965, p. 885), "the meaning of deprivation is a deprivation of meaning."

Lower levels of achievement motivation and expectation for lower-class children can also be assumed to occur from long-term social deprivation and to be passed along to the child by the parents (Rosen, 1956; 1959). Such differences are intimately linked to variations in the way the child learns to perceive the environment and its rewards for achievement. For example, lower-class children were found to perform more effectively for a material incentive, whereas a nonmaterial incentive is just as effective as a material one for middle-class children (Terrell, Durkin, & Wiesley, 1959). Battle and Rooter (1963) showed that lower-class Negro chlidren perceived themselves as having far less control over reinforcement in the environment than did middle-class white children. Such differences in perception of incentives could be a major factor in the focus and orientation of achievement behaviors.

A note of caution is in order for continued use of variables of parent-child interaction dependent upon social class distinctions. Bronfenbrenner (1961) has concluded, from an analysis of changes in parent-child relations over the past 25 years, that there are decreasing differences among classes with regard to such practices. More recently, Caldwell (1965) analyzed items that were used to rate the home environment and family interactions in homes classified as low or middle class on the basis of the customary criteria. Only a few of a large number of items differentiated lower- from middle-class homes, and these were entirely on the basis of physical environment. Hopefully, more specific and direct evidence relating parental practices to the child's intellectual growth is becoming available which will lessen dependence upon the grossly differentiating characteristics subsumed under the rubric of "social class."

TECHNIQUES FOR EARLY ENHANCEMENT OF COGNITIVE SKILLS

Systematically obtained evience (sic.) for parental use of specific instructional techniques to modify the young child's acquisition of cognitive skills is quite rare. A study by Irwin (reported in McCandless, 1961) indicated that working-class mothers who spent 10 minutes per day reading to the child, from 12 months to about 20 months of age, achieved improvement in "all phases of speech." Other available evidence of parental intervention is largely observational or anecdotal. Fowler (1962) summarizes a number of these "descriptive" surveys of gifted children who were early readers, including one with his own daughter. In such cases, children were generally exposed to instructional techniques developed by a parent, and the ability to read by age 3 was not uncommon. These same children often went on to outstanding intellectual achievement as adults.

One of the most extensive sources of potential didactic methods is the large number of studies by educators and psychologists who have evaluated techniques applied during the preschool years for modifying the child's intellectual development. The assumption is, essentially, that if such techniques have been effective they could constitute the framework for methods adaptable to parental use. The bulk of this evidence, to 1960, is covered in the comprehensive review by Fowler (1962) in which he summarizes the research which points to the possibility of modifying specific cognitive skills in children. His examination of the early studies, typified by those of Gesell (1954) and McGraw (1939), that attempted to support a maturational point of view, led him to conclude that the authors "often underplayed . . . the fact that specific training has invariably produced large gains regardless of whether training came early or late in development" (Fowler, 1962, p. 118). Studies cited on improvement of verbal memory and language, in that same review, point to the advantages of early verbal stimulation provided by oral, written, and pictorial material, as well as to the general experience gained in making observations and learning to discriminate between objects. Improvement in conceptual skills and increases in IQ scores were also shown to be amenable to early training attempts which teach higher-order verbal abstractions and provide broad verbal stimulation in play situations of the sort found in a nursery school setting.

Some of the more recent work, during the present decade, delves into the problem in broader scope, dealing largely with culturally deprived children of preschool age and the attempts to improve intellectual performance through specialized training methods (Deutsch, 1963; 1964). One such program by Gray and Klaus (1965) resulted in significant increases in IQ scores for deprived Negro children of preschool age following training programs over two summers and periodic visits to the home during the other months of the year. A control group showed the customary "cumulative deficit" in IQ scores over this same period of time. Further evidence from the Project Headstart Program of the U.S. Office of Economic Opportunity (Dobbin, 1965) has shown that preschool "enrichment" programs might reasonably improve intellectual and social skills. Evaluations of specific methods utilized in this program are now being undertaken and should constitute a rich source of instructional techniques.

Results in teaching young children from a variety of backgrounds to read at earlier ages than usual have been reported for a technique known as the Initial Teaching Alphabet (Downing, 1964) under large-scale evaluation in England. Attempts to apply programed instructional techniques as a means of hastening the acquisition of reading skills by the preschool child include those of Staats, Minke, Finley, Wolf, & Brooks (1964) and of Moore (reported in Hunt, 1964), who adapted the typewriter to a method of teaching letter recognition by having the child press the keys and observe the appropriate letter displayed. Unfortunately, this initial success has been dampened by Rosenhan's (1965) failure to duplicate Moore's results when the possible Hawthorne effect, resulting from the "publicity spotlight," is absent.

Although the programs that attempt to overcome environmental deficit seem certain to continue and expand, questions remain of just how extensively conceptual processes in the young child can be modified. Bruner's (1960) position is that almost any subject matter, if properly organized, can be taught at the grade-school or preschool level. At somewhat the other extreme is the essentially maturational position of Inhelder and Piaget (1958) who argue for specific levels of cognitive development that must be achieved before certain conceptual strategies can be learned (e.g., those basic to inductive reasoning). Ausubel (1965) would also doubt any likelihood of teaching certain concepts at the "pre-operational" stage in Piaget's system (i.e., to about age 7). However, he looks upon these conceptual stages as "nothing more than approximations" that are "susceptible to environmental influences" (Ausubel, 1965, pp. 11–12).

While it is not our intention to explore this controversy through all of the developmental stages, some noteworthy attempts have been made to deal with the teachability of "processes" or "central concepts" in Piaget's formulation at earlier age levels than Piaget (Inhelder & Piaget, 1958) had observed them to occur. With some reservations, trainability of young children on concepts of "conservation" and "transitivity" have been demonstrated by Smedslund (1961a; 1961b; 1963), but there is some question about the permanence of the results and whether the child is able to generalize the principles learned. Anderson (1964) achieved some degree of success with first-grade children in teaching problem solving that required a level of inductive reasoning usually reserved for much older children under the Inhelder and Piaget (1958) scheme. The learning was also shown to be relatively permanent and transferable. But the author believes that the children achieved this result using different strategies than those employed by adolescents or adults.

The major focus of research, stimulated by Piaget's work, seems to have shifted from attempts to support his postulated sequence of conceptual develop-ment, which appears to have been demonstrated reasonably well (Braine, 1959; Peel, 1959), to the more fruitful one of analysis of the strategies involved at such stages and appropriate programing of the material to be learned (Gibson, 1965).

SUMMARY AND NEEDED RESEARCH

The direction of recent research suggests that attempts to define parental influences on the child's acqusition of cognitive skills have begun to expand beyond the rather vague concepts of "enriched experience" and "widening of interests" that have served too often as explanations for poorly understood learning mechanisms. It is largely over the past decade that various aspects of parent-child interaction have been investigated in an attempt to define their influence upon specific modes of cognitive responses, with the most compelling lines of evidence pointing to a critical role for verbal patterns established by the parent. Included in these verbal patterns are the manner or "style" of communicating information to the child and the opportunities for verbal stimulation provided in the home (e.g., in the sheer amount of verbal activity and in the provision of books or other devices that supply a wide range of opportunity for language usage). Many of the social class distinctions in intellectual achievement, which consistently have been found, are likely to center around parental stimuli to the development of language skills as the mediating variable. But much more remains to be delineated regarding the dimensions of parental linguistic styles: the way in which these affect particular forms of verbal development and the patterns of parent-child communication which have an impact on specific verbal and problem-solving abilities.

Still other phases of parental practice

that indicate some promise for differentiating levels, as well as areas, of cognitive skill development have been dealt with in the framework of permissive-restrictive environments in the home and parental pressures for achievement. If these variables were to be more clearly defined operationally—so that present inconsistencies in research findings can be reconciled—the next steps would require determining their likely interaction with one another and their relation to the important role that seems to mark communication and language.

Any description of the processes by which parental behavior influences the development of cognition would be augmented considerably by knowledge of the parents' perception of their role in rearing practices and its influence on cognitive growth. One of the major research gaps has been the scarcity of information regarding parents' attitudes toward their own potential influence upon intellectual development—particularly for parents of different social classes. In a laboratory setting it has been found that inconsistencies in experimental results can occur if there is a failure to deal with data regarding the mother's feelings about interacting with the child in a problem-solving situation (Beller & Nash, 1965). Perhaps some appreciation of the child's views of the learning situation and of his mother's responses would also be in order.

The most pertinent and systematically obtained results dealing with relations between parental practices and the child's level of cognitive skill development have been (and likely to continue to be) achieved by observation in the laboratory setting as opposed to questionnaire methods. However, there remains the more ultimate validation that can only be derived from the broad range of daily rearing practices in a home or "homelike" setting. Data obtained from this source will be essential for defining the more

complex aspects of parental influences in the modification of the child's cognitive performance.

REFERENCES

ANASTASI, ANNE. Heredity, environment, and the question "How?" *Psychological Review*, 1958, 65, 197–208.

ANDERSON, R. C. Shaping logical behavior in six- and seven-year-olds. Cooperative Research Project No. 1790A. Chicago: University of Illinois, 1964.

AUSUBEL, D. P. Stages of intellectual development and their implications for early childhood education. In P. B. NEUBAUER (Ed.), *Concepts of development in early childhood education*. Springfield, Ill.: Charles C Thomas, 1965. Pp. 8–51.

BALDWIN, A. L., KALHORN, JOAN, & BREESE, FAY H. Patterns of parent behavior. *Psychological Monographs: General and Applied*, 1945, 58, No. 3 (Whole No. 268).

BATTLE, ESTHER S., & ROTTER, J. B. Children's feelings of personal control as related to social class and ethnic group. *Journal of Personality*, 1963, 31 (4), 482–490.

BAYLEY, NANCY. On the growth of intelligence. *American Psychologist*, 1955, 10, 805–818.

BEACH, F. A., & JAYNES, J. Effects of early experience upon the behavior of animals. *Psychological Bulletin*, 1954, 51, 239–263.

BELL, R. Q. Retrospective attitude studies of parent-child relations. *Child Development,,* 1958, 29, 323–338.

BELLER E. K., & NASH, A. Research with educationally disadvantaged preschool children. Paper presented at the annual meetings of the American Educational Research Association, Chicago, February 12, 1965.

BENNETT, E. L., DIAMOND, MARIAN C.,

KRECH, D., & ROSENZWEIG, M. R. Chemical and anatomical plasticity of brain. *Science*, 1964, 146, No. 3644, 610–619.

BERNSTEIN, B. Language and social class. *British Journal of Sociology*, 1960, 11, 271–276.

BIGLIN, J. E. The relationship of parental attitudes to children's academic and social performance. Unpublished doctoral dissertation, University of Nebraska, 1964.

BING, ELIZABETH. Effect of childrearing practices on development of differential cognitive abilities. *Child Development*, 1963, 34, (3), 631–648.

BLOOM, B. S. *Stability and change in human characteristics.* New York: Wiley, 1964.

BRAINE, M. D. S. The ontogeny of certain logical operations: Piaget's formulations examined by nonverbal methods. *Psychological Monographs: General and Applied*, 1959, 73, No. 5 (Whole No. 475).

BRONFENBRENNER, U. The changing American child: a speculative analysis. *Journal of social Issues* 1961, 17 (1), 6–17:

BRUNER, J. S. *The process of education.* Cambridge, Mass: Harvard University Press, 1960.

BRUNER, J. S. The course of cognitive growth. *American Psychologist*, 1964, 19, 1–15.

CALDWELL, BETTYE. Infant and preschool socialization in different social classes. Paper presented at the meetings of the American Psychological Association, Chicago, September, 1965.

CALLARD, ESTHER D. Achievement motive in the four-year-old child and its relationship to achievement expectancies of the motor. Unpublished doctoral dissertation, University of Michigan, 1964.

CHANCE, JUNE E. Independence training and first graders' achievement. *Journal of consulting Psychology*, 1961, 25, 149–154.

CRANDALL, V. J. Achievement. In H. W.

STEVENSON (Ed.), *Child psychology: the sixty-second yearbook of the National Society for the Study of Education.* Part I. Chicago: University of Chicago Press, 1963. Pp. 416–459.

CRANDALL, V. J., DEWEY, RACHEL, KATKOVSKY, W., & PRESTON, ANNE. Parents' attitudes and behaviors and grade-school children's academic achievements. *Journal of genetic Psychology*, 1964, 104, 53–66.

CRANDALL, V. J., & PRESTON, ANNE, Patterns and levels of maternal behavior. *Child Development*, 1955, 26, 267–277.

CRANDALL, V. J., PRESTON, ANNE, & RABSON, ALICE. Maternal reactions and the development of independence and achievement behavior in young children. *Child Development* 1960, 31, 243–251.

DAVE, R. H. The identification and measurement of educational process variables that are related to educational achievement. Unpublished doctoral dissertation, University of Chicago, 1963.

DENNIS, W., & NAJARIAN, PERGROUHI. Infant development under environmental handicap. *Psychological Monographs: General and Applied*, 1957, 71, No. 7 (Whole No. 436).

DEUTSCH, M. The disadvantaged child and the learning process: some social, psychological and developmental considerations. In A. H. PASSOW (Ed.), *Education in depressed areas.* Part II. New York: Bureau of Publications, Teachers College, Columbia University, 1963. Pp. 163–179.

DEUTSCH, M. Facilitating development in the preschool child: Social and psychological perspectives. *Merrill-Palmer Quarterly of Behavior and Development*, 1964, 10, (3), 249–263.

DEUTSCH M. The role of social class in language development and cognition. *American Journal of Orthopsychiatry*, 1965, 35 (1), 78–88.

DEUTSCH, M., & BROWN, B. Social influences in Negro-white intelligence differences. *Journal of Social Issues,* 1964, 20, (2), 24–35.

DOBBIN, J. E. Observations of Project Head Start: a report on 335 Project Head Start centers. Princeton, N.J.: Institute for Educational Development, October, 1965.

DOWNING, J. Teaching reading with i. t. a. in Britain. *Phi Delta Kappan,* 1964, 45, 322–329.

DREWS, ELIZABETH M., & TEAHAN, J. E. Parental attitudes and academic achievement. *Journal of Clinical Psychology,* 1957, 13, 328–332.

EELLS K., DAVIS, A., HAVIGHURST, R. J., HERRICK, V. E., & TYLER, R. *Intelligence and cultural differences.* Chicago: University of Chicago Press, 1951.

FOWLER, W. Cognitive learning in infancy and early childhood. *Psychological Bulletin,* 1962, 59, (2), 116–152.

FREEBERG, N. E., & PAYNE, D. T. A survey of parental practices related to cognitive development in young children. Princeton, N.J.: Institute for Educational Development, September, 1965.

GESELL, A. The ontogenesis of infant behavior. In L. CARMICHAEL (Ed.), *Manual of child psychology.* New York: Wiley, 1954.

GIBSON, ELEANOR J. Learning to read. *Science,* 1965, 148, 1066.

GRAY, SUSAN W., & KLAUS, R. A. An experimental preschool program for culturally deprived children. *Child Development,* 1965, 36, (4), 887–898.

HAVIGHURST, R. J., & DAVIS, A. A comparison of the Chicago and Harvard studies of social class differences in child rearing. *American sociological Review,* 1955, 20, 438–442.

HEBB, D. O. *The organization of behavior:* *a neuropsychological theory.* New York: Wiley, 1949.

HEFNER, LESLIE T. Realiability of mothers' reports on child development. Unpublished doctoral dissertation, University of Michigan, 1963.

HESS, R. D. Effects of maternal interaction on cognitions of pre-school children in several social strata. Paper presented at the meetings of the American Psychological Association, Chicago, September, 1965.

HESS, R. D., & SHIPMAN, VIRGINIA C. Early experience and the socialization of cognitive modes in children. *Child Development,* 1965, 36, (4), 869–886.

HUNT, J. McV. *Intelligence and experience.* New York. Ronald Press, 1961.

HUNT J. McV. The psychological basis for using pre-school enrichment as an antidote for cultural deprivation. *Merrill-Palmer Quarterly of Behavior and Development,* 1964, 10, 209–248.

HURLEY, J. R. Maternal attitudes and children's intelligence. *Journal of clinical Psychology,* 1959, 15, 291–282.

INHELDER, BARBEL, & PIAGET, J. *The growth of logical thinking.* New York: Basic Books, 1958.

JENSEN, A. R. Social class and verbal learning. Unpublished manuscript. Berkeley: University of California, 1964. (On file at Library, Educational Testing Service, Princeton, N.J.)

KAGAN, J., & MOSS, H. A. *Birth to maturity, a study in psychological development.* New York: Wiley, 1962.

KAGAN, J., MOSS, H. A., & SIGEL, I. E. Psychological significance of styles of conceptualization. *Monographs of the Society of Research in Child Development,* 1963, 28, No. 2 (Serial No. 86), 73–112.

KATKOVSKY, W., PRESTON, ANNE, & CRANDALL, V. J. Parents' attitudes toward their personal achievements and toward the achievement behaviors of their children. *Journal of genetic Psychology,* 1964, 104, 67–82. (a)

KATKOVSKY, W., PRESTON, ANNE, & CRANDALL, V. J. Parents' achievement attitudes and their behavior with their children in achievement situations. *Journal of genetic Psychology,* 1964, 104, 105–121. (b)

KLINEBERG, O. Negro-white differences in intelligence test performance: a new look at an old problem. *American Psychologist,* 1963, 18 (4), 198–203.

KOHN, M. L. Social class and parental values. *American Journal of Sociology,* 1959, 64, 337–351.

KRECH, D., ROSENZWEIG, M. R., & BENNETT, E. L. Relations between brain chemistry and problem-solving among rats raised in enriched and impoverished environments. *Journal of comparative and psysiological Psychology* 1962, 55, (5), 801–807.

McCANDLESS, B. *Children and adolescents: behavior and development.* New York: Holt, Rinehart & Winston, 1961.

McCORD, JOAN, & McCORD, W. Cultural stereotypes and the validity of interviews for research in child development. *Child Development,* 1961, 32, 171–185.

McGRAW, MYRTLE B. Later development of children specially trained during infancy; Johnny and Jimmy at school age. *Child Development,* 1939, 10, 1–19.

MANNINO, F. V. Family factors related to school persistence. *Journal of educational Sociology,* 1962, 35, 193–202.

MEDNICK, S. A., & SHAFFER, J. B. P. Mothers' retrospective reports in child-rearing research. *American Journal of Orthopsychiatry,* 1963, 33, 457–461.

MILNER, E. A. A study of the relationships between reading readiness in grade one school children and patterns of parent-child interactions. *Child Development* 1951, 22, 95–112.

MINTURN, L. & LAMBERT, W. *Mothers of six cultures: antecedents of child rearing.* New York: Wiley, 1964.

MORROW, W. R., & WILSON R. R. Family relations of bright high-achieving and under-achieving high school boys. *Child Development,* 1961, 32, 501–510.

MOSS, H. A., & KAGAN J. Maternal influences on early IQ scores. *Psychological Reports,* 1958, 4, 655–661.

NEWELL, A., SHAW J. C., & SIMON, H. A. Elements of a theory of human problem solving. *Psychological Review,* 1958, 65, 151–166.

OLIM, E. G., HESS, R. D., & SHIPMAN, VIRGINIA. Maternal language styles and their implications for children's cognitive development. Paper presented at the meetings of the American Psychological Association, Chicago, September, 1965.

PEEL, E. A. Experimental examination of some of Piaget's schemata concerning children's perception and thinking and a discussion of their educational significance. *British Journal of educational Psychology,* 1959, 29, 89–103.

PYLES, M. K., STOLZ, H. R., & MACFARLANC, J. W. The accuracy of mothers' reports on birth and developmental data. *Child Development,* 1935, 6, 165–176.

RIESEN, A. H. Plasticity of behavior: psychological aspects. In H. F. HARLOW and C. N. WOOLSEY (Eds.), *Biological and biochemical bases of behavior.* Madison: University of Wisconsin Press, 1958. Pp. 425–450.

ROBBINS, LILLIAN C. The accuracy of parental recall of aspects of child development and of child rearing practices. *Journal of abnormal and social Psychology.* 1963, 66, 261–270.

ROSEN, B. C. The achievement syndrome: a psychocultural dimension of social stratification. *American sociological Review*, 1956, 21, 203–211.

ROSEN, B. C. Race, ethnicity, and the achievement syndrome. *American sociological Review*, 1959, 24, 47–60.

ROSEN, B. C., & D'ANDRADE, R. The psychosocial origins of achievement motivation. *Sociometry*, 1959, 22, 185–218.

ROSENHAN, D. L. Cultural deprivation and learning: an examination of method and theory. Paper presented at the annual meetings of the American Educational Research Association, February, 1965.

SEARS, R. R., MACCOBY, ELEANOR E., & LEVIN H. *Patterns of child rearing.* Evanston, Ill.: Row, Peterson, 1957.

SENDEN, M. von., *Raum- und Gestaltauffassung bei operierten Blindgeborenen vor und nach der Operation.* Leipzig: Barth, 1932.

SHAW, M. C. Note on parent attitudes toward independence training and the academic achievement of their children. *Journal of educational Psychology*, 1964, 55, (6), 371–374.

SMEDSLUND, J. The acquisition of conservation of substance and weight in children, II: External reinforcement of conservation of weight and of the operations of addition and substraction. *Scandinavian Journal of Psychology*, 1961, 2, 71–84. (a)

SMEDSLUND, J. The acquisition of conservation of substance and weight in children, III: Extinction of conservation of weight acquired "normally" and by means of empirical controls on a balance. *Scandinavian Journal of Psychology*, 1961, 2, 85–87. (b)

SMEDSLUND, J. Patterns of experience and the acquisition of concrete transitivity of weight in eight-year-old children. *Scandinavian Journal of Psychology*, 1963, 4, 251–256.

SONTAG, L. W., BAKER, C. T., & NELSON, VIRGINIA L. Mental growth and personality development: a longitudinal study. *Monographs of the Society for Research in child Development*, 1958, 23, No. 2 (Serial No. 68).

SONTAG, L. W., & KAGAN, J. The emergence of intellectual achievement motives. *American Journal of Orthopsychiatry*, 1963, 33, (3), 532–535.

STAATS, A. W., MINKE, K. A., FINLEY, J. R., WOLF, M., & BROOKS, L. O. A reinforcer system and experimental procedure for the laboratory study of reading acquisition. *Child Development* 1964, 35, 209–231.

STEWART, R. S. Personality maladjustment and reading achievement. *American Journal of Orthopsychiatry*, 1950, 20, 410–417.

STODDARD, G. D. *The meaning of intelligence.* New York: Macmillan, 1943.

TAYLOR J. B. What do attitude scales measure? the problem of social desirability. *Journal of abnormal and social Psychology*, 1961, 62, 386–390.

TERRELL, G. JR., DURKIN, KATHRYN, & WIESLEY, M. Social class and the nature of the incentive in discrimination learning. *Journal of abnormal and social Psychology*, 1959, 59, 270–272.

WALTERS, J. Relationship between reliability of responses in family life research and method of data collection. *Marriage and family Living*, 1960, 22, 232–237.

WATSON, G. Some personality differences in children related to strict or permissive parental discipline. *Journal of Psychology*, 1957, 44, 227–249.

WHEELER, L. R. The intelligence of East Tennessee mountain children. *Journal of educational Psychology*, 1932, 23, 351–370.

WHITE, MARTHA S. Social class, child rearing practices, and child behavior. *American sociological Review*, 1957, 22, 704–712.

WIENER, G. G., RIDER, R. V., & OPPEL, W. Some correlates of IQ changes in children. *Child Development*, 1963, 34, (1), 61–67.

WINTERBOTTOM, MARIAN. The relation of need for achievement in learning experiences in independence and mastery. In J. ATKINSON (Ed.), *Motives in fantasy, action and society*. Princeton, N.J.: Van Nostrand, 1958.

WITKIN, H. A., DYK, RUTH, B., FATERSON, HANNA, GOODENOUGH, D. R., & KARP, S. A. *Psychological differentiation: studies of development*. New York: Wiley, 1962.

WITKIN, H. A., FATERSON, HANNA, GOODE-NOUGH, D., & BIRNBAUM, JUDITH. Cognitive patterning in high grade mentally retarded boys. Unpublished manuscript, Psychology Laboratory, Department of Psychiatry, State University of New York, Downstate Medical Center, 1965.

WOLF, R. M. The identification and measurement of environmental process variables related to intelligence. Unpublished doctoral dissertation, University of Chicago, 1964.

YARROW, L. J. Separation from parents during early childhood. In M. L. HOFFMAN and LOIS W. HOFFMAN (Eds.), *Review of child development research*. New York: Russell Sage Foundation, 1964. Pp. 89–136.

YARROW, MARIAN R. Problems of methods in parent-child research. *Child Development*, 1963, 34, 215–226.

ZINGG, R. M. Feral man and extreme cases of isolation. *American Journal of Psychology*, 1940, 53, 487–517.

ZUNICH, M. Relationship between maternal behavior and attitudes toward children. *Journal of genetic Psychology*, 1962, 100, 155–165.

SOCIAL CLASS,
PARENTAL ENCOURAGEMENT,
AND EDUCATIONAL ASPIRATIONS

William H. Sewell / Vimal P. Shah

INTRODUCTION

It is a sociological truism, evidenced by a number of studies, that children of higher social class origins are more likely to aspire to high educational and occupational goals than are children of lower social class origins.[1] This is true despite wide differ-

ences among the studies in the nature of their samples, the age level of their subjects, their measurement procedures, and the particular cutting points used to categorize the variables.[2] Even when other variables known to be related to both social class origins and aspirations—such

From: American Journal of Sociology, *1968, 73, 559–72. Copyright © 1968 by the University of Chicago Press, and reproduced by permission of the authors and the publisher.*

[1] There is a vast literature in this regard. References to these studies are given in: William H. Sewell, Archibald O. Haller, and Murray A. Straus, "Social Status and Educational and Occupational Aspiration," *American Sociological Review,* XXII (February, 1957), 67–73; William H. Sewell, "Community of Residence and College Plans," *American Sociological Review,* XXIX (February, 1964), 24–38; William H. Sewell and Alan M. Orenstein, "Community of Residence and Occupational Choice," *American Journal of Sociology,* LXX (March, 1965), 551–63; William H. Sewell and Archibald O. Haller, "Educational and Occupational Perspectives of Farm and Rural Youth," in Lee G. Burchinal (ed.), *Rural Youth in Crisis* (U.S. Department of Health, Education, and Welfare) (Washington, D.C.: Government Printing Office, 1965), pp. 149–69;

William H. Sewell and J. Michael Armer, "Neighborhood Context and College Plans," *American Sociological Review,* XXXI (April, 1966), 159–68; and William H. Sewell and Vimal P. Shah, "Socioeconomic Status, Intelligence, and the Attainment of Higher Education," *Sociology of Education,* XL (Winter, 1967), 1–23.

[2] Interesting evidence is provided by Haller and Miller, who attempted to test the hypothesis of a positive correlation between the level of occupational aspiration and social class status, race, parents' willingness to contribute financial support to help the youth, and post-educational work experience. They examined data from several published and unpublished studies. The hypothesis was confirmed in twenty-three instances, and the authors were somewhat doubtful about the validity of all of the remaining instances classified by them as contrary to the hypothesis. Archibald O. Haller and Irwin W. Miller, *The Occupational Aspiration Scale: Theory, Structure and Correlates* (East Lansing: Michigan State University Agricultural Experiment Station, 1963), pp. 28–55.

as sex, intelligence, high school achievement, value orientations, and contextual variables such as neighborhood and community of residence—have been controlled, social class origins have been found to have an independent influence on educational and occupational aspirations. The question is often raised as to what it is about social class that accounts for this relationship and through what intervening variables this relationship may be further explained. In other words, the need is emphasized for specifying the variables by which the social class characteristics of individuals are translated into differences in aspiration and subsequently into achievement.[3] One factor which has come in for considerable emphasis is the degree to which the child perceives his parents as encouraging or even pressuring him to have high educational and occupational goals.

Kahl first suggested the importance of parental encouragement in his study of the educational and occupational aspirations of "common-man" boys. After finding that intelligence and social class position accounted for the major variations in college aspirations of boys of common-man or working-class origins, he noted that the attitude of the parents regarding the importance of occupational success for personal happiness was the critical factor.[4]

Kahl's findings, although based on a very small sample of twenty-four common-man boys, have led many social scientists to emphasize the importance of parental encouragement and other social-psychological variables in explaining the relation of social stratification to aspirations. For example, in a critique of social structure and American education, Gross observes the following:

> It is frequently assumed that because children come from backgrounds, similar on such criteria as education, occupation, and religion of parents, that these children experience similar influences. However, as Kahl's paper suggests, in a setting of highly similar social status dimensions, quite disparate sociological and psychological influence, in this case parental pressure, may be operative on the child. This suggests that to type children simply on the basis of the characteristics of their socioeconomic environment or "social class" may provide an extremely inaccurate picture of the crucial influences affecting them. Social class typing of children, in short, may obscure more than it may reveal regarding influences operative on children.[5]

---

his study from a larger sample of 3,971 boys in public high schools in eight towns of the Boston metropolitan area. These twenty-four boys had intelligence scores in the top three deciles of their schools and therefore were considered intelligent enough to succeed in college. While most upper-status boys aimed toward college as a matter of course, most lower-status boys tended to be uninterested in college. Consequently, working-class boys who aimed high were exceptions, and Kahl's intensive study of this group was designed to discover the source of their higher aspirations (see Joseph A. Kahl, "Educational and Occupational Aspirations of 'Common-Man' Boys," *Harvard Educational Review*, XXIII (Summer, 1953), 186–203.

[5] Neal Gross, "A Critique of Social Class Structure and American Education," *Harvard Educational Review*, XXIII (Fall, 1953), 298–329.

[3] For example, Peter Rossi, in "Social Factors in Academic Achievement," in E. H. Halsey, Jean Floud, and C. Arnold Anderson (eds.), *Education, Economy and Society* (Glencoe, Ill.: Free Press, 1961), p. 269, in surveying the researches on social factors affecting the achievement of students in American elementary and high schools, observed that "it is characteristic of past researches on individual differences that they have not gone much beyond measuring the association between characteristics of individual students and their achievement scores, to specify the processes by which these characteristics are translated into differences in achievement."

[4] Kahl selected twenty-four subjects for

Bordua, in a study of 1,529 ninth through twelfth graders in two cities of Massachusetts, found that socioeconomic status was related positively to college plans at all school-year levels in both sexes and in Catholic, Protestant, and Jewish religious affiliations.[6] Since parental stress on college was positively and linearly related to college plans when sex and school year were controlled, Bordua asked whether these relationships were due to differential stress on college by the parents of boys as opposed to girls, to high socioeconomic status levels as opposed to low, and to Jews as opposed to Protestants and Catholics. He, therefore, controlled for parental stress on college and found that the effects of religious affiliation and socioeconomic status on college aspirations were reduced but not eliminated. Also, parental stress on college was related about equally to college plans whether or not socioeconomic status was controlled. However, Bordua's findings should be viewed with certain reservations because he did not control for all variables simultaneously, and particularly because he did not control for intelligence which has been found consistently related to both socioeconomic status and college plans. Similar limitations of methodology and data are characteristic also of Simpson's study of 743 boys in white high schools in two southern cities, in which it was concluded that "parental advice is a much better predictor of high ambition than is the boy's social class."[7]

In a study of 2,852 male sophomores in secondary schools in six middle-sized Pennsylvania cities, Rehberg and Westby found that the father's education and occupation influence educational expectancy both through parental encouragement and independent of it. Further, they found that the larger the family the greater the reduction not only in the frequency with which the parents encourage their children to continue their education beyond high school but also in the effectiveness of any given frequency level of parental educational encouragement.[8] Although family size was used as an additional control variable in their study, in the absence of data on intelligence Rehberg and Westby were unable to partial out the influence of ability on either parental encouragement or educational expectancy of the students. Further, they may have overstated the influence of parental encouragement in their top social status category when they suggested that "parental encouragement comes to being a *necessary* condition for the continuation of education beyond the high school level in *all* strata and not just in the lower classes."[9]

A critical review of these and other studies of the influence of parents' attitudes on youths' aspirations indicates not only major limitations of past studies but also the need for a clear formulation of a series of research questions. The purpose of this paper is to determine: (1) whether or not observed social class differences in the college plans of youth can be explained in terms of the differences in the level of perceived parental encouragement when intelligence is taken into account; (2) and if not, what additional influence parental

[6] David J. Bordua, "Educational Aspirations and Parental Stress on College," *Social Forces*, XXXVIII (March, 1960), 262–69.

[7] Richard L. Simpson, "Parental Influence, Anticipatory Socialization, and Social Mobility," *American Sociological Review*, XXVII (August, 1962), 517–22.

[8] Richard A. Rehberg and David L. Westby, "Parental Encouragement, Occupation, Education and Family Size: Artifactual or Independent Determinants of Adolescent Educational Expectations?" *Social Forces*, XLV (March, 1967), 362–74.

[9] *Ibid.*, p. 371.

encouragement has on college plans over and above the influence of social class and intelligence; (3) the direct and indirect influences that social class, intelligence, and parental encouragement have on college plans; (4) and, finally, whether or not there are any subpopulations of sex, intelligence, and parental encouragement in which social class differences in college plans might be eliminated.

THE DATA

The data for the present study come from a survey of graduating seniors in all public, private, and parochial schools in Wisconsin.[10] Information was obtained from the respondents, school authorities, and a statewide testing program on a number of matters, including the student's educational and occupational plans, the student's percentile rank in measured intelligence, the socioeconomic status of his family, his rank in his high school class, his course of study, and the educational attitudes of the student and his family. The analysis reported in this paper is based on 10,318 seniors who constituted about a one-third random sample of all 1957 seniors in Wisconsin.

The variable *socioeconomic status* (X_1) of the student's family is based on a weighted combination of father's occupation, father's formal educational level, mother's formal educational level, an estimate of the funds the family could provide if the student were to attend college, the degree of sacrifice this would entail for the family, and the approximate wealth and income status of the student's family. The sample was divided into four roughly

equal groups, labeled "High," "Upper Middle," "Lower Middle," and "Low" in socioeconomic status.[11]

The variable *intelligence* (X_2) is based on scores on the Henmon-Nelson Test of Mental Ability, which is administered annually to all high school juniors in Wisconsin.[12] The categories used represent the division of the sample into approximately equal fourths in measured intelligence, according to established statewide norms, labeled "High," "Upper Middle," "Lower Middle," and "Low" in intelligence.

The variable *paternal encouragement* (X_3) is based on the student's response to four statements intended to record his perception of his parents' attitude toward his college plans. The students were asked to check *any one* of the following four statements: (1) My parents want me to go to college; (2) My parents do not want me to go; (3) My parents do not care

[10] The over-all results of this survey are given in J. Kenneth Little, *A Statewide Inquiry into Decisions of Youth about Education beyond High School* (Madison: School of Education, University of Wisconsin, 1958).

[11] These six indicators of family socioeconomic status were factor analyzed using the principal-components method and were orthogonally rotated according to the varimax criterion. This produced a three-factor structure composed of a factor on which the three economic items were most heavily loaded, a factor on which the two educational items were most heavily loaded, and a factor on which the occupational item was most heavily loaded. The composite socioeconomic status index was developed by squaring the loadings of the principal items on each factor as weights, then multiplying students' scores on the items by the respective weights, and, finally, summing the weighted scores of the principal items on each factor. The three factors were combined into a composite socioeconomic status score after multiplying the scores of all students by certain constants which would produce approximately equal variances for each status dimension. The resulting sum of the weighted scores was then multiplied by a constant to produce a theoretical range of scores between 0 and 99.

[12] V. A. C. Henmon and M. J. Nelson, *The Henmon-Nelson Test of Mental Ability* (Boston: Houghton Mifflin Co., 1942).

whether I go; and (4) My parents will not let me go. For the purposes of this study, the students responding to the first statement are considered to have perceived positive parental encouragement to plan on college, while the students responding to the other three statements are considered not to have perceived positive parental encouragement to plan on college. The variable is dichotomized accordingly into high and low parental encouragement categories.

The variable *college plans* (X_4) is based on a statement by the student that he definitely plans to enroll in a degree-granting college or university (or one whose credits are acceptable for advanced standing by the University of Wisconsin). That these statements reflect realistic rather than vague hopes is supported by the fact that 87.3 per cent of the boys and 86.7 per cent of the girls who had stated that they planned on college actually attended college.[13]

STATISTICAL PROCEDURE

The principal purpose of this paper is to examine the relationship between socioeconomic status and college plans. The strategy followed is to partial out the influence of intelligence and parental encouragement prior to determining the relationship between socioeconomic status and college plans. Also, separate analysis is made for males and females because of known differences in their propensity to pursue higher education as well as likely

differences in the influence of socioeconomic status, intelligence, and parental encouragement on their college plans. Various statistical techniques are used to achieve the purpose of this study.

First, the gross relationships of socioeconomic status, intelligence, and parental encouragement to college plans and to one another are determined from their zero-order correlation coefficients. Second, the relationship of socioeconomic status to college plans, controlling for intelligence and parental encouragement, is determined by means of first- and second-order partial correlation coefficients. Third, the additional contribution of parental encouragement in predicting college plans, over and above the contribution of socioeconomic status and intelligence, is determined by means of stepwise multiple correlation coefficients. Fourth, the relative direct and indirect effects of socioeconomic status, intelligence, and parental encouragement on college plans are determined by using the method of path analysis.[14] And fifth, a multivariate cross-tabular analysis of the data is made to demarcate the differential influence of socioeconomic status on the college plans of various subgroups which differ by sex, intelligence, and degree of parental encouragement. The statistical significance of the relationships examined throughout the analysis is determined by appropriate tests using the .05 probability level.

---

[13] A follow-up survey was conducted by means of mailed questionnaires and telephone interviews, and responses were obtained from 9,007, or 87.2 per cent, of the students in the original one-third sample. For further information on the follow-up, see Sewell and Shah, *op. cit.* (see n. 2 above), pp. 6–7.

[14] Path analysis provides a convenient and efficient method for determining the direct and indirect effects of each of the independent variables in a causal chain composed of standardized variables in a closed system. These effects are expressed in path coefficients which are the β weights of all of the preceding independent variables on the successive dependent variables in the system. For a brief summary of the method of path analysis, see Otis Dudley Duncan, "Path Analysis: Sociological Examples," *American Journal of Sociology*, LXXII (July, 1966), 1–16.

RESULTS

The gross relationships of socioeconomic status, intelligence, and parental encouragement to college plans can be examined from the zero-order correlations given in the intercorrelation matrix of Table 1. The zero-order correlation coefficients of socioeconomic status, intelligence, and parental encouragement with college plans are all positive and statistically significant for males as well as for females. For males, socioeconomic status and intelligence each explains about 18 per cent of the variance in college plans. For females, socioeconomic status explains 22.9 per cent of the variance in college plans while intelligence explains only 12.6 per cent. Parental encouragement explains about one-fourth of the variance in the college plans of boys and about one-third of the variance in the college plans of girls. Thus, the zero-order correlation coefficients indicate that the relationship of parental encouragement to college plans is stronger than that of either socioeconomic status or intelligence to college plans and that the relationship of parental encouragement to college plans is stronger for females than for males. Socioeconomic status and intelligence have an equally strong relationship to the college plans of males, but socioeconomic status has a considerably stronger relationship to the college plans of females than does intelligence.

The stronger relationships of socioeconomic status and parental encouragement to the college plans of females than to those of males seem to reflect the differential pattern of role expectations from adult males and females in our society. College education is considered as desirable and increasingly necessary for fulfilling male occupational roles, but for females the situation is doubtless complicated by marital roles and economic considerations. Presumably, therefore, the family resources exert stronger influence on the college plans of females than on those of males, while ability exerts stronger influence on the college plans of males than on those of females.

Although the examination of various factors determining different levels of parental encouragement is outside the scope of this paper, the socioeconomic status of the family and the ability level of the children seem to be two of the most pertinent factors. Consequently, the relationship of parental encouragement to socioeconomic status and intelligence is examined.

Judging from the zero-order correla-

TABLE 1

INTERCORRELATION MATRIX

Variable	X_1	X_2	X_3	X_4
Males:				
X_1 (socioeconomic status)		.30	.40	.43
X_2 (measured intelligence)			.35	.42
X_3 (perceived parental encouragement) ...				.51
X_4 (college plans)				
Females:				
X_1 (socioeconomic status)		.32	.44	.48
X_2 (measured intelligence)			.29	.36
X_3 (perceived parental encouragement) ...				.57
X_4 (college plans)				

TABLE 2

FIRST-ORDER AND SECOND-ORDER
PARTIAL CORRELATION COEFFICIENTS OF
SOCIOECONOMIC STATUS WITH COLLEGE PLANS,
SEPARATELY FOR MALES AND FEMALES

Independent Variable	Dependent Variable	Control Variable(s)	Males		Female	
			Partial r	Variance Explained (%)	Partial r	Variance Explained (%)
Socioeconomic status...	College plans	Intelligence	.346	12.0	.412	17.0
Socioeconomic status...	College plans	Perceived parental encouragement	.283	8.0	.307	9.4
Socioeconomic status...	College plans	Intelligence and perceived parental encouragement	.240	5.8	.268	7.2

tion coefficients, for both males and females socioeconomic status indicates a stronger relationship with parental encouragement than does intelligence. Socioeconomic status explains about one-sixth of the variance in perceived parental encouragement for males and about one-fifth of the variance in perceived parental encouragement for females. But, intelligence explains about one-eighth of the variance in perceived parental encouragement for males and only about one-twelfth of the variance for females. Thus, as in the case of college plans, socioeconomic status is more strongly related to perceived parental encouragement for females than for males, but intelligence is more strongly related to perceived parental encouragement for males than for females.

An examination of the intercorrelation between socioeconomic status, intelligence, and parental encouragement indicates that these variables are related not only to college plans but also to each other and that their relationships are different for males and females. Conse-

quently, intelligence and parental encouragement should be controlled while the relationship of socioeconomic status to college plans is examined.

From the first-order partial correlation coefficients of socioeconomic status to college plans (Table 2), it is clear that when either intelligence or parental encouragement is controlled, the relationship between socioeconomic status and college plans of both males and females is reduced but not eliminated. When controlled for intelligence, socioeconomic status explains 12.0 per cent of the variance in the college plans of males, but it explains 17.0 per cent of the variance in the college plans of females. Similarly, when controlled for parental encouragement, socioeconomic status explains 8.0 per cent of the variance in the college plans of males, but it explains 9.4 per cent of the variance in the college plans of females. It should be noted that controlling for parental encouragement makes a greater reduction in the relationship of socioeconomic status to college plans than the reduction made in the relationship when intelligence is controlled. In either case, however, the relationship continues to be substantial and statistically significant. Also, the stronger relationship of socioeconomic status to the college plans of females than to those of males is evident when either intelligence or parental encouragement is controlled.

When intelligence and parental encouragement are both controlled in the second-order partial correlation coefficients (Table 2), the relationship of socioeconomic status to college plans is further reduced, but socioeconomic status still explains 5.8 per cent of the variance in the college plans of males and 7.2 per cent of the variance in the college plans of females. Thus, even after partialing out the effects of intelligence and parental encouragement, the relationship of socioeconomic status to college plans continues to be substantial and statistically significant.

The zero-order and partial correlation coefficients indicate that there is a positive and statistically significant relationship between socioeconomic status and

the college plans of both males and females, with or without controls for intelligence and parental encouragement, which are themselves related to each other and to both socioeconomic status and college plans. The analysis thus far demonstrates the independent relationship of socioeconomic status to college plans. The strength of parental encouragement for predicting college plans over and above the strength of socioeconomic status and intelligence will be determined by examining the multiple correlation coefficients.

The multiple correlation coefficient of socioeconomic status and intelligence to college plans is the same for both males and females ($R = .524$—Table 3); together they explain a little over one-fourth of the variance in college plans. This suggests that although socioeconomic status has a stronger relationship to the college plans of girls than of boys, and although intelligence has a stronger relationship to the college plans of boys than of girls, their combined strength is the same for both sexes.

TABLE 3

STEPWISE MULTIPLE CORRELATION COEFFICIENTS OF
SOCIOECONOMIC STATUS, MEASURED INTELLIGENCE,
AND PERCEIVED PARENTAL ENCOURAGEMENT WITH
COLLEGE PLANS, SEPARATELY FOR MALES AND FEMALES

Independent Variable(s)	*Dependent Variable*	*Males*		*Females*	
		r/R	*Variance Explained (%)*	*r/R*	*Variance Explained (%)*
Socioeconomic status	College plans	.426	18.2	.478	22.9
Socioeconomic status and measured intelligence	College plans	.524	27.5	.524	27.5
Socioeconomic status and perceived parental encouragement	College plans	.567	32.2	.620	38.4
Socioeconomic status, measured intelligence, and perceived parental encouragement	College plans	.607	36.8	.638	40.7

From Table 3, in addition to the variance explained by socioeconomic status, intelligence explains 9.3 (27.5 − 18.2) per cent of the variance in the college plans of males and 4.6 (27.5 − 22.9) per cent of the variance in the college plans of females, but parental encouragement explains 14.0 (32.2 − 18.2) per cent of the variance in the college plans of males and 15.5 (38.4 − 22.9) per cent of the variance in the college plans of females over and above that explained by socioeconomic status. Thus, both intelligence and parental encouragement add substantially to the variance explained by socioeconomic status, but the additional variance explained by parental encouragement is greater than the additional variance explained by intelligence. It should also be noted that the additional variance explained by parental encouragement is almost equal for males and females. Final-

ly, socioeconomic status, intelligence, and parental encouragement together explain 36.8 per cent of the variance in college plans for males and 40.7 per cent of the variance for females. Parental encouragement explains 9.3 (36.8 − 27.5) per cent of the variance in the college plans of males and 13.2 (40.7 − 27.5) per cent of the variance for females over and above that explained by both socioeconomic status and intelligence. In short, parental encouragement adds very substantially to the explained variance in the college plans of both males and females over and above that explained by socioeconomic status and intelligence.

In summarizing the correlational analysis, it is evident that social class differences in the college plans of Wisconsin high school seniors are not completely accounted for either by the level of students' intelligence or by perceived paren-

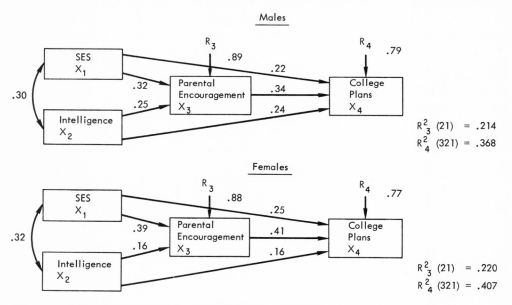

Figure 1. Path diagrams showing the influence of socioeconomic status, measured intelligence, and perceived parental encouragement on college plans (by sex).

tal encouragement, or both. Also, the relationship of parental encouragement to college plans is not simply an additive combination of the relationships of socioeconomic status and intelligence to parental encouragement. Its added independent contribution to the explained variance in the college plans of males as well as females is substantial. This demonstrates the usefulness of parental encouragement as an explanatory variable without undermining the importance of socioeconomic status and intelligence as explanatory variables. It is possible to determine and compare the direct and indirect effects of these variables on college plans by following the method of path analysis.

It is assumed in the path diagrams shown in Figure 1 that parental encouragement is determined by socioeconomic status and intelligence and that all three in turn determine college plans. The relationship between socioeconomic status and intelligence is not analyzed, and, consequently, no assumption is made regarding the causal link between them. The R_3 and R_4 indicate the residual factors determining parental encouragement and college plans, respectively. Although the path analysis generally corroborates the findings of the correlational analysis, several observations should be made from the path coefficients indicated in this figure.

First, neither parental encouragement nor college plans are completely accounted for by the variables explicitly included in this study. The magnitude of the effect of the residual factors on these variables is very large. Substantial proportions of the variance in parental encouragement (78.6 per cent for boys and 78.0 per cent for girls) cannot be accounted for by socioeconomic status and intelligence. Similar proportions of the variance in the college plans of males and females are not accounted for by socio-economic status, intelligence, and parental encouragement—63.2 per cent and 59.3 per cent, respectively. These large residuals indicate the need for bringing additional variables into the system.

Second, for both boys and girls the contribution of socioeconomic status to parental encouragement is greater than that of intelligence. But, while the effect of socioeconomic status on parental encouragement is greater for girls than for boys, the effect of intelligence on parental encouragement is greater for boys than for girls.

Third, the direct effect of parental encouragement on the college plans of boys as well as girls is greater than that of either socioeconomic status or intelligence. It should be noted in this connection that both socioeconomic status and intelligence also exert some indirect effect on college plans through their effect on parental encouragement. The direct effects of socioeconomic status and intelligence on the college plans of boys are almost equal, but the direct effect of socioeconomic status on the college plans of girls is much greater than the direct effect of intelligence on their college plans.

Finally, for boys as well as girls, while the direct effects of intelligence on parental encouragement and on college plans are almost equal, the direct effect of socioeconomic status on parental encouragement is much greater than its direct effect on college plans.

In summary, the correlational and the path analyses indicate very clearly that while there is some common component in socioeconomic status, intelligence, and parental encouragement which accounts for their relationship to college plans, all three variables have substantial independent relationships of their own to college plans. With particular reference to the major purpose of this study, neither intelligence

TABLE 4

PERCENTAGES OF STUDENTS WHO PLANNED ON COLLEGE, BY SOCIOECONOMIC STATUS, MEASURED INTELLIGENCE, AND PERCEIVED PARENTAL ENCOURAGEMENT, SEPARATELY FOR MALES AND FEMALES

	Perceived Parental Encouragement											
	Males						Females					
Socioeconomic Status	Low*		High*		Total*		Low*		High		Total*	
	%	N	%	N	%	N	%	N	%	N	%	N
Low Intelligence												
Low	1.1	353	16.8	77	4.0	430	1.1	459	17.0	53	2.7	512
Lower middle ..	0.8	234	24.3	111	8.4	345	3.7	296	32.2	90	10.4	386
Upper middle ..	4.6	174	34.1	138	17.6	312	4.1	170	33.3	108	15.5	278
High	7.6	52	40.6	96	29.0	148	10.7	56	38.3	94	28.0	150
Total	2.2	813	29.8	422	11.7	1,235	3.0	981	31.8	345	10.5	1,326
Lower Middle Intelligence												
Low	4.2	216	31.4	105	13.0	321	1.6	317	23.0	61	5.0	378
Lower middle ..	3.4	208	40.3	159	19.4	367	7.5	255	34.8	135	16.9	390
Upper middle ..	4.8	126	40.2	184	25.8	310	6.3	206	45.4	165	23.7	371
High	9.6	52	57.8	213	48.3	265	6.6	75	59.1	186	44.0	261
Total	4.4	602	44.5	661	25.4	1,263	4.9	853	45.0	547	20.6	1,400

Upper Middle Intelligence

	Low	High*	Total*	Low*	High*	Total*
Low	8.7 (138)	41.3 (92)	21.7 (230)	3.6 (224)	36.4 (55)	10.0 (279)
Lower middle	9.4 (127)	50.2 (185)	33.6 (312)	6.8 (176)	42.2 (147)	22.9 (323)
Upper middle	15.6 (109)	59.6 (248)	46.2 (357)	6.4 (186)	47.6 (191)	27.3 (377)
High	18.0 (50)	77.5 (289)	68.7 (339)	21.6 (60)	74.0 (311)	65.5 (371)
Total	11.8 (424)	61.8 (814)	44.7 (1,238)	7.0 (646)	57.2 (704)	33.2 (1,350)

High Intelligence

	Low	High*	Total*	Low	High*	Total*
Low	13.0 (77)	53.2 (92)	34.9 (169)	11.9 (109)	53.8 (52)	25.4 (161)
Lower middle	17.7 (96)	66.8 (178)	49.6 (274)	11.7 (128)	59.0 (122)	34.8 (250)
Upper middle	12.5 (48)	73.0 (271)	64.0 (319)	19.8 (101)	64.8 (219)	50.6 (320)
High	32.0 (25)	88.4 (468)	85.6 (493)	21.0 (62)	78.6 (458)	71.7 (520)
Total	16.6 (246)	77.3 (1,009)	65.4 (1,255)	15.2 (400)	70.7 (851)	53.0 (1,251)

Total

	Low*	High*	Total*	Low*	High*	Total*
Low	4.4 (784)	36.3 (366)	14.6 (1,150)	2.8 (1,109)	32.1 (221)	7.7 (1,330)
Lower middle	5.7 (665)	47.9 (633)	26.3 (1,298)	6.6 (855)	42.5 (494)	19.8 (1,349)
Upper middle	8.1 (457)	55.5 (841)	38.8 (1,298)	7.8 (663)	50.4 (683)	29.4 (1,346)
High	14.5 (179)	75.0 (1,066)	66.4 (1,245)	14.6 (253)	70.2 (1,049)	59.4 (1,302)
Total	6.5 (2,085)	58.6 (2,906)	36.9 (4,991)	6.2 (2,880)	55.6 (2,447)	28.9 (5,327)

* The χ^2 for each column designated is significant beyond the 0.5 level.

nor parental encouragement, individually or jointly, can completely account for the social class differences in the college plans of either males or females. This conclusion leads to the examination of a final question in this paper, namely, whether or not there are specific subpopulations of sex, intelligence, and parental encouragement in which social class differences in college plans are eliminated.

The multivariate cross-tabular data presented in Table 4 give the percentages of males and females planning on college, by socioeconomic status, intelligence, and parental encouragement. The separate relationships of socioeconomic status, intelligence, and parental encouragement to college plans can be examined from the marginals in this table. Each of these relationships is positive, monotonic, and statistically significant. The relationship of socioeconomic status to college plans, controlling only for intelligence, can be examined from the columns marked "Total" under the four intelligence categories. The control for intelligence reduces but does not eliminate the social class differences in the college plans of males and females in each category of intelligence. Similarly, from the bottom part of Table 4, the relationship of socioeconomic status to college plans continues to be positive, monotonic, and statistically significant when only parental encouragement is controlled. However, since the purpose of this multivariate cross-tabular analysis is to specify the subgroups in which the influence of social class on college plans is either markedly pronounced or markedly reduced, only the columns showing a simultaneous cross-tabulation of socioeconomic status, intelligence, and parental encouragement will be discussed here. Several observations can be made from these data.

First, the dictum—that the higher the level of socioeconomic status the higher the level of educational aspirations—is generally true, even after sex, intelligence, and parental encouragement are controlled. Except for some slight reversals in the two middle categories of socioeconomic status, the relationship between socioeconomic status and college plans is generally positive and monotonic. While only about 1 per cent of males and females with low intelligence and low parental encouragement from the low socioeconomic status category planned on college, 88.4 per cent of the males and 78.6 per cent of the females with high intelligence and high parental encouragement from the high socioeconomic status category planned on college. The proportions planning on college in the remaining socioeconomic status categories, by intelligence and parental encouragement, fall within this range. However, the difference in the percentage of students planning on college from the bottom and the top socioeconomic status categories of these subgroups varies over a wide range—from a minimum of 5 per cent to over 35 per cent.

Second, the socioeconomic status differences in the college plans of the seniors are almost four times as great for those who perceived parental encouragement as for those who did not: Further, these differences are generally greater for those who are in the two upper categories of intelligence than for those in the two lower categories of intelligence. Thus, differences in the levels of both intelligence and parental encouragement seem to increase the socioeconomic status differences in the college plans of youth. In other words, the socioeconomic status differences in college plans of youth are greater among the most able and the most encouraged than among the least able and the least encouraged.

Third, in most categories of socioeconomic status, intelligence, and parental encouragement, the proportion of students planning on college is greater for males than for females. This indicates the important influence of sex-role expectations on the college plans of youth. However, sex-role expectations seem to bear more heavily on those who are high in intelligence than on those who are low in intelligence. The greater proportions of females than of males planning on college in some of the subgroups within the two lower categories of intelligence support this conclusion.

Fourth, the socioeconomic status differences in college plans of the seniors in both categories of parental encouragement are greater among those who are most intelligent than among those who are least intelligent. On the one hand, among those who did not perceive parental encouragement and who are least able, only about 1 per cent of males and females from the low socioeconomic status category planned on college as against 7.6 per cent of males and 10.7 per cent of females from the high socioeconomic status category. On the other hand, among those who did not perceive parental encouragement but who are most able, 13.0 per cent of males and 11.9 per cent of females from the low socioeconomic status category planned on college as against 32.0 per cent of males and 21.0 per cent of females from the high socioeconomic status category. Similarly, among those who perceived parental encouragement and who are least able, about 17 per cent of both males and females from the low socioeconomic status category planned on college as against 40.6 per cent of males and 38.3 per cent of females from the high socioeconomic status category. Among those who perceived parental encouragement and who are most able, about 53 per cent of males and females from the low socioeconomic status category planned on college as against 88.4 per cent of males and 78.6 per cent of females from the high socioeconomic status category. Thus, ability continues to accentuate the social class differences in

aspirations of both males and females, regardless of whether or not they perceive parental encouragement to plan on college.

Finally, in each category of socioeconomic status and intelligence, the proportion of males and females planning on college is greater among those who perceived parental encouragement than among those who did not. In particular, in all categories of intelligence, the proportion of males and females planning on college is greater among the low socioeconomic status seniors who perceived parental encouragement than among the high socioeconomic status seniors who did not perceive parental encouragement. Consequently, parental encouragement seems to be a powerful factor in encouraging seniors who are low in socioeconomic status but high in ability to plan on college. In general, however, parental encouragement appears to have its strongest effect on the college plans of males and females who score relatively high on intelligence and come from families occupying relatively high socioeconomic positions.

In addition to providing the reader with an opportunity to see the effects of the several variables on college plans in familiar percentage terms, the multiple cross-tabular analysis tends mainly to emphasize and reinforce what was already known from the correlation analysis; namely, that (1) there are large differences between the socioeconomic status categories in college plans; (2) even though these differences are reduced when sex, intelligence, and parental encouragement are controlled, there are still large and important socioeconomic status differences in college plans, especially in the top two intelligence groups where college plans are most relevant in any case; (3) where parental encouragement is low, relatively few students, regardless of their intelligence or socioeconomic status levels, plan on college (even highly intelligent students with high social class origins who are not encouraged by their parents are not likely to plan on college); (4) where parental encouragement is high, the proportion of students planning on college is also high, even when socioeconomic status and intelligence levels are relatively low. Thus, it may be concluded that while social class differences cannot be entirely explained by differences in parental encouragement (or intelligence) among the various socioeconomic classes, parental encouragement makes an independent contribution to social class differences in college plans of both males and females; (5) the effects of sex-role expectations are such that girls' educational aspirations are generally lower than those of boys and are somewhat more sensitive to socioeconomic background than to ability or parental encouragement.

CONCLUSIONS

The correlational, causal, and cross-tabular analyses in this study substantiate, on the whole, the claim made by other investigators using less rigorous methods and less representative samples that parental encouragement is a powerful intervening variable between socioeconomic class background and intelligence of the child and his educational aspirations. While parental encouragement does not "explain" social class differences in aspirations, it contributes to the explanation of these differences. Because parental encouragement is a social-psychological variable, it is presumably subject to modification by means of programs of counseling directed at parents or parents and children, whereas the child's intelligence and family socioeconomic status are likely to be more difficult to influence at this point in the child's development.

At the same time there is still a good deal of variance in college plans of the socioeconomic classes that is not explained either individually or jointly by parental encouragement and intelligence. This leads to the question of what other factors may help to explain social class differences. Within the complex which is subsumed under socioeconomic status, the economic resources available for the support of college education must be an important determinant, and none of the studies reported to date have adequately assessed this aspect of socioeconomic level. Information regarding the economic resources of the families of the seniors under study is being currently collected from public sources which will make such an analysis possible. Other variables that should be considered include the student's knowledge of available opportunities for scholarships, loans, and jobs, and the student's self-conceptions —including his assessment of his chances for success in college, his reference groups, and various contextual influences such as the value climate and the opportunity structures of his school and community. All of these factors are in need of further study for increasing and strengthening the knowledge of the factors involved in social class differences in educational aspiration and for understanding more fully the contribution of nonintellectual factors to educational aspiration.

BEHAVIOR PROBLEMS OF CHILDREN AS VIEWED BY TEACHERS AND THE CHILDREN THEMSELVES

Dorothy D. Mutimer / Robert A. Rosemier

Although he might not be considered terribly profound, an individual could make the casual observation that certain behaviors of children are considered "problems," while others are not. He might also observe that it is the adult in our society who most frequently makes this discrimination and who dictates the ensuing treatments, educational or otherwise. To the degree that the adult perceives the seriousness of the behavior differently from the child exhibiting that behavior will the treatments he applies to that behavior be inappropriate in the eyes of the child. Consequently, the treatment applied may be of less than optimum effectiveness in changing that behavior.

The present study was undertaken to provide some data about the degree of consistency between children and teachers in terms of how they view the seriousness of "problem" behaviors. A number of earlier studies have attempted to assess the consistency between various adult sub-

From: Journal of Consulting Psychology, 1967, 31, 538–87. Copyright © 1967 by the American Psychological Association, and reproduced by permission of the authors and APA.

groups, such as teachers and mental hygienists (Wickman, 1929), elementary teachers and clinicians (Stouffer, 1952), secondary teachers and clinicians (Stouffer, 1956), and attitude changes between these groups over the years (Hunter, 1957; Schruppe & Gjerde, 1953). Other replications are presented in Beilen (1962). Little, if any, data are presently available concerning the degree of consistency between teachers and children themselves.

PROCEDURE

Four hundred children in Grades 7–12 in a northern Illinois town were administered a list of 50 behaviors which were used in the Wickman (1929) study and asked to briefly describe each behavior. The common description was then placed in parentheses after each original description so that the meaning of each behavior would be understood by the experimental Ss. The 50 behaviors with their common interpretations are listed in Table 1.

Fourteen female and 26 male teachers of Grades 7–12 in three northern Illinois towns and their 455

TABLE 1

RANK OF WICKMAN'S BEHAVIORS BASED ON
STUDENT FREQUENCIES

Behavior	Frequency in most serious categories	Total responses	Seriousness rank
1. Stealing	798	908	1
2. Cruelty, bullying (picking on others)	457	909	22
3. Heterosexual activity (making out)	354	899	35
4. Truancy (skip school)	513	901	13
5. Unhappy, depressed (sad)	287	903	43
6. Impertinence, defiance (talking back)	541	907	11
7. Destroying school property	747	909	2
8. Unreliableness (can't depend on)	506	907	14
9. Untruthfulness (lie)	717	908	3
10. Disobedience (not obey, not do as told)	612	906	7
11. Temper tantrums (temper outbursts)	550	905	9
12. Resentfulness (against—dislike)	348	903	37
13. Unsocial, withdrawing (not friendly)	364	905	31
14. Obscene notes/talk (dirty notes, talk)	551	908	10
15. Nervousness (jittery)	260	906	45
16. Cheating (copying)	617	910	6
17. Selfishness (not sharing)	284	905	44
18. Quarrelsomeness (argue, fight)	445	909	25
19. Domineering (bossy)	368	904	30
20. Lack of interest in school	490	910	17
21. Impudence, rudeness (not polite)	452	906	23
22. Easily discouraged (give up)	493	908	16
23. Fearfulness (afraid)	334	908	39
24. Suggestible (easily led)	495	903	15
25. Enuresis (wet the bed or the self)	644	906	5
26. Masturbation (sex-playing with the self)	692	909	4
27. Laziness (not active)	351	910	36
28. Inattention (not paying attention)	397	904	27
29. Disorderliness in class (acting up)	474	908	19
30. Sullenness (sulk, pout)	339	908	38
31. Physical coward (sissy)	379	906	28
32. Overcritical of others (finding fault)	461	909	20
33. Sensitiveness (easily hurt)	362	908	33
34. Carelessness in work (messy)	320	906	42
35. Shyness (bashful)	167	905	48
36. Suspiciousness (suspecting others)	376	902	29
37. Smoking (use of tobacco)	541	907	12
38. Stubbornness (bull-headed)	327	906	40
39. Dreaminess (day dream)	221	902	47
40. Profanity (swearing)	586	909	8
41. Attracting attention (cutting up in class)	459	908	21
42. Slovenly in personal appearance (sloppy)	450	906	24
43. Restlessness (over-active)	223	905	46
44. Tardiness (late)	325	906	41
45. Thoughtlessness (forgetting)	361	906	34
46. Tattling (telling on others)	478	902	18
47. Inquisitiveness (asking questions)	99	907	50
48. Interrupting (butting in)	363	906	32
49. Imaginative lying (exaggerating)	421	899	26
50. Whispering (talking softly)	100	907	49

male and 456 female students were asked to rate each behavior on a four-point scale. The number of Ss per grade ranged 115–198, and their ages ranged 12–20 years. The professional experience of the teachers ranged 1–25 years.

The three towns, somewhat semi-rural, each had less than 10,000 population and were within a 20-mile radius of a large metropolitan center. The communities were perceived by the authors to be somewhat above average in socioeconomic distribution, and the school physical plants were considered modern and up-to-date.

Neither students nor teachers were informed about comparisons to be made and were given only the following directions:

> Following this page, you will find a list of fifty behaviors which have been seen in children and adolescents. Some of these behaviors may never occur in some students, *but assuming that they did occur,* how serious would you consider them to be? Make your ratings according to *your own* personal opinion as to the seriousness of the behavior as you see it in *others.* Make your ratings quickly. Be sure to rate each of the fifty items. The words in parentheses may help you to better understand the meaning of each word or phrase.
>
> Please look at the first behavior of *Stealing.* If you think that stealing is *not at all serious,* place your check mark under that heading; if you think it is *slightly serious,* place your check mark in that column; and if you think that it is *serious* or *very serious,* place your check mark accordingly. Do the same for each behavior. There are no right or wrong answers. Be sure that your ratings represent your own opinions. Are there any questions?

Interactions between the dimensions of sex of student, grade level of student, and group status (teachers versus student) were analyzed by chi-square tests of independence on each behavior. The dimensions of sex, grade level, and academic specialty of the teachers were excluded from the analyses because of the restricted number participating.

Efforts were concentrated only on the 10 behaviors which showed the largest frequencies in the two most serious categories and the 10 items which showed the largest frequencies in the two least serious categories, as rated by the students. These are indicated by seriousness ranks of 1–10 and 41–50 in Table 1. Omitted from analysis were those behaviors showing a relatively rectangular frequency distribution in the four categories.

RESULTS

The results of the 500 chi-square tests of independence are reported in Table 2 for the 10 most serious and the 10 least serious behaviors.

DIFFERENCES AMONG STUDENTS

Sex Differences. Male students differed from female students on all 10 of the most serious behaviors and on 6 of the 10 least serious. The fewest number of disagreements between sexes occurred in Grade 8 (2 behaviors) and the greatest in Grade 9 (15 behaviors). At other grades the number of behaviors on which disagreements between sexes were observed ranged 5–7. Female students were inclined to rate both groups of extreme behaviors as more serious than boys (from raw frequencies).

Grade Differences. Disagreements were noted among grades on 7 each of the 10 most serious and the 10 least serious behaviors. Female students differed over grades more frequently than boys (girls differed over grades on 7 of the 10 most serious behaviors and on 5 of the least serious, while boys differed over grades on 3 of each).

TABLE 2

SUMMARY OF TESTS OF INDEPENDENCE FOR 10 MOST SERIOUS AND 10 LEAST SERIOUS BEHAVIORS

Comparison	Most serious										Least serious									
	Stealing	Destroying school property	Untruthfulness	Masturbation	Enuresis	Cheating	Disobedience	Profanity	Temper tantrums	Obscene notes/talk	Tardiness	Carelessness	Nervousness	Unhappy	Selfishness	Dreaminess	Restlessness	Shyness	Inquisitiveness	Whispering
Among grade levels																				
Male students	.01	.10	.05	.10		.10		.01		.01	.01	.01	.10	.05		.10	.01		.10	.01
Female students	.01	.10	.05				.05	.01		.01	.01	.05	.10			.05	.01		.01	.05
Between sexes of students																				
Grade 7	.01	.05	.10	.01	.01	.01	.01	.01	.01	.01	.01		.01	.01	.05	.05	.05		.10	.01
Grade 8		.05	.01	.01	.01	.01	.10		.05								.10			
Grade 9	.05	.05	.05	.01	.01	.05	.05	.05	.05	.01	.01	.10	.01	.10	.01		.10	.10	.10	.10
Grade 10				.01	.05		.05		.01	.10										
Grade 11				.01	.01												.10			.10
Grade 12	.10		.05	.01	.05			.01			.10		.01	.10	.01	.10	.05	.10	.01	
Status (student vs. teacher)				.01	.01	.10	.05	.01		.05	.05	.05	.05	.01	.05		.01	.05		.05
Male students vs. teachers																				
Grade 7	.05			.01	.01		.05	.05		.05	.05		.01	.01	.05		.01			
Grade 8				.01	.05		.05	.01		.05	.10		.05	.01	.05		.01			
Grade 9				.01	.05		.05	.01		.05			.01	.05			.10			
Grade 10				.01	.05		.10	.05		.10			.05	.05			.05			
Grade 11				.01	.01		1.0						.05	.05		.10	.01			.05
Grade 12				.01	.05		.05					.10	.01	.10			.05			
Female students vs. teachers																				
Grade 7	.10		.01	.01	.10		.01	.01		.05			.05	.05			.05	.05		
Grade 8	.10		.01	.01	.05		.10	.01		.05			.01	.01			.01		.10	
Grade 9	.10			.01	.01		.05	.01		.05			.05				.01			
Grade 10				.01	.01		.01	.01					.10				.05	.10		.10
Grade 11				.01	.01		.05	.10		.01			.10		.05		.05			.10
Grade 12	.10		.05	.01	.05		.10	.05			.10						.05		.10	.10

Sources of Disagreement. Most disagreements between the sexes of students occurred on the behaviors of masturbation (four of six grades), disobedience, untruthfulness, and temper tantrums (where sex differences occurred at three of the six grades in each).

DIFFERENCES BETWEEN STUDENTS AND TEACHERS

Differences by Sex of Student. Little distinction was noted between the sex of the students with regard to the number of disagreements they had with the teachers. Boys generally disagreed with the teachers on the same behaviors as did girls, at least on the 10 most serious behaviors. Of the 26 disagreements of boys with teachers on these behaviors, all but 1 was also in disagreement by girls and teachers. Of the least serious behaviors, only half the disagreements between boys and teachers were upheld by the girls. The boys appeared to have an approximately equal number of disagreements with the teachers on the 10 most serious behaviors and the 10 least serious (26 versus 27). Most of the disagreements between girls and teachers occurred on the most serious behaviors (31 versus 19). The total number of disagreements with teachers appeared equal for the two sexes (53 versus 50).

Differences by Grade Level. Although no single grade level appeared to have a greater number of disagreements between students and teachers than another, Grade 10 did appear to have fewer. Here, boys showed disagreements with teachers on 5 behaviors, while girls disagreed with teachers on 6. At other grades the number of behaviors on which disagreements with teachers occurred ranged 9–11 for boys and 8–10 for girls.

Sources of Disagreement. Students as a whole differed more frequently with teachers on the 10 most serious behaviors than on the 10 least serious (5 versus 3). This extent of disagreement with teachers was upheld when considering the sex and the grade level of the students (57 versus 46). Of the 10 most serious behaviors, the largest number of disagreements was observed on the behaviors of masturbation, enuresis, disobedience, profanity, and obscene notes/talk. The fewest number of disagreements within this extreme group was observed for the behaviors of destroying school property and temper tantrums. Of the 10 least serious behaviors, the largest number of disagreements was found on the behaviors of restlessness and nervousness. The smallest number of disagreements within this group was found for the behavior of dreaminess.

COMPOSITE TEACHER RANKING VERSUS COMPOSITE STUDENT RANKING

A composite teacher ranking of the seriousness of the 50 behaviors was derived by the same technique as that employed earlier in identifying the 10 most serious and 10 least serious behaviors on the basis of student responses. The 10 most serious and 10 least serious behaviors, as perceived by the teachers, as well as the comparable lists for students and for teachers in the Wickman (1929) study, are presented in Table 3.

Of the 10 most serious and the 10 least serious behaviors on the student list, 60% also appear on the present teacher list, while 60% and 50%, respectively, appear on Wickman's teacher list. Of the 10 most serious and the 10 least serious behaviors on the present teacher list, 60% also appear on Wickman's teacher list.

Four of the behaviors in each extreme of the student list did not appear in the same extreme of the present teacher list.

TABLE 3

TWENTY EXTREME RANKINGS OF BEHAVIORS BY
PRESENT STUDENTS AND TEACHERS AND BY
WICKMAN'S TEACHERS

Students	*Present teachers*	*Wickman teachers*
Most serious		
1. Stealing 2. Destroying school property 3. Untruthfulness 4. Masturbation 5. Enuresis 6. Cheating 7. Disobedience 8. Profanity 9. Temper tantrums 10. Obscene notes/talk	1. Destroying school property 2. Stealing 3. Untruthfulness 4. Cheating 5. Obscene notes/talk 6. Disobedience 7. Cruelty, bullying 8. Easily discouraged 9. Unreliableness 10. Impertinence, defiance	1. Heterosexual activity 2. Stealing 3. Masturbation 4. Obscene notes/talk 5. Untruthfulness 6. Truancy 7. Impertinence 8. Cruelty, bullying 9. Cheating 10. Destroying school property
Least serious		
41. Tardiness 42. Carelessness 43. Unhappy 44. Selfishness 45. Nervousness 46. Restlessness 47. Dreaminess 48. Shyness 49. Whispering 50. Inquisitiveness	41. Tardiness 42. Tattling 43. Selfishness 44. Smoking 45. Physical coward 46. Sensitiveness 47. Whispering 48. Inquisitiveness 49. Shyness 50. Restlessness	41. Dreaminess 42. Imaginative lying 43. Interrupting 44. Inquisitiveness 45. Over-critical 46. Tattling 47. Whispering 48. Sensitiveness 49. Restlessness 50. Shyness

Five of these eight behaviors had composite teacher ranks within a fifth adjacent to their location in the student list, while two others barely missed falling into an adjacent fifth. One behavior (unhappiness) nearly became one of the 10 most serious behaviors on the teacher list, while it was among the 10 least serious on the student list.

CONCLUSIONS

The data would suggest that considerable disagreements exist concerning the seriousness of certain behaviors. These disagreements were observed between teachers and students, as well as among students themselves with respect to sex and grade level.

At least 5 of the 10 most serious and 3 of the 10 least serious behaviors have been identified as those which appear to cause the greatest disagreement between students and teachers. Teachers in the present study rated the behaviors of masturbation, enuresis, profanity, and restlessness as being less serious than did students and tended to rate the behaviors of disobedience, obscene notes/talk, nervousness, and unhappiness as being more serious than did students.

To the degree that the above data

can be generalized to other school populations, teachers will need to consider the implications of these differing perceptions of seriousness when dealing with student behavior. Because of the apparent variation within this subgroup of junior high school and high school children, the teacher's task is made more difficult in selecting an "appropriate" treatment. These grade levels would appear to be no place for stereotyped reactions to student behavior patterns.

REFERENCES

BEILEN, H. Teachers' and clinicians' attitudes toward the behavior problems of children, a reappraisal. In V. NOLL & R. NOLL (Eds.), *Readings in educational psychology*. Macmillan, 1962. Pp. 361–379.

HUNTER, E. C. Changes in teachers' attitudes toward children's behaviors over the last thirty years. *Mental Hygiene,* 1957, 41, 3–11.

SCHRUPPE, M. H., & GJERDE, C. M. Teacher growth in attitudes toward behavior problems of children. *Journal of Educational Psychology,* 1953, 44, 203–214.

STOUFFER, G. A. W., JR. Behavior problems of children as viewed by teachers and mental hygienists. *Mental Hygiene,* 1952, 36, 271–285.

STOUFFER, G. A. W., JR. The attitudes of secondary school teachers toward certain behavior problems of children. *School Review,* 1956, 64, 358–362.

WICKMAN, E. K. *Children's behavior and teachers' attitudes.* New York: Commonwealth Fund, Division of Publishers, 1929.

SIMPLICIAL STRUCTURES OF MIDDLE-CLASS AND LOWER-CLASS PUPILS' ATTITUDES TOWARD TEACHERS

Albert H. Yee / Philip J. Runkel

Krech, Crutchfield, and Ballachey (1962, pp. 137–147) referred to an individual's total set of attitudes as his attitude constellation. Attitudes toward related objects can be perceived as clustered in interconnected patterns. In regard to one attitude and its "cognitive," "feeling," and "action tendency" components, the degree of "multiplexity" in a component's make-up varies from individual to individual (Krech et al., 1962, pp. 140–141).[1] Thus, a random sample of college students provides variation in attitudes toward learning, military conscription, and blondes. We expect people's attitudes toward such

From: Developmental Psychology, *1969*, 1, *646–52. Copyright* © *1969 by the American Psychological Association, and reproduced by permission of the authors and APA.*

[1] Krech et al. (1962, p. 178) defined multiplexity of attitude component as follows: The number and variety of the separate elements which make up the cognitive, feeling, or action tendency components of an attitude. A component which has a large number and variety of elements is referred to as a multiplex component; one with relatively few or highly similar elements, as a simplex component.

objects will vary in interconnectedness and multiplexity of components.

This study investigated the interconnected pattern and multiplexity among middle-class (MC) and lower-class (LC) pupils' attitudes toward their teachers' classroom effectiveness. The following questions were raised: (*a*) With a series of pupils' cognitive or evaluative attitude measurements directed at differing aspects of merit in a teacher's teaching, can an interconnected pattern be found? (*b*) Can differences be found between attitude patterns and the degree of multiplexity in MC and LC pupils' evaluative attitudes toward their teachers? Earlier results with the analysis of variance showed that MC and LC pupils' teachers contrasted significantly in their attitudes of warmth, sympathy, and permissiveness toward children (Yee, 1968a). Pupils' attitudes also differed significantly when classified by pupils' social class. Thus, the second question deals with greater explication and description of such differences.

Guttman's (1954, 1966) insightful writings on facet design and analysis inspired this study. In brief, facet design is a deductive approach to a domain of data and implies or hypothesizes certain intercorrelations in an overall configural structure. Facet analysis involves testing the predicted pattern by examining the correlational matrix of a given set of variables.

In facet design and analysis, a *simplex* matrix of intercorrelations is the simplest pattern that can provide useful psychological meaning. For example, Myers, McConville, and Coffman (1966) found simplex structuring of judgments on a number of criteria for grading essays greatly extended the explanation of their results. More complex structures, such as the circumplex and radex, have been described and tested (e.g., Foa, 1965; Guttman, 1957; Mori, 1965). Guttman (1966) described the simplex as follows:

> a simplex: the largest correlations are along the main diagonal, and the correlations tend to decrease in size as their positions approach the upper right or lower left corners. The closer two variables are in serial order, usually, the more highly are they correlated with each other [p. 447].

A simplicial structure reveals a hierarchial or serial order in a set of variables; "the general nature of the order is often empirically evident by inspection alone, without any calculation of parameters or precise mathematical specifications [Guttman, 1954, p. 279]." Discovery of a simplex "should spur efforts to reveal its nature in more detail, and may perhaps ultimately lead to an exact parametric theory for it [Guttman, 1954, p. 279]." In the interpretation phase of such procedures, the researcher attempts to explain the structure's content and meaning. In doing so, it can be said that one variable is on a lesser order of multiplexity than the next in series from the diagonals, and that the more multiplex variable encompasses the characteristics of the less multiplex variable and more.

METHOD

DATA

Pupils' attitudes toward their teachers were measured at the beginning of the school year and several months later with the 100-item "About My Teacher" (AMT) inventory developed by Beck (1964) under the direction of N. L. Gage. Beck and Gage constructed the AMT with five dimensions of teacher merit—affective, cognitive, disciplinary, innovative, and motivational. For the present study, eight factor subtests were compiled from Beck's factor analysis and the results of four later multiple-factor analyses (principal axis, rotated by Kaiser's 1958 Varimax method) by Yee (1966). The five factor analyses were each conducted with different data; further study of the results continues. The eight homogeneous factors formulated for this study do not represent exact results of any one factor analysis, contain no overlapping items, and represent a wide variety of pupils' perceptions of teacher-class behavior.

The eight factors are as follows:

P_1: Affective merit of teacher (9 items, such as "Is your teacher fun to be with?")

P_2: Cognitive merit of teacher (10 items written with positive statements, such as, "Does your teacher explain your lessons clearly?")

P_3: Cognitive merit of teacher (10 items written with negative statements, such as. "Is it sometimes hard to understand your teacher's explanations?")

P_4: Pupils' conduct (9 items, such as, "Do the children behave well for your teacher?")

P₅: Disciplining behavior of teacher (3 items, such as, "Does your teacher succeed in keeping the pupils under control?")

P₆: Innovative merit of teacher in use of audiovisual materials and field trips (3 items, such as, "Does your class go on field trips that help you understand what you are studying?")

P₇: Innovative merit of teacher in individualizing instruction (3 items, such as, "Do all the pupils in the class use the same books at the same time?")

P₈: Motivational merit of teacher (8 items, such as, "Does your teacher make you feel like learning a lot on your own?")

RELIABILITY OF MEASURES

The reliability of pupil agreement in rating their teacher on the AMT was estimated with Horst's (1949) formula. The Horst coefficient for the total score obtained at pretest was .86 for the 110 classes of LC pupils and .89 for the 99 classes of MC pupils; for total scores at posttest, the respective r's were .88 and .91. When separate Horst r's were computed for the various factor scores, the median r for the 110 classes of LC pupils was .85 with a high of .95 (P₇) and a low of .64 (P₈), and for the 99 classes of MC pupils, the median r was .86 with a high of .95 (P₇) and a low of .71 (P₈). Such results indicate strong within-class agreement and make it feasible to use class means as indexes of pupils' attitudes.

Horst r's computed separately for girls and boys were all lower than those for whole classes. Compared to findings for whole classes, Horst r's for girls were lower, with a median difference of .07 (high of .13 and low of .05), and boys' r's were lower, with a median difference of .11 (high of .15 and low of .09). The lower coefficients clearly indicate that classification of the data by pupil sex decreases reliability. Also, only minor differences can be found between girls' and boys' means and standard deviations. All of these findings indicate that agreement of pupils' attitudes toward their teacher are more accurately measured when girls' and boys' attitudes are considered together rather than separately. Thus, since girls' and boys' AMT measures do not differ in means or variability and offer less reliable data than what whole classes provide, it was decided that separate analyses by pupil sex would afford little gain in substantive knowledge.

Middle-class pupils' attitudes tend to be more stable than those of LC pupils; for example, for MC, the test-retest r for total AMT scores was .71 and for LC, it was .62. Since the Horst r's reported above for the total scores were greater than such test-retest r's, it appears there was greater variability between test occasions than within classes.

SUBJECTS

Ninety-nine classes of MC pupils and 110 classes of LC pupils in 52 Texas and California schools comprised the sample for this study. The sample was almost evenly divided among Grades 4, 5, and 6 (2 classes were Grade 7 in the LC group). The 40 male teachers in the sample were equally distributed between the MC and LC subsamples. The subsamples were roughly equivalent in levels of teachers' experience in classrooms: for LC, 0–1 year as a teacher (5 with 1 year's experience), $N = 25$; 2–8 years (average of 4.6 years), $N = 36$; 9+ years (average of 19.9 years), $N = 49$; and for MC, 0–1 year (4 with 1 year's experience), $N = 36$; 2–8 years (average of 5.5 years), $N = 31$; 9+ years (average of 17.2 years), $N = 32$.

Most of the teachers worked in school districts that were homogeneous in terms of pupils' social class background, that is, all MC or LC. If administrators of school districts heterogeneous in pupils' social class tended to assign novice teachers to LC schools and give MC assignments to experienced teachers, such bias would affect about one-fourth of the cases. Although such a tendency could not be verified if present, it is more likely that teachers' choices and administrators' recruitment and selection criteria influenced teacher placements. In the analysis of variance analyses mentioned earlier, teachers' attitudes toward children and teaching in general differed significantly by pupils' social class, but *not* across levels of teaching experience (Yee, 1968a).

Recruiting procedures conducted with school administrators created no known bias in the sample selected. The sample obtained is believed to be a fair representation of LC and MC pupils and their teachers, even though rigorous random selection was not possible. All classes were roughly equivalent in numbers of girls and boys and were homogeneous in pupils' social class status and ethnic background.

Social class status was determined by consultations with school administrators and follow-up validation by informal inspection of neighborhoods. The main criteria for establishing social class status were: (*a*) family income ($4,000 or less annually for LC; $6,000 or more for MC), and (*b*) father's occupation (blue collar and unskilled for LC; white collar and professional for MC). Such criteria ensured that classes were homogeneous in pupils' social class status.

Since within-class agreement of pupils' perceptions of their teacher was found to be strong and classes were either all MC or LC and not mixtures, the use of class means for this study's purposes seems feasible. For any class, the means obtained represent rather good estimates of how any randomly drawn pupil in the class, girl or boy, would score. Thus, the data do not pose the problems of inferring individual behavior as Robinson (1950) found in what he termed "ecological correlations."

ANALYSES

Class means were computed from the pupils' posttest scores and intercorrelated separately for the MC and LC groups. The resultant simplexes were found by visual inspection of the correlations.

Lingoes' (1965) smallest space analysis I (SSA-I) computer program, adapted by James C. Johnson for use at the University of Oregon Computer Center, was used to provide Euclidean distances between variables in a two-dimensional space.

RESULTS

Tables 1 and 2 present the simplexes found with visual inspection of the intercorrelations of pupils' posttest factor scores. Although the simplexes contain relatively minor imperfections, which are to be expected with actual data (Guttman, 1954, p. 278), definite simplicial structures appear for both sets of data. Definite gradients in the correlations can be seen and indicate meaningful rank orders. The order of the rankings appears to be logical, that is, increasing in multiplexity from left to right across the variables in Tables 1 and 2. The least complex attitude appears to be pupils' conduct (P_4), since P_4 cannot logically encompass the characteristics of all of the other attitudes. However, it makes good sense to say that the most complex attitude is teacher's innovative merit (P_7). The hierarchial ranking from P_4 to P_7 can be interpreted as a progressive increase in multiplexity from concrete, controlling behavior to more abstract, creative behavior.

The MC simplex structure incorporates more of the eight pupil variables than does the LC simplex and extends well through the motivational factor (P_8) up to P_6, one of the innovative factors, before it appears to collapse. The LC structure extends only strongly through the cognitive factors to the fifth level in series.

Comparison of Figures 1 and 2 helps to illustrate the nature of the two simplicial structures. The arrows in Figures 1 and 2 indicate the hierarchial order of the variables in the simplexes, as shown in Tables 1 and 2. SSA-I results, therefore, confirm the simplexes found through visual inspections of the intercorrelations. Such results show that MC pupils' attitudes toward their teacher's effectiveness were more multiplex, that is, more highly related and consistent, than LC pupils' attitudes. The most striking difference between the two sets of results is the closeness of the motivational factor (P_8) to the affective (P_1) and cognitive factors (P_2 and P_3) in the MC simplex and the contrasting result in the LC simplex.

Middle-class pupils in the study tended to associate motivational behavior

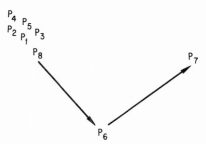

Figure 1. Smallest space analysis I results for middle-class pupils.

with affective and cognitive behaviors in a common package of meaning, while LC pupils perceived the motivational effects of the teacher as relatively dissociated from both his cognitive and affective merit. In the MC results, a highly interrelated set of variables appeared to comprise what may be termed a "traditional" clustering of instructional behavior common to the typical view of how MC pupils are taught and respond. In other words,

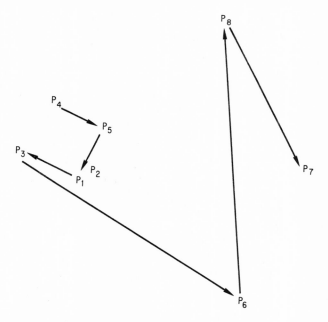

Figure 2. Smallest space analysis I results for lower-class pupils.

TABLE 1

SIMPLEX STRUCTURE OF MC PUPILS' FACTOR SCORES

Factor	P_4	P_5	P_2	P_1	P_3	P_8	P_6	P_7
P_4: Pupils' conduct		.74	.55	.56	.56	.38	.10	−.28
P_5: Teachers' disciplinary merit			.79	.71	.67	.36	.10	−.17
P_2: Teachers' cognitive merit				.88	.84	.35	.10	−.22
P_1: Teachers' affective merit					.76	.41	.10	−.22
P_3: Teachers' cognitive merit						.42	.14	−.13
P_8: Teachers' motivational merit							.21	−.16
P_6: Teachers' innovative merit								.32
P_7: Teachers' innovative merit								

Note.—$N = 99$ class means. MC = middle class.

TABLE 2

SIMPLEX STRUCTURE OF LC PUPILS' FACTOR SCORES

Factor	P_4	P_5	P_1	P_2	P_3	P_6	P_8	P_7
P_4: Pupils' conduct		.52	.47	.37	.50	.13	.11	−.07
P_5: Teachers' disciplinary merit			.56	.57	.41	.18	.17	−.02
P_1: Teachers' affective merit				.88	.77	.15	−.06	−.08
P_2: Teachers' cognitive merit					.77	.21	−.04	−.09
P_3: Teachers' cognitive merit						.08	−.13	−.14
P_6: Teachers' innovative merit							.03	.22
P_8: Teachers' motivational merit								.12
P_7: Teachers' innovative merit								

Note.—$N = 110$ class means. LC = lower class.

MC pupils perceived their own and teachers' effectiveness in the classroom in terms of conformity of conduct (P_4 and P_5), social-emotional warmth (P_1), understanding well what is taught (P_2 and P_3), and motivation to learn and perform (P_8).

In MC and LC results, the two innovative factors (P_6 and P_7) stand apart from each other and separate from what we termed the traditional cluster of instructional behavior. This may be because the factors were measures irrelevant to significant variance between classes, it may be that they measure aspects of teaching that differ from the traditional cluster and require further development. It may well be that items in the two innovative factors actually refer more to school policies and facilities than they do to teacher behavior. If so, it would explain the findings. Further thought and analysis of the present data must be given to the innovative factors.

Figure 2 shows that LC pupils' attitudes also tended to cluster around an instructional core, as the MC pupils' attitudes did. However, unlike MC results, the clustering of variables was much less positively interrelated and did not include the motivational factor. The proximity-relation of LC pupils' attitudes indicate less structural multiplexity than MC pupils' attitudes. Although LC pupils perceived the affective (P_1) and cognitive (P_2, items with positive statements) factors as highly related, they perceived more variance between their own conduct (P_4), teachers' disciplining merit (P_5), and teachers' cognitive merit (P_3, items with negative statements) than MC pupils did.

Thus, to answer the two questions posed earlier: (*a*) Interconnected patterns are evident in pupils' attitudes toward differing aspects of merit in a teacher's teaching; and (*b*) MC and LC pupils display sharp differences in attitude pattern and degree of multiplexity.

DISCUSSION AND CONCLUSIONS

The interconnected patterns found in this study greatly expand understanding of the significant analysis of variance results found previously with the same pupil data (Yee, 1968a). Such contrast between analysis of variance and structural results for MC and LC pupils' attitudes toward teachers may be attributed to the nature of schooling in this country and its emphasis on maintaining and reinforcing middle-class values and attitudes toward education. Traditional and socially satisfactory schooling, classroom behavior, and learning have long been recognized as middle-class attributes, but they may appear foreign and uncertain to children from disadvantaged neighborhoods. Since the most significant source of variance between teachers has been found to be pupils' social class background (Coleman, Campbell, Hobson, McPartland, Mood, Weinfeld, & York, 1966; Yee, 1968a), then such differences and those in pupils' attitude structure may also be attributed to teacher selection and retention rates that affect the teachers' behavior and characteristics (Gage, 1965).

One cannot safely conclude from these results that the differing attitude structures are due solely to the different characteristics of MC and LC pupils or that they are due to the fact that MC and LC pupils have different types of teachers. It seems safe to suggest that the differences are caused by both—that pupils' attitudes toward teachers are influenced by home and neighborhood as well as the teachers themselves.

By considering the solid, more multiplex structure of MC pupils' school attitudes a clue to such pupils' greater advantage in classroom achievement, then the loosely interconnected structure of LC pupils' attitudes may suggest approaches for remedial developments. The present results complement findings by Zigler and Kanzer (1962), who found significant interaction operating between the social class status of pupils and the type of reinforcer used. For LC pupils, praise reinforcers, such as "good" and "fine," were more reinforcing than correct reinforcers, such as "correct" and "right," while correct reinforcers were more effective than praise reinforcers for MC pupils. The researchers suggested such results indicated less growth in the developmental reinforcer hierarchy of LC children than MC children (e.g., Beller, 1955).

Preparatory programs for school routines and classroom learning need to be further developed and emphasized through the grades. Although many current efforts in this regard (such as Head Start) may be interpreted as ways to improve pupil-teacher communication by making the pupils more middle class, an alternative would be to build a "readiness program" that would help teachers become more understanding of and effective in teaching LC children (Riessman, 1967).

If we consider the results as reflections of the differences between teachers, research and development to improve teacher selection and preparation for interaction with LC pupils must be conducted to raise the quality as well as the favorability of teachers' attitudes. Significant differences found in teacher-pupil social interaction between levels of pupils' social class indicate that the characteristics and behavior of teachers are not similar for MC and LC classes (Yee, 1968b). The challenge of improving teacher effectiveness with LC pupils seems greater than typical teacher recruitment, selection, and preparation programs can realistically handle. Special training programs, such as the Teacher Corps, and changes in school policies for teacher placement, curriculum emphases, and extrinsic incentives seem essential to help provide more adequate teaching and guidance for LC pupils.

This study illustrates the feasibility and value of Guttman's (1954, 1966) facet design and analysis procedures. With conventional procedures, such as the analysis of variance, significant differences were found in pupils' attitudes; such information alone is highly limited in explaining and describing *why* such differences exist. Greater use of facet design and analysis when appropriate would help researchers overcome such limitations.

REFERENCES

BECK, W. H. Pupils' perceptions of teacher merit: A factor analysis of five hypothesized dimensions. Unpublished doctoral dissertation, Stanford University, 1964.

BELLER, E. Dependency and independence in young children. *Journal of Genetic Psychology*, 1955, 87, 25–35.

COLEMAN, J. S., CAMPBELL, E. Q., HOBSON, C. J., McPARTLAND, J., MOOD, A. M., WEINFELD, F. D., & YORK, R. L. *Equality of educational opportunity.* Washington, D.C.: National Center for Educational Statistics, United States Department of Health, Education, and Welfare, 1966. (Government Printing Office Documents No. FS5.238:38001).

FOA, U. G. New developments in facet design and analysis. *Psychological Review,* 1965, 72, 262–274.

GAGE, N. L. Psychological research on teacher education for the great cities. *Urban Education,* 1965, 1, 175–195.

GUTTMAN, L. A new approach to factor analysis: The radex. In P. F. LAZARSFELD (Ed.), *Mathematical thinking in the social sciences.* Glencoe, Ill.: Free Press, 1954.

GUTTMAN, L. Empirical verification of the Radex structure of mental abilities and personality traits. *Educational and Psychological Measurement,* 1957, 17, 391–407.

GUTTMAN, L. Order analysis of correlation matrics. In R. B. CATTEL (Ed.), *Handbook of multivariate experimental psychology.* Chicago: Rand McNally, 1966, pp. 438–458.

HORST, P. A generalized expression of the reliability of measures. *Psychometrika,* 1949, 14, 21–32.

KAISER, H. F. The Varimax criterion for analytic rotation in factor analysis. *Psychometrika,* 1958, 23, 187–200.

KRECH, D., CRUTCHFIELD, R. S., & BALLACHEY, E. L. *Individual in society.* New York: McGraw-Hill, 1962.

LINGOES, J. C. An IBM 7090 program for Guttman-Lingoes multidimensional scalogram analysis-I. *Behavioral Science,* 1965, 10, 183–184.

MORI, T. Structure of motivations for becoming a teacher. *Journal of Educational Psychology,* 1965, 56, 175–183.

MYERS, A. E., McCONVILLE, C. B., & COFFMAN, W. E. Simplex structure in the grading of essay test. *Educational and Psychological Measurement,* 1966, 26, 41–54.

RIESSMAN, F. Teachers of the poor: A five-point plan. *Journal of Teacher Education,* 1967, 18, 326–336.

ROBINSON, W. S. Ecological correlations and the behavior of individuals. *American Sociological Review,* 1950, 15, 351–357.

YEE, A. H. *Factors involved in determining the relationship between teachers' and pupils' attitudes.* (Cooperative Research Project No. 5–9346, United States Department of Health, Education and Welfare, Office of Education.) Austin: University of Texas, 1966.

YEE, A. H. Interpersonal attitudes of teachers and advantaged and disadvantaged pupils. *Journal of Human Resources,* 1968, 3, 327–345. (a)

YEE, A. H. The source and direction of causal influence in teacher-pupil relationships. *Journal of Educational Psychology,* 1968, 59, 275–282. (b).

ZIGLER, E., & KANZER, P. The effectiveness of two classes of verbal reinforcers on the performance of middle- and lower-class children. *Journal of Personality,* 1962, 30, 157–163.

3

Peer Groups

and Social Interaction

*The child participates in the life of many groups on
his way to maturity.*
Willard Waller

Peer groups are an unavoidable feature of modern educational settings. In the past, tutorial education for those who could afford it and simple (often one-room) schools for a predominantly agrarian society did not foster the peer groups we find so common throughout educational institutions today. Although the population of the United States has steadily increased, the number of school districts has declined because schools have greatly expanded their organizational structures and the scope of their operations. The populations of schools today make them fairly complex social systems. Thus, educational settings typically involve many peer groups—some arranged for instructional purposes and others that are informal and not necessarily directed to academic achievement.

The term *peer group* is generally meant to refer to students who are considered similar by chronological age or by some other factor or combination of factors, but it can also refer to groups of teachers, administrators, and other educational groups which bring together persons of similar positions, duties, and interests. By definition, therefore, peer groups can influence teaching-learning strategies in important ways and they can present a variety of personal and group conflict and need-satisfying possibilities. They can fulfill a variety of organizational and individual purposes, such as determining activities programs, comparing individual progress, and supplying reference groups.

Educational systems determine the characteristics of student peer groups in part by the organizational structures they form and put into practice. Such formal structures in schools as classes, teams, and units more or less define who may be members, determine how long, where, and how closely they work together, and dictate what activities they carry out. However, the peer groups developed and maintained informally by the members themselves may be as important or more influential than those arranged by the formal organizing structure. The "now generation" and "generation gap" concerns of recent times indicate that the influence and social impact of student peer groups are expanding.

Interestingly, educational settings have been deliberately organized to effect their greatest influence through "out of school" peer groups. Such traditions existed and continue to some extent today in England's public schools, such as Rugby, which Hughes (1857) described so admirably in *Tom Brown's School-Days*. He wrote:

> The object of all schools is not to ram Latin and Greek into boys, but to make them good English boys, good future citizens; and by far the most important part of that work must be done, or not done, out of school hours. To leave it, therefore, in the hands of inferior men, is just giving up the highest and hardest part of the work of education. Were I a private schoolmaster, I should say, let who will hear the boys their lessons, but let me live with them when they are at play and rest (p. 64).

As Arthur Wellesley, Duke of Wellington, reportedly put it so succinctly: "The battle of Waterloo was won in the playing fields of Eton."

Whether they are basically formal or informal arrangements, the significant nature of a peer group is determined by its members and their identity with it as a membership group. Members do so, first, through their perceptions of a peer group's purposes, its relevance to their own behavior and those of others, and its relationship to other groups. Second, what members do in a peer group, i.e., their activities and functions, influence the group's characteristics. Third, the individual and common motives, cost-rewards, goals of participating members, and so on must be assessed to understand any peer group. Thus, the nature of peer groups can be ascertained quite well in the study of the social interaction operating in them.

Newcomb's (1961) landmark study of two groups of 17 male students who lived together as housemates found that social attraction in groups was promoted by attitude similarity and influenced individuals' perceptions of other persons' preferences. However, what about social attraction in large groups such as typical college dormitories? Observing about 25,000 possible pairs of students residing in the same college dormitory for about four years, Priest and Sawyer tested the prediction, by way of Heider's balance theory, that students' proximity to each other and peership relate to interpersonal attraction. They found evidence to support the prediction, but it was found for more proximate persons that increasing time allowed friendships to compete with proximity and class peership. The strength of peership as a force for social attraction among students was found to be even greater than individual characteristics, such as interests, abilities, and attitudes (see footnote 44).

Priest and Sawyer's study, therefore, indicates that interpersonal attraction ("best friends") for students can be significantly affected by chance factors, that is, those persons one happens to find in physical proximity to him and in his college class. Such results are reminiscent of other studies that found accidental effects influencing propinquity and social attraction, for examples, Festinger, Schachter, and Back's (1950) study of a married students' housing project and Byrne's (1961) study of classroom seating arrangements in a college class.

To understand the relative importance of peer groups to students, let us contrast student and adult peer-group relationships. Simple reflection suggests that interpersonal attraction in adult social living differs from dormitory interaction. In comparison, college dormitory living is limited in the choice of associates, range of personality types, and activities. It is common in the adult life of modern American society to find almost anonymous attachments formed between most or some neighbors, a situation that indicates little positive attachment through proximity. It is not as simple to identify peership relations for adults as it is for young people. Typically, adults do associate in peer groups, such as service and country clubs, business, church, and social groups; but the restrictions of alternative choices and conformity do not seem to be as great as for students. Perhaps the major differences here between students and mature adults are the real needs and sources of primary-group relations, i.e., nurturance, intellectual-emotional acceptance and support, and informal interaction. For an adult, the family or living unit is his chief primary group and he may have a variety of other sources. For example, since the breadwinner's work occupies much of his attention and energy, he may form peer group attachments where he works.

Therefore, the needs of students for primary-group attachments usually differ considerably from those of adults; and such a contrast helps to clarify the factors influencing peer groups and social interaction within them. Students in college dormitories, somewhat like servicemen in barracks, perhaps away from home and familiar associations for the first time in their lives, have only each other to turn to for mutual support, guidance, and so on. Their abilities, interests, and backgrounds as well as their tentative status and position probably provide sufficient commonality and social-emotional need-dispositions to make their association as peers highly attractive and influential. However, once graduation passes and dormitory life ends, it is not surprising that college roommates and floormates, like military buddies, typically lose touch with each other and find little in common on meeting several years later. Yet their interaction over four or more years in dorms has had its effect upon their academic performance, values, attitudes, and so on. With increasing emphasis upon higher education, such peer-group relations of students require further study and understanding. We might wonder, for example, if results that Priest and Sawyer found for males would be the same for female students?

Utilizing interesting nonparametric procedures, the cleverly designed study by the Siegels of coeds' attitudes investigated the question: How do individuals behave when they perceive membership and reference groups as being similar or different? Their findings demonstrate that students' changes of attitude (authoritarianism) over time became consistent with their particular membership and reference group identification (with housing cooperatives, dormitories, or sororities). Implied in the Priest and Sawyer article, as well as in the one by Siegel and Siegel, is the suggestion that students seem to conform to the peer-group situations in which their housing arrangements place them.

It is uncertain how permanent such changes in attitude are; but given the potential influence of other reference group attachments, the relative instability of attitudes and values in American society, and the tendency of time and altered social conditions and roles to modify the views of capricious youth, we might expect more change than stability.

The third article in this chapter followed previous works that indicated sociometric preferences in pupil peer groups related to pupils' classroom behavior. Schmuck found two types of peer-group liking structure operating in classrooms—one termed *central* in which pupils selected a limited, small cluster of positive and negative nominations and another type of classroom termed *diffuse* in which pupils selected broadly among themselves and did not tend to form cliques. With an awareness of such differences in peer-group liking structure, Schmuck investigated their relationship to pupils' academic performance, accuracy in estimating actual status in peer-group affect, and involvement in the classroom setting. Such research helps to indicate the complex relations involved in peer-group behavior and the need to help teachers become aware of sociometric concerns and methods.

Studying the adolescent status systems in 10 American high schools, Coleman (1960) found that academic achievement was perceived to be of less concern than recognition as an athlete, good dresser, and being most popular among peers. Finding such adolescent norms contradictory to those of educators and the students' future roles as mature citizens, workers, and parents, Coleman argued that existing student peer groups should be guided or perhaps new ones formed to broaden students' norms to include and reinforce educational goals. The constant importance of ascertaining the patterns of adolescent peer-group behavior is emphasized further by Grinder's more detailed analyses. He also found strong evidence to support the hypothesis that students' relatively strong concern for the rewards of peer-group gratifications clash detrimentally with the students' academic performance. Professor Grinder graciously volunteered to revise his article for this book in order to include broader discussion of his study's background and implications.

In the chapter's fifth selection, Lott and Lott conducted a rather technical study to investigate the question: Is the degree of peer-group cohesiveness positively related to the drive level of individual members? In other words, does a class group's greater interpersonal relations help each member of the group achieve and produce more effectively? They found more than they had anticipated; one major finding was that peer-group cohesiveness was positively related to the verbal learning of high-IQ pupils, especially for girls, but not the low-IQ children. High-IQ girls in lower cohesive groups, therefore, are handicapped more than boys. The authors suggest that girls may have stronger affiliation needs and more intense social ties than boys, but the verbal learning tasks that Lott and Lott employed may be essentially 10- or 11-year-old girls' tasks. Further study, therefore, with learning tasks akin to boys' interests seems necessary (see Davis and Slobodian's article in Chapter 4). However, the present work should give pause to those who may have ignored the effect of interpersonal concerns in school achievement.

Thoresen and Krumboltz raised the question: Does the success level of peer social models affect their influence on students of differing abilities? Utilizing analysis of variance procedures, they found that adolescents in general tend to respond more readily to high-success athletic models instead of models similar to their self-concept. They also found that students' academic success was positively related to their information-seeking behavior and that the adult-counselor model and academic peer models were equally effective influences. However, the high-athletic success model was most effective in causing adolescent males to seek information concerning vocational planning. Thus, Thoresen and Krumboltz's work extended findings and conclusions, such as those of Coleman, by experimentally manipulating the variable of social model and finding effective means of utilizing peer-group modeling behavior.

Further utilization of peer-group relations in educational settings can be seen in Vriend's article which was awarded the American Personnel and Guidance Association's meritorious research award for 1970. Her successful demonstration program provided positive reinforcement to achieving disadvantaged students who were trained as model peer leaders and uplifted the educational and vocational orientations of the disadvantaged peer group. Certainly the effectiveness of such an educational program came about with direct utilization of social interaction theory and research approaches.

OTHER READINGS

BLAIN, M. J., & RAMIREZ, M. Increasing sociometric rank, meaningfulness, and discriminability of children's names through reinforcement and interaction. *Child Development,* 1968, *39*, 949–955.

BYRNE, D. The influence of propinquity and opportunities for interaction on classroom relationships, *Human Relations,* 1961, *14*, 63–69.

COLEMAN, J. S. The adolescent subculture and academic achievement. *American Journal of Sociology*, 1960, *64*, 337–349.

DUNCAN, O. D.; HALLER, A. O.; & PORTER, A. Peer influence on aspirations: A reinterpretation. *American Journal of Sociology*, 1968, *74*, 119–137.

FESTINGER, L.; SCHACTER, S.; & BACK, K. *Social pressures in informal groups: A study of human factors in housing.* New York: 1950.

GOLDBERG, M. H., & MACCOBY, E. E. Children's acquisition of skill in performing a group task under two conditions of group formation. *Journal of Personality and Social Psychology*, 1965, *2*, 898–902.

GRONLUND, N. *Sociometry in the classroom.* New York: Harper, 1959.

HUGHES, T. *Tom Brown's school-days.* London: Macmillan & Company Limited, 1857.

KELLEY, H. H. Two functions of reference groups. In H. PROSHANSKY & B. SEIDENBERG (Eds.), *Basic studies in social psychology.* New York: Holt, Rinehart & Winston, 1965. Pp. 210–214.

LIPPITT, R. & GOLD, M. Classroom social structure as a mental health problem. *Journal of Social Issues*, 1959, *15*, 40–49.

NEUGARTEN, B. L. Social class and friendship among school children. *American Journal of Sociology*, 1946, *51*, 305–313.

NEWCOMB, T. M. Varieties of interpersonal attraction. In D. CARTWRIGHT, & A. ZANDER (Eds.), *Group Dynamics.* (2nd ed.) Evanston, Ill.: Row, Peterson, 1960. Pp. 140–119.

SHELTON, J., & HILL, J. P. Effects of cheating achievement anxiety and knowledge of peer performance. *Developmental Psychology*, 1969, *1*, 449–455.

SHERIF, M., & SHERIF, C. W. *Reference groups: Exploration into conformity and deviation of adolescents.* New York: Harper and Row, 1964.

YAMAMOTO, K.; LAMBRIGHT, N. L.; & CORRIGAN, A. H. Intelligence, creative thinking, and sociometric choice among fifth-grade children. *Journal of Experimental Education*, 1966, *34*, (3), 83–89.

YARROW, M. R.; CAMPBELL, J. D.; & YARROW, L. J. Interpersonal dynamics in social integration. In E. E. MACCOBY, T. M. NEWCOMB, & E. L. HARTLEY (Eds.), *Readings in social psychology.* (3rd ed.) New York: Holt, Rinehart & Winston, 1958. Pp. 623–636.

PROXIMITY AND PEERSHIP:
BASES OF BALANCE IN
INTERPERSONAL ATTRACTION[1]

Robert F. Priest / Jack Sawyer

The theory of balance[2] in interpersonal relations is a deservedly popular model. By specifying relations between similarity of attitudes, similarity of status, and interpersonal sentiments, it offers a simple and general integration of interpersonal orientations.

Large-scale empirical verification of balance, however, has proved difficult. This is largely because balance is a phenomenon that attaches to a pair of persons, making this the unit of analysis. Pair analysis, though, is usually laborious and is infre-

quently employed in small-group research, despite its centrality in small-group theory.[3] The difficulty stems first from the problem of obtaining data on relations between all pairs in even a moderately sized group. The main problem, however, is the handling of such data once obtained. A small sample of persons means a large number of pairs, and it is thus not surprising that the major empirical basis for balance theory consists of just two groups of seventeen men each.[4]

Effective use of computers, though, permits analysis of much larger groups; the present study treats some 25,000 distinct pairs of persons. In doing so, this

From: American Journal of Sociology, 1967, 72, 633–49. Copyright © 1967 by the University of Chicago Press, and reproduced by permission of the author and publisher.

[1] This research was supported initially by the Social Science Research Committee of the University of Chicago, but predominantly by National Science Foundation grant G-19321.

[2] Fritz Heider, The Psychology of Interpersonal Relations (New York: John Wiley & Sons, 1958); Theodore M. Newcomb, "Individual Systems of Orientation," in Sigmund Koch (ed.), Psychology: Study of a Science. Vol. 3: Formulations of the Person and the Social Context (New York: McGraw-Hill Book Co., 1959), pp. 384–422; and Theodore M. Newcomb, The Acquaintance Process (New York: Holt, Rinehart & Winston, 1961), pp. 4–23.

[3] Current small-group theory strongly emphasizes the pair of persons as a basic unit. But of 166 variables employed in 83 demonstrated hypotheses from 6 major conceptual orientations (Bales, Cartwright and Zander, Homans, Moreno, Newcomb, and Thibaut and Kelley), only 25 variables required observation of exactly 2 persons, while 66 could be obtained from single individuals, and 75 required observing 3 or more persons or the entire group (see John DeLamater, Charles G. McClintock, and Gordon Becker, "Conceptual Orientations of Contemporary Small Group Theory," Psychological Bulletin, LXIV [December, 1965], 404).

[4] Newcomb, The Acquaintance Process.

research not only provides an unusually extensive test of balance but also illustrates the methodology that makes analysis on this scale feasible.

THEORIES OF BALANCE IN INTERPERSONAL RELATIONS

Both Heider's "theory of balance" and Newcomb's "system of interpersonal orientation" consider the sentiments two persons have for each other, their sentiments for third persons or objects, and other relations (such as proximity or similarity) that exist between the two persons.[5] Balance exists when these sentiments and relations are consistent. It is balanced for a pilot and co-pilot (proximate and similar) to like one another; it is imbalanced for a policeman and a thief to do so.

In general, the "balanced state designates a situation in which the perceived units and the experienced sentiments coexist without stress; there is thus no pressure toward change, either in the cognitive organization or in the sentiment."[6] A "perceived unit" consists of two entities that are seen to go together; two persons who are proximate form a unit (U); two who are distant do not (not U). Sentiments consist of liking (L) and disliking (DL). Then, more specifically, "A dyad is balanced if the relations between the two entities are all positive (L and U) or all negative (DL and not U). Disharmony results when relations of different sign character exist."[7]

The present research assesses balance on two characteristics that are basic in causing two persons to be seen as a unit: similarity of physical location (termed "proximity")[8] and similarity of college class (termed "peership"). Each pair of persons is characterized by a degree of proximity and peership; it is considered balanced to like a person who is proximate and to like a person who is a peer.[9]

Balance is also assessed, even more directly, by the reciprocation between person A's liking for person B, and B's liking for A. Thus, altogether, this research assesses balance in three ways: It compares A's liking for B with (1) B's liking for A,

5 The theory of cognitive dissonance characterizes both social and non-social perceptions, and so it too may be applied to interpersonal orientations (see Leon Festinger, *A Theory of Cognitive Dissonance* [Evanston, Ill.: Row, Peterson & Co., 1957]).

6 Heider, *op. cit.*, p. 176.

7 *Ibid.*, p. 202.

8 This concept is frequently called "propinquity" (e.g., in the reviews by John W. Thibaut and Harold H. Kelley, *The Social Psychology of Groups* [New York: John Wiley & Sons, 1959], pp. 39–42; and by Theodore M. Newcomb, Ralph H. Turner, and Philip E. Converse, *Social Psychology: The Study of Human Interaction* [New York: Holt, Rinehart & Winston, 1965], pp. 310–16), and in general "*Proximity, propinquity* are often used interchangeably because both denote nearness. Proximity, however, in good current use, commonly implies nearness in space.... [*Propinquity*] is more often used where *proximity* is not possible to imply nearness in relationship, closeness in association, in age, in tastes, or the like, or even closeness in time" (*Webster's Dictionary of Synonyms* [Springfield, Mass.: G & C. Merriam Co., 1951], p. 663). Because the present analysis sharply discriminates effects associated with similarity in physical location per se from effects of other similarities, it employs the term "proximity" throughout. Use of the term "peership," for similarity of status, is exactly parallel.

9 The primary basis for Heider's theory is cognitive; the tendency toward balance exists for an individual, in terms of *his* sentiments and the unit relations *as he perceives them*. It seems highly likely, however, that a person's perception of proximity and similarity of college class corresponds closely to reality. If so, then in the present research, where proximity and peership are *actual*, rather than perceived, Heider's theory should still hold. For Newcomb's theory, no extension is needed; he specifically treats not only "individual systems of orientation," which employ perceived relations, but also "collective systems of orientation," which employ actual relations (Newcomb, *The Acquaintance Process*, pp. 11–15).

(2) their similarity of location, and (3) their similarity of status. Each comparison is made both for a given time, and for change over time. This tests balance theory not only in its static aspect, which prescribes balance at a given time, but also in its dynamic aspect, which predicts that "if a balanced state does not exist, then forces toward this state will arise."[10] Testing the dynamic aspect is particularly valuable, since it evaluates the extent to which balance theory is able to predict changes in the behavior of individual pairs of persons over time.

Thus this research examines both static and dynamic balance of two basic characteristics—proximity and peership—that appear to condition much social interaction. It identifies their association with attraction, both singly and jointly, as they change over time in a newly established micro-society.[11]

PIERCE TOWER AND ITS RESIDENTS

In Autumn 1960, the newly constructed Stanley R. Pierce Hall opened to about 320 male students, nearly all of them freshmen and very few previously acquainted —thus creating an opportunity to study *de novo* the development and change of interpersonal attraction. Further, not only

the newness of the building and its occupants, but the physical design itself facilitated such a study. Indeed, the architecture virtually invited study, for unlike places like "Craftown," where Merton reported effects of proximity, little suspected by architects,[12] Pierce Tower was especially designed to provide social structure. As the *Architectural Record* notes in describing Pierce Tower, "The concept is that of 'house' groupings of approximately 80 men under a proctor, with each 'house' given identity. This was done by stacking four two-story 'houses' around their interior two-story lounges, with elevator access to lower floors only. . . . The rooms thus ring the central facilities which act as a core furthering the idea of identity."[13]

Thus, the residential part of the dormitory consists of a tower of eight floors, atop a larger two-story base containing a dining hall, lounge, and other common areas. Around the perimeter of the rectangular tower, as Figure 1 shows, are the rooms (mainly double) that house the forty occupants of each floor. The four corridors on which the rooms open describe a smaller rectangle, inside of which are various common rooms. The largest of these is the two-story lounge, which may be directly entered from either the lower or upper corridor, and is thus both central and proximate to all the rooms on both floors. The four lounges, as the architect intended, serve as foci of the four physically identical houses into which Pierce

10 Heider, *op. cit.*, p. 201.

11 This research thus takes as its starting point Berelson and Steiner's summary finding on face-to-face relations in small groups: "The more people associate with one another under conditions of equality, the more they come to share values and norms and the more they come to like one another" (Bernard Berelson and Gary A. Steiner, *Human Behavior: An Inventory of Scientific Findings* [New York: Harcourt, Brace & World, 1964], p. 327). The present research extends and amplifies this finding in both time and extent, by considering social organizations much larger than small groups and by following them over four years; thus to examine the changing role of proximity and peership over time further suggests the *process* by which these influences work.

12 Robert K. Merton, "The Social Psychology of Housing," in Wayne Dennis *et al.*, *Current Trends in Social Psychology* (Pittsburgh: University of Pittsburgh, 1948), pp. 163–217.

13 "Men's Dormitory, University of Chicago," *Architectural Record*, CXXVII (November, 1960), 138. Pierce Tower is further described and pictured in "Major Break-through on the Anti-Slab Front," *Architectural Record*, CXXVI (September, 1959), 171–75; and in Harold C. Riker, *College Students Live Here* (New York: Educational Facilities Laboratory, 1961), pp. 116–20.

Tower is organized. In this way, the physical and social structures reinforce one another. As this research shows, in exploring more generally the interaction of social and physical structure, the house is a highly prominent feature in the determination of friendship.

As a social entity, each of the four houses elects officers, plays athletics, gives parties, and conducts other group activities. The house members, however, like University of Chicago students generally, are unusually diverse, both in background and interest; their diversity makes the integration achieved by the houses the more remarkable.[14]

To explore the effects of social and physical structure, background and sociometric questionnaires were distributed to all residents, starting in Autumn 1960 and continuing each autumn and spring for the first four years of the Tower's existence.[15] Since only a few persons move out of the Tower during the year, the set of persons living in the Tower in the spring is nearly

the same as in the preceding autumn. Not everyone, however, responded both times, so the respondents are not completely comparable. Because of this, the present analysis employs only those who responded *both* autumn and spring of a given year; thus changes from autumn to spring are uncontaminated by sample differences. The persons responding both times number 143, 145, 134, and 135 for the four years, a total of 557, representing 471 different individuals, since some appeared in more than one year.[16] The number of persons in each year represents, on the average, 48 per cent of those still living in the dormitory in the spring.

I. MEASUREMENT OF INTERPERSONAL ATTRACTION

Each respondent first named his best friend, and his four next best friends, among all persons living in Pierce Tower (excluding the resident head and two assistants for each house). Then he checked, for each name on an alphabetical list of all 320 residents, whether he *recognized* the name (could immediately connect a face with the name), whether he *talked* to the man at least once a week on the average (carried on a conversion involving more than simply the exchange of greetings), and whether he *liked* him. These responses thus located the attraction of each person toward each other at one of six levels:

[14] An NORC report illustrates this diversity: Although 42 per cent of the fathers of the Class of 1961 were professionals (as high as that for a comparison group of seven "high-quality private" schools), another 20 per cent were blue-collar employees—twice as high as for the comparison schools. In religious preference, too, Chicago is more diverse: In most schools, Protestant preference predominates (60 per cent at time of college entry, in a national sample), and those with Jewish (8 per cent) and no preference (3 per cent) are rare; the University of Chicago, however, has a minority of Protestants (39 per cent), almost as many Jews (30 per cent), and a substantial proportion (13 per cent) with no preference (see Richard McKinley, Peter H. Rossi, and James A. Davis, "Students at the Midway" [University of Chicago, National Opinion Research Center, Report No. 86], June, 1962).

[15] Questionnaires were distributed, on the average, four weeks after the beginning of the autumn terms and four weeks before the end of the spring terms; thus the intervening period was about twenty-nine weeks.

[16] The number of persons appearing in more than one year is small because of the combined effect of an average response rate of 63 per cent and an average turnover of 71 per cent from one year to the next. According to information from the registrar, however, non-respondents differed no more than 10 per cent from respondents in the proportion who were Protestant, born in the Midwest, looking for a student job, majoring in physical science, or planning graduate study; the proportion of non-freshmen was about 15 per cent higher among non-respondents.

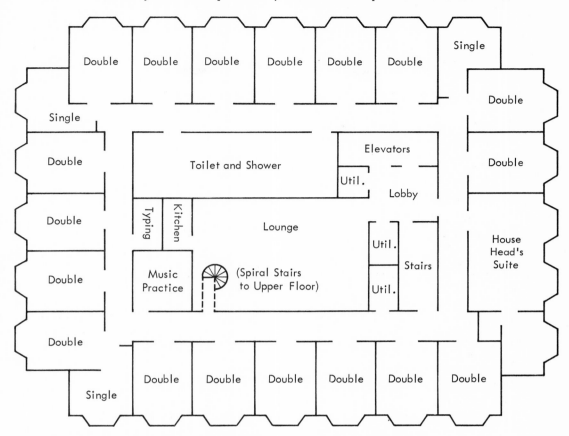

Figure 1. Lower floor of a house in Pierce Tower—the same for all four houses. (On the upper floor—otherwise largely identical to the lower—three student rooms replace the house head's suite.)

(0) non-recognition, (1) recognize, (2) talk, (3) like, (4) friend, and (5) best friend.[17]

STABILITY OF CHOICE

Of all those choices (between persons in the same house) in which one individual at least recognized another (levels 1

[17] Non-recognition is assumed when no other category is checked. Conceivably, this

might result from respondent fatigue at the end of a long list, but the correlation (for spring of year 3) between serial position on the list and number of recognitions received was only −.04. In years 3 and 4, levels 1, 2, and 3 of the attraction scale were dislike, neutral, like rather than recognize, talk, like; and the latter terms, where used in Tables 1, 6, 7, and Fig. 1, should be taken to imply also, for the last two years, the former set. The ordering is clearly the same for both sets, and separate tabulations for each year show the results obtained to be general over the two versions of the scale.

TABLE 1

RECIPROCATION: NUMBER OF PAIRS WITH EACH
COMBINATION OF ATTRACTION LEVELS*

Person A's Attraction toward B†	Person B's Attraction toward A				
	Recognize	*Talk*	*Like*	*Friend*	*Best Friend*
1. Recognize	1,425	1,564	625	37	0
2. Talk		1,897	2,756	182	13
3. Like			2,264	689	67
4. Friend				412	164
5. Best friend					139
Number of choices at this level	5,103	8,309	8,692	1,896	522

* These data comprise the 12,261 pairs, from all eight administrations, in which both persons at least recognize the other.
† These five levels of response are mutually exclusive; "recognize," for example, implies *mere* recognition and no more.

through 5) both autumn and spring, 48 per cent are at exactly the same level of attraction both times, and a total of 89 per cent are not more than one level disparate. Whereas little change or great change in reported attraction would produce suspicion of the measure, change of this order appears compatible with the relative fluidity of college life.

RECIPROCATION OF CHOICE

Reciprocation of choice provides a basic instance of balance. As Heider notes (here explicitly considering the sentiments of *two* persons rather than just the perception of a single individual): "a balanced state exists if both (p L o) [Person likes Other] and (o L p) [Other likes Person] are true."[18] Reciprocation of choice also provides another check on the measurement

18 Heider, *op. cit.,* p. 205.
19 Reciprocation can also be examined separately by level. For example, among the 522 choices of best friend, 278 (twice 139) are exactly

of attraction. Perfect reciprocation is of course not expected—if only because individuals may have different standards of what "like'" means, or because two persons may each call a third his best friend, while the latter can name only one of them. Still, reciprocation should be substantial, and Table 1 shows this to be so.

In 50 per cent of the 12,261 pairs where each person recognizes the other, their choices for one another are at exactly the same level. For 92 per cent of the pairs, the two choices are not more than one category disparate, and in less than 0.5 per cent are the choices more than two categories apart.[19] These non-reciprocated choices may involve different principles, and so further analysis disregards

reciprocated and 244 are not. By this rough standard, reciprocation is approximately equal at the various levels—around half the total choices at each level. Table 1 was also computed separately for each of the eight administrations. Patterns were highly similar, though in each of the four years there was somewhat higher reciprocation of choice in the spring.

the 8 per cent of the pairs that are not within one category of perfect balance. For the pairs where balance is perfect or nearly so, the following analysis determines how well attraction is predicted by proximity and peership.

II. BALANCE AND PREDICTION OF INTERPERSONAL ATTRACTION

To evaluate balance requires predicting the *relation* between two persons. Instead of the usual sociometric question, "Who is more attractive in general?" one must ask "Who is more attractive *to whom?*" Thus in all the following analyses, the dependent variable is some aspect of the attraction between two persons, and the number of observations is not the number of individuals but, rather, the number of pairs of persons. Further, this study examines the *complete matrix* of pair relations and so permits tests of balance that, even for large groups like these, consider the entire structure of interpersonal relations.[20]

In analyzing these pair relations, the strategy of prediction is to examine first the largest and framing effect—that of proximity. Then, within given levels of proximity, the effect of peership is demon-

[20] This was made feasible by a computer program constructed to produce pair matrices from individual responses (see Robert F. Priest, "Pair Similarities: An IBM 709–7090 Program for Scoring and Analyzing Similarities Between Pairs of Individuals," *Behavioral Science,* IX [July, 1964], 291). This program operates both upon data, like the attraction of one person for another, that are intrinsically *pair* characteristics, and upon data, like class in school, that are intrinsically *individual* characteristics. For individual characteristics, the program will combine values for two persons, through similarity or some other function, to *create* a pair characteristic, and then, as with intrinsically pair characteristics, sort these into matrix form.

strated. Finally, through use of multiple regression, their combined effect is ascertained.

PROXIMITY AND PAIR ATTRACTION

Based upon their location, each pair of persons in Pierce Tower was classified into one of the following categories, in order of decreasing proximity: (1) roommates—two persons occupying the same room, (2) floormates—non-roommates living on the same floor, (3) housemates—two persons on different floors of the same house, and (4) towermates—two persons in different houses.[21]

For each of these four groups, two summary measures of attraction were computed from the six levels previously described. The *recognition* composite sums the choices at the level of recognize *or higher* and divides this by the total possible number of choices. The *liking* composite sums choices at the level of like, friend, and best friend and divides this by the total number of recognitions. Thus, in terms of the levels 0 (non-recognition) through 5 (best friend), recognition equals $(1+2+3+4+5) / (0+1+2+3+4+5)$, and liking equals $(3+4+5)/(1+2+3+4+5)$. Conceptually, recognition defines the field within which attraction may occur, while liking identifies the relative intensity of the attraction that does occur. Empirically, too, the concepts are distinct: the total number of recognitions individuals receive correlates an average of only .20 with the proportion of these recognitions that are at the level of like or higher.

As Table 2 shows, the relation with

[21] Previously, it was found that two persons in different houses were no more likely to know or like one another when only one floor distant than when seven floors distant.

Table 2

Proximity: Recognition and Liking between
Roommates, Floormates, Housemates, and Towermates*

	Room-mates	Floormates	Housemates	Tower-mates†
Recognition (percentage of total possible):				
Autumn‡	96§	51	35	8
Spring‡	98§	85	77	20
Liking (percentage of total recognized):				
Autumn‡	92	52	42	25
Spring‡	93	45	37	16
Total number of possible choices (all eight administrations)	534	18,308	19,092	87,952†

  * Recognition as a percentage of total possible equals the total number of choices at the level of recognize or higher for all four autumn (or spring) administrations, divided by the total possible number of choices (based upon the number of respondents) for those same four administrations. Choices at the level of like or above are similarly summed over four administrations, then divided by the total number of recognitions for those four.

  † Percentages for towermates reflect only six administrations, since in year 4 respondents were asked only for in-house choices.

  ‡ Autumn and spring percentages compare choices among precisely the same set of persons at the two times: 143 in year 1, 145 in year 2, 134 in year 3, 135 in year 4. These 471 different individuals provide the basis for all the following tables.

  § Departure from 100 per cent indicates the magnitude of respondents' oversight in checking through the list of 320 names.

proximity is substantial and consistent, for both liking and recognition, in both autumn and spring. Not only are persons more distant less likely to be recognized, but even when they are, liking is less probable. Recognition, of course, increases sharply from autumn to spring, but much more within one's own house than outside.[22]

The absolute frequency of liking also increases, but less so than recognition; thus the proportion of those recognized who are also liked decreases. This suggests, if not an absolute limit to the number of persons one may like, at least a declining probability with increasing rec-

[22] The relations in Tables 2, 3, and 4 were computed separately for each of the eight administrations. For relations in each of the three tables, the general pattern was similar for all eight administrations, though as Tables 2 and 3 show, the level of relation differed systematically from autumn to spring. Table 5 provides a summary of the comparisons within and between years.

ognitions. Further, the previously demonstrated stability of choice implies that a person who was liked in the autumn is more probably liked in the spring than one who was not. Thus, it is the same interpersonal relations originally favored by proximity that continue to be favored. This is one of the ways in which relations originally associated with proximity are further promoted by other means.

The same relations hold when proximity is examined at a finer level—by the number of rooms separating a pair of persons who live on the same floor.[23] In Table

[23] Since rooms are numbered from 1 to 26 around the corridor, one person may be as many as thirteen rooms distant from another. Some of these are not student rooms but rooms for typing, music practice, laundry, etc.; student rooms total twenty on the lower floor of each house, twenty-three on the upper floor. Thus in comparison with the actual number of intervening students, or student rooms, the present measure of total rooms contains some random error, but no bias.

TABLE 3

PROXIMITY: RECOGNITION AND LIKING BETWEEN
FLOORMATES, BY NUMBER OF ROOMS DISTANT*

	Number of Rooms Distant			
	0†	1	2–7	8–13
Recognition (percentage of total possible):				
Autumn	96	66	52	46
Spring	98	90	85	83
Liking (percentage of total recognized):				
Autumn	92	65	53	47
Spring	94	53	48	42
Number of possible floormate choices (all eight administrations)	534	1,610	8,516	8,182

* Recognition and liking are computed as in Table.
† These 534 pairs are roommates, not floormates.

3, recognition (again computed as a percentage of the total possible) consistently decreases from roommates (zero rooms distant) to next-door neighbors to those farther distant.[24] Even in the spring, after more than half a year of living on the same floor, using the same elevator, bathroom, lounge, etc., those whose rooms are on the opposite side of the building are less frequently recognized.

Distance also continues, at this finer level of analysis, to be important for liking, and in the same way. In Table 3, as in Table 2, greater recognition in the spring is accompanied by a lower proportion of liking, suggesting that even when persons on the other side of the building come to be known, they are still less liked. Even among next-door neighbors, liking decreases as acquaintance increases. Thus, in general, the analysis of proximity at this finer level reinforces its initial and continuing importance in both recognition and liking.

This was not necessarily to be expected, even though the number of city blocks separating couples has been shown to be related to their probability of marriage,[25] and the distance between houses or even apartments to friendship choice.[26] These dormitory room doors, however, are only eight feet apart, and there are twenty such doors with a thirty-second's walk—

[24] For a very small minority of the pairs in Table 3—those involving upperclassmen who are roommates—distance should be considered the dependent rather than the independent variable. Non-freshmen who do not take a single room do typically select their roommates and, within restrictions, their rooms. The effect of such choices, however, is almost solely upon the roommate pairs and very little upon the relations between those who are simply on the same floor. Further, even among roommates, non-freshmen constitute a minority.

[25] First reported by James H. S. Bossard, in "Residential Propinquity as a Factor in Marriage Selection," *American Journal of Sociology,* XXXVIII (1932), 219–24, this phenomenon has been confirmed by several subsequent studies, referred to in Alvin M. Katz and Reuben Hill, "Residential Propinquity and Marital Selection: A Review of Theory, Method, and Fact," *Marriage and Family Living,* XX (February, 1958), 27–35.

[26] Leon Festinger, Stanley Schachter, and Kurt W. Back, *Social Pressures in Informal Groups* (New York: Harper & Bros., 1950).

all indoors, with no intervening stairways or doors. That proximity continues to predict attraction when distances are so small indicates that more than physical space is involved; later we suggest how developing friendship with a person whose room is farther may cost more than the added seconds.

PEERSHIP AND
PAIR ATTRACTION

Another important characteristic of the relation between a pair of persons is their relative tenure in the system in which they

Table 4 examines liking within each of these three groups, controlling for the effect of proximity by employing only floormates. Liking is distinctly less for mixed pairs than for the two types of homogeneous pairs, which differ little from one another. Thus peership, like proximity, tends toward balance with attraction.

PROXIMITY, PEERSHIP,
AND ATTRACTION

Because even within single floors, both proximity and peership related to attraction, it seems desirable not only to com-

TABLE 4

PEERSHIP: PERCENTAGE OF FLOORMATES LIKING EACH OTHER AMONG FRESHMEN PAIRS, NON-FRESHMEN PAIRS, AND MIXED PAIRS

	Freshman Pairs	Non-Freshmen Pairs	Mixed Pairs
Liking (percentage of total possible)*	31	33	14
Total number of floormate pairs (all four years)	3,757	621	2,368

* Each percentage is computed as follows: Count the number of pairs, at each administration separately, in which both persons at least like the other; add the eight numbers. Divide this by twice the sum (since each pair appears both autumn and spring) of the number of floormate pairs in all four years. By counting only pairs in which *both* persons like each other, and by dividing by the *total* number of floormate pairs, regardless of recognition, this measure differs from that of Tables 2 and 3. The differences cause the percentages to be lower, but do not greatly affect comparison among groups.

interact. In college, where tenure correlates highly with age, these combined to create rather strong status differences—so that similarity of college class best defines whether two students are or are not peers.

In Pierce Tower, the most important distinction in status is whether one is a first-year or older student. Because of this, and because the majority of all residents of Pierce Tower over the four years have been freshmen, that distinction is taken to define peership: any two freshmen are considered peers, as are any two non-freshmen; pairs consisting of one freshman and one non-freshman are mixed.

pare their contributions, but to determine their joint ability to predict attraction. Yet from Tables 3 and 4 it is by no means obvious whether proximity or peership is a better predictor of attraction among floormates. To examine their combined effect by constructing a larger cross-classification table, however, would encounter the usual problems of declining case bases and lack of a single statistic that states the magnitude of the combined relation.[27]

[27] One statistic summarizing the extent to which similarity predicts choice is the homophily coefficient (James S. Coleman, "Relational Analysis: The Study of Social Organizations with

A promising approach—feasible whenever categories may be ordered—is to employ each variable quantitatively rather than categorically. Such quantitative scaling permits computing correlations and multiple correlations, thus providing single summary statistics for the independent and joint prediction of attraction by proximity and peership.

For each of these variables, quantitative scaling is readily accomplished. For proximity, rooms distant is already a quantitative measure.[28] For peership, homogeneous pairs are scored as 0, mixed pairs as 1. For attraction, finer discriminations may be made. Levels of attraction are scored from 1 for recognize through 5 for best friend, with non-recognition scored 0.[29] Thus the levels best friend, friend, and

like—previously all combined into *liking* —are now distinguished. The attraction of a pair is taken as the sum of the two persons' scores, and ranges from 0 to 10— with 5, for example, indicating that one person reports talking with the other, who reports liking him in return.[30]

Thus each pair of floormates had values on three quantitative pair variables: proximity, peership, and attraction. These three variables, correlated separately for each administration, produce the results in Table 5. Each of these correlations summarizes a set of percentages, like the three presented in Table 4 or the four in each row of Table 3. As a result, comparison of proximity and peership is greatly facilitated. Further, the proximity correlations use more of the information in the data—since, unlike Table 3, they employ the exact number of rooms distant.

From the correlations of Table 5, it is apparent that among floormates peership is a better predictor of attraction than is proximity. Thus, while at greater distances the effect of proximity is paramount, when distances are small enough, its effect falls below that of a more strictly social characteristic. Among floormates, in fact, the prediction of peership is so much superior that adding proximity (even though this is essentially independent of peership) raises the correlation with at-

---

Survey Methods," *Human Organization,* XVII [1958], 28–36). This coefficient, easily computed from Table 4, permits a direct interpretation: the amount of in-class choice is 43 per cent of the way from a chance level to the maximum possible. Homophily could also be computed for the data of Table 3, though calculation for quantitative variables is more complicated, and in a 13 × 13 matrix of rooms distant, some cells would have small frequencies. Moreover, the homophily coefficient is intended for use on one predictor at a time, and in its usual form does not readily summarize the combined relations of two predictors.

[28] Number of rooms distant, because its relation to attraction is curvilinear, was transformed logarithmically, producing a more nearly linear regression. Its correlations with attraction were virtually unchanged, however, and those reported in Table 5 are for the untransformed number of rooms distant.

[29] To score levels of attraction from 0 to 5 is not meant to assert that the true positions of these levels on an underlying continuum are precisely equidistant. Rather, this procedure simply aims to extract greater information from the data than dichotomous distinctions permit. The "true" distribution on the continuum of attraction remains, of course, unknown, but seems unlikely to produce markedly different results. With a similar scale of attraction, a monotonic transformation that produced unequal intervals nonetheless did not substantially alter

correlations with other characteristics (see Jacqueline C. Massé, "Interpersonal Attraction and Similarity of Nationality, Tenure, and Location" [Ph.D. dissertation, University of Chicago, March 1965], p. 38).

[30] Original sociomatrices are, of course, in general asymmetric: the attraction of A for B need not equal the attraction of B for A. Each pair, then, needs two choices to characterize it, and the matrix contains $n(n-1)$ choices. All analyses except those in Tables 4 and 5 employ these $n(n-1)$ choices. These two tables, however, both employ the $n(n-1)/2$ pairs, where each pair is represented by a single value which is a combination of two separate choices.

TABLE 5

PROXIMITY AND PEERSHIP: CORRELATION AND
MULTIPLE CORRELATION WITH ATTRACTION,
FOR FLOORMATES

Administration	Number of Pairs*	Proximity†	Peership	Multiple Correlation
Autumn, year 1	934	.30	‡	‡
Spring, year 1	922	.18	‡	‡
Autumn, year 2	1,057	.17	.41	.44
Spring, year 2	979	.04	.35	.36
Autumn, year 3	746	.11	.33	.35
Spring, year 3	685	.09	.27	.29
Autumn, year 4	760	.17	.31	.35
Spring, year 4	726	.01	.14	.14

* The pairs in this table are largely the same as those in Table 4. The slight decrease here in number of pairs from autumn to spring reflects the exclusion in spring of pairs in which one person had moved to another floor.
† Signs have been changed so that a positive correlation means that friends are similar.
‡ The small number of non-freshmen in year 1 resulted in too few mixed pairs to provide a stable estimate of the correlation.

traction little if any over that of peership alone.

Further, since now a single number summarizes the relation to attraction, it is also easy to compare different administrations. Doing this reveals that among floormates, for both proximity and peership, the relation is always lower in the spring than in the preceding autumn, and it is generally also lower one year than at the same time the preceding year.[31]

The decline from autumn to spring found among floormates, in the relation between proximity and attraction, does not occur, however, when all pairs are considered together. When proximity is scored 0 for towermates, 1 for housemates, 2 for floormates, and 3 for roommates, the correlations *increase* from autumn to spring. Thus, between houses there exists a trend toward differentiation, but within houses, a trend toward integration, over distance and college class, both within an academic

[31] This same pattern is displayed by homophily coefficients for peership: .59, .51; .59, .44; .48, .13.

year and over the years the dormitory has been in existence.

III. BALANCE AND CHANGES IN INTERPERSONAL ATTRACTION

The previous analyses have shown several changes from autumn to spring. Among the entire set of residents, the relation of attraction to proximity increases, though for those already as proximate as floormates, its relation to both proximity and peership decreases. At the same time, attraction also becomes generally stronger: the average student recognizes about twice as many persons and likes a higher number (though a smaller proportion) of them. In addition, as attraction increases it also becomes more effective and realistic—in that more students choose those who choose them in return.

But these group changes—though important in themselves—do not say which kinds of interpersonal relations are likely to change more and which less. Balance theory, however, *does* prescribe exactly which individual pairs should change—those initially imbalanced. Indeed, the state of imbalance (for Heider), strain (for Newcomb), or dissonance (for Festinger) is the central motivating mechanism of consistency theories generally. Thus, analysis of change in individual pairs provides a critical test of the dynamic process of balance—a test much more stringent than analysis of static balance. Stability of attraction, it may be deduced, should be greater for those pairs initially in balance. The following sections show this critical test to hold for both proximity and peership.

PROXIMITY AND STABILITY OF ATTRACTION

Of all choices at the level of recognize or higher, among persons living in the same house, 48 per cent of those made in the autumn, as noted earlier, remain the same in the spring. But this percentage varies considerably by level of choice, by the proximity of the two persons, and most importantly, as shall be seen, by their combination. To examine the relation of stability and proximity, each autumn choice was classified by the level of attraction and by the proximity of the two persons; then within each of these classi-

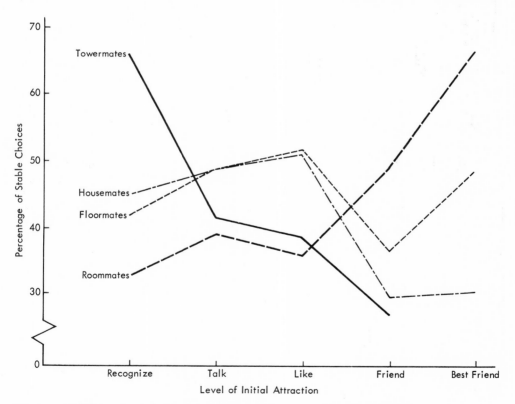

Figure 2. Stability of attraction as function of initial attraction and proximity. (Based upon 3,365 choices for towermates, 3,585 for floormates, 3,341 for housemates, and 260 for roommates.)

fications, the number of persons choosing at the same level in the spring was computed.

The results, in Figure 2, show a strong interaction between level of choice and proximity. For roommates, the higher the autumn attraction, the higher its stability from autumn to spring; for towermates, the higher the autumn attraction, the lower its stability; for floormates and housemates the relations are intermediate. Thus, higher levels of attraction are more stable only when they occur between proximate persons; at greater distances, lower levels of attraction are more stable than higher.

This is somewhat surprising, for one might reason that friendship over a greater distance must have had—in order to have been established in the first place—some special compensation making it in other ways a closer, and more enduring, friendship than more proximate ones.

The apparent anomaly disappears, however, when balance is considered. For proximate pairs, balance is implied by friendship; for distant pairs, by lack of friendship. Imbalance consists of distant friends or proximate strangers and mere acquaintances. In all cases, balanced relations are more stable. This illustrates again the importance of proximity—not only in the formation of friendships initially, but in their continued maintenance.

PEERSHIP AND STABILITY OF ATTRACTION

Attraction is also more stable when it is in balance with peership. In Table 6, where proximity is partially controlled by using only pairs of persons who live on the same floor, a similar interaction is found. For classmates, the higher the autumn attraction, the higher its stability from autumn to spring; for non-classmates, the higher the autumn attraction, the lower its stability.

TABLE 6

STABILITY OF ATTRACTION AS A FUNCTION OF PEERSHIP: PERCENTAGE OF STABLE CHOICES AT EACH LEVEL OF ATTRACTION, FOR CLASSMATES AND NON-CLASSMATES*

Level of Attraction	Class-mates	Non-Class-mates
1. Recognize	40	48
2. Talk	48	52
3. Like	54	46
4. Friend	38	32
5. Best friend	53	28
Number of choices	3,585	1,039

* For each percentage, the denominator is the number of choices at that level in the autumn (over all four years); the numerator is the number of those choices that were the same in the following spring. Data include choices among roommates and floormates.

The distinction is most apparent in the difference in stability at each level: when classmates initially just recognize one another, this choice is 8 per cent less stable than when non-classmates just recognize each other. At higher levels of attraction, stability of choice becomes higher for classmates: the differences increase from -8 to -4, $+8$, $+6$, and finally $+25$ for best friend choices. As with proximity, these changes are consistent with the theory of interpersonal balance. For classmates, balance is implied by friendship; for non-classmates, by lack of friendship. For both groups, the more balanced relations are more stable.

CHANGE IN ATTRACTION VERSUS CHANGE IN PROXIMITY

Attraction, it has been seen, changes more for pairs that are imbalanced. But in what direction does it change? If balance holds for *changes* as well as for the existing state at a given time, then one would expect a relation between change in attraction and change in proximity. Fortunately, changes

TABLE 7

CHANGE IN ATTRACTION VERSUS CHANGE IN PROXIMITY:
CORRELATION BETWEEN SPRING PROXIMITY AND
ATTRACTION AT FIXED AUTUMN LEVELS*

Autumn Level of Attraction	*Autumn Proximity*			
	Roommate	*Floormate*	*Housemate*	*Towermate†*
1. Recognize	‡	.01	.14	.26
2. Talk	‡	.10	.12	.14
3. Like	‡	.11	.16	.15
4. Friend	.30	.22	.05	.22
5. Best friend	.47§	.27	‡	‡

* Correlations were computed separately for each year, then averaged over the four years. Proximity was scored 0 for towermates, 1 for housemates, 2 for floormates, 3 for roommates. The fifty-one correlations summarized in this table are based upon a total of 10,080 spring choices.

† Towermate correlations are based upon only two years, since in the first year no one changed houses, and in the last year out-of-house choices were not collected.

‡ In one or more of the years, this particular combination of autumn attraction and proximity included fewer than ten pairs.

§ Based upon only three years, since during the first year no best-friend roommates changed rooms.

in proximity are sufficiently numerous to permit exploration of this relation: over one-fifth of the residents are in a different room in the spring than they were in the autumn. (Fourteen per cent moved to a different room on the same floor, 6 per cent to the other floor in the same house, and 1 per cent to a different house.)

To compare change in attraction and change in proximity, choices were separated into twenty groups, one for each combination of the five levels of autumn attraction and the four autumn proximities; this was done separately for each year, making a total of eighty groups.[32] In this way, autumn proximity and attraction were controlled, so that within each group of choices, differences in *spring* proximity or attraction reflected only the interim changes. Then for each of these eighty groups, a correlation was computed between spring attraction and spring proximity. This produced (much more easily) exactly the same result as if a change

score had been computed for each individual choice, and these correlated within groups.

For most of the groups, the modal combination of attraction and proximity is the same in spring as in the preceding autumn. But in all groups, many pairs changed proximity or attraction or both, and the correlation indicates whether when proximity changed, attraction also tended to change, and if so, in what direction.[33] The result, in Table 7, is uniformly positive correlation for all combinations of initial attraction and proximity: whenever either proximity or attraction increases, the other tends also to increase; when one

[32] Similar patterns appeared in the separate tables for each of the four years. This was true also of the separate tabulation for each year of the relations presented in Fig. 2 and in Table 6.

[33] The present approach, by computing separate correlations for each combination of initial attraction and proximity, effects literal control over initial values of these variables. A similar procedure effecting "statistical control" would compute for all the pairs a single partial correlation between the final values of the two variables, removing variance and covariance associated with the initial values of both (see Frederick W. Lord, "Elementary Models for Measuring Change," and Carl Bereiter, "Some Persistent Dilemmas in the Measurement of Change," both in Chester W. Harris (ed.), *Problems in Measuring Change* [Madison: University of Wisconsin, 1963]).

decreases, the other tends also to decrease.

Thus, when a change in attraction occurs (which is most probable, as Fig. 2 showed, with initial *im*balance), there is likely to be a corresponding change in proximity. For example, of those who in autumn chose their roommate as their best friend, about 70 per cent chose the same person in spring, too. But, as the correlation of .47 shows, when attraction did decrease, proximity also tended to decrease. The same relation holds for mere recognition of those living in other houses; as a balanced state, this was unlikely to change, but any increases in attraction or proximity tended to go together.

IV. PROCESSES UNDERLYING BALANCE IN INTERPERSONAL ATTRACTION

The preceding sections have provided unusually extensive support for balance theory, not only in its more commonly considered static aspects, but also in its crucial dynamic role. Balance is a useful theory partly because it includes such a range of sentiments and interpersonal relations, but this breadth also means that its verification for proximity and peership does not explain in detail the processes that make it work for these particular characteristics. This section examines possible processes, and in doing so suggests that even the operation of so apparently obvious a characteristic as proximity is somewhat subtle, and that it is in fact useful to distinguish among three types of distance: physical, functional, and phenomenal.

PROXIMITY

Physical Distance

Distance acts first as a physical screen in determining the probability of initial con-

tact. For any two individuals chosen at random from the residents of Pierce Tower, the city of Chicago, or the entire planet, the probability of their ever interacting is more a function of the distance between them than of any other characteristic.[34] For larger distances, this phenomenon is obvious. But it is striking that it should operate so strongly where distances are as small and diversity of interests as great as in Pierce Tower. Moreover, the balance between attraction and proximity of room location survives a mingling of persons at the common entrance, bank of mail boxes, dining hall, main lounge, and elevators that probably puts Pierce Tower resident within sight, at different times, of each other resident.

Between members of different houses, however, this mingling did not frequently result in recognition.[35] Further, the chance of recognizing a person from another house was little greater if he were but one floor distant than if he were seven floors distant. This uniformity represents a major depar-

[34] Similarity of age, race, or sex would also predict interaction highly, though these are also correlated substantially with proximity.

[35] Indeed, the probability of a student recognizing a given person from another house in the Tower was substantially less, autumn or spring, than the probability of a freshman at another midwestern college recognizing a given individual from his entire student population of one thousand—male and female, of all four classes, living in eight dormitories, seven fraternities, and local homes (Walter L. Wallace, *Student Culture: Social Structure and Continuity in a Liberal Arts College* [Chicago: Aldine Publishing Co., 1966], p. 49). This contrast in level of acquaintance partly reflects the fact that the College of the University of Chicago is numerically overwhelmed by its environment and in some ways merges into it, whereas a college in a small town is much more prominent. At Chicago, the twenty-one hundred students in the College constituted but one-third of the University—all of whose students made up but one in ten of those living in the neighborhood and one in a thousand of those in the metropolitan area.

ture from the rule of physical distance and suggests examining the functional distance that acts to segregate and integrate houses.

FUNCTIONAL DISTANCE

Festinger, Schachter, and Back, in their study of the Westgate married students' housing at M.I.T., incorporated the concept of functional distance, which reflects the actual patterns of traffic. They hypothesized that "friendships will depend upon the occurrence of passive contacts and that the pattern and frequency of passive contacts among particular people will depend upon the ecological factors of physical and functional distance."[36] In verifying the importance of functional distance, they showed that persons whose apartments were nearer stairways were more popular, as were those whose houses faced more directly into a court of other houses.

In Pierce Tower, functional distance contributes, as the architectural design intended, to segregation between houses and integration within. Use of the elevator by at least the upper three houses means that no student need ever set foot in another house. The elevator also promotes integration within houses, by stopping only at the lower floor of each house. The two-story lounge likewise affects functional distance; direct access from both levels makes it easier for residents of the two floors to meet.

The physical and functional aspects of distance, however, do not appear to account fully for the patterning of attraction according to the rooms of persons who live on the same floor. Here the physical distances are so small that to go one room farther takes only two seconds. The func-

tional distances associated with traffic patterns may differ for rooms, since these vary in their location relative to the lounge, toilet, elevators, stairs and telephones; but unlike Westgate, there are no systematic differences in popularity by room location. There is, however, this analysis suggests, an added relevant aspect of distance, which may be called "phenomenal distance"—the way distance is perceived and interpreted.

PHENOMENAL DISTANCE

The way the distance between two persons is pereceived appears to depend upon the number of others who intervene. In a rural area, for example, persons living a half-mile away may be considered neighbors, while in a city, those living one hundred feet away may not be. In Pierce Tower, a room five doors farther away represents more than ten added seconds of travel time; it represents five *closer* opportunities that must be passed by.[37] When distances are this small, the significance of the closeness, this analysis suggests, is less in the physical distance itself than in its perception. The farther a door is from one's own, the more purposive one's approach must be, and the more such approach tends to require justification. To borrow change for the Coke machine from someone five rooms away may raise the question, "Why didn't he ask someone closer?"

Thus it is not that the distance between rooms is large, but that it is discernible, and so furnishes an unmistak-

---

[36] Festinger, Schachter, and Back, *op. cit.*, p. 54.

[37] The concept of phenomenal distance resembles Stouffer's intervening opportunities, though the latter concerns perception less and macro-social units more (see Samuel A. Stouffer, "Intervening Opportunities: A Theory Relating Mobility and Distance," *American Sociological Review*, V [1940], 845–67).

able distinction as to what is closer and, hence, in Schelling's terms, more "prominent."[38] To pass over several closer opportunities is to manifestly seek another out. But this acknowledges that the other has something one wants—an admission that Blau points out may have a certain cost for the seeker.[39] Relations that are not obviously sought presume less and reduce this cost. Such relations are more likely with those who are proximate, and most of all with one's roommate. It is easy for roommates to interact without each encounter being an occasion. Their relation, almost certainly not the optimal combination of personalities,[40] is nonetheless attractive for its easy accessibility; its phenomenal distance is small. The high proportion of roommates who are friends suggests that the attractiveness of accessibility outweighs the costs of non-optimality.[41]

38 In *The Strategy of Conflict* (Cambridge, Mass.: Harvard University Press, 1960), pp. 53–80, Thomas C. Schelling presents prominence as a crucial determinant of perceived alternatives and hence of outcomes, in bargaining and negotiation. The present research suggests that prominence may be equally critical in the establishment of norms for interpersonal behavior generally.

39 Peter M. Blau, *Exchange and Power in Social Life* (New York: John Wiley & Sons, 1964).

40 The Student Housing Office does consider background in assigning roommates, but the matching procedure is limited by lack of information and the means to process it. The scheme, one year, was to assign roommates who were similar on field of study and dissimilar on region of the country. Thus, assignment of roommates is necessarily far from optimal, while matching of characteristics of students in adjoining rooms is not attempted.

41 This compromise with optimality is reflected by some students' difficulty in identifying a "best friend," or by comments like "I have no really good friends, these are only my buddies."

CHANGING PROCESSES

As time passes, and persons living on the same floor become generally better acquainted, the relation between proximity and attraction decreases—further indicating that more than physical distance is involved. Despite the decrease, however, distance remains important—for two reasons. First, the original physical costs and some of the phenomenal costs continue. Second, there is inertia from the original relations. Successful friendship reinforces itself; the longer it has been in existence, the more benefits it can offer. New acquaintances appear at first generally less able to provide reward than are old friends. When old friends are best, then, part of the reason may lie just in their oldness. In this way proximity continues to relate to friendship, though less as a primary agent and more as a correlate of the relations it originally facilitated.

For houses as a whole, the role of proximity probably also changes in a similar way. Initially it promotes the development of friendships within houses, but once the houses, thus aided, have developed as social entities, proximity probably becomes more of a correlate than a cause. This is consistent with the rise, from autumn to spring, of the integration within houses and segregation between them that the corresponding changes of balance imply.

PEERSHIP

For two persons who are sufficiently proximate so that they have a good chance of interacting, their relative statuses further predict the level of attraction that will actually develop. If proximity provides an initial physical screen for friendship, then peership provides a social screen. They act in different ways to make friendship attractive: proximity, by making friendship easier, reduces the costs; peership, through the benefits of similarity, increases the rewards.

Preference for peers, among underclassmen as well as upperclassmen, is not necessarily to be expected; one might reasonably assume that upperclassmen would be generally more popular, with *both* groups. Among undergraduates, year in college is highly prominent characteristic: it specifies just how far along one is in the system, and generally also tells his age and how many years he has been around. For all three of these, the more the better, and so upperclassmen have a combination of characteristics making them particularly desirable associates for freshmen to have.[42] For the reciprocity that constitutes friendship, however, there would need to be an equally good reason for upperclassmen to profit from the friendship of freshmen. Exchange theory[43] suggests that this could be provided by freshmen giving respect and deference to upperclassmen, and so provides an alternate hypothesis to that of balance between attraction and similarity in status.

That in fact freshmen associate with upperclassmen with no more than chance frequency indicates that freshmen are un-

willing or unable to pay a sufficient price. (Such unwillingness might stem, of course, from a perception that friendship with an upperclassman—contrary to the above assumption—is not worth much more than friendship with a classmate.) It also seems likely that the previously noted tendency toward a quota for the number of friends operates to segregate classes, for when freshmen enter in the autumn, upperclassmen tend to have their quotas already filled and hence are less eager candidates for friendship than are other freshmen. Thus, whatever the bases for original associations, they tend to persist along college class lines.

Strong ingroup norms may sometimes make it rewarding to like another on the basis of similarity alone, rather than its behavioral implications. For most students, however, the reward probably lies instead in the value of having a friend who is equally new or experienced, and who thus shares various interests that are correlated with college class. Both initial and continued association between classmates likely reflect more the correlates of status than status itself. For example, two freshmen are more likely to be taking the same courses, which both promotes their contact and provides more possibility of mutual reward.

But while college class correlates with several obvious interests, it fails to correlate at all with many others (e.g., interest in music, chess, or swimming) that become known only as students become better acquainted. As acquaintance grows, then, the use of peership as a general indicator of similarity can be replaced by more specific information about the interests, attitudes, activities, and background of particular individuals. When these factors cut across class lines, friendships that follow them will lead to decreasing balance on peership. At the same time, balance

[42] It thus seems likely that there should be a tendency toward a universalistic evaluation, by everyone, that upperclassmen are more desirable friends, rather than particularistic preferences of each group for its own. Such standards, however, concern evaluation, not association—which itself could at the same time be highly in-group, as has been pointed out by Peter M. Blau, in "Operationalizing a Conceptual Scheme: The Universalism-Particularism Pattern Variable," *American Sociological Review*, XXVII (April, 1962), 159.

[43] Blau, *Exchange and Power in Social Life;* George C. Homans, *Social Behavior: Its Elementary Forms* (New York: Harcourt, Brace & World, 1961).

may increase on these other individual characteristics. Indeed, it seems possible that relations always maintain a substantial degree of balance, but on predictably different characteristics as acquaintance progresses—a possibility that is explored in subsequent analyses.[44]

[44] Subsequent analysis of similarity of pairs of persons on over fifty individual characteristics, including abilities, attitudes, interests, activities, and background information, shows that none predicts attraction as well as does peership (see Jack Sawyer and Robert F. Priest, "Prediction of Interpersonal Attraction: Multivariate, Dyadic, Longitudinal" [Social Psychology Laboratory, University of Chicago, January, 1967]). Using a smaller number of characteristics, Anton S. Morton finds a similar predominance of college class in the interaction among members of two fraternities at an eastern college (see his *Similarity as a Determinant of Friendship: A Multi-dimensional Study* [Princeton, N.J.: Educational Testing Service, April 1959]).

REFERENCE GROUPS, MEMBERSHIP GROUPS, AND ATTITUDE CHANGE

Alberta Engvall Siegel / Sidney Siegel

In social psychological theory, it has long been recognized that an individual's *membership groups* have an important influence on the values and attitudes he holds. More recently, attention has also been given to the influence of his *reference groups,* the groups in which he aspires to attain or maintain membership. In a given area, membership groups and reference groups may or may not be identical. They are identical when the person aspires to *maintain* membership in the group of which he is a part; they are disparate when the group in which the individual aspires to *attain* membership is one in which he is not a member. It has been widely asserted that both membership and reference groups affect the attitudes held by the individual.[1]

From: Journal of Abnormal and Social Psychology, *1957, 55, 360–64. Copyright © 1957 by the American Psychological Association, and reproduced by permission of the authors and APA.*

[1] M. Sherif and C. Sherif, *Groups in Harmony and Tension* (New York: Harper & Row, Publishers, 1953).

The present study is an examination of the attitude changes which occur over time when reference groups and membership groups are identical and when they are disparate. The study takes advantage of a field experiment which occurred in the social context of the lives of the subjects, concerning events considered vital by them. The subjects were not aware that their membership and reference groups were of research interest; in fact, they did not know that the relevant information about these was available to the investigators.

The field experiment permitted a test of the general hypothesis that both the amount and the direction of a person's attitude change over time depends on the attitude norms of his membership group (whether or not that group is chosen by him) and on the attitude norms of his reference group.

This hypothesis is tested with subjects who shared a common reference group at the time of the initial assessment of attitudes. They were then randomly assigned to alternative membership groups, some being assigned to the chosen group and others to a nonchosen group. Attitudes were reassessed after a year of experience in these alternative membership groups with divergent attitude norms. During the course of the year, some subjects came to take the imposed (initially nonpreferred) membership group as their reference group. Attitude change after the year was examined in terms of the membership group and reference group identifications of the subjects at that time.

THE FIELD EXPERIMENT

The *S*s of this study were women students at a large private coeducational university. The study was initiated shortly before the end of their freshman year,

when they all lived in the same large freshman dormitory to which they had been assigned upon entering the university. At this university, all women move to new housing for their sophomore year. Several types of housing are available to them: a large dormitory, a medium-sized dormitory, several very small houses which share common dining facilities, and a number of former sorority houses which have been operated by the university since sororities were banished from the campus. These latter are located among the fraternity houses on Fraternity Row, and are therefore known as "Row houses." Although the Row houses are lower in physical comfort than most of the other residences for women, students consider them higher in social status. This observation was confirmed by a poll of students,[2] in which over 90 per cent of the respondents stated that Row houses for women were higher in social status than non-Row houses, the remaining few disclaiming any information concerning status differences among women's residences.

In the Spring of each year, a "drawing" is held for housing for the subsequent year. All freshmen must participate in this drawing, and any other student who wishes to change her residence may participate. It is conducted by the office of the Dean of Women, in cooperation with woman student leaders. Any participant's ballot is understood to be secret. The woman uses the ballot to rank the houses in the order of her preference. After submitting this ballot, she draws a number from the hopper. The rank of that number determines the likelihood that her preference will be satisfied.

In research reported earlier,[3] a random sample was drawn from the popula-

[2] S. Siegel, "Certain Determinants and Correlates of Authoritarianism," *Genetic Psychology Monographs*, 1954, *49*, pp. 187–299.
[3] S. Siegel, *op. cit.*

tion of freshman women at this university, several tests were administered to the *S*s in that sample, and (unknown to the *S*s) their housing preferences for the forthcoming sophomore year were observed by the investigator. The *S*s were characterized as "high status oriented" if they listed a Row house as their first choice, and were characterized as "low status oriented" if they listed a non-Row house as their first choice. The hypothesis under test, drawn from reference group theory and from theoretical formulations concerning authoritarianism, was that high status orientation is a correlate of authoritarianism. The hypothesis was confirmed: freshman women who listed a Row house as their first choice for residence scored significantly higher on the average in authoritarianism, as measured by the E-F scale,[4] than did women who listed a non-Row house as their first choice. The present study is a continuation of the one described, and uses as its *S*s only those members of the original sample who were "high status oriented" i.e., preferred to live in a Row house for the sophomore year. In the initial study, of the 95 *S*s whose housing choices were listed, 39 were "high status oriented," i.e., demonstrated that the Row was their reference group by giving a Row house as their first choice in the drawing. Of this group, 28 were available to serve as *S*s for the follow-up or "change" study which is the topic of the present paper. These women form a homogeneous subsample in that at the conclusion of their freshman year they shared a common membership group (the freshman dormitory) and a common reference group (the Row). These *S*s, however, had divergent experiences during

their sophomore year: nine were Row residents during that year (having drawn sufficiently small numbers in the housing drawing to enable them to be assigned to the group of their choice) and the other 19 lived in non-Row houses during that year (having drawn numbers too large to enable them to be assigned to the housing group of their choice).

E-F scores were obtained from each of the 28 *S*s in the course of a large-scale testing program administered to most of the women students at the university. Anonymity was guaranteed to the *S*s, but a coding procedure permitted the investigators to identify each respondent and thereby to isolate the *S*s and compare each *S*'s second E-F score with her first.

To prevent the *S*s from knowing that they were participating in a follow-up study, several procedures were utilized: (*a*) many persons who had not served in the earlier study were included in the second sample, (*b*) the testing was introduced as being part of a nation-wide study to establish norms, (*c*) the test administrators were different persons from those who had administered the initial tests, (*d*) *S*s who informed the test administrator that they had already taken the "Public Opinion Questionnaire" (E-F scale) were casually told that this did not disqualify them from participating in the current study.

The *S*s had no hint that the research was in any way related to their housing arrangements. Testing was conducted in classrooms as well as in residences, and all procedures and instructions were specifically designed to avoid any arousal of the salience of the housing groups in the frame of reference of the research.

The annual housing drawing was conducted three weeks after the sophomore-year testing, and, as usual, each woman's housing ballot was understood to be secret. In this drawing, each *S* had the opportunity to change her member-

---

[4] T. Adorno, *et al., The Authoritarian Personality* (New York: Harper & Row, Publishers, 1950); H. G. Gough, "Studies of Social Intolerance: I, Some Psychological and Sociological Correlates of Anti-Semitism," *Journal of Social Psychology,* 1951, *33,* pp. 237–246.

ship group, although a residence move is not required at the end of the sophomore year as it is at the end of the freshman year. If an *S* participated in this drawing, the house which she listed as her first choice on the ballot was identified by the investigators as her reference group. If she did not, it was evident that the house in which she was currently a member was the one in which she chose to continue to live, i.e., was her reference group. With the information on each *S*'s residence choice at the end of her freshman year, her assigned residence for her sophomore year, and her residence choice at the end of her sophomore year, it was possible to classify the subjects in three categories:

A. Women ($n = 9$) who had gained assignment to live on the Row during their sophomore year and who did not attempt to draw out of the Row at the end of that year;

B. Women ($n = 11$) who had not gained assignment to a Row house for the sophomore year and who drew for a Row house again after living in a non-Row house during the sophomore year; and

C. Women ($n = 8$) who had not gained assignment to a Row house for the sophomore year, and who chose to remain in a non-Row house after living in one during the sophomore year.

For all three groups of *S*s, as we have pointed out, membership group (freshman dormitory) and reference group (Row house) were common at the end of the freshman year. For Group A, membership and reference groups were disparate throughout the sophomore year. For Group B, membership and reference groups were disparate throughout the sophomore year. For Group C, membership and reference groups were initially disparate during the sophomore year but became identical because of a change in reference groups.

As will be demonstrated, the Row and the non-Row social groups differ in attitude norms, with Row residents being generally more authoritarian than non-Row residents. From social psychological theory concerning the influence of group norms on individuals' attitudes, it would be predicted that the different group identifications during the sophomore year of the three groups of *S*s would result in differential attitude change. Those who gained admittance to a Row house for the sophomore year (Group A) would be expected to show the least change in authoritarianism, for they spent that year in a social context which reinforced their initial attitudes. Group C *S*s would be expected to show the greatest change in authoritarianism, a change associated not only with their membership in a group (the non-Row group) which is typically low in authoritarianism, but also with their shift in reference groups, from Row to non-Row, i.e., from a group normatively higher in authoritarianism to a group normatively lower. The extent of attitude change in the *S*s in Group B would be expected to be intermediate, due to the conflicting influences of the imposed membership group (non-Row) and of the unchanged reference group (Row). The research hypothesis, then, is that between the time of the freshman-year testing and the sophomore-year testing, the extent of change in authoritarianism will be least in Group A, greater in Group B, and greatest in Group C. That is, in extent of attitude change, Group A < Group B < Group C.

RESULTS

GROUP NORMS.

From the data collected in the large-scale testing program, it was possible to determine the group norms for authoritarian attitudes among the Row and the non-Row women at the university. The E-F scale was administered to all available Row residents ($n = 303$) and to a random sample of residents of non-Row houses ($n = 101$). These Ss were sophomores, juniors, and seniors. The mean E-F score of the Row women was 90, while the mean E-F score of the non-Row was 81. The E-F scores of the two groups were demonstrated to differ at the $p < .001$ level ($x^2 = 11.1$) by the median test,[5] a nonparametric test, the data for which are shown in Table 7-12.

TABLE 7–12

FREQUENCIES OF E-F SCORES ABOVE AND BELOW COMMON MEDIAN FOR ROW AND NON-ROW RESIDENTS

	Residents of Non-Row Houses	Residents of Row Houses	Total
Above Median	36	166	202
Below Median	65	137	202
Total	101	303	404

ATTITUDE CHANGE.

The central hypothesis of this study is that attitude change will occur differentially in Groups A, B, and C, and that it will occur in the direction which would be predicted from knowledge of the group norms among Row and non-Row residents in general. The 28 Ss of this study had a mean E-F score of 102 at the end of their freshman year. The data reported above concerning authoritarianism norms for all women residing on campus would lead to the prediction that in general that Ss would show a reduction in authoritarianism during the sophomore year but that this re-

duction would be differential in the three groups; from the knowledge that Row residents generally are higher in authoritarianism than non-Row residents, the prediction based on social group theory would be that Group A would show the smallest reduction in authoritarianism scores, Group B would show a larger reduction, and Group C would show the largest reduction. The data which permit a test of this hypothesis are given in Table 7-13. The Jonckheere test,[6] a nonparametric k-sample test which tests the null hypothesis that the three groups are from the same population against the alternative hypothesis that they are from different populations which are ordered in a specified way, was used with these data. By that test, the hypothesis is confirmed at the $p < .025$ level.

DISCUSSION

Substantively, the present study provides experimental verification of certain assertions in social group theory, demonstrating that attitude change over time is related to the group identification of the person— both his membership group identification and his reference group identification. The hypothesis that extent of attitude change would be different in the three subgroups of Ss, depending on their respective membership group and reference group identifications, is confirmed at the $p < .025$ level; in extent of change in authoritarianism, Group A < Group B < Group C, as predicted.

Another way of looking at the data may serve to highlight the influence of membership groups and reference groups. At the end of the freshman year, the Ss in

[5] S. Siegel, *Nonparametric Statistics: For the Behavioral Sciences* (New York: McGraw-Hill Book Co., Inc., 1956).

[6] A. R. Jonckheere, "A Distribution-Free, k-Sample Test Against Ordered Alternatives," *Biometrika*, 1954, *41*, pp. 133–145.

TABLE 7–13

FRESHMAN-YEAR AND SOPHOMORE-YEAR
E-F SCORES OF SUBJECTS

	E-F Score		
Group	End of Freshman Year	End of Sophomore Year	Difference
A	108	125	−17
	70	78	−8
	106	107	−1
	92	92	0
	80	78	2
	104	102	2
	143	138	5
	110	92	18
	114	80	34
B	76	117	−41
	105	107	−2
	88	82	6
	109	97	12
	98	83	15
	112	94	18
	101	82	19
	114	93	21
	104	81	23
	116	91	25
	101	74	27
C	121	126	−5
	87	79	8
	105	95	10
	97	81	16
	96	78	18
	108	73	35
	114	77	37
	88	49	39

Groups A, B, and C shared the same membership group and the same reference group. During the sophomore year, the Ss in Group A shared one membership group while those in Groups B and C together shared another. From membership group theory, it would be predicted that the extent of attitude change would be greater among the latter Ss. This hypothesis is supported by the data (in Table 7-13); by the Mann-Whitney test,[7] the change scores of these two sets of Ss (Group A versus Groups B and C together) differ in the predicted direction at the $p < .025$ level. This finding illustrates the influence of *membership* groups on attitude change. On the other hand, at the conclusion of the sophomore year, the Ss in Groups A and B shared a common reference group while those in Group C had come to share another. From reference group theory, it would be predicted that attitude change would be more extensive among the subjects who had changed reference groups (Group C) than among those who had not. This hypothesis is also supported by the data (in Table 7-13); by the Mann-Whitney test, the change scores of these two sets of Ss (Groups A and B together versus Group C) differ in the predicted direction at the $p < .05$ level. This finding illustrates the influence of *reference* groups on attitude change. Any inference from this mode of analysis (as contrasted with the main analysis of the data, by the Jonckheere test) must be qualified because of the nonindependence of the data on which the two Mann-Whitney tests are made, but it is mentioned here to clarify the role which membership and reference groups play in influencing attitude change.

The findings may also contribute to our understanding of processes affecting attitude change. The imposition of a membership group does have some effect on an individual's attitudes, even when the imposed group is not accepted by the individual as his reference group. This relationship is shown in the case of Group B. If the person comes to accept the imposed group as his reference group, as was the case with the Ss in Group C, then the change in his attitudes toward the

[7] S. Siegel, *Nonparametric Statistics*, *op. cit.*, pp. 116–127.

level of the group norm is even more pronounced.

Methodologically, the study has certain features which may deserve brief mention. First, the study demonstrates that it is possible operationally to define the concept of reference group. The act of voting by secret ballot for the group in which one would like to live constitutes clear behavioral specification of one's reference group, and it is an act whose conceptual meaning can be so directly inferred that there is no problem of reliability of judgment in its categorization by the investigator. Second, the study demonstrates that a field study can be conducted which contains the critical feature of an experiment that is usually lacking in naturalistic stituations: randomization. The determination of whether or not a woman student would be assigned to the living group of her choice was based on a random event: the size of the number she drew from the hopper. This fact satisfied the requirement that the treatment condition be randomized, and permitted sharper inferences than can usually be drawn from field studies. Third, the test behavior on which the conclusions of this study were based occurred in a context in which the salience of membership and reference groups was *not* aroused and in which no external sanctions from the relevant groups were operative. This feature of the design permitted the interpretation that the E-F score represented the Ss' internalized attitudes.[8] Finally, the use of a paper-and-pencil measure of attitude and thus of attitude change, rather than the use of some more behavioral measure, is a deficiency of the present study. Moreover, the measure which was used suffers from a well-known circularity, based on the occurrence of pseudo-low scores.[9]

SUMMARY

In the social context of the lives of the subjects, and in a natural social experiment which provided randomization of the relevant condition effects, the influence of both membership and reference groups on attitude change was assessed. All subjects shared a common reference group at the start of the period of the study. When divergent membership groups with disparate attitude norms were socially imposed on the basis of a random event, attitude change in the subjects over time was a function of the normative attitudes of both imposed membership groups and the individual's reference groups. The greatest attitude change occurred in subjects who came to take the imposed, initially nonpreferred, membership group as their reference group.

    [8] Sherif and Sherif, *op. cit.,* p. 218.
    [9] Adorno, *op. cit.,* p. 771; S. Siegel, "Certain Determinants..." *op. cit.,* pp. 221–222.

SOME RELATIONSHIPS OF PEER LIKING PATTERNS IN THE CLASSROOM TO PUPIL ATTITUDES AND ACHIEVEMENT [1]

Richard Schmuck

Since the important research contributions of Whyte,[2] Newcomb,[3] Lewin, Lippitt, and White,[4] Reisman,[5] Coleman,[6] and others, laymen, youth workers, and social scientists have been interested in understanding the mechanisms by which peer groups influence their members. Some explorations of juvenile delinquents[7] and of industrial work groups[8] have focused systematically on these mechanisms. Also some current research concerning peer-group influences is being undertaken in the context of educational inquiry, especially in studies on school and classroom milieu. Along these lines, several new theoretical analyses[9] and empirical studies[10] directly relate peer-group processes to

From: School Review, *1963, 71, 337–59. Copyright © 1963 by the University of Chicago Press, and reproduced by permission of the author and publisher.*

[1] This article is based upon an unpublished doctoral dissertation, "Social-Emotional Characteristics of Classroom Peer Groups" (University of Michigan, 1962).

[2] W. Whyte, *Street Corner Society* (Chicago: University of Chicago Press, 1943).

[3] T. Newcomb, *Personality and Social Change* (New York: Dryden Press Co., 1943).

[4] K. Lewin, R. Lippitt, and R. White, "Patterns of Aggressive Behavior in Experimentally Created 'Social Climates,'" *Journal of Social Psychology,* X (1939), 271–99.

[5] D. Reisman, *The Lonely Crowd* (New Haven, Conn.: Yale University Press, 1950).

[6] J. Coleman, *The Adolescent Society: The Social Life of the Teenager and Its Impact on Education* (New York: Free Press of Glencoe, 1961).

[7] O. Moles, R. Lippitt, and S. Withey, *A Selective Review of Research and Theory on Delinquency* (Document Series No. 2, Inter-Center Program of Research on Children, Youth and Family Life, Institute for Social Research [Ann Arbor, Mich., 1959]).

[8] J. March and H. Simon, *Organizations* (New York: John Wiley & Sons, 1958).

[9] N. Gronlund, *Sociometry in the Classroom* (New York: Harper & Bros., 1959); B. Hudgins and L. Smith (eds.), "The Classroom as a Social System" (unpublished conference paper, Washington University, 1962); and E. Smith, *American Youth Culture* (New York: Free Press of Glencoe, 1962).

[10] W. Sewell, A. Haller, and M. Straus, "Social Status and Educational and Occupational Aspiration," *American Sociological Review,* XXII (February, 1959), 67–76, and A. Wilson, "Residential Segregation of Social Classes and Aspirations of High School Boys," *American Sociological Review,* XXIV (December, 1959), 836–45.

the academic motivations and successes of individual pupils. These contributions leave little doubt concerning the inter-relatedness of youth friendship patterns and norms on the one hand; and the school-related attitudes, self-concepts, and performances of individual pupils on the other. However, even with this current interest in school peer culture, few studies present in detail empirical associations between interpersonal processes of school peer groups, the psychological processes of individual pupils, and pupil behavior in the classroom.

In reviewing studies on classroom peer groups we have been able to derive social psychological organization and continuity among the results of research only by integrating findings from studies using various concepts and methods. Of course, when a number of different pieces of research are described side by side, they do tend to exhibit a conceptual thread. One problem in seeking continuity in this fashion, however, is that diverse populations of children might be construed as one. Nevertheless, we will integrate and summarize briefly some findings of several classroom studies to give the research presented below some initial perspective.

Studies completed recently by Echelberger,[11] Lippitt and Gold,[12] Van Egmond,[13] and Sears[14] on elementary-school

groups, as well as studies by Elkins,[15] and Keislar[16] on high-school youth, indicate that peer liking relations are associated with a pupil's classroom behavior, that over time these liking relations achieve stability, and that having low liking status in the peer group is associated both with negative manifestations of mental health and low utilization of academic abilities. Two of the studies cited above on elementary classroom groups are especially relevant for the analyses developed in this paper. In the first, Lippitt and Gold, assuming that one indicator of mental health is the facility for positive affect toward others, had pupils specify how much they liked each of their classmates. The results indicate that pupils low in peer-group liking status express less positive affect toward others than those high in liking status. In the second study, Van Egmond sought to link a pupil's sociometric status with his utilization of abilities (defined as how much each pupil was achieving in relation to his intelligence). He found that girls with high liking status utilize their abilities more highly than girls with low, and that boys with high influence status utilize their abilities more highly than boys with low.

Neither of these two studies focuses on the intervening cognitive processes connecting actual liking status with classroom performance; nor has either of them treated peer groups qua groups as units for analysis. Indeed, few studies analyze systematically the entire conceptual span connecting peer groups as social systems, through relevant perceptual-cognitive pro-

[11] E. Echelberger, "Relationships between Personality Traits and Peer Status" (unpublished doctoral dissertation, University of Michigan, 1959).

[12] R. Lippitt and M. Gold, "Classroom Social Structure as a Mental Health Problem," *Journal of Social Issues,* XV (1959), 40–49.

[13] E. Van Egmond, "Social Interrelationship Skills and Effective Utilization of Intelligence in the Classroom" (unpublished doctoral dissertation, University of Michigan, 1960).

[14] P. Sears, "A Look at Measures of Achievement Motivation" (paper read at APA symposium on "Achievement Motivation and Achievement Anxiety in Children," 1959).

[15] D. Elkins, "Some Factors Related to the Choice-Status of Ninety Eighth-Grade Children in a School Society," *Genetic Psychology Monographs,* LVII (2d Half, 1959), 207–72.

[16] E. Keislar, "Peer Group Rating of High School Pupils with High and Low Marks," *Journal of Experimental Education,* XXIII (1955), 369–373.

cesses of peer-group members, to the members' overt behaviors or performances. We attempted to do this conceptually and only partially empirically in an earlier paper.[17] In that paper, the social-psychological bonds between classroom informal peer processes and pupil performance were designated by specifying several assumptions connecting so-called "social space" factors, through life-space factors, to individual performance. The term, "social space," was employed to refer to group properties that are pre-perceptual for any given individual, while the term "life-space," was employed to refer to psychological events that are postperceptual and pre-behavioral. Performance was to designate overt behavioral events.

The several assumptions outlined in that paper were viewed as setting the stage for a program of research. The initial step in that program was the consideration of the differential effects of one important variable in the social space— peer-group sociometric structure. Two types of sociometric structures were conceptualized and examined. These were (1) centrally structured groups, characterized by a narrow focus of interpersonal acceptance and rejection, and (2) diffusely structured groups, characterized by a wide range of positive and negative choices— that is, little or no focus of interpersonal acceptance and rejection upon a few members. In other words, a large number of pupils agree in selecting a small cluster of their classmates as highly accepted or rejected in centrally structured groups. Diffusely structured groups, on the other hand, are not typified by small clusters of highly accepted and highly rejected pupils, that is, there are no distinct subgroups

[17] R. Schmuck, "Sociometric Status and Utilization of Academic Abilities," *Merrill-Palmer Quarterly of Behavior and Development,* VIII (1962), 165–72.

whose members receive most of the sociometric choices.

In a preliminary analysis of eight upper elementary-school classrooms we found that (1) pupils are more accurate in estimating their status positions in centrally structured groups than in diffusely structured groups, and (2) pupils who are accurate and have low status in the peer group are lower utilizers of their academic abilities than pupils who are accurate and have high status. The purpose of our presentation here is to report conceptualizations and empirical results that considerably refine and extend these preliminary findings.

THEORY AND VARIABLES

Pupils in a classroom can be viewed either as a group adjusting through patterns of informal relations to the formal organizational demands of the school or as a collection of parallel and co-operatively or competitively acting individuals engaged in intellectual and emotional change. We assume that informal relations among peers, in particular peer liking relations, have some effect on the way individual youngsters conceive of and carry out the more formal role requirements of being a pupil. This assumption holds especially when these peer likability patterns become intensely intimate and affective. Indeed, the more peer liking relations acquire importance for the individual pupil, the more they affect his definition and evaluation of self and the more psychologically threatening or supportive it is possible for them to become. Furthermore, the more threatening or supportive these relationships become, the more probability they have of effecting individual pupil's adjustments to the formalized learning and behavioral demands of the school.

In short, a pupil's academic performance is conditioned by emotional contents associated with his self-concepts as peer and pupil, and these self-concepts are formed, in part, by that pupil's liking relations with his peers. As was noted before, we assume from Van Egmond's study[18] that a pupil's actual sociometric status and his utilization of abilities are associated. We want to go beyond that finding here, looking for peer-group conditions that either enhance or mitigate that relationship, as well as some intervening psychological processes that link sociometric status to classroom performance.

In approaching a more refined analysis than those presented in previous studies concerning peer influences, several theoretical questions arise. The answers to each of these questions involve variables for empirical study. For instance, we ask: What peer-group conditions, beyond a pupil's liking status in the group, have impact on the ways he perceives himself in the classroom? Our tentative answer to this query involves two variables; the structure of peer-group liking choices, and a pupil's potency of involvement in the peer group. Further, we ask: What psychological processes intervene between these peer-group conditions and subsequent classroom behaviors? Here our answer involves three variables; cognized liking status in the peer group, attitude toward self, and attitude toward school. Finally, we ask: What performance factor makes sense conceptually as an outcome of these social psychological processes? We answer by making use of the variable, utilization of academic abilities. Each of these variables is elaborated on briefly below.

PEER-GROUP LIKING STRUCTURE.

Peer liking structure involves the way pupils of a classroom group distribute

their interpersonal preferences. We already have made reference to two types of sociometric structure—central and diffuse. Centrally structured peer groups are characterized by a large number of pupils who agree in selecting only a small cluster of their classmates as pupils they like. Along with this narrow focus on a small number of pupils, many other pupils are neglected entirely. Diffusely structured peer groups, on the other hand, are distinguished by a more equal distribution of liking choices; by no distinct subgroups whose members receive a large proportion of preferences; and by fewer entirely neglected pupils.

The theoretical basis for these two varieties of sociometric structure emanates from two diverse perspectives in social science, Gestalt perceptual theory,[19] and group dynamics.[20] From the former, for instance, an important assumption is that at least one significant determinant of perceptual veridicality lies in the structure of the distal stimulus object, that is, its "good form," clarity, symmetry, distinctiveness, etc. Here we argue that the centrally structured sociometric situation represents a clearer and more distinct distal stimulus for individual pupils than the diffusely structured situation. From group dynamics, studies on communication nets and group structure[21] indicate that task leadership is recognized more quickly and easily in centrally structured groups. It can be argued from this work that social-emotional status might also be more easily recognized in groups with centrally structured sociometric dimensions. In any case,

---

[18] *Op. cit.*

[19] W. Kohler, *Gestalt Psychology* (New York: Liveright Publishing Corp., 1947).

[20] D. Cartwright and A. Zander, *Group Dynamics* (Evanston, Ill.: Row, Peterson & Co., 1960).

[21] H. Leavitt, "Some Effects of Certain Communication Patterns on Group Performance," *Journal of Abnormal and Social Psychology,* XLVI (1951), 38–50.

both of these perspectives represent the theoretical and empirical bases for our thinking on group sociometric structuring and individual cognition of the classroom environment.

Pupil Potency of Involvement in the Peer Group

The amount of psychological investment a pupil has in his peer relations represents his potency of involvement in the classroom peer group. More specifically, we define potency of involvement in the classroom peer group as the degree that a pupil is limited to his classmates for like-age friendship ties.

Actual Liking Status in the Peer Group

Actual liking status refers to the preferential position that an individual pupil actually holds within his classroom peer group.

Cognized Liking Status in the Peer Group

Cognized liking status is defined as the preferential position that an individual pupil conceives of himself as holding within his classroom peer group.

Attitude toward Self

Attitude toward self is defined as those general cognitions and associated feelings a pupil has regarding himself.

Attitude toward School

Attitude toward school is defined simply as an individual pupil's cognitions and associated feelings, both positive and negative, concerning aspects of the school environment.

Utilization of Abilities

Utilization of abilities is the degree a pupil's performance is congruent with his academic abilities, or how well he fulfils the formal learning demands of the classroom, taking his intelligence level into consideration.

Ten hypotheses involving these variables arise out of our theoretical scheme. These are stated formally, along with relevant data, in the "Hypotheses and Results" section below.

METHODS

The data reported in this study were derived from public school classrooms, in rural, industrial, suburban, and university communities. The data about each classroom were obtained from three sources: (1) questionnaires and group interviews with pupils, (2) questionnaires and interviews with teachers, and (3) a brief period of classroom observation. Pupil and teacher responses to selected items on these questionnaires are used as data in this study.

A sample of twenty-seven teachers was selected from those who volunteered to participate in the research. The final selections were made with the objective of sampling diverse types of communities and grade levels. As a result, a subject pool comprising 727 children was available from the classrooms of these teachers. These twenty-seven classrooms included eighteen elementary-school and four junior high and five senior high school groups. Our analyses here involve the elementary-school classrooms primarily. The fathers' occupations for the pupils in the sample differ significantly from classroom to classroom. For instance, in one classroom 90 per cent of the fathers are professional, while in another 97 per cent are classified as unskilled. The racial composition ranges from predominantly Negro in one class to all White in others.

All the questionnaires were administered by members of the research staff in the spring of 1961. The only exceptions to this general procedure were a short family-background information form and a sentence-completion test that were administered by the classroom teacher. Each teacher was instructed carefully in the standard administration procedure.

Nearly all the pupils had filled out a shorter but similar pilot questionnaire in the fall of the school year. Children who did not have adequate reading skills to follow the questionnaire (which was read to all pupils by the examiner) were eliminated from the sample. Approximately 2 per cent of the original sample did not complete their questionnaires. The generalizations made in this study, therefore, must be restricted to those children without severe academic disabilities.

The following operational definitions of our variables are used in this study.

PEER-GROUP LIKING STRUCTURE

Every pupil nominates four classmates he likes most and four he likes least. Each pupil is awarded one "choice-status" score whenever he is nominated by another pupil as highly liked and one "rejection-status" score whenever he receives a low liking nomination. Since each pupil chooses four pupils as high in liking and four others as low, the mean "choice" and "rejection" scores for each class are both equal to four. Centrality of the peer group liking structure increases, and diffuseness decreases, as the variability of the "choice" and "rejection" score distributions increase. Three types of peer group structures are studied here. Peer groups referred to as having *bimodal centrality* have high variability (above median of all class-

rooms studied) in both the "choice" and "rejection" distributions. Peer groups of *monomodal centrality* have one score distribution of high variability and one of low. Finally, groups characterized by *diffuseness* have low variability in both score distributions.

PUPIL POTENCY OF INVOLVEMENT IN THE PEER GROUP

Each pupil designates how many peers outside the classroom he likes the same or better than his classmates. A classroom median is used to distinguish high involvement from low involvement for each pupil.

ACTUAL LIKING STATUS IN THE PEER GROUP

The pupils in each class are rank-ordered according to their liking "choice-status" scores. This distribution is split at the median in deriving high- and low-status pupils.

COGNIZED LIKING STATUS IN THE PEER GROUP

Each pupil is asked to estimate whether he is in the first, second, third, or fourth quarter of his class in liking. Each pupil is then designated as holding either high (first and second quarter) or low (third and fourth quarter) cognized liking status.

ATTITUDE TOWARD SELF

The measurement of attitude toward self is obtained from a sentence completion test. The test as a whole consists of forty-six sentence stems, three of which relate to feelings about the self, as, for example, "When I look in the mirror I ———," "Sometimes I think I am ———," or "When I look at other boys and girls and then look at myself I feel ———." The completed sentences are rated on a seven-point scale and combined into an index concerning attitude toward self.

This technique yields rich and interesting personal data. For instance, a sixth-grade boy, scored as having a very positive attitude toward self by our scoring system, answered in the following ways:

> When I look in the mirror I *see a nice face.*
> Sometimes I think I am *a great man in sports.*
> When I look at other boys and girls and then look at myself I feel *I'm glad I am myself.*

A much different psychological picture is exhibited by a tenth-grade boy. His protocol is scored low for attitude toward self:

> When I look in the mirror I *look like Mike—ugly.*
> Sometimes I think I am *Bob M. and Dick S. who are no good farmers and wastes.*
> When I look at other boys and girls and then look at myself, I feel *very different.*

An internal consistency check for this measure indicates that each single item contributes about the same to the over-all index. For instance, the item, "When I look in the mirror I ———" is in agreement with the index 77 per cent of the time, for high and low designations. The other two items both agree with the total measure 72 per cent of the time. These moderately high and consistent percentages indicate a fair amount of internal consistency and imply that each item is contributing in its own right to the total index. An analysis of the inter-item associations also supports this latter point. Each of the items is moderately and positively correlated with every other item at levels ranging from +.36 to +.58.

ATTITUDE TOWARD SCHOOL

Five items from the sentence completion test, "Studying is ———," "This school ———," "My schoolwork ———," "Homework is ———," and "Learning out of books is ———," are used to obtain an index of attitude toward school by rating each completed sentence on a seven-point scale and computing the mean of the five.

A fifth-grade girl, scored as having a positive attitude toward school, wrote the following:

> Studying is *good for me because it helps me learn things.*
> This school is a *very very pretty place.*
> My schoolwork is *more important than playing around and wasting time.*
> Homework is *better than playing around.*
> Learning out of books is *about as much fun as learning from the teacher.*

On the other hand, another fifth-grade girl, scored as low in school adjustment, wrote the following contrasting material:

> Studying is *awful.*
> This school is *awful, I don't like it.*
> My schoolwork *is good enough.*
> Homework is *terrible.*
> Learning out of books is *lousy—you don't learn much.*

Analyses of both internal consistency and inter-item associations for the index of attitude toward school are quite similar to those for the index of attitude toward self. Single-item per cent agreement with the total index ranges from 68 per cent to 77 per cent, while inter-item correlations range from +.36 to +.54.

Preliminary analyses of rater reliability for both the attitude toward self and the attitude toward school indexes indicated 95 per cent agreement for high-low scoring. Thus, it appears that our scoring procedure affords very high reliability especially for high-low estimates.

UTILIZATION OF ABILITIES

Each class is split at the median into a high-intelligence group and low-intelligence group by scores from standard intelligence tests. The teacher then divides each of these groups into high-achieving and low-achieving subgroups. Thus, the class is divided into four ability-achievement groups; high ability-high achievement, high ability-low achievement, low ability-high achievement, and low ability-low achievement. The two high-achieving groups are considered to be utilizing their abilities more completely and are designated as the "high utilizers" while the two low-achieving groups are considered to be "low utilizers."

A comparison of the mean I.Q. scores yielded no difference for these two groups of utilizers. I.Q. mean for the "high utilizers," for instance, is 109.38, while that of the "low utilizers" is 109.00.

GROUP AFFECT

Our one remaining variable, group affect, is measured by each pupil designating on a nine-point scale how much he values every pupil in the class. Peer groups with higher mean scores on this measure have more positive group affect than those with lower scores.

HYPOTHESES AND RESULTS

All data reported below, except those concerning hypotheses one and ten, are derived from upper elementary-school classrooms (Grades 3–6). When appropriate, however, the generalizability of these findings to other developmental levels will be mentioned. Hypothesis 1 (which involves the proposed association between two group variables) and hypothesis 10 (which involves one added control variable) require a population larger than that afforded by our eighteen elementary classrooms for statistical analysis. In light of this, the full sample of twenty-seven classrooms is used for testing these two hypotheses.

Hypothesis 1 states:

> 1. Classroom peer groups distinguished by more liking diffuseness exhibit more positive group affect than groups with more centrality.

This hypothesis involves the general assumption that as interpersonal support increases its scope in a group, the effects tend to be circular in nature. That is, the more affective support, personal esteem, and personal well-being become evident in a peer group, the more easily a diffuse distribution of interpersonal attraction is perpetuated.

A rank-order correlation of $\rho = -.33$ ($p < .05$) indicates a negative association between the centrality of liking "choice" scores and group affect. As predicted, group affect decreases as a narrow focus of liking choices increases. Further, a correlation of $\rho = -.26$ ($p < .10$) indicates a probable negative association between the centrality of liking "rejection" scores and group affect. These correlations, though small, indicate at least a tendency for peer groups with diffuse liking structures to have more supportive social-emotional atmospheres.

Hypothesis 2 is:

> 2. The more liking choices are centrally structured in the peer group, the more accurate pupils are when estimating their actual liking status in the group.

In other words, pupils should more accurately judge where they stand in relation to their peers as the relationships among pupils approach a clear status hierarchy. Peer-group situations like this, in which interpersonal choices tend to be narrowly and distinctly focused, make shared awareness of this situation more probable. As we noted above, this pro-

pupils accurately estimate their status in the peer group. These results were also substantiated for high-school classrooms ($x^2 = 15.51$, $df = 2$, $p < .001$).

TABLE 1

LIKING STRUCTURAL TYPES AND
PUPILS' ACCURACY IN ESTIMATING STATUS*

	Estimate of Status			
	Accurate Pupils		Inaccurate Pupils	
Liking Structural Type	*No.*	*Per Cent*	*No.*	*Per Cent*
Bimodal centrality	97	66	51	34
Monomodal centrality†	83	64	46	36
Diffuseness	75	51	72	49

* $x^2 = 7.85$; $p < .02$.
† Includes either "choice" or "rejection" centrality.

position of "accuracy" received empirical support in a previous study.[22]

Table 1 delineates the results relevant to this hypothesis. These data indicate a positive association between structural centrality and accuracy of per-

A more refined analysis further supports hypothesis 2. Table 2 indicates that pupils who have low actual liking status in elementary-school peer groups tend to cognize their low status more accurately in the centrally structured situations. In

TABLE 2

PUPIL ACCURACY IN COGNIZING LOW STATUS IN
THREE LIKING STRUCTURES*

	Cognition of Low Status			
	Accurate Pupils		Inaccurate Pupils	
Liking Structural Type	*No.*	*Per Cent*	*No.*	*Per Cent*
Bimodal centrality	44	58	32	42
Monomodal centrality	29	45	35	55
Diffuseness	29	40	44	60

* $x^2 = 14.65$ $p < .001$.

sonal status in the peer group. The results show, moreover, that as the liking dimension approaches a more narrowly focused distribution, bimodal centrality, more

[22] Schmuck, *op. cit.*

the diffusely structured classrooms about 60 per cent of those pupils with low actual status cognize themselves as being highly liked in the group. We contend that the profusion of emotional support for individuals in the diffusely structured peer group accounts for this condition. Similar results were obtained for a combined analysis of the junior and senior high age levels, $(x^2 = 9.95, df = 2, p < .01)$.

Some ramifications of having low liking status and knowing it become evident in analyses of the results for hypotheses 3 and 4. Hypothesis 3 states:

> 3. Pupils with low actual liking status are lower utilizers of their abilities than pupils with higher actual liking status.

cognized status into studies relating sociometric status to performance.

The data for hypotheses 5 and 6 emphasize again the importance of considering cognized liking status along with actual status in studies of classroom peer groups. Hypotheses 5 and 6 state:

> 5. Pupils who cognize themselves as holding low liking status have more negative attitudes toward self than pupils with higher cognized status.

TABLE 3*

ACTUAL LIKING STATUS, COGNIZED LIKING STATUS, AND UTILIZATION OF ABILITIES†

Actual Liking Status	Cognized Liking Status	High Utilizers (N = 210)		Low Utilizers (N = 214)		Total Cognized Status	Total Actual Status
		No.	Per Cent	No.	Per Cent		
High	High	100	65	53	35	153⎫	
	Low	25	43	33	57	58⎭	211
Low	High	53	48	58	52	111⎫	
	Low	32	31	70	69	102⎭	213

* The x^2 partitioning statistic used in Table 3–5 is explained by William Hays in notes from his statistics course entitled, "Analyses of Qualitative Data" (University of Michigan, Spring, 1955), pp. 24–33.
† x^2 (actual status-cognized status) = 18.77, $p < .001$; x^2 (actual status-utilization) = 15.85, $p. < .001$; x^2 (cognized status-utilization) = 19.87, $p < .001$; x^2 (interaction) = .02, N.S.; x^2 (actual status-cognized (status-utilization) = 54.51, $p < .001$.

Hypothesis 4 is:

> 4. Pupils who cognize themselves as holding low liking status are lower utilizers of their abilities than pupils with higher cognized status.

The data shown in Table 3 strongly support both hypotheses. Furthermore, an inspection of the percentages in Table 3 shows that pupils who cognize themselves as being liked, though they have low actual liking status, are utilizing their abilities more highly than those who have low status and know it. Results for older pupils are essentially the same. These results emphasize the importance of introducing

> 6. Pupils who cognize themselves as holding low liking status have more negative attitudes toward school than pupils with higher cognized status.

The results in Tables 4 and 5 show that cognized liking status is related positively and significantly to both attitude toward self and attitude toward school, while actual liking status shows no such relation to these variables.

Thus, one could be misled if he were to conclude from previous studies that peer-group sociometric relations are not related to pupil attitudes toward self and school on the basis of an analysis of actual

TABLE 4

ACTUAL LIKING STATUS, COGNIZED LIKING STATUS,
AND ATTITUDE TOWARD SELF*

| | | Attitude toward Self | | | | | |
| | | Positive (N = 212) | | Negative (N = 209) | | | |
Actual Liking Status	Cognizer Liking Status	No.	Per Cent	No.	Per Cent	Total Cognized Status	Total Actual Status
High	High	90	60	61	40	151 ⎱	
	Low	24	40	36	60	60 ⎰	211
Low	High	63	58	46	42	109 ⎱	
	Low	35	35	66	65	101 ⎰	210

* x^2 (actual status-cognized status) $= 17.22$, $p < .001$; x^2 (actual status-attitude toward self) $= 2.28$, N.S.; x^2 (cognized status-attitude toward self) $= 19.60$, $p < .001$; x^2 (interaction) $= .57$, N.S.; x^2 (actual status-cognized status-attitude toward self) $= 39.67$, $p < .001$.

TABLE 5

ACTUAL LIKING STATUS, COGNIZED LIKING STATUS,
AND ATTITUDE TOWARD SCHOOL*

| | | Attitude toward School | | | | | |
| | | Positive (N =206) | | Negative (N = 216) | | | |
Actual Liking Status	Cognized Liking Status	No.	Per Cent	No.	Per Cent	Total Cognized Status	Total Actual Status
High	High	82	54	69	46	151 ⎱	
	Low	24	40	36	60	60 ⎰	211
Low	High	62	56	48	44	110 ⎱	
	Low	38	38	63	62	101 ⎰	211

* x^2 (actual status-cognized status) $= 16.88$, $p < .001$; x^2 (actual status-attitude toward school) $= .34$, N.S.; x^2 (cognized status-attitude toward school) $= 11.06$, $p < .001$; x^2 (interaction) $=.56$, N.S.; x^2 (actual status-cognized status-attitude toward school) $= 28.84$, $p < .001$.

liking status alone. Cognized liking status as well as actual liking status should be analyzed together when making a complete social psychological analysis of the classroom peer group. Indeed our data indicate that one important conditioner of attitudes toward self and school is the liking status a child cognizes himself as holding in relation to his peers. Presumably, the group-structured properties that were highlighted in our results for hypothesis 2 represent at least one dynamic aspect of this.

The data for the first six hypotheses support the notion that peer-group sociometric diffuseness, extensity of interpersonal support for the individual pupil, attitudes toward self and school, and academic productivity vary together in a systematic fashion. The remaining hypotheses involve another significant variable in analyzing the impact of peer-group liking patterns on individual pupils: pupil potency of involvement in the peer group.

Hypotheses 7–9 deal with the predicted differential effects on the individual pupil of high or low involvement in his classroom peer group. The general proposition underlying each of these hypotheses is that peer-group status should have a greater impact on those pupils who are highly involved in classroom life (those with few additional alternatives for interpersonal gratifications) than on those pupils lacking such involvement. The results for hypotheses 7 and 8 are quite clear, while those for hypothesis 9 are less so.

Hypothesis 7 states:

> 7. Associations exist between actual liking status and one's utilization of abilities, only for pupils with high potency of involvement in the peer group.

ability utilization of those pupils most involved in the classroom peer group is more highly associated with actual liking status than is true for those pupils less involved. Hypotheses 8 and 9 state:

> 8. Associations exist between actual liking status and one's attitude toward self only for pupils with high potency of involvement in the peer group.

> 9. Associations exist between actual liking status and one's attitude toward school only for pupils with high potency of involvement in the peer group.

Hypothesis 8, concerning attitude toward self, is supported by our data, while hypothesis 9 is not. A comparison of the

TABLE 6

ACTUAL LIKING STATUS AND UTILIZATION WITH POTENCY OF INVOLVEMENT

Liking Status	High Utilizers		Low Utilizers	
	No.	Per Cent	No.	Per Cent
*High Potency of Involvement**				
High	73	65	47	45
Low	39	35	58	55
Low Potency of Involvement†				
High	48	49	44	40
Low	50	51	67	60

* $x^2 = 9.14$, $p < .005$.
† $x^2 = 1.84$, N.S.

A comparison of the x^2 analyses in Table 6 supports this hypothesis. For pupils with high potency of involvement condition, there is a positive association between actual liking status in the peer group and the utilization of academic abilities. However, this association does not hold for those pupils with low potency of involvement. Thus, it appears that the

x^2 analyses in Table 7 does confirm the proposition that actual liking status is associated more highly with attitude toward self for pupils highly involved in the peer group than for those with less involvement. The results for hypothesis 9 concerning potency of involvement, actual liking status, and attitude toward school are not significant.

TABLE 7

ACTUAL LIKING STATUS AND ATTITUDE TOWARD SELF
WITH POTENCY OF INVOLVEMENT

Liking Status	Positive Attitude		Negative Attitude	
	No.	*Per Cent*	*No.*	*Per Cent*
*High Potency of Involvement**				
High	65	61	53	46
Low	42	39	62	54
Low Potency of Involvement†				
High	46	44	46	45
Low	59	56	57	55

* $x^2 = 4.78$, $p < .05$.
† $x^2 = .02$, N.S.

Finally, combining the variables of structure and involvement, hypothesis 10 states:

> 10. Attitude toward self of pupils with high potency of involvement in the peer group is more positive as peer group structure increase in diffuseness.

Hypothesis 10, analyzed with the entire sample, is supported by our data. Table 8 shows that the attitude toward self of pupils with high potency of involvement in the classroom group is higher as group structure increases in diffuseness.

Briefly, then, the bulk of the em-pirical data reported here concerning relations among peer-group, attitudinal, and academic-performance variables support our hypotheses. These data point out, among other things, that peer groups characterized by a wide spread of liking relations among members have more positive emotional climates; that peer-group liking structure and pupil involvement in the group help to fashion a pupil's cognition of himself in relation to the peer group; that this cognition of self in relation to others is associated with a pupil's attitudes toward self and school; and that a pupil's personal conception of his place in the

TABLE 8

ATTITUDE TOWARD SELF OF PUPILS HIGHLY INVOLVED
IN THE PEER GROUP FOR THREE LIKING STRUCTURES†

Liking Structural Type	Positive Attitude		Negative Attitude	
	No.	*Per Cent*	*No.*	*Per Cent*
Bimodal centrality	56	41	82	59
Monomodal centrality	67	46	79	54
Diffuseness	50	58	36	42

* $x^2 = 6.63$, $p < .05$.

peer group is related also to his utilization of abilities.

IMPLICATIONS FOR FURTHER RESEARCH

In most systematic studies in social science, data are considered to support hypotheses when legitimate statistical devices indicate that little possibility exists that the results occurred by chance. Of course, many negative cases always are present in tables of data, even though we formally consider a hypothesis as generally confirmed. Certainly one reason that these negative cases occur is that most complex social psychological phenomena are multidetermined, and in studies such as this one, is not always able to conceptualize and measure all of the significant variables while making a prediction. This means, then, that negative cases in the tables should give impetus to ideas for future research.

For example, consider pupils who are highly liked in the classroom peer group and who view themselves as being liked. Our data indicate that fifty-three pupils in this category in the elementary grades are low utilizers of their academic abilities. How might one begin to explain the occurrence of the negative cases? One explanation is that the crude measures of socioeconomic status, cognized status, and utilization were invalid for some individual cases. This is undoubtedly true to some extent. Another explanation is that these pupils are receiving so much satisfaction in their social relations and using so much energy in that area of life that they have little left for classroom learning. On the other hand, what about the thirty-two high-utilizing pupils who are not liked and who know it? It could be that these pupils are not much concerned with social relations; perhaps classroom learning presents them with the most satisfying school condition and all of their energies are exerted here. In any case, we should point out that our theoretical framework is quite simple and that many variables must be introduced into it before it reflects completely the realities of classroom peer-group life.

Consider the pupil who has a high affiliation motive; will not being disliked by his peers affect his academic work more than a pupil who has little desire for affiliation? Consider the pupil who has a much stronger achievement than affiliation motive; perhaps for him social relations can be disregarded except with relevant authorities such as the teacher. Consider the pupil with little power motive; will it matter much to him if he is not influential with his peers? Probably many other psychosocial motives, attitudinal clusters, and personal values could be presented here to show the need for more elaboration on the framework presented in this report. One impetus for future study comes from a systematic investigation of negative cases and some speculating on the reasons for these.

Some other relevant areas for future research concerning classroom peer groups include:

1. A statistical partitioning of the relative impact of several social psychological variables on the utilization of abilities, attitude toward self, and attitude toward school. Variables could include social class, sex, cognized peer liking status, attitudes toward the teacher, and cognized home support for school.

2. An investigation of the determinants of different sociometric structures. We might ask, for instance: Can one predict to types of sociometric structures by knowing some relevant personality characteristics of children, by knowing something about the social backgrounds of the children, by analyzing teacher values and behavior, or by analyzing some other set of variables?

3. A laboratory experiment would be appropriate to test whether peer-group rejection leads to a decrement in intellectual performance and attitude toward self under controlled conditions. Also important would be experimentation indicating the conditions under which learning and attitude toward self decrements do not occur even when peer rejection is present.

4. And finally, some research is needed on alternative ways of conceptualizing and measuring the utilization of abilities. The utilization of academic abilities has been central throughout this study, yet, just as there are various kinds of ability, there may also be different forms of utilization. Extended conceptualization and empirical work is needed here for a more complete delineation of this concept.

SUMMARY

This study was undertaken in an attempt to fill some social psychological gaps left by recent studies on peer relations, learning, and mental health in the classroom. Indeed, most research on classroom groups does not deal systematically with the interrelationships between interpersonal peer-group variables and intrapersonal individual variables. Our research professes to delineate some of these relations both conceptually and empirically.

The framework of conceptual linkages considered in this analysis ranged from peer-group conditions through intervening psychological processes to individual performance. Specific empirical variables studied under the rubric of *peer-group conditions* include liking sociometric structure, group affect, potency of involvement in the classroom group, and actual liking status in the peer group. The *intervening psychological processes* include cognized liking status, attitude toward self, and attitude toward school, while the

performance indicator is the pupil's utilization of his abilities. The central problems for this study involved how social-situational factors shape emotional-personal factors; and how these latter factors related to a pupil's utilization of his academic abilities.

A sample of 727 pupils representing Grades 3–12 was drawn from twenty-seven classrooms. Our analyses here centered on the elementary classrooms primarily—Grades 3–6. The sample included classrooms from rural, suburban, industrial, and university communities in southeastern Michigan. The occupational categories of the father of each pupil were quite diverse, ranging from professional to unskilled. The pupils and teachers were administered questionnaires and interviews by the research staff and data were drawn also from school files. The data were collected as part of a broader study concerning classroom group dynamics, teacher in-service training, and educational innovation.

Our theoretical framework proposed that an individual's academic performance is conditioned to some extent by the emotional and cognitive contents associated with his self-concepts as peer and pupil. Furthermore, we argued that these self-concepts are formed, at least in part, by one's social relations in the classroom peer group; and that they have some effect on the way in which a pupil carries out the more formal learning requirements of the classroom. Ten hypotheses were delineated systematically using this general framework.

In general, our empirical findings supported the major hypothesized associations between peer-group conditions, intervening psychological processes, and individual performance in the classroom. Among the important findings confirming our hypotheses were the following:

1. Classroom peer groups with a wide

range of liking choices (diffuse liking structures) tend to have more positive group affect than classrooms with narrowly focused liking distributions (central liking structures).

2. Pupils are more accurate in estimating their actual liking statuses in peer groups characterized by bimodal centrality (both positive and negative dimensions of liking area narrowly focused) than in groups characterized by diffuseness (both positive and negative dimensions widely focused). Specifically, pupils who have low liking status in elementary classrooms tend to cognize their low position more accurately in the centrally structured situation than in the diffusely structured one.

3. Pupils who are accurate when estimating their position in a liking structure and who are negatively placed in that structure are lower utilizers of academic abilities and have less positive attitudes toward self and school than pupils who are accurate and positively placed. Furthermore, pupils who cognize themselves as being liked, though they have low actual liking status, are utilizing their abilities more highly and have more positive attitudes toward self and school than those pupils who have low status and know it.

4. For elementary-school pupils who are highly involved in the classroom peer group (high potency of involvement), significant relationships exist between actual liking status on the one hand and utilization of abilities, attitude toward self, and attitude toward school on the other hand. These same associations do not exist under condition of low potency of involvement in the classrom peer group.

5. The attitude toward self of pupils with high potency of involvement in the peer group is more positive as peer-group liking structure increases in diffuseness.

SOCIAL DATING ATTRACTIONS OF THE YOUTH CULTURE AND THEIR ASSOCIATION WITH ASPECTS OF ACADEMIC ORIENTATION AND PEER RELATIONS '

Robert E. Grinder

The youth-culture literature suggests that adolescents who lean heavily upon peer functions for support are likely to be diverted from attaining adult-approved objectives of socialization (Allport, 1961; Coleman, 1961; Erikson, 1962; Parsons, 1962; Wilfert, 1963). The available evidence indicates that youth-culture activities may offer the sole passageway to heterosexual popularity and peer status for many adolescents, and the prompt and forcible operation of the peer reward-and-punishment system heightens their effect (Parsons, 1962; Hollingshead, 1949; Smith, 1962). One might expect, therefore, that adjustment to high-school responsibilities would be affected adversely by the extent to which adolescents strive for the attractions of the youth culture. The assumption is highly general, and the present study attempts to evaluate empiri-

cally the degree to which it holds for both boys and girls in the 10th, 11th, and 12th grades by comparing interest in certain specific attractions of social dating with various aspects of orientation toward high school and toward peer relations.

The belief that youth-culture and adult goals may be incompatible stems traditionally from psychoanalytic theory. This viewpoint holds that youth-culture refractoriness represents a necessarily hostile reaction that occurs when biological propensities, surging anew, drain ego-strength, displace dependency from parent to peer-group figures, and produce through reaction-formation a compulsive independence and defiance of adult standards (Blos, 1962; Parsons, 1950). The venerable psychoanalytic outlook has provided a firm basis for the widely adopted belief that participation in the youth culture serves primarily as an outlet for adolescent rebelliousness (Hurlock, 1955, Keniston, 1962; Pearson, 1958).

A more beneficent view of youth culture activities has emerged recently through the influence of social learning theory, which in contrast, stresses the

205

formative influence of reward-and-punishment features of familial and cultural functions rather than the dynamics of internal variables (Bandura, 1964; Elkin and Westley, 1955; Parsons, 1962). Presumably, children acquire degrees of dependency upon their parents on the basis of the ways in which rewards and punishments are manipulated. Parents tend to relax their control with the advent of adolescence, while concurrently, peer reference groups, high school leaders, and teenage heroes burgeon in their salience as administrators of rewards and punishments. As a consequence, adolescents master age-graded expectations associated with autonomy, independence, and delay of gratification, largely as a function of the way in which they experience social reinforcements. This viewpoint, significantly, asserts that adolescents may be more interested in participating in activities of the youth culture than of their families or schools if they perceive its attractions and privileges to be more appealing. The theory implies also that the adolescent who underachieves in school may be obtaining abundant satisfactions from the youth culture. If the adolescent, in addition, seems defiantly independent (rebellious) of adult-sponsored goals, it may be that he is attempting to preserve his peer status and to maintain a flow of rewards from his youth-culture cohorts. Hence, social learning theory leads to the belief that adolescent involvement in the youth culture is a function of individual differences and is only one of the many possible *rites de passage.*

The two interpretations of youth culture functions differ primarily in that psychoanalytic theory in contrast to social learning theory envisages frustration, hostility, alienation, and rebellion as an inevitable consequence of development. One may reason from both theories that extensive interest and involvement in youth culture attractions would be associated with unsatisfactory adjustment to high school responsibilities. However, the social learning theory view holds that youths' diversion from their obligations may be, in part, a result of the powerful appeal of youth-culture rewards, satisfactions, and comforts. This viewpoint, therefore, offers a basis for analyses of individual differences and provides the basic framework for the present study.

The present investigation of youth culture functions is restricted, in order that it might be reduced to manageable proportions, to the appeal of social dating. For present purposes, the dating system has been framed expansively, *i.e., social dating is viewed as encompassing all situations in which the principal actors constitute a heterosexual pair or dyad, are unmarried, and are unchaperoned, free agents.* The range of attractions that dating functions may offer as competition for youth's attention depends arbitrarily upon how inclusively social dating is defined. For example, dating patterns appear distinguishable; moreover, narrowly restricted operational definitions seem justifiable in the sense that the interactions of a couple who has recently met are likely to be different from a couple who is engaged. Waller (1937), Burgess and Locke (1951), Smith (1962), and Delora (1963) argue that a firm commitment to marriage differentiates dating and courtship and that the two types of couples represent unlike systems. Delora (1963) has further distinguished casual, steadily, steady, engaged to be engaged, and engaged systems of social dating. The investigator whose interests *per se* are in the cultural norms, role behaviors, and social systems probably would find the restricted definition of dating especially suitable. The aims of the present study, however, are upon pervasive and basic reward patterns, and the broad conceptualization presented here is required.

The dating patterns encompassed by

the definition offered above appear to share several common attractions (cf. *Method,* below). One finds that gaining affection and sexual gratification (Waller, 1937; Lowrie, 1951; Ehrmann, 1959), asserting independence of adult institutions and norms (Waller, 1937; Lowrie, 1948, 1951), developing poise, sophistication, and status (Waller, 1937; Lowrie, 1948, 1951; Cuber, 1943; Delora, 1963), and simply enjoying dating either as an end in itself or as a means of avoiding loneliness (Burgess and Locke, 1940; Cuber, 1943; Lowrie, 1951) are readily discernible gratifications and rewards that appear regularly in social dating situations. The rewards most easily obtained through social dating surely appear in various contexts and in countless other configurations; as defined here, social dating merely is one of many systems through which they are obtained. However, the dating social system provides an excellent entré to the mysteries of the youth culture because maturation of sexual propensities and cultural emphases upon heterosexual associations are likely to make the rewards of social dating especially compelling for most youth.

The interpretation drawn from social learning theory and the analysis of social dating presented above suggest that adolescents should find strong motivation for the rewards of dating to be incompatible with dedication to high school responsibilities. The rewards for social dating are promptly and tangibly acquired from peers, and their consistent attainment requires investment of considerable time; the rewards for discharging high school obligations entail postponement of gratification, intangibleness, and consumption of vast amounts of time. The two systems apparently compete for youths' attention, and many youths seemingly forsake one for the other. Specifically, then, one might expect that orientation toward the incentives of social dating would be inversely related to better-than-average grades, at-

tention to homework, and vocational aspirations. Since school extracurricular activities are adult-sponsored, controlled, and reflect essentially adult-oriented rewards, one would also expect an inverse relationship to prevail between motivation for social dating and participation in extracurricular activities such as school clubs and councils. Further, the adolescents who seek the attractions of dating should be those who have a coterie of friends, inasmuch as peers are the primary administrators of youth-culture rewards.

METHOD

SUBJECTS

Subjects were 393 boys and 346 girls from the 10th, 11th, and 12th grades, drawn in fairly equal numbers from "college," "general," and "basic" curricular groupings of an urban public high school, which enrolled some 2,000 pupils who were widely diversified in terms of social class, academic skills, and vocational aspirations.

QUESTIONNAIRE

A comprehensive list of the attractions offered by social dating was compiled primarily from the descriptive interpretations of sociologists, the replies of several adolescents when queried as to why they dated, and from various articles in newspapers and teenage magazines. Analysis of the data from these sources led to the postulation of the following four incentive categories:

1. *Sexual Gratification* (SG). Dating offers sanctioned opportunities to make physical contact with members of the opposite sex, for example, to dance cheek to cheek, to hold hands at the theater, to stroll with an arm around the consort's waist, to caress, to neck in a parked car or in some secluded place, etc.

2. *Independence Assertion* (IA). Dating provides a context in which to achieve autonomy of adult authorities and of generally accepted standards of society. Drag racing on lonely streets, fudging one's age in order to gain admittance to an "adults-only" movie, and dating members of the opposite sex whose reputations are tarnished are among the possibilities. Dating may also be a vehicle for deviating from family religious practices, disdaining family political beliefs, ignoring parental strictures on curfew hours and sex-conduct rules, and being heedless of family propriety in crossing of social class lines, in smoking, and drinking.

3. *Status Seeking* (SS). Dating offers occasions for associating with prestigious members of the opposite sex. One may prefer consorts who are champions or leaders in debating, athletics, or dramatics. Dating may be a vehicle for entering an "in group." Dating partners may be sought who are excellent models for developing social etiquette, grace, and sophistication.

4. *Participative Eagerness* (PE). Rewards notwithstanding, dating sometimes is appealing for the sake of the activity it provides, for example, obtaining an identifiable reward may be of less concern than avoiding loneliness, boredom, anxiety, work-role responsibilities, and functions with parents or same-sex peers.

Each of the above categories provided the basis for an unidimensional Likert-type scale. Separate scales, employing similar, sex-appropriate items, were prepared for each sex. Each scale is comprised of items or statements that purport to describe a choice that a same-sex protagonist has made between two discernible alternatives: one, the attraction of social dating, and the other, either a desirable nondate goal or adherence to cultural norms, mores, parental strictures, etc. Each item recreates the situational dynamics of a double approach-avoidance conflict (Miller, 1944). The subjects (Ss) are asked to evaluate the protagonist's behavior in each item—whether or not they have ever been in the situation—on the basis of five degrees of agreement and disagreement. The summation of each S's responses to the items of the separate scales yields for each category a total score, which is interpreted as representing an indication of S's motivation for that particular category of social dating incentive (Selltiz, Jahoda, Deutsch, & Cook, 1962).

In constructing the items, an attempt was made to provide simple and realistic conflicts, to avoid response set by reversing the direction of the items, and to minimize arousal of self-consciousness and defensiveness. Also, efforts were aimed at writing median items in order to maximize variance and, very importantly, to provide a safeguard against including items that adolescents—and school officials who must sanction them before they can be administered—might regard as bizarre and/or irrelevant.

Initially, 15 items for each scale were randomized for presentation in a 60-item booklet and were pilot tested upon two high school populations of 220 and 406 Ss, respectively. After the second revision, each scale was reduced to 10 items. The final form of the questionnaire, therefore, comprised 40 items. An example of boys' *Sexual Gratification, Independence Assertion, Status Seeking,* and *Participative Eagerness, respectively,* is given below:

1. A boy and girl are parked in his car beside the lake. She is shy but they have necked before. He would like to neck again, but she hints about leaving. He tries to change her mind.

2. A couple have stayed out once or twice beyond the girl's curfew hour, as set by her parents. They are at an interesting party and they decide to stay longer since her parents don't enforce the curfew.

3. A boy is eager to make the "honor" service society, but he must know more of the top members. Being

TABLE 1

INTERCORRELATIONS AMONG SEXUAL-GRATIFICATION (SG),
INDEPENDENCE-ASSERTION (IA), STATUS-SEEKING (SS),
AND PARTICIPATIVE-EAGERNESS (PE) SCALES FOR
BOYS AND GIRLS

Scale	*Boys (N = 393)*				*Girls (N = 346)*			
	SG	*IA*	*SS*	*PE*	*SG*	*IA*	*SS*	*PE*
SG	.87[a]	.31	.16	.22	.81[a]	.32	.21	.31
IA		.76[a]	.16	.22		.78[a]	.24	.35
SS			.58[a]	.12			.64[a]	.40
PE				.70[a]				.66[a]

[a] Diagonal entries are Hoyt reliability values.

a member will make him a school leader, too. He dates an interesting and attractive girl who is a member, *just* so he will be invited to the society's parties—thus he will get to know the members and be asked to join the society.

4. A famous sports star is coming to town to make a public appearance for one night only. A boy is eager to see him. He knows his buddies are going and he plans to go with them. But then he finds out that a girl he has wanted to date would like him to ask her out to another show. He gets the date.

Table 1 shows the intercorrelations among the four scales for each sex. The dimensions under study were not expected to be entirely unrelated, and forcing the independence of the scales further seemed unwarranted; moreover, the existence and nature of the relationships are themselves worthy of scrutiny. The correlation between the Status Seeking and Participative Eagerness scales for girls is .40 whereas the corresponding comparison for boys is .12, and it may be that participation itself represents acquisition of status for girls. The differences among the reliability measures reported in the diagonals of Table 1 reflect in part differences among the items for each of the scales.

The SS items for example, are relatively more dissimilar than the SG items, and the phenomenon probably mirrors the real-life scene; for example, *S*s are less likely to diffuse the focus of sexual symbols and inclinations than of status symbols.

PERSONAL INFORMATION

The personal information items were grouped into three categories: *validity,* including such items as frequency of dating, age beginning dating, curfew hour, nights out per week, and access to car; *academic,* including grades received in school, hours spent studying, and academic degree aspirations; *peer relations,* including number of close friends, participation in high school activities, and membership in cliques. Each of the personal information items was followed with a list of appropriate responses, one of which was to be checked.

PROCEDURE

*S*s were administered the questionnaire and personal information items in their classrooms by one of four experimenters, none of whom was a teacher. *S*s were asked to raise their hands upon completing the questionnaire; then, as each *S* finished, he was handed the personal information items, and his questionnaire was collected. The two parts together consumed approximately 30 minutes. Only the most general instructions were given to *S*s. They were told that all the data would be the confidential property of the university researchers; moreover, *S*s were explicitly told not to put their names on the papers. However, in order that the two sets might be matched, they were asked to use their birth dates. Serious cooperation on the part of *S*s was stressed. All *S*s were cooperative, and most appeared to be highly interested in participating in the project.

STATISTICAL ANALYSIS

Major statistical evaluation in this study was accomplished through use of a two-way analysis of variance design. Unequal frequencies in the subclasses necessitated the use of a special procedure described by Scheffé (1959). Each of the four scales of the questionnaire was treated as a dependent variable, and the personal information items were employed as classificatory factors in a univariate analysis of variance. Three sets of analyses were computed for each sex. Frequency of dating was cross-partitioned with each of several validity measures; additionally, frequency of dating and grade in school, respectively, were cross-partitioned with each of the academic and peer-relations variables.

RESULTS AND DISCUSSION

The results presented in Tables 2 and 3 include only main effects since none of the interactions with the frequency-of-dating and grade-in-school classifications were significant. Further, a main effect for the grade-in-school classification, by 10th, 11th, and 12th grades, did not appear, and these data also are not reported.

The data offered in Table 2 pertain mainly to construct validation. One would expect, for example, that adolescents expressing relatively greater interest in the attractions represented by the scales would participate more frequently in the dating system and would be more likely to possess opportunities with which to pursue the rewards. The findings of Table 2 confirm the expectation in respect to frequency of dating. Mean scores on the scales increase as dating becomes more active. The main effect is significant for boys on the four scales, that is, SG ($p < .001$), IA ($p < .001$), SS ($p < .05$), and PE ($p < .001$); for girls on the SG ($p < .001$) and IA ($p < .001$) scales. It is noteworthy that the Status-Seeking and Participative-Eagerness scales yielded nonsignificant main effects for adolescent girls on the frequency-of-dating classification. Girls who actively date and girls who seldom date appear either equally eager or equally disinclined to pursue the rewards of the dating system. The image of the present population of adolescent girls as being reluctant to engage in dating is palpably incongruent with the facts of contemporary life, and it would seem that the appropriate interpretation is that all girls, whether they date frequently, are eager to participate in the system and to seek the peer status it proffers.

The findings presented in Table 2 offer scant support for the notion that opportunity to acquire the attractions of dating is associated with enhanced interest in them. Possession of freedom to participate in the dating system, however, appears to exert a differential effect upon the two sexes. In the instance of every classificatory variable shown in Table 2, the main effect on the Independence-Assertion scale is significant. Inspection of the means shows that given more or less unrestrained liberty, boys rather than girls seem more likely to assert their individuality in the

TABLE 2

MEAN SCORES AND RESULTS OF ANALYSES OF VARIANCE FOR SEXUAL GRATIFICATION (SG), INDEPENDENCE ASSERTION (IA), STATUS SEEKING (SS), AND PARTICIPATIVE EAGERNESS (PE) IN TERMS OF FREQUENCY OF DATING AND OTHER ASPECTS OF SOCIAL DATING

Antecedent	Boys					Girls				
	N	SG	IA	SS	PE	N	SG	IA	SS	PE
Frequency of dating										
No dates yet	81	27.4	24.7	24.9	27.9	48	25.4	25.5	23.7	25.3
1 per wk.	123	32.0	29.0	26.1	29.1	96	28.0	25.8	23.9	27.3
1 per mo.	106	34.2	31.0	27.2	31.0	97	29.8	27.0	23.6	26.4
3 + per wk.	83	36.7	32.5	27.0	32.4	105	32.8	29.7	24.1	27.3
F ratio		27.46***	24.30***	3.50*	10.68***		14.11***	5.86***	ns	ns
Age dating began										
13 or younger	85	35.9	32.5	28.1	32.4	45	31.6	28.4	23.1	26.3
14	99	34.2	31.3	26.4	30.4	106	30.2	28.2	24.1	27.9
15	74	34.0	29.8	26.6	30.2	101	30.2	27.0	23.3	26.5
16 or older	54	32.4	28.1	25.9	30.0	46	29.8	26.6	23.6	26.7
F ratio		ns	4.95**	ns	ns		ns	ns	ns	ns
Curfew										
12 P.M.	119	33.8	29.5	27.1	30.5	190	30.0	27.1	23.8	27.0
2 A.M.	72	35.3	31.3	25.6	30.6	50	32.3	29.7	23.0	27.3
Anytime	121	34.4	32.8	27.1	31.4	58	29.4	27.1	23.3	26.7
F ratio		ns	5.20**	ns	ns		ns	3.50*	ns	ns
Nights allowed out per wk.										
1	60	31.7	27.7	26.3	28.9	69	30.9	27.7	25.4	28.3
2–3	177	34.6	31.2	27.1	30.8	206	30.9	28.0	23.6	27.1
4 or more	75	36.2	33.2	27.1	32.5	23	32.4	27.2	22.7	30.2
F ratio		4.92**	9.58***	ns	4.46*		ns	ns	ns	ns
Car availability										
Always	130	35.1	32.4	26.7	30.5	162	30.4	27.7	23.1	27.2
Sometimes	119	34.0	30.4	26.7	31.3	92	30.5	27.7	24.4	26.6
Seldom/never	63	32.9	28.0	26.9	30.8	44	29.2	26.3	23.7	26.4
F ratio		ns	11.04***	ns	ns		ns	ns	ns	ns

* $p < .05$.
** $p < .01$.
*** $p < .001$.

TABLE 3

MEAN SCORES AND RESULTS OF ANALYSES OF VARIANCE FOR SEXUAL GRATIFICATION (SG),
INDEPENDENCE ASSERTION (IA), STATUS SEEKING (SS), AND PARTICIPATIVE EAGERNESS (PE)
IN TERMS OF ACADEMIC AND PEER-RELATIONS VARIABLES

Antecedent	Boys					Girls				
	N	SG	IA	SS	PE	N	SG	IA	SS	PE
I. Academic variables										
Grade-point average										
A	77	31.4	27.2	25.4	29.1	116	27.3	25.3	23.5	26.1
B	99	31.8	28.7	25.9	28.1	91	30.9	27.1	23.2	27.0
C	147	32.9	29.7	26.5	30.9	102	31.3	29.1	24.1	27.6
D	70	34.6	32.1	28.2	32.2	37	29.9	28.1	24.8	26.2
F ratio		2.62*	6.82*	4.16**	5.54***		3.61*	3.46*	ns	ns
Hrs. of study at home per wk.										
3–4	154	34.5	31.4	26.8	32.6	74	32.5	30.4	24.1	28.2
4–5	141	31.7	28.9	25.9	28.9	132	29.3	27.3	23.9	26.8
7+	98	30.3	26.5	25.3	28.5	140	28.5	25.6	23.4	26.1
F ratio		10.84***	16.88***	ns	18.54***		8.46***	13.38***	ns	3.38***
Aspirations										
High school degree	92	33.5	30.7	27.2	31.4	76	32.8	29.1	22.8	28.3
Vocational school	89	32.8	30.1	26.7	31.3	95	30.2	28.3	24.0	27.5
College	212	32.0	28.9	25.9	29.2	175	28.1	25.8	24.0	25.8
F ratio		ns	3.09*	ns	2.99*		10.50***	6.64**	ns	5.27**
II. Peer-relations variables										
Extracurricular participation										
0	135	32.8	30.2	27.2	31.7	68	29.5	28.4	22.5	26.7
2–3 per mo.	138	32.5	29.2	26.3	30.1	173	30.3	27.8	23.9	27.6
3 + per wk.	120	32.4	28.6	25.3	28.6	95	29.2	25.8	24.2	26.2
F ratio		ns	ns	4.10*	8.38**		ns	3.23*	ns	ns
No. friends										
0	51	29.6	26.1	25.2	28.9	64	29.1	27.0	23.6	26.2
1–2	136	32.2	29.1	25.6	29.7	91	30.4	28.7	24.7	27.4
3–4	108	32.0	28.9	26.2	29.8	97	29.5	26.7	23.8	26.4
5+	98	35.0	31.6	28.3	31.7	94	29.2	26.9	23.1	26.4
F ratio		6.91***	9.35***	5.88***	3.41*		ns	ns	ns	ns
Clique membership										
yes	151	34.0	30.7	27.8	31.1	159	29.9	27.1	23.9	27.0
no	55	32.1	28.9	25.7	30.6	32	27.6	26.0	21.2	26.0
F ratio		ns	ns	4.97*	ns		4.32*	ns	10.83***	ns

* $p < .05$. ** $p < .01$. *** $p < .001$.

context of the dating system. It appears also that boys' zeal for participating in dating and for seeking physical gratifications are associated with the number of evenings they are allowed out per week, but not by whether they enjoy an early or late curfew or by whether they have access to a car. Of what avail, after all, are a late curfew and a car if opportunities to capitalize upon these advantages are highly limited? On the whole, girls who have relatively greater autonomy and opportunity would also be expected to be especially interested in the attractions of dating since, by and large, the inducements are there for the taking. As in the instance of frequency of dating, however, impositions and restrictions notwithstanding, girls appear equally zealous to acquire the rewards of the dating system.

The belief that youths' enthusiasm for the incentives of social dating would be associated inversely with academic performance is supported by the data presented in Table 3, Part I. The means based upon grade-point average show that high scores on the dating scales tend to be associated with low grades. The main effect is significant for boys on each of the four scales (SG, $p < .05$; IA, $p < .05$; SS, $p < .01$; PE, $p < .001$), and for girls on the SG ($p < .05$) and IA ($p < .05$) scales. Two measures associated with academic performance corroborate the interpretation. The data of Table 3, Part I, also show that the means of the dating scales that showed significant main effects decreased for both sexes as study time and aspirations increased.

The data presented in Table 3, Part II, suggest, as expected, that an inverse relationship exists between participating in adult-sponsored extracurricular activities and certain of the social dating attractions. For the extracurricular-participation classification, involving school clubs and councils, significant main effects appeared for

boys on the SS ($p < .05$) and PE ($p < .001$) scales, and for girls, on the IA ($p < .05$) scale. Also, the expectation that adolescents' interests in dating may be associated with peer interaction, on the assumption that peers are the primary administrators of youth-culture rewards, was largely confirmed. On the number-of-friends classification, the analyses of variance yielded a significant main effect for boys on each of the four scales (SG, $p < .001$; IA, $p < .001$; SS, $p < .001$; PE, $p < .05$). The mean scores for each scale increased with the possession of a greater number of friends. Tests for the number-of-friends measure were nonsignificant for girls. However, when the girls who reported having three or more friends are separated in terms of whether or not they share secrets with one another, following Hollingshead's (1949) analysis of clique behavior, the expectation receives some support. The main effects are significant for the SG ($p < .05$) and SS ($p < .001$) scales, and the discrepancies between the means indicate that the girls with close-knit peer relations scored higher on the scales. This comparison holds only for boys on the SS scale ($p < .05$).

To the extent that the variables employed in the present study discriminate among adolescents in terms of their eagerness to obtain the rewards of the social dating system, it appears that the interpretation drawn from social learning theory is affirmed. Although negative, punitive, frustrating aspects of school life may propel adolescents away from campus, the data of the present investigation suggest that, also, there may exist inducements that entice them away. Moreover, it appears that the various attractions of social dating are equally influential across the 10th, 11th, and 12th grades. On the whole, poor academic performance is consistently related to interest in sexual gratification and in asserting independence. Nearly every adolescent is imbued with the cultural imperative to find a mate, and it seems that adolescents who have been sidetracked from fulfilling school responsibilities find solace in sexual gratifications and refractoriness, the rewards for which are peer-culture administered.

Yet, for boys at least, peer relations appear to exert less influence upon motivation for the physical and libertarian aspects of dating than upon the status-seeking and participative features. Boys who are nonparticipants in extracurricular activities seem especially eager to participate in dating and to use the dating system for seeking status. Sex differences also emerge in respect to peer relations. Having friends *per se* is an important factor in boys' motivation for all the resources of dating whereas having close, intimate friends appears to be of critical concern to girls.

One cannot discern from the data of the present study whether adolescents seek the attractions of social dating because they find high school responsibilities excessively difficult to fulfill or whether they neglect them because they find the rewards of dating especially compelling; yet one general point clearly emerges: the adolescent who finds school nonmotivating is likely to find youth-culture functions, such as social dating, highly alluring. Thus, it seems that many underachieving adolescents who must change their attitudes toward school must also learn to turn away from youth-culture fascinations.

REFERENCES

ALLPORT, G. W. Values and our youth. *Teachers College Record*, 1961, 63, 211–219.

BANDURA, A., & WALTERS, R. H. *Social learning and personality development.* New York: Holt, 1963.

BANDURA, A. The stormy decade: Fact or Fiction? *Psychology in the Schools*, 1964, 1, 224–231.

BERKOWITZ, L. *Aggression: A social psychological analysis.* New York: McGraw-Hill, 1962.

BLOS, P. *On adolescence.* New York: Free Press of Glencoe, 1962.

BURGESS, E. W., & LOCKE, H. J. *The Family.* New York: American Book Co., 1940.

COLEMAN, J. S. *The Adolescent Society.* New York: Free Press, 1961.

CUBER, J. F. Changing courtship and marriage customs. *Ann. Amer. Acad. pol. & soc. Sci.*, 1943, 229, 30–38.

DELORA, J. Social systems of dating on a college campus. *Marriage fam. Living*, 1963, 25, 81–84.

EHRMANN, W. W. *Premarital dating behavior.* New York: Holt, 1959.

ELDER, G. H. Achievement orientations and career patterns of rural youth. *Sociology of Education*, 1963, 37, 29–58.

ELKIN, F., & WESTLEY, W. A. The myth of adolescent culture. *American Sociological Review*, 1955, 20, 680–684.

ERIKSON, E. H. Youth: fidelity and diversity. *Daedalus*, 1962, 91, 5–27.

HOLLINGSHEAD, A. B. *Elmtown's youth.* New York: Wiley, 1949.

HURLOCK, ELIZABETH B. *Adolescent development.* New York: McGraw-Hill, 1955.

JACKSON, P. W., & STRATTNER, NINA. Meaningful learning and retention: Noncognitive variables. *Review of Educational Research*, 1964, 34, 513–529.

KENISTON, K. Social change and youth in America. *Daedalus*, 1962, 91, 145–171.

LOWRIE, S. H. Dating: A neglected field of study. *Marriage fam. Living*, 1948, 10, 90–91.

LOWRIE, S. H. Dating theories and students' responses. *Amer. sociol. Rev.*, 1951, 10, 334–340.

MILLER, M. E. Experimental studies of conflict. In J. McV. Hunt (Ed.), *Personality and the Behavioral Disorders*, Vol. I. New York: Ronald Press, 1944.

Parsons, T. Age and sex in the social structure of the United States. *Amer. sociol. Rev.*, 1942, 7, 604–616.

Parsons, T. Psychoanalysis and the social structure. *Psychoanalytic Quarterly*, 1950, 19, 371–384.

Parsons, T. Youth in the context of American society. *Daedalus*, 1962, 91, 97–123.

Pearson, G. H. J. *Adolescence and the conflict of generations*. New York: Norton, 1958.

Scheffe, H. *The analysis of variance*. New York: Wiley, 1959.

Selltiz, Claire, Johoda, Marie, Deutsch, M., & Cook, S. W. *Research methods in social relations.* New York: Holt, 1962.

Smith, E. A. *American youth culture: Group life in a teenage society*. New York: Free Press of Glencoe, 1962.

Waller, W. The rating-dating complex. *Amer. J. Sociol.*, 1937, 2, 727–734.

Wilfert, O. Youth-adult relationships: the social milieu. *Int. J. adult youth Educ.*, 1963, 15, 43–49.

GROUP COHESIVENESS AND INDIVIDUAL LEARNING

Albert J. Lott / Bernice E. Lott

In an attempt to coordinate small-group behavior to more general behavior principles, the concept of cohesiveness has been formulated in terms of reinforcement

From: Journal of Educational Psychology, *1966, 57, 61–73. Copyright © 1966 by the American Psychological Association, and reproduced by permission of the authors and APA.*

learning theory. The present approach assumes that the primary source of a group's attractiveness to its members is the attractiveness of fellow members. The concept of attitude is substituted for that of attraction because the former has a precise and particular meaning within reinforcement learning theory (an anticipatory response with cue and drive properties—Doob, 1947), and cohesiveness is then defined as that group property which is inferred from the number and strength of mutual positive attitudes among the members (Lott, 1961).

The authors have previously tested hypotheses regarding antecedents of cohesiveness (James & Lott, 1964; Lott & Lott, 1960). Theoretically derived predictions regarding the consequences of cohesiveness also follow from placement of the concept within a Hullian framework. In an earlier investigation, degree of group cohesiveness was shown to be positively related to both intragroup level of communication and the tendency of members to conform to a dominant group opinion (Lott & Lott, 1961). The present study was designed to test another predicted consequence of variations in cohesiveness. Since attitudes are presumed to have drive value, the greater the degree of intermember liking (group cohesiveness), the higher should be the general drive level in individual members. Since learning is ordinarily a positive function of drive, the authors predict that better individual learning will take place in high- than in low-cohesive groups (other things being equal), or that individuals who are in the presence of highly liked others will perform better on learning tasks than individuals who are in the presence of less-liked others.

Little previous research has been concerned with learning as a function of interpersonal attraction per se. Perkins (1950) and Rehage (1951) investigated the consequences of different classroom "climates" for learning or problem solving, but in these studies manipulation of leadership (teaching) techniques constituted the independent variable. More relevant to the present study is the finding by Shaw and Shaw (1962) that early spelling scores were positively correlated with the degree of liking among members of second-grade study groups.[1]

In the present study we compared high- and low-cohesive groups of fourth- and fifth-grade children of similar tested general intelligence on a verbal learning task, retention, relearning, and a second verbal learning task. The authors' expectation that children in high-cohesive groups will learn better and retain more than children in low-cohesive groups presupposes that the children being compared are similar in general learning ability, and it was assumed that the latter is validly reflected by IQ scores. Specifically, the authors predicted that among children who are similar in tested intelligence, either high or low, those who are in small groups with other children whom they like a great deal will learn and retain new material better than those who are with children they like less.

Since it was assumed that objects or persons which evoke positive attitudes can serve as secondary reinforcers (Hull, 1952; Lott & Lott, 1961), that is, can strengthen behavior when they are presented contingent upon that behavior, it was necessary to eliminate as far as possible chances of this occurring. Such direct intermember reinforcement would confound the effects of increased drive based on the

[1] A number of recent investigations have tested hypotheses which relate verbal conditioning to the relationship between *S* and *E,* or simply to the attractiveness of *E* (e.g., Binder, McConnell, & Sjoholm, 1957; Reece & Whitman, 1962; Sapolsky, 1960). Although these studies are theoretically relevant to the present hypothesis, discussion of them will be omitted since the focus here is on learning within a group context where the group is composed of individuals who are mutually attracted to one another to a high or low degree.

mere presence of liked group members. If the group members were permitted to freely interact, then the children in high-cohesive groups could reinforce a variety of one another's behaviors, related or unrelated to the learning tasks. Consequently, the experimental situations were carefully planned to control and channel member interaction. Both verbal and nonverbal communication among members of all groups was strictly structured and confined to task essentials.

METHOD

Subjects

Four elementary schools, three predominantly white and one entirely Negro in student body, cooperated in this investigation. Within each school, subjects (*S*s) were obtained from one fourth- and one fifth-grade class. For Learning Task I (LTI) a total of 206 children (97 boys, 109 girls) was selected on the basis of sociometric and IQ-score considerations to participate in three- or four-person same-sex groups.

One week after LTI, the same *S*s (reduced in number to 155; 71 boys, 84 girls) were tested, within the same small groups, on Retention (RET), Relearning (REL), and Learning Task II (LTII). *S* losses are accounted for by absences: In the case of three-person groups, the absence of one child climinated the other two; if one child was absent from a four-person group, however, the group simply became a three-person group for the remaining tasks.

Procedure

Experimental Formation of Groups. Two days prior to presentation of LTI, all members of each of the eight participating classes were given a sociometric test (Socio I) by their regular teacher. This consisted of a Friendship Book in which each child rated all other same-sex children in his class on the following scale:

——I like him very, very much.
——I like him. He's alright, but I like some other boys better.
——Sometimes I like him a little bit and sometimes I don't like him.
——Most of the time I don't like him.
——I never liked him and don't think I ever will.

Each teacher employed the same simple instructions and, with the aid of a large cardboard model of a Friendship Book page, demonstrated how to place an X in front of the one sentence which best described how an *S* felt about the boy (or girl) whose name appeared at the top of the page. These ratings were then converted to numbers ranging from 5 ("I like him very, very much.") to 1.

High-cohesive (HiCo) and low-cohesive (LoCo) same-sex groups of three or four children were formed on the basis of similar mutual ratings. A single score, indicating the cohesiveness level of a group (its group-cohesiveness index—GCI), was calculated by the formula $\Sigma X / N (N-1)$, where X = a rating, and N = the number of group members who rated each other. This formula takes into account the rating of each group member by every other member and is, thus, an operational measure of our conceptual definition of cohesiveness (Lott & Lott, 1961). Thirty-five HiCo groups were formed, ranging in GCI from 5.0–4.2 (M = 4.59), and 27 LoCo groups were formed, ranging in GCI from 3.3–2.2 (M = 2.91). Of the total of 62 groups, 37 had 3 members and 25 had 4.

In addition to the sociometric ratings made and received, *S*s' IQ scores were also taken into account in placing them in groups. The *California Short-Form Test of Mental Maturity, Ele-*

TABLE 1

Summary of Experimental Conditions

Condition	No. groups	Mean GCI	Total No. Ss	Mean IQ
Learning Task I				
HiI-HiCo	18	4.63	64	120.98
HiI-LoCo	12	2.97	39	120.46
LoI-HiCo	17	4.53	54	99.35
LoI-LoCo	15	2.86	49	96.89
Total	62		206	
Retention, Relearning, and Learning Task II				
HiI-HiCo	14	4.62	47	121.21
HiI-LoCo	10	2.93	28	120.96
LoI-HiCo	15	4.53	47	99.32
LoI-LoCo	10	2.91	33	98.47
Total	49		155	

mentary Form, 1957 (CTMM) had been administered several weeks prior to Socio I. A child with a total IQ score of 116 or above was eligible for placement only in a high-IQ (HiI) group; a child with a score of 100 or below was eligible for placement only in a low-IQ (LoI) group. Those with scores between 115 and 101 could be placed in either HiI or LoI groups, but the authors tried to avoid putting an *S* into a LoI group if his IQ score was above 108 and putting an *S* into a HiI group if his score was below 108. It must be kept in mind that *S*s had to be placed in groups with other children of a compatible IQ level as well as with other children whom they rated highly and were highly rated by (HiCo groups), or whom they rated poorly and were poorly rated by (LoCo groups).

Table 1 describes the independent-variable conditions, HiI-HiCo, HiI-LoCo, LoI-HiCo, and LoI-LoCo groups in terms of number of groups, mean cohesiveness index, total number of *S*s, and mean individual IQ score. Since some *S*s (and groups) were present for LTI but absent for the subsequent tasks (RET, REL, and LTII), the independent-vari-

able conditions are also described for the latter. It is clear from Table 1 that *S* losses produced only minor changes in average cohesiveness and IQ-score characteristics.

Learning Task I. The experimenter (*E*), when introduced by the classroom teacher, explained that he wanted to find out how easily children can learn words in a foreign language. The previously formed small groups were then called to the experimental room in a random, predetermined order and given identical task instructions.

LTI consisted of learning Spanish equivalents of English words. *S*s first worked as a group in arranging and assembling the materials: 12 6¼ × 5⅛ inch plastic-covered cards, each containing a four-word Spanish sentence (e.g., *"Este es un vaso."*) and an appropriate india-ink illustration, and 12 plastic-covered 5 × 2 inch cards, each containing a four-word English sentence, equivalent to one of the Spanish sentences (e.g., "This is a glass."). Each English card could be fitted onto a Spanish card by sliding it under a paper clip on top of the latter. *S*s were told that they would each receive three or four cards (depending upon the group size) with a picture and Spanish sentence on each, and were instructed as follows:

In the center of your table I will place a stack of smaller cards. These will not have pictures on them. Instead, each will have just an English sentence on it. . . .

Your job will be to match up each English card. . .with one of the Spanish picture cards. . . . You can do the matching job best if each one of you, in order, will turn up an English card on the top of the stack, read the sentence out loud, and then see who has the Spanish picture card that goes with it. . . . [Whoever] has the right Spanish picture card gets the matching English card [and]. . .can then put the two cards together. . . .

When you have matched each Spanish picture card with the correct English one, let me know. . . .

The amount of time it took each group to assemble the materials was recorded by an assistant.

Following the group matching procedure, *S*s were told that they would be tested on their knowledge of the English meanings of Spanish words after a period of studying the materials individually. They were instructed to:

Study your own [cards]. . .first. When Miss Briscoe rings this bell, pass your pairs to the. . .right. Study [the new cards you've received]. . . until the bell rings again. Then pass your cards again to the. . .right. We'll keep doing this until you've all had a chance to study all the. . .cards twice. . . . Study quietly. . . .

The interval between bells was either 1½ or 2 minutes, depending upon whether there were four or three *S*s in the group (and thus, upon whether each S had three or four cards).

After 12 minutes of study the cards were collected, and a mimeographed answer sheet with 15 spaces on it was distributed to each *S*. Each Spanish test word was presented once, one at a time on a printed card held in front of *S*s for 15 seconds. *S*s were told to write the English meaning or to draw a line in the appropriate space before going on to the next test word.

Retention and Relearning. One week after LTI, *E* reported to the class that they had done well on the previous learning task, and he once more solicited cooperation for additional language learning. The same groups were again called to the experimental room in a predetermined random order where they were given instructions for a retention test on 10 of the 15 Spanish words on which they had been tested in LTI. On the retention test each Spanish test word was exposed on a card to the group for 10 seconds; *E* then turned the card over to expose the English equivalent for approximately 3 seconds, saying the English word aloud as he flipped over the card.

After the RET trial, *S*s were given three relearning trials. The same words were presented by the same technique, but in a new randomly determined order on each trial. *S*s were instructed to stop if they got all 10 words correct on any trial and to sit with the group while the others went on. A new answer booklet was distributed prior to each trial.

Learning Task II. Immediately after the last REL trial, *S*s were introduced to another task, the learning of 10 new Spanish nouns and their English equivalents (e.g., *"silla"*-"chair"). Each *S* was given his own list of the 10 Spanish-English pairs, while the group as a whole received a stack of 10 cards, each with one of the Spanish words on it. *E* suggested the following study procedure:

Starting with you. . .why don't you turn over the first card when I say "Begin." Place it on the table so that everyone can see it and all of you try to find on your list what the Spanish word means in English. Call out the correct English answer as soon as you know it. Then take turns turning up a Spanish card from the center pile. After a few minutes I'll. . . give you the same kind of test that I just gave you on the old words.

After Ss had gone through the stack of cards four times, E gave four trials on the new words, using the same procedure as that followed previously for RET and REL.

Sociometric Test II. Approximately 2 weeks after RET, REL, and LTII, a second sociometric test (Socio II) was given in each class by the regular teacher, following the same procedure as that described for Socio I.

RESULTS

LEARNING TASK SCORES

The mean scores earned under the four different experimental conditions were calculated for each learning task, separately for each trial. These results are presented in Figure 1. Figures 2 and 3 show mean scores made by high-IQ and low-IQ Ss, respectively, under HiCo and LoCo conditions, separately for each sex.[2] On the LTI test, the maximum possible score was 15 correct words; the maximum score on all subsequent tests was 10. (In REL and LTII, an S who scored 10 on any trial was given the same score on any remaining trials.)

The IQ variable, high versus low, made a significant difference on every learning test, except for the last trial of LTII, with HiI Ss scoring reliably higher than LoI Ss in every case. The results of

[2] Preliminary analyses indicated that the number of persons in a group, three or four, had no reliable effect on the learning-task scores so data from both types of groups were combined.

median test analyses using two-tailed probabilities (Siegel, 1956) are as follows; LTI, $\chi^2 = 19.93$, $p < .001$; RET, $\chi^2 = 7.17$, $p < .01$; REL, Trial 1, $\chi^2 = 10.95$, $p < .001$; REL, Trial 2, $\chi^2 = 9.06$, $p < .01$; REL, Trial 3, $\chi^2 = 4.92$, $p < .05$; LTII, Trial 1, $\chi^2 = 10.96$, $p < .001$; LTII, Trial 2, $\chi^2 = 5.63$, $p < .02$; LTII, Trial 3, $\chi^2 = 5.50$, $p < .02$; LTII, Trial 4, $\chi^2 = 3.72$, $p < .10$. Since these findings justify separate treatment of high- and low-IQ Ss, an analysis of variance for frequency data (Wilson, 1956) was performed separately for HiI and LoI Ss, for each set of learning scores, to test the effects of cohesiveness and sex. This analysis compares conditions in terms of the number of individuals within each who scored at or above the median and the number who scored below the median. The results of these analyses are given in Table 2.

Examination of Figure 1 will show that in the HiI condition HiCo Ss did better than LoCo Ss, as was predicted, in every case except for LTII, Trial 1. The relationship between learning-task scores made by HiI Ss and cohesiveness is statistically reliable on RET, and on the first two REL trials, and is close to the standard level of significance on the third REL trial, and on the third LTII trial (see Table 2).

The analyses of variance summarized in Table 2 indicate that among HiI Ss, sex is not reliably associated with the scores (except on LTII, Trial 2, on which the girls did significantly better), and there is little indication of significant cohesiveness-sex interactions. What is not revealed in Table 2, however, but can be clearly seen by inspecting Figure 2, is that the differences in learning between HiCo and LoCo high-IQ Ss are contributed to primarily by the girls. Separate median tests were performed for girls and boys to evaluate

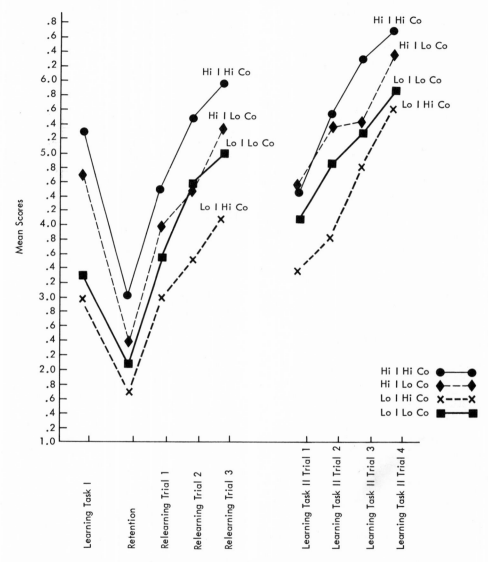

Figure 1. The experimental conditions (total sample) compared on the learning tasks.

the significance of HiCo-LoCo differences on each learning test. For the high-IQ girls, a significant χ^2 (i.e., $p < .05$) was obtained, indicating a reliable relationship between cohesiveness and learning,

on six of the nine measures; LTI ($\chi^2 = 5.97$); RET ($\chi^2 = 5.67$); REL, Trial 1 ($\chi^2 = 3.92$); REL, Trial 2 ($\chi^2 = 5.24$); LTII, Trial 3 ($\chi^2 = 5.67$); and LTII, Trial 4 ($\chi^2 = 5.67$). In contrast, among

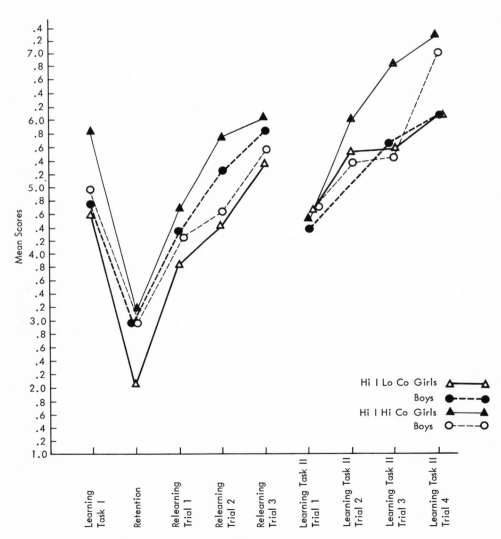

Figure 2. HiI Ss compared, by cohesiveness condition and sex, on the learning tasks.

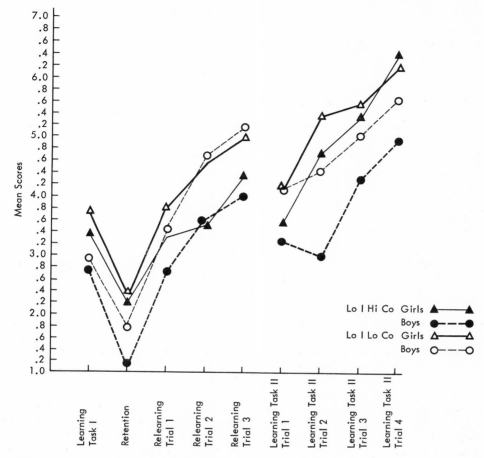

Figure 3. LoI *S*s compared, by cohesiveness condition and sex, on the learning tasks.

the high-IQ boys, conditions of high and low cohesiveness made no reliable difference on any learning measure.[3]

[3] We may look at the same data in another way. On every one of the nine learning measures, HiI-HiCo girls did better, on the average, than HiI-LoCo girls. Using the sign test (Siegel, 1956), we find that the probability that such results are due to chance is .004 (two tailed). This test is not strictly applicable since measures are all taken on the same *S*s, but it is suggestive. For the HiI boys, on the other hand, average HiCo scores exceeded LoCo scores on

Turning now to the low-IQ *S*s, we find a strikingly different pattern of results. It can be seen in Figure 1 that on every one of the learning-task measures the average score of LoCo *S*s is greater than the average score of HiCo *S*s, in direct opposition to the authors' prediction and to the results obtained on HiI *S*s. The relationship, however, between cohesive-

only five out of nine measures; the two-tailed probability that this is a chance phenomenon is 1.00.

TABLE 2

SUMMARY OF ANALYSES OF VARIANCE (FOR FREQUENCY DATA) ON LEARNING-TASK SCORES

Task	HiI Ss χ^2 for source of variance[a]			LoI Ss χ^2 for source of variance[a]		
	Cohesiveness	Sex	Interaction	Cohesiveness	Sex	Interaction
LTI	2.47	2.57	3.34*	—	—	—
RET	4.01**	—	—	2.79*	6.13**	—
REL, Trial 1	5.28**	—	—	1.99	—	—
REL, Trial 2	5.07**	—	—	3.45*	—	—
REL, Trial 3	3.33*	—	—	—	—	—
LTII, Trial 1	—	—	—	3.12*	—	—
LTII, Trial 2	2.11	4.25**	1.03	3.09*	2.55	3.83*
LTII, Trial 3	3.54*	—	—	—	—	—
LTII, Trial 4	.43	1.66	2.85*	1.30	2.46	2.25

Note.—For HiI Ss, $N = 103$ on LTI, 75 on subsequent tasks; for LoI Ss, $N = 103$ on LTI, 80 on subsequent tasks.
a $df = 1$ in every case. If there was no possibility of obtaining a significant χ^2 (determined by the magnitude of the total χ^2), further analyses were not performed. This was the case wherever χ^2 figures are not given in the table.
* $p < .10 > .05$.
** $p < .05$.

ness and the learning measures is not reliable ($p > .05$), as is indicated in Table 2, although significance is approached on RET, REL Trial 2, and LTII Trials 1 and 2.

Separate analyses were performed on the scores made by boys and girls. Among the LoI girls, the average LoCo score exceeds the average HiCo score in every case except for the last trial of LTII, but none of these cohesiveness-score relationships is statistically reliable (median tests). On REL Trial 2, a χ^2 of 2.92 was obtained, which approaches significance ($p < .10 > .05$).[4] For the LoI boys, the average LoCo score is greater than the average HiCo score in every case.[5] Median test analyses of the data on each learning test yielded a

[4] Using the sign test, it is found that a pattern of eight results out of nine in one direction (LoCo > HiCo) has a two-tailed chance probability of .04.
[5] The probability is .004 that nine out of nine results in one direction is a chance phenomenon (sign test).

χ^2 of 3.36 ($p < .10 > .05$) on RET, and a χ^2 of 6.87 ($p < .01$) on LTII Trial 2. All other chi-squares are nonsignificant.

TIME MEASURE

On LTI a record was kept of the time that it took for each group of children to match the Spanish sentences to their English equivalents. This was a group activity, preliminary to individual study.

The results are shown in Table 3. Differences between means were evaluated with the t test (McNemar, 1949). HiCo groups were found to have worked significantly faster than LoCo groups within the total HiI sample, that is, boy and girl groups considered together, and within the HiI sample of girls. The difference between HiCo and LoCo groups of HiI boys was in the same direction, but not statistically reliable. For the LoI groups, the results are quite different; there are no reliable differences between HiCo and LoCo groups within the total sample, or for girls or

TABLE 3

TIME TAKEN BY GROUPS TO MATCH SPANISH TO
ENGLISH SENTENCES IN LEARNING TASK I

Condition	No. groups	Mean time (in sec.)	s	t
Total sample				
HiI-HiCo	18	112.78	19.1	
HiI-LoCo	12	147.33	51.9	2.20*
LoI-HiCo	17	135.53	48.5	
LoI-LoCo	15	127.00	26.3	—
Girls				
HiI-HiCo	10	111.00	19.3	
HiI-LoCo	8	134.12	27.1	2.12*
LoI-HiCo	8	130.88	66.3	
LoI-LoCo	8	117.88	16.6	—
Boys				
HiI-HiCo	8	115.00	19.8	
HiI-LoCo	4	173.75	82.3	1.41
LoI-HiCo	9	139.67	28.8	
LoI-LoCo	7	137.43	32.5	—

* $p < .05$ (two-tailed test).

TABLE 4

CHANGES IN AVERAGE RATINGS OF OTHER GROUP MEMBERS
FOLLOWING INTERACTION IN THE LEARNING TASKS

Condition	No. Ss	Mean ratings on Socio I	Mean ratings on Socio II	M_d	s_d	t
Girls						
HiI-HiCo	30	4.76	4.41	−.36	.08	−4.50***
HiI-LoCo	16	2.97	4.00	1.03	.23	4.48***
LoI-HiCo	21	4.53	4.58	.05	.11	.45
LoI-LoCo	15	2.95	3.74	.79	.29	2.72**
Boys						
HiI-HiCo	18	4.38	4.56	.18	.14	1.29
HiI-LoCo	15	2.84	3.35	.51	.22	2.32**
LoI-HiCo	22	4.53	4.50	−.03	.08	−.38
LoI-LoCo	17	2.95	3.40	.45	.22	2.05*

* $p < .10 > .05$ (two-tailed test).
** $p < .05$ (two-tailed test).
*** $p < .001$ (two-tailed test).

boys considered separately. In each case, moreover, the LoCo groups were slightly faster, on the average, than the HiCo groups, in reverse of the findings for the HiI groups.

It is of considerable interest that on this time measure, as one would expect, the HiI groups were faster than the LoI groups, on the average, under HiCo conditions, but under LoCo conditions, LoI groups were faster than HiI groups. In neither case is the difference between the

IQ conditions statistically reliable ($t =$ 1.80, $df = 33$; $t = 1.23$, $df = 25$—for HiCo and LoCo, respectively), but under the HiCo condition the two-tailed probability approaches significance ($p < .10 >$ .05).

Changes in Sociometric Ratings

By comparing Ss' ratings of their fellow group members on Socio II (subsequent to group interaction) with ratings on Socio I it could be determined whether any changes were related to the experimental conditions.

The data shown in Table 4 are taken from those Ss who were present in their groups for RET, REL, and LTII and who were also present when Socio II was given. It can be seen that the children in LoCo groups rated fellow group members significantly more favorably after their group experience than before; this is true of HiI girls and boys, as well as LoI girls and boys. Children who had been in HiCo groups, on the other hand, tended not to change their ratings of one another (which were initially high), except in the case of HiI girls who rated each other on Socio II significantly lower than they had on Socio I. Although the average decrease is small, it is highly reliable.

DISCUSSION

The results on all the learning tests, considered together, indicate that high-IQ children who were in high-cohesive groups did generally better than high-IQ children who were in low-cohesive groups. For low-IQ children, however, cohesiveness, or degree of interpersonal attraction among group members, made no difference, although there was a tendency for such children to do slightly better in low-cohesive than in high-cohesive groups. The

findings for high-IQ children thus confirm our hypothesis, while those for low-IQ children do not and suggest an opposite trend. A similar phenomenon was reported by Calvin, Hoffman, and Harden (1957). Trends in three experiments indicated that for Ss of high intelligence, group problem solving is better in a permissive than in a traditional group "climate," whereas for Ss of average or below-average intelligence, a permissive climate is a handicap.

Post-hoc consideration of our data has suggested a possible explanation. The authors predicted that children under high-cohesive conditions would learn better than children under low-cohesive conditions because the former, working in the presence of liked others, would be more highly motivated, or have greater "drive." Since attitudes are presumed to have a drive component, individuals with highly positive attitudes toward other group members should, it was reasoned, have a higher general drive level, other things being equal, than individuals with more neutral or slightly negative attitudes toward their fellow group members. While it is true that the higher the drive, the better the learning for simple tasks where alternative responses are few, it is also known that when a complex task is to be learned, high drive will strengthen incorrect competing responses as well as correct ones, thus impeding the learning process (Farber & Spence, 1953; Taylor, 1956). The authors suggest that this phenomenon has implications for the present experimental conditions. High-IQ children were reliably superior to low-IQ children on all the learning tests, indicating that our tasks were relatively more simple for the former than the latter. Among the former, then, increased drive (assumed to be associated with being in high-cohesive groups) should have improved test performance, while it should have served to depress it among the latter.

Within the high-IQ sample, the cohesiveness conditions made less difference to the boys than to the girls. Why this should be the case is not immediately clear. Perhaps girls have stronger affiliation needs and more intense social ties than boys. Or, the type of verbal learning tasks which the authors employed may be essentially girls' tasks at the developmental period represented by ages 10 and 11. High-IQ girls may be especially at ease in such learning situations, in which case the heightened drive provided by the high-cohesive condition should serve to improve learning for the girls, but not for the boys. Observations of boy and girl groups made by *E* and his assistant during the learning sessions support the view that the former were less at ease and more distractable.

Within the low-IQ sample, the average scores of children in high-cohesive groups tended to be somewhat lower than those of children in low-cohesive groups regardless of sex, although the differences appear to be greater for boys. This is congruent with our assumption that the learning tasks were more difficult (complex) for low-IQ children and for boys.

The results obtained on a time measure in Learning Task I are in line with, and support, the data obtained on the learning tests. HiCo groups were significantly faster than LoCo groups within the high-IQ sample; again, this was especially true of the girls. Within the low-IQ sample, however, the LoCo groups worked faster than the HiCo groups, although not reliably. Thus, for the high-IQ *S*s, the condition of working with liked others facilitated performance in the sense of increasing task speed, while for the low-IQ *S*s this same condition seemed to interfere with performance.

The authors' findings on changes in sociometric ratings of fellow group members following interaction in the learning

tasks are also interpretable, post hoc, within a learning-theory framework. In all conditions except one the children tended either to increase their ratings of other group members or to rate them the same as they had previously; this is generally expected following neutral or positive interaction. Increased favorability of ratings was statistically reliable for LoCo *S*s, both boys and girls, and both HiI and LoI. Since HiCo *S*s started with ratings of group members which were close to the maximum, the only possibilities following interaction were no change or decreased favorability. The former result was obtained for HiCo boys, both HiI and LoI, and for LoI-HiCo girls. Among HiI-HiCo girls, however, sociometric ratings decreased significantly. In attempting to understand this latter finding, it is important first of all to keep in mind that feedback from the learning tasks was similar for all *S*s. *E* told all *S*s, 1 week after LTI, that they had done well, but no evaluation was given after the other learning tasks. *S*s did know each time they got a word right or wrong on REL and LTII, but they could not compare themselves with other children to determine relative success or failure. The HiI-HiCo girls were superior to all other experimental conditions on every learning measure, but how well they thought they were doing is not known. The fact that their ratings of fellow group members declined may be explainable on the basis of effort, using the concept of reactive inhibition (Hull, 1951). It is reasonable to infer that the HiI-HiCo girls exerted more effort than children in the other experimental conditions both from their superior performance on the learning tests and from the fact that they worked fastest on LTI where a time measure was obtained. It has been suggested (Lott, 1963) that perhaps stimuli (other group members) associated with effort come to evoke avoidance tendencies just as reward-associated stimuli come to signal approach.

In general, findings of the present study can be said to have provided qualified support for the authors' initial hypothesis and to have raised new questions of broader scope for subsequent investigation.

REFERENCES

BINDER, A., MCCONNELL, D., & SJOHOLM, NANCY A. Verbal conditioning as a function of experimenter characteristics. *Journal of Abnormal and Social Psychology*, 1957, 55, 309–314.

CALVIN, A. D., HOFFMAN, F. K., & HARDEN, E. L. The effect of intelligence and social atmosphere on group problem solving behavior. *Journal of Social Psychology*, 1957, 45, 61–74.

DOOB, L. W. The behavior of attitudes. *Psychological Review*, 1947, 54, 135–156.

FARBER, I. E., & SPENCE, K. W. Complex learning and conditioning as a function of anxiety. *Journal of Experimental Psychology*, 1953, 45, 120–125.

HULL, C. L. *Essentials of behavior*. New Haven: Yale Univer. Press, 1951.

HULL, C. L. *A behavior system*. New Haven: Yale Univer. Press, 1952. Ch. 5.

JAMES, ANNA G., & LOTT, A. J. Reward frequency and the formation of positive attitudes toward group members. *Journal of Social Psychology*, 1964, 62, 111–115.

LOTT, A. J., & LOTT, BERNICE, E. Group cohesiveness, communication level, and conformity. *Journal of Abnormal and Social Psychology*, 1961, 62, 408–412.

LOTT, BERNICE E. Group cohesiveness: A learning phenomenon. *Journal of Social Psychology*, 1961, 55, 275–286.

LOTT, BERNICE E. Secondary reinforcement and effort: Comment on Aronson's "The effect of effort on the attractiveness of rewarded and unrewarded stimuli." *Journal of Abnormal and Social Psychology*, 1963, 67, 520–522.

LOTT, BERNICE E., & LOTT, A. J. The formation of positive attitudes toward group members. *Journal of Abnormal and Social Psychology*, 1960, 61, 297–300.

MCNEMAR, Q. *Psychological statistics*. New York: Wiley, 1949.

PERKINS, H. V., JR. The effects of climate and curriculum on group learning, *Journal of Educational Research*, 1950, 44, 269–286.

REECE, M. M., & WHITMAN, R. N. Expressive movements, warmth, and verbal reinforcement. *Journal of Abnormal and Social Psychology*, 1962, 64, 234–236.

REHAGE, K. J. A comparison of pupil-teacher planning and teacher-directed procedures in eighth grade social studies classes. *Journal of Educational Research*, 1951, 45, 111–115.

SAPOLSKY, A. Effect of interpersonal relationships upon verbal conditioning. *Journal of Abnormal and Social Psychology*, 1960, 60, 241–246.

SHAW, M. E., & SHAW, LILLY MAY. Some effects of sociometric grouping upon learning in a second grade classroom. *Journal of Social Psychology*, 1962, 57, 453–458.

SIEGEL, S. *Nonparametric statistics for the behavioral sciences*. New York: McGraw-Hill, 1956.

TAYLOR, JANET A. Drive theory and manifest anxiety. *Psychological Bulletin*, 1956, 53, 303–320.

WILSON, K. V. A distribution-free test of analysis of variance hypotheses. *Psychological Bulletin*, 1956, 53, 96–101.

SIMILARITY OF SOCIAL MODELS AND CLIENTS IN BEHAVIORAL COUNSELING : TWO EXPERIMENTAL STUDIES

Carl E. Thoresen / John D. Krumboltz

Learning can occur vicariously through observation of the behavior of social models. While there are different theories of imitative or observational learning (Bandura, 1962; Holt, 1931; Miller & Dollard, 1941; Mowrer, 1960), recent evidence does suggest that modeling can be an effective procedure for transmitting and controlling certain behaviors (Bandura & Walters, 1963). Investigations in social modeling have stimulated research in the use of modeling procedures in several areas, including counseling (Krumboltz & Thoresen, 1964; Krumboltz & Schroeder, 1965; Krumboltz, Varenhorst, & Thoresen, 1967; Thoresen, 1966; Thoresen, Krumboltz, & Varenhorst, 1967; Thoresen & Stewart, 1967), teacher training (Acheson, 1964; Olivero, 1964; Orme, McDonald, & Allen, 1966; Schueler & Gold, 1964), and in related areas (Barber & Calverley, 1964; Lazarus, in press; Sherman, 1965; Truax & Carkhuff, 1965; Wilson & Walters, 1966).

From: Journal of Counseling Psychology, *1968,* 15, *393–401. Copyright © 1968 by the American Psychological Association, and reproduced by permission of the authors and APA.*

One rather consistent finding of counseling investigations using modeling procedures has been that some client-observers are more influenced by the modeling procedure than others. It is not clear why this has occurred although observational learning theory (Bandura & Walters, 1963) submits that many observer, model, and situational factors influence the extent to which an observer will match the model's behavior. In the present study two variables and their interrelationship are investigated: (*a*) characteristics of the social model, and (*b*) characteristics of the observer.

Research has suggested that social models which are perceived as attractive and rewarding (Bandura & Huston, 1961), prestigeful (Asch, 1948; Krumboltz, Varenhorst, & Thoresen, 1967; Maccoby, 1959; Mussen, 1959), competent (Mausner & Bloch, 1957), high in status (Lefkowitz, Blake, & Mouton, 1955), and powerful (Bandura, Ross, & Ross, 1961; Grusec & Mischel, 1966; Mischel & Grusec, 1966) result in increased imitative behaviors by observers. However, the specific model characteristics that will promote imitation by different types of observers is not at all clear. Some evidence (Coleman, 1961; Gordon, 1957; Havighurst & Neugarten, 1962) suggests that high school students are very responsive to the academic, athletic, and social success of their peers. These studies suggest that students tend to emulate behaviors of students perceived as having comparable social status, but experimental evidence on adolescents is meager. Some research (Burnstein, Stotland, & Zander, 1961; Kagan, 1958) with elementary-school-age children supports the importance of perceived similarity between observer and model.

Several studies have claimed more counseling success when counselor and client were at least somewhat similar. Tuma and Gustad (1957) concluded that a close client-counselor resemblance on personality tests was associated with more accurate client self-ratings; however, about as many negative as positive correlations were reported. Mendelsohn and Geller (1963) found that clients tended to return for more interviews if their personality test scores were similar to those of their counselors. Whether these clients solved their problems more effectively remains unknown. Bare (1967) found that dissimilarity between several counselor and client characteristics (e.g., original thinking, responsibility) appeared more highly related to success of counseling. Success criteria, however, were restricted to client ratings such as how helpful was counseling and how empathic was the counselor.

Carson and Heine (1962) found a curvilinear relationship. A moderate degree of dissimilarity between Minnesota Multiphasic Personality Inventory (MMPI) profiles of medical student therapists and psychiatric patients yielded the highest supervisor ratings. However, having an MMPI profile either very similar or very dissimilar to a psychiatric patient's profile might also be associated with the quality of therapy; conceivably the best adjusted therapists were also those moderately dissimilar to patients. More evidence of a curvilinear relationship was found by Cook (1966). A moderate degree of similarity between Study of Values profiles was associated with the most improvement in clients' semantic differential evaluations of "my future occupation" and "education." Such correlational evidence leaves unanswered whether other characteristics of the clients and counselors who happened to fall in the "medium similarity" group contributed to the differences found.

Do adolescents tend to imitate models most like themselves or models highest in prestige? To what extent will the degree of similarity between the characteristics of a social model and observers influence the amount of behavior emulated?

METHOD

SUBJECTS

The studies were conducted in five suburban high schools in the vicinity of Stanford University. All male eleventh-grade students were asked to indicate if they would be interested in speaking with a counselor about their educational and vocational plans, especially about ways of seeking information relevant to plans. All male junior students in two high schools completed a High School Sports Survey. Male junior students in three other high schools completed the High School Academic Survey. The relevant question was similar in both surveys: "If you divided students into three groups in terms of (athletic success)/(academic success) where would you place yourself?" Three groups of names were formed based on the resulting self-estimates. Eight students who had volunteered for counseling in each school were then randomly selected from each group (high, middle, or low success). Of these eight *S*s two were randomly assigned to each of four treatment groups. The total *N* for the athletic study was 48; the total *N* for the academic study was 72. Students were informed that it might not be possible to provide this counseling for everyone who requested it. Approximately 50% of the students in each high school volunteered, but in each school only 24 boys were selected at random from those who volunteered.

TREATMENTS

Four model-reinforcement treatment groups were formed in each high school: (*a*) low-success model, (*b*) middle-success model, (*c*) high-success model, and (*d*) adult-counselor model.[1] The *S*s with self-estimates of low, middle, or high academic or athletic success were equally distributed among the four treatments. For example, of the eight high-academic-success *S*s, two received the low-success academic model treatment; two, the middle-success model; two, high-success; and two, the adult-counselor model.

High academic model. After the counselor introduced himself he said, in effect:

> The purpose of our getting together is to discuss your ideas about your plans after high school, especially about how to go about getting information as to your plans. Before we start discussing this I thought you might be interested in hearing a tape recording of a student who recently faced a problem similar to yours. He was concerned about how best to make some decisions about what he was going to do after he graduated from high school. He has been really pleased with his decision and he gave

me permission to let other high school students listen to this recorded interview. Let's listen to it, especially to what he says about how he is going to find out things about his plans. You might have some questions to ask about it when it is over.

A brief prerecorded introduction about Chris, the student model, was then played. The introduction stated:

> Although you may not have the same interests and concerns of Chris, the interview will provide you with concrete suggestions of how you can get information which will help you in making plans. Chris is a junior who is in the college prep program. He is an excellent student with an overall grade average of A⁻. Chris is a member of the Honor Society and is highly thought of by his teachers because he can often contribute good ideas to class discussions. On a general abilities test he took recently, Chris scored in the highest group. He does a lot of reading and plans to enter one of the professions. Chris feels that his studies come first.

A 12-minute tape recording of a model counseling interview similar to that used in previous studies (Krumboltz & Schroeder, 1965; Krumboltz & Thoresen, 1964) was then played. During the first 2 minutes of the model interview the model counselor commented that he had just heard about Chris' election to membership in CSF (California Scholarship Federation). Chris stated he was very pleased about this and planned to do well enough in school to become a lifetime CSF member. In the interview Chris mentioned many different ways he has sought plans to seek career information. Chris asked questions about possible outcomes and alternatives. The model counselor verbally reinforced his question asking and information seeking, occasionally offering additional suggestions of ways to get information.

---

[1] A no-treatment control group was not included. Several preceding studies (Krumboltz & Thoresen, 1964; Krumboltz & Schroeder, 1965; Thoresen, Krumboltz, & Varenhorst, 1967) have established the effectiveness of this type of counseling in comparison to no treatment.

After playing the model tape the counselor said to his own counselee, "Well, why don't you tell me what you've been thinking about in terms of *your* plans." The counseling session continued for 30 minutes with the counselor verbally reinforcing any information-seeking response by the student. An information-seeking response was any indication that the student had sought, was presently seeking, or intended to seek information relevant to his own educational or vocational plans.

The counselor closed the interview by asking *S* to summarize the specific things which he might do to get information about his future plans. The counselor verbally reinforced each summary statement and added any additional steps not mentioned by *S*. The counselor asked *S* if he might begin acting on some of these specific steps this week. Only one interview was held.

Middle academic model. This treatment was virtually identical to the above except that the prerecorded introduction to the model interview described Chris, the model student as:

...taking a number of courses required for college and some electives. His grade-point average is 2.7 and on a test of general ability he took recently he scored in the high average group. Chris is a reliable student in that he regularly prepares his written assignments but he seldom does any work for extra credit. He participates in class discussions when called upon and occasionally volunteers a comment. When he completes his studies in the evening, Chris finds something to do that has nothing to do with school.

During the first 2 minutes of the model interview the counselor mentions that he was glad to see that Chris received an A in one of his classes. Chris states that it was "sort of amazing" that he got the A in his business class and that if he would try harder he probably could get better grades in other classes too.

Low academic model. This treatment followed the above except that the prerecorded introduction described Chris as follows:

He is taking a general studies program and his grades for the most part are Cs and Ds. Because he failed one course required for high school graduation, Chris is trying to decide whether or not to go to summer school or to repeat the course in his senior year. On a general ability test Chris scored in the low average group. Chris usually prepares his assignments about half the time. Some evenings he watches TV or goes over to see his girl friend. He seldom participates in class discussions and doesn't like to be called upon because he might not have a good idea to contribute.

During the first 2 minutes of the model interview the counselor mentions that he was very pleased to see that Chris had brought his grade of D up to a C in his history class.

High athletic model. This treatment was identical to the above except that the student model, Chris, was introduced as:

...very much interested in athletics and has earned four block letters. He is well-built and well-coordinated and scored very high on a physical fitness test recently given in gym class. Chris seems to get along well with students and teachers. Last fall Chris was first string end on the football team and voted the Most Inspirational Player Award. This was rather unusual in that the award is usually given to a senior. In addition he was named to second string of the All-City Team. Currently Chris is a guard on the varsity basketball team and plans to turn out for track in the spring.

In the first 2 minutes Chris mentions that his best friend has been having interviews with college representatives about getting an athletic scholarship.

Middle athletic model. Here Chris is described as follows:

> Chris is interested in athletics and considers himself to be an average athlete. Though he is not what one would call a natural athlete Chris does work to stay physically fit. He turned out for football and baseball for three years in a row. Last fall he was second string guard on the football team and earned a varsity letter. He hopes to make the first team in his senior year. Usually Chris enjoys gym class and manages to do well, although he's never really a standout.

During the first 2 minutes the counselor asks if Chris plans to turn out for baseball in the spring. Chris mentions that he probably will.

Low athletic model. In this treatment Chris is described in the prerecorded introduction as follows:

> Chris doesn't care much for athletics although he occasionally watches athletic events on television. Though he turned out for football in his freshman year he decided he'd probably never make the team so he hasn't turned out since. Because he tends to be a bit heavy for his size and somewhat awkward, he doesn't really enjoy his gym class. Just recently he had a "barely pass" score on his physical fitness test. Chris has said in the past that often he'd rather watch athletic events than take part in them.

During the beginning 2 minutes Chris mentions that gym class is going all right but that the gym tests kind of get to him as he never does very well.

Counselor model. Designed to serve as an active control procedure, the counselor-model treatment permitted exploration of whether any type of a peer model was necessary. Perhaps the suggestions for seeking information, not the source of those suggestions, constitute the effective ingredient. The treatment was identical in length and specific content to the academic and athletic models. The same model counselor was involved. A prerecorded introduction identified the model counselor as a very experienced high school counselor who was especially interested in assisting students to learn how to make good decisions. The model counselor's tape-recorded monolog covered the same content in the same sequence as in the other treatments. Identical concrete ways of seeking information were presented (e.g., reading college guides, writing for catalogs, visiting a campus).

SPECIAL COUNSELORS

The five counselors were graduate students enrolled in the Counseling Practicum course at Stanford University during the 1964–65 academic year. All were female. Four were experienced teachers with an average of 5 years of classroom experience. One counselor had no teaching experience and one had completed student teaching.

One counselor was assigned to each high school in October of 1964 on the basis of convenience of location and matching of time schedules. The experiment was conducted in February and March of 1965. For purposes of statistical analysis, these five special counselors and the five participating schools are considered a fixed constant factor and will be referred to as the counselor-school effect.

CRITERIA

The criterion behavior consisted of the frequency and variety of student information-seeking behaviors which occurred outside the counseling interview during a 3-week period of time after the counseling interview. Approximately 3 weeks after the counseling interview each of the 118 *S*s was interviewed by a member of the evaluation team. These interviewers were not the counselors involved in the study and did not know the type of treatment each *S* received. During the interview each *S* was asked a series of predetermined questions some of which were designed to elicit self-reports of information-seeking behavior. Buffer questions were used to disguise the purpose of the interview and to vary the interview format. Each affirmative information-seeking report was followed by other questions to find out precisely how much and what kind of information-seeking behavior was performed by each *S* during the specified 3-week interval. The following are examples of information-seeking behavior covered by the interview question: (*a*) writing to request a college pamphlet, catalog, or an occupational pamphlet; (*b*) reading books, magazine articles, or other material about occupations or educational institutions; and (*c*) talking to parents, teachers, or other relevant persons who have worked or are working in an occupation or school being considered.

To verify the accuracy of the self-reported information seeking, 15 evaluation interviews were randomly selected for investigation. All reported information-seeking behaviors by these 15 *S*s were checked insofar as possible. Of 51 information-seeking behaviors, 44 were verified and 7 were unconfirmable. No false reports were reported.

RESULTS

For the academic-model study, which was conducted in three of the five high schools, a fixed effects 3 × 3 × 4 analysis of variance was computed using counselor-schools, students success level, and social-model type as the independent variables. A 2 × 3 × 4 analysis of variance was computed for the athletic-model study, which took place in the other two high schools. Separate analyses were computed for the two criterion behaviors: frequency and variety of information-seeking behaviors outside the interview setting. Summaries of both analyses for the academic and athletic study are presented in Tables 1 and 2, respectively. In the study using academic models (Table 1), the main effect for student success level was significant

TABLE 1

ACADEMIC STUDY: ANALYSES OF VARIANCE OF FREQUENCY AND VARIETY OF EXTERNAL INFORMATION-SEEKING BEHAVIOR

| Source | df | Frequency | | Variety | |
		MS	F	MS	F
Student type (A)	2	30.47	5.454*	6.85	8.319*
Model level[a] (B)	3	2.62	.432	1.20	1.460
Counselor-school (C)	2	31.74	5.681*	1.64	1.990
A × B	6	3.44	.615	.71	.865
A × C	4	.47	.084	1.23	1.498
B × C	6	3.15	.564	1.74	2.114
A × B × C	12	4.21	.753	.97	1.175
Within Cells	34	5.59		.82	
Total	69				

[a] Treatment.
* $p < .01$.

TABLE 2

ATHLETIC STUDY: ANALYSES OF VARIANCE OF FREQUENCY
AND VARIETY OF EXTERNAL INFORMATION-SEEKING BEHAVIOR

Source	df	Frequency		Variety	
		MS	F	MS	F
Student type (A)	2	5.65	2.42	1.19	2.375
Model level[a] (B)	3	23.39	10.02**	2.73	5.00*
Counselor-school (C)	1	36.75	15.75**	6.75	13.5**
A × B	6	2.20	.94	.937	1.875
A × C	2	1.19	.51	1.187	2.375
B × C	3	2.47	1.06	.14	.278
A × B × C	6	3.58	1.53	.66	1.319
Within Cells	24	2.33		.5	
Total	47				

[a] Treatment.
* $p < .01$.
** $p < .001$.

for both criterion behaviors. The counselor-school effect was significant for frequency of information-seeking behaviors. The interaction (A × B) between student type and model level which would provide support for the comparability or similarity of student- and social-model view was clearly not significant.

In the study using athletic models (Table 2), the main effect for treatment was significant for both criteria as was the main effect for counselor-schools. The main effect for student type approached but did not reach the .05 level of statistical significance for either criterion.

Table 3 presents the means for counselor-schools, model levels, and student types on both criteria. The students rating themselves high academically did more information-seeking on the average than students rating themselves middle or low academically. A significant treatment effect occurred only in the athletic study where the high-success athletic model produced more information-seeking than any other treatment. The significant main effects for counselor-schools may be attributed to the

lower means for counselor-schools A and E. In both of these schools the counselors were relatively young and inexperienced, but of course unknown systematic differences between school environments could also have been a factor.

Table 4 presents the cell means for the frequency of information seeking by student type and model success level. The high academic student is more responsive on the average to all models. However, in the athletic study the high-success model clearly appears on the average to be the most influential for all three student types. The high athletic model is particularly effective for high-success athletic students who apparently were unimpressed by the low- and middle-athletic-success models.

Post hoc comparisons between levels of student type and of model success level were tested for both criteria. Since differences were not hypothesized beforehand, the Scheffé procedure (Hays, 1963; Scheffé, 1959) for unplanned comparisons was used.

In the academic study the mean differences between the high academic stu-

TABLE 3

MEANS OF FREQUENCY AND VARIETY OF EXTERNAL
INFORMATION-SEEKING BY MODEL LEVEL, STUDENT
TYPE, AND COUNSELOR-SCHOOL

Source	Academic study		Athletic study	
	Frequency	Variety	Frequency	Variety
Model level (treatment)				
Low	4.69	2.81	3.25	2.17
Middle	4.29	2.35	2.42	1.92
High	4.78	2.89	5.67	2.92
Counselor	5.24	2.94	3.33	2.00
Student type				
Low	4.55	2.50	4.25	2.56
Middle	3.77	2.41	3.69	2.13
High	5.83	3.29	3.06	2.06
Counselor-schools				
A	3.43	2.48		
B	5.78	2.83		
C	4.91	2.92		
D			4.54	2.63
E			2.79	1.88

TABLE 4

MEANS OF FREQUENCY OF INFORMATION-SEEKING
BEHAVIORS FOR STUDENT TYPE AND MODEL LEVEL

Student type	Academic model study[a]				Athletic model study[b]			
	Low	Middle	High	Counselor	Low	Middle	High	Counselor
Low	3.83	3.00	5.00	5.30	4.25	3.25	6.50	3.00
Middle	4.00	3.33	3.50	3.66	3.75	2.25	5.50	3.25
High	5.33	6.33	5.83	5.83	1.75	1.75	5.00	3.75

[a] $N = 6$ per cell.
[b] $N = 4$ per cell.

dents and the middle and low students were significant for the variety of information sought ($p < .05$). The same mean differences for the frequency of information sought approached significance ($p < .10$), especially for the middle versus high student. None of the unplanned comparisons between treatment models were significant.

In the athletic study the mean differences between the high-athletic-success model and all other models were significant for both frequency and variety of information-seeking behavior ($p < .05$).

DISCUSSION

Findings of these studies appear to support these conclusions:

1. Variations in the athletic success level attributed to social models produced differ-

ences in the amount of information seeking by male high school students.

2. The high-success athletic model was most effective for students rating themselves in all three categories of athletic success: high, middle, and low. Students of middle and low athletic success did not tend to emulate models like themselves.

3. Variations in academic success attributed to the models was not found to produce significant differences in amount of information seeking.

4. The more academically successful students sought considerably more information on the average than middle- and low-academic-success students, regardless of treatment model.

5. The counselor model proved about as effective in encouraging information seeking as the academic peer models but not as effective as the high-athletic-success model.

6. Different counselors and/or school settings were associated with significantly different frequencies and varieties of information seeking by students.

The results might be interpreted as supportive of the view that people emulate high-status models, not necessarily models similar to themselves. Of course, the issue is far more complicated. All the models were similar to Ss in at least one important respect—all were male. To maximize the effectiveness of a model, it might be desirable for S and model to be quite similar on some characteristics, but quite different on others. Many experiments would be needed to test feasible combinations.

Why, for example, were the high athletic students responsive only to the high athletic model whereas the high academic students appeared to be equally responsive to all academic models? It may be that the gradations between the three athletic models were perceived by Ss as more distinct than between the academic models. The high athletic model, for ex-

ample, was presented as a very outstanding athlete. Even students who rated themselves as highly successful athletically might have perceived the high athletic model student as of higher status. The high success academic model was not presented as being outstanding to the same degree. Kagan (1967) has argued that it is the *distinctiveness* of a model which causes Ss to attend and thus learn from it. The model displays certain cues which draw the attention of the individual. He reported an experiment in which Radcliffe girls recalled poems better when they were recited by girls with personality characteristics similar to their own. Both models were depicted as of high accomplishment: one socially; the other academically. The novelty of discovering someone like herself, not similarity per se, presumably focused attention on the poem and enhanced recall. Kagan's argument could be used to support the present findings since it was the truly unusual model (lousy athletes and A students are not unusual) who was imitated the most. Further experimentation could determine what are the distinctive cues for particular clients. What facets of prestige and similarity, for example, function to produce attention to social models and subsequent imitation. (Lee Harvey Oswald certainly drew the attention of many but how many would use him as a model to be emulated?)

Another explanation is that for Ss represented in these experiments athletic success is probably more highly reinforced than academic success. Academic success therefore might not be highly valued, and thus models representing different degrees of academic success would not produce differential degrees of effectiveness.

Furthermore, information seeking probably seems a natural and expected extension of behavior for an academically-oriented person. But for a star athlete to gather career information—that is unexpected and newsworthy. The relevance of the criterion to the characteristics of the model is another possibly fruitful area for experimentation.

The methodology of determining student success level also merits further study. Approximately 70% of the students in these studies rated themselves in the "middle" category. Thus, the high- and low-student-success groups tended to represent more extreme and possibly more homogeneous groups while students in the middle group were proportionally more heterogeneous. This might explain in part why there was a tendency among low- and high-success students to be more differentially responsive to particular models. Future studies could use several selection criteria such as peer ratings and behavioral observations as well as more comprehensive self-report procedures in determining success levels.

The reason for significant differences between counselor-schools in both studies remains unexplained. All counselors were female and received identical training. Some, however, were older and had had more classroom teaching experience; the two youngest female counselors were at schools with the lowest criterion means. Subsequent studies should include at least two treatment counselors at each school to permit separation of the relative effect of counselor and school. In addition, a variety of counselor assessment procedures might provide data as to which types of counselors are effective in using certain kinds of modeling procedures with particular kinds of students.

The specific effects of modeling procedures were confounded in these studies with the reinforcement counseling in the interview. Presently a series of studies are underway to ascertain the effect of using only a social model without subsequent verbal interaction.

As initial explorations these studies provide encouraging evidence that specific characteristics of students and of social models do make a difference in the outcomes of counseling. The value of developing and experimentally testing different types of social models for different kinds of students in counseling is supported. Subsequent research need not be limited to studies using information-seeking behaviors as criteria. Modeling procedures in counseling possess a tremendous potential for assisting clients with many kinds of personal, social, vocational, and educational problems. Optimally, social-modeling procedures could be individually tailored for each client and his problem.

REFERENCES

ACHESON, K. A. The effects of feedback from television recordings and three types of supervisory treatment on selected teacher behaviors. Unpublished doctoral dissertation, Stanford University, 1964.

ASCH, S. E. The doctrine of suggestion, prestige, and imitation in social psychology. *Psychological Review*, 1948, **55**, 250–277.

BANDURA, A. Social learning through imitation. In M. R. Jones (Ed.), *Nebraska symposium on motivation*. Lincoln: University of Nebraska Press, 1962.

BANDURA, A., & HUSTON, A. C. Identification as a process of incidental learning. *Journal of Abnormal and Social Psychology*, 1961, **63**, 311–318.

BANDURA, A., ROSS D., & ROSS, S. A. Transmission of aggression through imitation of aggressive models. *Journal of Abnormal and Social Psychology*, 1961, **63**, 575–582.

BANDURA, A., & WALTERS, R. H. Aggression. In *Child psychology: The sixty-second yearbook of the National Society for the Study of Education*, Part 1. Chicago:

The National Society for the Study of Education, 1963.

BARBER, T. X., & CALVERLEY, D. S. Comparative effects on "hypnotic-like" suggestibility of recorded and spoken suggestions. *Journal of Consulting Psychology*, 1964, **28**, 384.

BARE, C. E. Relationship of counselor personality and counselor-client personality similarity to selected counseling success criteria. *Journal of Counseling Psychology*, 1967, **14**, 419–425.

BURNSTEIN E., STOTLAND, E., & ZANDER, A. Similarity to a model and self-evaluation. *Journal of Abnormal and Social Psychology*, 1961, **62**, 257–264.

CARSON, R. C., & HEINE, R. W. Similarity and success in therapeutic dyads. *Journal of Consulting Psychology*, 1962, **26**, 38–42.

COLEMAN, J. S. *The adolescent society.* New York: Free Press of Glencoe, 1961.

COOK, T. E. The influence of client-counselor value similarity on change in meaning during brief counseling. *Journal of Counseling Psychology*, 1966, **13**, 77–81.

GORDON, C. W. *The social system of the high school.* Glencoe, Ill.: Free Press, 1957.

GRUSEC, J., & MISCHEL W. Model's characteristics as determinants of social learning. *Journal of Personality and Social Psychology*, 1966, **4**, 211–215.

HAVIGHURST, R. J., & NEUGARTEN, B. L. *Society and education.* Boston: Allyn & Bacon, 1962.

HAYS, W. L. *Statistics for psychologists.* New York: Holt, Rinehart & Winston, 1963.

HOLT, E. C. *Animal drive and the learning process.* Vol 1. New York: Holt, 1931.

KAGAN, J. The concept of identification. *Psychological Review*, 1958, **65**, 296–305.

KAGAN, J. On the need for relativism. *American Psychologist*, 1967, **22**, 131–142.

KRUMBOLTZ, J. D., & SCHROEDER, W. W. Promoting career exploration through reinforcement. *Personnel and Guidance Journal*, 1965, **44**, 19–26.

KRUMBOLTZ, J. D., & THORESEN, C. E. The effect of behavioral counseling in group and individual settings on information-seeking behavior. *Journal of Counseling Psychology*, 1964, **11**, 324–333.

KRUMBOLTZ, J. D., VARENHORST, B., & THORESEN, C. E. Non-verbal factors in the effectiveness of models in counseling. *Journal of Counseling Psychology*, 1967, **14**, 412–418.

LAZARUS, A. A. Behavior therapy in groups. In G. M. GAZDA (Ed.), *Theories and methods of group psychotherapy and counseling.* New York: Charles C Thomas, in press.

LEFKOWITZ, M., BLAKE, R. R., & MOUTON, J. S. Status factors in pedestrian violation of traffic signals. *Journal of Abnormal Social Psychology*, 1955, **51**, 704–705.

MACCOBY, E. E. Role-taking in childhood and its consequences for social learning. *Child Development*, 1959, **30,** 239–252.

MAUSNER, B., & BLOCH, B. L. A study of the additivity of variables affecting social interaction. *Journal of Abnormal and Social Psychology*, 1957, **54,** 250–256.

MENDELSOHN, G. A., & GELLER, M. H. Effects of counselor-client similarity on the outcome of counseling. *Journal of Counseling Psychology*, 1963, **10,** 71–77.

MILLER, N. E., & DOLLARD, J. *Social learning and imitation.* New Haven: Yale University Press, 1941.

MISCHEL, W., & GRUSEC, J. Determinants of the rehearsal and transmission of neutral and oversize behaviors. *Journal of Personality and Social Psychology*, 1966, **3**, 197–205.

MOWRER, O. H. *Learning theory and the symbolic process.* New York: Wiley, 1960.

MUSSEN, B. H., & DISTLER, L. Masculinity

identification and father-son relationships. *Journal of Abnormal and Social Psychology*, 1959, **59**, 350–356.

OLIVERO, J. L. Video recordings as a substitute for live observations in teacher education. Unpublished doctoral dissertation, Stanford University, 1964.

ORME, M. E. J., McDONALD. F., & ALLEN, D. The effects of modeling and feedback variables on the acquisition of a complex teaching strategy. Paper presented at the American Educational Research Association Convention, Chicago: February, 1966.

SCHEFFÉ, H. *The analysis of variance*. New York: Wiley, 1959.

SCHUELER, H., & GOLD. M. J. Video recordings of student teaching. *Journal of Teacher Education*, 1964, **15**, 358–361.

SHERMAN, J. A. Use of reinforcement and imitation to reinstate verbal behavior in mute psychotics. *Journal of Abnormal and Social Psychology*, 1965, **70**, 155–164.

THORESEN, C. E. Using appropriate models. *American Psychologist*, 1966, **21**, 688.

THORESEN, C. E., KRUMBOLTZ, J. D., & VARENHORST, B. Sex of counselors and models: Effect on client career exploration. *Journal of Counseling Psychology*, 1967, **14**, 503–508.

THORESEN, C. E., & STEWART, N. S. Counseling in groups: Using group social models. Paper presented at the American Educational Research Association Convention, February 1967.

TRUAX, C. B., & CARKHUFF, R. R. Personality change in hospitalized mental patients during group psychotherapy as a function of the use of alternate sessions and vicarious therapy pretraining. *Journal of Clinical Psychology*, 1965, **21**, 225–228.

TUMA, A. H., & GUSTAD, J. W. The effects of client and counselor personality characteristics on client learning in counseling. *Journal of Counseling Psychology*, 1957, **4**, 136–141.

WILSON, F. S., & WALTERS, R. H. Modification of speech output of near-mute schizophrenics through social learning procedures. *Behaviour Research and Therapy*, 1966, **4**, 59–67.

HIGH-PERFORMING INNER-CITY ADOLESCENTS ASSIST LOW-PERFORMING PEERS IN COUNSELING GROUPS

Thelma J. Vriend

Underachievement is an important concern of counselors, especially counselors of disadvantaged students (Clark, 1963; Deutsch, 1963; Stewart & Warnath, 1965; Torrance, 1966). Counselors continue to seek a variety of strategies for helping the underachieving student develop greater academic competence. Research studies of the adolescent today describe him as living in a society of his own, with peer approval being a major aspect of this adolescent subculture (Coleman, 1961; Gordon, 1957). Unresolved conflicts between peer and adult values are often related to low achievement. Peer group membership is especially a problem for the socially disadvantaged youth who may find his only source of security in close identification with members of his own racial or ethnic group (Stewart & Warnath, 1965).

Although peer influence is often channeled in directions that are not conducive

From: Personnel and Guidance Journal, *1969,* 47, *897–904.* © *1969 by the American Personnel and Guidance Association, Washington, D.C. and reproduced by permission of the author and APGA.*

to school achievement, the peer influence model in education reveals examples where peer groups have been utilized to influence school achievement positively (Brown, 1965; Engle & Szyperski, 1965; Valley View School District, 1967–68). Commitment to change is enhanced by helping students discover affiliation with other students who wish to make similar changes. Research in group procedures and group counseling suggests that the group is an important setting in which students who already demonstrate the desired behaviors can provide leadership for the development of other students (Brown, 1965; Mezzano, 1968; Ofman, 1963). When a shift in behavior is supported by a group standard, the new behavior of students in the group will be reinforced by the group members.

In search of effective methods of utilizing the peer group as a positive force for school achievement among inner-city high school students, the investigator (also the counselor) developed a demonstration program of supervised peer leadership in counseling and study groups. A method was developed of training students to be peer leaders in the group, and the program's effects on the academic performance of the selected students were evaluated.

It was hypothesized that the academic achievement of students in the demonstration program would be greater than that of students in the control group, and that students in the demonstration program would show improved classroom skills. It was further hypothesized that the educational and vocational aspirations and expectations of students in the demonstration program would show a greater increase than those of students in the control group.

METHOD

SUBJECTS AND PROCESS OF SELECTION

The demonstration study was conducted with a group of selected eleventh grade students at a high school in Detroit, Michigan. The demonstration high school area ranks in the lowest quintile of Detroit sub-communities in regard to socioeconomic level when measured by such characteristics as families with incomes under $3,000, number of unemployed persons, Aid to Dependent Children families,

and family disorganization (United Community Services, 1962). The student population is comprised predominantly of Negroes from lower socioeconomic circumstances. The parental socioeconomic levels of the selected students were rated according to the Hamburger Revised Occupational Scale for Rating Socio-economic Status (Hamburger, 1958). Eighty percent of the parents were employed at the two levels requiring little or no post-high school training (T. J. Vriend, 1968).

An achievement typology was used to identify and categorize second-semester, eleventh grade students into achievement types. This typology utilized teacher recommendations (High Nomination [HN] or Low Nomination [LN]) to supplement the measures of grade point average (High Performance [HP] or Low Performance [LP]), and standardized test scores (High Testing [HT], or Low Testing [LT]), in the identification of achievement types. Only those students who were high in one or more of the three categories were selected. There is more than the average probability that the school performance—and, in many cases, the standardized test scores—of the educationally disadvantaged student do not represent

TABLE 1

COMPOSITION OF GROUPS

	Number of Groups				
Group	Counseling	Study	Activity	Ratio of Types	Total
Demonstration	4	12	2	3 Peer leaders (HP) 9 Student participants (LP)	48
Control	—	—	—	3 Peer leaders (HP) 9 Student participants (LP)	48

the full measure of his potential learning ability (CEEB, 1965). However, intelligent or creative behavior is often apparent to teachers, and in these cases the teacher's judgment is a primary criterion (Miller, 1961).

Students identified by achievement types were randomly selected and assigned to groups as shown in Table 1.

THE DEMONSTRATION GROUPS

Each student selected for participation in the demonstration group was scheduled to meet for one 40-minute period of each school day for counseling groups, study groups, and guidance activities.

Students who had been classified in the high-performing categories of the achievement typology were trained as peer leaders. It was assumed that because of prior successful experiences in school, they possessed classroom skills which would enable them to help low-performing students become more achievement-oriented and improve their achievement levels.

Four groups of 12 students each—3 peer leaders and 9 student participants—met each week with the counselor for 40 minutes of group counseling. The focus of the counseling groups was the utilization of peer leaders in the group to support the desired behavior of becoming more achievement-oriented and improving achievement.

Each counseling group was divided into three study groups—each containing one peer leader and three student participants—which met to implement activities planned during group counseling sessions. The function of the group was flexible in that it was based on differences in the members' problems and needs. Each group was directed by a peer leader and met for three 40-minute periods weekly. Although the counselor did not meet with the groups, the group leader could request special assistance from her, as well as from a teacher or another student.

Guidance activities that involved an entire group of 24 students and supplemented the counseling and study groups were conducted one day per week. These activities provided information about the world of work, educational and vocational planning, self-evaluation, and self-improvement.

The demonstration groups were conducted for two semesters of 20 weeks each. Except for the aforementioned scheduled daily activities, the school programs for the students in both the demonstration and control groups were alike.

INSTRUMENTS AND PROCEDURES OF DATA COLLECTION

Evaluative criteria to determine changes in academic achievement, classroom skills, and vocational and educational aspirations and expectations were applied to all groups as indicated in Table 2.

TABLE 2

EVALUATIVE CRITERIA

Pre-	During	Post-
School and College Ability Test (SCAT) 10B	Teacher evaluation of personal characteristics	SCAT, 12B
Sequential Tests of Educational Progress (STEP), 10B	Anecdotal material	STEP, 12B
Grade point averages (GPA), 10A–11B	Tape-recorded observations	GPA, 11A–12B
Planning questionnaire	Attendance and punctuality data	Planning questionnaire

Grade point averages were computed for each student in the demonstration and control groups using all course subjects except physical education. SCAT-STEP tests are a part of the testing program for students in the Detroit Public Schools, and the scores were available from the students' cumulative records. These measures were used to determine changes in academic achievement.

An Aspiration and Planning Questionnaire was used to evaluate pupil goals and aspirations and to note changes over a period of time. This questionnaire was a modification of a planning questionnaire developed for use in the Career Pattern Study (Hamburger, 1958), with adaptations from a questionnaire used to study the vocational aspirations of inner-city youth (Sain, 1965).

A five-point descriptive scale was provided for teachers to rate the selected students on seven characteristics that describe specific classroom behaviors in the areas of: (a) ability to get along with others; (b) work habits; (c) manners; (d) emotional maturity; (e) leadership, (f) study habits; and (g) class participation. These ratings were secured from teachers of students in the demonstration group.

Records of school attendance and punctuality were secured from each student's permanent record. Comparisons were made between the 11B-grade and 12B-grade attendance and punctuality records of students in both the demonstration and control groups.

As an aid to the current and continuous evaluation of the demonstration program activities, and as a supplement to the objective evaluation of the program, anecdotal reports were kept. These included student weekly logs and periodic evaluations of individual and group progress, counselor logs and process reports, teacher reports of student behavior, and tape evaluations by judges of counseling sessions.

ANALYSES OF DATA

Analysis of covariance was used to analyze the pre- and post-data on SCAT-STEP converted scores. Analysis of variance was used to determine whether the pre- and post-mean grade point averages of the demonstration and control groups were significantly different. *T*-tests for related observations were used to determine mean differences (a) in the analysis of teacher ratings of personal characteristics of the demonstration group, (b) between responses of the control and demonstration groups on the aspiration and planning questionnaire, and (c) between attendance and punctuality scores of the control and demonstration groups.

RESULTS

HYPOTHESIZED FINDINGS

The results relevant to the hypothesis about academic achievement are presented in Tables 3, 4, and 5. Table 3 presents the results of the analysis of STEP scores.

On each of the five subscores of the STEP, the mean scores of the demonstration group are significantly higher than those of the control group.

Table 4 presents the results of analysis of covariance on the SCAT scores of both groups.

The mean scores of the demonstration group are higher than those of the control group on two of the SCAT scores. The SCAT-Verbal and SCAT-Total show differences statistically significant at the .05 level. The mean scores of the control group are slightly higher than those for the demonstration group on the SCAT-Quantitative subscore; however, the difference is not statistically significant. There

TABLE 3

COMPARISONS OF 10B AND 12B STEP SCORES OF
DEMONSTRATION AND CONTROL GROUPS
(N = 48 FOR EACH GROUP)

Test	Group	Pre-Score Mean	SD	Post-Score Mean	SD	F
Math.	Dem.	261.27	14.02	271.81	12.02	
	Control	263.04	12.35	266.46	13.93	7.26†
Science	Dem.	268.60	10.56	BGG.VG	10.18	
	Control	270.08	9.45	274.13	11.44	4.12*
Soc. stud.	Dem.	269.88	9.14	277.06	12.09	
	Control	267.52	9.02	269.98	10.93	8.06†
Reading	Dem.	281.52	12.41	293.04	12.48	
	Control	279.23	14.04	284.67	15.02	10.31†
Writing	Dem.	275.15	12.86	285.35	12.13	
	Control	271.15	13.10	276.40	14.89	7.67†

* Significant at .05 level for 1, 95 d.f.
† Significant at .01 level for 1, 95 d.f.

TABLE 4

COMPARISONS OF 10B AND 12B SCAT SCORES OF
DEMONSTRATION AND CONTROL GROUPS
(N = 48 FOR EACH GROUP)

Test	Group	Pre-Score Mean	SD	Post-Score Mean	SD	F
Verbal	Dem.	272.58	12.65	280.77	11.26	5.20*
	Control	273.00	10.55	277.89	12.20	
Quan.	Dem.	282.73	11.94	283.92	14.43	
	Control	284.58	11.58	284.02	14.40	0.51
Total	Dem.	278.42	9.06	284.02	9.93	
	Control	279.19	7.51	281.64	10.04	6.76*

* Significant at .05 level for 95 d.f.

were gains in the mean score of the demonstration group although it remains slightly lower than the mean SCAT-Quantitative score of the control group. It will be noted that group mean scores are relatively low considering that a process was used to identify the more able student. The fact that the achievement typology utilized high test scores as only one of three selection criteria is reflected in lower mean test scores.

Table 5 presents data on the criterion of grade point average.

The mean pre-grade point averages yield F-values that show no significant differences between the demonstration and control groups. The post-grade point average means, however, show a difference

table 5

Comparisons of Pre- and Post-Grade
Point Averages of Demonstration and
Control Groups
(n = 48 for Each Group)

Group	Mean	SD	F
Pre-11B GPA			
Demonstration	2.07	0.78	
Control	2.19	0.77	0.58
Post-12B GPA			
Demonstration	2.88	0.50	
Control	1.88	0.68	66.22*

* Significant at .001 level for 1, 94 d.f.

significant at the .001 level of confidence.
The demonstration group showed a gain
of .81 point during the two-semester period

of the program, while the control group
showed a decrease of .31 point in mean
grade point average.

The results of the analyses of the
three criteria of academic achievement
permit the acceptance of the hypothesis
that the academic achievement of the demonstration group is greater than that of
the students in the control group.

It was hypothesized that in addition
to greater academic achievement the demonstration group would also exhibit improved classroom skills. An analysis of
teacher ratings of personal characteristics
related to classroom skills by the related
t-test showed statistically significant increases in these ratings at the .05 level or
above (see T. J. Vriend, 1968, for tables
and instrument). Students who participate in a program organized to reinforce

table 6

Comparison of Pre- and Post-Measures of
Vocational and Educational Aspirations
and Expectations of Demonstration and
Control Groups

Variable[1]	Pre-		Post-		t-Value
	Mean	SD	Mean	SD	
Demonstration (N = 48)					
VA	5.42	1.11	6.08	0.61	4.74†
VE	4.77	1.36	5.77	0.80	5.31†
SC	4.98	1.26	5.42	0.92	2.30*
EA	5.54	1.35	6.73	1.10	6.77†
EE	4.65	1.48	5.98	1.31	5.97†
Control (N = 27)					
VA	5.59	1.18	4.96	1.16	−2.85†
VE	4.56	1.28	4.52	1.16	−0.18
SC	4.63	1.57	4.56	1.28	−0.39
EA	5.30	1.88	4.41	1.84	−2.73†
EE	4.52	1.65	3.70	1.81	−2.88†

* Significant at .05 level.
† Significant at .005 level.
1 References to the aspiration and expectation variables are abbreviated as follows: VA = Vocational Aspiration;
VE = Vocational Expectation; SC = Vocational Self-Concept; EA = Educational Aspiration; and EE = Educational Expectation.

related positive behaviors can be helped to develop better classroom skills. The pattern of change indicated that while these behaviors can be influenced in a relatively short period of time, they seem to require regular practice and support over a longer period of time to sustain them.

Table 6 presents comparisons of pre- and post-mean scores on the variables related to vocational and educational aspirations and expections of the demonstration and control groups. The reversed occupational rating scale (Hamburger, 1958) ranges from 7, representing the highest socioeconomic level, to 1, representing the lowest level. The educational rating scale runs from 8, representing the highest level of education, to 1, representing the lowest level.

There were significant increases in the demonstration group mean scores on all five variables when examined by the related *t*-test. There were significant decreases in the control group mean scores on three variables—VA, EA, and EE. The variables VE and SC show decreases in mean scores that are not statistically significant.

Students who participated in the demonstration program were helped to increase their levels of vocational aspiration and, at the same time, to show an increase in vocational expectations. An important aspect of the vocational maturity of students is that vocational goals be accompanied by educational goals at the same level (J. Vriend, 1968). While students in the control group possess school ability comparable to those in the demonstration group, they aspire to and expect to attain lower levels of education and vocation. The hypothesis that the vocational and educational aspirations and expectations of students in the demonstration group would show a greater increase than those in the control group was supported.

ADDITIONAL FINDINGS

Attendance and punctuality data are important factors in the evaluation of school performance, since both contribute to school grades and teacher judgments. Statistical analysis of these data for the demonstration and control groups revealed that the demonstration group showed significant improvement in attendance and punctuality records, while the control group showed significant changes in a negative direction.

Group counseling effectiveness was evaluated by judges who listened to selected taped group sessions. From a total of 16 sessions evaluated, only 18 out of 240 minutes, or 7.5 per cent of the total time, were rated as including behavior unrelated to the goals of the group.

Summary statements from student evaluations tended to report positive feelings about the effectiveness of student logs, counseling and study groups, and guidance activities. The counseling group and student logs were reported to be very important tools in promoting self-understanding and goal-setting. Study groups offered an opportunity to implement plans, and guidance activities were reported to be inspirational and informative.

DISCUSSION

The findings and conclusions of this study demonstrate that achieving disadvantaged students can be trained as peer leaders to serve as models for fellow students, and to help them to develop attitudes and behaviors that improve school performance. Because the peer group is especially important to the minority group youth, ties with peer groups who value achievement are essential if optimum school performance is to be reached. In the demonstration program, the example of achieving peers and the support and reinforcement of a group with similar goals provided the impetus for students to develop better classroom skills, higher grades, and higher levels of vocational and educational aspirations and expectations.

The counseling group was an important medium for the development of leadership skills for the peer leaders and for the practice of these skills in aiding student participants make plans for developing new directions and behaviors. The opportunity to work with peers in study groups and guidance activities in addition to the counseling groups, and to do this on a daily basis over a period of time, helped peer leaders to establish closer and more meaningful relations with the students they helped. The group, however, did not replace the need for individual counseling for some students with special problems. The experience, however, did encourage many students to seek individual assistance from teachers and counselors.

The transition from high school to work or further schooling is a critical period for students. The decisions and adjustments they necessarily have to make require a high degree of reliance on personal skills and resources if the move is to be regarded as successful. One of the goals of the demonstration program was to develop attitudes, skills, and plans that are essential for successful post-high school training. The study groups and guidance activities of the demonstration program attempted to invest more meaning into the learning program and experiences of the students involved.

In addition to other demands for student competence, it was important to raise the level of school performance for the demonstration group to correspond with their higher levels of vocational and educational aspirations. To encourage students to raise aspirations and expectations without helping them to increase the knowledge

and skills with which to implement these hopes and desires is a questionable, if not unethical, counseling practice.

The use of peer leadership in counseling groups is seen as a practice that not only holds promise for high school, but can also be considered as a developmental program at all levels. It has been suggested that because disadvantaged students are more apprehensive about their chances for success, and because their environment has caused and perpetuated this apprehension, they need the kind of counseling that is more active, more directive, and more supportive. Guidance for these students should be a process taking place on a continuum between directed and supported involvement and independent behavioral commitment (Gordon & Wilkerson, 1966). Peer leadership in peer groups could provide this support in a manner acceptable to the student.

In the peer influence model there is inherent an enormous potential for educational improvement. There is a need to develop better ways of utilizing the resourceful ability of students to help other students become more successful in the school setting. The findings of this study indicate that peer leaders can be trained to assist their fellow students to improve school performance. This practice seems to hold promise for the disadvantaged student who generally needs more attention and more direction, and whose margin for error is small.

REFERENCES

BROWN, W. F. Student-to-student counseling for academic adjustment. *Personnel and Guidance Journal,* 1965, 48, 811–816.

CLARK, K. B. Educational stimulation of racially disadvantaged children. In A. H. PASSOW (Ed.), *Education in depressed areas.* New York: Teachers College, Columbia University, 1963. Pp. 142–161.

COLEMAN, J. S. *The adolescent society.* New York: The Free Press, 1961.

College Entrance Examination Board. Interpreting SAT scores of educationally disadvantaged students. New York: College Entrance Examination Board, 1965.

DEUTSCH, M. P. The disadvantaged child and the learning process. In A. H. PASSOW (Ed.), *Education in depressed areas.* New York: Teachers College. Columbia University, 1963. Pp. 163–179.

ENGLE, K., & SZYPERSKI, T. A demonstration study of significant others in producing change in self-concept and achievement in Kalamazoo Secondary School underachievers. Kalamazoo, Mich.: Kalamazoo Public Schools, 1965. (Mimeo)

GORDON, C. W. *The social system of the high school: A study in the sociology of adolescence.* Glencoe, Ill.: The Free Press, 1957.

GORDON, E., & WILKERSON, D. *Compensatory education for the disadvantaged.* New York: College Entrance Examination Board, 1966.

HAMBURGER, M. Realism and consistency in aspirations and expectations of early adolescents. Unpublished doctoral dissertation, Teachers College, Columbia University, 1958.

MEZZANO, J. Group counseling with low-motivated male high shool students— Comparative effects of two uses of counselor time. *Journal of Educational Research,* 1968, *61,* 222–224.

MILLER, L. H. *Guidance for the underachiever with superior ability.* Washington, D.C.: U.S. Office of Education, 1961.

OFMAN, W. Evaluation of a group counseling procedure. Unpublished doctoral dissertation, University of California at Los Angeles, 1963.

SAIN, L. F. Occupational preferences and expectations of Negro students attending a high school located in a lower socioeconomic area. Unpublished doctoral dissertation, Wayne State University, 1965.

STEWART, L. H., & WARNATH C. *The counselor and society.* Boston: Houghton Mifflin, 1965.

TORRANCE, E. P. Motivating the creatively gifted among economically and culturally disadvantaged children. In J. GOWAN and G. DEMOS (Eds.), *The disadvantaged and potential dropout.* Springfield, Ill.: Charles C. THOMAS, 1966. Pp. 302–309.

United Community Services. *Quintile values of sub-communities in Detroit.* (Based on 1960 census figures) Detroit: United Community Services, 1962.

Valley View School District. *Cadet teacher program,* 1967–1968. Overland Park, Ka.: Valley View School District No. 49, 1968.

VRIEND, J. The vocational maturity of seniors in two inner-city high schools. Unpublished doctoral dissertation, Wayne State University, 1968.

VRIEND, T. J. Utilizing peer leaders in counseling and study groups to modify academic achievement: A demonstration study in an inner-city high school. Unpublished doctoral dissertation, New York University, 1968.

4

Social Interaction Involving Learners, Teachers, and Administrators

For teaching is a superb way of learning.
J. S. Bruner

There is a popular, romantic assumption abroad, that is mostly false—it says that there is a classical, ideal type of teacher who is effective with all pupils, from recalcitrant to indifferent types. This simplex perception and strategy often regards teaching as transmitting knowledge logically and clearly to learners, and it views learning as passively but willingly accepting what teachers prescribe. On the other hand, fables such as *Goodbye, Mr. Chips* would have us pretend that all that really matters in teaching is finding teacher-learner affective rapport, the irrelevance of Latin and Greek drill and recitation notwithstanding.

Unfortunately, there is strong tradition for narrow, one-sided conceptions of teaching and learning, and many teachers have sought out those premises conducive to their biases and have attempted to practice them in classrooms. What merit any one point of view or any one technique may possess cannot accommodate the entire complex of teaching and learning contingencies and needs. Historical patterns of scholarship, including inter-personal patterns stemming from archaic traditions, tend to portray the role of teacher as omniscient and that of learner as docile. Over-simplified generalizations in teacher education and instructional writings have also supported the naive perceptions of teacher predominance against pupil receptivity by over-emphasizing affective concerns and neglecting systematic, cognitive strategies (Yee, 1970). It is sad to see the classic by Lewin, Lippitt, and White (1939) dealt with in such an over-simplified, pseudo-philosophical manner. The simple criterion-of-effectiveness model placed an unrealistic burden on countless teachers and pupils and, in general, it hindered the advance of pedagogy.

Theories and studies of human interaction would tend to refute the superficial romantic view and say that the nature of interpersonal behavior events is the result of all personality structures interacting together (Della Piana and Gage, 1955; Yee, 1968). The normal practice has been to compliment and reward the teacher who has a well-functioning, achieving group of learners for her warm personality and effective teaching methods. In the opposite situation, problems in classrooms such as the children's lack of discipline, responsiveness, and background tend to be blamed upon the children rather than upon the teacher. We would not overlook the teacher's influence upon the social setting and, therefore, we must not overlook the learners' initiations and responses in the interactive process. The learners may be more influential in the process of developing a classroom's interpersonal behavior patterns and general "social climate" than is generally assumed. At any rate, what matters is *more* than one or the other set of behaviors and characteristics taken separately; what really matters is what takes place when teachers and pupils interact (e.g., Halpin and Croft, 1963).

To begin the chapter's readings, Dewey's statement from his chapter on "Thinking in Education" expresses quite well the social interactional view of teaching and learning. In his inimitable style, Dewey helps clarify the view that social interaction in education is logically sound and realistic in terms of human behavior.

Newcomb's article relates well to the last chapter on peer-group relationships, but is placed in this chapter since the Bennington community he studied involved faculty and students and several reference groups. This classical work emphasizes the possible socio-psychological effects of a reference group's majority attitudes upon everyone involved. According to Newcomb, the faculty felt "one of the foremost duties of the college was to acquaint its somewhat oversheltered students with the nature of the contemporary world." Through four years of investigations of the students' attitude change in such an educational setting by means of psychological tests and interviews, Newcomb concluded that "the individual's attitude development is a function of the way in which he relates himself both to the total membership group and to one or more reference groups."

Conducted in educational settings quite different from Newcomb's, the study reported in the third selection investigated teachers' attitudes toward children and pupils' attitudes toward their teacher with analysis of variance procedures. Results consistent with Newcomb's indicated great variance between the characteristics of teachers of advantaged pupils and teachers of disadvantaged pupils. A number of factors were found to be significant sources of variation and some significant interaction effects were found. The researcher concluded that to improve educational opportunities, it is essential to consider administrative-community factors and the personality-pedagogical characteristics of teachers. Investigating teacher-pupil interpersonal attitudes as contributors to variance in classroom operations, Yee's study strongly indicates teacher-pupil interaction cannot be overlooked for advantaged and/or disadvantaged pupils. The nature of teachers' interpersonal attitudes in schools with disadvantaged pupils raises serious concern, since the study found their attitudes to be more negative, punitive, and authoritarian than the attitudes of teachers working with socially advantaged pupils.

There has been some concern that school teachers, typically females, may not be as effective in their social interaction with boys as they are with girls. However, Davis and Slobodian found evidence that conflicted with the charge, especially supported by McNeil's (1964) study. Investigating first-grade pupils' perceptions of teacher-pupil interaction during reading instruction, teachers' ratings of pupils' motivation and readiness, and comparative reading achievement in auto-instruction versus classroom instruction, McNeil concluded that teachers tend to reinforce the feminine-oriented behavior of girls and discriminate against the natural behavior of boys.

Davis and Slobodian replicated McNeil's research with some refinements; in particular, they added use of a systematic observation schedule of teacher-pupil verbal interactions during reading (ROR). Largely on the basis of finding nonsignificant differences in teachers' treatment of boys and girls, observed with ROR, they suggested that "explanations of boys' lower reading achievement under classroom teaching, if real, probably should be focused on the specific teacher-pupil interactions in the situation of classroom reading instruction." However, four days of observing reading instruction in 10 classrooms may be considered inconclusive by some. Also, the greater achievement of boys with auto-instruction versus their lower reading progress under teacher instruction was not refuted by Davis and Slobodian who felt the issue of teacher favoritism remains ambiguous and that further study merits attention.

If the interpretative review of studies in this area by Sears and Feldman (1966) does lead them to valid inferences, it appears that teachers have been unprepared to, and do not, accommodate essential behavioral differences—not only between boys and girls but among individuals. Such findings suggest that teachers need to overcome single-method, simplex instructional approaches applied universally to every pupil. They conclude that teacher education and schools need to recruit more "men who carry some of the 'feminine' characteristics of sensitivity to other people and responsiveness to emotion, as well as tougher 'masculine' characteristics . . . . and women who are somewhat tougher in their thinking processes than they now are, more confident of their own ability to solve problems, less conforming to social pressures" (p. 35).

Such concerns indicate that the issue is greater than the possibility that teachers favor the behavior of girls and discriminate against boys. The present controversy suggests that teachers may lack and are unable to apply basic concepts from differential psychology as well as simple social-psychological understandings. However, there appears to be ample evidence that teacher education provides little positive effect on teachers' classroom behavior, and that many serious, innovative changes are needed in teacher education to prepare the professionally competent teachers that modern, urban society requires (Yee, 1969 & 1970). Davis and Slobodian's use of social interaction in their study of a problem in reading instruction, therefore, helps to illustrate the value of giving classroom social interaction greater central attention in studies and development of teaching and learning.

The work by Runkel investigated the general question: Does similarity between two person's cognitive structures increase their ability to communicate? Runkel developed an index of colinearity as an objective estimate of information exchange between individuals. His research found that "the colinearity index predicts a difference among quiz grades which is not attributable to the relation between A.C.E. scores and quiz grades, to response to an attribute norm, or to a preference for the stimulus-statements preferred by the teacher."

Runkel's conceptual framework, which stems from Newcomb's theory of communicative acts and Coombs' thinking on "unfolding" processes in social measurement, perceives the cognitive structure as an individual's set of potential responses and considers its significant mediation in social interaction. The carefully conceived views and the positive results of Runkel's study seriously challenge teachers' abilities to communicate effectively with their students. The following concerns seem to be raised by such provocative work: Is colinearity a relatively fixed attribute or can it be experimentally manipulated? If the latter, how can teachers and learners maximize their ability to be colinear with each other? Much educational thought and work, such as that by Taba and Elzey's (1964) and Hoetker and Ahlbrand (1969), assume educators can improve their teaching-learning strategies through more effective social interaction. Thus, Runkel's work with co-linearity carries important implications for pre- and in-service teacher education.

We need to know if there is a developmental process involved in teaching-learning interaction. Can we say that elementary school pupils and their teachers should be more colinear than older students and their instructors, because youngsters have cognitive fields that are less structured and thus can be more easily influenced by their elementary school teachers? Are there other teacher and learner characteristics that mediate their communicative interaction, such as sex, race, socio-cultural background, values, etc. (Della Piana and Gage, 1955; Drabek, 1966; Gilliland, 1966; Yee, 1968)? Does generality of colinearity exist such that individuals can be classified more or less colinear in comparison with others? Much further research needs to be conducted to follow up the fifth selection's lead.

The chapter's sixth article reports a study of the interpersonal relationships involving student teachers, college supervisors, and cooperating teachers. The importance of laboratory experiences in teacher education makes the social interaction in such a triad extremely worthy of study and improvement. Results of the study raised serious concerns that the student-teaching triad functions negatively against the objectives of the laboratory experiences. Once again, the greater development of the educational setting appeared to be far less than possible, because socio-psychological variables had not been taken into consideration.

The work by Daw and Gage sought answers to the question: Does feedback from teachers regarding the behavior of their principals influence the principals' behavior? Previous research by Gage, Runkel, and Chatterjee (1960) had shown that pupils could influence teachers' behavior, and the present study further supports the view this book wishes to stress: that social interaction is a vital aspect of what takes place in educational setttings, between teachers and principals as well as teachers and students. Daw and Gage's research design is exemplary and it alone makes study of their article worthwhile.

The chapter's last article considers the interpersonal relationship involving pupils, teachers, and principals. Concerned with their social interaction, the researcher asked if there were certain dyadic patterns of agreement and disagreement operating in such interpersonal relationships. Significant agreement between principals' and teachers' attitudes toward children was found with noteworthy differences resulting for middle- and lower-class pupils. Principals' and pupils' ratings of teacher merit were found to lack agreement, and this sort of finding seems to reflect the increasing social distance between learners and administrators in most educational settings. Perhaps the major finding of the study indicated that teacher-principal attitudes were negative and discriminatory toward lower-class pupils and positive and advantageous toward middle-class pupils.

OTHER READINGS

DELLA PIANA, G. M., & GAGE, N. L. Pupils' values and the validity of the Minnesota Teacher Attitude Inventory. *Journal of Educational Psychology,* 1955, *46,* 167–78.

DRABEK, T. E. Student preferences in professor-student classroom role relations. *Sociological Inquiry,* 1966, *36,* 87–97.

GAGE, N. L. Theories of teaching. In E. R. HILGARD (Ed.), *Theories of learning and instruction.* The 63rd Yearbook of the National Society for the Study of Education, Part I. Chicago: University of Chicago Press, 1964. Pp. 268–285.

GAGE, N. L., & CHATTERJEE, B. B. Changing teacher behavior through feedback from pupils: An application of equilibrium theory. In W. W. CHARTERS and

N. L. GAGE (Eds.), *Readings in the social psychology of education.* Boston: Allyn & Bacon, 1963. Pp. 173–181.

GILLILAND, B. E. Small group counselling with Negro adolescents in a public high school. *Journal of Counselling Psychology,* 1966, *15,* 147–152.

HALPIN, A. W., & CROFT, D. B., *Organizational climate of schools.* Chicago: Midwest Administration Center, University of Chicago, 1963.

HOETKER, J., & AHLBRAND, W. P. The persistence of the recitation. *American Educational Research Journal,* 1969, *6,* 145–167.

HUGHES, M. M. Teaching is interaction. *Elementary School Journal,* 1958, *58,* 457–464.

KOUNIN, J. S., & GUMP, P. V. The ripple effect in discipline. *Elementary School Journal,* 1958, *59,* 158–162.

LEWIN, K., LIPPITT, R., & WHITE, R. K. Patterns of aggressive behavior in experimentally created "social climates." *Journal of Social Psychology,* 1939, *10,* 271–299.

McNEIL, J. D. Programed instruction versus usual classroom procedures—teaching boys to read. *American Educational Research Journal,* 1964, *1,* 113–119.

SEARS, P. S., & FELDMAN, D. H. Teacher interaction with boys and girls. *National Elementary Principal,* 1966, *46,* 30–35.

TABA, H., BRADY, E. H., & ROBINSON, J. T. *Intergroup education in public schools.* Washington, D. C.: American Council on Education, 1952.

TABA, H., & ELZEY, F. F. Teaching strategies and thought processes. *Teachers College Record,* 1964, *65,* 524–534.

YEE, A. H. Source and direction of causal influence in teacher-pupil relationships. *Journal of Educational Psychology,* 1968, *59,* 275–282.

YEE, A. H. Teacher education: Rube Goldberg or systems management *Educational Technology,* 1969, *9,* 36–41.

YEE, A. H. What should modern, urban society expect of teacher education. *Education and Urban Society,* 1970, *2,* 277–294.

DEMOCRACY AND EDUCATION

John Dewey

The educational moral I am chiefly concerned to draw is not, however, that teachers would find their own work less of a grind and strain if school conditions favored learning in the sense of discovery and not in that of storing away what others pour into them; nor that it would be possible to give even children and youth the delights of personal intellectual productiveness—true and important as are these things. It is that no thought, no idea, can possibly be conveyed as an idea from one person to another. When it is told, it is, to the one to whom it is told, another given fact, not an idea. The communication may stimulate the other person to realize the question for himself and to think out a like idea, or it may smother his intellectual interest and suppress his dawning effort at thought. But what he *directly* gets cannot be an idea. Only by wrestling with the conditions of the problem at first hand, seeking and finding his own way out, does he think. When the parent or teacher has provided the conditions which stimulate thinking and has

Reprinted with permission of The Macmillan Company from Democracy and Education *by John Dewey, pp. 187–88. Copyright © 1916.*

taken a sympathetic attitude toward the activities of the learner by entering into a common or conjoint experience, all has been done which a second party can do to instigate learning. The rest lies with the one directly concerned. If he cannot devise his own solution (not of course in isolation, but in correspondence with the teacher and other pupils) and find his own way out he will not learn, not even if he can recite some correct answer with one hundred per cent accuracy. We can and do supply ready-made 'ideas' by the thousand; we do not usually take much pains to see that the one learning engages in significant situations where his own activities generate, support, and clinch ideas—that is, perceived meanings or connections. This does not mean that the teacher is to stand off and look on; the alternative to furnishing ready-made subject matter and listening to the accuracy with which it is reproduced is not quiescence, but participation, sharing, in an activity. In such shared activity, the teacher is a learner, and the learner is, without knowing it, a teacher—and upon the whole, the less consciousness there is, on either side, of either giving or receiving instruction, the better.

257

ATTITUDE DEVELOPMENT AS A FUNCTION OF REFERENCE GROUPS: THE BENNINGTON STUDY

Theodore M. Newcomb

Membership in established groups usually involves the taking on of whole patterns of interrelated behavior and attitudes. This was one of the hypotheses pursued in the study which is reported here in part. The group selected for study consisted of the entire student body at Bennington College—more than 600 individuals—between the years 1935 and 1939. One of the problems to be investigated was that of the manner in which the patterning of behavior and attitudes varied with different degrees of assimilation into the community.

Not all of the attitudes and behaviors that are likely to be taken on by new members, as they become absorbed into a community, can be investigated in a single study. A single, though rather inclusive, area of adaptation to the college community was therefore selected for special study, namely, *attitudes toward*

From Readings in Social Psychology *edited by E. E. Maccoby, T. M. Newcomb, and E. L. Hartley, Third Edition. Copyright 1947, 1952, © 1958 by Holt, Rinehart and Winston, Inc. Reprinted by permission of Holt, Rinehart and Winston, Inc.*

public affairs. There were two reasons for this selection: (1) methods of attitude measurement were readily available; and (2) there was an unusually high degree of concern, in this community at this time, over a rather wide range of public issues. This latter fact resulted partly from the fact that the college opened its doors during the darkest days of the depression of the 1930's, and its formative period occurred in the period of social change characterized by the phrase "the New Deal." This was also the period of gathering war clouds in Europe. Underlying both of these circumstances, however, was the conviction on the part of the faculty that one of the foremost duties of the college was to acquaint its somewhat oversheltered students with the nature of their contemporary social world.

In a membership group in which certain attitudes are approved (i.e., held by majorities, and conspicuously so by leaders), individuals acquire the approved attitudes to the extent that the membership group (particularly as symbolized by leaders and dominant subgroups) serves as a positive point of reference. The findings of the Bennington study seem to be better understood in terms of this thesis than any other. The distinction between membership group and reference group is a crucial one, in fact, although the original report did not make explicit use of it.

The above statement does not imply that no reference groups other than the membership group are involved in attitude formation; as we shall see, this is distinctly not the case. Neither does it imply that the use of the membership group as reference group necessarily results in adoption of the approved attitudes. It may also result in their rejection; hence the word *positive* in the initial statement. It is precisely these variations in degree and manner of relationship between reference group and membership group which must be known in order to explain individual variations in attitude formation, as reported in this study.

The essential facts about the Bennington membership group are as follows: (1) It was small enough (about 250 women students) so that data could be obtained from every member. (2) It was in most respects self-sufficient; college facilities provided not only the necessities of living and studying, but also a cooperative store, post office and Western Union office, beauty parlor, gasoline station, and a wide range of recreational opportunities. The average student visited the four-mile-distant village once a week and spent one week end a month away from the college. (3) It was self-conscious and enthusiastic, in large part because it was new (the study was begun during the first year in which there was a senior class) and because of the novelty and attractiveness of the college's educational plan. (4) It was unusually active and concerned about public issues, largely because the faculty felt that its educational duties included the familiarizing of an oversheltered student body with the implications of a depression-torn

America and a war-threatened world. (5) It was relatively homogeneous in respect to home background; tuition was very high, and the large majority of students came from urban, economically privileged families whose social attitudes were conservative.

Most individuals in this total membership group went through rather marked changes in attitudes toward public issues, as noted below. In most cases the total membership group served as the reference group for the changing attitudes. But some individuals changed little or not at all in attitudes during the four years of the study; attitude persistence was in some of these cases a function of the membership group as reference group and in some cases it was not. Among those who did change, moreover, the total membership group sometimes served as reference group but sometimes it did not. An oversimple theory of "assimilation into the community" thus leaves out of account some of those whose attitudes did and some of those whose attitudes did not change; they remain unexplained exceptions. A theory which traces the impact of other reference groups as well as the effect of the membership group seems to account for all cases without exception.

The general trend of attitude change for the total group is from freshman conservatism to senior nonconservatism (as the term was commonly applied to the issues toward which attitudes were measured). During the 1936 presidential election, for example, 62 percent of the freshmen and only 14 percent of the juniors and seniors "voted" for the Republican candidate, 29 percent of freshmen and 54 percent of juniors and seniors for Roosevelt, and 9 percent of freshmen as compared with 30 percent of juniors and seniors for the Socialist or Communist candidates. Attitudes toward nine specific issues were measured during the four years of the study, and seniors were less conservative in all of them than freshmen; six of the nine differences are statistically reliable. These differences are best shown by a Likert type scale labeled Political and Economic Progressivism (PEP) which dealt with such issues as unemployment, public relief, and the rights of organized labor, which were made prominent by the New Deal. Its odd-even reliability was about .9, and it was given once or more during each of the four years of the study to virtually all students. The critical ratios of the differences between freshmen and juniors-seniors in four successive years ranged between 3.9 and 6.5; the difference between the average freshman and senior scores of 44 individuals (the entire class that graduated in 1939) gives a critical ratio of 4.3.

As might be anticipated in such a community, *individual prestige was associated with nonconservatism.* Frequency of choice as one of five students "most worthy to represent the College" at an intercollegiate gathering was used as a measure of prestige. Nominations were submitted in sealed envelopes by 99 percent of all students in two successive years, with almost identical results. The nonconservatism of those with high prestige is not merely the result of the fact that juniors and seniors are characterized by both high prestige and nonconservatism; in each class those who have most prestige are least conservative. For example, ten freshmen receiving 2 to 4 choices had an average PEP score of 64.6 as compared with 72.8 for freshmen not chosen at all (high scores are conservative); eight sophomores chosen 12 or more times had an average score of 63.6 as compared with 71.3 for those not chosen; the mean PEP score of five juniors and seniors chosen 40 or more times was 50.4 and of the fifteen chosen 12 to 39 times, 57.6, as compared with 69.0 for those not chosen. In each

class, those intermediate in prestige are also intermediate in average PEP score.

Such were the attitudinal characteristics of the total membership group, expressed in terms of average scores. Some individuals, however, showed these characteristics in heightened form and others failed to show them at all. An examination of the various reference groups in relation to which attitude change did or did not occur, and of the ways in which they were brought to bear, will account for a large part of such attitude variance.

Information concerning reference groups was obtained both directly, from the subjects themselves, and indirectly, from other students and from teachers. Chief among the indirect procedures was the obtaining of indexes of "community citizenship" by a guess-who technique. Each of twenty-four students, carefully selected to represent every cross section and grouping of importance within the community, named three individuals from each of three classes who were reputedly most extreme in each of twenty-eight characteristics related to community citizenship. The relationship between reputation for community identification and nonconservatism is a close one, in spite of the fact that no reference was made to the latter characteristic when the judges made their ratings. A reputation index was computed, based upon the frequency with which individuals were named in five items dealing with identification with the community, minus the number of times they were named in five other items dealing with negative community attitude. Examples of the former items are: "absorbed in college community affairs," and "influenced by community expectations regarding codes, standards, etc."; examples of the latter are: "indifferent to activities of student committees," and "resistant to community expectations regarding codes, standards, etc." The mean senior PEP score of fifteen individuals whose index was + 15 or more was 54.4; of sixty-three whose index was + 4 to − 4, 65.3; and of ten whose index was − 15 or less, 68.2.

To have the reputation of identifying oneself with the community is not the same thing, however, as to identify the community as a reference group for a specific purpose—e.g., in this case, as a point of reference for attitudes toward public issues. In short, the reputation index is informative as to degree and direction of tendency to use the total membership group as a *general* reference group, but not necessarily as a group to which social attitudes are referred. For this purpose information was obtained directly from students.

Informal investigation had shown that whereas most students were aware of the marked freshman-to-senior trend away from conservatism, a few (particularly among the conservatives) had little or no awareness of it. Obviously, those not aware of the dominant community trend could not be using the community as a reference group for an attitude. (It does not follow, of course, that all those who are aware of it are necessarily using the community as reference group.) A simple measure of awareness was therefore devised. Subjects were asked to respond in two ways to a number of attitude statements taken from the PEP scale: first, to indicate agreement or disagreement (for example, with the statement: "The budget should be balanced before the government spends any money on social security"); and second, to estimate what percentage of freshmen, juniors and seniors and faculty would agree with the statement. From these responses was computed an index of divergence (of own attitude) from the estimated majority of juniors and

seniors. Thus a positive index on the part of a senior indicates the degree to which her own responses are more conservative than those of her classmates, and a negative index the degree to which they are less conservative. Those seniors whose divergence index more or less faithfully reflects the true difference between own and class attitude may (or may not) be using the class as an attitude reference group; those whose divergence indexes represent an exaggerated or minimized version of the true relationship between own and class attitude are clearly not using the class as an attitude reference group, or if so, only in a fictitious sense. (For present purposes the junior-senior group may be taken as representative of the entire student body, since it is the group which "sets the tone" of the total membership group.)

These data were supplemented by direct information obtained in interviews with seniors in three consecutive classes, just prior to graduation. Questions were asked about resemblance between own attitudes and those of class majorities and leaders, about parents' attitudes and own resemblance to them, about any alleged "social pressure to become liberal," about probable reaction if the dominant college influence had been conservative instead of liberal, etc. Abundant information was also available from the college personnel office and from the college psychiatrist. It was not possible to combine all of these sources of information into intensive studies of each individual, but complete data were assembled for (roughly) the most conservative and least conservative sixths of three consecutive graduating classes. The twenty-four nonconservative and nineteen conservative seniors thus selected for intensive study were classified according to their indexes of conservative divergence and of community reputation. Thus eight sets of seniors were identified, all individuals within each set having in common similar attitude scores, similar reputations for community identification, and similar degrees of awareness (based upon divergence index) of own attitude position relative to classmates. The following descriptions of these eight sets of seniors will show that there was a characteristic pattern of relationship between membership group and reference group within each of the sets.

1. *Conservatives, reputedly negativistic, aware of their own relative conservatism.* Four of the five are considered stubborn or resistant by teachers (all five, by student judges). Three have prestige scores of 0, scores of the other two being about average for their class. Four of the five are considered by teachers or the psychiatrists, or by both, to be overdependent upon one or both parents. All of the four who were interviewed described *their major hopes,* on entering college, *in terms of social rather than academic prestige;* all four felt that they had been defeated in this aim. The following verbatim quotations are illustrative:

E2: "Probably the feeling that (my instructors) didn't accept me led me to reject their opinions." (She estimates classmates as being only moderately less conservative than herself, but faculty as much less so.)

G32: "I wouldn't care to be intimate with those so-called 'liberal' student leaders." *(She claims to be satisfied with a small group of friends.* She is chosen as friend, in a sociometric questionnaire responded to by all students, only twice, and reciprocates both choices; both are conservative students.)

F22: "I wanted to disagree with all the noisy liberals, but I was afraid and I couldn't. *So I built up a wall inside me against what they said. I found I couldn't compete, so I decided to stick to my father's*

ideas. *For at least two years I've been insulated against all college influences."* (She is chosen but once as a friend, and does not reciprocate that choice.)

Q10: (who rather early concluded that she had no chance of social success in college) "It hurt me at first, but now I don't give a damn. *The things I really care about are mostly outside the college.* I think radicalism symbolizes the college for me more than anything else." (Needless to say, she has no use for radicals.)

For these four individuals (and probably for the fifth also) the community serves as reference group in a *negative* sense, and the home-and-family group in a positive sense. Thus their conservatism is dually reinforced.

2. *Conservatives, reputedly negativistic, unaware of their own relative conservatism.* All five are described by teachers, as well as by guess-who judges, to be stubborn or resistant. Four have prestige scores of 0, and the fifth a less than average score. Each reciprocated just one friendship choice. Four are considered insecure in social relationships, and all five are regarded as extremely dependent upon parents. In interviews four describe with considerable intensity, and the fifth with more moderation, precollege experiences of rebuff, ostracism, or isolation, and all describe their hopes, on entering college, in terms of making friends or avoiding rebuff rather than in terms of seeking prestige. All five felt that their (rather modest) aims had met with good success. Each of the five denies building up any resistance to the acceptance of liberal opinions (but two add that they would have resented any such pressure, if felt). Three believe that only small, special groups in the college have such opinions, while the other two describe themselves as just going their own way, *paying no*

attention to anything but their own little circles and their college work. Typical quotations follow:

Q47: "I'm a perfect middle-of-the-roader, neither enthusiast nor critic. I'd accept anything if they just let me alone.... I've made all the friends I want." (Only one of her friendship choices is reciprocated.)

Q19: *"In high school I was always thought of as my parents' daughter.* I never felt really accepted for myself.... I wanted to make my own way here, socially, but independence from my family has never asserted itself in other ways." (According to guess-who ratings, she is highly resistant to faculty authority.)

L12: "What I most wanted was to get over being a scared bunny.... I always resent doing the respectable thing just because it's the thing to do, but I didn't realize I was so different, politically, from my classmates. At least I agree with the few people I ever talk to about such matters." (Sociometric responses place her in a small, conservative group.)

Q81: "I hated practically all my school life before coming here. I had the perfect inferiority complex, and I pulled out of school social life—out of fear. I didn't intend to repeat that mistake here.... I've just begun to be successful in winning friendships, and I've been blissfully happy here." (She is described by teachers as "pathologically belligerent"; she receives more than the average number of friendship choices, but reciprocates only one of them.)

For these five individuals, who are negativistic in the sense of being near-isolates rather than rebels, the community does not serve as reference group for public attitudes. To some extent, their small friendship groups serve in this capacity, but in the main they still refer such areas of their lives to the home-and-family group. They are too absorbed in their own pursuits to use the total membership group as a reference group for most other purposes, too.

3. *Conservatives, not reputedly negativistic, aware of their own relative conservatism.* Three of the five are described by teachers as "cooperative" and "eager," and none as stubborn or resistant. Four are above average in prestige. Four are considered by teachers or by guess-who raters, or both, to retain very close parental ties. All four who were interviewed had more or less definite ambitions for leadership on coming to college, and all felt that they had been relatively successful—though, in the words of one of them, none ever attained the "really topnotch positions." All four are aware of conflict between parents and college community in respect to public attitudes, and all quite consciously decided to "string along" with parents, feeling self-confident of holding their own in college in spite of being atypical in this respect. Sample quotations follow:

Q73: *"I'm all my mother has in the world. It's considered intellectually superior here to be liberal or radical. This puts me on the defensive,* as I refuse to consider my mother beneath me intellectually, as so many other students do. Apart from this, I have loved every aspect of college life." (A popular girl, many of whose friends are among the nonconservative college leaders.)

Q78: *"I've come to realize how much my mother's happiness depends on me, and the best way I can help her is to do things with her at home as often as I can.* This has resulted in my not getting the feel of the college in certain ways, and I know my general conservatism is one of those ways. But it has not been important enough to me to make me feel particularly left out. If you're genuine and inoffensive about your opinions, no one really minds here if you remain conservative." (Another popular girl, whose friends were found among many groups.)

F32: *"Family against faculty has been my struggle here.* As soon as I felt really secure here I decided not to let the college atmosphere affect me too much. Every time I've tried to rebel against my family I've found out how terribly wrong I am, and so I've naturally kept to my parents' attitudes." (While not particularly popular, she shows no bitterness and considerable satisfaction over her college experience.)

Q35: "I've been aware of a protective shell against radical ideas. When I found several of my best friends getting that way, I either had to go along or just shut out that area entirely. I couldn't respect myself if I had changed my opinions just for that reason, and so I almost deliberately lost interest—really, *it was out of fear of losing my friends."* (A very popular girl, with no trace of bitterness, who is not considered too dependent upon parents.)

For these five the total membership group does not serve as reference group in respect to public attitudes, but does so serve for most other purposes. At some stage in their college careers the conflict between college community and home and family as reference group for public attitudes was resolved in favor of the latter.

4. *Conservatives, not reputedly negativistic, not aware of their own relative conservatism.* All four are consistently described by teachers as conscientious and cooperative; three are considered overdocile and uncritical of authority. All are characterized by feelings of inferiority. All are low in prestige, two receiving scores of 0; all are low in friendship choices, but reciprocate most of these few choices. Two are described as in conflict about parental authority, and two as dependent and contented. All four recall considerable anxiety as to whether they would fit into the college community; all feel that they have succeeded better than

they had expected. Sample statements from interviews follow:

D22: "I'd like to think like the college leaders, but I'm not bold enough and I don't know enough. So the college trend means little to me; I didn't even realize how much more conservative I am than the others. *I guess my family influence has been strong enough to counterbalance the college influence."* (This girl was given to severe emotional upsets, and according to personnel records, felt "alone and helpless except when with her parents.")

M12: "It isn't that I've been resisting any pressure to become liberal. The influences here didn't matter enough to resist, I guess. *All that's really important that has happened to me occurred outside of college,* and so I never became very susceptible to college influences." *(Following her engagement to be married, in her second year, she had "practically retired" from community life.)*

Q68: "If I'd had more time here I'd probably have caught on to the liberal drift here. But I've been horribly busy making money and trying to keep my college work up. *Politics and that sort of thing I've always associated with home instead of with the college."* (A "town girl" of working-class parentage.)

Q70: "Most juniors and seniors, if they really *get excited about their work, forget about such community enthusiasms as sending telegrams to Congressmen.* It was so important to me to be accepted, I mean intellectually, *that I naturally came to identify myself in every way with the group which gave me this sort of intellectual satisfaction."* (One of a small group of science majors, nearly all conservative, who professed no interests other than science and who were highly self-sufficient socially.)

For none of the four was the total membership group a reference group for public attitudes. Unlike the nonnegativistic conservatives who are aware of their relative conservatism, they refer to the total membership group for few if any other purposes. Like the negativistic conservatives who are unaware of their relative conservatism, their reference groups for public attitudes are almost exclusively those related to home and family.

5. *Nonconservatives, reputedly community-identified, aware of their relative nonconservatism.* Each of the seven is considered highly independent by teachers, particularly in intellectual activities; all but one are referred to as meticulous, perfectionist, or overconscientious. Four are very high in prestige, two high, and one average; all are "good group members," and all but one a "leader." None is considered overdependent upon parents. All have come to an understanding with parents concerning their "liberal" views; five have "agreed to differ," and the other two describe one or both parents as "very liberal." All take their public attitudes seriously, in most cases expressing the feeling that they have bled and died to achieve them. Interview excerpts follow:

B72: *"I bend in the direction of community expectation*—almost more than I want to. I constantly have to check myself to be sure it's real self-conviction and not just social respect." (An outstanding and deeply respected leader.)

M42: "My family has always been liberal, but the influences here made me go further, and for a while I was pretty far left. Now I'm pretty much in agreement with my family again, but it's my own and it means a lot. It wouldn't be easy for me to have friends who are very conservative." (Her friendship choices are exclusively given to nonconservatives.)

E72: "I had been allowed so much independence by my parents that I needed desperately to identify myself with an institution with which I could conform

conscientiously. Bennington was perfect. I drank up everything the college had to offer, including social attitudes, though not uncritically. I've become active in radical groups and constructively critical of them." (Both during and after college she worked with C.I.O. unions.)

H32: "I accepted liberal attitudes here because *I had always secretly felt that my family was narrow and intolerant, and because such attitudes had prestige value.* It was all part of my generally expanding personality—*I had never really been part of anything before.* I don't accept things without examining things, however, and I was sure I meant it before I changed." (One of those who has "agreed to differ" with parents.)

Q43: "It didn't take me long to see that liberal attitudes had prestige value. But all the time I felt inwardly superior to persons who want public acclaim. Once I had arrived at a feeling of personal security, I could see that it wasn't important—it wasn't enough. *So many people have no security at all. I became liberal at first because of its prestige value.* I remain so because the problems around which my liberalism centers are important. What I want now is to be effective in solving the problems." (Another conspicuous leader, active in and out of college in liberal movements.)

The total membership clearly serves as reference group for these individuals' changing attitudes, but by no means as the only one. For those whose parents are conservative, parents represent a negative reference group, from whom emancipation was gained via liberal attitudes. And for several of them the college community served as a bridge to outside liberal groups as points of reference.

6. *Nonconservatives, reputedly community-identified, not aware of their own relative nonconservatism.* The word *enthusiastic* appears constantly in the records

of each of these six. All are considered eager, ambitious, hard-working, and anxious to please. Four are very high in prestige, the other two about average. None is considered overdependent upon parents, and only two are known to have suffered any particular conflict in achieving emancipation. Each one came to college with ambitions for leadership, and each professes extreme satisfaction with her college experience. Sample quotations follow:

Qx: "Every influence I felt tended to push me in the liberal direction: my underdog complex, *my need to be independent of my parents, and my anxiousness to be a leader here.*"

Q61: "I met a whole body of new information here; I took a deep breath and plunged. When I talked about it at home my family began to treat me as if I had an adult mind. *Then too, my new opinions gave me the reputation here of being open-minded and capable of change.* I think I could have got really radical but I found it wasn't the way to get prestige here." (She judges most of her classmates to be as nonconservative as herself.)

Q72: "I take everything hard, and so of course I reacted hard to all the attitudes I found here. I'm 100-percent enthusiastic about Bennington, and that includes liberalism (but not radicalism, though I used to think so.) Now I know that you can't be an *extremist if you're really devoted to an institution,* whether it's a labor union or a college." (A conspicuous leader who, like most of the others in this set of six, *judges classmates to be only slightly more conservative than herself.)*

Q63: *"I came to college to get away from my family,* who never had any respect for my mind. Becoming a radical meant thinking for myself and, figuratively, thumbing my nose at my family. *It also meant intellectual identification with the faculty and students that I*

most wanted to be like." (She has always felt oppressed by parental respectability and sibling achievements.)

Q57: "It's very simple. *I was so anxious to be accepted that I accepted the political complexion of the community here.* I just couldn't stand out against the crowd unless I had many friends and strong support." (Not a leader, but many close friends among leaders and nonconservatives.)

For these six, like the preceding seven, the membership group serves as reference group for public affairs. They differ from the preceding seven chiefly in that they are less sure of themselves and are careful "not to go too far." Hence they tend to repudiate "radicalism," and to judge classmates as only slightly less conservative than themselves.

7. Nonconservatives, not reputedly community-identified, aware of own relative nonconservatism. Each of the six is described as highly independent and critical-minded. Four are consistently reported as intellectually outstanding, and the other two occasionally so. All describe their ambitions on coming to college in intellectual rather than in social terms. Four of the five who were interviewed stated that in a conservative college they would be "even more radical than here." Two are slightly above average in prestige, two below average, and two have 0 scores. Three have gone through rather severe battles in the process of casting off what they regard as parental shackles; none is considered overdependent upon parents. Sample interview excepts follow:

Q7: *"All my life I've resented the protection of governesses and parents.* What I most wanted here was the intellectual approval of teachers and the more advanced students. Then I found you can't be reactionary and be intellectually respectable." (Her traits of independence became more marked as she achieved academic distinction.)

Q21: "I simply got filled with new ideas here, and the only possible formulation of all of them was to adopt a radical approach. *I can't see my own position in the world in any other terms. The easy superficiality with which so many prestige-hounds here get 'liberal' only forced me to think it out more intensely.*" (A highly gifted girl, considered rather aloof.)

C32: "*I started rebelling against my pretty stuffy family before I came to college.* I felt apart from freshmen here, because I was older. Then I caught on to faculty attempts to undermine prejudice. I took sides with the faculty immmediately, against the immature freshmen. I crusaded about it. *It provided just what I needed by way of family rebellion,* and bolstered up my self-confidence, too." (A very bright girl, regarded as sharp tongued and a bit haughty.)

J24: "*I'm easily influenced by people whom I respect,* and the people who rescued me when I was down and out, intellectually, gave me a radical intellectual approach; they included both teachers and advanced students. *I'm not rebelling against anything.* I'm just doing what I had to do to stand on my own feet intellectually." (Her academic work was poor as a freshman, but gradually became outstanding.)

For these six students it is not the total membership group, but dominant subgroups (faculty, advanced students) which at first served as positive reference groups, and for many of them the home group served as a negative point of reference. Later, they developed extracollege reference groups (left-wing writers, etc.). In a secondary sense, however, the total membership group served as a negative point of reference—i.e., they regarded their nonconservatism as a mark of personal superiority.

8. *Nonconservatives, not reputedly community-identified, not aware of own*

relative nonconservatism. Each of the five is considered hard-working, eager, and enthusiastic but (especially during the first year or two) unsure of herself and too dependent upon instructors. They are "good citizens," but in a distinctly retiring way. Two are above average in prestige, and the other three much below average. None of the five is considered overdependent upon parents; two are known to have experienced a good deal of conflict in emancipating themselves. All regard themselves as "pretty average persons," with strong desire to conform; they describe their ambitions in terms of social acceptance instead of social or intellectual prestige. Sample excerpts follow:

E22: "*Social security is the focus of it all with me.* I became steadily less conservative as long as I was *needing to gain in personal security, both with students and with faculty.* I developed some resentment against a few extreme radicals who don't really represent the college viewpoint, and that's why I changed my attitudes so far and no further." (A girl with a small personal following, otherwise not especially popular.)

D52: "*Of course there's social pressure here to give up your conservatism.* I'm glad of it, because for me this became the *vehicle for achieving independence from my family.* So changing my attitudes has gone hand in hand with two *very important things: establishing my own independence and at the same time becoming a part of the college organism.*" (She attributes the fact that her social attitudes changed, while those of her younger sister, also at the college, did not, to the fact that she had greater need both of family independence and of group support.)

Q6: "I was ripe for developing liberal or even radical opinions because so many of my friends at home were doing the same thing. So it was really wonderful that I could agree with all the people

I respected here and the same time move in the direction that my home friends were going." (A girl characterized by considerable personal instability at first, but showing marked improvement.)

Qy: "I think my change of opinions has given me *intellectual and social self-respect at the same time.* I used to be too timid for words, and I never had an idea of my own. As I gradually became more successful in my work and made more friends, I came to feel that it didn't matter so much whether I agreed with my parents. It's all part of the feeling that I really belong here." (Much other evidence confirms this; she was lonely and pathetic at first, but really belonged later.)

These five provide the example *par excellence* of individuals who came to identify themselves with "the community" and whose attitudes change *pari passu* with the growing sense of identity. Home-and-family groups served as supplementary points of reference, either positive or negative. To varying degrees, subgroups within the community served as focal points of reference. But, because of *their need to be accepted, it was primarily the membership group as such which served as reference group for these five.*

SUMMARY

In this community, as presumably in most others, all individuals belong to the total membership group, but such membership is not necessarily a point of reference for every form of social adaptation, e.g., for acquiring attitudes toward public issues. *Such attitudes, however, are not acquired in a social vacuum. Their acquisition is a function of relating oneself to some group or groups, positively or negatively.* In many cases (perhaps in all) the referring of social attitudes to one group negatively leads to referring them to another group positively, or vice versa, so that the attitudes are dually reinforced.

An individual is, of course, "typical" in respect to attitudes if the total membership group serves as a positive point of reference for that purpose, but "typicality" may also result from the use of other reference groups. It does not follow from the fact that an individual is "atypical" that the membership group does not serve for reference purposes; it may serve as negative reference group. Even if the membership group does not serve as reference group at all (as in the case of conservatives in this community who are unaware of the general freshman-to-senior trend), it cannot be concluded that attitude development is not a function of belonging to the total membership group. The unawareness of such individuals is itself a resultant adaptation of particular individuals to a particular membership group. The fact that such individuals continue to refer attitudes toward public issues primarily to home-and-family groups is, in part at least, a result of the kind of community in which they have membership.

In short, the Bennington findings seem to support the thesis that, in a community characterized by certain approved attitudes, the individual's attitude development is a function of the way in which he relates himself both to the total membership group and to one or more reference groups.

INTERPERSONAL ATTITUDES OF TEACHERS AND ADVANTAGED AND DISADVANTAGED PUPILS

Albert H. Yee

According to Gage (1965), three basic areas of psychological research require attention in order to improve teacher education for the Great Cities: (1) pupils' characteristics, (2) teachers' methods and characteristics, and (3) teacher education. Only the first area, however, has been given much study. According to Gordon (1965, p. 375), chairman of a comprehensive review of research on education for socially disadvantaged youth, researchers have emphasized the "ways in which [such children] differ from their more privileged peers and into the nature of evaluation and remedial approaches to problems of the disadvantaged. Striking is the dearth of studies which attack basic problems in learning and instruction... and are radically experimental." As far as this writer can ascertain, the situation that Gordon decried continues today. Much needed research remains to be done in what Gage suggested in areas (2) and (3), i.e., teachers' characteristics, classroom interaction, effective school strategies, and desirable classroom procedures.

A massive study in this area recently completed by Coleman *et al.* (1966) must be considered the most important single contribution to this field of educational research (reviewed by Nichols, 1966, and Bowles and Levin, 1968). However, it has serious limitations where the above needs are greatest. Even though Coleman *et al.* investigated the characteristics of teachers and pupils, their report discussed teachers' and pupils' characteristics separately and considered schools as the unit of analysis. Thus, conclusions and implications do not focus upon classrooms and what may well be the greatest source of variance—teacher-pupil interaction (Withall and Lewis, 1963). Examples of some of the report's important conclusions regarding the education of minority group (disadvantaged) pupils are as follows:

> ...children from a given family background, when put in schools of different social composition, will achieve at quite different levels. This effect is again less for white pupils than for any minority group other than Oriental. Thus, ...if a minority pupil from a home without

From: Journal of Human Resources, *1968, 3, 327–45. Copyright © 1968 by the Regents of the University of Wisconsin.*

much educational strength is put with schoolmates with strong educational background, his achievement is likely to increase (p. 22).

Also,

...the effect of good teachers is greatest upon the children who suffer most educational disadvantage in their background and that a given investment in up-grading teacher quality will have most effect on achievement in underprivileged areas (p. 317).

However, the researchers concluded that:

...schools bring little influence to bear on a child's achievement that is independent of his background and general social context; and that this very lack of an independent effect means that the inequalities imposed on children by their home, neighborhood, and peer environment are carried along to become the inequalities with which they confront adult life at the end of school (p. 325).

This writer wishes the Coleman report had given more consideration to teacher-pupil interpersonal relationships by obtaining greater information on teachers' and pupils' characteristics together. For, without such information and analysis, what steps can best improve educational settings, especially for disadvantaged youth, are difficult to specify and investigate. Relevant to this point, Charters (1963) has suggested that greater understanding of the social forces affecting teaching will be found when researchers focus more upon the "functional connections" of a community's social and cultural forces, the teacher's personality and characteristics, and the teaching-learning processes.

The Coleman report recommended that for equality of educational opportunity, schools must provide 'strong effects" independent of disadvantaged children's immediate social environment. Thus, we ask: What can be done to provide the necessary "strong effects"? One major inference made by the report was that the greatest contribution schools can offer as "strong effects" would be integrating disadvantaged with advantaged pupils. Such is the implication in the first quotation from the report above. But what is the causal factor that provides such effects —association with advantaged classmates, the teachers of advantaged pupils, the interaction of both factors, or the effect of other factors? Can we specify what variables are crucial in promoting the school achievement of disadvantaged pupils when integration is provided them?

Another inference made by the report was that disadvantaged pupils require "good teachers." But then the question is raised: What are the characteristics of a good teacher? Are the characteristics the same for disadvantaged as well as for advantaged pupils? Providing teachers who are college graduates, are professionally trained, and perform well on vocabulary tests is obvious, but the report admits insufficient data were collected on teachers' characteristics to be conclusive on the matter of teacher quality (p. 22).

Research on the question of what relevant variables effect the achievement of disadvantaged pupils in integrated classes is badly needed. On the question of what is a good teacher, Ryans (1960) has shown how complex this concern can be to investigate. After much rigorous research, he was able to describe most of the behavior of teachers by three major dimensions:

TCS Pattern X_0—warm, understanding, friendly *vs.* aloof, egocentric, restricted teacher behavior.

TCS Pattern Y_0—responsible, business-like, systematic *vs.* evading, unplanned, slip-shod teacher behavior.

TCS Pattern Z_0—stimulating, imaginative, surgent *vs.* dull, routine teacher behavior. (p. 382)

Ryans found that the three dimensions were highly intercorrelated among elementary school teachers and appeared to be highly correlated with pupils' classroom behavior. Viewed together, the dimensions appear to be quite similar to teacher characteristics indicated by the Minnesota Teacher Attitude Inventory and the "About My Teacher" inventory. Utilizing data on these inventories, this article provides further information on the characteristics of advantaged and disadvantaged pupils and their teachers. Results of other analyses of the same body of data dealing with interpersonal influence operating between teacher and pupils are reported in Yee (1968).

BACKGROUND OF THE STUDY

SAMPLE

The two-year study (Yee, 1966) providing the data for this report was mainly concerned with interpersonal influence operating between teachers and pupils and the effect upon teacher-pupil relationships by a variety of factors.

Data were first obtained in the 1964–65 school year from 100 intermediate-grade teachers and their pupils (pretest N = 2,952; post-test N = 2,871) in 34 public elementary schools located mainly in middle-class (MC) neighborhoods of San Francisco, California; Austin, Texas; and San Antonio, Texas.

In the 1965–66 school year, data were collected from 112 teachers and their pupils (pretest N = 2,824; post-test N = 2,777) in 16 public schools located in lower-class (LC) neighborhoods of cities in central Texas. Some classrooms in four schools located in MC neighborhoods were tested so that data could be exchanged between the two years' testings to form roughly equal-sized samples homogeneous in social class. Recruiting procedures conducted with school administrators created no known systematic bias in the sample selected. The sample obtained is believed to be a fair representation of LC and MC pupils and their teachers, even though rigorous random selection was not possible.

Social-class status and ethnic background was determined by consultation with school administrators and informal inspection of neighborhoods. Family income ($4,000 or less annually for lower class; $6,000 or more for middle class) and father's occupation (blue-collar and unskilled for lower class; white-collar and professional for middle class), as ascertained from school administrators, were the main criteria for establishing social-class status.

Thus, by the end of the fall semester, 1965–66, data had been secured for 102 teachers and their pupils in 32 schools situated in MC neighborhoods (in Grade 4, N = 33; Grade 5, N = 36; Grade 6, N = 33) and 110 teachers and pupils in 18 schools situated in LC neighborhoods (in Grade 4, N = 39; Grade 5, N = 38; Grade 6, N = 31; Grade 7, N = 2). The two Grade 7 classes were combined with the Grade 6 classes. Three levels of teaching experience were established; for LC: 0–1 year (5 with one year's experience), N = 25; 2–8 years (average of 4.6 years), N = 36; 9 + years (average of 19.9 years), N = 49; and for MC: 0–1 year (4 with one year's experience), N = 39; 2–8 years (average of 5.5 years), N = 31; 9 + years (average of 17.2 years), N = 32.

DATA

Pretests were administered about the second week of school and post-tests were administered toward the end of the first semester.

Teachers' attitudes were measured with the Minnesota Teacher Attitude Inventory (MTAI) and a semantic-differential (Osgood, Suci, and Tannenbaum, 1957) prepared for this study with "My Class" as the concept and 17 bipolar adjectives highly loaded on the evaluative dimension. In using the MTAI, we do not overlook concerns for its validity (Yee, 1967). We use the MTAI for its research value as an "indicant" of teachers' affective attitudes toward children. Pupils' attitudes were measured with the 100-item "About My Teacher" inventory (AMT) developed by Beck (1964) under the direction of N.L. Gage. Factor analyses provided 11 measures of pupils' affective, cognitive, disciplinary, innovative, and motivational attitudes toward their teachers to supplement the total AMT measures. Because of space limitations, this article will refer only to total MTAI scores (T_0, T_0'; unprimed symbols indicate pretests and primed symbols indicate post-tests); the first factor with 17 items, "Traditionalistic versus Modern Beliefs about Child Control" (T_1, T_1'), from Horn and Morrison's (1965) factor analysis of the MTAI; and total scores from the pupil inventory (P_0, P_0').

ANALYSES OF TEACHERS' AND PUPILS' ATTITUDES

Analyses of variance were first computed using two statistical computer programs developed by D. J. Veldman (1967, pp. 246–58). One program allowed unequal N's in multiple analysis of variance (MANOVA) for subject groups, and the other provided one-factor analysis of variance for unequal group N's. Veldman's MANOVA program accommodates unequal numbers of subjects in multiple groups according to the method of unweighted means described by Winer (1962, pp. 222-24).

Since Winer considers the unweighted means analysis less powerful than a least-squares analysis (p. 224), a MANOVA program[1] providing a least-squares solution for the sums of squares was also applied to the data. Results obtained with the two MANOVA programs were found to compare favorably with more conservative F ratios obtained in the second series of computations. This article, therefore, reports results obtained with the MANOVA program providing the least-squares analyses.

The one-factor ANOVA program by Veldman and the STATJOB program available at the University of Wisconsin Computer Center utilize similar conventional procedures and were found to provide the same results.

FACTORIAL ANALYSES

Table 1, 2, and 3 present the means and standard deviations found for the multiple groups analyzed in three factorial analyses. Each contained two levels of pupils' social-class background as discussed earlier. The three factorial analyses varied in the second factor considered, i.e., (1) three levels of teacher's experience; (2) three levels of class grade level; and (3) two levels of teacher sex.

The standard deviations shown in Tables 1, 2, and 3 indicate that the assumption of homogeneity of variance across cell observations may not have been met in

[1] Developed by D. J. Clyde, E. M. Cramer, and R. J. Sherin at the Biometric Laboratory of the University of Miami; on file at the Social Science Data and Computation Center, University of Wisconsin, Madison.

TABLE 1

MEANS AND STANDARD DEVIATIONS FROM ANALYSES
WITH PUPILS' SOCIAL CLASS AND TEACHER'S
EXPERIENCE AS FACTORS

Factor levels										
Pupil's social class	Teacher's years of experience	N		T_0	T_1	P_0	T_0'	T_1'	P_0'	
Middle-class	0–1	39	M	43.36	7.54	128.39	36.21	6.54	126.10	
			SD	28.63	6.55	15.40	36.73	8.03	17.78	
	2–8	31	M	48.00	5.61	129.05	43.71	4.13	129.84	
			SD	28.53	6.95	12.95	33.74	9.12	15.74	
	9+	32	M	38.75	5.84	125.23	44.56	6.41	124.04	
			SD	34.19	8.79	14.43	35.12	9.26	20.97	
Lower-class	0–1	25	M	27.76	4.68	126.20	30.36	5.28	121.62	
			SD	32.90	9.02	10.23	42.36	9.04	15.87	
	2–8	36	M	30.95	3.83	121.84	32.06	3.72	119.65	
			SD	29.18	8.20	11.38	32.72	8.78	14.53	
	9+	49	M	21.86	0.41	117.21	15.47	0.45	117.86	
			SD	33.05	8.22	11.83	39.95	9.90	16.11	

TABLE 2

MEANS AND STANDARD DEVIATIONS FROM ANALYSES
WITH PUPILS' SOCIAL CLASS AND GRADE LEVEL AS FACTORS

Factor levels										
Pupils' social class	Grade	N		T_0	T_1	P_0	T_0'	T_1'	P_0'	
	5	36	M	35.36	5.91	122.27	30.42	4.58	121.47	
			SD	32.79	6.94	11.58	38.68	8.51	12.77	
Middle-class	4	33	M	47.22	7.42	125.90	45.14	6.67	125.16	
			SD	28.50	8.55	15.29	32.50	9.08	19.60	
	6	33	M	47.03	5.85	134.78	47.40	5.97	133.28	
			SD	29.17	6.61	13.17	32.93	8.74	19.81	
	4	39	M	26.49	3.77	118.80	31.03	4.46	120.48	
			SD	28.64	8.61	12.08	35.13	9.08	11.85	
Lower-class	5	38	M	25.50	0.66	120.71	24.24	0.92	118.24	
			SD	36.42	8.64	12.94	40.23	9.29	15.65	
	6	33	M	26.58	3.12	123.17	16.36	2.40	119.11	
			SD	30.47	8.22	9.81	40.84	10.06	19.07	

TABLE 3

MEANS AND STANDARD DEVIATIONS FROM ANALYSES
WITH PUPILS' SOCIAL CLASS AND TEACHER'S SEX AS FACTORS

Factor levels									
Pupils' social class	*Teacher's sex*	N		T_0	T_1	P_0	T_0'	T_1'	P_0'
Middle-class	Female	82	M	41.17	6.40	125.74	39.74	5.72	124.49
			SD	32.23	7.71	13.73	37.05	8.88	17.80
	Male	20	M	52.15	6.50	135.20	46.70	5.95	135.20
			SD	19.30	6.21	14.61	26.38	8.40	17.95
Lower-class	Female	90	M	28.93	3.22	119.75	28.71	3.50	118.10
			SD	31.60	8.46	12.18	37.34	9.27	15.97
	Male	20	M	13.75	−.75	125.35	4.35	−1.35	124.67
			SD	30.23	8.31	8.74	39.90	9.66	11.96

all analyses, such as seen for the dependent variables of T_0 in Table 3. According to statisticians such as Hays (1965, p. 408), the homogeneity requirement is unimportant with a "relatively large number of observations per cell." When there are equal cell N's, "the requirement ... may also be violated without serious risk." All results, therefore, were compared with the same factorial analyses with cell N's made equal to the smallest cell N utilizing a table of random numbers.[2] Means were similar and the assumption of equal error variance in combinations was satisfied. The F tests of such data produced results comparable to results found with analyses of all the observations; conclusions based on either set of F ratios would be the same. Also, the very significant results to be discussed lessen concern for the problem of heterogeneity (Lindquist, 1953, p. 86). We now proceed to discuss the results of analyses with unequal N's.

[2] With computer program, N-Way Analysis of Variance, written by T. Houston, Laboratory of Experimental Design, Wisconsin Research and Development Center for Cognitive Learning.

Table 4 summarizes findings for analyses with pupils' social-class background as a source of variation in teachers' and pupils' interpersonal attitudes. Testing the effect of this factor with each of three different factors on the six dependent variables, we see that all 18 analyses result in highly significant F ratios. The uniform, unequivocal findings strongly indicate the magnitude of differences between the attitudes of teachers and pupils in the two groups. Reference to Tables 1–3 shows that the attitudes of MC pupils and their teachers are consistently more favorable than those for counterpart teachers and pupils in the LC pupil group. These findings, therefore, support the belief that pupils' social-class background is a major influence in the nature of teachers' and pupils' attitudes toward each other.

Table 5 summarizes results for factors other than pupils' social class. Only five of the 18 F ratios are statistically significant which indicates that the factors considered in Table 5 are less potent sources of variance than pupils' social class, especially for teachers' attitudes.

TABLE 4

RESULTS FOR PUPILS' SOCIAL CLASS AS SOURCE OF VARIATION

Factor analyzed with pupils' social class	Variable	Mean square	F Ratio	$p <$
Teacher's years of teaching experience (df = 1,206)	T_0	14,056.12	14.48	.001
	T_1	621.09	9.83	.002
	P_0	1,856.58	11.16	.001
	T_0'	13,977.04	10.26	.002
	T_1'	389.41	4.73	.031
	P_0'	2,499.12	8.73	.003
Grade level (df = 1,206)	T_0	15,246.01	15.70	.001
	T_1	819.98	12.76	.001
	P_0	2,310.37	14.49	.001
	T_0'	14,905.60	10.98	.001
	T_1'	529.22	6.33	.013
	P_0'	2,721.33	9.79	.002
Teacher's sex (df = 1,208)	T_0	15,620.02	16.46	.001
	T_1	825.25	12.97	.001
	P_0	2,388.82	14.62	.001
	T_0'	15,204.05	11.35	.001
	T_1'	534.94	6.49	.012
	P_0'	2,721.66	9.89	.002

TABLE 5

RESULTS FOR FACTORS OTHER THAN PUPILS' SOCIAL CLASS AS SOURCES OF VARIATION

Factor	Variable	Mean square	F Ratio	$p <$
Teacher's years of teaching experience (df = 1,206)	T_0	2,316.97	2.39	.094
	T_1	270.79	4.28	.015*
	P_0	977.76	5.88	.003*
	T_0'	2,124.87	1.56	.213
	T_1'	190.57	2.31	.101
	P_0'	411.80	1.44	.240
Grade level (df = 1,206)	T_0	825.46	.85	.429
	T_1	12.26	.19	.826
	P_0	1,307.68	8.20	.001*
	T_0'	255.72	.19	.828
	T_1'	11.73	.14	.869
	P_0'	588.08	2.01	.137
Teacher's sex (df = 1,208)	T_0	107.20	.11	.737
	T_0'	112.68	1.77	.185
	T_1	1,907.58	11.67	.001*
	P_0	2,314.98	1.73	.190
	T_1'	165.48	2.01	.158
	P_0'	2,501.40	9.09	.003*

* Statistically significant.

Pupils' Attitudes. Since four of the significant F ratios in Table 5 were found in analyses of pupils' attitudes, such factors appear to be important contributors to variance pupil groups, even though they are less potent effects than pupils' social class.

The factor of teacher's sex provides significant F ratios for the pre- and post-test attitudes of pupils. MC and LC pupils clearly favored male teachers over female teachers at both test occasions. This finding is particularly interesting when there is such contrast between the attitudes of male teachers teaching MC pupils and males teaching LC pupils, as can be seen in Table 3. More will be said of this contrast when teachers' attitudes are discussed.

With the factors of teachers' years of experience and grade level, the pretest attitudes of pupils, especially LC pupils, are significantly different. Pupils perceived or anticipated differences between levels of teachers' experience and grade level at the beginning of the school year. However, several months later when pupils were more familiar with their teachers, their P_0' scores did not differ significantly. Examination of pupils' attitude means in Tables 1 and 2 shows that the last result was brought about by substantial increases in variation from pre- to post-test within all groups rather than substantial changes in means. In MC and LC groups, pupils expressed less variation in their attitudes toward their teachers with moderate experience and Grade 4 teachers than they did toward other types of teachers. Whether teacher's experience, grade level, or any other factor is important to the variance of pupils' attitudes toward their teacher and may reflect a teacher's ability to communicate and express a common impression to every pupil in the class requires further study.

Mean pre- and post-test attitudes of LC pupils decline as teachers' years of experience increase, while MC pupils' attitudes are highest for teachers with moderate experience and lower for novice and senior teachers. The greatest change of pupils' attitudes from pre- to post-test was in the lowering of LC pupils' attitudes toward their beginning teachers. This should not be surprising since those teachers had a low T_0 mean score of 27.76 at the beginning of the semester, compared to the higher mean of 43.36 for beginning teachers of MC pupils. The more negative attitudes of their beginning teachers probably influenced LC pupils to lower their attitudes.

Pupils' pretest attitudes are higher from Grade 4 to Grade 6 in both social-class groups. However, while this progression holds true for the MC pupils' post-test attitudes, it does not for the post-test attitudes of LC pupils. Table 2 helps explain this difference by showing the contrast again between the teachers of MC and LC pupils, such as the T_1' mean of 6.67 for Grade 6 teachers of MC pupils and .92 for Grade 6 teachers of LC pupils. There are generally lower teacher attitudes for all three grade levels in the LC group than in the MC group. It would be well to note the decline from the T_0 mean of 26.58 to 16.36 for Grade 6 teachers of LC pupils.

Teachers' Attitudes. Table 4 results clearly demonstrate that the factor of pupils' social class determines strong differences in teachers' attitudes toward children. Only one significant result in Table 5 for teacher's measures suggests that other factors this study investigated are less influential single effects upon teachers' attitudes.

The significant F ratio for T_1 deserves attention, since in pre- and post-test means for this measure (MTAI Factor I), the senior teachers of LC pupils scored so much lower than their counterpart teachers of MC pupils and all other teacher groups in general. The T_1 factor contains items such as "Pupils should be required to do more studying at home," "Pupils have it too easy in the modern school," "Too much nonsense goes on in many classrooms today," and "Children are too carefree." In such views toward children and their proper control, teachers of MC pupils were more "modern" and tolerant, and were inclined to be more positive-minded and lenient toward children than those who taught LC pupils. Scoring significantly lower, the latter expressed more "traditionalistic," punitive, and blameful perceptions. The more negative attitudes of teachers with 9 + years' experience (with MC pupils such teachers' means are: $T_1 = 5.84$, $T_1' = 6.41$; with LC pupils: $T_1 = .41$, $T_1' = .45$) teaching lower-class pupils raises serious questions concerning such teachers' effectiveness with LC pupils and teaching in general.

Three significant F ratios were found for interaction variance in teacher's measures. Interaction involves the combinatory effect of two or more factors upon the dependent variable.

Figure 1 presents a graph of the T_0' means in the analysis of the factors—pupils' social class and grade level (F ratio of 3.34, $p < .037$).

We see in Figure 1 that Grade 4 teachers varied little and fifth and six grade teachers differed considerably. The significant departure of curves from parallelism clearly shows the interaction effect: teachers of MC pupils improved upward in T_0' scores from Grade 4 to Grade 6, and teachers of LC pupils correspondingly decreased in T_0' scores. For these analyses, the factor of teachers' years of experience was fairly well controlled, except for sixth grade (MC: 7.8 years, 8.3, 5.1; LC: 9.0, 10.7, 11.5, Grades 4–6, respectively). Teachers' sex did not provide statistically significant variance in teachers' attitudes, although there are outstandingly low scores for male teachers of LC pupils. Strong interaction effect (for T_0, $F = 5.85$, $p < .016$; for T_0', $F = 5.94$, $p < .016$) was found in teachers' attitudes and is shown graphically in Figures 2 and 3.

In Figures 2 and 3, the effect of

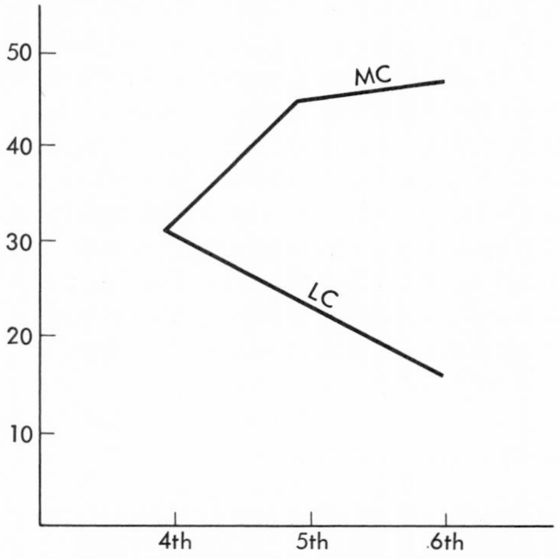

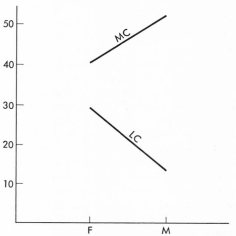

Figure 1. Plot of cell means for T_0' from Table 2 showing interaction of pupils' social class and grade level.

Figure 2. Plot of cell means for T_0 from Table 3 showing interaction of pupils' social class and teachers' sex.

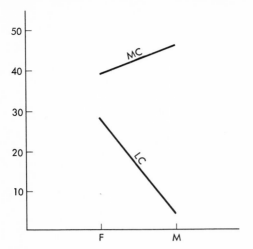

Figure 3. Plot of cell means for T_0' from Table 3 showing interaction of pupils' social class and teachers' sex.

pupils' social class can be seen to provide two highly separate curves. Differences in teachers' sex across levels of pupils' social class run in opposite directions and tend to cancel out column variance; hence the lack of statistical significance for female-male differences in Table 5. Departing significantly from parallelism, the curves in Figures 2 and 3 clearly depict interaction operating between the two main effects.

In other words, MC and LC pupils in this study were exposed to contrasting trends in teachers' affective characteristics. MC pupils enjoyed significantly more positive teacher attitudes in general, and their male teachers scored higher than female teachers who taught them. LC pupils were taught by teachers with more negative affective attitudes toward children and their male teachers scored much lower than their female teachers. The sharp contrast between the male teacher groups differing by their pupils' social-class background can be seen in T_0' means of 46.70 and 4.35 and T_1' means of 5.95 and -1.35, MC and LC, respectively.

In general, pupils, whether MC or LC, perceived the merit of male teachers higher than that of female teachers. Since the male teachers of LC pupils had very low attitudes, as discussed above, LC pupils' attitudes toward such teachers cannot be overlooked. In further data not reported here, the same pattern is consistent in other pupil attitudes with one exception. With 3-item factor scores on teachers' merit in individualizing instruction, post-test attitudes of LC pupils toward their male teachers were lowest of all four groups in results showing significant row, column, and interaction variance. Pretest scores on the same factor provide similar, though statistically less significant, results.

Of further interest is the fact that most of the male teachers teach sixth graders—for MC pupils: Grade 4, N = 2; Grade 5, N = 1; Grade 6, N = 17; for LC pupils in the same grade level order: N's = 2, 4, and 14. The 20 males teaching MC pupils had an average of 5.9 years of teaching experience and the 20 males teaching LC pupils averaged 7.6 years of experience. The significant interaction effect found for T_0' in Figure 1 may be due to more complex interaction operating between pupils' social class, grade level, teachers' sex, and teachers' years of experience. Certainly further research to provide more complex analyses is necessary to determine with greater certainty what differences in teacher-pupil relations are influenced by various factors investigated in this study and others not dealt with here.

ONE-FACTOR ANOVA

Table 6 provides results of a one-factor ANOVA conducted to see if there are significant differences between teacher-class groups classified by pupils' environmental background. In this regard, we

TABLE 6

RESULTS OF ONE-WAY ANALYSIS OF VARIANCE FOR
PUPILS' ENVIRONMENTAL BACKGROUND

Pupil's background		Means of the variables						
Social class	Ethnic background	N	T_0	T_0'	T_1	T_1'	P_0	P_0'
Middle class	Anglo	102	43.32	41.11	6.42	5.76	127.60	126.59
Lower class	Anglo	23	28.00	31.96	5.09	4.43	123.46	119.73
	Mexican	64	27.83	23.80	2.81	3.20	120.35	118.55
	Negro	23	19.74	17.96	− .96	− .83	119.27	120.94
df	3 and 208							
	F Ratio	5.76	4.17		6.63	3.61	5.24	3.39
	$p <$	.001	.007		.001	.014	.002	.019

assigned subjects by four levels of pupils' ethnic and social-class characteristics.

Significant *F* ratios were found for teachers' and pupils' attitudes at pre- and post-test occasions, with the greatest variance resulting at pretest.

Attitude means of MC pupils and their teachers are highest and indicate more positive and warmer interpersonal relations in classrooms. Examining the means for groups of Anglo (English-speaking whites) pupils differentiated only by social-class background, we see how the characteristics of lower class depresses the positivity of teachers' and pupils' attitudes.

Most Anglo and Mexican (primary language is Spanish) pupils were taught by Anglo teachers, the exceptions being one Japanese-American teacher who taught MC pupils and 13 teachers of Mexican descent who taught LC pupils. Thus, it is interesting to note that all teacher means follow a consistent pattern of descending pupil order from MC, Anglo; LC, Anglo; LC, Mexican; and LC, Negro. At pretest, the order of pupils' means (P_0) corresponds with the teacher pattern; but the order is changed at post-test, as LC means (P_0') became more equivalent. As one would expect, the fact a teacher is Anglo tells little. The very low T_1 tnd T_1' means for Negro teachers of LC Negro pupils indicate that such teachers in this study were extremely traditionalistic and negative in their views of children and child control. Yet such significant variance between teachers' attitudes is not reflected in pupils' attitudes.

It should be pointed out that no general inferences concerning these findings can be made, since data for classifications of MC pupils of minority groups were lacking.

DISCUSSION AND CONCLUSIONS

The results discussed above indicate that there are great differences between the teachers who instruct children differing in environmental background. Analyses of teachers' affective attitudes toward children indicate that warm, trustful, and sympathetic teachers instruct middle-class (MC) pupils, and lower-class (LC) pupils face old teachers who tend to blame and fault them. Since pupils' attitudes were found to reflect most of these differences between teachers, pupils' attitudes would probably show even greater group variance if pupils realized the range of teachers' affective behavior.

The characteristic of pupils' social-class background stands out as the most potent source of variance in this study's analyses. Other factors studied were also found to be important sources of variance. Teachers' sex provided strong differences in teachers' pre- and post-test MTAI scores, with significant interaction operating between it and the factor of pupils' social class. Female teachers of MC or LC pupils were more similar in attitudes than male teachers. Of the four teacher-sex groups, the male teachers of MC pupils scored highest and the male teachers of LC pupils scored lowest. With such results, it was surprising to find LC pupils' attitudes toward their male teachers significantly more favorable than their attitudes toward female teachers. This interesting result calls for further investigation to ascertain if there is a real issue of pupil preference for male teachers over female teachers, and if so, why. Pupils' pretest attitudes showed significant variance with the factors of grade level and teachers' years of experience. Significant interaction between pupils' social class and grade level was found for teachers' post-test MTAI scores.

Coleman *et al.* (1966) found that disadvantaged children, unlike advantaged children, were uncertain that they could affect or change their environmental conditions. Can pupils with such characteristics be effectively taught by teachers who tend to be negative toward children and attempt to dictate and penalize rather than explain and guide? The very negative attitudes of teachers with 9+ years' experience working with LC pupils and

the low attitudes pupils have toward such teachers raise serious questions concerning such teachers' placement and length of service with LC pupils or, perhaps, in teaching in general.

Results of this study suggest need for further research of possible personality and pedagogical variables that can ascertain what teachers are more favorably suited to teach disadvantaged pupils, such as values (e.g., Rosenberg, 1957; Spindler, 1955), commitment to teaching as a career (Mason, Dressel, and Bain, 1963), explaining ability (Gage, 1966), leadership traits (White and Lippitt, 1960), and experiential background (Ryans, 1960). We need to know what personal and social choices really determine whether a teacher works in schools serving a disadvantaged or an advantaged neighborhood. Does a teacher's attitude toward children reflect the type of pupil the teacher sees herself teaching? How much success can be expected in attempts to modify teachers' attitudes toward children through information and training? Would more qualified teachers teach LC pupils if they were specially prepared for such work and paid salary incentives?

Since groups of beginning and experienced teachers differentiated by pupils' social class differed so in teachers' attitudes, the relationship of institutional and teachers' characteristics should be pursued. If we assess equality of opportunities in schools from the point of view of adequacy in meeting the chief educational needs of pupils, this study's results suggest that LC pupils receive teachers whose attitudes toward children are inadequate and contrary to such pupils' needs. Studying teachers' academic preparation, job satisfaction, and teaching performance, Herriott and St. John (1966) were not able to find clear evidence to support the hypothesis that LC pupils are discriminated against with respect to the teachers

Interpersonal Attitudes of Teachers and Advantaged and Disadvantaged Pupils 281

assigned them. Our study of teachers' attitudes does seem to provide support for the hypothesis. If school integration becomes America's major method of improving educational opportunities for disadvantaged pupils, then this question should be raised and investigated: What relevant variables operate in integrated classes to effect achievement and satisfaction on the part of disadvantaged pupils?

If what this study indicates and what many have suggested concerning the more critical needs of disadvantaged pupils is true, then teachers of greater ability and capacity to meet such needs should teach disadvantaged pupils. Perhaps the problem of adequately staffing schools in LC neighborhoods is of such magnitude that only concerted programs specially designed for such purposes, such as the National Teacher Corps, can begin to help school districts meet the necessary special teacher selection and training, and the incentive required. Riessman's (1967) five-point plan to provide effective "teachers of the poor" calls for extensive pre- and in-service training for teachers of disadvantaged pupils.

Findings of Turner (1965) and Kliebard (1967) also suggest that attention be given to administrative policies of schools which may be providing curriculum emphases contradictory to the primary needs of disadvantaged pupils. Such policies may very well determine the characteristics and methods of teachers that teach disadvantaged pupils. This concern is reinforced by Herriott and St. John's (1966) finding that the principal's influence on his teachers in "planning for the school, smoothing office routine, handling students, and upgrading the performance of teachers, especially those who are inexperienced" is greater in schools serving LC pupils than in those with MC pupils.

The greater contrasts in attitudes found in this study emphasize the importance of considering the characteristics and behaviors of both teachers and pupils in classroom interaction. The results indicate that very different types of teachers enter and remain in schools serving MC and LC neighborhoods. Insofar as teachers' attitudes can be brought into the classroom through selection and training procedures, the effort should especially be made to place the teachers with more positive attitudes toward children in schools located in LC neighborhoods.

REFERENCES

W. H. BECK. "Pupils' Perception of Teacher Merit: A Factor Analysis of Five Hypothesized Dimensions." Unpublished dissertation, Stanford University, 1964.

S. BOWLES and H. M. LEVIN. "The Determinants of Scholastic Achievement—An Appraisal of Some Recent Evidence," *Journal of Human Resources*, 3 (1968), pp. 3–24.

W. W. CHARTERS, JR. "The Social Background of Teaching," *Handbook of Research on Teaching*, ed. N. L. GAGE. Chicago: Rand McNally & Co., 1963. pp. 715–813.

J. S. COLEMAN *et al. Equality of Educational Opportunity*. Washington: U.S. Office of Education, 1966. Documents Nos. FS5.238:38001.

N. L. GAGE. "Psychological Research on Teacher Education for the Great Cities," *Urban Education*, 1 (1965), pp. 175–95.

———. "Research on Cognitive Aspects of Teaching," *The Way Teaching Is* (ASCD-NEA monograph). Washington: National Education Association, 1966, pp. 29–44.

E. W. GORDON. "Foreword: Education for Socially Disadvantaged Children," *Review of Educational Research*, 35 (1965), p. 375.

W. L. HAYS. *Statistics for Psychologists*. New York: Holt, Rinehart, & Winston, 1965.

R. E. HERRIOTT and NANCY H. ST. JOHN. *Social Class and the Urban School*. New York: JOHN WILEY & SONS, Inc., 1966.

J. L. HORN and W. E. MORRISON. "Dimensions of Teacher Attitudes," *Journal of Educational Psychology*, 56 (1965), pp. 118–25.

H. KLIEBARD. "Curriculum Differentiation for the Disadvantaged," *Educational Forum*, 31 (1967), pp. 47–54.

E. F. LINDQUIST. *Design and Analysis of Experiments in Psychology and Education*. Boston: Houghton-Mifflin Co., 1953.

W. S. MASON, R. J. DRESSEL, and R. K. BAIN. "Sex Role and the Career Orientations of Beginning Teachers," *Readings in the Social Psychology of Education*, eds. W. W. CHARTERS, JR., and N. L. GAGE. Boston: Allyn and Bacon, Inc., 1963, pp. 278–86.

R. C. NICHOLS. "Schools and the Disadvantaged," *Science*, 154 (1966), pp. 1312–14.

C. E. OSGOOD, G. J. SUCI, and P. H. TANNENBAUM. *The Measurement of Meaning*. Urbana: University of Illinois Press, 1957.

F. RIESSMAN. "Teachers of the Poor: A Five-Point Plan," *Journal of Teacher Education*, 18 (1967), pp. 326–38.

M. ROSENBERG. *Occupations and Values*. Glencoe, Ill.: The Free Press, 1957.

D. G. RYANS. *Characteristics of Teachers*. Washington: American Council on Education, 1960.

G. D. SPINDLER. "Education in a Transforming American Culture," *Harvard Educational Review*, 25 (1955), pp. 145–56.

R. L. TURNER. "Characteristics of Beginning Teachers: Their Differential Linkage with School-System Types," *School Review*, 73 (1965), pp. 48–58.

D. J. VELDMAN. *Fortran Programming for the Behavioral Sciences*. New York: Holt, Rinehart & Winston, 1967.

R. K. WHITE and R. LIPPITT. *Autocracy and Democracy: An Experimental Inquiry*. New York: Harper & Bros., 1960.

B. J. WINER. *Statistical Principles in Experimental Design*. New York: McGraw-Hill Book Co., 1962.

J. WITHALL and W. W. LEWIS. "Social Interaction in the Classroom," *Handbook of Research on Teaching*, ed. N. L. GAGE. Chicago: Rand McNally & Co., 1963, pp. 683–714.

A. H. YEE. *Factors Involved in Determining the Relationship Between Teachers' and Pupils' Attitudes*. Austin: The University of Texas, 1966. U.S. Department of Health, Education, and Welfare, Office of Education, Cooperative Research Project No. 5–8346.

———. "Is the Minnesota Teacher Attitude Inventory Valid and Homogeneous?" *Journal of Educational Measurement*, 4 (1967), pp. 151–61.

———. "The Direction and Source of Causal Influence in Teacher-Pupil Relationships," *Journal of Educational Psychology*, 1968, *59*, 275-282.

TEACHER BEHAVIOR TOWARD BOYS AND GIRLS DURING FIRST GRADE READING INSTRUCTION

O. L. Davis, Jr. / June Jenkinson Slobodian

The observation that girls demonstrate superior achievement in reading is generally acknowledged by teachers and substantiated in the research literature on school achievement. Girls seem to gain in reading achievement over boys during initial instruction (Gates, 1961; Stroud and Lindquist, 1942) and their superiority appears to persist through the secondary school (Loughlin and others, 1965; Stroud and Lindquist, 1942). More boys attend reading clinics than do girls (Durrell, 1956; Newton, 1959). Even so, systematic research on sex differences is not as conclusive as expert opinion and some representative studies would suggest. Stroud and Lindquist (1942), in their review, noted "a conspicuous absence of significant differences," and some recent studies (Kowitz, 1964; Parsley and others, 1963; Sinks and Powell, 1965) have reported generally non-significant sex differences.

From: American Educational Research Journal, *1967, 4, 261–69. Copyright © 1967 by the American Educational Research Association, and reproduced by permission of the authors and the AERA.*

In this ambiguous situation, belief in girls' superiority in reading, and efforts to both account for this difference and to act on it continue. Various factors such as growth and maturation have been advanced to explain girls' higher reading achievement (Chronister, 1964; Clark, 1959; Kowitz, 1964; and Nicholson, 1957). Elements of the general culture, expectations, and attitudes have been suggested (Dechant, 1964; Gates, 1961; Mazurkiewicz, 1960; and Preston, 1962). Also, for many years, the nature of the school and teacher behaviors have been asserted to contribute to boys' lower scholastic achievement in general, and reading achievement in particular. Ayres (1909) commented that "our schools as they now exist are better fitted to the needs and natures of the girl than of the boy pupils." The *feminized* school was attributed to the behaviors of women teachers by St. John (1932). He observed that boys' generally lower academic performance was "due chiefly to a maladjustment between the boys and their teachers which is the result of interests, attitudes, habits, and general behavior tendencies

283

of boys to which the teachers fail to adjust themselves and their school procedures as well as they do to the personality traits of girls." While general observations such as these have appeared from time to time, McNeil (1964) has presented evidence which indicated that first grade (female) teachers do not treat boys and girls equally under reading instruction. Boys in his study had achieved higher than girls under programmed instruction during kindergarten, but had been surpassed by the girls after a period of classroom instruction in first grade. The evidence employed by McNeil demonstrated teachers' apparent discrimination against boys by uses of pupil and teacher reports of their perceptions. Thus, McNeil (1964) suggested "an association between teacher behavior and performance in beginning reading."

Do female first grade teachers in fact discriminate against boys and favor girls in the situation of reading instruction? That is, do these teachers actually behave differently toward boys and girls during reading instruction? In the presence of meager, and, as yet only indirect evidence, the present study was designed as a portion of the continued inquiry that is obviously warranted.

PROCEDURE

This study was designed to incorporate a) collection and analysis of pupil perceptions of teacher behaviors in the setting of the reading instruction, b) collection and analysis of observed teacher-pupil interaction data gathered during regular reading instruction, and c) analysis of sex differences in reading achievement, if any, and the relation of these data to teacher-pupil interaction data.

SUBJECTS

Ten first-grade teachers and their pupils provided data for this study. These classes were chosen from the first-grade sections in a large public school system in the Detroit, Michigan, suburban area. Eligible for selection were only those classes whose teachers had experience at the first-grade level, were on tenure in the system, and would agree to participate in the study. These teachers ranged in age from 23 to 38 years (median: 27.5). All teachers held baccalaureate degrees; one possessed a master's degree. Their teaching experience ranged from 2 to $9\frac{1}{2}$ years (median: 4 years). Nine of the ten teachers were married; three had children of their own. All classes were heterogeneously grouped and used a system-wide-adopted basal reading series. In the ten classes, 276 pupils were enrolled. Since complete data were available on 238 (122 boys and 116 girls), this total served as the study population. Boys and girls in this study did not differ significantly with respect to age (boys: 82.3 months; girls: 82.4 months) and to reading achievement (Harrison-Stroud Readiness Test) (boys: $M = 95.30$, $SD = 23.25$; girls: $M = 97.71$; $SD = 22.14$). Data were collected during the Spring, 1965.

DATA COLLECTION

Pupil perceptions of pupil-teacher interactions during reading instruction were gathered in individual interviews employing a standard structured schedule. Questions asked pupils by McNeil (1964) were included in addition to three additional items. The pupils were told, "pretend you are in your reading group. To whom is the teacher talking when she says: a) Read that page out loud for us? b)[1] Sit up and pay attention? c) You did a fine job of reading? d)[1] Who doesn't get to read very much in your group? e) Who doesn't read well? and f) Who is the best reader in your group?" Pupils could name themselves if they so desired.

Following McNeil (1964), teachers

---

[1] Items used by McNeil (1964).

were asked to rate each pupil in the class-room according to his motivation and readiness for reading, "considering the child's ability to pay close attention to explanations, stay with a task, and ask relevant questions." Instead of a five-point scale as used by McNeil, a graphic rating scale (Guilford, 1954) was employed.

To guide the observation and sys-tematic recording of teacher-pupil verbal interactions in the setting of reading in-struction, a Reading Observation Record (ROR) was developed following proce-dures outlined by Medley and Mitzel (1963). The ROR makes possible the sequential recording of verbal discourse segments, similar to the cycles of Bellack and Davitz (1963), and elements within these segments. Provided by the ROR, consequently, were data on the number of call-on response units, acceptance-response units, rejection-response units, interruption-response units, interruption-acceptance units, and interruption-rejec-tion units. The sequence of interaction was also noted. The ROR also provided data regarding time spent by teachers on various standard reading instructional activities. Five experienced special read-ing teachers were trained as observers for this study. All reached a criterion of 95 per cent agreement on all observations made during training. The reading instruc-tion in each of the first grade classes participating in the study was observed, employing the ROR, on four different days by different observers. Each reading group in a class was observed on the same day and data over all reading groups were pooled for analysis.

The Stanford Achievement Test, Primary Battery, Form X, provided data on pupils' general reading achievement. The raw score for reading was employed. This incorporated raw scores from the subtests of word meaning, paragraph meaning, word study skills, vocabulary, and spelling.

FINDINGS

To check on the possibility of interview-item overlap for each class, the difference was calculated between the percentage-of-boys-nominated to all-pupils-nominated and the percentage of boys in the class. These differences for each class were ranked for each question and intercorrelated (Spear-man *rho* coefficients). The results, displayed in Table 1, indicate that the percentage of boys nominated in each class was not con-sistent across questions and that the inter-view items evoked different percentages of boy nominations. Nonsignificant item over-lap was revealed.

Analyzing the total number of nominations received by boys and girls, following McNeil (1964), boys were per-ceived as receiving more negative com-ments from the teacher ($X^2 = 43.94$, $p < .01$), as having little opportunity to read ($X^2 = 12.76$, $p < .01$), and as being poor readers ($X^2 = 9.98$, $p < .01$). Non-significant sex differences were obtained on analysis. of nominations as receiving much opportunity to read, as receiving praise from the teacher, and as best read-er. This number (three) of significant differences is itself significant ($p < .01$) (Sakoda, Cohen, and Beall, 1954).

These results, while consistent with those reported by McNeil, are suspect and conclusions based on them, as were Mc-Neil's, seem unwarranted. Based on the total number of nominations, they do not take into account the fact that multiple nominations received by an individual and credited to a sex group would exaggerate the real situation. For example, several nominations of the same boy as having little opportunity to read might exceed the number of single nominations of sev-eral girls. The assumption of independence underlying the chi-square tests employed is doubtful. While their use, therefore, may be questionable (Lewis and Burke, 1949), obtained results are particularly

TABLE 1

INTERCORRELATIONS (SPEARMAN *rho*)
OF INTERVIEW QUESTIONS

Item[a]	1	2	3	4	5	6
1	—	.56	.15	.54	.50	.20
2		—	.35	.72*	.38	.13
3			—	.18	.16	.54
4				—	.22	.12
5					—	.00
6						—
* p .05						

1—receiving more negative comments from the teacher.
2—little opportunity to read.
3—much opportunity to read.
4—receiving praise from the teacher.
5—being "best" reader.
6—being poor readers.

useful here in that they may be related to those obtained by McNeil. Consequently, nomination data were reexamined.

First, an analysis was performed on the number of individual boys and girls nominated on each interview item. As a result of this reanalysis, boys were still perceived as receiving more negative comments from the teacher ($X^2 = 7.50$, $p < .01$) and as being poor readers ($X^2 = 4.16$, $p < .05$). On each of the other four analyses, no significant sex difference was noted. This number of obtained significant differences (two of six) still being significant, the earlier conclusion of pupils' perceiving teachers' differentially treating boys and girls is supported.

Inasmuch as the results of these chi-square analyses were suspect because of the doubtful assumption of independence, a second and probably more appropriate set of analyses was performed. For each question, the percentage of boys nominated to all pupils nominated in each class was contrasted to the percentage of boys in that class. (Classes in which boys nominated/all pupils nominated > boys/class members were assigned "1"; classes in

which boys nominated/all pupils nominated < boys/class assigned "0.") These data were then subjected to sign tests. For none of the six interview items was a significant difference ($p = .05$) obtained. Thus, pupils in the classes did not nominate a significantly higher percentage of boys of those named than the percentage of boys in the classes.

Inspection of the nomination data further suggested that nominations on some of the items were sex-linked. Subsequent analysis revealed sex-linking in a significant number of contrasts. Boys were found to choose other boys and girls to select other girls when asked who received the most opportunity to read ($X^2 = 65.91$, $p < .01$), who was told he did a fine job after finishing reading ($X^2 = 7.18$, $p < .01$), and who read the best ($X^2 = 39.03$, $p < .01$). Boys were nominated significantly more by both boys and girls on the item relating to negative comments from the teacher ($X^2 = 5.52$, $p, < .05$). On the items relating to who did not read well and who did not read much, nominations were not sex-linked.

Teachers' estimates of pupils' motivation and readiness for reading were treated by two analyses. Pupils rated at or above the mean were categorized as "motivated and ready for reading" while pupils rated below the mean were classified as being perceived by their teachers as having little motivation and readiness to read. Teachers were found to have assessed more boys as "less motivated and ready" than girls ($X^2 = 6.75$, $p < .01$). Teachers did not so assess a higher proportion of boys than the percentage of boys in the class. Non-significant differences were also obtained between teachers' mean assessment of boys and girls ($t < 1.0$).

Tables 2 and 3 present summary results of the analyses of variance (Lindquist Type I) performed on the observation (ROR) data. A nonsignificant difference was noted between the number of times boys and girls were called on to respond by their teachers (See Table 2); too, teachers were not found to react differentially to boys' and girls' responses. A significant difference in the nature of teachers' reactions to pupils' responses was revealed; teachers employed more "acceptance" and "neutral" than "rejection" reactions. Boys were found to interrupt the reading group significantly more than

TABLE 2

SUMMARY OF ANALYSIS OF VARIANCE (LINDQUIST TYPE I) OF OBSERVED CALL-ON RESPONSE/TREATMENTS

Source	d.f.	Sum of Squares	Mean Square	F	F.05
Between (class and sex)	19	457.65			
Between Sex	1	34.12	34.12	1.45	4.41
Error between	18	423.53	23.53		
Within (classroom and sex and response)	40	810.48			
Nature of response	2	712.12	356.06	134.36	3.28
Response × sex	2	3.35	1.68	.64	3.28
Error within	36	95.01	2.65		

TABLE 3

SUMMARY OF ANALYSIS OF VARIANCE (LINDQUIST TYPE I) OF OBSERVED INTERRUPTION/TREATMENTS

Source	d.f.	Sum of Squares	Mean Square	F	F.05
Between (class and sex)	19	56.63			
Between Sex	1	25.58	25.58	14.79	4.41
Error between	18	31.05	1.73		
Within (classroom and sex and response)	40	66.13			
Nature of response	2	4.41	2.21	1.38	3.28
Response × sex	2	4.02	2.01	.796	3.28
Error within	36	57.70	1.60		

girls (see Table 3), but teachers did not react differently to boys' interruptions than to girls'. Apparently, teachers were '(accepting" or "rejective" of interruptions without regard to whether the interruptions originated with boys or girls. In addition, teachers did not react (acceptance, rejection, or neutral) in one way more frequently than another to interruptions.

General reading achievement of boys ($M = 92.74$, $SD = 30.48$) and of girls ($M = 93.86$, $SD = 26.99$) was not significantly different ($t < 1.0$). Subsequently, comparisons were made of the reading achievement of all pupils and of those nominated on the six interview items. Each of the comparisons revealed nonsignificant differences.

DISCUSSION

Results of this investigation do not support the hypothesis that female first grade teachers discriminate against boys and favor girls in reading instruction. In particular, these findings conflict sharply with those presented by McNeil (1964), provide empirical confirmation of several questions raised by Ingle and Gephart (1966), and suggest that explanations of boys' lower reading achievement under classroom teaching, if real, probably should be focused on the specific teacher-pupil interactions in the situation of classroom reading instruction.

Pupils' perceptions of teacher behavior toward pupils during reading instruction, at least in this study, must not be admitted as evidence of teachers' differential behavior toward boys and girls. Analyses of the interview data according to individuals nominated rather than the total number of nominations received by boys and girls yielded generally nonsignificant results. Had McNeil also analyzed

the data in these ways, results quite different from those reported might well have been obtained. In addition, the finding of sex-linked nominations on a significant number of interview items, a possibility unexamined by McNeil, further points out the general unsuitability of these data on which to base conclusions about teachers' treatment of pupils during reading instruction.

More damaging to the notion of teachers' discrimination against boys, because it is more direct and relevant, is the observation evidence presented. Teachers were not found to call on girls more and boys less frequently or to direct more negative comments toward boys during reading instruction. Rather, teachers were observed as giving boys and girls essentially equal opportunity to read and/or respond during reading instruction. Teachers, further, did not treat (accept, reject, ignore) boys' responses differently than girls'. Even though boys interrupted the reading group more frequently than girls, teachers reacted to these interruptions essentially no differently than when the interruptions were originated by girls. Teachers' reactions to interruptions, in all likelihood, were framed primarily by the demands of the situation itself and not by noting if the interrupting pupil was a boy or a girl. These results obviously indicate that the female first grade teachers in this study did not act (at least, in their verbal behavior) differently toward boys and girls. Apparently, the teachers worked at the task of teaching pupils to read, without considering the sex of the pupil relevant in this instructional setting.

These results underscore the importance of obtaining direct, behavioral evidence whenever possible in studies of teaching. Such data about the teaching behaviors of the teachers in McNeil's study might also have contributed to a different conclusion than that advanced.

In such an event, an hypothesis other than teacher differential treatment would have been necessary to explain the achievement differences noted under the two situations (auto-instruction and classroom).

In light of these findings, continued inquiry is clearly dictated. A matter of basic concern is the reality or fiction of important sex differences in school achievement, reading in particular. The situation is ambiguous at present, to say the least. The value of auto-instructional procedures in reading instruction, demonstrated by McNeil (1964), merits attention. If replications reveal a consistent finding of boys' higher achievement than girls' under auto-instruction, explanations should be sought that lie more directly within the context of these procedures. Obviously, additional studies of classroom teachers' behaviors, particularly during reading instruction and including attention to more than verbal behavior, and employing refined observational schedules, will be valuable.

REFERENCES

AYRES, L. P. *Laggards In Our Schools*. New York: Russell Sage Foundation, 1909. 286 pp.

BELLACK, ARNO, and DAVITZ, JOEL R. *The Language of the Classroom*. U.S.O.E. Cooperative Research Project No. 1497. New York: Institute of Psychological Research, Teachers College, Columbia University, 1963. 200 pp.

CHRONISTER, GLENN M. "Personality and Reading Achievement." *Elementary School Journal* 64: 253–260; February 1964.

CLARK, WILLIS W. "Boys and Girls—Are There Significant Ability and Achievement Differences?" *Phi Delta Kappan* 41: 73–76; November 1959.

DECHANT, EMERALD V. *Improving the Teaching of Reading*. Englewood Cliffs, N.J.: Prentice-Hall, Inc., 1964. 568 pp.

DURRELL, D. D. *Improving Reading Instruction*. Chicago: World Book Company, 1956. 402 pp.

GATES, ARTHUR I. "Sex Differences in Reading Ability." *The Elementary School Journal* 61: 431–434; May 1661.

GUILFORD, J. P. *Psychometric Methods*. Second edition. New York: McGraw-Hill Book Company, 1954, 597 pp.

INGLE, ROBERT B., and GEPHART, WILLIAM J. "A Critique of a Research Report: Programed Instruction Versus Usual Classroom Procedures in Teaching Boys to Read." *American Educational Research Journal* 3: 49–53; January 1966.

KOWITZ, GERALD T. and MAHONEY, LEO. G. "Sex-Linked Factors in Reading and Arithmetic Achievement." Paper presented at the American Educational Research Association convention, Chicago, Illinois, February 10–14, 1964. 10 pp. (Mimeographed)

LEWIS, DON, and BURKE, C. J. "The Use and Misuse of the Chi-Square Test." *Psychological Bulletin* 46: 433–489; November 1949.

LOUGHLIN, LEE J.; O'CONNOR, HENRY A.; POWELL, MARVIN; and PARSLEY, KENNETH M., JR. "An Investigation of Sex Differences by Intelligence, Subject-Matter Area, Grade, and Achievement Level on Three Anxiety Scales." *Journal of Genetic Psychology* 106: 207–215; June 1965.

MAZURKIEWICZ, ALBERT J. "Social-Cultural Influences and Reading." *Journal of Developmental Reading* 1: 235–240; Summer 1960.

McNEIL, JOHN D. "Programed Instruction Versus Usual Classroom Procedures in Teaching Boys to Read." *American Educational Research Journal* 1: 113–119; March 1964.

MEDLEY, DONALD M., and MITZEL, HAROLD E. "Measuring Classroom Behavior by Systematic Observation." *Handbook of Research on Teaching.* (Edited by N. L. Gage) Chicago: Rand-McNally and Co., 1963, pp. 247–328.

NEWTON, EUNICE SHAED, and others. "Empirical Differences Between Adequate and Retarded Readers." *The Reading Teacher* 13: 40–44; October 1959.

NICHOLSON, ALICE K. *Background Abilities Related to Reading Success in First Grade.* Unpublished doctoral dissertation. Boston University, 1957. 201 pp.

PARSLEY, KENNETH M.; POWELL, MARVIN; O'CONNOR, HENRY; and DEUTSCH, MURRAY. "Are There Really Sex Differences in Achievement?" *Journal of Educational Research* 57: 210–212; December 1963.

PRESTON, RALPH C. "Reading Achievement of German and American Children." *School and Society* 90: 350–54; October 1962.

SAKODA, J. M.; COHEN, B. H.; and BEALL, G. "Test of Significance for a Series of Statistical Tests." *Psychological Bulletin* 51: 172–175; March 1954.

SINKS, NAOMI B., and POWELL, MARVIN. "Sex and Intelligence as Factors in Achievement in Reading in Grades Four through Eight." *Journal of Genetic Psychology* 106: 67–79; March 1965.

ST. JOHN, C. W. "The Maladjustment of Boys in Elementary Grades." *Educational Administration and Supervision* 18: 649–672; December 1932.

STROUD, J. B., and LINDQUIST, E. F. "Sex Differences in Achievement in the Elementary and Secondary Schools." *Journal of Educational Psychology* 33: 657–667; December 1942.

COGNITIVE SIMILARITY
IN FACILITATING COMMUNICATION

Philip J. Runkel

It has long been commonly observed that the meaning of any spoken phrase or any gesture depends upon the expectations within which it is embedded. Another way to say this is that the stimuli comprised by a communication impinge upon a set of potential responses belonging to the listener. This set of potential responses, being a limited selection of all human acts and being organized by a hierarchy of probabilities, must mediate every communicative process by presenting a framework, or mechanism, within which any communicated message will find its effect. It is this framework of potentialities upon which are engraved expectations of culture and role and the demands of the situation. In the terms of this framework any communication finds its resultant.

Clearly, an act of communication is itself a response. The possibilities of response are the possibilities of communication. The transmitter as well as the receiver of communication acts within a

From: Sociometry, *1965, 19, 175–91. Copyright © 1956 by the American Sociological Association, and reproduced by permission of the author and ASA.*

limiting framework. Using the term "cognitive field" to designate the possibilities of response, we may conceive the total communication process as an interaction between cognitive fields. The stimuli which impinge upon each field bring about alterations of response not only to the stimuli explicit in the situation but also to stimuli which are carried implicitly in the field; and further, the response which we see as communication arises not only from the stimuli offered by the other communicator, but also from the many stimuli implicitly associated in the cognitive field of the speaker and from the hierarchy of potential responses which organize them.

It follows from this view that communication cannot fruitfully be conceived as a sequence in which self-contained packets of information are exchanged. It is not a process in which one person merely adds to the belongings of another by "giving" him information. It is rather a kind of guessing game. Each person carries with him his cognitive field as a map of the world. He responds not to the world, but to the map. When he receives the stimulus of a communication, the meaning it has is the way it can be fitted into the map. When the communication fits readily, one's confidence in his map of the world is increased.

Since the effects of a communication depend on the manner in which it "meshes" with an existing cognitive map, we might entertain the notion that these effects will take place more readily when the cognitive maps of the communicators are similar in structure. In fact, the general hypothesis of this paper is that *similarity of structure between two cognitive fields increases the efficacy of communication between them*. In its general form, this hypothesis is no doubt as old as communication. The contribution of this paper to the problems of communication lies not in the general terms of the problem chosen for study, but rather in the forms by means of which quantification has been applied to similarity of cognitive structure. In the present study, the particular index which furnishes operations for assessing similarity of cognitive structure is one which I have labeled "colinearity" and which will be explained below.

THEORY

The theoretical framework supporting this investigation of the mediation of communication is a deliberate attempt to utilize in one consistent scheme Newcomb's (4) theory of communicative acts and some of the ideas of C. H. Coombs, particularly as the latter are represented in the monograph by Coombs and Kao (3). Because of space limitations, only those theoretical concepts necessary for explaining the experimental operations will be presented here.

We define an *orientation* toward a stimulus A as the set of all potential responses which the individual might at some moment make toward stimulus A or a set of stimuli containing stimulus A. There may at any moment be a number of possible respects in which the individual might respond to stimulus A. That is, there may be a number of *attributes* of stimulus A and the other stimuli in the situation which are relevant at that moment. These *relevant attributes* serve as reference vectors and define a multidimensional space within which the individual's potential responses to stimulus A are determined.

Although the space in which an orientation occurs may be multidimensional, the individual may simplify the interrelations of his judgments or potential responses by combining in some way the attributes of the objects to which he responds. By weighting or ordering the relevant attributes in some way, the individual can frequently put a number of stimuli into a simple (or linear) order. When an orientation involving a set of stimuli is so highly structured that the individual responds to the stimuli as if they were simply ordered, an important consequence is that *certain responses to the stimuli will be impossible* to him as long as he maintains the cognitive structure within which the simple order is defined. This assertion is not so complicated as it may sound, and illustrations are easy to find. Most men, for example, perceive the "fit" of clothing to correspond to the sizes in which the clothing is manufactured. Suppose a man is trying on suits of sizes 36, 38, 40, 42, and 44. If he decides that size 42 fits him best, it would be impossible for him to report that the size 40 suit was a *worse* fit than the size 36.

But now the reader may object. "Is it inconceivable," he may ask, "that some man might be found who would give such an unusual opinion?" Let us put ourselves in the shoes of such an unusual fellow. We would feel, I believe, that he had found some characteristic or attribute of the suits which made it reasonable for him most to prefer the size 42, next the size 36, and least the size 40. Whatever this attribute might be, it would certainly be above and beyond the characteristics determining the usual order of the sizes. In other words, the response of our deviant would enable us no longer to interpret the preferences of individuals within the unidimentional space indicated by the simple ordering of sizes, but would require us to admit a multidimensional response space. This illustration points up the two parts of the assertion made earlier that the individual will find certain responses impossible *as long as he maintains a cognitive structure which puts a simple (unidimensional) order on the stimuli.*

Now let us suppose that person B is communicating with person A about a set of stimuli. Suppose that a clothing salesman is communicating with a customer about suits. "Try on this size 40," the salesman suggests. "Not quite right? Well, let's try a size 42. There, that looks just fine, doesn't it? You'd like to try a size 44? All right, here you are. Yes, I agree, this one is a little too large. The size 42 is just right for you."

Let us now ask the customer what the salesman would say about a size 38 or a size 36, or about a size 46 or a size 48. Obviously, the customer can predict very well what sizes the salesman would consider too small and too large. The point is that in providing the customer with an attribute in terms of which his judgments are being made, the salesman is giving the customer his opinions about stimuli which are not mentioned explicitly. From a sample of observed stimuli, the customer *gets information about other stimuli which can be judged according to the same attribute* as that underlying the judgments among the sampled stimuli. The important qualification here is that

both communicators must be making their judgments, and interpreting the communication which occurs, according to the same attribute. If this is the case, each person can make correct predictions about responses the other would make to stimuli not yet communicated about explicitly.

But the customer might be purchasing a suit to wear to a fancy-dress ball, and the order of sizes might not be at all the order in which he judges how funny the suits are. If the customer with such a purpose does not let the salesman know what attribute is underlying his judgments, we can only feel sorry for the salesman when we imagine the communication which might take place.

When two communicating individuals utilize the same underlying attribute in forming their judgments, we shall say that their orientations are *co-linear*. When they utilize attributes which would give at least some conflicting judgments, we shall say that their orientations are *non-co-linear*. These terms are chosen for their metaphorical reference to the unidimensional requirement and serve to suggest that the individuals are "on the same line" or "not on the same line," respectively.

CO-LINEARITY

The concepts so far presented have brought us to the point of being precise about a way of investigating the proposition that similarity of structure between two cognitive fields increases the efficacy of communication between them. If, in a multidimensional space, two individuals select the same attributes as relevant, they may then (or they may not) compose or weight these attributes so as to resolve their judgments into a simple order. If they do this, thus resolving a multidimensional space into a unidimensional, they may or may not do so similarly. The resulting simple orders, in brief, may or may not be co-linear. But if the two individuals do form orientations which are co-linear, then communication from one to the other transmits information about stimuli *in addition* to those stimuli which are explicitly mentioned in the communication as was illustrated earlier. We can now state our central hypothesis more precisely. We can assert that *communication about a sample of stimuli will convey more information about the stimuli from which the sample is drawn if the orientations of the communicators are co-linear, and less information if they are non-co-linear.*

The index of co-linearity used in the present research is built on the unfolding technique of Coombs (1, 2). In terms of the illustration of the customer looking for a suit, the preferences of most men in regard to fit would "unfold" into the order in which sizes fall. A man on the small side of size 42 might prefer five suits in the order of the sizes 42, 40, 44, 38, 36. And a man near size 36 might have the preference order 36, 38, 40, 42, 44. But we can call out both these orders because we are aware of the underlying attribute which organizes the preferences. There are some permutations of these five numbers which cannot be called off by standing in the shoes of a man of some one size and calling off the sizes in order of best fit to worst.

Orders of five stimuli which can

TABLE 1

CO-LINEARITY TABLE FOR FIVE STIMULI

Given two rank orders, re-label the stimuli of one order A B C D E, respectively. Then label each stimulus of the second order with the letter assigned to that stimulus in the first order. If the resulting second rank order appears below, the two given rank orders are non-co-linear.

A	B	E	D	C		C	E	D	B	A
A	C	E	D	B		D	A	C	B	E
A	D	C	B	E		D	A	C	E	B
A	D	C	E	B		D	A	E	C	B
A	D	E	C	B		D	B	C	A	E
A	E	B	D	C		D	B	C	E	A
A	E	C	B	D		D	B	E	C	A
A	E	C	D	B		D	E	A	C	B
A	E	D	B	C		D	E	B	C	A
A	E	D	C	B		E	A	B	D	C
B	A	E	D	C		E	A	C	B	D
B	C	E	D	A		E	A	C	D	B
B	D	C	A	E		E	A	D	B	C
B	D	C	E	A		E	A	D	C	B
B	D	E	C	A		E	B	A	D	C
B	E	A	D	C		E	B	C	A	D
B	E	C	A	D		E	B	C	D	A
B	E	C	D	A		E	B	D	A	C
B	E	D	A	C		E	B	D	C	A
B	E	D	C	A		E	C	A	D	B
C	A	E	D	B		E	C	B	D	A
C	B	E	D	A		E	C	D	A	B
C	E	A	D	B		E	C	D	B	A
C	E	B	D	A		E	D	A	C	B
C	E	D	A	B		E	D	B	C	A

unfold with A B C D E into *no* underlying order are given in Table 1. This table is used to compare the rank orders yielded by the responses of two subjects. Every rank order in the table is non-co-linear with the rank order A B C D E. For five stimuli, there are fifty rank orders which are non-co-linear with any given order, and seventy which are co-linear.

PROCEDURES

Students in the introductory course in psychology at the University of Michigan were presented with five statements which could be seen as related to the content of the course but which were not assertions of the kind that would be made as a part of the material to be learned in the course or given as items on tests. The five statements used are these:

1. The conditions of living in the United States tend to narrow the range of things we are able to decide to do, think about, etc.

2. People who have a firm moral code are in general better adjusted than those who have not.

3. The biggest weakness of present-day psychology is that it is too theoretical.

4. Individuals could be changed in practically any way one might wish if the environment could be appropriately controlled.

5. The strongest influence in shaping a person into the kind of person he becomes is his mother.

For reasons which will appear shortly, the Method of Rank Order was not used in collecting responses to these statements. The method used was the Method of Triads (2, p. 502). The statements were presented in groups of three, all ten of the possible combinations being used. The subject was instructed to mark, in each triad, the statement with which he *most* agreed

and the statement with which he *least* agreed. Data were collected in this way from the classes of five teachers during the first week of the semester, and the identical procedure was repeated during the last week but one of the semester. The same questionnaire given to the students was also given to each of the five teachers. The preferences of teacher and student among the five statements were tallied, and a rank order inferred in each case where there was no evidence of a multidimensional response. Each teacher's rank order was then compared with the rank order given by each of his students by means of the co-linearity table, and the teacher-student pair was then categorized as co-linear or non-co-linear.

Since we have asserted that co-linear pairs of persons should exchange information more efficiently, and since quizzes on the course work can be taken as a measure of the degree to which the student has received the information which the teacher has given, we are ready to state hypotheses in operational terms. Since reliability or stability of a unidimensional orientation is one of the postulated requirements for a prediction based on co-linearity, two hypotheses will be advanced for testing, so that the results for each, when compared, will provide a check on the postulated effect of stability of the orientation.

Hypothesis 1: Among students who yield reliable rank orders of attitude items pertinent to the course, those who from pretest to posttest maintain rank orders co-linear with that of the instructor will receive higher grades on quizzes than those whose rank orders remain non-co-linear with those of the instructor.

Hypothesis 2: The difference in quiz grades predicted by Hypothesis 1 will be at least as pronounced when only those students are considered whose pretest and posttest rank orders are co-linear.

It is now appropriate to gather together a few loose threads; these will concern the selection of stimulus-statements for indexing co-linearity and the method of selecting stable and unidimensional responses from the responses obtained.

We have already mentioned that a direct sample of quiz material was avoided in choosing the stimulus-statements for indexing co-linearity. Obviously, no elaborate theory would be required to predict quiz grades from a sample of quiz material. A further word, however, needs to be said about the way in which the stimulus-statements should be "related" to the content of the introductory psychology course. Briefly, the statements were chosen so as to "represent," in a special sense, the cognitive fields (or response spaces) which would mediate the communication between teacher and student. In order for a set of stimuli to be "representative," each statement should be multidimensional. That is, it should be possible for one subject to judge the statement on the basis of one attribute, and for another subject to judge the same statement on the basis of another attribute. With such stimuli, the order of preference given by the subject can reflect the attributes, and his weighting of them, which the subject brings to the stimulus situation.

To select a group of multidimensional statements, a long list of statements was first put together in which each statement, in the judgment of the experimenter, seemed interpretable from more than one viewpoint. These statements were then carried to a number of teachers of the introductory course in psychology, and each teacher was asked to state reasons which students might have for agreeing or disagreeing with the statements. The objective was to find a set of statements (a) which could be judged from a variety of reasons or viewpoints, and (b) could be discriminated from each other in regard to degree of agreement or disagreement with the statement. It will be seen that the search was for a highly heterogeneous set of items, rather than for a homogeneous set. The final selection rested on the judgments of the experimenter and the teachers. (A similar procedure was used in an earlier pilot study done with classes in zoology, which gave results substantially the same as those to be described here.) According to the theory, any set of stimulus-statements which was representative in the sense indicated, and discriminable, would have done as well as the set chosen.

We now turn to the method of selecting stable and unidimensional responses. The selection of subjects for whom co-linearity with the teacher was computed went through the following stages:

(1) Out of seven classes in introductory psychology (taught by five teachers), some students responded only to the pretest or only to the posttest. The number responding to both administrations of the questionnaire was 145.

(2) Of 145 subjects responding at both pretest and posttest, 15 gave responses at one time or the other which were intransitive, indicating that they were "unwilling" to compose the stimuli into a simple (or unidimensional) order. This left 130.

(3) The 130 transitive subjects gave responses which contained varying degrees of inconsistency. The Method of Traids presents each pair of stimuli to the subject three times when five stimuli are used. It is therefore possible for the subject to express a preference for stimulus A over stimulus B at one moment and for B over A at a later moment. If a subject is highly inconsistent, there is some ponderable possibility that the weight of his responses would have yielded an *intransitive* relation among the stimuli, had he responded a moment later than he did.

In this sense, inconsistency may be interpreted as "uncertainty" on the part of the subject about putting a simple order on the stimuli. An arbitrary criterion was established at 70 per cent of the paired comparisons. Subjects who gave inconsistencies in 30 per cent or more of the pairs of stimuli were dropped from consideration. This removed 54 subjects, leaving 76. All five teachers gave transitive responses containing at least 80 per cent consistency.

(4) Hypothesis 1 makes explicit the next step in selection. Once the co-linearity index is applied to two rank orders, it provides in itself evidence for change of viewpoint between the two responses. (I shall frequently from here forward use the term "viewpoint" as a synonym for the cognitive structure underlying a rank ordering.) Subjects whose pretest responses were co-linear with the teacher's, but whose posttest responses were non-co-linear, or conversely, would have been exposed to one condition and then to the other in some unknown proportion and could not reliably be used to test the hypothesis. Using only those subjects who were co-linear with the teacher at both pretest and posttest, or non-co-linear at both, reduced the number of subjects by 34 of the 76, leaving 42. At this level of "purity," so to speak, I judged that the co-linearity index should be effective enough to separate sheep from goats.

(5) Hypothesis 2 specifies a further step in selection. If the co-linearity index is applied to the subject's own two responses, one at pretest and one at posttest, non-co-linearity "pre-to-post" would imply that the subject has changed his viewpoint in the interim, even though the viewpoints at both times are co-linear (or non-co-linear) with that of the teacher. Of the 48 students used in testing Hypothesis 1, 6 gave non-co-linear pre-to-post responses, leaving 36 subjects in the test of Hypothesis 2.

QUIZ GRADE z-SCORES

Co-linearity, then, applied in the manner described, is the independent variable for Hypotheses 1 and 2. The dependent variable is the mean grade made by the subject on quizzes written and graded by his teacher. Within each of the seven classes, each quiz was given equal weight in the total score. In order to compare quiz grades across classes, z-scores were then computed for each class. The z-scores were used as data in all further computations.

RESULTS FOR HYPOTHESIS 1

Dividing the 42 subjects used to test Hypothesis 1 into those co-linear with the instructor at both pretest and posttest (21 subjects) and those non-co-linear with the instructor at both tests (also 21 subjects) the finding is in the proper direction (t-test, satisfies $\alpha > .07$).[1] Statistics pertinent to this result are shown in Table 2.

Although this result would make acceptance of this hypothesis dubious by itself, it will be seen that this result is entirely consistent with the result of the test of Hypothesis 2, which reaches traditionally acceptable levels of significance.

RESULTS FOR HYPOTHESIS 2

Hypothesis 2 stated that the difference in quiz grades predicted by Hypothesis 1 will be at least as pronounced when only those students are considered whose pre-

[1] All probability figures in this paper are two-tailed probabilities.

TABLE 2

DIFFERENCE BETWEEN Z-SCORES ON QUIZZES FOR
STUDENTS CO-LINEAR AND NON-CO-LINEAR
WITH THE INSTRUCTOR

| | N | Z-scores | | |
		Mean	Range	S.D.
Co-linear with instructor	21	.51	−1.16 to 2.77	1.18
Non-co-linear with instructor	21	−.15	−2.56 to 1.74	1.18

TABLE 3

DIFFERENCE BETWEEN Z-SCORES ON QUIZZES FOR
STUDENTS CO-LINEAR AND NON-CO-LINEAR WITH
THE INSTRUCTOR, FOR STUDENTS WHO WERE CO-LINEAR
WITH THEMSELVES FROM PRETEST TO POSTTEST

| | N | Z-scores | | |
		Mean	Range	S.D.
Co-linear with instructor	17	.60	−1.16 to 2.77	1.38
Non-co-linear with instructor	19	−.25	−2.56 to 1.74	1.17

test and posttest rank orders are co-linear.

In the test of Hypothesis 2, there were 17 subjects in the group co-linear with the instructor and 19 in the non-co-linear group. The t-test applied to the quiz scores of these two groups yields a significance level beyond .05. Statistics for this test are shown in Table 3.

It should be pointed out that the t-test is not entirely appropriate for testing these hypotheses. When the co-linearity index gives a value of non-co-linear, it may be said according to the theory that the subject could not, from any position on the attribute underlying his response, give a rank order of the stimuli which would unfold with that of the other person. But when the index gives a value of co-linear, the converse cannot be said. An index value of "co-linear" indicates only that it *cannot be said,* according to

the theory, that the subject's viewpoint is *not* co-linear with that of the other person. It *may or may not* unfold with his. For this reason, a test of co-variation such as product-moment correlation, chi square, or the t-test demands more of the data than can be predicted.

For the reason that a test such as the t-test is treating the data more stringently than the prediction undertakes, the probability of .07 given by the t-test for Hypothesis 1 becomes more acceptable. As was suggested earlier, the result of Hypothesis 1, when compared to that for Hypothesis 2, argues for the correctness of the theoretical derivations, since it was expected on theoretical grounds that the criteria for the co-linearity index used in Hypothesis 2 would give better results than the less stringent criteria used in Hypothesis 1.

TESTS OF ALTERNATIVE HYPOTHESES

It will now be well to raise a few questions about the findings so far given. The first of these has to do with the effect of co-linearity, as contrasted with similar preferences among the stimuli on the part of teacher and student, in predicting mean grades.

PREFERENCES AMONG THE STIMULI

It may occur to the reader to wonder whether it might be that the co-linearity index has picked out, among the data, co-linear rank orders which contain the same stimuli in preferred positions. That is, it might be that co-linear persons are those who agree that certain stimuli are *most preferable*. If this were the case, it might be argued that the theoretical derivations were unnecessary, and that agreement with the teacher on quiz answers was foreshadowed by agreement with the teacher on the choice of the most preferred among the five attitude statements.

The tau statistic, which measures rank order similarity, was used as a measure of the degree to which a student and his teacher chose the same stimulus-statements as best. Since the scatter-diagrams suggested that both the tau values and the quiz z-scores were distributed symmetrically, the product-moment correlation was computed between them. The correlation figure was .23 for 34 degrees of freedom, which is far short of a value at which the null hypothesis of no association could reasonably be rejected. In short, the data fail to give evidence that quiz grades follow a preference for the same stimulus-statements preferred by the teacher. It is not agreement with the teacher on which statements are the best which makes the difference in quiz grades; rather it is judging the statements according to the *same*

underlying attribute, regardless of whether the student agrees with the teacher about the most desirable point on the attribute.

EXISTENCE OF AN ATTITUDE NORM

Another possibility which should be examined is that co-linearity with one's particular teacher is not the determining factor, but rather co-linearity with a *normative* ordering of the stimuli. That is, it might not be the interaction of cognitive fields of teacher and student which accounts for the difference in grade-achievement, but rather the sensitivity of the student to a more general "cultural" frame of reference which is merely mediated by the teacher. If this were the case, the data should show a tendency for mutual co-linearity among the responses of the teachers. That this is not the case is shown in Table 4. This table shows that while teachers 1 and 2 are co-linear, and teachers 3 and 4 are co-linear, neither 1 nor 2 is co-linear with either 3 or 4. This indicates that at least two incompatible viewpoints exist among the five teachers. A tendency toward a single viewpoint is not found.

SCHOLASTIC APTITUDE

In any investigation where symbolic responses are being studied, the possibility can always be entertained that the performance of the subjects may be related to performance on some measure of symbolic skill such as a test of intelligence, scholastic aptitude, or scholastic achievement. If a relation were found between such an ability and the quiz z-score, the novelty of the present findings would be weakened to the extent that co-linearity with the instructor was not independent of the symbolic skill.

The American Council on Education test of scholastic aptitude seemed an ap-

TABLE 4

CO-LINEARITY OF VIEWPOINT BETWEEN PAIRS OF TEACHERS

Margins of the table show identification numbers of the teachers. Each cell shows whether the responses of the two indicated teachers are co-linear or non-co-linear

2	3	4	5	
Co-lin.	Non-co.	Non-co.	Co-lin.	1
	Non-co.	Non-co.	Co-lin.	2
		Co-lin.	Non-co.	3
			Co-lin.	4

propriate measure with which to examine this possible relationship. A.C.E. scores were available for 100 of the subjects who responded both to pretest and posttest, including 26 of the 36 subjects used in testing Hypothesis 2.

A t-test was carried out to see whether the co-linearity index somehow selected groups which differed in A.C.E. scores. No difference was demonstrable between the group co-linear with the teacher and the group non-co-linear with the teacher in regard to mean A.C.E. score. One would conclude from this result that members of the co-linear group were drawn from the same level of A.C.E. scores as members of the non-co-linear group. The difference in z-scores between the two groups can be attributed to the co-linearity condition and not to any difference in scholastic aptitude. To check whether scholastic aptitude could in any case have differentiated among quiz grades, A.C.E. scores for the 100 available cases were correlated with quiz grades, and a positive correlation of .42 was found, which is significant beyond the .05 level. The nonsignificant result of the t-test of the 26 cases in the co-linearity groups, nevertheless, argues that the co-linearity effect on quiz grades was not due to differential selection of scholastic ability.

In sum, it seems clear that the co-linearity index predicts a difference among quiz grades which is not attributable to the relation between A.C.E. scores and quiz grades, to response to an attribute norm, or to a preference for the stimulus-statements preferred by the teacher.

DISCUSSION

This research examines the relation between an interaction variable (co-linearity) and an individual variable (success in choosing "correct" answers in quizzes). It examines the effect on individual responses when a certain kind of "meshing" exists or does not exist between the viewpoints which shape the communicative acts of two or more persons.

In describing the intent and implications of this research it is important to make clear the structural difference between an interaction variable such as co-linearity (or deviation from a group norm, or certain kinds of power relations, to give other examples) and experimental variables which are constructed by comparing individuals on some specific attribute. Examples of the latter would be found in selecting pairs or groups of persons according to how they compared with each other on liking for dancing, years of education, authoritarianism, or some other particular attribute. A variable constructed in this fashion enables hypotheses to be made of this type: if individuals who are high (or low, or the same, or different) on attribute x are put in communication with each other, then these individuals will show certain behaviors rather than others.

An hypothesis concerning an interaction variable such as co-linearity has a different form: if individuals communicate on the basis of the same attribute x, regardless of what attribute it may be and regardless of whether the individuals are high, low, the same, or different on this attribute, then they will show certain behaviors rather than others.

In ascertaining co-linearity between pairs of persons in the present research no attempt was made to put a label on the attribute which two co-linear individuals used in common in organizing their responses to the stimuli. Nor was any attempt made to find out whether one co-linear teacher-pupil pair was responding according to the same attribute utilized by another co-linear teacher-pupil pair. The "content" of the attribute mediating the responses of any pair was unknown. Further, there was good evidence that some co-linear pairs must have been judging the stimuli on the basis of different attributes from other pairs, as indicated by Table 4. The predictions and analyses of this research were made with regard only to the *structural* similarity of orientations toward the stimuli as reflected in the co-linearity index, and without regard to the content character of the orientations, indeed without any knowledge of their content character.

Many investigations of social process require the study of communication, of the transmission of information, of the "understanding" of stimuli presented by some persons to others. The effects of this

communication depend on the abilities of the individuals involved, and often upon the agreement or disagreement which exists between the communicators in regard to the content of the communication. But beyond these factors the present research argues that whatever the abilities of the individuals and whatever the extent of their agreement, the effects of the communication also depend on the structural similarity of the viewpoints which mediate "sending" and "receiving" in the communicative interaction.

SUMMARY

This paper has been concerned with the proposition that similarity of structure between two cognitive fields increases the efficacy of communication between them.

Communication or interaction between two persons is conceived as being mediated by the cognitive structure, or space of potential responses, associated with each individual. The response spaces, in turn, can be described in terms of the attributes which mediate the responses; that is, the attributes of the objects in respect to which the individual makes his responses. Further, an individual may combine the attributes mediating his responses into one composite attribute. This composite attribute is compounded in different ways by different individuals, and such a composite attribute underlying the responses of an individual permits some responses and precludes others. I have described criteria for deciding whether or not a composite attribute can be inferred reliably to underlie the responses, and if so, whether or not the composite attributes being used by two communicating individuals might be permitting or precluding the same responses.

If responses of two individuals can be interpreted to be mediated by the same underlying attribute, the responses are termed "co-linear," and "non-co-linear" if they cannot. Computation of an index of co-linearity rests upon the "unfolding technique" of Coombs.

In these terms, we can index similarity of cognitive structure with the co-linearity index and put into more precise terms the proposition with which we began; namely, where changes in orientations occur as a result of communication, the changes will be more pronounced for co-linear communicating pairs and less pronounced for non-co-linear pairs.

This hypothesis was tested by presenting statements to teachers and students concerning the introductory course in psychology in which they interacted for the period of a semester. It was predicted that students co-linear with the teacher would get higher grades on quizzes than students non-co-linear with the teacher. This prediction was well supported by the results. Further examinations of the data provided evidence that the higher grades on the part of co-linear students could not be accounted for by differences in scholastic ability as measured by A.C.E. scores, nor by conformity to a common attitude norm, nor by a preference for the same attitude position as that held by the teacher.

The results of this research imply that differences in abilities between communicators and differences in agreement concerning the content of communication must fail to account for certain effects of communication which can be accounted for by similarity of cognitive structure between the communicators.

REFERENCES

1. COOMBS, C. H., "Psychological Sealing without a Unit of Measurement," *Psychological Review*, 1960, 57, 145–158.

2. COOMBS, C. H., "Theory and Methods of Social Measurement," in L. FESTINGER and D. KATZ (eds.), *Research Methods in the Behavioral Sciences*. New York: Dryden, 1953.

3. COOMBS, C. H., and R. C. KAO, *Nonmetric Factor Analysis,* Ann Arbor, Michigan: University of Michigan Press, Engineering Research Bulletin No. 38, 1955.

4. NEWCOMB, T. M., "An Approach to the Study of Communicative Acts," *Psychological Review*, 1953, 60, 393–404.

5. RUNKEL, P. J., "Cognitive Facilitation of Communication Effects," unpublished doctoral dissertation, University of Michigan, 1956.

INTERPERSONAL RELATIONSHIPS IN THE STUDENT-TEACHING TRIAD

Albert H. Yee

In the nearly twelve hundred teacher education programs of the United States, laboratory experiences in student teaching are normally required of all candidates. To culminate their professional preparation, more than two hundred thousand teachers currently work with more than one hundred and fifty thousand cooperating teachers (39:1). No group or authority calls for the deemphasis of student teaching, and its continuance and expansion are taken for granted. Many believe that student-teaching experiences comprise the most important aspect of teacher preparation; support for this view can be found in statements by students (5, 64), professional educators (2), and critics of teacher education programs. In his much-discussed book, *The Education of American Teachers,* Conant (9:142) wrote: "As we have seen, the one indisputably essential element in professional education is practice teaching."

From: Journal of Teacher Education, *1968,* 19, *95–112. Copyright © 1968 by the National Commission on Teacher Education and Professional Standards, National Education Association, and reproduced by permission of the author and NCTEPS, NEA.*

Yet, with increased emphasis being given to this facet of teacher education, what do we know empirically about the effect of student teaching on future teachers? Does it really provide a qualitative difference in teacher product? Reviewing research on preservice and in-service education of teachers, Reynard (48:375) lamented the lack of investigation in the area of professional laboratory experiences: "Professional laboratory experience seems to be the area least challenged in teacher education." Such comment indicated no change since Michaelis (36: 1473) wrote: "The general status of critical, evaluative research on student teaching is poor."

Little attention has been given to the identification of factors that significantly determine the nature of outcomes in student-teaching experiences. Not knowing for sure *what* really matters in student teaching, very little empirical research has been conducted to explain *how* it affects the candidate in his professional development. Until much greater knowledge is sought and found concerning what variables really matter and how they affect behavior, systematic improvements in student-teaching programs will be unlikely.

APPROACHES TO THE STUDY OF STUDENT TEACHING

In an attempt to provide greater understanding of student teaching and indicate ways to improve its operations, a pilot study was conducted to investigate interpersonal behavior events in student-teaching settings. A preliminary review of relevant literature was made to find a meaningful approach to such a study, and the following areas reviewed:

(1) New Trends in Teacher Education

New programs are being developed to improve teacher education, such as those reported by Allen (1), Ort (43), and Ward and Suttle (60). The programs attempt to provide learnings and supervision more directly related to classroom purposes and requirements. With such objectives, these innovations emphasize and enhance the interactive relationship between the student teacher and those who direct and supervise his work and learning.

(2) Individual Differences

The need to consider individual differences has often been expressed in regard to young learners. Writings, such as those of MacDonald and Doll (35), Sharpe (53), Symonds (56), and Walberg (59) remind us that the individual characteristics of *all* persons interacting in educational situations must be considered.

Although few professional educators need to be convinced that the individual differences of student teachers require attention, many may not apply the same principle to the personality and behavior of cooperating teachers and college super-

visors; they may assume an ideal, normative type of leader that is effective with most student teachers. Such assumptions place considerable burden on the candidates, who must then accept major responsibility for personal adjustments and interpersonal problems. A study by Stager (55) on the effect of group members' conceptual structure level helps to emphasize the importance of considering the individual differences of leaders as well as of student teachers. Stager found that groups' interpersonal conflict increased as the percentage of members with high conceptual structures increased. Regarding the student-teaching leaders as being high in educational conceptual structure and the candidates as being low, we are reminded of the adage about too many Indian chiefs.

(3) Interpersonal Relations

Interaction processes that influence teaching-learning outcomes in educational settings have been illustrated by Della Piana and Gage (14), Flanders (18), Halpin and Winer (24), Hughes (30), Miller (37), White and Lippitt (61), and Withall and Lewis (63). Bass (4:5) and Sanford (50:329) have suggested that the search for leadership traits will not be successful unless a study is made of the relations between leader and follower and the demands each makes upon the other. Lindsey (33) has made the same suggestion for the student-teaching situation.

In student teaching, the candidate's personality and behavior become significant factors relative to others around him. Unlike other course work where the students are mostly passive and absorbing whatever the instructors say and do, student teaching is conducted in an interaction setting that has no equivalent in most teacher-training programs. It is a time for candidates to perform, evaluate, act, react, and adapt in relationship with and in response to others also involved in the setting. Unfortunately, little is known about these relationships of personality and behavior in student teaching.

(4) DYADIC RELATIONSHIPS

Two-person relationships between the student teacher and one of his leaders have been given much attention, e.g., 11, 52, and 49. A good example of such concerns is a dissertation study completed under the supervision of W. W. Charters, Jr., where R. L. Holemon (28) used Newcomb's ABX model to investigate change in pre- and posttest attitudes of student teachers toward leaders' attitudes measured at pretest.

Such studies, however, were more concerned with change in student teachers' perceptions than with the actual study of interactive relationships. As suggested by Sarason, Davidson, and Blatt (54:116), "what are desperately needed are studies which have as their aims a detailed description of what goes on between neophyte and supervisor. . . ."

(5) EQUILIBRIUM IN INTERPERSONAL RELATIONS

Equilibrium theory offers a framework to consider the alternative courses of action and the psychological resolutions open to persons faced with conflicting perceptions and to understand better their choices among them. The general theory is a combination of contributions by Festinger (17), Heider (27), Newcomb (41), and Osgood and Tannenbaum (44). Central to all models is the notion that human nature abhors "dissonance—imbalance—incongruity" and continually strives to eliminate it in some way. Studies such as 3, 8, 13, and 20 suggest that there may be practical value in applying equilibrium theory to the study of student-teaching relationships.

(6) SOCIAL ORGANIZATION

The study of small group systems (e.g., 25) helps us perceive the student-teaching setting from the view of functioning social units created and set into operation for special objectives and activities. Within such units, we can find the interplay of normative system-influences. For example, we can consider the manner in which member participation is brought about and concluded; organizational structure and task dependency, e.g., differentiation of roles, statuses, and functions; communication, e.g., who talks how much to whom and how; motivation processes, e.g., individuals' purposes and reward—cost alternatives and outcomes; and group cohesiveness, e.g., attractiveness of the group to members and their desire to maintain group relationships. The combination of such system-influences with individual differences provide potential for commonality as well as variation among units in student teaching. Boyd (6) provides a needed review of such concerns.

Discussions of three-person or triad relationships, such as 27:179; 38; 42: 308–309; 54; 57:191–221; 58; and 62 have indicated that the maintenance of positive attraction may often be difficult for triad members. This is especially so when they do not have complete control over the choice of the other two members, as usually found in student teaching. Under such conditions, chances are strong that a coalition between two triad members may form at the expense of the third member.

Group cohesiveness may be far more important in its effects in student teaching than the actual concern given it today. Guetzkow (22) found that task-oriented groups performed more effectively in communication nets when there was clear role differentiation and an interlocking organizational structure. Studying decision-making in a management game, Hutte (31) found groups to be more effective in decision making when there was less leadership. French (19) has noted that group performance is positively related to equivalent participation by group members. In a review of studies which indicated how groups developed lowered cohesiveness, Cartwright and Zander (7:83–86) listed these reasons: (1) possible reduction of needs group has been satisfying; (2) disagreement over the way to solve a group problem; (3) unpleasant experiences of a member of the group, such as assumption of responsibilities that may provide stress, opportunity for failure, and demand for greater ability than he feels himself capable of; (4) other members are too dominating or have unpleasant characteristics; (5) limitation of satisfaction and other activities; (6) failure or lack of communication; (7) negative status ascribed by others to group members; (8) competition between different groups for members.

THE STUDENT-TEACHING TRIAD AS A UNIT OF ANALYSIS

The review of literature briefly outlined above leads us to consider the interaction operating among student teacher, college supervisor, and cooperating teacher. We decided to focus upon the interpersonal relations of this three-person group for which the term, *student-teaching triad,* was formulated. The triad can be viewed as being comprised of two dyads between the student teacher and each of his leaders, and a dyadic relationship between the two leaders. Such a focus can encompass significant features of each category reviewed above. Approaching any student-teaching concern, such as objectives, personnel, motivation and morale, evaluation, activities, etc., we can start from the triad

framework and develop approaches and operational procedures to handle the concern.

The relevance of the triad model to a search for better ways to understand and improve student-teaching programs is further described in Figure 1, where the possible interpersonal relationships are depicted for the student-teaching setting.

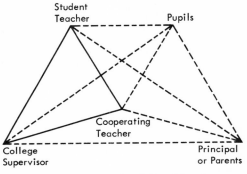

Figure 1. Interpersonal relationships in the student-teaching situation.

The solid lines in Figure 1 indicate connections for what are considered the most significant interpersonal behavior events, i.e., where interaction is of most importance for the purposes and outcomes of student teaching. The dotted lines indicate other relationships that operate in the student-teaching setting but are less influential in their effects on student teachers or are less likely to be formed and carried on beyond superficial interaction. Of the dotted connections presented, the pupils are probably more significant factors than the principal and the parents.

Not much is known beyond speculation about the pupil factor in student teaching. Although their attention and efforts are directed to the education of learners, student teachers seem to credit their cooperating teachers' and supervisors' influences as more significant. Although pupils must determine the setting to some degree, their overall effect on the relationships of triad members may not be very great. Supervisors seldom deal with the learner; accordingly the cooperating teacher and student teacher form a leadership team or coalition to facilitate daily classroom activities. In other words, the adults, including student teacher, form a unit separate from the children. Interaction concerning the purposes of student teaching prevails in this unit where the student teacher is a follower and the cooperating teacher and supervisor act as leaders. In this study, therefore, we have restricted our attention to this triad.

Typically, each member of the triad enters the group from two distinct systems—the student teacher and supervisor from the college, and the cooperating teacher from the school. Assignments to triads are hardly ever completely voluntary and of free choice. The college supervisor may be assigned a list of student teachers and certain schools in which to place them, or he may be given the assignments already made by a director of student teaching. The cooperating teacher may or may not have the option of accepting or refusing a student teacher, but seldom does he have much information about the student teacher with whom he may work. For the candidate, the few options generally available in choosing grade-level interests, and perhaps college supervisor, do not provide him with much control of the cooperating teacher to whom he will be assigned. As for the leaders, familiarity and choice of each other may range somewhat. Thus, there is sufficient reason to consider the manner in which triads are formed.

In some institutions, the supervisor assumes responsibility in matching the other two members. However, with the increasing number of student teachers each year, many institutions find it difficult to locate sufficient classroom placements for students, and as a consequence, candidates must often accept assignments to grade levels other than those preferred and count themselves fortunate just to be in student teaching.

Such problems, of course, decrease the ability to be selective in choosing cooperating teachers. Findings suggesting that cooperating teachers strongly influence the future teaching methods of their student teachers (34, 45) emphasize the importance of imposing qualitative screening criteria and adequate preparation for cooperating teachers (26).

From Thibaut and Kelley (57:12–50), we would expect differences in reward-cost conditions for each triad member, i.e., what outcomes each expects and gets out of the relationship and what he must sacrifice or give up for such work. The student desires fulfillment of much discursive preparation in working with pupils and favorable grades and references, for which he expends time, effort, and probably anxiety. According to Goodlad (21), student teachers are often more concerned with survival than with principles of pedagogy. Each leader desires satisfactory outcomes in the candidate's development in terms of his own perceptions of effective teaching performance and commitment to the profession. These perceptions of leaders may be quite diverse and in conflict, and student teachers must often balance the disequilibrium by themselves.

The costs for the leaders are not equivalent; for the supervisor's occupation, analagous to the student's purposes, requires that there be a functioning triad. But not so for the cooperating teacher. The reward-cost outcomes for the teacher, who already carries primary responsibilities for his class or classes, may be more wide-ranged than for the supervisor. Many colleges, often under pressure from cooperating school districts, have had to increase stipends paid to cooperating teachers to provide greater recognition and reward for their services. Without the professional sanctions cooperating teachers would face for not fulfilling or completing the student-teaching assignment, we might expect more cooperating teachers dissolving student-teaching relationships. For as Thibaut and Kelley (57:192) pointed out: "Like any group, a triad is viable only if all of its members are dependent on its continued existence...." The question may be raised, Does compliance to the organizational structure maintain the existence of the student-teaching triad more than group cohesiveness?

The main concern of the present study, therefore, was focused on the relationship of interpersonal attitudes among student teachers, college supervisors, and cooperating teachers. We raised the following questions: What patterns in triad attitude relationships are there at the beginning and toward the end of the student-teaching period? Are there trends in the shifting of attitude relationships from pre- to posttest occasions? If so, what interpretations concerning triad cohesiveness can be made from such trends?

THE METHOD

Subjects. The sample involved 44 elementary and 80 secondary student teachers, their 124 cooperating teachers, and 4 elementary and 8 secondary college supervisors. The selection of subjects was made according to the availability of such student teachers and supervisors for testing at The University of Texas and assignment of seminars to the study by the director of student teaching. Information regarding the candidates' characteristics, obtained from the National Teacher Examinations and periodically during professional training, indicates that candidates

in this University are similar to typical students elsewhere. Means and standard deviations of teachers' and student teachers' attitudes measured with the *Minnesota Teacher Attitude Inventory,* modified to refer to "young people" instead of "children," resembled MTAI norms (10).

This study's subsample of supervisors may not be entirely representative of supervisors at institutions where there is less diversity in status and experience among supervisors, and especially where clinical professors (9) have been deliberately screened and prepared for such roles. It is felt, however, that such diversity among college supervisors prevails in most student-teaching programs that handle more than one hundred and fifty student teachers each semester. All of the supervisors had had extensive classroom teaching experience (an average of 12.5 years).

Procedures. Attitudes of each triad member toward the other two members were obtained with inventories and questionnaires specially prepared for this study. Student teachers' attitudes toward leaders' affective, cognitive, and general merit were measured with respective items such as, "Does this cooperating teacher or supervisor understand your feelings?" "Has this cooperating teacher or supervisor discussed many interesting facts and theories concerning teaching with you?" "Would you recommend working with this cooperating teacher or supervisor to another student?" Leaders' perceptions were ascertained with responses to questions concerning other triad members and scores of seven-point scales between the extremes of "inferior-superior" for nine items, such as student teacher's "relation with pupils" and "teaching skills."

Pretests were administered during the first and second weeks of the 1966 spring semester, and posttests toward the end of the semester; there were about 16 weeks between tests. Satisfactory Guttman (23) and Spearman-Brown split-half reliability coefficients in the .90's were found for student teachers' measures. It is assumed that assurances of anonymity helped provide reliable responses to fill-in questionnaires.

In reference to the measures, we classified a student teacher's attitude toward each of his two leaders as positive if his score for a leader was above the median, or negative if it was below the median. For the attitude of each leader toward each of the other two members of the triad, we ascertained from their fill-in questionnaire responses whether their attitudes were positive or negative. It should be pointed out that the 124 triads are not completely independent from each other, since college supervisors were necessarily involved in several triads. The planned follow-up work to this pilot study will attempt to provide independent triads and determine how much this problem affects the results.

In analyses of the data, a dyad relationship was considered positive $(+)$ if each member's attitude toward the other was positive $(+ +)$. A dyad was considered negative $(-)$ if members reported negative attitudes toward each other $(- -)$, or contrasting attitudes toward the other $(+ -)$ or $(- +)$. Thus, a triad can be viewed as balanced (in a state of equilibrium) or unbalanced (in a state of disequilibrium) from its combination of dyadic relationships. Frequencies of the following types of triads were tabulated at pre- and posttest occasions:

(1) Balanced triad composed of all positive dyads: $(+ + +)$.

(2) Balanced triads with two negative dyads: $(+ - -)$, $(- + -)$, and $(- - +)$.

(3) Unbalanced triad composed of all negative dyads: $(- - -)$.

(4) Unbalanced triads with one negative dyad: $(+ + -)$, $(+ - +)$, and $(- + +)$.

RESULTS AND DISCUSSION

Total sample (N = 124 triads). Table 1 presents the frequencies for each type of triad which occurred at pre- and posttest occasions, showing 75 triads balanced at pretest, and 62 at posttest. Imbalanced triads numbered 49 at pretest, and 62 at posttest. Specific types of pre- and posttest shifts in triad relationships will be examined before the overall pattern of change is discussed more fully.

Beginning with the first row on Table 1, we find a total of 42 triads balanced with all-positive dyads $(+ + +)$ at pretest. At posttest, only 18 of these triads remained balanced and only 4 were still in the form of $(+ + +)$. Of these 18 triads balanced at posttest, the majority (14) shifted to $(- - +)$.

Twenty-four $(+ + +)$ triads found at pretest shifted to the following types of imbalance at posttest: 4 $(- - -)$, 8 $(+ - +)$, one $(+ + -)$, and 11 $(- + +)$. Almost half (11) of these shifts had developed a negative dyad between the college supervisor and student teacher, while T-S and C-T dyads remained positive $(- + +)$. Eight triads became imbalanced when the dyad between cooperating teacher and student teacher became negative $(+ - +)$.

The 19 cases of $(+ - +)$ and $(- + +)$ indicate some tendency for coalitions to form between the student teacher and one of the leaders. Because supervisor and cooperating teacher interact infrequently with each other and may maintain a positive dyadic relationship from a distance, it is conceivable that more of these imbalanced cases of $(+ - +)$ and $(- + +)$ would be balanced as $(+ - -)$ and $(- + -)$, respectively, if interaction between C-T was greater. With only

TABLE 1

TRIAD RELATIONSHIPS AT PRE- AND POSTTEST

(N = 124 TRIADS)

Dyad Relationships:			Posttest								
(C-S)	(T-S)	(C-T)*	+++	+-+	+--	++-	---	--+	-++	-+-	Totals
+	+	+	4	8	0	1	4	14	11	0	42
+	-	+	1	7	2	2	1	7	7	1	28
+	-	-	0	0	0	0	0	0	0	0	0
-	+	-	0	0	0	0	0	0	0	0	0
-	-	+	2	1	4	0	8	14	4	0	33
-	-	+	1	1	1	1	3	9	3	2	21
-	+	-	0	0	0	0	0	0	0	0	0
		Totals	8	17	7	4	16	44	25	3	124

(Pretest rows shown at left.)

* (C-S) denotes the college supervisor-student teacher dyad, (T-S) denotes the cooperating teacher-student teacher dyad, and (C-T) denotes the college supervisor-cooperating teacher dyad. A "+" sign indicates positive attitudes between members of dyads; a "−" sign indicates negative attitudes in dyads.

four posttest cases out of 42 at pretest actually remaining in the all-positive state of $(+ + +)$, we begin to see that the student-teaching triad shifts away from all-around unity toward triadic arrangements of positive and negative dyad relationships.

In the second row of Table 1, 28 $(+ - +)$ triads were imbalanced at pretest. At the posttest occasion, 17 remained imbalanced with only 7 remaining in the same state of imbalance $(+ - +)$; one became $(- - -)$, 7 $(- + +)$; and 2 shifted to $(+ + -)$. Eleven of the 28 $(+ - +)$ were found to be balanced at posttest in the following forms: only one shifted to $(+ + +)$, 2 to $(+ - -)$, 7 to $(- - +)$, and one became $(- + -)$. Instead of shifting toward positive triad unity $(+ + +)$, this initial group arrangement shows considerable instability in the two dyads involving the student teacher. The persistence of the C-T dyad to remain stable can be seen again in noting that only 6 of these 28 dyads changed to negative compared with 14 of the C-S dyad which changed to $(-)$ and 17 of the T-S dyad which shifted to $(+)$.

In the sixth row, 33 triads were balanced as $(- - +)$ at pretest. At posttest, 20 were found to be balanced in the form of 14 still $(- - +)$, 2 $(+ + +)$, and 4 $(+ - -)$. The remaining 13 triads were imbalanced at posttest; 8 became $(- - -)$, one $(+ - +)$, and 4 $(- + +)$. Since these triads began the semester with negative cohesiveness as a group, it is not surprising that only 2 became $(+ + +)$ and that this unstable arrangement continued and moved toward greater breakdown of the group.

In the seventh row, we find 21 $(- + +)$ triads imbalanced at pretest. At posttest, only one of these triads had shifted to $(+ + +)$. One had become $(+ - -)$, 9 $(- - +)$, and 2 $(- + -)$, resulting in 13 out of 21 $(- + +)$

triads achieving balance between pre- and posttests. Among the 8 triads which were still imbalanced at posttest, 3 remained $(- + +)$, one became $(+ - +)$, one $(+ + -)$, and 3 $(- - -)$. Here again, we see the tendency for stability in C-T coalitions. Unlike the pre- to posttest shifts from $(+ - +)$ discussed above, there is strong stability in how the C-S dyad remained negative; only 4 out of 21 changed and became $(+)$. However, 14 out of the T-S dyads changed to $(-)$ in keeping with the instability between student teacher and cooperating teacher noted above.

Among the 62 triads which were balanced at the posttest occasion, 44 were formed as $(- - +)$, 8 $(+ + +)$, 7 $(+ - -)$, and 3 $(- + -)$. The question arises as to why more triads (44) found balance in the form of $(- - +)$ than in any other triadic relationship. There were only 10 other triads where balance was achieved as a result of one dyad coalition, 7 of which were coalition formations between college supervisor and student teacher $(+ - -)$. For the total sample, therefore, the predominant pattern for triadic balance is in the condition of $(- - +)$ where a coalition exists between the leaders and there are negative dyadic relations between leaders and student teachers.

Triadic balance achieved with a $(- - +)$ relationship may be the result of coalition formation between the leaders in order to exercise mutual control and influence over the student teacher. In their discussion of coalition formation, Thibaut and Kelley (57: 205) wrote:

This joint action is presumably based upon common interest, or, in our technical terms, correspondence of outcomes. Insofar as the outcomes of all the individuals in a given subset are affected in the same way by another individual, the basis exists for their forming a coalition against him.

A cooperating teacher and college supervisor share common interests in the performance of a student teacher, since the quality of work done by a student teacher reflects, in part, the quality of leadership given by the cooperating teacher and the college supervisor. Common personal characteristics, such as age and background, may also help the two leaders coalesce.

Among the 124 triads studied in the total sample, patterns of shift were found from pre- to posttest occasion. First, there is a trend toward greater triadic inbalance. Although the differences between the frequencies of triads balanced at pretest and at posttest were not significant $(75 \rightarrow 62)$, the reduction from 42 pretest cases of $(+ + +)$ triads to 8 such triads at posttest is significant. Also, at pretest there were no $(- - -)$ triads; at posttest, there were 16. The difference between balanced and unbalanced triads at pretest (75 to 49) is statistically significant at well above the .05 level $(x^2 = 5.04,$ 2×1 contingency table, two-tailed with 1 df). However, because of the increased shift toward imbalance, posttest frequencies are exactly equal to chance expectations of N.

Another method of viewing such shift is to note the few cases in the diagonal from the northwest corner to the southeast corner of Table 1. This diagonal passes through the cells that are identical from pre- to posttest. In Table 1, those cells contain a total of only 28 out of 124 possible triads, indicating considerable instability. Simmel (54: 135–36) considered the three-person group to be inherently unstable.

Second, the student-teaching triad becomes much less cohesive as a positive-attractive group to its members. What ap-

parently happens over time, as the triad members work longer and become more familiar with each other, is that coalitions are formed, especially between the leaders; and C-S and T-S dyads exhibit strong tendencies toward negative outcomes. Thus, triadic balance of the form $(- - +)$ is most outstanding among outcomes and seems to represent the student-teaching triad's overall movement toward equilibrium.

Elementary and Secondary Subsamples. Elementary cooperating teachers and student teachers involved in this study were found to have more positive attitudes toward young people and teaching than did their secondary counterparts. Since such results suggested characteristic differences between elementary and secondary triads, we analyzed results of triad shifts for the two levels of school. Tables 2 and 3 show frequencies of triadic shifts from pre- to posttest among elementary and secondary triads separately.

As in Table 1, few cases are found in the "stable" cells by diagonals running from the northwest corner to the southeast corner in both tables. The three sets of results are similar to each other. In Tables 2 and 3, we find that triadic balance is achieved more through arrangements with negative dyads and coalitions than through positive triadic balance, i.e., $(+ + +)$. Twenty-six of 44 elementary triads were balanced at pretest; 23 were balanced at posttest with 13 $(- - +)$, 3 $(+ - -)$, and only 7 $(+ + +)$. Among the 80 secondary triads, 42 were balanced at posttest with 30 cases $(- - +)$, 4 $(+ - -)$, 4 $(- + -)$, and only 4 $(+ + +)$. The majority of triad relationships, therefore, show negative dyads operating between student teacher and both leaders, i.e., $(- - -)$ and $(- - +)$. Of this majority, the latter situation where the leaders formed a positive coalition and had negative dyadic rela-

TABLE 2

ELEMENTARY TRIAD RELATIONSHIPS AT PRE- AND POSTTEST (N = 44)

Dyad Relationships:			Posttest								
(C-S)	(T-S)	(C-T)*	+++	+−+	+−−	++−	−−−	−−+	−++	−+−	Totals
+	+	+	5	0	1	0	1	5	2	0	14
+	−	+	0	1	1	0	2	3	3	0	10
+	−	−	0	0	0	0	0	0	0	0	0
−	+	−	0	0	0	0	0	0	0	0	0
−	−	−	1	0	1	0	5	4	1	0	12
−	−	+	1	1	0	1	3	1	1	0	8
−	+	+	0	0	0	0	0	0	0	0	0
Totals			7	2	3	1	11	13	7	0	44

(Pretest rows at left.)

* (C-S) denotes the college supervisor-student teacher dyad, (T-S) denotes the cooperating teacher-student teacher dyad, and (C-T) denotes the college supervisor-cooperating teacher dyad. A "+" sign indicates positive attitudes between members of dyads; a "−" sign indicates negative attitudes in dyads.

TABLE 3

SECONDARY TRIAD RELATIONSHIPS AT PRE- AND POSTTEST (N = 80)

Dyad Relationships:			Posttest								
(C-S)	(T-S)	(C-T)*	+++	+-+	+--	++-	---	--+	-++	-+-	Totals
+	+	+	2	4	1	1	2	13	3	0	26
+	-	+	1	9	0	2	0	2	3	0	17
+	-	-	0	0	0	0	0	0	0	0	0
-	+	-	0	0	0	0	0	0	0	0	0
-	-	+	1	2	2	0	6	8	3	1	23
-	+	+	0	0	1	0	2	7	1	3	14
-	+	-	0	0	0	0	0	0	0	0	0
Totals			4	15	4	3	10	30	10	4	80

Pretest

* (C-S) denotes the college supervisor-student teacher dyad, (T-S) denotes the cooperating teacher-student teacher dyad, and (C-T) denotes the college supervisor-cooperating teacher dyad. A "+" sign indicates positive attitudes between members of dyads; a "—" sign indicates negative attitudes in dyads.

tionships with student teacher was most predominant, especially in the secondary subsample.

In the elementary subsample (Table 2), 13 triads in the form of $(- - +)$ materialized at posttest as opposed to 12 at pretest. In the secondary subsample (Table 3), there were 30 $(- - +)$ triads against 23 at pretest, approximately 10 percent more cases than elementary triads so balanced. No $(- - -)$ outcomes were found for either subsample at pretest; however, at posttest, striking increases from none to 13 outcomes of $(- - -)$ for elementary triads and 10 for secondary triads do provide significant differences.

CONCLUSIONS

The student-teaching triad appears to seek greater dyadic balance at the cost of decreased triad cohesiveness. Balance is found in dyadic coalitions, especially between the leaders; and negative dyads between leaders and the student teacher. The student-teaching triad seems to degenerate and become less of a viable group as time passes; the greatly increased numbers of triads with only negative dyads $(- - -)$ help to emphasize this conclusion.

The primary objective of student teaching is supposedly to help prepare the student teacher for future independent classroom teaching and evaluate his potential worth as a teacher. The results of this study for attitude relationships in student-teaching triads indicate very great need to find means of improving what is essentially the educational setting in student teaching—the interpersonal relationships in the triad.

Triad relationships more often resemble competitive triad settings than cooperative triad situations (15, 47, 12). In the competitive situation, triad members perceive each other as "contriently inter-

dependent" with respect to their goals, and coalitions are more likely to form than in the cooperative situation. In the cooperative type triad, members perceive each other as "promotively interdependent" with respect to their goals (16).

The reason that the student-teaching triad shifts toward negative relationships and resembles competitive rather than cooperative situations may very well be that typical student-teaching programs provide little opportunity and purpose for meaningful triad interaction. The primary objective of student teaching would seem to require meaningful and sustained cooperation among triad members. Therefore, to achieve the objective for most student teachers, sufficient conditions for cooperative type triads should be provided.

One step to foster positive interaction and morale would be to consider better methods of matching triad members than the random methods now commonly used. This could be best accomplished when more is known about triad members: we need to know more about cooperating teachers' and college supervisors' leadership styles and effects of special training for their work with student teachers. These are important considerations since, within the limits of administrative policies, it is the cooperating teacher and supervisors who mostly control the destiny of the student-teaching triad once it is formed and operating. Also required for developing such methods would be much more information and thought about student teachers.

With greater knowledge of triad members, interaction patterns in triads can be given further investigation. Then, understanding more about the operations of triads and having better notions of criterion behavior for effective teaching than are available today, we can relate triad formation to objectives on the more certain basis of systematic input-output re-

quirements. Thus, deliberate triad formation can provide more maximum positive
effects for student teachers' personal and
professional growth. However, because
the study of interaction processes in educational settings is only now taking root
(6, 63), all of these developments will require much time and effort. Nevertheless,
before such understanding is available,
triad formation can be better handled
than it is today by using existing information on personality characteristics,
teacher behavior, and group interaction.

Probably the most important step in
enhancing the effectiveness of the student-
teaching triad would be increased emphasis
on the triad itself. Each potential member, whether he be student teacher, supervisor, or cooperating teacher, should
perceive the student-teaching experience
as an interaction of three working coop-
eratively together. Such an emphasis would
require that the triad actually function
as an interacting unit and that time and
purpose for triad members to meet and
work together be provided by administrative sources. As Cartwright and Zander
(7:83) have written:

> ...the attractiveness of a group may be
> increased by making it better serve the
> needs of people. A group will be more
> attractive the more it provides status
> and recognition, the more cooperative
> the relations, the freer the interaction,
> and the greater security it provides for
> members.

Realistically, many present problems, such as conflicting responsibilities
and overcrowded schedules for all triad
members, do not easily lend themselves to
sweeping administrative changes; yet,
these problems need to be overcome to
help create professional, primary-group
arrangements in triads today. However,
a real sense of the potential in these relationships by triad members will help

prevent the predominant negativity so
common in this study's findings. This
awareness alone may help enhance communication and cooperation among triad
members. If support is given this important emphasis on developing the effectiveness of triads by providing time and
policies for triad operations and special
selection and training for leaders, then
there should be far less likelihood of or
excuse for triads with all negative dyads
occurring.

The college supervisor is the key
person in the triad (46, 40); student-
teaching supervision should be his specialization and dedication. In the triad framework, the college supervisor carries the
greatest potential for influencing the nature of interaction. However, given the
typical burdens of a college supervisor's
work, such as too many students to supervise adequately and the low prestige and
narrow academic background associated
with such work in many teacher education centers, the supervisor is always
working against tremendous disadvantages
and frustration. Many supervisors perceive
good things they would like to pursue in
their work, but there are often too many
handicaps, especially in establishing meaningful interaction. Often, their chief functions become handling administrative
routines, providing superficial conciliation
and facilitation of the relationships between cooperating teacher and student
teacher, and taking responsibility for final
evaluation of the student teacher.

The greater appeal at this time,
therefore, is to the administrative sources
responsible for the organization and implementation of student-teaching programs
rather than to the triad leaders. With the
greater enrollments in colleges and univer-
sities today and the increasing teacher
shortage, teacher education centers have
attempted to handle conflicting quantitative and qualitative program demands at

the same time. Often, there are only enough time, resources, and inclination to handle the quantitative needs, e.g., the major goals being the number of education majors and B. E. degrees awarded. However, never have professional educators realized more than they do today that qualitative program changes must be made in teacher education (39, 32).

For improvements in student teaching, therefore, we recommend the greater qualitative development of the student-teaching triad, even if such changes are at the cost of decreasing the number of triads an institution can provide at one time. If student-teaching requirements really do matter in the preparation of effective teachers, then the student-teaching triad should become an integral, cooperative team. By building upon today's loosely connected triad structure, we can make systematic, qualitative changes to provide meaningful interaction among student teacher, college supervisor, and cooperating teacher. In these changes, we can create a higher level of professionalism in student teaching and more often obtain the desired result of high-quality teachers.

REFERENCES

1. ALLEN, D. W. "A New Design for Teacher Education: The Teacher Intern Program at Stanford University." *The Journal of Teacher Education* 17: 296–300; Fall 1966.

2. ANDREWS, L. O. "Theory Underlying Proposed State and Federal Support To Promote High-Quality Student Teaching." *Action for Improvement of Teacher Education.* Eighteenth Yearbook. Washington, D.C.: American Association of Colleges for Teacher Education, National Education Association, 1965, pp. 203–15.

3. BALES, R. F. "The Equilibrium Problem in Small Groups." *Small Groups: Studies in Social Interaction.* (Edited by A. P. HARE, E. F. BORGATTA, and R. F. BALES.) Revised edition. New York: Knopf, 1965, pp. 444–76.

4. BASS, B. M. *Leadership, Psychology and Organization Behavior.* New York: Harper, 1960.

5. BENNIE, W. A. "Campus Supervision of Student Teaching—A Closer Look." *Teachers College Journal* 36: 131–33; 1964.

6. BOYD, R. D. "The Group as a Sociopsychological Setting for Learning." *Review of Educational Research* 35: 209–17; June 1965.

7. CARTWRIGHT, D., and ZANDER, A. F., editors. *Group Dynamics: Research and Theory.* Second edition. New York: Harper, 1960.

8. CHAPMAN, L. J., and CAMPBELL, D. T. "An Attempt To Predict the Performance of Three-Man Teams from Attitude Measures." *Journal of Social Psychology* 46: 277–86; 1957.

9. CONANT, J. B. *The Education of American Teachers.* New York: McGraw-Hill, 1963.

10. COOK, W. W.; LEEDS, C. H.; and CALLIS, R. *Minnesota Teacher Attitude Inventory: Manual.* New York: Psychological Corp., 1951.

11. CORRIGAN, D., and GRISWOLD, K. "Attitude Changes of Student Teachers." *Journal of Educational Research* 57: 93–95; October 1963.

12. CROMBAG, H. F. "Cooperation and Competition in Means-Interdependent Triads: A Replication." *Journal of Personality and Social Psychology* 4: 692–95; 1966.

13. CRUTCHFIELD, R. S. "Conformity and Character." *American Psychologist* 10: 191–98; 1955.

14. DELLA PIANA, G. M., and GAGE, N. L. "Pupils' values and the Validity of the *Minnesota Teacher Attitude Inventory.*" *Journal of Educational Psychology* 46: 167–78; March 1955.

15. DEUTSCH, M. "An Experimental Study of the Effects of Cooperation and Competition upon Group Process." *Human Relations* 2: 199–231; 1949.

16. ———. "A Theory of Cooperation and Competition." *Human Relations* 2: 129–52; 1949.

17. FESTINGER, L. *A Theory of Cognitive Dissonance.* Stanford, Calif.: Stanford University Press, 1957.

18. FLANDERS, N. A. *Teacher Influence, Pupil Attitudes, and Achievement.* U. S. Department of Health, Education, and Welfare, Office of Education, Cooperative Research Monograph No. 12. Washington, D.C.: Government Printing Office, 1965.

19. FRENCH, I. R. P. "Group Productivity." *Groups, Leadership and Men: Research in Human Relations* (Edited by H. S. Guetzkow.) Pittsburgh, Pa.: Carnegie Institute of Technology Press, 1951, pp. 44–54.

20. GAGE, N.L.; RUNKEL, P.J.; and CHATTERJEE, B. B. "Changing Teacher Behavior Through Feedback from Pupils: An Application of Equilibrium Theory." *Readings in the Social Psychology of Education.* (Edited by W. W. CHARTERS, JR., and N. L. GAGE.) Boston, Mass.: Allyn & Bacon, 1963, pp. 173–81.

21. GOODLAND, J. I. "An Analysis of Professional Laboratory Experiences in the Education of Teachers." *The Journal of Teacher Education* 16: 263–70; September 1965.

22. GUETZKOW, H. "Differentiation of Roles in Task-Oriented Groups." *Group Dynamics: Research and Theory.* (Edited by D. CARTWRIGHT and A. ZANDER.)

Second edition. New York: Harper, 1960, pp. 683–704.

23. GUTTMAN, L. "A Basis for Analyzing Test-Retest Reliability." *Psychometrika* 10: 255–82; 1945.

24. HALPIN, A. W., and WINER, B. J. "A Factorial Study of Leader Behavior Descriptions." *Leader Behavior: Its Description and Measurement.* (Edited by R. M. STOGDILL and A. E. COONS.) Bureau of Business Research Monograph No. 88. Columbus: Ohio State University, 1957.

25. HARE, A. P. *Handbook of Small Group Research.* New York: Free Press of Glencoe, 1962.

26. HAYES, R. B. "A Study of Programs of Preservice and In-Service Education for Cooperating School Supervising Teachers Used by Selected Teacher Education Institutions." Doctor's thesis. Lawrence: University of Kansas, 1960. (Unpublished)

27. HEIDER, F. *The Psychology of Interpersonal Relations.* New York: Wiley, 1958.

28. HOLEMON, R. L. "Attitude Change of the Student Teacher: A Test of the ABX Model." Doctor's thesis. Saint Louis, Mo.: Washington University, 1963. (Unpublished)

29. ———. "An Investigation of Attitudes of Student-Teaching Advisers and Student Teacher Attitude Change." Albuquerque: University of New Mexico, 1966. (Unpublished)

30. HUGHES, MARIE M., and others. "Teaching Is Interaction." *The Elementary School Journal* 58: 457–64; May 1958.

31. HUTTE, H. "Decision-Making in a Management Game." *Human Relations* 18: 5–20; 1965.

32. JOINT COMMITTEE ON STATE RESPONSIBILITY FOR STUDENT TEACHING. *A New Order in Student Teaching; Fixing Re-*

sponsibilties for Student Teaching. Washington D.C.: National Commission on Teacher Education and Professional Standards, National Education Association, 1967.

33. LINDSEY, MARGARET, editor. *New Horizons for the Teaching Profession.* Washington, D.C.: National Commission on Teacher Education and Professional Standards, National Education Association, 1961. Chapter 4, "Preparation of Professional Personnel."

34. McAULAY, J. D. "How Much Influence Has a Co-operating Teacher?" *The Journal of Teacher Education* 11: 79–83; March 1960.

35. MacDONALD, J. B., and DOLL, R. C. "Who Is Ready for Teacher Education?" *Journal of Educational Sociology* 35: 123–27; November 1961.

36. MICHAELIS, J. U. "Student Teaching and Internship." *Encyclopedia of Educational Research.* (Edited by C. W. HARRIS.) New York: Macmillan, 1960, pp. 1473–81.

37. MILLER, G. L. "Collaborative Teaching and Pupil Thinking." *The Journal of Teacher Education* 17: 337–58; Fall 1966.

38. MILLS, T. M. "Power Relations in Three-Person Groups." *Group Dynamics: Research and Theory.* (Edited by D. CARTWRIGHT and A. ZANDER.) Second edition. New York: Harper, 1960. pp. 766–80.

39. NATIONAL EDUCATION ASSOCIATION, NATIONAL COMMISSION ON TEACHER EDUCATION AND PROFESSIONAL STANDARDS. *Who's in Charge Here? Fixing Responsibilities for Teacher Education.* Washington, D.C.: the Commission, 1966.

40. NEAL, C. D.; KRAFT, L. E.; and KRACHT, C. R. "Reasons for College Supervision of the Student-Teaching Program." *The Journal of Teacher Education* 18: 24–27; Spring 1967.

41. NEWCOMB, T. M. "Individual Systems of Orientation." *Psychology: A Study of a Science.* Vol. 3—*Formulations of the Person and the Social Context.* (Edited by S. KOCH.) New York: McGraw-Hill, 1959, pp. 384–422.

42. NEWCOMB, T. M.; TURNER, R. H.; and CONVERSE, P. E. *Social Psychology: The Study of Human Interaction.* New York: Holt, Rinehart and Winston, 1965.

43. ORT, E. P. "New Dimensions in Pre-Student Teaching Laboratory Experiences." *Teachers College Journal* 36: 167–68; 1965.

44. OSGOOD, C. E., and TANNENBAUM, P. H. "The Principle of Congruity in the Prediction of Attitude Change." *Psychological Review* 62: 42–55; 1955.

45. PRICE, R. D. "The Influence of Supervising Teachers." *The Journal of Teacher Education* 12: 471–75; December 1961.

46. PURPEL, D. E. "Student Teaching." *The Journal of Teacher Education* 18: 20–23; Spring 1967.

47. RAVEN, B. H., and EACHUS, H. T. "Co-operation and Competition in Means-Interdependent Triads." *Journal of Abnormal and Social Psychology* 67: 307–16; 1963.

48. REYNARD, H. E. "Pre-Service and In-Service Education of Teachers." *Review of Educational Research* 33: 369–80; 1963.

49. SANDGREN, D. L., and SCHMIDT, L. G. "Does Practice Teaching Change Attitude Toward Teaching?" *Journal of Educational Research* 49: 673–80; 1956.

50. SANFORD, F. H. "The Follower's Role in Leadership Phenomena." *Readings in Social Psychology.* (Edited by G. S. SWANSON, T. M. NEWCOMB, and E. G. HARTLEY.) Second edition. New York: Holt, Rinehart and Winston, 1952, pp. 328–40.

51. SARASON, S. B.; DAVIDSON, K. S.; and BLATT, B. *The Preparation of Teachers: An Unstudied Problem in Education.* New York: Wiley, 1962.

52. SCHUELER, H.; GOLD, M. J.; and MITZEL, H. E. *The Use of Television for Improving Teacher Training and for Improving Measures of Student-Teaching Performance. Phase I: Improvement of Student Teaching.* U.S. Department of Health, Education, and Welfare, Office of Education. New York: Hunter College, City University of New York, 1962.

53. SHARPE, D. M., and others, "Suggestions for Supervised Teaching." *Teachers College Journal* 35: 119–22; 1964.

54. SIMMEL, G. *The Sociology of Georg Simmel.* (Translated and edited by K. H. WOLFF.) New York: The Free Press of Glencoe, 1950.

55. STAGER, P. "Conceptual Level as a Composition Variable in Small-Group Decision Making." *Journal of Personality and Social Psychology* 5: 152–61; 1967.

56. SYMONDS, P. M. "Teaching as a Function of the Teacher's Personality." *The Journal of Teacher Education* 5: 79–83; March 1954.

57. THIBAUT, J. W., and KELLEY, H. H. *The Social Psychology of Groups.* New York: Wiley, 1959.

58. VON NEUMANN, J., and MORGENSTERN, O. *Theory of Games and Economic Behavior.* Princeton, N.J.: Princeton University Press, 1944.

59. WALBERG, H. J. "Personality, Role Conflicts, and Self-Conception in Student Teachers." Research Bulletin. Princeton,

N.J.: Educational Testing Service, 1966. (Unpublished)

60. WARD, W., and SUTTLE, J. "The Oregon Plan To Improve the Induction Process: The Program To Prepare Supervising Teachers and the Organization of Schools and Colleges To Accommodate the Process." *The Journal of Teacher Education* 17: 444–51; Winter 1966.

61. WHITE, R. K., and LIPPITT, R. *Autocracy and Democracy: An Experimental Inquiry.* New York: Harper, 1960.

62. WILLIS, R. H., and LONG, NORMA J. "An Experimental Simulation of an Internation Trial." *Behavioral Science* 12: 24–32; 1967.

63. WITHALL, J., and LEWIS, W. W. "Social Interaction in the Classroom." *Handbook of Research on Teaching.* (Edited by N. L. GAGE.) Chicago: Rand McNally, 1963, pp. 683–714.

64. WROBLEWSKI, C. "A Student Teacher Views the Supervising Teacher." *The Journal of Teacher Education* 14: 333; September 1963.

65. YEE, A. H. *The Student-Teaching Triad: The Relationship of Attitudes Among Student Teachers, College Supervisors, and Cooperating Teachers.* U.S. Department of Health, Education, and Welfare, Office of Education, Cooperative Research Project No. 5–8354. Austin: The University of Texas, 1967.

66. ZAJONC, R. B. "The Effects of Feedback and Probability of Group Success on Individual and Group Performance." *Human Relations* 15: 149–61; 1962.

EFFECT OF FEEDBACK
FROM TEACHERS TO PRINCIPALS

Robert W. Daw / N. L. Gage

It is highly plausible that feedback regarding how others feel about one's behavior will affect one's behavior. Whether this maxim will hold under a given set of practical circumstances must, however, be determined empirically. In the present experiment, elementary school principals were told how their teachers rated them and an ideal principal; other principals, similarly rated, were not given this information.

One theoretical justification for hypothesizing that feedback of this kind changes behavior has been developed by Gage, Runkel, and Chatterjee (1960). In brief, the rationale is that the fedback will inform some principals that their teachers evaluate their behavior less favorably than the principals might desire. If we assume that principals respect their teachers' opinions, we can expect this information to create in the principals a condition of imbalance (Heider, 1958), asymmetry

(Newcomb, 1959), incongruity (Osgood and Tannenbaum, 1955), or dissonance (Festinger, 1957). To remove or reduce this condition, that is, to restore a condition of equilibrium or consistency, the principals are likely to change the behaviors concerned in the directions desired by the teachers. After enough time has elapsed to allow such behavior changes to occur and to be perceived by the teachers, a second description of the principals' behaviors by their teachers will reflect such changes.[1]

Positive results in experiments on the effect of feedback of ratings have previously been obtained (Bryan, 1963; Gage, 1963; Gage, Runkel, and Chatterjee, 1963). In those experiments, teachers were rated by their pupils and then, on a sub-

[1] William McGuire (personal communication, August 15, 1966) has suggested that self-esteem theory—that is, that persons behave so as to maximize self-esteem, not to minimize inconsistencies, or discrepancies—is more relevant to our experiment. This kind of alternative to consistency theory has been outlined by Deutsch, Krauss, and Rosenau (1962), Steiner and Rogers (1963), and McGuire and Millman (1965).

From: Journal of Educational Psychology, *1967, 58, 181–88. Copyright © 1967 by the American Psychological Association, and reproduced by permission of the authors and APA.*

sequent rating by the same subjects, were found to differ significantly, and in the direction of the raters' ideals, from a control group not given the ratings.

The present experiment was aimed at determining whether the same effects would be found with feedback from teachers to principals. It also incorporated some refinements in design that permitted testing rival hypotheses as to the cause of the change in rated behavior. In addition, data were gathered concerning different time intervals, forms of feedback, and personal characteristics of the principals.

METHOD

SUBJECTS

The subjects were 455 elementary school principals in all the counties in California in the fall of 1962. Because they were assigned at random, the principals in the experimental and control groups had about the same number of pupils and teachers, and were similar in sex, age, educational level, and years of experience as a principal, as shown in Table 1. Besides the experimental (E) group, there were two control groups:

TABLE 1

DISTRIBUTIONS, MEANS, AND RANGES ON VARIABLES FOR EXPERIMENTAL AND CONTROL GROUPS

Variable	Experimental group (E)	Control group 1 (C_1)	Control group 2 (C_2)
Kind of district			
District with superintendent other than principal	105	111	115
District where the principal also acts as the superintendent	46	32	46
Sex			
Male	137	130	146
Female	14	13	15
Education			
No. B.A. degree	1	0	1
B.A. degree	49	40	44
M.A. degree	97	100	115
Ed.D. degree	3	3	1
Ph.D. degree	1	0	0
Number of students in the school			
M	509	512	507
Range	185–1011	185–1157	200–1175
Age			
M	42	43	41
Range	27–63	29–63	27–63
Number of years of experience as a principal			
M	8.3	8.6	7.9
Range	1–36	1–32	1–35
Number of teachers in the school			
M	14.8	15.3	15.5
Range	8–34	8–37	8–39

Note.—For the Experimental Group, $N = 151$; for Control Group 1, $N = 143$; for Control Group 2, $N = 161$.

Control Group C_1, which was rated on both the first and second occasions, and "posttest only" Control Group C_2, which was rated only on the second occasion.

Each superintendent of an elementary school district (including unified districts) in California with more than one principal was invited to send the name of the first principal in the alphabetical listing of principals in his district, and then that principal was invited to participate. In districts with a single principal who also acted as superintendent, the superintendent-principal was directly invited to participate. Although initial attrition was about 25%, the subsequent rate of participation was never less than 93% of the principals invited. That is, of the 1007 original contacts, 752 yielded the name of the person who participated. To insure the anonymity of the teacher responses, all schools with less than eight teachers were eliminated, leaving 500 principals. Of these, 455 completely met all other requirements for inclusion in the experiment. Obviously, this final group may have been biased toward containing superintendent-principals (*a*) interested in what their teachers thought of their actions or (*b*) reluctant to refuse to participate.

METHODS AND SCHEDULE OF DATA COLLECTION

The study was made in the school year 1962–63. Letters of invitation were sent on November 30. To minimize the possibility that principals would discuss the project with one another, only one principal was invited from each district. By January 5, 752 principals' names had been received; of these, 252 were excluded because their schools had less than eight teachers. Between January 2 and 9, booklets entitled "What Do They Expect?" (WDTE) were mailed to 340 principals in Groups E and C_1. These booklets, presenting the research as the tryout of a "Principal's Information Project," required the principal to rate himself and his ideal principal on 12 items. In addition, the principal was asked to provide the information summarized in Table 1 and to indicate how many Teacher Opinion Booklets would be needed to collect ratings of the principal from his teachers. (The WDTE booklet was mailed to Group C_2 just prior to the mailing of the posttest materials.) Principals were randomly assigned to Groups E, C_1, and C_2 prior to the mailing of the WDTE booklet. The rate of return of these booklets for the three groups ranged from 94.0 to 98.7%.

Teacher Opinion Booklets were mailed to the principals on January 21; only eight of the 336 booklets mailed were not returned. In these booklets, the teachers rated their actual and ideal ("best imaginable") principal on the same 12 items.

On February 11, booklets entitled "Report on Your Teachers' Opinions" (RYTO) were mailed to the principals in Group E. In these booklets, as shown in Figure 1, the principal was given, for each of the 12 items, histograms showing the percentages of his teachers who described him and their ideal principal with each of the six response-alternatives. A randomly chosen half of the experimental group (the "a + h" group) received both the histograms and the medians (indicated by arrows) of the ratings of the actual and ideal principal; the remaining principals (the "a" group) were given only the medians of the ratings by their teachers. These RYTO booklets were withheld from Groups C_1 and C_2 until after the second round of ratings of principals by their teachers.

A follow-up questionnaire, designed to encourage careful reading of the RYTO's, was mailed on February 25 to all principals in Group E. This questionnaire and a reminder elicited responses concerning the RYTO from 93% of the experimental group.

The second round of Teacher Opinion Booklets was mailed to a ran-

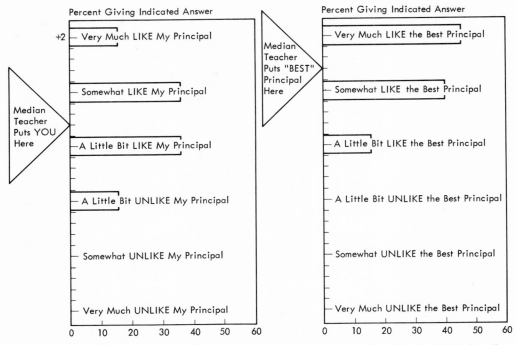

Figure 1. From of feedback, arrow-plus-histogram, in "Report on Your Teachers' Opinions."

domly chosen half of Groups E and C_1 on March 25. A letter had been mailed a week in advance asking the principal to set aside a specific day for the administration of these instruments. They were returned with little delay. Teacher Opinion Booklets were mailed to the second half of Groups E and C_1 on May 6. The use of two posttest dates permitted determining whether the effect of the feedback changed with the length of interval between feedback and posttest.

ITEMS CONCERNING PRINCIPAL BEHAVIOR

The teachers described their actual principal and their ideal principal on the following 12 items concerning principal behavior:

1. Encourages teachers with a friendly remark or smile.

2. Gives enough credit to teachers for their contributions.

3. Does not force opinions on teachers.

4. Enforces rules consistently.

5. Criticizes without disparaging the efforts of teachers.

6. Informs teachers of decisions or actions which affect their work.

7. Gives concrete suggestions for improving classroom instruction.

8. Enlists sufficient participation by teachers in making decisions.

9. Demonstrates interest in pupil progress.

10. Interrupts the classroom infrequently.

11. Displays much interest in teachers' ideas.

12. Acts promptly in fulfilling teacher requests.

The items were based on ideas obtained from Campbell and Gregg (1957), Gross, Mason, and McEachern (1958), Guba and Bidwell (1958), Medsker (1956), and various elementary school teachers. Each item was worded in both positive and negative directions in Forms A and B, respectively. Forms A_1 and B_1 placed the items in reverse order from that in Forms A_2 and B_2.[2]

The items were intended to deal with behaviors that could be expected to occur frequently, could be briefly described without qualifying phrases, and could be changed by the principal within the time span of the research in a way that could be recognized by the teachers.

The 70 items originally written were reduced to the final 12 on the basis of ratings of their importance, improvability, and noticeability; the ratings were made by psychologists, professors of educational administration, teachers, and principals.

TEACHER OPINION BOOKLET

In the Teacher Opinion Booklet, the teacher was asked to rate his principal on each item using one of the six alternatives shown in Figure 1. Then he was asked to rate his ideal principal on the same 12 items. The teachers read the directions silently while the principal read them aloud. The teacher wrote his responses on a card, put the card in an envelope, and sealed the envelope. On the cover of his booklet, the teacher read: "Your answers will be sealed in an envelope by you and sent directly to Stanford University. No one at your school or in your district will know how you answered these questions." Further to insure the teachers' privacy, the principal was directed to stand far enough away from his teachers to prevent him

[2] The various forms—A_1, A_2, B_1, and B_2 —were randomly assigned across schools; that is, every teacher in a given school received the same form.

from seeing their papers, to make certain that all teachers' answer cards were sealed in the envelope, to require the teachers to put their sealed envelopes into the large mailing envelope, to permit his teachers to see him moisten and close the clasp of the large envelope, and finally to ask one of his teachers to drop the envelope in a United States mail box. The administration of the questionnaires was standardized as fully as possible with printed directions to the principals and teachers so as to assure both groups that their anonymity would be preserved. It is noteworthy that all answer cards came back in sealed envelopes.

"REPORT ON YOUR TEACHERS' OPINIONS"

The "Report on Your Teachers' Opinions" consisted of a booklet containing two charts for each of the 12 items, as shown in Figure 1. The discrepancy between the teachers' descriptions was implicit in the vertical distance between the two arrows indicating medians. If the two arrows were at the same point on these scales, the principal could infer that his teachers saw no difference between him and their ideal principal in that kind of behavior. In proportion to the distance between the two arrows, the principal could infer that he departed in the given direction from his teachers' ideal for that kind of behavior.

To determine the principal's reaction to the RYTO and to encourage him to review these reports, he was asked to answer six questions on a reaction sheet. The responses indicated that high percentages (85–95%) of Group E found the RYTO interesting, understandable, and informative.

EXPERIMENTAL DESIGN

The experimental design is shown in Figure 2. Here, X represents the experimental treatment (feedback), O

	Group	Pretest	Treatment	6 Weeks	12 Weeks
B	a–short	O_1	X_a	O_2	
B	a–long	O_3	X_a		O_4
B	a+b–short	O_5	X_{a+b}	O_6	
B	a+b–long	O_7	X_{a+b}		O_8
C	1–short	O_9		O_{10}	
C	1–long	O_{11}			O_{12}
C	2–short			O_{13}	
C	2–long				O_{14}

Figure 2. The experimental design.

refers to the process of observation (ratings), Xs and Os in a given row are applied to the same subjects, the left-to-right dimension indicates temporal order, and the rows represent equivalent samples of persons. X_a represent "arrow-only" feedback; X_{a+b} represents "arrow-plus-histogram" feedback. Group C_2 (posttest only) was used to allow comparisons free of any effect attributable to unintended feedback received by Group C_1 through participating in the pretest; these comparisons would show whether the pretest itself produced changes in behavior.

RESULTS

In describing the results, we shall refer to the protocols obtained from the teachers as follows:

Pre-ACT—the teacher's description of his *actual* principal on the *pre*test.

Post-ACT—the teacher's description of his *actual* principal on the *post*test.

Pre-IDL—the teachers' description of his *ideal* principal on the *pre*test.

For each item, the mean of the ratings received by a group of principals was computed over the medians of the ratings of each principal by his teachers. The ratings of all items, regardless of whether they were originally worded posi-

tively or negatively, were converted to a scale in which 1 signified the desirable end, and 6 the undesirable end, of the continuum.

PRE-ACT

The random assignment of principals to Groups E and C_1 should have made them equivalent. But the pre-ACT means of these groups differed at the .05 level on five of the 12 items and on the mean of the 12 items. Also, the direction of the difference was the same for all 12 items, namely, the direction favoring Group E. Presumably, however, the analysis of covariance, to be described below, eliminated this pretest bias to the extent that the pretest scores were reliable.

The difference between Groups E and C_1 in pre-ACT means might have resulted from a greater tendency of subjects receiving unfavorable feedback on pre-ACT to drop out of Group E. In that event, the remaining members of Group E would be those who had received more favorable pre-ACT ratings. But when this possibility was investigated, it was found that, in fact, the few drop-outs from Groups E and C_1 did not differ on pre-ACT in this way, and the difference remained unexplained.

The two experimental subgroups differing in the type of feedback provided (arrow-only and arrow-plus-histogram) did not differ significantly on any of the 12 pre-ACT means. Nor were there any significant differences in pre-ACT means among the subgroups given forms differing in the direction of wording or the sequence of the items.

ADJUSTED POST-ACT

The effect of the feedback was measured by the difference between Groups E and C_1. To adjust for the pre-ACT differences between the groups, analysis of covariance was used. The pre-ACT rating served as the control variable, the post-ACT rating as the dependent variable, and the feedback as the independent variable. Although the 12 items are correlated, it is considered worthwhile to examine results for each item individually as well as for the mean over all 12 items. Analyses of covariance for each of the 12 items and for the mean over Items 1–12 yielded the results shown in Table 2. The difference between the adjusted post-ACT means was significant at the .05 level or better for all but two of the 12 items; for the mean over Items 1–12, it was significant at the .01 level. In all cases, the difference between the adjusted post-ACT means favored the experimental group. Only on Items 9 and 10 did the adjusted post-ACT

means not differ at even the .05 level of significance. But even on these items, the difference favored the experimental group. Item 9, "Demonstrates interest in pupil progress," may have been too difficult for the teachers to perceive in the period allowed. Item 10, "Interrupts the classroom infrequently," may have been rated too favorably on the pretest to allow sufficient room for improvement; the pre-ACT means on Item 10 were the most favorable (had the lowest numerical value) of all 12 items.

POSTTEST-ONLY CONTROL GROUP

The "posttest-only" control group (C_2) was used to eliminate certain possible attenuating effects on the comparisons.

TABLE 2

MEANS OF TEACHERS' RATINGS OF ACTUAL PRINCIPALS IN EXPERIMENTAL GROUP AND CONTROL GROUPS C_1 AND C_2

Item	pre-ACT		post-ACT			Adjusted post-ACT		Difference between adjusted post-ACT Means	F
	E	C_1	E	C_1	C_2	E	C_1		
1	1.32	1.39	1.31	1.50	1.44	1.38	1.43	.05	11.6**
2	1.47	1.57	1.45	1.63	1.60	1.50	1.58	.08	5.0*
3	1.54	1.61	1.50	1.77	1.77	1.61	1.66	.05	15.5**
4	1.68	1.75	1.59	1.84	1.96	1.69	1.74	.05	13.5**
5	1.34	1.51	1.36	1.56	1.56	1.42	1.49	.08	6.7*
6	1.42	1.46	1.38	1.61	1.67	1.48	1.51	.03	17.0**
7	1.72	1.84	1.64	2.04	1.93	1.81	1.87	.06	25.1**
8	1.58	1.63	1.50	1.80	1.86	1.63	1.67	.04	19.0**
9	1.28	1.37	1.27	1.36	1.38	1.30	1.34	.04	2.2
10	1.19	1.26	1.20	1.29	1.30	1.23	1.26	.03	3.3
11	1.40	1.55	1.40	1.59	1.57	1.45	1.54	.09	4.4*
12	1.51	1.61	1.44	1.66	1.71	1.52	1.57	.05	8.7**
1–12	1.45	1.55	1.42	1.64	1.65	1.49	1.57	.08	19.4**

Note.—In this and all other tables, means refers to a scale in which a score of 1 was assigned to "Very much LIKE" rating scale alternative, 2 to "Somewhat LIKE," etc., to 6 for "Very much UNLIKE." For the Experimental Group (E), $N = 151$; for Control Group 1 (C), $N = 143$; for Control Group 2 ( ), $N = 161$.
* $p < .05$.
** $p < .01$.

TABLE 3

ADJUSTED MEAN POST-ACT AND PRE-IDL
RATINGS FOR THE EXPERIMENTAL GROUP AND
CONTROL GROUP C_1

Item	*Adjusted post-ACT* M		*Pre-IDL* M		*Adjusted Post-ACT minus pre-IDL*	
	E	C_1	E	C_1	E	C_1
1	1.38	1.43	1.09	1.08	.29	.35
2	1.50	1.58	1.13	1.14	.37	.44
3	1.61	1.66	1.21	1.22	.40	.44
4	1.69	1.74	1.20	1.17	.49	.57
5	1.42	1.49	1.13	1.17	.29	.32
6	1.48	1.51	1.09	1.10	.39	.41
7	1.81	1.87	1.19	1.25	.62	.62
8	1.63	1.67	1.20	1.23	.43	.44
9	1.30	1.34	1.10	1.13	.20	.21
10	1.23	1.26	1.15	1.19	.08	.07
11	1.45	1.54	1.13	1.18	.32	.36
12	1.52	1.57	1.13	1.16	.39	.41
1–12	1.49	1.57	1.14	1.17	.35	.40

Note.—For the Experimental Group, $N = 151$; for Control Group C_1, $N = 143$.

Such effects might have resulted from any feedback, or sensitization to the items of behavior, that might have been received by the pretested control group (C_1) as a result of their participation in the pretest. If such sensitization occurred, Group C_1 would differ less from Group E than would a nonpretested control group (C_2) which received neither the feedback nor the pretest. Here the comparisons must be made in terms of unadjusted posttest means, since there were no pretest means with which to adjust the posttest means of Group C_2

Table 2 also shows the means for Group C_2. The means for Group C_1 and C_2 did not differ significantly. Both of these groups did differ, in the same direction, from Group E. Hence, the pretest in itself did not affect Group C_1, and the improvement in Group E must be ascribed to the feedback alone, not to the feedback plus the pretest.

ADJUSTED POST-ACT MINUS PRE-IDL

The teachers' initial ratings of their ideal principal (pre-IDL) make possible an interpretation of the direction of the difference between adjusted post-ACT means. It should be recalled that the feedback informed Group E as to how their teachers rated the ideal principal. The feedback should influence the principal to change in that direction. Hence, the difference between adjusted post-ACT and pre-IDL should be smaller for Group E than for Group C_1. As Table 3 shows, most of these differences were indeed smaller for the experimental group. At the time of the posttest, the principals who received feedback came closer to their teachers' desires. Since the items are interdependent, they do not, of course, provide 12 separate tests of the overall hypothesis. But the means over all 12 items also differed in the expected direction.

INTERVAL, FORM OF FEEDBACK, AND
OTHER VARIABLES

In the experiment by Gage, Runkel, and Chatterjee (1960), experimental group subjects changed more if they had a longer interval between feedback and posttest. But the time interval was relatively short, ranging from 18 to 59 days. In the present experiment, the experimental and control groups were assigned at random to either a 6-week or a 12-week interval group. Analysis of covariance revealed no significant difference in the two groups' adjusted post-ACT means. Further, there was no significant effect due to the Feedback × Interval interaction. In short, the effect of the feedback was not a function of the interval over which it was measured.

One randomly chosen half of the experimental groups received feedback in the form of median ratings (arrows) only, and the other half received median ratings plus the frequency distributions (histograms) of the ratings. Either kind might reasonably be predicted to be the more effective: The median-only might be sharper, less ambiguous; on the other hand, the median-plus-distribution might be more convincing. But no significant difference was found for any item between the adjusted post-ACT means of the subgroups receiving these two kinds of feedback.

When the principals were divided into subgroups on the basis of age (40 or younger versus 41 or older), experience (5 years or less as elementary school principal versus 6 years or more), and form (A_1, A_2, B_1, B_2) of the Teachers' Opinion Booklet, analyses of covariance yielded no significant difference at the .05 level due to main effects or interactions. Thus, the significant results that occurred due to feedback did not seem to vary with age, experience, or form. The latter findings show that positional or directional

sets did not significantly affect the teachers' responses.

DISCUSSION

All in all, the results indicate that the feedback affected changes in the principals' behavior. Various questions remain, however, for subsequent research. First, we must recall the unexplained pretest differences between the experimental and control groups despite their random assignment. Second, we must ask whether methods of measuring behavior other than reratings by the same teachers would reveal the same kinds of behavior change. Would observations by trained observers produce confirming evidence? Would interviews of the principals reveal the process by which feedback operates, and show whether the principals were consciously attempting to change their behavior? Would disguised tests of teacher "morale" reflect the desirable changes in rated principal behavior?

Third, we should determine better whether the improvements in the post-ACT ratings reflect mere improved "halo effect" or actual changes in specific behaviors. One way to proceed on this question would be to collect post-ACT ratings on uncorrelated items not dealt with in the feedback; if behavior also improves on such items, the significance of the feedback on specific items must be questioned. Similarly, items differing widely in 'changeability" could be compared as to the amount of change principals exhibit in them; presumably, if the ratings reflect more than general impressions, relatively unchangeable behaviors should be rated as changing less.

If research allays the skepticism implicit in these suggestions, further attention should be given to ways of enhancing the effectiveness of feedback. The behavior of teachers, principals, and persons in many similar roles could be made more effective by applying the results of such a program of research.

REFERENCES

BRYAN, R. C. *Reactions to teachers by students, parents and administrators.* (United States Office of Education, Cooperative Research Project No. 668) Kalamazoo: Western Michigan University, 1963.

CAMPBELL, R. F., & GREGG, R. T. (Eds.) *Administrative behavior in education.* New York: Harper, 1957.

DEUTSCH, M., KRAUSS, R. M., & ROSENAU, N. Dissonance or defensiveness? *Journal of Personality,* 1962, **30,** 16–28.

FESTINGER, L. *A theory of cognitive dissononce.* Evanston, Ill.: Row, Peterson, 1957.

GAGE, N. L. A method for "improving" teacher behavior. *Journal of Teacher Education,* 1963, **14,** 261–266.

GAGE, N. L., RUNKEL, P. J., & CHATTERJEE, B. B. *Equilibrium theory and behavior change: An experiment in feedback from pupils to teachers.* (Report No. 6 in Studies in the generality and behavioral correlates of social perception.) Urbana: Bureau of Educational Research, College of Education, University of Illinois, 1960.

GAGE, N. L., RUNKEL, P. J., & CHATTERJEE, B. B. Changing teacher behavior through feedback from pupils: An application of equilibrium theory. In W. W. CHARTERS & N. L. GAGE (Eds.), *Readings in the social psychology of education.* Boston: Allyn & Bacon, 1963, Pp. 173–181.

GROSS, N., MASON, W., & MCEACHERN, A. W. *Explorations in role analysis: Studies of the school superintendency role.* New York: Wiley, 1958.

GUBA, E. G., & BIDWELL, C. E. *Administrative relationships.* Chicago: Midwest Administration Center, University of Chicago, 1958.

HEIDER, F. *The psychology of interpersonal relationships.* New York: Wiley, 1958.

MCGUIRE, W. J., & MILLMAN, S. Anticipatory belief lowering following forewarning of a persuasive attack. *Journal of Personality and Social Psychology,* 1965, **2,** 471–479.

MEDSKER, L. L. The job of the elementary school principal as viewed by teachers. Unpublished doctoral dissertation, Stanford University, 1956.

NEWCOMB, T. M. Individual systems of orientation. In S. Koch (Ed.), *Psychology: A study of a science.* Vol. 3. New York: McGraw-Hill, 1959. Pp. 384–422.

OSGOOD, C. E., & TANNENBAUM, P. H. The principle of congruity in the prediction of attitude change. *Psychological Review,* 1955, **62,** 42–55.

STEINER, I. D., & ROGERS, E. D. Alternative responses to dissonance. *Journal of Abnormal and Social Psychology,* 1963, **66,** 128–136.

DO PRINCIPALS' INTERPERSONAL ATTITUDES AGREE WITH THOSE OF TEACHERS AND PUPILS?

Albert H. Yee

Do principals and pupils agree when they evaluate teacher merit? How well do principals' and teachers' attitudes toward pupils agree?

The importance of the first question becomes obvious if principals' and pupils' ratings are regarded as valid criteria by which teacher effectiveness can be ascertained. To a certain extent, principals and pupils observe the same teacher behavior, but their differing roles and viewpoints provide great possibilities for contrasting expectations and perceptions (e.g., Spindler, 1955). The second question concerns the development and maintenance of school atmosphere by teachers and principals and consequent pupil response. The common assumption that principals' and teachers' attitudes toward pupils determine the manner in which learners are handled and react seems valid, but how much agreement is there between principals' and teachers' attitudes?

Sophisticated concepts of education, some proposed more explicitly than others, assume that analyzable processes of social interaction characterize the most relevant elements of teaching and learning (Gage, 1963; Withall and Lewis, 1963). Thus, investigation into the characteristics and processes of a school's social interaction can provide specific facts and greater understanding of the strengths and weaknesses affecting the school's life-style. However, such study is not simple. Surely the complexity of social interaction in schools becomes apparent as one considers the many independent variables which can affect it, such as the background characteristics and leadership styles of principals and teachers and the developmental, ethnic, and social-class characteristics of learners (e.g., Clark, 1965; Flanders, 1967; Jensen, 1968; White and Lippitt, 1960; and Yee and Runkel, 1969).

Prevalent educational thinking may assume too easily that all relevant observers—administrators, teacher colleagues,

From: Educational Administration Quarterly, *1970, 6, 1–13. Copyright © 1970 by the University Council for Educational Administration, and reproduced by permission of the author and UCEA.*

teacher educators, parents, and pupils— perceive effective teaching and professionalism in the same way. In other words, when a principal recognizes a teacher as superior or inferior, many assume the teacher's pupils will agree with the principal. Quite often, the principal bases his evaluation on his estimate of the pupils' perceptions. As for the teacher, pupil behavior as well as his principal's behavior influence his attitudes toward pupils and one might wonder which is most influential. Certainly the decisions of principals as to what teachers are hired, retained, and rewarded, influence teacher behavior; but the effectiveness of even the most skilled teacher remains subject to learner response and the nature of his return response.

Previous research (e.g., Gross, 1958; Lipham, 1964) indicates that educational roles, such as those of school-board members and superintendents, express differing attitudes which affect the decisions made. However, little is known empirically about the relationship of the interpersonal attitudes of principals, teachers, and pupils.

Recent studies have found insignificant or low correlations between principals' and pupils' ratings of teachers (Leeds, 1969; Robbins, 1967; Yee, 1967). However, lack of statistical independence obfuscates the correlations reported, since principals in previous studies rated more than one teacher. Thus, this study was conducted to overcome that problem and better ascertain: (1) the relationship between the perceptions of principals and pupils toward the same teachers, and (2) the relationship of principals' and teachers' attitudes toward children.

Particular attention was given the independent variable of pupils' social-class backgrounds, since it has been found to be a highly significant factor influencing classroom behavior (e.g., Coleman *et al.*, 1966; Yee, 1968a).

METHOD

DATA AND SAMPLE

The data included 206 teachers' responses to the Minnesota Teacher Attitude Inventory (MTAI); perceptions of those teachers by the teachers' intermediate-grade pupils, as measured by the "About My Teacher" attitude inventory developed by Beck (1964) under the direction of N. L. Gage; and 47 principals' MTAI responses and perceptions of the 206 teachers. The pupils' and principals' rating instruments provided attitudes toward teachers' affective, cognitive, disciplinary, innovative, and motivational merit.

The following sample items illustrate the nature of the 100-item "About My Teacher" inventory and were used to ascertain teachers' affective, cognitive, disciplinary, innovative, and motivational merit, respectively: "Is your teacher fun to be with?"; "Does your teacher explain your lessons clearly?"; "Do the children behave well for your teacher?"; "Do all the pupils in the class use the same book at the same time?"; and "Does your teacher make you feel like learning a lot on your own?"

Principals' ratings were made with an unpublished five-point scale developed by W. H. Beck for each of the five dimensions of teacher merit with descriptions such as the following for the highest and lowest, respectively: "In this respect, he is one of the most outstanding teachers you have known," and "In this respect, he is of less value than most of the teachers you have known." The total score from each pupil's responses and the mean of each principal's five teacher ratings were used in the analyses.

The reliability of pupils' agreement within classes in rating their teacher was estimated with Horst's (1949) formula. Horst coefficients in the high .80s indicated that the pupils' measures were reliable, thus pupils' class means were deemed quite adequate estimates of pupil sentiments. Principals' and teachers' measures provided Guttman (1945) split-half (odd-even) coefficients of .94 and .89, respectively, and were judged reliable in internal consistency.

This study used data from 96 classes of middle-class (MC) pupils and 110 classes of lower-class (LC) pupils, their principals and their self-contained classroom teachers in 51 California and Texas elementary schools. The classes were almost evenly divided among Grades 4, 5, and 6 (2 were Grade 7 in the LC group) and the two social-class sub-samples were roughly equivalent in levels of teachers' experience in classrooms, with the average number of years in teaching for all teachers being 8.8. Each sub-sample included 20 male teachers. Of the 47 principals, four were female. Five principals administered two school buildings each; data from pupils and teachers in each of such principals' schools were analyzed together.

PROCEDURES

As has been mentioned, correlations between principals' measures and pupils' or teachers' measures lack statistical independence, since such data usually include more than one teacher-class set of data for each principal. To overcome the problem, medians of teachers' and pupils' measures were used in correlations with principals' measures. In other words, the data from each principal's teachers and classes were considered together and medians of such data were used in computing correlations with principals' measures. Thus, we reduced the 206 sets of teacher-class measures to 47 (total sample), including 33 with MC pupils and 14 with LC pupils. The median number of teacher-class sets per principal was three with a range of one (eight schools) to 14.

RESULTS AND DISCUSSION

Table 1 presents correlations computed for the total sample.

Since previous research has shown pupils' social class to be a very significant factor in such data, only brief comment will be given Table 1 results. It can be seen that pupils' and principals' ratings tend to correlate negatively, though the *r* of −.18 is statistically nonsignificant. However, principals' and teachers' attitudes toward children correlate positively and significantly. It is interesting to note that the most positive *r*s result when the principals' perceptions of teachers and MTAI attitudes are correlated with teachers' MTAI attitudes.

Table 2 presents results for the sub-

TABLE 1
CORRELATIONS OF PRINCIPALS', PUPILS', AND TEACHERS' MEASURES FOR TOTAL SAMPLE (N = 47)

Measures	Mean	SD	1	2	3	4
1. Principals' teacher ratings	3.52	.55		−.18	.17	.24
2. Pupils' teacher ratings	126.28	10.43			−.15	.14
3. Principals' MTAI scores	41.06	35.74				.39**
4. Teachers' MTAI scores	37.94	23.43				

** *p* < .01

TABLE 2

CORRELATIONS OF PRINCIPALS', PUPILS', AND TEACHERS'
MEASURES FOR MIDDLE-CLASS SUB-SAMPLE (N = 33)

Measures	Mean	SD	1	2	3	4
1. Principals' teacher ratings	3.52	.61		−.25	.22	.42**
2. Pupils' teacher ratings	128.43	11.06			−.18	.11
3. Principals' MTAI scores	44.91	36.74				.37*
4. Teachers' MTAI scores	41.64	23.12				

* $p < .03$.
** $p < .01$.

TABLE 3

CORRELATIONS OF PRINCIPALS', PUPILS', AND TEACHERS'
MEASURES FOR LOWER-CLASS SUB-SAMPLE (N = 14)

Measures	Mean	SD	1	2	3	4
1. Principals' teacher ratings	3.54	.41		.19	.10	−.38
2. Pupils' teacher ratings	121.20	6.65			−.41	−.14
3. Principals' MTAI scores	32.00	32.72				.33
4. Teachers' MTAI scores	29.21	22.58				

sample with MC pupils. Two significant rs were found; both involving principals' measures and teachers' MTAI attitudes. In the $r_{1 vs. 4}$ of .42, principals' ratings of teacher merit relate fairly strongly with teachers' MTAI attitudes. Such a finding means: teachers that express warm, sympathetic, permissive, non-punitive attitudes toward children tend to be rated highest by principals in all-around classroom behavior. Principals did not know the teachers' MTAI scores, and therefore, based their ratings for this study strictly on their own normal school observations. The $r_{3 vs. 4}$ of .37 indicates that principals' and teachers' attitudes in schools with MC pupils relate positively.

Results show that MC pupils' and principals' perceptions of teacher merit do not correlate significantly. The rs suggest little likelihood that pupils and principals agree in ratings of teachers' merit. The positive relationship of principals' and teachers' measures and their low and negative relationships with pupils' ratings indicate an important difference in evaluation of teachers' merit. In analyses with principals' ratings of each dimension of teacher merit taken separately, the highest and only significant r between principals' and pupils' ratings was found with principals' ratings of teachers' disciplinary merit ($r = -.43$, $p < .01$). Such a result indicates that MC pupils disagree strongly with their principals in teachers' disciplinary merit. The teachers that MC pupils rate high in overall merit are perceived by principals as poorest in discipline and vice versa.

Table 3 presents interesting similarities and contrasts to Table 2 results. A negative r of $-.25$ was found between principals' and MC pupils' teacher ratings; but with principals' and LC pupils' ratings, a positive *r* of .19 was found. The highest *r* in principal-LC pupil data, that of .37, p < .20, was found in correlations of the principals' ratings of teachers' disciplinary merit with pupils' overall rating. Note the similarity and contrast to MC results discussed above, for testing the difference between those *r*s with Fisher's z_r transformation found a significant *z* of 2.71, p < .01. Such results suggest special emphasis on orderliness and disciplinary merit by principals in their ratings of teacher merit, especially in LC schools. They also suggest that pupils perceive the disciplinary role and behavior of teachers quite differently in MC and LC schools. However, no statistically significant relationship appeared between the ratings of LC pupils and principals toward teachers. Further study with data from additional subjects can tell how the small LC sub-sample size here affects findings. With significant MC result contrasting with the LC tendency, the relationship of principals' and pupils' perceptions of teachers' disciplining behavior and merit seems worthy of speculation and study.

Results for the MC and LC sub-samples also differ importantly in the correlation between principals' ratings and teachers' MTAI scores. In Table 3 results for the LC sub-sample, the correlation is negative; but in Table 2, we see that the result is significantly positive (*r* = .42, p < .01). Testing the difference between the *r*s with Fisher's z_r transformation, we found a significant *z* of 2.71, p <.01. In rating teacher merit, therefore, principals in schools with LC pupils tend to rate higher those teachers who have negative, authoritarian, punitive, dogmatic, and rigid attitudes toward children, which principals in schools with MC pupils would perceive as inferior. Reflecting such a contrast, the MTAI means are lower for

principals and teachers working with LC pupils than those teaching MC pupils. It is important to see that the positive *r*s found with principals' and teachers' MTAI measures show that principals and teachers they work with agree fairly well in their attitudes toward children.

The correlational analyses above have been concerned with principal-pupil-teacher measures by schools. Thus we have discussed the relationship of such measures for what may be termed the between-schools view. In other words, ordering the measures from high to low provides a ranking of schools by obtained measures, the total set of school data representing the target population—elementary schools in the USA. Comparing the rankings of the measures is a simplified way of perceiving the main question of this study, that is, how do principal-pupil-teacher interpersonal attitudes relate?

However, another question may be raised, that is, How do such variables relate *within* schools? Within one school, teacher merit may be evaluated relative to the teacher behavior principals and pupils know and can observe. Yet it seems debatable that principals and even pupils would rate inferior teacher behavior high or vice versa mainly on the basis of rankings in the same building or system. The attitude inventories used in this study did not call for within-school comparison, which could be done quite easily, but they referred to or implied evaluations of teachers and pupils against a background of all teachers and children. At any rate, to probe the interesting question, correlations were computed school by school and averages of the *r*s were found.

School *r*s were used in the averaging only when a school had five or more sets of teacher-class data. For the MC pupil groups (8 schools), a *r* of .18 was found for principals' and pupils' perceptions of teacher merit, while the same relationship for LC pupils (8 schools) produced a *r* of .27. Principals' perceptions of teacher merit correlated with teachers' MTAI scores produced *r*s of .04 and .38 for MC and LC groups, respectively. Teachers' MTAI scores and pupils' attitudes toward teachers correlated with results of .07 and .17, MC and LC groups, respectively.

None of these results are statistically significant, and the averaged *r*s are probably spurious due to the inadequate sample sizes and the evident variability. Further study should be pursued to see if such findings hold. With more adequate sample Ns, it would be interesting to see if there is greater relationship between principals' perceptions to teacher merit and teachers' attitudes toward children within LC pupils' schools than in those for MC pupils. The between-school analyses indicate no such contrast.

SUMMARY AND IMPLICATIONS

This study found that pupils' and principals' ratings of teachers lack significant relationship. However, teachers' and principals' attitudes toward children correlate positively. In schools with MC pupils, principals' ratings of teachers correlate positively with teachers' MTAI attitudes toward children. In schools serving LC pupils, such variables tend to correlate negatively. The significant differences between such *r*s and those dealing with principals' rating of teachers' disciplining merit and pupils' teacher rating suggest that principals value and reward contrasting teacher behavior. In the MC situation, principals rate superior those teachers who express positive affective attitudes toward pupils. In the LC situation, principals rate superior those teachers who

express negative affective attitudes toward pupils.

What principals regard as superior or inferior teacher behavior seems to depend on whether their school serves MC or LC pupils. How does this come about? Do varying pupil characteristics and behavior account for such differences? Or do they result from variation not only in the characteristics and behavior of pupils but also from differences in principals and teachers?

Perhaps one would agree with the first possibility if he could assume that there is little bias in the recruitment and placement of principals and teachers and that differences in principal-teacher behavior toward pupils may be explained through impartial, professional response to contrasting pupil behavior and needs. However, social interaction theory and research does not support such assumptions; the second, more complex social arrangement is more plausible and recent research related to this study by Herriott and St. John (1966) lends further support.

Herriott and St. John did not include pupils' perceptions of teachers in their analyses, but they did investigate a number of factors that could affect the impact of pupils' social-class background on teachers and principals. Some of their major findings support what has been well known, e.g., teachers in schools situated in neighborhoods of lowest socioeconomic status (SES) generally seek horizontal mobility—assignment to a "better neighborhood" where schools serve more advantaged pupils (Becker, 1952). Principals in low SES schools seek both vertical and horizontal mobility, i.e., assignments offering greater "responsibility" and "prestige." Teachers and principals in the highest SES schools expressed the greatest satisfaction with their roles and current positions, and those in the lowest SES schools were most dissatisfied.

Consistent with the above and important to note, Herriott and St. John also found that principals and teachers in the lowest SES schools were younger and less experienced than counterparts in high SES schools. Teachers and principals come from similar social-class and geographical origins; the lower a school's SES, the greater the proportion of teachers and principals reporting lower SES and urban backgrounds. In educational performance, teachers, but not principals, in lowest SES schools were found to be poorer than in schools of highest SES. However, principals in lower SES schools were found to have significantly greater administrative influence and control over their teachers in planning, smoothing office routines, student management, and upgrading teacher performance. All of these findings indicate that real differences exist in the characteristics of principals and teachers in MC versus LC schools and supposedly, their behavior and work patterns too. And within schools, there appear to be strong general similarities in the characteristics of principals and their teachers.

The relationship of principals and teachers as an alliance or coalition in respect to pupils and other persons involved in schools bears attention. Although Foskett (1969) and Foskett and Wolcott (1967) detected variation between teachers' and principals' perceptions of their educational roles within some schools, they found little actual difference between principals' and teachers' perceptions when analyzed between schools and communities. Also, principals were found to be quite accurate in their perceptions of how teachers would respond. Compared to all other group combinations, which also included citizens in general, parents, community leaders, school board members, and super-

intendents, teachers and principals were found to be in highest common agreement. Pupils' perceptions were not obtained; but if they had been, one would not expect their views of principals and teachers would be greater than parents, etc., however, it would have been interesting to see how much and what contrast existed between the views of principals and teachers and those of pupils in Foskett's samples. In the present study, the attitudes of principals and teachers toward children were found to correlate well, but little agreement materialized between principals' and pupils' ratings of teacher merit.

Viewing the principal-teacher-pupil interpersonal relationships as a triad, we can conceive of a triangle drawn with a short line, representing common agreement and alliance between principal and teacher, and relatively longer lines separating each of them and pupils. Social exchange theory (e.g., Nord, 1969; Thibaut and Kelley, 1959) helps us predict such relationships. Coalitions are to be expected in triads and there would seem to be greater potential for cost-reward outcomes to influence relations between principals and teachers, especially inexperienced and untenured teachers, than between pupils and principals or teachers. Since teacher-pupil relations are more informal and persistent than those between principal and pupils, which usually involve nomothetic rather than idiographic contacts and perceptions, a scalene rather than an isosceles triangle might best represent the typical principal-teacher-pupil triad. The teacher would be intermediary in relation to principal and pupils but closer to the principal.

By classifying our data by school SES, we found a critical difference between the nature of agreement in the principal-teacher coalition of MC versus LC schools. Thus, despite the social distance separating pupils from their principals and teachers, MC pupils face principal-teacher coalitions that tend to be positive, warm, sympathetic, and permissive toward children, a condition conducive to effective learning, motivation, and mutual understanding. On the other hand, LC pupils must confront principal-teacher coalitions that seem to be characterized by negative, cold, inflexible, and punitive attitudes toward children. Certainly all that has been expressed about effective teacher qualities (e.g., *X, Y, Z* characteristics reported by Ryans, 1960) and the extraordinary needs of LC pupils and how educators should relate to them (e.g., Riessman, 1967) conflict with such findings.

Much has been said and written about the effect of social class upon pupils, and it is almost vernacular today to speak of the "advantaged" versus the "disadvantaged" child. Unfortunately, such distinctions often tend to be over-simplified and stereotypic, as they assume too easily that the pupil or the educator is the main and only source of significant variance between schools of differing social class levels. Use of a social interaction frame of reference has helped this writer probe the complex interpersonal relationships involving teachers and pupils (Yee, 1969). Such an approach leads naturally into the present study of principal-teacher-pupil interpersonal relationships.

Further study should be given to the principal-teacher coalition as it relates to pupils and others involved in schools. Studies by Della Piana and Gage (1955); Flanders (1965); Gage, Runkel and Chatterjee (1963); and Yee (1968b) show that teacher-pupil relations involve reciprocal influence and complex interaction. In a brilliant experiment, Daw and Gage (1967) demonstrated the significant effect of teacher feedback on the behavior of principals. Further study should now be given the processes and relative effects involved in principal-teacher-pupil interpersonal relations.

REFERENCES

1. BECK, W. H. Pupils' perceptions of teacher merit: A factor analysis of five hypothesized dimensions. Unpublished doctoral dissertation, Stanford University, 1964, *Dissertation Abstracts,* 1965, 25, 5668.

2. BECKER, H. S. The career of the Chicago public schoolteacher. *American Journal of Sociology,* 57, (1952), 470–477.

3. CLARK, K. B. *Dark ghetto.* (New York: Harper and Row, 1965.)

4. COLEMAN, J. S.; CAMPBELL, E. Q.; HOBSON, C. J.; MCPARTLAND, J.; MOOD, A. M.; WEINFELD, F. D.; & YORK, R. L. *Equality of educational opportunity.* Washington, D. C.: National Center for Educational Statistics, U. S. Department of Health, Education, and Welfare, 1966. (Government Printing Office Documents No. F55.238:38001).

5. DAW, R. W., & GAGE, N. L. Effect of feedback from teachers to principals. *Journal of Educational Psychology.* 58, (1967), 181–188.

6. DELLA PIANA, G. M., & GAGE, N. L. Pupils' values and the validity of the Minnesota Teacher Attitude Inventory. *Journal of Educational Psychology,* 46, (1955), 167–178.

7. FLANDERS, N. A. Teacher influence in the classroom. In E. J. AMIDON & J. B. HOUGH (Eds.), *Interaction analyses: Theory, research and application.* (Reading, Mass.: Addison-Wesley, 1967), pp. 103–116.

8. FLANDERS, N. A. *Teacher influence, pupil attitudes, and achievement.* Washington,

D. C.: U.S. Office of Education, 1965. (Government Printing Office Document No. FS 5.225:25040).

9. FOSKETT, J. M. *Role consensus: The case of the elementary school teacher.* Eugene, Oregon: Center for the Advanced Study of Educational Administration, 1969.

10. FOSKETT, J. M., & WOLCOTT, H. F. Self-images and community images of the elementary school principal. *Educational Administration Quarterly,* 3, (1967), 162–182.

11. GAGE, N. L. Paradigms for research on teaching. In N. L. GAGE (Ed.), *Handbook for research on teaching.* (Chicago: Rand McNally, 1963), pp. 94–141.

12. GAGE, N. L., RUNKEL, P. J., & CHATTERJEE, B. B. Changing teacher behavior through feedback from pupils: An application of equilibrium theory. In W. W. CHARTERS, JR. & N. L. GAGE (Eds.), *Readings in the social psychology of education.* (Boston: Allyn and Bacon, 1963), pp. 173–181.

13. GROSS, N. *Who runs our schools?* (New York: Wiley, 1958.)

14. GUTTMAN, L. A basis for analyzing test-retest reliability. *Psychometrika,* 10, (1945), 255–282.

15. HERRIOTT, R. E., and ST. JOHN, N. H. *Social class and the urban school: The impact of pupil background on teachers and principals.* (New York: Wiley, 1966.)

16. HORST, P. A generalized expression of the reliability of measures. *Psychometrika,* 14, (1949), 21–32.

17. JENSEN, A. R. Social class, race, and genetics: Implications for education. *American Educational Research Journal,* 5, (1968), 1–42.

18. LEEDS, C. H. Predictive validity of the Minnesota Teacher Attitude Inventory.

Journal of Teacher Education, 20, (1969), 51–56.

19. LIPHAM, J. M. Organizational character of education: Administrative behavior. *Review of Educational Research,* 34, (1964), 435–454.

20. NORD, N. R. Social exchange theory: An integrative approach to social conformity. *Psychological Bulletin,* 71, (1969), 174–208.

21. RIESSMAN, F. Teachers of the poor: A five-point plan. *Journal of Teacher Education,* 18, (1967), 326–336.

22. ROBBINS, C. B. The principal and his knowledge of teacher behavior. In E. J. AMIDON & J. B. HOUGH (Eds.), *Interaction analysis: Theory, research and application.* (Reading, Mass.: Addison-Wesley, 1967), pp. 176–185.

23. RYANS, D. G. *Characteristics of teachers.* (Washington, D.C.: American Council on Education, 1960.)

24. SPINDLER, G. D. Education in a transforming American Culture. *Harvard Educational Review,* 25, (1955), 145–156.

25. THIBAUT, J. W., & KELLEY, H. H. *Social Psychology of groups* (New York: JOHN WILEY, 1959.)

26. WHITE, R. K., & LIPPITT, R. *Autocracy and democracy: An experimental inquiry.* (New York: Harper, 1960.)

27. WITHALL, J., & LEWIS, W. W. Social interaction in the classroom. In N. L. GAGE, (Ed.), *Handbook of research on teaching* (Chicago: Rand McNally, 1963), pp. 683–714.

28. YEE, A. H. Is the Minnesota Teacher Attitude Inventory valid and homogeneous? *Journal of Educational Measurement,* 4, (1967), 151–161.

29. YEE, A. H. Interpersonal attitudes of teachers and advantaged and disadvantaged pupils, *Journal of Human Resources,* 3, (1968), 327–345. (a)

30. YEE, A. H. Source and direction of causal influence in teacher-pupil relationships. *Journal of Educational Psychology,* 59, (1968), 275–282. (b)

31. YEE, A. H. Social interaction in classrooms: Implications for the education of disadvantaged pupils. *Urban Education,* 4, (1969), 201–219.

32. YEE, A. H., & RUNKEL, P. J. Simplicial structure of middle-class and lower-class pupils' attitudes toward teachers. *Developmental Psychology,* 1, (1969), 646–652.

5

Methods and Problems

of Studying Social Interaction

in Educational Settings

*The important question about
methods is not "How" but "Why."*
John W. Tukey

The ten chapters of Volume V, *Handbook of Social Psychology* (Lindzey
and Aronson, 1968) devoted to research methods attest to social psychology's
great need for and use of research procedures. Readings in the previous
chapters indicate that the study of social interaction in education requires
a formidable arsenal of varied research procedures. That is only proper
since social-psychological problems in education are of wide range and
involve many variables and their arrangements. An interesting and instructional exercise for the student would be to list the independent and dependent
variables of the preceding readings and the research designs and techniques
the authors utilized. Such listings lead naturally to categorization and
reflection upon central theoretical and research concerns. The student might
ascertain how well this book's sample of research studies and those published
in relevant journals relate to the conceptual framework presented in the
first chapter.

No one area of study in education commands a monopoly of research
design and method. There are many textbooks (e.g., Campbell and Stanley,
1966; Cattell, 1966) that the student of social interaction can consult for
detailed information on research design and techniques, and we need not
go into them here. This chapter deals with some central methodological
issues in the study of social interaction in education.

As we would not be able to classify social psychologists by the type
of automobiles they might drive, we cannot reasonably say that technical
procedures and their use should distinguish between fields of study.

Areas are better distinguished one from the other by the relevant
variables their theoretical and research interests focus upon and interrelate.

The social interactional variables the studies in this book focus upon, of which interpersonal attitudes are particularly prominent, are usually theoretical constructs that are inferred through considerable observation, deduction, and shrewd insight. Often the variables are intangible, abstract conceptions of something that the researcher believes there is sufficient justification to define and label.

Although relatively tangible variables, such as age, time, and income can be measured without much bother, variables such as attitudes require clear operational definitions and their measurement must stand the tests of reliability and validity. Thus, it is difficult to avoid giving attention to the special requirements of psychometric tests and measurement and the test of hypotheses through inferential statistics. Hays (1967) provides an excellent introduction to such concerns. However, refinements in psychometrics should be sought without forgetting the variables to be measured (Anastasi, 1967).

This chapter's readings require little introduction. Their descriptions of methods and problems relevant to the study of social interaction in educational settings are self-explanatory. All of us need to appreciate differences in researchers' methodological needs and approaches to the study of social behavior. Note carefully how the first two articles contrast with each other, yet remain relevant to the study of social interaction.

As an educational anthropologist, Wolcott studies social behavior through longitudinal observations of his subjects in their natural environment. Using the method of participant observation, as William Foote Whyte did in his classical study of *Street Corner Society* (Chicago, University of Chicago Press, 1943), Wolcott observes and records in field notes as much as he can without setting a priori inferences. His aim is to adequately describe and explain human behavior in educational settings. As time passes, he concentrates upon behavioral features that he finds pertinent; after a long span of time, perhaps years of study, he interprets and finally describes what he has observed in written form. Reflecting upon his own ethnographic study of elementary school classrooms, Smith (1967) characterized his study as "micro-ethnographic" in scope and said the data he obtained was more concrete and vivid than expected. However, he concluded that "the approach seems to us to be very fruitful in developing rather than verifying hypotheses" (p. 221).

Little if any work of ethnographers is intended to lead directly to specific prescriptive and developmental changes. If research such as Wolcott's is to affect schools and their teaching-learning operations, analytical studies of the type Gage describes need to follow-up their inferences, a move which may involve anthropological procedures to test hypotheses (e.g., Burnett, 1969). Ethnographers are serious about their field work and attempt to be as objective and unobtrusive as possible. Yet, they are aware of possible bias effects influencing their findings and constantly attempt to overcome them.

Thus, they conduct their field work for long periods of time and do not attempt to manipulate the subjects and conditions they are studying, i.e., research, *yes*, but little or no development and intent to change subjects and conditions.

In contrast, Gage's analytical approach pursues a far less global view of behavior than does Wolcott's. It is primarily mission-oriented and involves research *and* development, i.e., it is concerned with understanding and improving educational processes, while the holistic approach aims at descriptive objectives. Wolcott would probably say that his concern is not with modifying educational processes so much as with describing them as he sees them. To better develop teacher competence in working with learners, Gage and his associates attempt to identify relevant variables, i.e., specific behavior skills which Gage termed micro-criteria. Once a relevant micro-criterion of desired behavior is identified and defined adequately in measurement terms, controlled experiments can be conducted to see what conditions, such as micro-teaching, help achieve the desired behavior best.

Thus, by delimiting the scope of observation and quantifying analysis, Gage seeks minimum risk-high yield results in contrast to Wolcott's admittedly "high risk-low yield" outcome possibilities that accrue from his holistic perspective. One could say, however, that the analytical approach could lead one to mistaken an ear, trunk, or tail for an elephant. There is an assumption underlying the analytical approach that should be made more explicit because of its importance that delimitation of scope is possible only after a broad survey of the problem area and development of an inference structure leading to the needed chains of studies (Platt, 1964).

Empirical workers in education, such as Gage, seek maximum conceptual understanding, prediction of future outcomes, and control of effects in their scientific endeavors. That others can replicate their findings is a desideratum. Gage explained the analytical approach quite well with his example of research on the technical skill of explaining ability. More and more educational researchers pursue studies today much as Gage and his associates do (e.g., Denny, 1970). To provide the broad perspective and inferential insights so necessary to complement the work of analytical researchers, more researchers are needed to study social behavior as Wolcott and Smith do and apparently there is excellent progress in this area (Sindell, 1969). Although ethnographic and related methods cannot help us decide with probability estimates which teaching method among many should be favored, or what specific characteristics predict behavior in social interaction, they can provide valuable insight into the operations of educational environments and promote the generation of theory and hypotheses to be tested and developed with analytical approaches. The practical exigencies of decision-making and improvement of educational systems and processes will probably lead more researchers to use analytical approaches.

The remaining articles in this chapter deal with various analytical methods and problems inherent in the study of social interaction in educational settings. The Kennedy and Vega article emphasizes the need to consider the "nature of interactions between Negro students and white teachers, or examiners." Their article also illustrates the modern application of multivariate analyses in the study of social interaction. Separate articles by Kliebard and Flanders provide considerable background information on the systematic observation of classroom behavior. The reader might consider the advantages and disadvantages such systematic schedules provide as seen from the ethnographic or analytical view. Interestingly, the development and use of "social interaction" schedules attracted so much attention through the last decade that many persons in education equated the study of social interaction with the technique. It seems that such a narrow impression grew out of a greater general concern for methodological refinements and wide application of the observation schedules than the theoretical aspects of social interaction in educational settings. The programs for the annual meetings of the American Educational Research Association record the rise of such an emphasis to about 1967 and the decline of paper sessions devoted to it since. As Kliebard and Flanders show in their articles, the general method is feasible and useful when related to relevant issues and theory. Therefore, why a technique is used is a more important and primary concern than how the method works.

In the sixth selection, the researcher illustrates through an intensive examination of the Minnesota Teacher Attitude Inventory many of the problems involved in developing an adequate scale to measure attitudes. It and Damrin's (1959) article indicate the complexities and importance of adequate test construction and validation in the study of social interaction. Lott and Lott, however, show that the study of interpersonal attraction need not be restricted by the use of verbal self-report measures and can be promoted by indirect behavioral measures (also, see Webb, Campbell, Schwartz, and Sechrest, 1966).

The work by Yee and Gage concerns the need to deal explicitly with causality in the social sciences, especially in social interaction. Their article describes four techniques for estimating the source and direction of causal influence in panel data, and applies them to hypotheses on teacher-pupil interpersonal relationships. Such techniques, if found feasible and applicable through further study, may supplement multivariate procedures, such as path analysis, a technique Sewell and Shah used in their article presented in Chapter 2 and recently demonstrated with sociological examples by Duncan (1966) and with psychological examples by Werts and Linn (1970).

In Hollander and Julian's critical review of recent theory and research in the area of leadership, much of what they find significant concerning the interpersonal involvement between leader and followers supports the relevance of social interaction in education, e.g., "the key to an understanding of leadership rests in seeing it as an influence process, involving an implicit exchange relationship over time."

OTHER READINGS

ANASTASI, A. Psychology, psychologists, and psychological testing. *American Psychologist*, 1967, *22*, 297–306.

BALES, R. F. *Personality and interpersonal behavior*. New York: Holt, Rinehart and Winston, 1970.

BOYLE, R. P. Algebraic systems for normal and hierarchial sociograms. *Sociometry*, 1969, *32*, 99–110.

BURNETT, J. H. Ceremony, rites, and economy in the student system of an American high school. *Human Organization*, 1969, *28*, 1–10.

CAMPBELL, D. T., & STANLEY, J. C. *Experimental and quasi-experimental designs for research*. Chicago: Rand McNally, 1966.

CATTELL, R. B. (Ed.) *Handbook of multivariate experimental psychology*. Chicago: Rand McNally, 1966.

DAMRIN, D. E. The Russell Sage social relations test: A technique for measuring group problem solving skills in elementary school children. *Journal of Experimental Education*, 1959, *28*, 85–99.

DENNY, T (Ed.) Educational evaluation. *Review of Educational Research*, 1970, *40*, 181–320.

DUNCAN, O. D. Path analysis: sociological examples. *American Journal of Sociology*, 1966, *72*, 1–16.

GUMP, P. V. Intra-setting analysis: The third grade classroom as a special but instructive core. In E. P. WILLIAMS & H. L. RAUSH (Eds.), *Naturalistic views in psychological research*. New York: Holt, Rinehart & Winston, 1969. Pp. 200–220.

HAYS, W. L. *Quantification in psychology*. Bemont, California: Wadsworth, 1966.

LINDZEY, G., & ARONSON, E. (Eds.) Handbook of social psychology. Vol. 2, *Research Methods*. Reading, Mass.: Addison-Wesley, 1968.

MEDLEY, D. M., & MITZEL, H. E. Measuring classroom behavior by systematic observation. In N. L. GAGE (Ed.), *Handbook of research on teaching*. Chicago: Rand McNally, 1963. Pp. 247–328.

PLATT, J. R. Strong inference. *Science*, 1964, *146*, 347–353.

SINDELL, P. S. Anthropological approaches to the study of education. *Review of Educational Research*, 1969, *39*, 593–605.

SMITH, L. M. The micro-ethnography of the classroom. *Psychology in the Schools*, 1967, *4*, 216–221.

WEBB, E. J.; CAMPBELL, D. T.; SCHWARTZ, R. D.; & SECHREST, L. *Unobtrusive measures: Nonreactive research in the social sciences*. Chicago: Rand McNally, 1966.

WERTS, C. E., & LINN, R. L. Path analysis: psychological examples. *Psychological Bulletin*, 1970, *74*, 193–212.

AN ETHNOGRAPHIC APPROACH TO THE STUDY OF SCHOOL ADMINISTRATORS

Harry F. Wolcott

The ethnographer's task is the selective recording of human behavior in order to construct explanations of that behavior in cultural terms. The standard ethnography thus provides an account of the way of life of some special human process (say, law or more narrowly, divorce) or of some particular group of people, such as the Tikopia or the Children of Sanchez. My approach in this paper is ethnographic in that the purpose of the research project is to describe and analyze in cultural terms the behavior of one elementary school principal and the behavior of those who interact with him, such as teachers, pupils, spouse and family, and other principals.

There are, of course, other ways to study the life style of school administrators. One alternative is to obtain such a position oneself, but there are limitations on the ability to observe objectively processes in which one is deeply involved as a participant. A second alternative is to draw upon existing literature. Unfortunately, the literature in educational administration is disappointing as a source of data for learning about the real world of the principal, since it tends to be hortatory or normative in content. It tells principals (or superintendents, or other administrators) how they *ought* to act. It is prescriptive rather than descriptive. Thus while it is an excellent source of information for learning about the ideal world of formal education, it fails to provide an account of what actually goes on or how the ideals are translated into real behavior.

The literature in educational administration that *is* empirically based, on the other hand, provides factual data which tell us too little about too many. For example, we can readily learn from current studies[1] that the average American elementary school principal is a married male between the ages of 35 and 49, has

From: Human Organization, *1970, 29, 115–122. Copyright* © *1970 by the Society for Applied Anthropology, and reproduced by permission of the author and publisher.*

[1] See, for example, the recent survey of the elementary school principalship completed by the Department of Elementary School Principals of the National Education Association, Washington, D. C. *The Elementary School Principalship in 1968,* the fourth such report completed since an initial survey conducted in 1928.

had between 10 and 19 years' total experience in schools, and was an elementary classroom teacher just prior to assuming his administrative post. However useful such data are as a source of census information, they provide virtually no insight into what it is like to be one of these people. Similarly, the ubiquitous questionnaires which plague public school people are constantly inventorying their training, habits and preferences; but because the people who compose them typically fail to do careful preliminary fieldwork, the information obtained (to questions like "Should a principal attend church regularly?") may reveal more about the tendency of school administrators to give "expected" responses than about their actual practices. Furthermore, such questionnaires often ignore the consequences of the fact that if the questions asked are not crucial, differences in responses are not crucial either. The closest approximation to sources of data on the actual behavior of school administrators are various studies based on self-reporting techniques,[2] an approach beset with problems of subject reliability.

There is at least one facet in the literature on school administrators which to date has received little serious and sustained attention. This needed facet is a series of careful and detailed descriptive studies of the actual behavior of principals, viewed not only in the context of the formal educational system but also in terms of their lives as human beings living out their experience in the context of a total cultural milieu. It was to provide an

in-depth study of one elementary school principal seen in the perspective of the cultural context in which he lives that the present research project was begun.

The most intensive period of fieldwork occurred during the first year of the two-year study. During that first year I attempted to spend some part of at least three days a week with the principal. Most, but by no means all, of this time was spent with him while he was at school. The school was an average-size suburban elementary school with a faculty of 18 classroom teachers, three teachers at each grade level from first through sixth, plus a staff including several additional certificated personnel (counselor, resource teacher, nurse) and noncertificated personnel (secretary, cooks, custodians). The school is located in a unified school district of some 20,000 pupils in a metropolitan area in the Pacific Northwest.

Over the period of two years I focused my attention on the principal's actual behavior, both in word and in deed, and on the real situations which occurred in both his professional and personal life as these impinged on his behavior as a school administrator. I assumed that every aspect of his life had some relevance for the study. When I was asked (somewhat facetiously, I suppose) whether I planned to take his body temperature each day, I replied, not at all facetiously, that were it readily available I would like such information, just as it might be interesting to know what he ate for dinner each Sunday. Obviously, it was not possible to be quite so eclectic, and it was necessary to establish priorities in data gathering. My attention was drawn primarily to such aspects of a principal's life as the who, what, where, and when of his personal encounters; the cultural themes manifested in his behavior and in his attempts to influence the behavior of those about him; and what it is about the position of principal that those

[2] The four national surveys conducted by the Department of Elementary School Principals cited above are based exclusively on self-reporting techniques. An unpublished doctoral dissertation by Bill Jay Ranniger, "A Summary of the Job Responsibilities of the Elementary School Principal," University of Oregon, 1962, describes a number of such studies conducted typically as doctoral studies or as research surveys made by statewide organizations of school principals.

occupying it find more and less satisfying.

The purpose of this article is to examine the field methods employed to arrive at "The Ethnography of a Principalship"; the substantive content of the study will be reported elsewhere.[3] But first let me dispose of one surprising question several people have asked, "Did the principal know you were making the study?" I can assure readers that he did. I spent several weeks searching for a suitable and willing subject, and I did not proceed with formal permission to conduct the study until I had the personal permission and commitment of the individual selected. His family, his faculty and staff, his fellow principals, and many visitors to the school knew something about the project. Even a few pupils learned the nickname ("The Shadow") which members of the faculty assigned me as a semi-humorous acknowledgment of my presence and purpose at their school.

THE FIELDWORK METHODS

Although the ethnographic approach implies commitment to a special perspective in regard to both the gathering of data in field research and the subsequent handling of data in research writing, it does not always explicate the methods for doing either. As a brief descriptive label for the methodology, Zelditch's term "field study" is perhaps the most useful, primarily be-

cause he makes an excellent case for the participant-observer approach without going to the extreme of insisting that participant observation entails only participating and observing.[4] Zelditch argues that "a field study is not a single method gathering a single kind of information";[5] in fact, the participant-observer employs three methods: "enumeration to document frequency data; participant observation to describe incidents; and informant interviewing to learn institutionalized norms and statuses."[6] The three elements of the field study which he identifies provide a useful framework for describing my research activities. The following account of data gathering and data handling in the ethnographic study of a school principal makes use of these three categories—enumeration, participant observation, and interviewing.

ENUMERATION.

Census data of various sorts as well as a wide variety of other numerical or potentially numerical data are available in virtually every public school. Not all such data are equally relevant, of course, but a few examples will illustrate the ways and the ethnographic purposes for which frequency data were gathered in this study.

It was possible, for instance, to collect all official notices issued at the school or distributed at school on behalf of the school district's central office. Collecting these items was facilitated by having an assigned mailbox in the school office; like the regular members of the staff, I received copies of a great deal of memoranda simply as a matter of office routine. For correspondence and reports originating from the school office, the secretary often

[3] Harry F. Wolcott, *The Ethnography of a Principalship* (in preparation). An overview of the study appears in a chapter, "The Elementary School Principal: Notes from a Field Study," in George D. Spindler (ed.), *Education and Cultural Process: Approaches to an Anthropology of Education,* Holt, Rinehart and Winston, New York (forthcoming). A brief statement on methodology in that chapter is based on the same original paper as the discussion presented here. The chapter also contains one detailed episode and analysis from the field study, an episode dealing with the selection of new principals in the school district.

[4] Morris Zelditch, Jr., "Some Methodological Problems of Field Studies," *American Journal of Sociology,* Vol. 67, 1962, pp. 566–576.
[5] *Ibid.,* p. 567.
[6] *Ibid.,* p. 566.

made an extra carbon copy for me. At the end of the school year in June, some of the year's records (for example, the daily notices written in a faculty notebook, and a personal log of incidents which the principal kept during part of the year) were turned over to me simply because they had no further use at school and would ordinarily have been discarded had I not expressed an interest in them.

Such data made possible frequency counts of the kinds and content of messages and interactions which were otherwise recorded in my daily journal entries as single rather than as recurring events. Official reports also provided a permanent record of attendance and other changes accountable to the school district central office during the year. Even the *lack* of personal correspondence emanating from the principal's office (in contrast to the number of formal announcements addressed collectively to all pupils, parents, or staff) provided useful data by supporting the observation that most of the "business" of the principal was conducted verbally.

Another source of enumeration data was tapped through a "time and motion" study: notation was made, at 60-second intervals over a carefully sampled period of two weeks at school, of what the principal was doing, where he was, with whom he was interacting, and who was doing the talking at the time. Had I not been strongly encouraged to include attention to this type of data by one of my colleagues in sociology, I might well have missed an excellent opportunity to get "hard" data with which to support the more content-oriented field notes. In organizing the field notes I have been impressed with the utility of being able to lend quantitative support regarding the relative amount of time the principal spent in various parts of the school building as well as to the frequency of his interactions with certain categories of people and the extent to which he was the person doing the talking.

Another quantitative aspect of the fieldwork included the projects of mapping and photographing the school and the neighborhood. Initially these procedures helped to orient me within the school building and within the school's attendance area. Mapping the attendance area has led to two further independent but related studies carried on by my research assistant, one exploring how a school administrator can use a map as a way of organizing the census data available to him at school,[7] the other a critical examination of the concept of "community" as used in the familiar phrase "school and community."[8] It is hoped that in the monograph (now being prepared), photographs taken of the school and of homes and businesses in the immediate neighborhood will help educators and other readers assess for themselves the extent to which the setting of this study is similar and dissimilar to other elementary schools with which they are familiar.

PARTICIPANT OBSERVATION.

The initial phase of participant observation began with the search for a willing and likely subject. My search was initiated on a personal and informal basis by asking friends and colleagues familiar with the general region in which I wished to con-

[7] John A. Olson, "Mapping: A Method for Organizing Data About Your School Attendance Area," Bulletin of the Oregon School Study Council, College of Education, University of Oregon, Vol. 12, No. 7, March 1969.

[8] Mr. Olson, an experienced geographer, is completing a study of the ecology of the school attendance area to compare the "school community" as the principal and other school personnel perceive it with the community as perceived through the perspective of a geographer. Mention should be made of Mr. Olson's important contribution in the analyses of other enumeration and interview data in the study. His lesser involvement in the school setting was undoubtedly important in insuring that the analyses were objectively restricted to the data at hand.

duct the study to recommend principals who might be helpful in my search. These initial contacts recommended persons whom they felt would be likely as well as "representative" subjects. I sought a principal who would fit the description of the average American elementary school principal given previously, with the obvious added qualification that he be willing to work closely with an observer over an extended period of time. I was able to identify several likely prospects and to spend some time in trial runs with them as a test for them and for myself. Finally, I extended an invitation to one principal and asked him to take whatever time he needed and to consult with anyone he wished before making a decision. Several days later I received his personal commitment to take part in the study. Until that time no attempt had been made to secure the formal permission that was ultimately obtained from the school district. I had been concerned that had I worked initially through formal channels some school superintendent might have "assigned" a school and principal to me, thus making the project dependent on administrative fiat rather than on volunteered cooperation.

Particularly during the first year— once the study was formally underway— my primary methodology was that of participant observation. As often as necessary the principal introduced me as being "from the university and doing some research in which I'm involved." It was usually possible to maximize the opportunity to observe and record while minimizing my participation (other than by my very presence), by standing or sitting just far enough from the principal that those with whom he was interacting could not easily engage us both. I made it a practice to carry my notebook with me and to make entries in it as often as possible. My intent was to create a precedent for constant note-taking so that it would

seem natural for me to be writing regardless of the topic or event at hand.

Regarding the taking of notes, several guidelines proved helpful. Notes were taken in longhand in complete and readable form. When the nature of the events was such that I could not take notes as completely as I wished and yet thought it essential to continue a period of observation, I jotted brief notes in the margins of my note book and completed my full account later. I never returned to the school until all the notes from the previous visit were completed. I felt that nothing was gained by my mere presence as an observer; until my notes from one visit were a matter of record, there was no point in returning to school and reducing the impact of one set of observations by imposing a more recent one. Customarily I did not attempt to do an intense job of notetaking for more than two hours at a time.[9] When a single event (e.g., the regular meetings of all the elementary

[9] In a paper entitled "Issues in Anthropological Fieldwork in Schools," presented at the annual meeting of the American Anthropological Association, New Orleans, November 1969, Professor Bud Khleif argued that the fieldworker in the school or classroom cannot be a participant. Although I would hold that by the very nature of his approach the fieldworker always functions in both participant and observer roles to some extent, participant observation in schools does indeed provide far more extensive opportunity for observing and ordinarily makes minimum demands on one as participant. The fact of long, virtually uninterrupted periods of observation helps account for the problem of observer fatigue noted here, after blocks of time that might otherwise be considered brief in utilizing a participant-observer approach. For further discussions of fieldwork problems in schools and classrooms see Peter S. Sindell, "Anthropological Approaches to the Study of Education," *Review of Educational Research,* Vol. 39, No. 5, December 1969; and Louis M. Smith and J. A. Brock, " 'Go, Bug, Go!': Methodological Issues in Classroom Observational Research," Occasional Paper Series, No. 5, Central Midwestern Regional Educational Laboratory, Inc., St. Ann, Mishouri, January 1970.

school principals in the school district) extended much beyond two hours I noticed a considerable diminishing in my attention and an increasing succinctness in the notes.

Ultimately the longhand entries were transcribed onto 5 × 8 papers in duplicate. Each entry describes one single event to facilitate sorting and organizing the data. Here are two brief examples from notes made in October, 1967:

October 4. Lunchtime. The principal and an all-woman faculty group [none of the three male teachers happened to be present] are in the faculty room finishing lunch when I arrive at school. The principal is watching the World Series on a classroom TV set he has brought into the room. The volume is rather loud. One teacher jokes with me about whether I had realized there were "so many ball fans" on the faculty. Another teacher tells me to write down that the principal is "practically useless when the World Series is on," but she hastens to add that "he doesn't have time to watch as intently as he used to— he just used to sit there and never leave the set." No one gave evidence of displeasure at the TV dominating the lunchroom. Later, however, when the principal returned after being called out to the hall by some upper-grade boys and went to shut off the TV he asked, "Does anyone mind if I turn this off?" and a cheer went up in approval. But by then the game was over and only the commercials were being shown. As the principal switched the set off he turned to me and quipped, "Put it in your notes as a day of my sick leave." At 12:15 he left the faculty room to set up the TV for the older pupils in the cafeteria as he had promised them earlier [on the assumption that the day's game would still be going during their lunch period].

October 19. The principal briefed me on an argument he had yesterday with the night custodian, precipitated over where the custodian should park his car. The principal reported: "He got so mad I

thought he was going to fight me. But I told him I wasn't afraid of him; I'm from the 'show-me' country, too. We're having a meeting on Monday with the maintenance supervisor. Maybe we'll let him go. This has been building up. He seems to resent any authority. If a teacher asks him to do something, he does it, but if I tell him, he gets all in a huff. We can't keep him around if he won't take directions. It'll be tough on him, too. He's pretty old, and he can't do hard labor. And we won't be able to give him a recommendation."

One of the objectives of this study was to see the principal in as many different settings as possible. A table and chair (more symbolic than functional) were moved into the principal's office for my use. At the school I was excluded, by prior arrangement, only from a few "touchy" parent conferences. I had opportunity for extended observations at all school activities and meetings, at district-wide meetings of teachers and administrators, at meetings of local, regional, and state educational associations, and at formal and informal staff gatherings, at school and away.

The meetings which I attended with the principal were seldom so large that I could accompany him unnoticed, but in the long duration of the fieldwork I was present often enough that I believe most of his professional colleagues conducted business-as-usual in my presence. One individual who seemed to remain ever conscious of my presence as a note-taker was the superintendent of schools; he never conducted a meeting which I attended without at least once directing some comment to me in the manner one might use with a newspaper reporter.

Except for engaging in light social banter, I minimized my interaction in the field settings to avoid being pressed for feedback regarding what I was recording or how I felt about it. Thus I felt somewhat at a loss in terms of being able to "give" in exchange for the cooperation I was getting from the principal and his colleagues. I discovered that by offering to provide transportation to meetings in my automobile, I was able to perform a service much appreciated by the principal and his fellow administrators. Serendipitously I discovered that the usually free-wheeling conversation of a group of principals riding together to and from a meeting provided another source of information.

I was concerned lest I should be overidentified at the school with the principal, particularly since he was the formally appointed status leader of the school. Therefore, I expressed interest in the lives and work of the teachers and other staff members, and made a point of visiting the school on days when I knew the principal was away. "Oh, checking up on us, eh?" someone would inevitably comment, leading me to feel that the possibility of being overidentified with "the boss" was not too remote. Such visits also provided an opportunity to observe the school as it operated during the frequent periods when the principal was away from the building.

In those settings where I observed the principal acting outside his formal administrative role, I had no apprehension about being overidentified with him, but there are very few guidelines to direct a research while accompanying a subject to see about a new battery for his car or to attend his service-club luncheon. Nevertheless I was able to include observations of the principal's life at home with his family, at business meetings at his church, teaching his weekly Sunday School class, during trips to local businesses for school and personal reasons, and at Kiwanis luncheons. I was present during occasional brief meetings with old friends and neighbors. A family wedding provided an opportunity for me to meet more family and friends as well as to discuss with the

principal a guest list which served research interests by providing a sort of family sociogram. These out-of-school observations provide the data necessary to place the principal within the broader cutural context of his life as a human being who happens to be a school administrator rather than as a principal viewed only incidentally as a human and cultural being.

INFORMANT INTERVIEWING

In the context of a long-term field study, interviewing can provide not only for learning about institutionalized norms and statuses, but also a means of obtaining systematic data about the range of perceptions among a group of people regarding both persons and events. For example, taped interviews of approximately one hour duration, structured but open-ended, provided excellent data concerning the principal's family life (interviews with his wife and mother) and in the perceptions of him as a school administrator (interviews with thirteen faculty and two staff members). The typescripts of these interviews have proved extremely valuable for uncovering the range of perceptions and for the extent of the affective content expressed by the teachers regarding their work and the people with whom they are associated professionally. The fact that each interview was requested as a personal favor and that no interviewing was done until I had spent over half a year at the school undoubtedly contributed to the ease with which these interviews were held. Collectively the interviews provide a basis for content analysis in terms of what people talked about and how strongly they felt about it. More importantly for this study, they provide illustrative material about the problems of those whose lives are enmeshed personally or professionally with the principal. Recognizing as they did how my study focused on the principal, it was fascinating to me to see how quickly and directly many teachers began discussing their perceptions about administration or their specific points-of-view as they reflected their own successes and problems of the year during the interview sessions.

Toward the end of the school year I asked all the puplis in each fifth and sixth grade classroom to write (anonymously, if they wished) what they thought they would remember about the principal. The phrases which I suggested to them to start their writing were "What kind of a principal is he?"; "Pleasant memories are...";
and "One time I won't forget...." The comments I received ran the gamut of opinion, from the succinct response of one pupil who wrote that his principal is "a Dam stopit one," to "He is the kind of a principal who helps you figure it out." Like the teacher interviews, these statements lent themselves to content analysis (e.g., positive *vs.* negative responses of boys and girls) and provide a source of data for illustrative purposes.

The principal naturally served as a primary informant, since he was not only the focus of the research but was indeed a colleague and partner in the fieldwork. I was never too explicit about what data I was gathering, nor did I share my hunches or tentative analyses with him, but he correctly assumed that a brief recounting of what had occurred at school since my last visit would be helpful to the study. He enjoys talking and visiting (I found him to be doing the talking one-third of the total school day during the "time and motion" part of my study), so this self-imposed task came easily to him. At times he reflected on his personal feelings and philosophy and these statements provided valuable insights into his "ideal world." The juxtaposition of actual behavior and ideal behavior provides excellent means for describing and analyzing a cultural system, because it helps point out the satisfactions, the strains, and the paradoxes between real

and ideal behavior. I was fortunate in having an informant who talked easily about aspects of his ideal world.

On a few occasions I formalized the informant role and asked the principal to relate specific accounts. Plans were always discussed in advance when these sessions were to be taped. Three important tapes of this "informant" type were a session in which the principal summarized the opening of school and gave a forecast of the coming year, the session mentioned previously in which he discussed from the wedding list the people who had been invited to his daughter's wedding and reception, and a session recorded in my automobile as we drove through the school attendance area while the principal described the neighborhood to three new teachers accompanying us. In each of these cases he was providing me with perceptions of his universe and/or of his personal value system, each bit of information fitting or challenging the developing ethnographic picture as I have attempted to organize it following the fieldwork.

One final task of informant interviewing was the development of a ten-page questionnaire designed for and distributed to the faculty and staff at the end of the fieldwork. The questionnaire was particularly valuable because it enabled me to obtain systematic data about all the staff, since it had not seemed possible, practical, or even necessary to hold a long taped interview with all 29 members of the regular and part-time staff. This questionnaire provided standard census data and information concerning each teacher's perceptions of the school, the community, and his own classroom. It also provided an opportunity for every staff member to comment on his feelings about his principal, about principals in general, and about his feelings of what an ideal principal should be.

The use of the questionnaire also provided me with a chance to thank the staff for their patience and help during the study. I felt that the questionnaire might give me an opportunity to elicit staff reaction to the research project, and the last statement was an open-ended one: "Some things the researcher may never have understood about this school are ...." The question did not evoke much response, but it was flattering to read, "I think you probably understand more than we may think," and I delighted in the humor of one teacher who assumed (correctly) that I did not know "there is no Kotex dispenser in the [women's] restroom."

COMMENT

A small but growing body of literature gives indication that more attention is being given to anthropologically-oriented field studies in education of the kind described in this paper.[10] That educators are becoming interested in drawing on a broader

10 For a summary of this literature see, e.g., Harry F. Wolcott, "Anthropology and Education," *Review of Educational Research,* Vol. 37, No. 1, February 1967, pp. 82–92. More recent publications include Jacquetta Hill Burnett, "Ceremony, Rites, and Economy in the Student System of an American High School," *Human Organization,* Vol. 28, No. 1, Spring 1969, pp. 1–10; Estelle Fuchs, *Teachers Talk: Views from Inside City Schools,* Anchor Books, Doubleday and Company, New York, 1969; Philip W. Jackson, *Life in Classrooms,* Holt, Rinehart and Winston, New York, 1968; A Richard King, *The School at Mopass,* Holt, Rinehart and Winston, New York, 1967; Eleanor Burke Leacock, *Teaching and Learning in City Schools,* Basic Books, New York, 1969; Louis M. Smith and William Geoffrey, *The Complexities of an Urban Classroom: An Analysis toward a General Theory of Teaching,* Holt, Rinehart and Winston, New York, 1968; Harry F. Wolcott, "Concomitant Learning: An Anthropological Perspective on the Utilization of Media," in Raymond V. Wiman and Wesley C. Meierhenry (eds.), *Educational Media: Theory into Practice,* Charles E. Merrill Publishing Company, Columbus, Ohio, 1969, pp. 217–247.

research base than that provided by either experimental psychology or sociological survey methods is a heartening sign, especially as it means that what actually goes on in classrooms and schools has become a legitimate focus for research efforts.

The purpose of this paper has been to discuss an ethnographic approach to the study of a school administrator. The research has been described here as a field study approach, the specific methodology entailing a major effort in participant observation, complemented by the extensive collection of enumeration and interview data. The potential of being able to provide a substantial ethnographic account of a principalship has provided the *raison d'être* for the study.

I should conclude this discussion by pointing out at least some of the pitfalls in this approach, lest this study and others like it should suddenly and inadvertently precipitate a deluge of field studies in education research by students dissatisfied with methods which appear to be more "rigorous."

Participant observation is not intended to be an apology for an absence of method. It is an excellent method for obtaining certain kinds of data—its proponents argue its superiority to any other single method—but it cannot by itself provide the whole picture. My detractors constantly plague me with the question, "But what can you prove by studying only *one* principal?" An administrator of an elementary school in Harlem has already warned me, "If you had really wanted to learn about administering an elementary school, you would have come to mine." One always faces the problem of generalizability in pursuing an in-depth study of a single case.

The participant-observer approach is a high risk, low yield adventure. It is high risk because unless the fieldwork is eventually translated into a significant, readable (and read) monograph, the only possible gain is in the experiential repertoire of the researcher himself. It is low yield because of the great investment in time and personal effort to obtain basic and often rather commonplace data. The researcher who adopts this approach must face the problems common to participant observation in any setting, especially including a confrontation with oneself as a research instrument.

In educational settings, a researcher contemplating the ethnographic approach faces certain rather unique problems as well, for he undertakes not only a cross-cultural and comparative approach to studying events within his own society, but he must also attempt the difficult task of suddenly assuming the role of formal observer within an institutional framework with which he has probably been in continuous contact since the age of six. Perhaps cross-cultural field experience should be an ordinary prerequisite for conducting ethnographically-oriented research within the narrow cultural boundaries of our American educational system. Even if such a prerequisite cannot always be met, calling attention to it serves the useful function of requiring the researcher to consider the crucial nature of himself as instrument in collecting data through participant observation and interviewing techniques.

AN ANALYTICAL APPROACH TO RESEARCH ON INSTRUCTIONAL METHODS

N. L. Gage

Instructional method constitutes one of the most important and promising but also the most frustrating of the areas of

From: Phi Delta Kappan, *1968, 49, 601– 16. Copyright © 1968 by Phi Delta Kappa, and reproduced by permission of the author and publisher.*

educational research and development. Compared with the areas of learning, subject matter, instructional materials, and organization for instruction, instructional method appeals to the classroom teacher as closest to the heart of his problem. It is all right for a teacher to know about learning, to know his subject matter, to have appropriate instructional materials, and to fit into a given organization for instruction. But what a teacher really wants to know is, "What should I do in the classroom?" If you ask prospective teachers or teachers on the job "Where do you really want help?," I think the reply will deal with some aspect of instructional methods.

Unfortunately, the urgency of this demand has not been accompanied by corresponding success in meeting the demand. Research on teaching has yielded relatively few solid and usable results. The stature of theory and research in, say, learning puts it well ahead of the study of teaching in the struggle for scientific maturity.

Implicit in what I am saying is a basic distinction between research on learning and research on teaching. The former deals with all the conditions under which learning, or a change in behavior due to experience, takes place. And as I have already indicated, the study of learning is relatively mature, well established, with many volumes of substantial literature to its credit. Research on teaching, on the other hand, deals with a subset of the conditions under which learning occurs in one person, namely, the conditions established by the behaviors of another person, called the teacher. As our schools have developed during the past two or three millennia, we have always attempted to promote and improve the learning process through the intermediation of such another person. Until very recently, the assumption that teachers were helpful or even necessary for many important kinds of learning that society wanted to promote went unchallenged. Even today, the challenge of independent study or computer-assisted instruction and other devices is a mere whisper against the thunder of the assumption that teachers are necessary, that teachers are here to stay. My discus-

sion of instructional methods is going to be based on that assumption. It is the relatively neglected, undernourished, and underachieving subset of research on learning which I call research on teaching that I shall deal with here.

The Stanford Center for Research and Development in Teaching is devoted to this problem area. In its conceptual framework, teaching, or the behaviors and characteristics of teachers, stands at the center. This domain contains variables that serve as both independent and dependent variables in the center's program. When the teachers' behaviors and characteristics serve as independent variables, and the pupils' learning and behaviors serve as the dependent variables, then we have research on teacher effectiveness, or, more neutrally, research on teacher effects. On the other hand, when teachers' behaviors and characteristics serve as the dependent variables, and teacher education programs and procedures serve as the independent variables, then we have research on teacher education. Taking both research on teacher education and research on teacher effects as our domain, we have research on teaching, as it is understood in the Stanford Center. The subject of this paper is the center's program of research and development on instructional methods, and my procedure will be to work from the past to the present, from the general to the specific, and then to try for a look at where we are going. When I get down to specifics, I shall be talking primarily about research in which I am involved, rather than all of the research under way in our center.

A FRUITLESS PARADIGM

But first let us look at where research on teaching has been. As the behavioral sciences go, it has a respectably long history but a regrettably inglorious one. Research on teaching has been going on almost as long as research on learning. Some studies were made in the 1910's and 1920's, and quite a few were made during the 1930's, By the early 1950's, substantial reviews and bibliographies of research on teaching began to appear. And during the last decade, the flow of research on teaching has indeed become significant. But the early years did not pay off in solid, replicable, meaningful results that had considerable theoretical or practical value. Positive and significant results were seldom forthcoming, and they survived replication even less often. The research yielded many findings that did not make sense, that did not hang together in any meaningful way.

Under these conditions, as Kuhn[1] has pointed out, research workers are impelled to re-examine their first principles, the paradigms by which they guide their efforts. The model problems and solutions of the community of researchers on teaching were accordingly subjected to more and more reappraisal. Licking the wounds inflicted by their negative results, researchers on teaching built up a modest literature of new conceptual frameworks, approaches, and paradigms for research on teaching.

To illustrate, let me refer to one of the dominant paradigms that even today leads many discussions and research projects into the wilderness. This is the paradigm that says that what we need above all, before we can select and train better teachers, is *the* criterion of teacher effectiveness. Here is one example of that kind of approach:

> The lack of an adequate, concrete, objective, universal criterion for teaching ability is thus the primary source of trouble for all who would

measure teaching. One typical method of attack used in rating scales is to compile a list of broad general traits supposedly desirable for teachers, with respect to which the rater passes judgment on each teacher. This amounts to an arbitrary definition of good teaching, which is subjective and usually vague, but it does not necessarily lead to an identification of it. Only if the traits themselves can be reliably identified can their possessor be identified as a "good teacher" according to the definition laid down in the scale. Even when the scale is made quite specific, relating not to general traits but to concrete procedure, the fundamental difficulty remains, that there is no external and generally accepted criterion against which the scale can be validated to establish the significance of its items.[2]

This kind of writing implies that there is some magic variable that applies to all of teaching, for all pupils, at all grade levels, in all subject matters, and in all objectives. The phrase "the criterion of teacher effectiveness" betokens a degree of generality that has seldom been found in any branch of the behavioral sciences. It also reflects the mistaken notion that such a criterion, largely a matter of values, can be established on the basis of scientific method alone.

The so-called criterion problem misled a whole generation of researchers on teaching, embroiled them in endless and fruitless controversy, and lured them into hopelessly ambitious attempts to predict teacher effectiveness over vast arrays and spans of outcomes, teacher behaviors, time intervals, and pupil characteristics, all on the basis of predictive variables that had only the most tenuous theoretical justifica-

---

[1] T. S. Kuhn, *The Structure of Scientific Revolutions.* Chicago: University of Chicago Press, 1962.

[2] Helen M. Walker, Preface, W. H. Lancelot, *et al., The Measurement of Teaching Efficiency.* New York: Macmillan, 1935, pp. ix–xiv.

tion in the first place. It is little wonder that, when Berelson and Steiner dealt with the subject of teachers' behaviors and characteristics in their inventory of scientific findings in the behavioral sciences, they dismissed the "large number of studies" with the single dismal sentence that "there are no clear conclusions."[3]

MICRO-CRITERIA AND MICRO-TEACHING.

If the global criterion approach had proved to be sterile, what was the alternative? The answer was to take the same path that more mature sciences had already followed: If variables at one level of phenomena do not exhibit lawfulness, break them down. Chemistry, physics, and biology had, in a sense, made progress through making finer and finer analyses of the phenomena and events they dealt with. Perhaps research on teaching would reach firm ground if it followed the same route.

Apparently, a number of students of the problem had this general idea at about the same time. In 1962, writing my chapter on paradigms for the *Handbook of Research on Teaching,* I coined the term, "micro-criteria" of effectiveness. As I said in that chapter:

> ...One solution within the "criterion-of-effectiveness" approach may be the development of the notion of "micro-effectiveness." Rather than seek criteria for the over-all effectiveness of teachers in the many, varied facets of their roles, we may have better success with criteria of effectiveness in small, specifically defined aspects of the role...a sufficient number of laws applying to relatively pure aspects of the teacher's role, if such laws could be developed, might

eventually be combined,...to account for the actual behavior and effectiveness of teachers with pupils under genuine classroom conditions."[4]

A group of workers at Stanford University, to which I was to move a few months later, took a similar view. In the Stanford program for training secondary school teachers, Robert Bush, Dwight Allen, and their co-workers adopted what is now known as the technical skills approach. Technical skills are specific instructional techniques and procedures that a teacher may use in the classroom. They represent an analysis of the teaching process into relatively discrete components that can be used in different combinations in the continuous flow of the teacher's performance. The specific set of technical skills adopted in the teacher education program at Stanford may be quite arguable. Indeed, the list of skills has been revised a number of times over the past few years. What is important is the approach—the attempt to analyze teaching into limited, well-defined components that can be taught, practiced, evaluated, predicted, controlled, and understood in a way that has proven to be altogether impossible for teaching viewed in the larger chunks that occur over a period of an hour, a day, a week, or a year.

When analyzed-teaching in the form of technical skills, is made the focus of our concern, we find it possible to do fairly satisfying research both on teacher education and on teacher effects. The satisfaction comes from being able to measure or manipulate relevant independent variables, perform true experiments, or make careful analyses and measure relevant dependent variables.

[3] B. Berelson and G. Steiner, *Human Behavior: An Inventory of Scientific Findings.* New York: Harcourt, Brace, and World, 1964.

[4] N. L. Gage, "Paradigms for Research on Teaching," in N. L. Gage (ed.), *Handbook on Research on Teaching.* Chicago: Rand, McNally, 1963, pp. 94–141.

The idea of technical skills may be illustrated by the terms used in a recent list of such skills. One was called "establishing set," or the establishment of cognitive rapport between pupils and teacher to obtain immediate involvement in the lesson; one technique for inducing a positive set is the use of relevant analogies. A second technical skill is that called "establishing appropriate frames of reference," or points of view. A third technical skill is that of "achieving closure," or pulling together major points, linking old and new knowledge, at appropriate points within a teaching episode as well as at the end. A fourth technical skill is that of "using questions" in such a way as to elicit the kinds of thought processes and behaviors desired, such as simple recall, or concept formation, or evaluation. Other technical skills are those in "recognizing and obtaining attending behavior," "control of participation," "providing feedback," "employing rewards and punishments," and "setting a model."

These technical skills into which important aspects of the teaching job have been analyzed are not merely the subjects of lectures and discussions in the teacher education program. Rather, they form the basis for the intern's practice teaching prior to his entrance into actual classrooms. This procedure, well known by now as "micro-teaching," consists in getting the trainee to teach a scaled-down teaching exercise. It is scaled down in terms of time because it lasts only five to 10 minutes. It is scaled down in terms of class size, because the intern teaches a group of not more than five pupils, who are brought in and paid to serve as pupils in the micro-teaching clinic. It is scaled down in terms of the task, since the trainee attempts to perform only one of the technical skills in any single micro-teaching session. The sessions are recorded on video tape, and the trainee gets to see

and hear himself immediately after the session. While he looks at and listens to himself, he receives criticisms and suggestions from supervisors trained to be both perceptive and tactful. Then he "reteaches" the same lesson to a new small group of pupils in an attempt to improve on his first performance of the specific technical skill that is his concern in that session.

Obviously, the general idea is subject to many variations. The size of the class can be manipulated, the number of trainees teaching a given group of children can be increased, the duration of the lessons can be lengthened, and the nature of the teaching task can be made more complex so as to embrace a group of technical skills in their real-life combinations. But the idea of analyzing teaching into technical skills remains the heart of the method and provides its power as a paradigm for research.

The research on micro-teaching and technical skills in the Stanford teacher education program has taken the form of experiments in which various procedures for feedback to the trainee are manipulated. Professors Dwight Allen and Frederick McDonald have organized a program of research on variables hypothesized to influence the learning of the technical skills of teaching. Their independent variables fall into three categories: practice variables, feedback variables, and demonstration variables. A practice variable may consist in micro-teaching versus teaching in an actual classroom. A feedback variable may be the positive or negative character of the feedback, or the mediation of the feedback by another person rather than the trainee himself. Finally, a demonstration variable may take the form of the symbolic demonstration, consisting of written or spoken words, or perceptual demonstration, consisting in either live or video taped portrayals of the desired behavior; and each of these can consist either of self-modeling or modeling by others. Other independent variables have been identified, such as the timing of a reinforcement, the amount of practice, and the amount of feedback.

This condensed description of the Allen-McDonald research program can suffice to illustrate the use of the analytic approach in research on teacher education. Their research takes the form of true experiments in which subjects are randomly assigned to different values of the independent variable.

*EFFECTIVENESS
IN EXPLAINING*

I should like to turn now to an example of the way in which the technical skills approach can be applied to the study of teacher effects. This research has dealt with a technical skill that I call "explaining," or the skill of engendering comprehension—usually orally, verbally, and extemporaneously—of some process, concept, or generalization. Explaining occurs in all grade levels and subject matters, whether it is a fifth-grade teacher explaining why the time in New York differs from that in San Francisco or a geologist explaining how the ice age may have been caused by volcanic eruptions. Everyday observation tells us that some people explain aptly, getting to the heart of the matter with just the right terminology, examples, and organization of ideas. Other explainers, on the contrary, get us and themselves all mixed up, use terms beyond our level of comprehension, draw inept analogies, and even employ concepts and principles that cannot be understood without an understanding of the very thing that is being explained. To some of us, it has seemed that explaining comes very close to being the inner essence of instruction, so that

when a teacher is attempting to explain proportionality to his geometry class or irony to his English class, he is behaving more purely as a teacher than when he is attempting, say, to motivate, promote discussion, or maintain discipline. At any rate, we have made some studies of explaining ability in the attempt to determine some of the characteristics of effective explanations.

The first study was made in the micro-teaching clinic at Stanford during the summer of 1965 by J. C. Fortune, R. F. Shutes, and me. We attempted to determine the generality of explaining ability, that is, the degree to which the ability to explain one topic was correlated with the ability to explain another topic, and the degree to which the ability to explain a topic to one group of pupils on one occasion was correlated with the ability to explain the same topic to another group of pupils on another occasion. We also were able to design the study so as to determine the degree to which there was generality over both pupils and topics, or the degree to which the ability to explain one topic to one group of pupils on one day correlated with the ability to explain another topic to another group of pupils on another day. Because there were only 60 pupils to be shared in groups of five among approximately 40 interns in the micro-teaching clinic, the design became quite complex in order to avoid having any intern teach a given topic to the same group of pupils more than once and to avoid having a given group of pupils receive an explanation of the same topic more than once. Accordingly, the 40 social studies interns—and we chose to work with the social studies interns only because there were more of them than any other kind of intern—were divided into five clusters of eight interns each. The lectures dealt with 20 different topics, each consisting of an "Atlantic Report" from *The*

Atlantic. The correlations that we obtained were thus medians of five correlations, each based on four, six, six, six, and eight interns, respectively (10 of the 40 interns being lost to the study for one reason or other).

The index of lecture effectiveness, or what I would like to call the micro-criterion of teacher—explaining ability, was the pupils' mean score on a 10-item test of their comprehension of the main ideas of the lecture, which was presented by each intern in 15 minutes under somewhat standardized conditions. This mean score was adjusted for the mean ability of the pupils in the given group as measured by their scores on all of the other topics. Similarly, any given mean score was adjusted for the difficulty of the topic as measured by the mean score of all groups of pupils on that topic. Thus, the variance of the adjusted mean post-test comprehension scores was attributable not to the ability of the pupils or the difficulty of the topic, but rather to the differences among the teachers. We then investigated the question of the various kinds of generality by determining the median intercorrelations among the various means. The upshot of this part of the study was that generality over topics was nonexistent, and generality over groups was about .4. In other words, the interns were moderately consistent in their ability to explain the same topic to different groups on different occasions, but they were not consistent in their ability to explain different topics.

This study also dealt with the correlations between explaining effectiveness and the pupils' ratings of various aspects of the explanations. The pupils rated the interns' performance with respect to 12 items, such as clarity of aims, organization of the lesson, selection of material, and clarity of presentation. To us it seemed that some of these dimensions should correlate more highly than others with explaining ability. In particular, we hoped that such discriminant validity would be manifest in the form of a higher correlation between the mean rating of the lecture for "clarity of presentation" than for any of the other items of the Stanford Teacher Competence Appraisal Guide. Our hope was borne out; the correlation of the adjusted mean post-test comprehension scores with pupils' ratings of "clarity of presentation" was .56, higher than that with any of the other rating scale items. This result seems to us to support the validity of both the index of lecture effectiveness and the mean ratings by the pupils.

During the school year 1965–1966, I was able, in collaboration with Barak Rosenshine, to undertake a replication and extension of this study in the public schools. Because there was no lack of students in the high school classes, taught by their own teachers, we did not become involved in the complexities of design necessary in the micro-teaching clinic. To put it very briefly, we got 40 eleventh-grade social studies teachers each to deliver a 15-minute lecture on an "Atlantic Report" on Yugoslavia taken from *The Atlantic*. The teachers had been given the article several days in advance, and had been told to prepare a lecture that would enable their pupils to answer a 10-item multiple-choice test of comprehension of the article's main ideas. To guide them in preparing their lecture, they were given five of the multiple-choice questions that would be asked, while the other five questions were withheld. After the 15-minute lecture, in which the teachers were permitted to use the blackboard but no other aids, their students took the 10-item test. They also rated the teacher's lecture on items similar to those I have already described. The next day, the same teachers and classes did the same things, except that the subject matter was an "Atlantic Report" on Thailand; again the teachers had been given five of the 10 items as a guide to the kind of lecture that they should prepare and had been told to focus on the explanation of the major ideas, concepts, and principles brought out in the article, which constituted the curriculum for this bit of teaching. On the third day, the classes heard a third lecture, one that was the same for all classes, an audiotape-recorded 15-minute lecture on Israel, a verbatim reading of an "Atlantic Report." Then the pupils took a 10-item test based on that article.

The class mean on the Israel test was used to adjust the class means on Yugoslavia and Thailand for between-class differences in ability. Our reasoning was that the score on such a test of comprehension of a uniform lecture would be more useful in controlling relevant kinds of ability than would the usual scholastic aptitude test. The class means on Yugoslavia and Thailand were also adjusted for teacher differences in the content-relevance of the lecture, as determined by scoring the transcript of the lecture for relevance to the 10 items on the comprehension test. We then assumed that the variance that still remained in the adjusted comprehension test means of the classes would reflect differences between the teachers in what we were concerned with, namely, the intellectual style and process of the teacher's lecture. In this study, the teacher's adjusted effectiveness index on Yugoslavia correlated .47 with his effectiveness on Thailand; i.e., there was considerable generality of effectiveness over topics, even after student ability and content relevance had been partialed out.

It should be noted that we were using the micro-teaching idea in this investigation. The teaching was restricted to just one aspect of the teacher's role, namely, ability to explain the current social, political, and economic situation in another country. The curriculum was also scaled down. We also used another major feature of the micro-teaching clinic, the video tape recorders, which made it possible for us to study the teacher's behavior, verbal and nonverbal, at leisure.

One major question was that of whether our criterion, or micro-criterion, of teacher effectiveness in explaining, namely, the mean comprehension score of the pupils, adjusted for both mean pupil ability and content-relevance, contained variance that would be manifested in something about the lecture that was visible or audible. In other words, was there some difference between good and poor explanations that was worth trying to analyze? So W. R. Unruh picked two lectures on Yugoslavia that were extremely high on our index of effectiveness and two that were extremely low. He had eight judges read the article on Yugoslavia, take the comprehension test, and then watch and listen to all four of these lectures. Then the judges ranked the lectures in terms of perceived effectiveness in engendering comprehension as measured by the 10-item test. It turned out that the judges' postdictions were quite significantly more accurate than could have been expected on the basis of chance, and we were accordingly reassured that our micro-criterion was indeed reflected in something that could be seen or heard in the lecture.

Rosenshine's concern in this investigation was to determine the cognitive and stylistic correlates of the lecture's effectiveness. For this purpose, he used extreme groups to minimize the labor of scoring a host of variables about which we had no great conviction. So the 10 most effective explanations on Yugoslavia were identified and also the 10 least effective. From these he chose at random five of the most effective and five of the least effective. Then groups of judges and content analysts worked over the transcripts of the lectures, scoring and rating them on a host of variables. Some of these were sentence fragments, the average sentence length, the number of prepositional phrases per sentence, and so on. Other variables dealt with the number of self-references by the teacher, or with various aspects of syntax, or instructional set, familiarization, uses of previous knowledge, mobilizing sets, attention focusing procedures, organization, emphasis, amount of repetition and redundancy, the number of words per minute, and so on.

The variables that discriminated between the five best and the five worst lectures on Yugoslavia were then tried out on the other set of five best and five worst lectures on Yugoslavia to see if they still discriminated. Those that survived this first cross-validation were then tried out on the best and worst lectures on Thailand. At the last accounting, two characteristics of the lectures had survived this kind of validation and cross-validation procedure. These variables were what Rosenshine calls "explaining links," or the degree to which the teacher describes the how, why, or effect of something, and the "rule-eg-rule" pattern, or the degree to which the teacher states a generalization, gives examples of it, and then summarizes a series of illustrations at a higher level of generality than the illustrations themselves. These two variables not only seem to be valid in our data but also are reliably rated by independent judges. Nonetheless, these must not be considered to be firmly established findings; they are merely examples of the kinds of conclusions to which research of this kind can lead.

Currently, we are in the process of scoring all of the explanations on all of the variables that appear to hold any promise, and we will then undertake studies of the complete correlation matrices involving not only the indices of explanation effectiveness, but also all of the characteristics of the explanations, and the ratings of the lectures by the pupils who heard them. Such a complete correlational study will throw light on the consistency from one lecture to another of the indices of lecture effectiveness, and the stylistic characteristics of the lectures, and also their intercorrelations.

LIVE AND PROGRAMMED TEACHING

What I have been describing is of course a correlational study. Along with its advantages in permitting the exploration of a wide variety of possible correlates of explaining ability as they occur under fairly normal conditions, it also has the disadvantage of making causal interpretations hazardous. For this reason, studies of this kind ought to proceed fairly rapidly into experiments in which the different ways of explaining will be based, at least in part, on leads obtained from our correlational studies.

Such experimental research may lead toward quite novel methods of teaching that could never be developed on the basis of studies of teaching the way teaching is. Stolurow has contrasted the approach of "modeling the master teacher" with that of "mastering the teaching model." The first approach is that of studying the most effective teachers we can find in order to find out how they behave and what they are like so that we can attempt to produce more teachers like them. Many research workers see little promise in this approach. They recommend that we undertake instead to develop wholly new models of the teaching process designed for optimal effectiveness, regardless of their similarity to the way teaching now goes on in the normal classroom.

The teaching model that many advocates of this approach have in mind is that of programmed instruction, particularly computer-assisted programmed instruction. As Suppes[5] and Atkinson and others have described this revolutionary undertaking in research and development on instruction, it holds out great promise indeed. Before too long, the annoying problems in the hardware will have been solved. After a somewhat longer time, we may expect substantial and well-validated programmed curricular materials to have been developed in all the subject matters and grade levels. As one who has seen the highly developed installations at the Brentwood School in East Palo Alto, California, I must share the optimism of Suppes and Atkinson, and other developers of computer-assisted instruction.

Their very success, or coming success, raises problems for the kind of instructional methods with which we have been concerned. Upon superficial examination, at least, certain major problems of ordinary classroom teaching seem to be clearly surmounted by computer-assisted instruction. For example, the problem of the cognitive complexity in the teacher's task, of how the teacher can say just the right thing at the right time to develop a concept or formulate a theory, is apparently well handled, at least in principle, by computer-assisted instruction. Its programs can be worked out and tried out in meticulous detail, well in advance, at leisure, by the most skilled curriculum experts in the land, and then made available in all their subtlety and complexity to every teacher who uses the program. Another major problem in the ordinary classroom is that of individualizing instruction. No matter how we group our pupils between schools,

within schools, or within classrooms, we still have the problem of adjusting the rate and direction of the teaching and learning process to the needs and abilities of the individual pupil; here again, at least in principle, computer-assisted instruction seems at first glance to have the better of the live teacher.

While pondering these problems, I got some help from a restatement of the idea of individualized instruction in a recent paper by Philip Jackson.[6] As he put it,

> Individualizing instruction, in the educator's sense, means injecting humor into a lesson when a student seems to need it, and quickly becoming serious when he is ready to settle down to work; it means thinking of examples that are uniquely relevant to the student's previous experience and offering them at just the right time; it means feeling concerned over whether or not a student is progressing, and communicating that concern in a way that will be helpful; it means offering appropriate praise, not just because positive reinforcers strengthen response tendencies, but because the student's performance is deserving of human admiration; it means, in short, responding *as* an individual *to* an individual.

Individualization in this sense is much more than allowing for differences in speed of moving through a program or providing different branches or routes through the material.

Jackson's analysis of this kind of limitation in computer-assisted instruction should be placed alongside of the indications by Suppes that tutoring and dialogue, which are higher levels of instruction than drill-practice, are still well in the

---

[5] P. Suppes, "The Uses of Computers in Education," *Scientific American*, 1966, pp. 207–20. See also Suppes' April, 1968, KAPPAN article, "Computer Technology and the Future of Education."

[6] P. W. Jackson, *The Teacher and the Machine: Observations on the Impact of Educational Technology.* (Mimeographed, University of Chicago, 1966).

future as capabilities of computer-based instruction. Hence any fears about the rapid obsolescence of live teachers, even where narrowly defined cognitive objectives are concerned, are quite unwarranted. That is, there will be a need for teachers to use the kinds of technical skills, including explaining, with which the analytic approach being developed at Stanford and elsewhere is concerned. We shall have to continue to grapple with the problems of cognitive complexity and individualization through the medium of the live, human teacher even in the realm of the well-formulated cognitive objectives. And there will always be the indispensable role of teachers in assisting pupils in attaining various kinds of affective and social learnings in the classroom.

Accordingly, group discussions, role playing, teaching for divergent thinking, as well as the technical skills I have already mentioned, are all the subject of various research and development projects now under way in the Stanford Center for Research and Development in Teaching. We are also looking at the way in which the organizational context influences the teacher's choices among ways to teach.

IN ONE WORD ...

In conclusion, let me refer again to what I see as one basic new theme in the research and development in teaching that is now under way at Stanford and elsewhere. If it were necessary to sum it up in one word, my word would be *analysis*, breaking down the complexities that have proven to be so unmanageable when dealt with as a whole.

We are no longer crippled by the notion that because there is the one word "teaching," there is one, single, overall criterion of effectiveness in teaching that will take essentially the same form wherever teaching occurs. Even if the present analyses prove not to be viable, they will not be replaced by the old, global, conceptually impossible, complex variables that I see as one reason for the fruitlessness of so much of research on teaching in the past. Instead, they will be replaced by other analyses of teaching, perhaps even finer analyses, until we get the sets of lawful relationships between variables that will mark the emergence of a scientific basis for the practice of teaching. It may well be that a 15-minute explanation of a five-page magazine article is still too large a unit of teaching behavior to yield valid, lawful knowledge. It may well be that the mean score on a 10-item test of comprehension, adjusted for student ability and content relevance of the lecture, is still too large and complex a dependent variable. But, compared with the massive, tangled, and unanalyzable units that have typically been studied in the past—in research on the lecture method, the discussion method, and class size, for example—such units seem precise and manageable indeed. And eventually, of course, we shall have to put teaching back together again into syntheses that are better than the teaching that goes on now. I think it would be safe to say that there is abundant hope of our being able to develop a scientifically grounded set of answers to every teacher's central question, "What should I do in the classroom?"

NEGRO CHILDREN'S PERFORMANCE ON A DISCRIMINATION TASK AS A FUNCTION OF EXAMINER RACE AND VERBAL INCENTIVE

Wallace A. Kennedy / Manuel Vega

As the pattern of integration unfolds across the country, it is apparent that the number of Negro students having white teachers, counselors, and examiners will greatly increase. Katz (1964) has suggested that these changes, inherent in the desegregation process, are likely to cause detrimental changes in the performance of Negro students if they are rejected by white classmates or teachers, whereas acceptance by white peers and adults should "endow scholastic success with high incentive value [p. 396]." It would seem appropriate, therefore, to gather information about the nature of interactions between Negro students and white teachers, or examiners.

Perhaps one of the most relevant variables in the educational process is the use of verbal praise and blame as incentives for performance and as means of informing students of the quality of their work. The Human Development Clinic of Florida State University, study-

From: Journal of Personality and Social Psychology, *1965, 2, 839–43. Copyright* © *1965 by the American Psychological Association, and reproduced by permission of the authors and APA.*

ing these incentives under various experimental conditions, has been interested in the performance of Negro children, as well as that of white children. Tiber and Kennedy (1964), studying the effects of these verbal incentives on intelligence test performance of different social groups (480 second- and third-graders divided into middle-class white, lower-class white, and lower-class Negro), found no significant difference between incentive groups, and no significant interaction between type of incentive and social group.

Kennedy and Willcutt (1963), investigating the effects of praise and blame on a discrimination task under the variables of grade, intelligence, sex, race, social class, school, and differences between white examiners (720 second-, fourth-, seventh-, and tenth-graders equally divided between white and Negro races), found praise to be more effective for both Negro and white children, than was blame, which was actually detrimental to performance.

Although Shuey (1958) implies that the race of the examiner has no significant influence on the performance of Negro subjects, other suggestions in the literature

(Dreger & Miller, 1960; Katz, 1964; Trent, 1954) that the race of the examiner might effect Negro performance led to the current study, for it would seem important for the psychologist working in the field to know the nature of the effect of his race upon the performance of Negro children whom he meets in his daily routine. The logical first step to more accurate interpretation and prediction of the behavior of Negro children under white examiners would be to determine whether a significant difference exists in the performance of Negro children tested under white and Negro examiners.

METHOD

Task

Due to the well-known discrepancy between the performance of Negro and white children (Dreger & Miller, 1960; Garth, 1931; Kennedy, Van De Riet, & White, 1963; Klineberg, 1935; Pintner, 1931; Shuey, 1958), a discrimination task which all subjects could solve in time was chosen as appropriate for the purposes of this study. The task (conceived by Turner, 1962, after Chalmers[1]) consisted of 24 oddity-problem stimulus cards presenting four patterns, one of which was different from the other three, at eight levels of difficulty involving the distribution of 32 black squares on a 64-square white checkerboard. Each square was divided into four quadrants of 16 squares each, 8 black. Each quadrant was subdivided into subquadrants of 4 squares each, 2 black, the placement of which was done randomly. The most difficult discrimination was formed by moving 1 of the 64 squares from one quadrant to another, according to a table of random numbers. The second most difficult involved mov-

[1] E. L. Chalmers, unpublished data, Florida State University.

ing 2 squares, and so on down to the least difficult problem where 8 squares were moved. On the easier levels a restriction of random placement was upheld in order to keep a balance between the remaining three quadrants. Thus, when 3 squares were being moved from one quadrant, 1 each was assigned to the other three quadrants.

The discrimination task was administered through an apparatus designed along with the task. The stimulus cards appeared on a viewing screen below which were four momentary switches corresponding to the four patterns on the card. The apparatus timed, in one hundredths of a second, the period between the appearance of the stimulus card on the screen and the subject's pressing of the switch. A trial consisted of the same-order presentation of all 24 of the stimulus cards to each subject.

Normative data, using 1,042 subjects, has been gathered on this task by four studies under the auspices of the Human Development Clinic (Kennedy, Turner, & Lindner, 1962; Kennedy & Willcutt, 1963; Turner, 1962; Willcutt & Kennedy, 1963).

Subjects

Selected from the second-, sixth-, and tenth-grades, the 324 Negro subjects were public school pupils at the Pine Park and Northside schools in Havana, Florida (Gadsden County). Half of them were tested by Negro examiners, half by white examiners.

Materials

The Short Form A of the 1957 California Test of Mental Maturity was used to determine the intellectual level: high, range = 85–140, $M = 89.61$, $SD = 9.84$; medium, range = 73–84, $M = 79.19$, $SD = 5.77$; low, range = 47–72, $M = 70.60$, $SD = 6.37$. This represented a random sample of the Negro children in these grades in Gadsden County.

The definition of intelligence

poses some problems in that obviously the definition at the second-grade level is somewhat different from that at the tenth-grade level. However, the mean and standard deviation were virtually identical at the three grade levels: Grade 2, $M = 81.98$, $SD = 1.20$; Grade 6, $M = 78.81$, $SD = 1.13$; Grade 10, $M = 78.61$, $SD = 1.03$.

EXAMINERS

Six examiners, male graduate students in psychology, three white from Florida State University and three Negro from Florida A and M University, trained in the use of the apparatus and uniform delivery of the verbal incentives, were periodically checked in the field to keep procedures as uniform as possible.[2]

PROCEDURE

The subjects, tested individually at their schools, were given the first trial on the discrimination task, the experimental incentive condition, and a second trial on the discrimination task. Each examiner worked with the same number of subjects in each of the experimental incentive treatment groups—praise, blame, control.

All subjects were read the following instructions:

This game is to see if you can tell the difference between designs. When I turn on the light, you will see four designs there in front of you. [Examiner shows subject where to look.] You are to find the one that is not the same as the others. Three of the designs will be the same, but one will be different. As soon as you find the one that is different, press the switch handle underneath it. For

[2] Statistical tests of significant differences run on within-race variations of the six examiners indicated nonsignificant differences between same-race examiners.

example, if the first design on the left is different from the rest, you press the first switch on the left. If the second design is different, press the second switch. And so on. Have you any questions?

The examiner then demonstrated a sample card to make sure that the subject understood the design-switch combination. Although the difficulty of instructions was perhaps too high for second-graders, the combination of instructions and demonstration was effective: the error variable was virtually nonexistent. Following the demonstration, instructions were continued:

Now, you try the switches yourself. Press number one, please, two, three, and four. OK. The first card is just for practice so you can see what the designs look like. You press the switch under the design that is different from all the rest. Ready? [If the subject pressed the correct switch, the examiner said, "good."]

All the cards will not be the same, but the problem will be the same. That is, to find the one design that is different from all the rest on the card. Any questions?

Put both of your hands palm down on the table in front of the switches. Keep them on the table until you are ready to press the switch. Do not jump ahead. Press the switch as quickly as you can, but be sure to press the one under the design that is different. Ready?

If the subject had further questions, the appropriate portion of the directions was reread. If necessary, a second sample card was used. The examiner was as active as necessary to assure that the subject fully understood what was required of him.

A trial consisted of 24 stimulus cards randomly ordered at each difficulty level, but in sequence as far as difficulty was concerned. That is, the easier discrimination problems were presented first, building up to the more difficult. Or more specifically, the subjects started at Difficulty Level 1, worked up to Level 8, and then back to Level 1, to repeat the pattern through the 24 cards.

At the end of Trial 1 reproof was administered to subjects assigned to the reproof group as follows:

> Well, that's it. [Pause] Your scores are not nearly as good as I thought they would be. I'm really disappointed. I think these are the worst scores I've gotten yet. [Pause] But perhaps if we ran through the cards again. I'll tell you what. Just forget these scores. Let's go through the cards again. Do you understand the directions? Let me repeat them once more.

The directions were then reread verbatim and the same 24 cards readministered in the same order.

Subjects in the praised group were told:

> Well, that's it. [Pause] Your scores are very good. I knew you would do well, but you did even better than I expected. I am really pleased. These look like the best scores I have gotten yet. [Pause] Now, I'd like you to go through the cards again. To get the time the same, I'll repeat the directions.

Subjects in the control group were asked questions of a biographical nature during the interval between trials. The time to do this was equated as closely as possible with that used to present the verbal incentives.

At the end of the second trial all subjects were asked not to discuss the experiment with anyone. Those who served in the reproof group were detained and given high praise for their two performances to counteract any adverse effect resulting from the reproof.

CRITERION MEASURE

The reaction time between the stimulus card appearing on the screen and the depression of the subject switch was the criterion measure for the experiment. The major variance studied was the mean reaction time of Trials 1 and 2 and the mean reaction time difference between Trials 1 and 2.

The discrimination task used for this study was such that all subjects, given time, could solve the problem. A check was kept on the error responses, which were so few as to be only a random effect. No correction was made for the few errors which appeared.

STATISTICAL DESIGN

A general linear hypothesis analysis was performed using as a criterion the difference scores (mean reaction time score difference between Trial 1 and Trial 2).

This was a $2 \times 3 \times 3 \times 3$ analysis of variance with 2 examiner races, 3 grade levels, 3 intelligence levels, and 3 reward conditions. A difference score was used because, although there was no significant difference between the means of the 54 cells on Trial 1, there was a considerable amount of variability within the cells.

The reaction time of the subject was the dependent measure. That is, it was the time in seconds intervening between the stimulus onset and the subject's pressing the response switch. The individual reaction time for each card was converted into trial means for each subject.

Because the BI-MED 5 program used for the statistical analysis would not handle signs, a constant (7) was added to the difference score means. However, in the table of means the constant value has been removed and the signs restored for clarity of presentation.

RESULTS

Table 1 illustrates the significant *F* ratios for the statistical analysis of the mean difference scores between Trials 1 and 2. Significant were examiner race, experimental incentive, and the interaction between the two, as well as their combined interaction with grade level.

TABLE 1

SIGNIFICANT *F* RATIOS FOR MEAN SCORE DIFFERENCES BETWEEN TRIALS 1 AND 2

Variable	df	F
Examiner race (A)	1/270	15.90***
Grade level (B)	2/270	2.19
Intelligence (C)	2/270	.53
Reward (D)	2/270	9.30**
A × B	2/270	.61
A × C	2/270	1.61
A × D	2/270	6.00*
A × B × C	4/270	.64
A × B × D	4/270	3.06*
A × C × D	4/270	1.05
A × B × C × D	8/270	.71
B × C	4/270	2.00
B × D	4/270	1.50
B × C × D	8/270	.77
C × D	4/270	1.40

* $p = .05$.
** $p = .01$.
*** $p = .001$.

Illustrated in Table 2 are the significant mean differences and their standard deviations. For examiner race, subjects working under white examiners showed an improvement of .67 from Trial 1 to Trial 2, while subjects under Negro examiners improved their overall performance on Trial 2 by 1.33.

Praise and control resulted in a greater decrease in speed of performance for all subjects, than did blame (praise, 1.40; control, 1.33; blame, .27).

Working under white examiners, subjects reacted to praise and control with improvements of 1.37 and 1.16, respectively, while they suffered a decrement of −.53 under white-examiner blame. On the contrary, subjects working under Negro examiners reacted to blame with a 1.06 improvement in score (praise, 1.43; control, 1.51). In other words, all Negro subjects reacted to praise and control with decreased reaction time on Trial 2 with no

TABLE 2

MEAN AND STANDARD DEVIATION FOR MEAN SCORE DIFFERENCES BETWEEN TRIALS 1 AND 2 BY EXAMINER RACE (A), GRADE LEVEL (B), AND EXPERIMENTAL INCENTIVE (D)

A × B × D	Praise		Blame		Control		Total	
	M	SD	M	SD	M	SD	M	SD
White								
2	1.63	1.58	−1.21	2.13	1.07	2.06		
6	.76	1.57	.09	1.75	.87	1.05		
10	1.73	.93	− .47	1.75	1.54	.78		
Total	1.37	1.46	− .53	1.96	1.16	1.44	.67	1.85
Negro								
2	1.59	1.62	.99	3.70	1.35	1.40		
6	.82	1.74	.77	1.24	1.86	1.76		
10	1.87	.96	1.43	1.58	1.33	1.10		
Total	1.43	1.55	1.06	2.45	1.51	1.46	1.33	1.88
Grand total	1.40	6.66	.27	2.35	1.33	1.46	1.00	

TABLE 3

NEWMAN-KEULS SEQUENTIAL RANGE TEST SIGNIFICANT
MEAN SCORE DIFFERENCES BETWEEN GROUPS AS
DIVIDED BY EXAMINER RACE, EXPERIMENTAL
INCENTIVE, AND GRADE LEVEL

Experimental group			White/blame/2		White/blame/6		White/blame/10	
	M	SD	M	SD	M	SD	M	SD
Negro/praise/2	1.59	1.62	−1.21	2.13	.09	1.75	−.47	1.75
Negro/praise/6	.82	1.74	−1.21	2.13			−.47	1.75
Negro/praise/10	1.87	.96	−1.21	2.13	.09	1.75	−.47	1.75
Negro/blame/2	.99	3.70	−1.21	2.13			−.47	1.75
Negro/blame/6	.77	1.24	−1.21	2.13			−.47	1.75
Negro/blame/10	1.43	1.58	−1.21	2.13	.09	1.75	−.47	1.75
Negro/control/2	1.35	1.40	−1.21	2.13	.09	1.75	−.47	1.75
Negro/control/6	1.86	1.76	−1.21	2.13	.09	1.75	−.47	1.75
Negro/control/10	1.33	1.10	−1.21	2.13	.09	1.75	−.47	1.75
White/praise/2	1.63	1.58	−1.21	2.13	.09	1.75	−.47	1.75
White/praise/6	.76	1.57	−1.21	2.13			−.47	1.75
White/praise/10	1.73	.93	−1.21	2.13	.09	1.75	−.47	1.75
White/blame/2	−1.21	2.13	−1.21	2.13	.09	1.75		
White/blame/6	.09	1.75	−1.21	2.13	.09	1.75		
White/blame/10	− .47	1.75					−.47	1.75
White/control/2	1.07	2.06	−1.21	2.13			−.47	1.75
White/control/6	.87	1.05	−1.21	2.13			−.47	1.75
White/control/10	1.54	1.44	−1.21	2.13	.09	1.75	−.47	1.75

Note.—No group differences, other than those listed in table, were significant.

difference in response according to examiner race. However, reaction to blame was different under white and Negro examiners, with a resulting decrement in performance under white examiners and in improvement under Negro examiners.

A Newman-Keuls sequential range test run on the data for the interaction between examiner race and verbal incentive indicated that subjects working under white examiners in the blame group reacted significantly differently from every other experimental group. No other groups differed significantly from each other.

The significant results of the Newman-Keuls sequential range test performed on the significant interaction data between examiner race, verbal incentive, and grade level are illustrated in Table 3. It is only at the sixth-grade level that blame administered by white examiners does not consistently produce mean score differences between Trials 1 and 2 which are significantly different from other experimental group mean score differences.

DISCUSSION

It is apparent that the only significant difference between Negro subjects working under white and Negro examiners is the differential reaction to blame. Under white examiners Negro students react to blame in the same manner as white students under white examiners: with a decrement in performance (as demonstrated in Kennedy & Willcutt, 1963, pp. 43–44). Under Negro examiners Negro students react to blame with an increment in performance similar to that under praise and no incentive. Thus the fact that Negro students showed a greater improvement in performance under Negro examiners is directly related to the detrimental effect of blame from white examiners.

It appears then, that the verbal incentive, blame, will have an increasingly detrimental effect on simple learning tasks as Negro children encounter white examiners, teachers, and administrators.

REFERENCES

DREGER, R. M., & MILLER, K. S. Comparative psychological studies of Negroes and whites in the United States. *Psychological Bulletin*, 1960, 57, 361–402.

GARTH, T. A. *Race psychology: A study of racial mental differences*. New York: McGraw-Hill, 1931.

KATZ, I. Review of evidence relating to effects of desegregation on the intellectual performance of Negroes. *American Psychologist*, 1964, 19, 381–399.

KENNEDY, W. A., TURNER, A. J., & LINDNER, R. Effectiveness of praise and blame as a function of intelligence. *Perceptual and Motor Skills*, 1962, 15, 143–149.

KENNEDY, W. A., VAN DE RIET, V., & WHITE, J. C., JR. A normative sample of intelligence and achievement of Negro elementary school children in the southeastern United States. *Child Development Monographs*, 1963, 28 (6, Ser. No. 90).

KENNEDY, W. A. & WILLCUTT, H. C. *Motivation of school children*. (United States Department of Health, Education, and Welfare Cooperative Research Project No. 1929) Tallahassee: Florida State University, 1963.

KLINEBERG, O. *Race differences*. New York: Harper, 1935.

PINTNER, R. *Intelligence testing: Methods and results*. New York: Holt, 1931.

SHUEY, AUDREY M. *The testing of Negro intelligence*. Lynchburg, Va.: Bell, 1958.

TIBER, N., & KENNEDY, W. A. The effects of incentives on the intelligence test performance of different social groups. *Journal of Consulting Psychology*, 1964, 28, 187.

TRENT, R. D. The color of the investigator as a variable in experimental research with Negro subjects. *Journal of Social Psychology*, 1954, 40, 281–287.

TURNER, A. J. *Discrimination reaction time as a function of anxiety and task difficulty*. (Doctoral dissertation, Florida State University) Ann Arbor, Mich.: University Microfilms, 1962, No. 62–3520.

WILLCUTT, H. C., & KENNEDY, W. A. Relation of intelligence to effectiveness of praise and reproof as reinforcers for fourth-graders. *Perceptual and Motor Skills*, 1963, 17, 695–697.

THE OBSERVATION
OF CLASSROOM BEHAVIOR

Herbert M. Kliebard

Writing in 1904 on the relationship between theory and practice, Dewey recommended that a basic element in teacher training should be the observation of classroom behavior. He stressed that this observation "should not be too definitely practical in aim." Rather, it should be done "with reference to seeing the interaction of mind, to see how teacher and pupils react to each other—how mind answers mind" (p. 26). Obviously, Dewey was not concerned here with the commonsense notion of the experienced teacher passing on the "tricks of the trade" to the novice. Instead, he saw the observation of teaching as contributing to a sense of the nature of teaching—to an insight into the special kind of world that one finds in the classroom.

Implicit in Dewey's proposal is a kind of framework or system of analysis through

From: The Way Teaching Is, *Washington, D.C., 1966, 45–76. Copyright © 1966 by the Association for Supervision and Curriculum Development and the National Education Association, and reprinted with permission of the Association for Supervision and Curriculum Development, the National Education Association, and the author.*

which this observation could be carried on. Although observation schedules and systems appeared in the literature of the early part of this century, they frequently took the form of supervisors' checklists designed to rate teachers rather than to study teaching. It has been largely within the past decade that descriptive studies involving the observation of classroom teaching and the development of instruments of analysis have become prominent. Medley and Mitzel (1963) have ably reviewed this trend and discussed its implications.

While the studies involving the observation of classroom behavior all reflect, in a sense, a common research orientation, they tend to differ in other respects. Essentially, what all the investigators undertaking such research share are a desire to understand the nature of teaching and a feeling that it can be best understood by studying it directly as it goes forward in the classroom. The variety that is reflected in these studies stems generally from the predilections and interests of the investigators, but more particularly from three basic decisions which they are called upon

373

to make. It is their approach to these decisions that tends to give each study its distinctive character.

Probably the most critical decision is that of determining the range of behaviors that will be observed. Observing everything that happens in a classroom is an obviously futile task. Any observer finds it necessary to single out certain dimensions of behavior and to ignore others. The choice reflects a central focus which may be based on philosophical, sociological, or psychological considerations. It is, of course, possible to select a completely unrelated congeries of behaviors to observe, but most investigators choose to focus on a set of behaviors which represents a given perspective. Thus one set of observations is concerned with the logic of teaching while others focus on classroom climate, or critical thinking, or communication patterns.

A second decision is concerned with the setting and population being observed. Not only are population samples drawn from various grade levels, but they frequently are selected in terms of other special interests of the investigators. Certain studies, for example, observe classes grouped only in given subject areas; other investigators are interested in observing gifted students or underachievers. At times the setting and population samples are central to the overall framework of the study and sometimes more or less incidental to the research design.

The third source of variety in investigations of classroom behavior is the observational technique or procedure. Basically, there are two alternatives here: to record the observations directly in the classroom while the lesson is going on; or to perform this task indirectly through tape recordings, kinescopes, or typescripts. Sometimes a combination of both methods is used. As a rule, observational procedures tend to be a function of the kinds of behavior being observed and the complexity of the system of analysis. Obviously, if such factors as facial expression and physical movement are to be observed, then tape recordings and typescripts alone would be inadequate. On the other hand, if a complex analysis is attempted involving several dimensions of a particular unit of behavior, this would preclude direct and immediate observation as the only procedure.

If the studies reviewed here, then, share one perspective, it is that some understanding of the process of teaching can be gained through observation of what goes on in the classroom. This shared perspective, however, does not preclude wide differences in such matters as which behaviors will be observed and which will be ignored, what students and teachers will be observed in what kind of classroom setting, and what techniques or procedures will be used in making the observations. The decisions that investigators make with respect to such questions as these cannot normally be described as good or bad, right or wrong. These decisions simply reflect basic interests and concerns of those who make them.

In *The Language of the Classroom: Meanings Communicated in High School Teaching,* Bellack, Davitz, Kliebard, and Hyman (1963) are concerned primarily with various kinds of meaning as they are conveyed through the language that teachers and pupils use. Their decision to focus on this dimension of teaching is based on at least two assumptions. The first is that the principal function of language is the communication of meaning. Analysis of the language of the classroom, therefore, offers the most promising way of studying the communication of meaning. This, they point out, is consistent with Wittgenstein's notion that "the meaning of a word is its use in the language" (1953, p. 20). Second, they use Wittgenstein's description of various kinds of verbal activity as "language games" as a basis for treating teaching as a game in the sense that it is a form of rule-governed behavior. Much of the study, therefore, is concerned with delineating the ground rules of teaching and with describing the respective roles that the teacher and student players play when engaged in the game of teaching.

The classes studied were drawn from seven high schools in the New York metropolitan area. Fifteen tenth- and twelfth-grade classes in problems of American democracy comprised the final sample. The teacher in each of these classes was asked to teach a four-day unit on international trade basing his lessons on the first four chapters of the pamphlet, *International Economic Problems,* by Calderwood. All of the 60 class sessions were recorded on tape from which typescripts were later prepared. Estimates of verbal intelligence were obtained for all of the students involved, and pretests and posttests of knowledge of international trade were administered.

With language as the central focus of the study, a key methodological problem was that of devising the unit of language behavior which would serve as the basis for the analysis. On the basis of studying sample tape recordings and typescripts of class sessions, Bellack (1965) conceived of four basic verbal maneuvers which describe what the teachers and pupils do pedagogically when engaged in the game of teaching. These maneuvers were called *pedagogical moves,* a term consistent with the game metaphor. Further analysis of the tape recordings and typescripts indicated that all of the observed verbal behavior by both teachers and pupils could be classified in terms of these moves. The four pedagogical moves are described as follows (p. 4):

> *Structuring.* Structuring moves serve the pedagogical functions of setting the context for subsequent behavior by launching or halting-excluding interaction between students and teachers. For example, teachers frequently begin a class period with a structuring move in which they focus attention on the topic or problem to be discussed during that session.

> *Soliciting.* Moves in this category are designed to elicit a verbal response, encourage persons addressed to attend to something, or elicit a physical response. All questions are solicitations, as are commands, imperatives and requests.

> *Responding.* These moves bear a reciprocal relationship to soliciting moves and occur only in relation to them. Their pedagogical function is to fulfill the expectation of soliciting moves. Thus, students' answers to teachers' questions are classified as responding moves.

> *Reacting.* These moves are occasioned by a structuring, soliciting, responding, or another reacting move, but are not directly elicited by them. Pedagogically, these moves serve to modify (by clarifying, synthesizing, or expanding) and/or to rate (positively or negatively) what has been said previously. Reacting moves differ from responding moves, in that while a responding move is always directly elicited by a solicitation, preceding moves serve only as the occasion for reactions. Rating by a teacher of a student's response, for example, is designated a reacting move.

Pedagogical moves not only provided the basic unit of analysis but served to describe the first of the dimensions of meaning with which Bellack and his associates were concerned, pedagogical meaning. This refers to the distinctively didactic sense of the verbal unit. In addition, pedagogical moves are combined into larger units of discourse called *teaching cycles.* This is done by viewing two of the moves, structuring and soliciting, as initiatory moves, and the other two, responding and reacting, as reflexive. A typical teaching cycle, then, might consist of a teacher solicitation followed by a pupil response which in turn is followed by the teacher's reaction to the responding move. A new cycle begins when a new initiatory move is made.

A second dimension of meaning with which the investigators were concerned was the content of what was being said. Two basic subdivisions were identified: substantive meanings—that is, the subject matter under discussion (international trade)—and instructional meanings—the routine managerial statements such as those concerned with assignments and procedures. The substantive and the instructional meanings were observed and recorded along with their associated logical meanings. Thus if a pupil replied to a teacher's question by giving a definition of tariffs, the pedagogical meaning is recorded as *responding,* the substantive meaning as *tariffs,* and the logical process as *defining.* In addition, the pupil is designated as the speaker, and the length of his utterance, in lines of transcript, is also recorded.

The complete system of analysis is presented below in summary form (pp. 10–13):[1]

(1) SPEAKER: indicates source of utterance

Teacher (T); Pupil (P); Audio-Visual Device (A)

(2) TYPE OF PEDAGOGICAL MOVE: reference to function of move

Initiatory Moves
  Structuring (STR): sets context for subsequent launches, halts / excludes
  Soliciting (SOL): directly elicits verbal, physical or mental response; coded in terms of response expected

[1] Underlining indicates actual coding terminology.

Reflexive Moves
  Responding (RES): fulfills expectation of solicitation; bears reciprocal relation only to solicitation
  Reacting (REA): modifies (by clarifying, synthesizing, expanding) and/or rates (positively or negatively); occasioned by previous move but not directly elicited; summaries or reactions to more than one previous move coded REA
  Not Codable (NOC): function uncertain because tape inaudible

(3) SUBSTANTIVE MEANING: Reference to subject matter topic. (Based on a content analysis of the pamphlet by Calderwood)

Trade (TRA)
  Trade—Domestic and International (TDI)
  Trade—Money and Banking (TMB)
  Trade—Who Trades with Whom (TWH)
Factors of Production and/or Specialization (FSP).
  Factor of Production—Natural Resources (FNR)
  Factor of Production—Human Skills (FHS)
  Factory of Production—Capital Equipment (FCE)
  Factors Other Than Natural Resources, Human Skills, and Capital Equipment Occurring in Discussion of Reasons for Trade (FRE)
Imports and/or Exports (IMX)
Foreign Investment—General (FOR)
  Foreign Investment—Direct (FOD)
  Foreign Investment—Porfolio (FOP)
Barriers to Trade (BAR)
  Barrier—Tariffs (BAT)
  Barrier—Quotas (BAQ)
  Barrier—Exchange Control (BAE)
  Barrier—Export Control (BAX)
  Barrier—Administrative Protectionism (BAA)

Promoting Free Trade (PFT)
Relevant to Trade (REL)
Not Trade (NTR)

(4) SUBSTANTIVE-LOGICAL MEANING: reference is cognitive process involved in dealing with the subject matter under study

Analytic Process: proposed use of language or established rules of logic
  Defining-General (DEF): defining characteristics of class or term with example of items within class explicitly given
    Defining-Denotative (DED): object referent of term
    Defining-Connotative (DEC): defining characteristics of class or term
  Interpreting (INT): verbal equivalent of a statement, slogan, aphorism, or proverb
Empirical Process: sense experience as criterion of truth
  Fact Stating (FAC): what is, was, or will be without explanation or evaluation; account, report, description, statement of event or state of affairs
  Explaining (XPL): relation between objects, events, principles, conditional inference; cause-effect; explicit comparison-contrast; statement of principles; theories or laws
Evaluative Process: set of criteria or value system as a basis for verification
  Opining (OPN): personal values for statement of policy, judgment or evaluation of event, idea, state of affairs; direct and indirect evaluation included
  Justifying (JUS): reasons or argument for or against opinion or judgment
  Logical Process Not Clear (NCL): cognitive process involved not clear

(5) NUMBER OF LINES IN (3) AND (4) ABOVE

(6) INSTRUCTIONAL MEANINGS: reference to factors related to classroom management

Assignment (ASG): suggested or required student activity; reports, tests, readings, debates, homework, etc.
Material (MAT): teaching aids and instructional devices
Person (PER): person as physical object or personal experiences
Procedure (PRC): a plan of activities or a course of action
Statement (STA): verbal utterance, particularly the meaning, validity, truth or propriety of an utterance
Logical Process (LOG): function of language or rule of logic; reference to definitions or arguments, but not presentation of such
Action-General (ACT): Performance (vocal, nonvocal, cognitive, or emotional) the specific nature of which is uncertain or complex
Action-Vocal (ACV): physical qualities of vocal action
Action-Physical (ACP): physical movement or process
Action-Cognitive (ACC): cognitive process, but not the language or logic of a specific utterance; thinking, knowing, understanding, listening
Action-Emotional (ACE): emotion or feeling, but not expression of attitude or value
Language Mechanics (LAM): the rules of grammar and/or usage

(7) INSTRUCTIONAL-LOGICAL MEANING: reference to cognitive processes related to the distinctly didactive verbal moves in the instructional situation

Analytic Process: see (4) above
  Defining-General (DEF)
    Defining-Denotative (DED)

Defining-Connotative (DEC)
Interpreting (INT)
Empirical Process: see (4) above
Fact Stating (FAC)
Explaining (XPL)

Evaluative Process
Opining (OPN): see (4) above
Justifying (JUS): see (4) above
Rating: reference to metacommunication; usually an evaluative reaction (REA)
Positive (POS): distinctly affirmative evaluation
Admitting (ADM): mild or equivocally positive evaluation
Repeating (RPT): implicit positive evaluation when statement (STA) is repeated by another speaker; also for SOL to repeat vocal action (ACV)
Qualifying (QUAL): explicit reservation stated in evaluation; exception
Not Admitting (NAD): evaluation which rejects by stating the contrary; direct refutation or correction excluded
Negative (NEG): distinctly negative evaluation
Positive/Negative (PON): SOL requesting positive or negative evaluation
Admitting/Not Admitting (AON): SOL asking to permit procedure or action

Extralogical Process: SOL expecting physical action or when logical nature of verbal response cannot be determined
Performing (PRF): asking, demanding; explicit directive or imperative
Directing (DIR): SOL with or without stated alternatives; asking for directive, not permission for specific action

(8) NUMBER OF LINES IN (6) AND (7) ABOVE

Each pedagogical move is coded as follows:
(1) / (2) / (3) / (4) / (5) / (6) / (7) / (8)

(1) Speaker
(2) Type of Pedagogical Move

(3) Substantive Meaning
(4) Substantive-Logical Meaning
(5) Number of Typescript Lines in (3) and (4)
(6) Instructional Meaning
(7) Instructional-Logical Meaning
(8) Number of Typescript Lines in (6) and (7)

The following is an example of the coding system applied to a verbal exchange:

#1 T: What is a tariff?
     T/SOC/BAT/DEF/1/-/-/-/
#2 P: A Tax.
     P/RES/BAT/DEC/1/-/-/-/
#3 T: Good.
     T/REA/BAT/-/-/STA/POS/1

The coding could be interpreted as follows:

Move #1—Teacher solicitation calling for definition of a term relating to tariffs—one line
Move #2—Pupil responding move giving connotative definition relating to tariffs—one line
Move #3—Teacher reacting move giving positive rating of previous statement—one line

To determine reliability of the coding system, 12 five-page samples of transcript were selected at random. Two teams of two members coded each of the samples, and their results were compared. The percentage of agreement was calculated for each of the basic categories of the system of analysis: pedagogical moves, substantive meanings, substantive-logical meanings, instructional meanings, and instructional-logical meanings. In terms of moves, the percentage of agreement ranged from 0.87 to 0.95. In terms of lines of transcript, the range was from 0.84 per cent to 0.96 percent.

The development of the system of analysis was the primary task of the early stages of this research. Nevertheless, once processed by the IBM 7090 computer, the analysis of the 60 class sessions yielded some interesting descriptive data. The 15 teachers, for example, made about 50 percent more moves than the 345 pupils and spoke three times as many lines. Soliciting, responding, and reacting moves accounted for roughly 90 percent of the moves, and structuring about 10 percent. By and large, it was the teachers who made the structuring, soliciting, and reacting moves, and the pupils' role was confined largely to responding. Of 21 possible teaching cycles or patterns of moves, only two, solicitation-response-reaction and solicitation-response, accounted for more than half of the total of 4,592 teaching cycles. Approximately three-quarters of the discourse in terms of lines was given over to substantive as opposed to instructional meanings. About half of all moves were classified in the substantive-empirical mode (fact stating and explaining) rather than analytic (defining and interpreting) or evaluative (opening and justifying). The analysis is designed to provide not only a picture of linguistic behavior in the sample classes as a whole, but some clues as to how teaching styles differ from one classroom to another.

Like the work of Bellack and his associates, Jackson's research (1965), "Teacher-Pupil Communication: An Observational Study," provides some basis for describing and analyzing patterns communication in the classroom. Jackson's study, however, is more restricted in its focus and uses a different type of population sample.

One of the first tasks was that of grouping or categorizing the various communications that take place between teach-

ers and pupils. Jackson identified three types of verbal communication between teachers and pupils:

1. Instructional messages—communications referring to content or intended to attain educational objectives

2. Group management messages—communications having to do with setting procedures and rules

3. Classroom control messages—communications having to do with maintaining discipline and keeping order.

Aside from the type of communication, two other dimensions of the activity were identified: (a) the recipient of the teacher's message (whether a boy, a girl, or a group), and (b) the initiator of the message (whether a boy, a girl, or the teacher). In addition, the type of activity in which the class was engaged (e.g., recitation, group work, and so on) was recorded as well as when shifts took place from one type of activity to another.

Jackson's population sample was drawn from a private elementary school and included one first-grade, one second-grade, and two fourth-grade classes. The observations were made and recorded directly in the classrooms themselves rather than through tape recordings or transcripts. Over the two-month period during which data were collected, each classroom was visited at least 15 times for periods ranging from a few minutes to a whole day. The four classes were observed for a total of 1,467 minutes.

Over this period, an entry was made each time there was a verbal exchange between the teacher and pupils in the class. Confirming the impression gained by casual observation of classroom activity, Jackson's study shows that the rate of verbal communications is remarkably high. Communication rates ranged from 3.08 communications per minute for the second-grade class to 3.66 for the first-grade class. Although the differences seem significant at first glance, Jackson's analysis also shows that the rate of communications during any given class activity was very much the same from class to class. Differences in the overall rate of communication tended to be a function of the proportion of time devoted to seatwork as opposed to activities involving the class as a whole. Since seatwork usually involves fewer teacher-pupil communications than whole class work, those classes which devoted a proportionally greater amount of time to seatwork tended to have slower overall rates. Taking only the rates for whole class activity, the four classes were remarkably similar in the average rate of communications per minute (3.64, 3.80, 3.83, 3.65). Further examination of the data also revealed that communications which lasted for as much as one minute accounted for a small percentage of the total time. Typically, then, these classes were characterized by short and frequent communication between teachers and pupils.

Another matter of concern to observers of classroom behavior is the extent to which a class is "teacher-dominated" or "pupil-dominated." Although Jackson's sample was drawn from a private school with a reputation for being child-centered, the four classes he observed tended to be "teacher-dominated" in terms of the initiator of verbal communication. In the most "pupil-dominated" class, 55.2 percent of the communications were initiated by the teacher; in the most "teacher-dominated" class, the percentage was 80.7. The percentages of teacher-initiation in the two fourth-grade classes were 67.2 and 65.2.

In terms of the type of communication, Jackson found that the range for instructional communications was 50.4 to 69.1; for management it was 20.0 to 33.5, and for control, the range was 10.9 to

16.6 percent. Taking management and control communications together, it was found that they account for at least 30 percent of all communications in each of the four classes. In the first-grade class, the percentage of instructional communications was only 50.4.

The picture that emerges from this study is one where teachers and pupils engage in a series of rapid-fire verbal interchanges (about 200 an hour) and that about one-half to one-third of these communications are other than instructional in character. The similarity in communication rates in the four classes suggests the hypothesis that this rapid pace is characteristic of teaching in elementary schools generally rather than a peculiarity of a limited number of classes. This similarity in rate and pattern of verbal behavior from one class to another is consistent with the findings of Bellack and his associates in their study of high school classes.

Increasing attention has been given lately to the observation of classroom behavior as a basis for teacher training (LaGrone, 1964). Although the typical professional sequence of education courses provides for the study of the schools as a social institution, for development of skills in use of materials, for planning for teaching, comparatively little attention is given to direct and systematic study of teaching itself as it occurs in the classroom. The research study, "A Conceptual System for Prospective Teachers To Study Teaching Behavior," by Waimon and Hermanowicz (1965) attempts to fill this gap by providing prospective teachers with a system for analyzing classroom behavior and training in the use of that system.

The basic framework for the system was derived largely from Miller's conception of learning as comprising drive, cue, response, and reward. Since the investigators regard teaching as the obverse of learning, their system focused on the teacher's attempts to induce learning "by developing a predisposition (drive), helping students acquire, comprehend, or use subject matter (cue and response), and giving evaluative reactions to pupil responses (reward)."

Using this approach, three major types of verbal behavior by teachers were identified:

1. Procedural statements, in which teachers set goals, gain attention, and so on.

2. Substantive statements, which have to do with subject matter. This includes such operations as fact stating and explaining.

3. Rating statements, which are the teacher's evaluations of the student responses.

The complete observation schedule including subcategories is summarized by the investigators as follows (pp. 18–19):

1. PROCEDURAL (PRO) The teacher develops and maintains a predisposition for learning.

  1.1 *Activating* (Act) The teacher makes pupil goals similar to his own.

    1.11 teacher gains attention

    1.12 teacher gives instruction

    1.13 teacher states goals

    1.14 teacher poses a problem

    1.15 teacher points out importance of goals

    1.16 teacher invites pupils to react to goals

  1.2 *Maintaining* (Mai) The teacher keeps pupil goals similar to his own.

    1.21 teacher prevents pupil from moving class in a new direction

    1.22 teacher reminds pupil to continue to pay attention

    1.23 teacher comments on the cause of unsatisfactory progress

    1.24 teacher offers encouragement

    1.25 teacher points out progress being made

    1.26 teacher invites questions or acknowledges pupil with a question

2. SUBSTANTIVE (SUB) The teacher helps pupil acquire, comprehend, or use subject matter.

  2.1 *Informing* (Inf) The teacher tells pupil subject matter to be remembered.

    2.11 teacher defines terms

    2.12 teacher states facts or generalizations

    2.13 teacher explains facts or generalizations

    2.14 teacher evaluates a subject

  2.2 *Cuing* (Cu) The teacher asks pupil questions requiring a substantive response.

    2.21 teacher helps pupil recall subject matter

    2.22 teacher helps pupil demonstrate comprehension of subject matter

    2.23 teacher helps pupil discover new subject matters

    2.24 teacher helps pupil apply subject matter to problem solving

  2.3 *Reacting Informing* (R. Inf) The teacher improves a pupil substantive response.

    2.31 teacher rephrases, or restates pupil response

    2.32 teacher adds new information to pupil response

    2.33 teacher relates various pupil responses

  2.4 *Reacting Cuing* (R. Cu) The teacher helps a pupil improve a substantive response.

    2.41 teacher helps pupil to rephrase, or restate response

    2.42 teacher helps pupil add new information to a response

    2.43 teacher solicits additions to a response from other pupils

3. RATING (RAT) The teacher gives an evaluative reaction to a substantive response.

  3.1 *Positive* (Po) The teacher lets pupil know a substantive response is correct.

    3.11 teacher gives an explicitly positive rating (Yes, Right, A good answer)

    3.12 teacher gives a mild or equivocally positive rating (Alright, O.K., Uh-huh)

3.2 *Negative* (Neg) The teacher lets pupil know a substantive response is incorrect.

    3.21 teacher gives an explicitly negative rating (No, Wrong, That's a terrible answer)

    3.22 teacher indicates a reservation (Yes, but . . . however . . . nevertheless . . . That's one way of saying it)

    3.23 teacher disagrees with a response (England is *not* in the Common Market)

3.3 *Neutral* (Neu) The teacher acknowledges a pupil response but does not let the pupil know it is correct or incorrect.

    3.31 teacher gives a positive reaction to part of a response, a negative reaction to another part

    3.32 teacher acknowledges having heard the response without evaluating it (repeats the response)

    3.33 teacher gives an ambiguous evaluation to response (Oh).

In addition to the teacher categories, two categories of pupil responses were identified: adequacy and magnitude. The former is based on a judgment as to whether the response fulfills the expectation of the teacher. The latter, which is limited to substantive responses, is based on whether the response requires knowledge, comprehension, or reasoning.

Waimon and Hermanowicz also identified larger verbal units which they called teaching episodes. These were defined as verbal units which are initiated by activating, cuing, or informing and terminate with a flexite move. Essentially, each episode represents an effort on the part of the teacher to elicit an appropriate response. Once these episodes are identified, they are classified in terms of the difficulty that was encountered in eliciting that response. Type A is assigned to those episodes where no difficulty is encountered,

type B where some difficulty is encountered, and type C where great difficulty is encountered.

In computing reliability, the investigators compared their own coding of a three-page segment of a lesson with the coding of the 28 students involved in the study. In terms of lines of transcript, the coefficients of agreement ranged from 0.32 to 1.00, with a mean of 0.82. A second reliability estimate using paired student teams and the formula developed by Smith, Meux, and their associates (1962) yielded a mean coefficient of agreement of 0.62 and a range of 0.49 to 0.72.

In attempting to assess the effect of their training in the observation of teaching, the investigators administered pretests and post-tests to the 28 students using five different instruments designed to measure critical thinking (*Watson-Glaser Critical Thinking Appraisal*), knowledge of research procedures (Patton-Barnes Cognitive Inventory), the meanings which students associate with various concepts inherent in the coding system (semantic differential), general attitudes to research in curriculum (Patton-Barnes Attitude Inventory), and the students' attitudes toward teaching (*Minnesota Teacher Attitude Inventory*).

No significant changes were found in terms of critical thinking, curriculum research methodology, or attitudes toward curriculum research. However, in rating 20 concepts selected by the investigators as important to their analysis system, the subjects, using a semantic differential scale, differed significantly in the meanings they attached to the concepts. Significant changes were also observed on the post-test scores of the *Minnesota Teacher Attitude Inventory*. In none of the five areas was change related to relibility in using the system. Some of the items from *The Purdue Rating Scale for Instruction* were used to obtain further reactions from the students. The most frequent response indicated a high value attached to direct observation of classroom behavior as opposed to the analysis of typescripts.

Perkins' study of classroom behavior and underachievement (1964, 1965) uses adaptations of observation schedules by Flanders (1960), Kowatrakul (1959), and Sears (1963) to determine whether the classroom behavior of underachieving pupils differs from that of achievers. The study is described by the investigator as based on the assumptions that "(1) an individual responds to a situation in accordance with the way he perceives it; (2) areas, events, and activities that have special significance for an individual are those that facilitate or threaten his maintenance and enhancement of self; (3) behaviors that are reinforced tend to be repeated" (p. 3). As such, the kinds of behavior that are the focus of this study deal with types of ongoing class activities (e.g., large-group discussions, seatwork, small-group or committee work, and so on) and with students' behavior (e.g., high activity or involvement, intent on work of nonacademic type, withdrawal, and so on) in the context of these activities. One observation schedule was developed for student behavior and another for teacher behavior.

Perkins' study lists student categories as follows (p. 251):

LISWAT: Interested in ongoing work: listening and watching—passive.

REWR: Reading or writing: working in assigned area—activity.

HIAC: High activity or involvement: reciting or using large muscles—positive feeling.

WOA: Intent on work in another curricular area: school activity not assigned to be done right then.

WNA: Intent on work of nonacademic

type: preparing for work assignment, cleaning out desk, etc.

SWP: Social, work-oriented—PEER: discussing some aspect of schoolwork with classmate.

SWT: Social, work-oriented—TEACHER: discussing some phase of work with teacher.

SF: Social, friendly: talking to peer on subject unrelated to schoolwork.

WDL: Withdrawal: detached, out of contact with people, ideas, classroom situation; daydreaming.

DISC: Large-group discussion: entire class discusses an issue or evaluates an oral report.

REC: Class recitation: teacher questions, student answers—entire class or portion of it participating.

IND: Individual work or project: student is working alone on task that is not a common assignment.

SEAT: Seatwork, reading or writing, common assignment.

GRP: Small-group or committee work: student is part of group or committee working on assignment.

REP: Oral reports—individual or group: student is orally reporting on book, current events, or research.

The teacher categories were designed to describe the teacher's role in terms of these activities (e.g., leader-director, resource person, and so on) as well as the specific activities in which the teacher is engaged (listens, lectures, gives directions, and so forth.)

The teacher categories are as follows (p. 251):

1. Does not accept student's idea, corrects it: rejection or correction of student's response.

2. Praises or encourages student or behavior: enthusiastic acceptance of student's response.

2A. Listens to, helps, supports, nurtures student: accepting, helping response; also listening to recitation.

3. Accepts or uses student's answer or idea.

4. Asks questions about content (what? where? when?): wants to find out whether student knows and understands material.

4A. Asks questions that stimulate thinking (why? how?): encourages student to seek explanations, to reason, to solve problems.

5. Lectures, gives facts or opinions about content: gives information in discussion, recitation, or committee meeting.

6. Gives directions, commands, or orders with which student is expected to comply.

7. Criticizes or justifies authority: disapproves of conduct or work of student or group of students.

10. Is not participating in class activities: is giving test or is out of room—class silent or in confusion.

LDR: Leader-director—teacher initiative—active: conducts recitation or discussion, lectures, works with small groups.

RES: Resource person—student-centered, lesser role than leader: helps group or committee, brings material, suggests.

SUPV: Supervisor—teacher initiative, passive, role during seatwork: circulates to observe and help.

SOC: Socialization agent: points to and reinforces social expectancies and rules; criticizes behavior.

EVL: Evaluator: listens and gives mark for oral report, individual or group; asks, "How many did you get right?"

The population sample consisted of 72 fifth-grade pupils and their teachers. Pupils were identified as either under-achievers or achievers by obtaining a regression equation for each pupil using IQ and grade point averages. Then 36 underachievers were paired with 36 achievers in terms of scores on the "Reading Vocabulary" and "Reading Comprehension" sections of the *California Achievement Test*. Using an electrically powered Bales-Gerbands recorder (1948), two-man teams categorized the behavior of pupils and teachers in two-minute units. In all, 2,410 two-minute samples were observed. To obtain a measure of interobserver reliability, each of the number of seconds for each category during the same observation was compared. A mean product-moment coefficient of 0.97 was obtained for the student categories and of 0.94 for the teacher categories.

Perkins' data indicate that the behavior of underachievers in the classroom tends to be characterized by involvement in nonacademic work and/or work in another academic area and that underachievers also exhibit distinctly more withdrawal behavior than achievers. Low academic achievement seems to be related to withdrawal on the part of the student and criticism on the part of the teacher. High academic achievement is associated with academic work-oriented behavior on the part of the student and role behavior on the part of the teacher which is designed to facilitate learning. The finding that underachievers and achievers differ significantly in three combined categories—intent on work in another curricular area (WOA), intent on work of nonacademic type (WNA), and withdrawal (WDL)—seems to indicate a kind of withdrawal syndrome which is consistent with less formal observation of underachievers. When seen in relation to the teacher categories, it was found that this syndrome is related to the *teacher lecture-criticizer* factor for both achievers and underachievers.

Smith and associates' study, *A Ten-*

tative Report on the Strategies of Teaching (1964), extends and broadens earlier research into classroom behavior by Smith and associates. The new study, however, differs from the earlier one in some significant respects. For one thing, the basic units of analysis in the earlier study were the episode and the monologue; in the present one, a newly conceived verbal unit, the strategy, forms the basis of the analysis. In addition, two other units, the venture and the move, are used to help identify and clarify the concept of teaching strategies. The population sample is the same as in the study of logical operations, and the data are drawn from transcripts of tape recordings of 17 high school class sessions. The sample includes ninth-, tenth-, eleventh-, and twelfth-grade classes in English, mathematics, science, and social studies.

The first unit of discourse to be identified was the venture. A venture is defined as "a segment of discourse consisting of a set of utterances dealing with a single topic and having a single overarching content objective." Usually five or six such units of discourse may be found in a lesson. Since each venture is, in a sense, a self-contained unit, the identification of these units ensures that the strategies therein will not be fragmented as would be the case if time units were used. The identification of these units of discourse, however, constituted a possible source of unreliability which the investigators sought to minimize by developing a carefully worded set of criteria for identification. To determine reliability, four judges who were not involved in the development of the research were divided into two teams and presented with nine transcripts of class sessions. Each team identified the ventures in each lesson and the judgments of the two teams were compared. The coefficients of agreement for the nine classes ranged from 0.56 to 0.89, with a median of 0.70.

In order to facilitate the identification of strategies, ventures were classified as to their cognitive import, that is, their central meaning or theme. The investigators are careful to point out that in using the term *content objective* to describe the import of the venture they are referring neither to the teacher's intent in initiating the unit of discourse nor to the learning that the student may acquire. Judgments of this kind would be highly speculative and, in all likelihood, quite unreliable.

The nine types of ventures identified by the investigators were described by Coombs[2] thusly:

> *Causal ventures.* The overarching content objective of this type of venture is a cause-effect relationship between particular events or between classes of events. A cause of an event, in the sense in which 'cause' is used here, need be neither necessary nor sufficient to bring the event. It may be only one factor contributing to or facilitating the event's occurrence.
>
> *Conceptual ventures.* The overarching objective of this type of venture is a set of conditions either governing, or implied by, the use of a term. These conditions constitute criteria for determining whether something is or is not a member of the class of things and the criteria by which members of the class are identified together with a term that names the class.
>
> *Evaluative ventures.* The objective of this type of venture is a rating of an action, object or event, policy, or practice, or a rating of a class of such things with respect to its worth, goodness, correctness, and the like. Discussion in ventures of this type usually attempts to determine whether or not

[2] Adapted from *Teaching Strategies and the Teaching of Concepts,* by Jerrold R. Coombs. Unpublished doctor's dissertation, University of Illinois, 1964, pp. 22–40.

some action, etc., is to be placed in a particular value category.

Informatory ventures. The informatory venture has as its objective a body of information which clarifies or amplifies a specified topic or group of related topics. The central concern of the discussion in this type of venture is the answering of questions such as "What happened?" "When did it happen?" "What did it do?" "Who or what did it?" or "What is it like?"

Interpretive ventures. The objective of this type of venture is the meaning or significance of a set of words or symbols.

Procedural ventures. A venture of this type discloses a sequence of actions by which an end may be achieved. The sequence of actions may be related to solving a problem, making a product, or bringing about a certain type of event.

Reason ventures. A venture falling into this category discloses the reason or reasons for an action, decision, policy, or practice. As used here, the term 'reason' refers to a consideration which leads a person to perform an action or which justifies his performing the action.

Rule ventures. The objective of this type of venture is a rule or several related rules. The term 'rule' as it is used here refers to conventional ways of doing things and to analytic relationships which may be used to guide actions.

System ventures. This type of venture focuses on the functional relations of the parts of a mechanism that produces a given end.

The procedure for assessing reliability in classifying ventures into these categories was essentially the same as for identifying ventures in the transcripts of the discourse. Independent judges were trained in identi-

fication procedures and were presented with 28 ventures to classify. The two teams were in agreement on 22 of the ventures. Taking each of the types of ventures separately, the coefficients of agreement ranged from 0.67 to 1.00 with the exception of causal ventures where there was no agreement between the two teams. The median coefficient was 0.75.

Once a system for identifying and classifying ventures had been developed, the next task was to define and clarify the concept of strategy as a unit of classroom behavior. Essentially a strategy was seen as "a set of verbal actions that serves to attain certain results and to guard against others."[3] Two basic dimensions of strategy were identified. The first, called the treatment dimension, involves those classroom operations which are designed to present and structure what is to be learned. The focus here is essentially substantive in the sense that the presentation of content is central to the activity. The second dimension, the control dimension, is concerned essentially with the teacher's attempts to guide or control student behavior. In pursuing the analysis of teaching strategies, Smith and his associates choose to concentrate on the treatment dimension.

Initially, the conceptual venture was singled out for analysis in terms of the treatment dimension. One task was the identification of the kinds of content that are characteristic of a conceptual venture. In this type of venture, the emphasis is upon definition, the ways in which the term may be used. Ten kinds of content were identified as contributing to this objective:[4]

1. A part the referent has
2. A characteristic of the referent

[3] *Ibid.*, p. 50.
[4] *Ibid.*, p. 55.

3. A function of the referent

4. A characteristic use of the referent

5. A characteristic treatment accorded the referent

6. A physical relationship between the referent and something else

7. The way in which the referent compares to something else with respect to a particular characteristic

8. The evaluative rating implied by the use of the term

9. A condition necessary or required to produce or cause the referent

10. The results of an operation involving the referent.

The second task was identifying and classifying the kinds of verbal maneuvers that are used in conjunction with these aspects of content. Such a verbal maneuver was described as a move and defined as "a verbal activity which logically or analytically relates terms of the proposition set forth by the strategy to some event or thing or to some class of events or things." For conceptual ventures, 18 types of moves were identified:[5]

1. *Criterion description.* Individual criteria are simply noted or discussed. The criteria are not implied in the course of some more complex maneuver such as comparing or contrasting the referent with something else or proving something to be an instance of the referent.

2. *Analysis.* A set of parts which, together, constitute the referent is noted or discussed.

3. *Enumeration.* The instances to which the term applies are noted or an exhaustive set of sub-classes of the referent is noted or discussed.

4. *Classification.* The referent is identified as a sub-class of a larger class of things.

[5] *Ibid.*, pp. 56–59.

5. *Classificatory description.* The referent is classified as a sub-class of a more inclusive class of things and is uniquely identified within that class.

6. *Analogy.* The way in which the referent is like something else is noted or discussed. In some cases, however, the way in which the referent is like the other thing may not be discussed. The similarity is simply noted.

7. *Differentiation.* The difference between the referent and something else is noted or discussed.

8. *Negation.* That the referent is not something else or not the same as something else is noted, but there is no discussion of why the referent is not the same as the other thing.

9. *Opposition.* The opposite of the referent is noted or discussed.

10. *Sufficient conditions.* A set of conditions represented as being sufficient to identify something as an instance of the referent is noted or discussed.

11. *Instance production.* The way in which an instance of the referent may develop or be produced is noted or discussed.

12. *Positive instance.* A particular instance of the referent is noted or discussed.

13. *Negative instance.* A particular object, situation or event which is not an instance of the referent, but which is similar enough to the instance to be easily mistaken for it is noted or discussed.

14. *Instance substantiation.* A positive or negative instance is pointed out, named, or described and the reasons or evidence for concluding that it is a positive or negative instance are discussed.

15. *Instance comparison.* Two or more instances to which the term applies are named or described and the similarities or differences between the instances are noted or discussd.

16. *Instance variance.* One or more positive instances and one or more negative in-

stances, each negative instance differing from a positive instance with respect to only one condition, are noted or discussed.

17. *Operation variance.* This sort of move establishes a criterion involving an empirical correlation. Suppose the term refers to a relationship between two factors. In an operation variance move an operation involving these factors is performed. In this operation the values of the independent variables are known and the values of the dependent variables are noted. The operation is repeated, but with one independent variable, call it variable *A*, having a different value. Changes in the values of the variables involved in a relationship referred to by the term are noted. This same operation may be repeated several times, with variable *A* having a different value each time. Finally, a conclusion is reached concerning the effect a change in the value of *A* has on the relationship or on the value of the variables in the relationship.

18. *Meta distinction.* In this sort of move the different uses of a term, the kinds of meaning a term can have, the types of conditions which may be associated with the term are noted or discussed.

This list may be divided into two broad categories of moves: instancing moves and abstract moves. The former includes positive instance, negative instance production, instance substantiation, operation variance, instance variance, instance comparison, and enumeration. The latter includes criterion description, classification, analogy, differentiation, classificatory description, negation, opposition, sufficient conditions, and meta distinction. Strategies consist essentially of combinations of various kinds of moves but may occasionally comprise only a single move. Smith and his associates have tentatively identified four types of strategies representing certain groupings of conceptual moves. Their descriptions in abridged form are listed below (1964, pp. 60–84):

TYPE I STRATEGIES

Strategies of this type consist entirely of abstract moves.
Sub-type A.
These are strategies which contain only one move.
Sub-type B.
A strategy of this type contains an initial abstract move (other than a criterion description move) supplemented by one or more criterion description moves.
Sub-type C.
This strategy is one which begins with a series of criterion description moves and culminates with a different type of abstract move.
Sub-type D.
Strategies of this type contain both criterion description moves and other abstract moves. However, rather than being grouped at the beginning or at the end of the strategy, the criterion description moves are interespersed with other abstract moves.

TYPE II STRATEGIES

In Type II, one or more abstract moves are followed by one or more instancing moves.

TYPE III STRATEGIES

These strategies consist of one or more instancing moves followed by one or more abstract moves.

TYPE IV STRATEGIES

Type IV consists of mixed strategies.

Each of these strategies, then, represents a different patterning of moves within a conceptual venture. Taken together, they may be seen as four different tactics for achieving the same kind of content objective.

In this preliminary stage of their research, Smith and his associates have developed a framework and set of concepts which may be used to describe and analyze the classroom discourse associated with achieving content objectives. The notion of strategies provides a means of conceptualizing the verbal maneuvers that are involved in this aspect of teaching behavior. Further research may be directed toward establishing relationships between certain kinds of strategies and of measurable outcomes.

Like the researchers in the study just reviewed, Taba, Levine, and Elzey in *Thinking in Elementary School Children* (1964) are concerned with cognitive processes, but their approach is considerably different. Taba and her associates are interested in assessing the role of curriculum organization and teacher training instituted for achieving a higher level of thinking in elementary school children than is usually the case.

In addition, Taba and her associates developed a concept of thinking and instruments by which cognitive processes could be measured, analyzed, and observed. They began with the notion that thinking is "an active transaction between the individual and the demands of his environment, which is neither fully controlled by environmental stimulation, nor wholly independent of some mediating intervention" (p. 21). Also basic to their concept of thinking is the idea that thinking may be seen as occurring in sequential steps, which suggests that there may be an optimum sequence of learning experiences in the development of thinking processes. After an exhaustive study of the research and literature in this area, the investigators identified three clusters of cognitive processes: "1) grouping and classification of information; 2) interpretation of data and the making of inferences; and 3) the application of known principles and facts to explain new phenomena, to predict consequences from known conditions and events, or to develop hypotheses

by using known generalizations and facts" (p. 30).

These cognitive processes were analyzed from two different points of view: their basic elements and the ways of mastering them. The first of these processes, concept development, is seen as comprising three basic operations: differentiation as to the properties of the objects or events, grouping or assembling these properties as to certain characteristics, and labeling the categories. In terms of parallel classroom operations, differentiation involves enumerating on the basis of previous experience or a classroom presentation; grouping may take the form of putting together items with varying characteristics; and labeling can occur as a form of decision making involving the hierarchy of concepts as to their generality.

The second process, interpreting data and making inferences, is seen as involving the operations of gathering or collecting the information, offering reasons or explaining, establishing relationships among certain kinds of information, and, finally, generalizing on the basis of these relationships.

In analyzing the third cognitive task, involving the application of principles, predicting consequences, and using generalizations and facts, Taba and her associates identify two basic operations: prediction itself and the development of appropriate ways to test the validity of prediction.

In spite of these differences in operation, the three cognitive tasks are seen as having certain things in common. In the first place, these tasks all involve a series of steps. Second, these steps may be seen as a kind of hierarchy of abstraction and complexity. Third, each of the operations involves different levels of intuitive as well as conscious awareness of the operational principles.

This conceptualization of cognitive

tasks provided the framework for much of the training of the 20 teachers involved in the study. Each teacher was given 10 days of training, during which special attention was given to the development of cognitive skills in elementary social studies classes. The 20 classes involved included grades 2 through 6. In all, 481 students were involved representing a range in IQ of 88 to 121 and a broad range as to socioeconomic status.

Two instruments were developed for the purpose of measuring and analyzing aspects of cognitive skills. The first is the Social Studies Inference Test which is designed to test the students' ability to draw inferences from new data. Four sub-areas were identified: discrimination, inference, overgeneralization and caution, and error.

The second instrument is a coding system designed to analyze tape recordings of the class sessions. Four tape recordings were taken for each class. The first was of the discussion involving grouping and classification; two others involved interpretation of data; the fourth involved predicting consequences. Thought units in the typescripts of the class sessions were subjected to a threefold analysis which included *designation,* whether the source was a teacher or a pupil and whether information was sought or given; *function,* whether the unit was related to managerial matters or involved content and thought processes; and *levels,* the relative concreteness or abstraction of the unit. One of the major purposes for devising the coding system was to provide for the tracing of patterns in the development of cognitive skills as it actually occurs in the classroom. Using the system, it became possible to map teaching strategies on a flow chart and to determine, for example, where the teacher sought to extend one level of thought and to "lift" it to another and higher level.

Taba and her associates (1964) summarize their system as follows (pp. 118–19):

COGNITIVE TASK: GROUPING AND LABELING[6]
(giving or seeking)

10 specific or general information outside of focus

11 specific or general information within focus

12 specific or general information with qualifications[6]

30 grouping information without basis

31 grouping information with implicit basis

32 grouping information with explicit basis

40 categorizing information without basis

41 categorizing information with implicit relationships between items

42 categorizing information with explicit relationships between items

COGNITIVE TASK: INTERPRETING AND MAKING INFERENCES
(giving or seeking)

10 specific or general information outside of focus

11 specific or general information within focus

12 specific or general information with qualifications and relationships

50 specific reason or explanation that does not relate to the information

51 specific reason or explanation that relates or organizes the information

52 specific reason or explanation that states how it relates or organizes the information

60 irrelevant or incorrect inference which is derived from information

[6] Categories in the 20 series were originally reserved for "general information" but were later combined with the 10 series.

61 relevant inference which is derived from information

62 relevant inference which is derived from information and expresses a cause-and-effect relationship, explanation, consequence, or contrast

70 relationship between information which implies an irrelevant or incorrect principle or generalization

71 relationship between information which implies a principle or generalization

72 principle or generalization which is derived from information

Cognitive task: Predicting consequences
(giving or seeking)

90 correcting the cause or condition

Establishing parameters of information

100 irrelevant information

101 relevant information for establishing the parameter (if-then) for a particular hypothesis or prediction

102 relevant information for the parameter or any particular prediction with appropriate explanation

Establishing parameters of conditions

110 irrelevant or untenable condition for the logical parameter or for the particular prediction or hypothesis

111 relevant condition without connecting it with relevant information

112 relevant condition and information and plus a logical connection between them

Prediction: (Level one, (100), immediate consequences)
(Level two, (200), remote consequences)

120–220 incorrect or out of focus prediction

121–221 prediction with no elaboration

122–222 prediction accompanied by explanation, qualification, differentiation, comparison, or contrast

123–223 prediction accompanied by a stated or implied principle.

To determine reliability, two members of the staff coded a transcript independently. After an adjustment in the system involving the collapsing of certain categories, 90 percent agreement was achieved between the two coders.

The results of the analysis are in terms of changes in the measures of cognitive skill and are also descriptive of the teaching strategies that were employed to bring about these changes. Taba points out, for example, that although the emergence of formal thought appears earlier than at first believed (second grade), a continued emphasis on concrete operations in the early grades serves as a foundation for the more complex operations to follow. Appropriate teaching strategies seem to ease the transition from concrete to formal operations considerably, and the fact that there is a low correlation between cognitive performance and IQ indicates that effective teaching strategies may be developed for both high- and low-ability students. Probably most significant here is the conclusion that the development of higher levels of cognition is an attainable educational objective.

The six research studies reviewed here share a kind of common perspective. It is that some insight and understanding may be gained into the nature of teaching by studying it in the classroom setting. Despite this common orientation, considerable diversity is represented here as well. This diversity results in part from the predilections of the investigators and partly from the many-faceted nature of teaching itself. Something of the range represented in these six studies may be seen in terms of the dimensions of focus, population and setting, and technique or observational procedure.

It is difficult at this early stage of

Principal Investigator	Focus	Population and Setting	Procedure
Bellack	classroom language; meaning	high school social studies	typescripts; tape recordings
Jackson	teacher-pupil communication	private elementary school	direct observation
Waimon	observation as teacher training	upper elementary grades	direct observation, tapes; typescripts
Perkins	role behavior; class activity	fifth-grade underachievers	direct observation
Smith	teacher strategies	high school	typescripts
Taba	congnitive skills	elementary social studies	typescripts

the game to evaluate these studies in terms of the ultimate contribution they will make to a useful description of the teaching process—a description which, it is hoped, will provide some basis for teaching theory. But it is in these terms, rather than in terms of the narrowly practical, that these studies must be seen. It may be that our insistence on research which has immediate practical application has kept us from conducting the kind of patient and painstaking analyses of teaching that can shed light on that highly complex human activity. If so, the fact that these studies raise more questions than they attempt to answer is a highly desirable turn of events.

REFERENCES

BALES, R. F., and GERBRANDS, H. "The Interaction Recorder, an Apparatus and Check List for Sequential Content Analysis of Social Interaction." *Human Relations* 14: 238–43; 1948.

BELLACK, ARNO A., and DAVITZ, JOEL R., in collaboration with KLIEBARD, HERBERT M., and HYMAN, RONALD T. *The Language of the Classroom: Meanings Communicated in High School Teaching.* U.S. Department of Health, Education, and Welfare, Office of Education, Co-operative Research Project No. 1497. New York: Institute of Psychological Research, Teachers College, Columbia University, 1963.

BELLACK, ARNO A., in collaboration with HYMAN, RONALD T.; SMITH, FRANK L., JR.; and KLIEBARD, HERBERT M. *The Language of the Classroom: Meanings Communicated in High School Teaching. Part Two.* U.S. Department of Health, Education, and Welfare, Office of Education, Cooperative Research Project No. 2023. New York: Institute of Psychological Research, Teachers College, Columbia University, 1965.

DEWEY, JOHN. *The Relation of Theory to Practice in Education.* Yearbook of the National Society for the Study of Education, Part I, 1904.

FLANDERS, NED A. *Teacher Influence, Pupil Attitudes, and Achievement.* U.S. Department of Health, Education, and Welfare, Office of Education, Cooperative Research Project No. 397. Minneapolis: University of Minnesota, 1960.

JACKSON, PHILIP W. "Teacher-Pupil Communication in the Elementary Classroom: An Observational Study." Paper read at the American Educational Research Association Convention, Chicago, February 1965.

KOWATRAKUL, SURANG. "Some Behaviors of

Elementary School Children Related to Classroom Activities and Subject Areas." *Journal of Educational Psychology* 50: 121–28; June 1959.

LaGrone, Herbert F. *A Proposal for the Revision of the Preservice Professional Component of a Program of Teacher Education.* U.S. Department of Health, Education, and Welfare, Office of Education, Educational Media Branch, Contract No. OE 3–16–006. Washington, D.C.: American Association of Colleges for Teacher Education, 1964.

Medley, Donald M., and Mitzel, Harold F. "Measuring Classroom Behavior by Systematic Observation." *Handbook of Research on Teaching.* (Edited by N. L. Gage.) Chicago: Rand McNally & Co., 1963. pp. 247–328.

Perkins, Hugh V. "A Procedure for Assessing the Classroom Behavior of Students and Teachers." *American Educational Research Journal* 1: 249–60; November 1964.

Perkins, Hugh V. "Classroom Behavior and Underachievement." *American Educational Research Journal* 2: 1–12; January 1965.

Sears, Pauline S. *The Effect of Classroom Conditions on the Strength of Achievement Motive and Work Output of Elementary School Children.* U.S. Department of Health, Education, and Welfare, Office of Education, Cooperative Research Project No. 873. Stanford, Calif.: Stanford University, 1963.

Smith, B. Othanel, and Meux, Milton O., in collaboration with Coombs, Jerrold; Eierdam, Daniel; and Szoke, Ronald. *A Study of the Logic of Teaching.* U.S. Department of Health, Education, and Welfare, Office of Education, Cooperative Research Project No. 258(7257). Urbana: Bureau of Educational Research, College of Education, University of Illinois, 1962.

Smith, B. Othanel, and others. A Tentative *Report on the Strategies of Teaching.* U.S. Department of Health, Education, and Welfare, Office of Education, Cooperative Research Project No. 1640. Urbana: Bureau of Educational Research, College of Education, University of Illinois, 1964.

Taba, Hilda; Levine, Samuel; and Elzey, Freeman F. *Thinking in Elementary School Children.* U.S. Department of Health, Education, and Welfare, Office of Education, Cooperative Research Project No. 1574. San Francisco: San Francisco State College, 1964.

Waimon, Morton D., and Hermanowicz, Henry J. "A Conceptual System for Prospective Teachers To Study Teaching Behavior." Paper read at the American Educational Research Association convention, Chicago, February 1965.

Wittgenstein, Ludwig. *Philosophical Investigations.* New York: Macmillan Co., 1953. 232 pp.

INTENT, ACTION AND FEEDBACK:
A PREPARATION FOR TEACHING

Ned A. Flanders

THE PROBLEM

The point is that much of what is learned in education courses is neither conceptualized, quantified, nor taught in a fashion that builds a bridge between theory and practice. Education students are only occasionally part of an exciting, systematic, exploration of the teaching process, most infrequently by the instructor's example. How can we create, in education courses, an active, problem-solving process, a true sense of inquiry, and a systematic search for principles through experimentation? At least one factor favors change and that is the lack of solid evidence that anything we are now teaching is clearly associated with any index of effective teaching, with the possible exception of practice teaching.

A great many factors resist curriculum change in teacher education. Perhaps the most important is that genuine cur-

From: Journal of Teacher Education, *1963,* 14, 251–60. *Copyright* © *1963 by the National Commission on Teacher Education and Professional Standards, National Education Association, and reproduced by permission of the author and publisher.*

riculum innovation, to be distinguished from tinkering with content and sequence, would require that existing faculty members, old and new alike, think differently about their subject matter, act differently while teaching, and relate differently to their students. For some this is probably impossible, for all it would be difficult. Yet changes do occur when enough energy is mobilized and convictions are strongly held.

It is a serious indictment of the profession, however, to hear so many education instructors say that their students will appreciate what they are learning *after* they have had some practical teaching experience. What hurts is the obvious hypocrisy of making this statement and then giving a lecture on the importance of presenting material in such a way that the immediate needs and interests of the pupils are taken into consideration. Such instances reveal a misunderstanding of theory and practice. To be understood, concepts in education must be verified by personal field experiences; in turn, field experiences must be efficiently conceptualized to gain insight. With most present practices, the gorge between theory and practice grows deeper and wider, excavated by the very individuals who are pledged to fill it.

One stumbling block is our inability to describe teaching as a series of acts through time and to establish models of behavior which are appropriate to different kinds of teaching situations. This problem has several dimensions. First, in terms of semantics, we must learn how to define our concepts as part of a theory. We also need to organize these concepts into the fewest number of variables necessary to establish principles and make predictions. Too often we try to teach the largest number of variables; in fact, as many as we can think of for which there is some research evidence. Second, in terms of technology, we must develop procedures for quantifying the qualitative aspects of teaching acts so that our students will have tools for collecting empirical evidence. Third, in terms of philosophy, we must decide whether our education students are going to be told about teaching in lectures and read about it in books or if they are going to discover these things for themselves. This paper will be devoted to these three issues, in reverse order.

A PHILOSOPHY OF INQUIRY

When Nathaniel Cantor (5) published his nine assumptions of orthodox teaching, there was little evidence to support his criticisms. Must pupils be coerced into working on tasks? In what way is the teacher responsible for pupils' acquiring knowledge? Is education a preparation for later life rather than a present, living experience? Is subject matter the same to the learner as it is to the teacher? The last decade has provided more evidence in support of Cantor's criticism than it has in defense of existing practice.

H. H. Anderson and his colleagues (1,2,3,4) first demonstrated that dominative teacher contacts create more compliance and resistance to compliance, that dominative teacher contacts with pupils spread to the pupil-to-pupil contacts even in the absence of the teacher, and that this pattern of teaching creates situations in which pupils are more easily distracted and more dependent on teacher initiative.

Flanders and Havumaki (8) demonstrated that dominative teacher influence was more persuasive in changing pupil opinions but that such shifts of opinion were not stable since inner resistance was so high.

A research team in Provo, Utah (9) believes that patterns of spontaneous teacher action can be identified and that more effective patterns can be distinguished from less effective patterns. The difference is that more dominative patterns are less effective.

Our own eight-year research program which involved the development of interaction analysis as a tool for quantifying patterns of teacher influence lends further support to Cantor. The generalizations to follow are based on all teachers observed in our different research projects. This total is only 147 teachers, representing all grade levels, six different school districts in two countries; but these teachers came from the extremes of a distribution involving several thousand teachers. The total bits of information collected by interaction analysis are well in excess of 1,250,000.

The present, average domination of teachers is best expressed as the rule of two-thirds. About two-thirds of the time spent in a classroom, someone is talking. The chances are two out of three that this person is the teacher. When the teacher talks, two-thirds of the time is spent by many expressions of opinion and fact, giving some direction and occasionally criticizing the pupils. The fact that teachers are taking too active a part for effective learning is shown by comparing superior with less effective classrooms. A superior classroom scores above average on constructive attitudes toward the teacher and the classwork. It also scores higher on achievement tests of the content to be learned, adjusted for initial ability. In studies (7) of seventh grade social studies and eighth grade mathematics, it was found that the teachers in superior classrooms spoke only slightly less, say 50 to 60 per cent of the time, but the more directive aspects of their verbal influence went down to 40 to 50 per cent. These teachers were much more flexible in the quality of their influence, sometimes very direct, but on more occasions very indirect.

To describe the classrooms which were below average in constructive pupil attitudes and in content achievement (they are positively correlated), just change the rules of two-thirds to the rule of three-fourths plus.

The foregoing evidence shows that no matter what a prospective teacher hears in an education course, he has, on the average, been exposed to living models of what teaching is and can be that are basically quite directive. After fourteen or so years he is likely to be quite dependent, expecting the instructor to tell him what to do, how to do it, when he is finished, and then tell him how well he did it. Now it is in this general context that we turn to the question of how we can develop a spirit of inquiry with regard to teaching.

Thelen (10) has described a model of personal inquiry, as well as other models, and the question is whether teacher education can or should move toward this model. He describes this model as follows (*ibid.*, p. 89):

...(personal inquiry) is a process of interaction between the student and his natural and societal environment. In this situation the student will be aware of the process of which he is a part; during this process he will be aware of many choices among ways he might behave; he will make decisions among these ways; he will then act and see what happens; he will review the process and study it with the help of books and other people; he will speculate about it, and draw tentative conclusions from it.

Returning to the education course, the student will be aware of the learning process of *that* classroom, he will confront choices, he will make decisions among the choices, he will act and then evaluate his actions, and then he will try to make some sense out of it with the help of books, the instructor, and his peers. This is a tall order, but who knows, it may be the only route to discovery and independence for the prospective teacher.

Occasionally we hear of exciting learning experiences in which education students attain a sort of intellectual spirit of inquiry. A unit on motivation can begin with an assessment of the motivation patterns of the education students. The same assessment procedures can then be used at other grade levels, permitting comparisons and generalizations. Principles of child growth and development can be discovered by observation and learned more thoroughly, perhaps, than is possible with only lecture and reading. But this is not what is meant by inquiry.

Inquiry in teacher education means translating understanding into action as part of the teaching process. It means experimenting with one's own behavior, obtaining objective information about one's own behavior, evaluating this information in terms of the teacher's role; in short, attaining self-insight while acting like a teacher.

Procedures for obtaining self-insight

have been remarkably improved during the last decade in the field of human relations training. Two characteristics of these training methods seem relevant to this discussion. First, information and insights about behavior must become available in a way that can be accepted and in a form that is understood. Second, opportunities to utilize or act out these insights must be provided. Our ability to accept information about ourselves is a complex problem, but it helps if we believe the information is objective, valid, and given in an effort to help rather than hurt. Our understanding of this information will depend a great deal on our ability to organize the information conceptually. Freedom to act at least requires freedom from threat or embarrassment.

From all of these things, a spirit of inquiry develops.

THE TECHNIQUE OF INTERACTION ANALYSIS

Interaction analysis is nothing more and nothing less than an observation technique which can be used to obtain a fairly reliable record of spontaneous verbal statements. Most teacher influence is exerted by verbal statements, and to determine their quality is to approximate total teacher influence. This technique was first developed as a research tool, but every observer we ever hired testified that the process of learning the system and using it in classrooms was more valuable than anything else he learned in his education courses. Since interaction analysis is only a technique, it probably could be applied to teacher education in a fashion that is consistent or even totally inconsistent with a philosophy of personal inquiry. How it is used in teacher preparation is obviously as important as understanding the procedure itself.

The writing of this manuscript followed the completion of a terminal contract report of a U.S. Office of Education-sponsored, inservice training program based on interaction analysis as a tool for gathering information. How we used interaction analysis is illustrated by the conditions we tried to create for the fifty-five participating teachers, most of whom represented about one-half of the faculties of two junior high schools:[1]

1) Teachers developed new (to them) concepts as tools for thinking about their behavior and the consequences of their behavior. These concepts were used to discover principles of teacher influence. Both types of concepts were necessary: those for describing actions and those for describing consequences.

2) Procedures for assessing both types of concepts in practical classroom situations were tried out. These procedures were used to test principles, to modify them, and to determine when they might be appropriately applied.

3) The training activities involved in becoming proficient in the assessment of spontaneous behavior, in and of themselves, increased the sensitivity of teachers to their own behavior and the behavior of others. Most important, teachers could compare their intentions with their actions.

4) By avoiding a discussion of right and wrong ways of teaching and emphasizing the discovery of principles of teacher influence, teachers gradually became more independent and self-directing. Our most successful participants investigated problems of their own choosing,

[1] Interaction analysis as a research tool has been used ever since R. F. Bales first developed a set of categories for studying groups. Most of our research results can be found in the references at the end of this paper. Its use as a training device is more recent. Projects have taken place in New Jersey, Philadelphia, Chicago, and Minneapolis. Systematic evaluation is available in only the Minneapolis project.

designed their own plans, and arranged collaboration with others when this seemed advantageous.

Five filmstrips and one teacher's manual have been produced and written. These materials would have to be modified before they could be used with undergraduate students. Before asking how interaction analysis might be used in teacher preparation, we turn next to a description of the procedures.

THE PROCEDURE OF OBSERVATION

The observer sits in a classroom in the best position to hear and see the participants. At the end of each three-second period, he decides which category best represents the communication events just completed. He writes this category number down while simultaneously assessing communication in the next period and continues at a rate of 20 to 25 observations per minute, keeping his tempo as steady as possible. His notes are merely a series of numbers written in a column, top to bottom, so that the original sequence of events is preserved. Occasionally marginal notes are used to explain the class formation or any unusual circumstances. When there is a major change in class formation, the communication pattern, or the subject under discussion, a double line is drawn and the time indicated. As soon as the total observation is completed, the observer retires to a nearby room and completes a general description of each separate activity period separated by the double lines, including the nature of the activities, the class formation, and position of the teacher. The observer also notes any additional facts that seem pertinent to an adequate interpretation and recall of the total visit.

The ten categories that we used for interaction analysis are shown in Table 1.

The numbers that an observer writes down are tabulated in a 10×10 matrix as sequence pairs, that is, a separate tabulation is made for each overlapping pair of numbers. An illustration will serve to explain this procedure.

Teacher: "Class! The bell has rung. May I have your attention please!" [6] During the next three seconds talking and noise diminish. [10]

Teacher: "Jimmy, we are all waiting for you." [7] Pause.

Teacher: "Now today we are going to have a very pleasant surprise, [5] and I think you will find it very exciting and interesting. [1] Have any of you heard anything about what we are going to do?" [4]

Pupil: "I think we are going on a trip in the bus that's out in front." [8]

Teacher: "Oh! You've found out! How did you learn about our trip?" [4]

By now the observer has written down 6, 10, 7, 5, 1, 4, 8, and 4. As the interaction proceeds, the observer will continue to write down numbers. To tabulate these observations in a 10×10 matrix, the first step is to make sure that the entire series begins and ends with the same number. The convention we use is to add a 10 to the beginning and end of the series unless the 10 is already present. Our series now becomes 10, 6, 10, 7, 5, 1, 4, 8, 4, and 10.

These numbers are tabulated in a matrix, one pair at a time. The column is indicated by the second number, the row is indicated by the first number. The first pair is 10–6; the tally is placed in row ten, column six cell. The second pair is 6–10; tally this in the row six, column ten cell. The third pair is 10–7, the fourth pair is 7–5, and so on. Each pair overlaps with the next, and the total number of observations, "N," always will be tabulated by N-1 tallies in the matrix. In this case we

TABLE 1

CATEGORIES FOR INTERACTION ANALYSIS

Teacher Talk	Indirect Influence	1.* Accepts Feeling: accepts and clarifies the feeling tone of the students in a nonthreatening manner. Feelings may be positive or negative. Predicting or recalling feelings are included. 2.* Praises or Encourages: praises or encourages student action or behavior. Jokes that release tension, not at the expense of another individual, nodding head or saying, "um hm?" or "go on" are included. 3.* Accepts or Uses Ideas of Student: clarifying, building or developing ideas suggested by a student. As teacher brings more of his own ideas into play, shift to category five. 4.* Asks Questions: asking a question about content or procedure with the intent that a student answer.
	Direct Influence	5.* Lecturing: giving facts or opinions about content or procedures; expressing his own ideas, asking rhetorical questions. 6.* Giving Directions: directions, commands, or orders with which a student is expected to comply. 7.* Criticizing or Justifying Authority: statements intended to change student behavior from nonacceptable to acceptable pattern; bawling someone out; stating why the teacher is doing what he is doing; extreme self-reference.
Student Talk		8.* Student Talk—Response: talk by students in response to teacher. Teacher initiates the contact or solicits student statement. 9* Student Talk—Initiation: talk by students which they initiate. If "calling on" student is only to indicate who may talk next, observer must decide whether student wanted to talk. If he did, use this category.
		10.* Silence or Confusion: pauses, short periods of silence and periods of confusion in which communication cannot be understood by the observer.

* *There is no scale implied by these numbers. Each number is classificatory; it designates a particular kind of communication event. To write these numbers down during observation is to enumerate, not to judge a position on a scale.*

started a series of ten numbers, and the series produced nine tallies in the matrix.

Table 2 shows our completed matrix. Notice that in a correctly tabulated matrix the sums of the corresponding rows and columns are equal.

The problem of reliability is extremely complex, and a more complete discussion can be found in two terminal contract reports (6,7) one of which will be published as a research monograph in the 1963 series of the Cooperative Research Program. Education students can learn how to make quick field checks of their reliability and work toward higher reliability under the direction of an instructor.

THE INTERPRETATION OF MATRICES

A matrix should have at least 400 tallies, covering about twenty minutes or more of a homogeneous activity period, before attempting to make an interpretation.

TABLE 2

Category	1	2	3	4	5	6	7	8	9	10	Total
1				1							1
2											0
3											0
4								1		1	2
5	1										1
6										1	1
7				1							1
8				1							1
9											0
10						1	1				2
Total	1	0	0	2	1	1	1	1	0	2	9

Certain areas within the matrix are particularly useful for describing teacher influence. Some of these areas will now be discussed by making reference to Table 3.

The column totals of a matrix are indicated as Areas "A," "B," "C," and "D." The figures in these areas provide a general picture by answering the following questions: What proportion of the time was someone talking compared with the portion in which confusion or no talking existed? When someone was talking, what proportion of the time was used by the students? By the teacher? Of the time that the teacher talked, what proportion of his talk involved indirect influence? Direct influence?

The answers to these questions form a necessary backdrop to the interpretation of the other parts of the matrix. If student participation is about 30 or 40 per cent, we would expect to find out why it was so high by studying the matrix. If the teacher is particularly direct or indirect, we would expect certain relation-ships to exist with student talk and silence.

The next two areas to consider are areas "E" and "F." Evidence that categories 1, 2, and 3 were used for periods longer than three seconds can be found in the diagonal cells, 1–1, 2–2, and 3–3. The other six cells of Area E indicate various types of transitions between these three categories. Sustained praise or clarification of student ideas is especially significant because such elaboration often involves criteria for praise or reasons for accepting ideas and feelings. The elaboration of praise or student ideas must be present if the student's ideas are to be integrated with the content being discussed by the class.

Area F is a four-cell combination of giving directions (category 6) and giving criticisms or self-justification (category 7). The transition cells 6–7 and 7–6 are particularly sensitive to difficulties that the teacher may have with classroom discipline or resistance on the part of students. When criticism follows directions or

TABLE 3

MATRIX ANALYSIS

Category	Classification		Category	1	2	3	4	5	6	7	8	9	10	Total
Accepts Feelings	Teacher Talk	Indirect Influence	1	Area E										
Praise			2											
Student Idea			3											
Asks Questions		Direct Influence	4	"Content Cross"							Area I			
Lectures			5											
Gives Directions			6							Area F				
Criticism			7											
Student Response	Student Talk		8	Area G					Area H		Area J			
Student Initiation			9											
Silence			10											
			Total	Area A			Area B			Area C		Area D		
				Indirect Teacher Talk			Direct Teacher Talk			Student Talk				

direction follows criticism, this means that the students are not complying satisfactorily. Often there is a high loading on the 6–9 cell under these circumstances. Excessively high frequencies in the 6–6 cell *and* 7–7 cells indicate teacher domination and supervision of the students' activities. A high loading of tallies in the 6–6 cell alone often indicates that the teacher is merely giving lengthy directions to the class.

The next two areas to be considered are Areas G and H. Tallies in these two areas occur at the instant the student stops talking and the teacher starts. Area G indicates those instances in which the teacher responds to the termination of student talk with indirect influence. Area H indicates those instances in which the teacher responds to the termination of student talk with direct influence. An interesting comparison can be made by contrasting the proportion G to H versus the proportion A to B. If these two proportions are quite different, it indicates that the teacher tends to act differently at the

instant a student stops talking compared with his overall average. Often this is a mark of flexible teacher influence.

There are interesting relationships between Area E and Area G and between Area F and Area H. For example, Area G may indicate that a teacher responds indirectly to students at the instant they terminate their talk, but an observer may wish to inspect Area E to see if this indirect response is sustained in any way. The same question with regard to direct influence can be asked of Areas F and H. Areas G and H together usually fascinate teachers. They are often interested in knowing more about their immediate response to student participation.

Area I indicates an answer to the question, What types of teacher statements trigger student participation? Usually there is a high tally loading in cells 4–8 and 4–9. This is expected because students often answer questions posed by the teacher. A high loading on 4–8 and 8–4 cells alone usually indicates classroom drill directed by the teacher. The contrast of tallies in columns 8 and 9 in this area gives a rough indication of the frequency with which students initiate their own ideas versus respond to those of the teacher.

Area I is often considered in combination with Area J. Area J indicates either lengthy student statements or sustained student-to-student communication. An above-average frequency in Area C, but not in Area J, indicates that short answers, usually in response to teacher stimulation, have occurred. One would normally expect to find frequencies in Area E positively correlated with frequencies in Area J.

We turn next to concepts and principles of teacher influence before speculating about how this technique can be applied to teacher education.

CONCEPTS AND PRINCIPLES OF TEACHER INFLUENCE

It may be too early to determine what are the *fewest* number of concepts which, if organized into logically related principles, can be used by a teacher to plan how he will use his authority. Surely he will need concepts that refer to his authority and its use. He will need concepts to describe learning goals and pupil tasks. He will need concepts to classify the responses of students. He may also need concepts to characterize class formations and patterns of classroom communication. These concepts are at least the minimum.

CONCEPTS THAT REFER TO TEACHER BEHAVIOR

INDIRECT INFLUENCE

Indirect influence is defined as actions taken by the teacher which encourage and support student participation. Accepting, clarifying, praising, and developing the ideas and feelings expressed by the pupils will support student participation. We can define indirect behavior operationally by noting the per cent of teacher statements falling into categories 1, 2, 3, and 4.

DIRECT INFLUENCE

This concept refers to actions taken by the teacher which restrict student participation. Expressing one's own views through lecture, giving directions, and criticizing with the expectation of compliance tend to restrict pupil participation. We can define direct behavior operationally by noting the per cent of teacher statements falling into categories 5, 6, and 7.

Other concepts which we do not have the space to discuss include: flexibility of teacher influence, dominance or sustained direct influence, and intervention.

CONCEPTS THAT REFER TO LEARNING GOALS

CLEAR GOALS

Goal perceptions are defined from the point of view of the pupil, not the teacher. "Clear goals" is a state of affairs in which the pupil knows what he is doing, the purpose, and can guess at the first few steps to be taken. It can be measured by paper-and-pencil tests, often administered at different points in a problem-solving sequence.

AMBIGUOUS GOALS

"Ambiguous goals" describes a state of affairs in which a pupil is not sure of what he is expected to do, is not sure of the first few steps, or is unable to proceed for one reason or another. It can be measured as above.

Other concepts in this area include:

attractive and unattractive clear goals, pupil tasks, task requirements, and similar concepts.

CONCEPTS THAT REFER TO PUPIL RESPONSES

DEPENDENT ACTS

Acts of dependence occur when a pupil not only complies with teacher influence but solicits such direction. A pupil who asks a teacher to approve of his work in order to make sure that it is satisfactory, before going on to the next logical step, is acting dependently. This type of response can be measured by observation techniques and by paper-and-pencil tests on which he indicates what kind of help he would like from the teacher.

INDEPENDENT ACTS

Acts of independence occur when the pupils react primarily to task requirements and are less directly concerned with teacher approval. The measurement of this concept is the same as for dependent acts.

Other concepts include: dependence proneness—a trait, compliance, conformity, counterdependence, and similar concepts.

SOME PRINCIPLES THAT CAN BE DISCOVERED

We discovered in our research (7) that, during the first few days of a two-week unit of study in seventh grade social studies and when introducing new material in eighth grade mathematics, superior teachers (as previously defined, page 252) are initially more indirect, becoming more direct as goals and associated tasks become clarified. We also suspect that these same teachers are more indirect when helping

pupils diagnose difficulties, when trying to motivate pupils by arousing their interest, and in other situations in which the expression of pupil perceptions is helpful. On the other hand, the average or below average teacher did exactly the opposite.

Now the problem in teacher education is not only to create a situation in which education students could verify these relationships but could practice controlling their own behavior so as to become indirect or more direct at will. One place to begin is to have two, six-man groups work on a task under the direction of a leader. One task is something like an assembly line; it has a clear end product and sharp role differentiation. The other task is much more difficult to describe and does not have clear role differentiation. Now let the class superimpose different patterns of leader influence. Let them interview the role players, collect interaction analysis data by some simplified system of categories, and discuss the results. When undergraduate students first try to classify verbal statements, it sometimes helps to use only two or three categories. In one instance, the issue was the effect of using broad questions versus narrow questions. A broad question was one to which it was hard to predict the type of answer. A narrow question was one to which it was easy to guess at the type of answer. Which type of question was more likely to increase pupil participation? The students role-played this and kept a record of broad questions, narrow questions, and the length of the response. The fact that they verified their prediction correctly for this rather superficial problem was much less important compared with the experience that they gained. They learned how to verify a prediction with empirical evidence, and some had a chance to practice control of their own behavior for professional purposes.

There is no space here to list a

complete set of principles that can be investigated by systematic or intuitive data-collecting procedures. The following questions might stimulate useful learning activities. Does dependence always decrease as goals become clear? Is the final level of dependence determined by the pattern of teacher influence when goals are first formulated? Are measures of content achievement related to the pupils' attitudes toward the teacher and the schoolwork? What effects can you expect from excessive and pedantic clarification of pupil ideas and feelings? And many others.

APPLICATIONS OF INTERACTION ANALYSIS TO TEACHER EDUCATION

Suppose that before education students were given their practice teaching assignment, they had been exposed to a variety of data-collecting techniques for assessing pupil perceptions, measuring achievement, and quantifying spontaneous teacher influence. Suppose, further, that these skills had been taught in a context of personal inquiry as described earlier. What effect would this have on their approach to practice teaching?

One of their suggestions might be that two students should be assigned as a team to the first assignment. While one took over the class the other could be collecting information; the next day or so, the roles could be reversed. Together they would work out a lesson plan, agree on the data to be collected, go over the results with the help of the supervising teacher who might also have the same data-collecting skills. This situation could approach the inquiry model described earlier. The practice teacher might discover that his failure to clarify the pupils' ideas restricted the development of curiosity or that his directions were too short when he was asked for further help; both

of these inferences can be made from an interaction matrix with reasonable reliability and objectivity.

Later on a student may wish to take a practice teaching assignment by himself and turn to the supervising teacher for aid in feedback. In either case, the requirement is that the learner be able to compare his intentions with feedback information about his actions and analyze this information by using concepts which he found useful in his earlier courses in education.

There are some precautions that can already be stated with regard to the use of interaction analysis in such a situation.

First, no interaction analysis data should be collected unless the person observed is familiar with the entire process and knows its limitations.

Second, the questions to be answered by inspecting the matrix should be developed before the observation takes place.

Third, value judgments about good and bad teaching behavior are to be avoided. Emphasis is given to the problem being investigated so that cause-and-effect relationships can be discovered.

Fourth, a certain amount of defensive behavior is likely to be present at the initial consultation; it is something like listening to a tape recording for the first time.

Fifth, a consultation based on two observations or at least two matrices helps to eliminate value judgments or at least control them. Comparisons between the matrices are more likely to lead to principles.

Just how experiences of the type we have been discussing will fit into the present curricula is difficult to know. If activities of the sort described in this paper are valuable, are they to be superimposed on the present list of courses or is more radical surgery necessary?

Perhaps this is the point to risk a prediction, which is that teacher education will become increasingly concerned with the process of teaching itself during the next few decades. Instead of emphasizing knowledge which *we think* teachers will need in order to teach effectively, as we have in the past, we will turn more and more to an analysis of teaching acts as they occur in spontaneous classroom interaction. We are now at the point in our technology of data collecting at which procedures for analyzing and conceptualizing teaching behavior can be developed. Systems for doing this will become available regardless of whether they are similar or dissimilar to the procedures described in this paper. When this fine day arrives, the role of the education instructor will change, and the dichotomy between field and theory will disappear. The instructor's role will shift from talking about effective teaching to the rigorous challenge of demonstrating effective teaching. The process of inquiry will create problem-solving activities that will produce more independent, self-directing teachers whose first day on the job will be their worst, not their best.

These changes will be successful to the extent that the graduates of teacher education can learn to control their own behavior for the professional purpose of managing effective classroom learning. It will be the responsibility of the education instructor to help prospective teachers discover what their teaching intentions should be and then create training situations in which behavior gradually matches intentions with practice. Teaching will remain an art, but it will be studied scientifically.

REFERENCES

1. ANDERSON, HAROLD H. "The Measurement of Domination and of Socially Integrative Behavior in Teachers' Contacts with Children." *Child Development* 10: 73–89; June 1939.

2. ———, and BREWER, HELEN M. *Studies of Teachers' Classroom Personalities,* I: *Dominative and Socially Integrative Behavior of Kindergarten Teachers.* Applied Psychology Monographs of the American Psychological Association. No. 6. Stanford, California: Stanford University Press, July 1945.

3. ———, and BREWER, JOSEPH E. *Studies of Teachers' Classroom Personalities,* II: *Effects of Teachers' Dominative and Integrative Contacts on Children's Classroom Behavior.* Applied Psychology Monographs of the American Psychological Association. No. 8 Stanford, California: Stanford University Press, June 1946.

4. ———; BREWER, J. E.; and REED, M. F. *Studies of Teachers' Classroom Personalities,* III: *Follow-up Studies of the Effects of Dominative and Integrative Contacts on Children's Behavior.* Applied Psychology Monographs of the American Psychological Association. No. 11. Stanford, California: Stanford University Press, December 1946.

5. CANTOR, NATHANIEL. *The Teaching-Learning Process.* New York: Dryden Press, 1953. pp. 59–72.

6. FLANDERS, N. A. A terminal contract report on using interaction analysis for the inservice training of teachers. To be submitted to the U.S. Office of Education N.D.E.A., Title VII. Available from the author. University of Michigan, after April 1963.

7. ———. *Teacher Influence, Pupil Attitudes, and Achievement.* Dittoed manuscript to be published in 1963 as a Research Monograph, Cooperative Research Program, U.S. Office of Education. Available from author, University of Michigan, 1962. 176 pp.

8. ———, and HAVUMAKI, S. "Group Compliance to Dominative Teacher Influence." *Human Relations* 13:67–82.

9. ROMNEY, G. P.; HUGHES, M. M.; and

others. *Progress Report of the Merit Study of the Provo City Schools.* Provo, Utah, August 1958. XIX + 226 pp. See also *Patterns of Effective Teaching: Second Progress Report of the Merit*

Study of the Provo City Schools. Provo, Utah, June 1961. XII + 93 pp.

10. THELEN, H. A. *Education and the Human Quest.* New York: Harper Brothers, 1960, pp. 74–112.

IS THE MINNESOTA TEACHER ATTITUDE INVENTORY VALID AND HOMOGENEOUS?

Albert H. Yee

Reviews of research on teachers' characteristics and on the measurement and prediction of teaching success (e.g., Ryans, 1963; Stinnett and Clarke, 1960) have noted investigators' concern with teachers' affective behavior. In such reviews, the Minnesota Teacher Attitude Inventory (MTAI) has been given special attention, because so many studies have employed it. Getzels and Jackson (1963) devote 14 pages of their *Handbook* review of research on teachers' personality and characteristics to studies using the MTAI. They conclude: "The importance of understanding teacher atti-

From: Journal of Educational Measurement, *1967, 4, 151–61. Copyright © 1967 by the National Council on Measurement in Education, and reproduced by permission of the author and publisher.*

tudes would certainly justify any efforts to make the MTAI more meaningful" (p. 522). *The Sixth Mental Measurements Yearbook,* (Buros, 1965) lists 155 references for the MTAI, but few of the studies were conducted to provide greater understanding of the inventory and increase its usefulness.

BACKGROUND OF THE MTAI

First developed about 1946 and published in standardized form in 1951, the inventory was designed by its test authors (Cook, Leeds & Callis, 1951, p. 3):

...to measure those attitudes of a teacher which predict how well he will get along with pupils in interpersonal relationships, and indirectly how well satisfied he will be with teaching as a vocation. The most direct use to which the MTAI can be put is in the selection of students for teacher preparation and the selection of teachers for teaching positions. A parallel use is in counseling students about a vocational choice.

Validation of the MTAI proceeded as follows (Cook et al., 1951; Leeds, 1950): (1) principals' selection of 100 "superior" teachers characterized as maintaining good relations with pupils and 100 "inferior" teachers characterized as maintaining poor relations with pupils; (2) responses of the 200 teachers to 756 items presented to them in two forms were examined by statistical item analysis; (3) selection of 164 items which were believed to be differentiating between the superior and inferior teachers; (4) cross-validation of the inventory with another group of 100 teachers selected without prior information as to their relations with pupils; (5) obtaining principals', pupils', and observer's ratings of each teacher's affective merit; (6) finding validity coefficients by computing correlations between teachers' scores and criterion scores, which were $\rho = .45$ with principal's ratings, $\rho = .46$ with pupils' ratings, $\rho = .49$ with observer's ratings, and $\rho = .60$ with combined criteria; and (7) final formulation of an empirical scoring key and selection of 150 items for publication.

In 1953, *The Fourth Mental Measurements Yearbook* provided reviews of the inventory by Arnold and Cronbach which praised the painstaking development of the MTAI but raised questions concerning its recommended use. Arnold requested further norms for different stages and backgrounds in teachers' experience. Cronbach wrote: "The central question is whether the inventory is valid for the recommended (predictive) uses of teacher selection and guidance" (p. 798). Recom-

mending that the MTAI be used only for research purposes until the question was investigated, Cronbach suggested, however, that the "studies reported in the manual make one optimistic that the validity of the test will prove satisfactory" (p. 798). Gage (1965) suggested that the MTAI required further study to be useful in providing better understanding of teachers working with culturally deprived students.

Others, such as Rabinowitz (1954), Scott and Brinkley (1960), Sheldon (1959), and Sorenson (1956), have questioned the MTAI's susceptibility to faking.

PREDICTIVE VALIDITY OF THE MTAI

The predictive validity of the MTAI is based on the important thesis "that the attitudes of a teacher are the key to the problem of predicting the type of classroom atmosphere he will be able to maintain" (Cook et al., 1951, p. 4). Relatively high correlations found between teachers' scores and criteria have been the primary evidence for the validity of the MTAI (Callis, 1953; Cook, Kearney, Rocchio, and Thompson, 1956; Leeds, 1950; Leeds, 1952; Stein and Hardy, 1957). Since concurrent comparisons were used to obtain the validity coefficients, the test authors further assume that such correlations will remain essentially the same over time. For example, they wrote:

> It is assumed that the attitudes of pupils toward their teachers and school work are a reflection of their teachers' attitudes toward them and toward teaching procedures. Hence, if the attitudes of teachers and of pupils are reliably measured there should be a high relationship between them (p. 10).

This assumption may be questionable in light of findings concerning the relationship between teachers' and pupils' attitudes. Della Piana and Gage (1955) found that the validity of the MTAI in correlating with the favorability of a teacher's ratings by his pupils varied according to the value-orientation of his pupils. For pupils with strong cognitive values, teachers' MTAI scores did not correlate as highly with pupils' ratings ($\rho =$ .05), as they did for pupils with strong affective values ($\rho = .57$, p $< .01$). In another study, Yee (1966) found differences in teacher-pupil interaction according to levels of teaching experience and pupils' social-class background. It was also found that teachers' attitudes influence pupils' attitudes in the *in*congruent direction, i.e., to reduce the correlation between attitudes, as well as in the congruent direction, i.e., to raise the correlation between attitudes.

Additional problems raised by other studies also create uncertainty in the MTAI's predictive validity. Findings, such as those by Cook and Medley (1955) and Gage and Chatterjee (1960) indicate the possible influence of response sets in MTAI scores. The inventory's Likert-type format for item responses, "Strongly agree . . . Strongly disagree," may make the MTAI susceptible to response biases. Relevant to such concerns are Hudson's (1966, pp. 64–68) findings of differences in responding emphatically between "converger" and "diverger" types of English schoolboys.

Significant changes have been found in MTAI scores over time (Cook, Hoyt, & Eikaas, 1956; Day, 1959; Hoyt & Cook, 1960; Rabinowitz & Rosenbaum, 1960). Scores of teacher candidates tend to improve from the beginning of their junior year to their senior year and begin to decline in student teaching. Through the early years of teaching, teachers' MTAI scores continue to fall until they approximate scores at the beginning of professional preparation.

Uncertainty in the MTAI's predictive validity increases when dissimilar group scores are evident for students preparing for differing specialities in education (Callis, 1950), for teachers in this country and England (Evans, 1966), in public and parochial schools (Burkard, 1965), from various teacher preparation centers (Kearney & Rocchio, 1956), and according to differences in pupils' and teachers' personality and characteristics (Gage & Suci, 1951; Teigland, 1966; Yee, 1966). Also, the large variances typical of MTAI results make it difficult to classify types of teachers.

A REVALIDATION OF THE MTAI

A study of the MTAI was conducted to test its validity and homogeneity. Data were available from a study of teacher-pupil attitude relationships (Yee, 1966). The data included 212 teachers' MTAI responses, attitudes of their 4th, 5th, and 6th grade pupils measured by the 100-item "About My Teacher" inventory (Beck, 1964) and 51 principals' ratings for 206 of the 212 teachers. The pupils' and principals' instruments provided perceptions of teachers' affective, cognitive, disciplinary, innovative, and motivational merit.

CORRELATIONS

Table 1 presents the product-moment correlations obtained between teachers' MTAI scores and criterion and between different criterion scores.

All but one of the principals' ratings correlate higher with teachers' MTAI scores than do pupils' ratings, and all principals' ratings correlate significantly with the MTAI. The highest validity coefficients appear with principals' and pupils' innovative merit ratings, but they are much lower than .45, the lowest coefficient found by the test authors. Unlike the pupils'

TABLE 1

CORRELATIONS OBTAINED BETWEEN TEACHERS' MTAI
SCORES, PUPILS' CLASS MEANS, AND PRINCIPALS' RATINGS

Criterion	Pupils' Ratings vs. MTAI (N = 212)	Principals' Ratings vs. MTAI (N = 206)	Pupils' vs. Principals' Ratings (N = 206)
Affective merit	.16*	.21**	.18*
Cognitive merit	.07	.15*	.05
Disciplinary merit	.04	.14*	.13
Innovative merit	.26**	.24**	.19**
Motivational merit	.21**	.23**	.15*
Composite merit	.17*	.24**	.28**

*$p < .05$.
**$p < .01$.

ratings, the principals' ratings lack independence, since most principals evaluated several teachers. Discounting this possible problem in the validity coefficients against principals' criterion ratings (which is also present in the authors' validation), we see that there is moderate relationship between teachers' MTAI scores and principals' ratings. However, there are fewer statistically significant relationships with pupil criteria, and correlations between principals' and pupils' ratings are lower than expected. These indefinite results, therefore, do not yield conclusive support for the concurrent validity of the MTAI.

ITEM ANALYSES

The MTAI was also subjected to item analysis. We used the same statistical formula employed by the test authors (Garrett, 1937, pp. 385–386) to test the significance of item discrimination. For a test of the MTAI, it would be in the following form:
Where,

$$\chi^2 = \frac{\sum_{i=1}^{5} \left[\frac{1}{a + a'} (aN' - a'N)^2 \right]}{NN'}$$

a and a' are the five pairs of column entries found under responses to an item, N and N' be the corresponding row totals, i.e., totals for contrasted groups.

For example, in Table 2, Item 1, under "Strongly agree," a = 18, a' = 4, N = 60, and N' = 60. Following Guilford's (1965, pp. 240–241) procedures for computing chi square in which either rows or columns, or both, exceed two, we obtain the same χ^2 value as with the above formula.

This study's item analyses differ from the test authors' by the establishment of extreme criterion groups with Kelley's (1939) 27% rule for the selection of contrasted groups (Ns of 60) in validating test items. Twelve separate item analyses conducted with different pupil attitudes as validating criterion found most of the MTAI items deficient in discriminating between upper and lower teacher groups. With such criteria, the average proportion of discriminating items was about .07 or less than 11 items out of 150. With pupils' attitudes toward teacher's innovative merit as the criterion, a high of 29 discriminating items (.19) was found, and the index of discrimination calculated with "Right" scores (Ebel, 1965, pp. 352–359) was found to be only .07.

TABLE 2

Examples of Upper and Lower Teacher Groups'
Response Distribution (Principals' Combined
Affective-innovative Ratings as Criterion)

	Strongly Agree	Agree	Undecided	Disagree	Strongly Disagree	Right	Wrong
Item 1. Most children are obedient.							
Group	1*	2**	3	4**	5		
Superior	18	42	0	0	0	18	42
Inferior	4	50	3	2	1	4	52
Difference	14	−8	−3	−2	−1	$\chi^2 = 15.60$	
Item 98. Pupils can be very boring at times.							
Group	1**	2**	3*	4*	5		
Superior	0	8	1	30	21	31	8
Inferior	2	18	8	30	2	38	20
Difference	−2	−10	−7	0	19	$\chi^2 = 26.99$	
Item 14. Young people are difficult to understand these days.							
Group	1**	2**	3**	4	5*		
Superior	0	5	0	44	11	11	5
Inferior	0	12	7	36	5	5	19
Difference	0	−7	−7	8	6	$\chi^2 = 12.93$	

* denotes "Right" response.
** denotes "Wrong" response.

One item analysis was conducted with principals' combined ratings of teachers' affective and innovative merit as the criterion. Less than half the items discriminated between the responses of the contrasted groups, although the 70 items that did discriminate provided differences with chi-square values often significant at the .01 level. However, the item index of discrimination averaged only .15.

Results of these item analyses agree with the correlational findings discussed in the last section. Pupils' and principals' ratings as criteria provide differing results. MTAI scores appear to be poor indicators of teachers' rapport with pupils, but better, if only modest, indicators of principals' satisfaction with teachers' affective-innovative merit in classrooms. Perhaps this finding, which suggests better concurrent validity for MTAI scores with principals' ratings than with pupils' ratings, should not be surprising since principals' ratings were the only criterion in selecting superior and inferior teachers to try-out the original list of 756 items.

Discrepancies in Scoring. Examining the scoring of "Right" and "Wrong" responses for items discriminating significantly between superior and inferior teachers, we found very few items providing clear-cut polarity of "Rights" for superior teachers and "Wrongs" for inferior teachers. Of the 70 discriminating items found with principals' ratings as the criterion, only 15 items provided more "Right" responses than "Wrong" responses for superior teachers and more "Wrong" than "Right" responses for inferior teachers. Often the significant contrast between groups is in only the "Right" or "Wrong" scores. Sometimes inferior teachers score more "Right" responses than superior teachers and vice versa. Examination of the few examples of item analysis provided by the developers (Cook et al., 1951, p. 11; Leeds, 1950, pp. 8–9), however, show that this possible discrepancy in scoring may have been present in the original construction of the inventory. Table 2 presents some examples of our findings.

Deriving the scoring key for the MTAI purely through empirical means has been questioned in the past (Cronbach, 1953; Gage, 1957), mainly because of the illogical and contradictory weighting often found for MTAI items. Whatever advantage such scoring provides, however, the key should be consistently valid in giving superior teachers more "Right" scores and less "Wrong" scores than inferior teachers, i.e., in predicting the criterion.

As can be seen for Item 1 in Table 2, more of the teachers in both groups responded "Agree," which is scored "Wrong," but more of the superior teachers correctly responded "Strongly Agree' than did inferior teachers. Thus, we have most of the difference between groups in the first column. Since only six inferior teachers responded in the logical direction of wrongness, this item should probably be rejected. In Item 98, the response "Strongly Disagree" clearly discriminates between groups, but is scored neutral. Responses three and four do not actually discriminate, but are scored "Right." Responses one and two apparently do the job they are supposed to do. Such empirical scoring, however, produces more "Right" scores for the inferior teachers. By scoring only "Strongly Agree" as correct, this item would be more useful than it is at present. Satisfactory results were obtained with Item 14.

More than 15 years have passed since the first publication of the MTAI. The test authors' samplings of teachers' attitudes toward children and principals' perceptions of teaching effectiveness strongly influence its items and scoring key now available from the test publishers. Domi-

nant philosophical and methodological practices of the 1940's may be much less relevant in classrooms of the late 1960's. In documenting the demise of the "progressive movement," Cremin (1961) wrote that many problems and issues arising in the 40's and culminating in the 50's "held the makings of the deepest educational crisis in the nation's history" (p. 339). Kandel (1957) wrote that a new era in American education began with the start of the second half of the twentieth century. Therefore, to improve its usefulness in testing today, the validity of the MTAI's scoring as well as its items require extensive retesting and revision.

HOMOGENEITY OF THE MTAI

The developers of the MTAI estimated the inventory's internal consistency or homogeneity by the Spearman-Brown split-half method with odd-even correlations. Our findings of .89 with the Spearman-Brown and Guttman (1945) split-half (odd-even) formulas and also with the Kuder-Richardson formula 21 agree exactly with the test authors' results (Cook et al., 1951, pp. 12 & 14).

Using total MTAI scores as criterion, we also conducted item analyses for contrasted groups of 60 teachers each. Only 29 items did not discriminate between superior and inferior teachers, and the average difference obtained provided Chi-square values significant above the .001 level. However, scores for the discriminating items lacked logical "Right" and "Wrong" polarization, as was found in results from the item analyses with external criteria.

Using another approach to the question of test homogeneity, Horn and Morrison (1965) factor-analyzed the MTAI to test the developers' claim that the inventory measures a unifactorial attitude. They extracted five factors, but intercorrelations indicated "the five factors ... fall into a positive manifold (thus giving some credence to the authors' claim for unidimensionality), but are largely independent . . . ." (p. 124).

Since the Horn-Morrison factor analysis was somewhat contrived due to computer limitations, we conducted a factor analysis of all 150 items together. The 46 factors extracted and the resulting positive factor intercorrelations agree basically with the hypothesis and findings of Horn and Morrison. Our first factors, which account for most of the variance extracted, are very similar. Horn and Morrison titled their Factor I, "Traditionalistic versus Modern Beliefs about Child Control."

CONSTRUCT VALIDITY OF THE MTAI

According to the test authors, the theoretical variable the MTAI is intended to measure is teacher's future rapport with pupils or the affective relationship between teacher and pupils. The problems discussed above with the inventory's predictive and concurrent validity may stem from a serious, basic weakness in the MTAI's construct validity. In assessing what factors determine classroom atmosphere, the test authors over-emphasize teachers' attitudes and neglect other determinants. By claiming predictive validity and not just concurrent validity, the test authors assert MTAI scores predict future relationships in classroom interaction.

Social interaction in classrooms, however, involves more variables than the MTAI or similar teacher inventories can ascertain. For interactional concerns in classrooms, we may want to consider relationships of variables, such as school neighborhood, grade level, and the characteristics and behavior of the teacher, other teachers, parents, pupils, and the principal. By studying the nature of their interaction

over time, we may be better prepared to understand and predict the behavior of a teacher in future classroom interpersonal behavior events. No teacher scale could be devised to encompass such complex relationships in its measurements.

The MTAI is a throwback to the earlier days when the criterion-of-effectiveness paradigm (Gage, 1963) was in vogue and "the approach to the analysis of . . . interaction in the learning situation was that of examining and quantifying certain 'monadic' variables. . . ." (Withall & Lewis, 1963, p. 708). It was developed without benefit of the *Technical Recommendations for Psychological Tests and Diagnostic Techniques* published by APA in 1954 and the more recent *Standards for Educational and Psychological Tests and Manuals* published in 1966 by a joint APA-AERA-NCME committee. Statements C4.41 and C7.1 in *Standards,* which consider it essential that manuals *not* substantiate predictive validity only with concurrent criteria (pp. 17–18) and that manuals "indicate the extent to which the proposed interpretation has been substantiated" (p. 23), would have been helpful to the MTAI's authors and publisher. Perhaps fair evaluation of the inventory must provide consideration of these disadvantages and appreciation of the extensive development underlying the test.

To conclude this effort to provide better understanding of the MTAI, we refer to Stevens (1951, p. 29):

> We conclude . . . that the most liberal and useful definition of measurement is the assignment of numerals to things so as to represent facts and conventions about them. The problems of what is and what is not measurement then reduces to the simple question: what are the rules, if any, under which numerals are assigned? If we can point to a consistent set of rules, we are obviously concerned with measurement

of some sort, and we can then proceed to the more interesting question: what kind of measurement is it?

Because we were able to question the basic premises or "rules" upon which the MTAI was developed, we must conclude that the MTAI does not adequately measure what it is supposed to measure, even though the MTAI appears to be homogeneous. With Stevens' distinction between "measures" as defined above and "indicants," i.e., " . . . *effects* or *correlates* related to psychological dimensions by *unknown* laws" (p. 47), we conclude that the MTAI is useful, especially for research purposes, as an indicant of teachers' attitudes toward pupils. This suggested limitation in the use of the MTAI is in keeping with the precept of Cronbach and Meehl (1955, p. 291) that " . . . *unless* (theory) *makes contact with observations, and exhibits explicit, public steps of inference, construct validation cannot be claimed.*"

REFERENCES

American Psychological Association. *Technical recommendations for psychological tests and diagnostic techniques.* Washington, D.C.: American Psychological Association, 1954.

American Psychological Association, American Educational Research Association, and National Council on Measurement in Education, Joint Committee on Test Standards. *Standards for educational and psychological tests and manuals.* Washington, D.C.: American Psychological Association, 1966

ARNOLD, D. L. Minnesota Teacher Attitude Inventory. In O. K. BUROS (Ed.), *The fourth mental measurements yearbook.* Highland Park, N.J.: Gryphon Press, 1953, pp. 797–798.

BECK, W. H. Pupils' perceptions of teacher merit: a factor analysis of five hypothe-

sized dimensions. Unpublished dissertation, Stanford University, 1964.

BURKARD, SISTER M. INNOCENTIA. Effectiveness of the MTAI in a parochial school setting. *Journal of Experimental Education,* 1965, **33**, 225–229.

BUROS, O. K. (Ed.) *The sixth mental measurements yearbook.* Highland Park, New Jersey: Gryphon Press, 1965.

CALLIS, R. Change in teacher-pupil attitudes related to training and experience. *Educational and Psychological Measurement,* 1950, **10**, 718–727.

CALLIS, R. The efficiency of the MTAI for predicting interpersonal relations in the classroom, *Journal of Applied Psychology,* 1953, **37**, 82–85.

COOK, W. W., HOYT, C. J., & EIKAAS, A. Studies of predictive validity of the Minnesota Teacher Attitude Inventory. *Journal of Teacher Education,* 1956, **7**, 167–172.

COOK, W. W., KEARNEY, N. C., ROCCHIO, P. D., & THOMPSON, A. Significant factors in teachers' classroom attitudes. *Journal of Teacher Education,* 1956, **7**, 274–279.

COOK, W. W., LEEDS, C. H., & CALLIS, R. *Minnesota teacher attitude inventory: Manual.* New York: Psychological Corp., 1951.

COOK, W. W., & MEDLEY, D. M. The relationship between Minnesota Teacher Attitude Inventory scores and scores on certain scales of the Minnesota Multiphasic Personality Inventory. *Journal of Applied Psychology,* 1955, **39**, 123–129.

CREMIN, L. A. *The transformation of the school.* New York: Alfred A. Knopf, 1961.

CRONBACH, L. J. Minnesota Teacher Attitude Inventory. In O. K. BUROS (Ed.), *The fourth mental measurements yearbook.* Highland Park, New Jersey: Gryphon Press, 1953. Pp. 798–802.

CRONBACH, L. J., & MEEHL, P. E. Construct validity in psychological tests. *Psychological Bulletin*, 1955, **52**, 281–302.

DAY, H. P. Attitude changes of beginning teachers after initial teaching experience. *Journal of Teacher Education*, 1959, **10**, 326–328.

DELLA PIANA, G. M. & GAGE, N. L. Pupils' values and the validity of the Minnesota Teacher Attitude Inventory. *Journal of Educational Psychology*, 1955, **46**, 167–178.

EBEL, R. L. *Measuring educational achievement*. Englewood Cliffs, N.J.: Prentice-Hall, 1965.

EVANS, K. M. The Minnesota Teacher Attitude Inventory. *Educational Research*, 1966, **8**, 134–141.

GAGE, N. L. Psychological research on teacher education for the great cities. *Urban Education*, 1965, **1**, 175–196.

GAGE, N. L. Paradigms for research on teaching. In N. L. GAGE (Ed.) *Handbook for research on teaching*. Chicago: Rand McNally, 1963. Pp. 94–141.

GAGE, N. L. Logical versus empirical scoring keys: the case of the MTAI. *Journal of Educational Psychology*, 1957, **48**, 213–216

GAGE, N. L., & CHATTERJEE, B. B. The Psychological meaning of acquiescence set: further evidence. *Journal of Abnormal and Social Psychology*, 1960, **60**, 280–283.

GAGE, N. L., & SUCI, G. J. Social perception and teacher-pupil relationships. *Journal of Educational Psychology*, 1951, **42**, 144–152.

GARRETT, H. E. *Statistics in psychology and education*. New York: Longmans, Green, 1937.

GETZELS, J. W., & JACKSON, P. W. The teacher's personality and characteristics. In N. L. GAGE (Ed.). *Handbook of research on teaching*. Chicago: Rand McNally, 1963. Pp. 506–582.

GUILFORD, J. P. *Fundamental statistics in psychology and education*. (4th ed.) New York: McGraw-Hill, 1965.

GUTTMAN, L. A basis for analyzing test-retest reliability. *Psychometrika*, 1945, **10**, 255–282.

HORN, J. L., & MORRISON, W. E. Dimensions of teacher attitudes. *Journal of Educational Psychology*, 1965, **56**, 118–125.

HOYT, C. J., & COOK, W. W. The stability of MTAI scores during two to seven years of teaching. *Journal of Teacher Education*, 1960, **11**, 487–491.

HUDSON, L. *Contrary imaginations*. New York: Schocker, 1966.

KANDEL, I. L. *American education in the twentieth century*. Cambridge, Massachusetts: Harvard University Press, 1957.

KEARNEY, N. C., & ROCCHIO, P. D. The effect of teacher education on the teacher's attitudes. *Journal of Educational Research*, 1956, **49**, 703–708.

KELLEY, T. L. The selection of upper and lower groups for the validation of test items. *Journal of Educational Psychology*, 1939, **30**, 17–24.

LEEDS, C. H. A scale for measuring teacher-pupil attitudes and teacher-pupil rapport. *Psychological Monographs: General and Applied*, 1950, **64**, 1–24.

LEEDS, C. H. A second validity study of the Minnesota Teacher Attitude Inventory. *Elementary School Journal*, 1952, **52**, 398–405.

RABINOWITZ, W. The fakability of the Minnesota Teacher Attitude Inventory. *Educational and Psychological Measurement*, 1954, **14**, 657–664.

RABINOWITZ, W., & ROSENBAUM, I. Teaching experience and teachers' attitudes. *Ele-*

mentary School Journal, 1960, **60**, 313–319.

RYANS, D. G. Assessment of teacher behavior and instruction, *Review of Educational Research*, 1963, **33**, 415–441.

SCOTT, O., & BRINKLEY, S. G. Attitude changes of student teacher and the validity of the Minnesota Teacher Attitude Inventory. *Journal of Educational Psychology*, 1960, **51**, 76–81.

SHELDON, M. S. Conditions affecting the fakability of teacher-selection inventories. *Educational and Psychological Measurement*, 1959, **19**, 207–219.

SORENSON, A. G. A note on the "fakability" of the MTAI. *Journal of Applied Psychology*, 1956, **40**, 192–194.

STEIN, H. L., & HARDY, J. A validation study of the Minnesota Teacher Attitude Inventory in Manitoba. *Journal of Educational Research*, 1957, **50**, 322–338.

STEVENS, S. S. Mathematics, measurement, and psychophysics. In S. S. STEVENS (Ed.), *Handbook of experimental psychology.* New York: Wiley, 1951. Pp. 1–49.

STINNETT, T. M., & CLARKE, C. M. Teacher education—programs. In C. W. HARRIS (Ed.), *Encyclopedia of educational research.* (3rd ed.) New York: Macmillan, 1960. Pp. 1461–1471.

TEIGLAND, J. J. The relationship between measured teacher attitude change and certain personality characteristics. *Journal of Experimental Research*, 1966, **60**, 84–85.

WITHALL, J., & LEWIS, W. W. Social interaction in the classroom. In N. L. GAGE (Ed.) *Handbook of research on teaching.* Chicago: Rand McNally, 1963. Pp. 683–714.

YEE, A. H. *Factors involved in determining the relationship between teachers' and pupils' attitudes.* U. S. Dept. of Health, Education, & Welfare, Office of Education, Cooperative Research Project No. 5–8346, Austin, Texas: The University of Texas, 1966.

SOME INDIRECT MEASURES
OF INTERPERSONAL ATTRACTION
AMONG CHILDREN

Albert J. Lott / Bernice E. Lott

As part of a program of research on the antecedents and consequents of attitudes toward persons, we have been concerned with the problem of obtaining behavioral indexes of attitudes, beyond the verbal self-report measures which are typically used.

Employing a reinforcement theory model (Lott & Lott, 1968), a positive attitude (liking) is defined as an implicit anticipatory goal response and a negative attitude (disliking) is defined as an implicit anticipatory pain or frustration response. Once an attitude toward a person has been acquired, as a result, primarily, of relatively consistent association between that person and satisfying or aversive events, the attitude should function as a mediator (r-s) which can evoke a variety of both unlearned and learned responses. Application of the simple Pavlovian paradigm leads to the expectation that responses typically made to satisfying or aversive events (because of unlearned con-

From: Journal of Educational Psychology, *1970,* 61, *124–35. Copyright* © *1970 by the American Psychological Association, and reproduced by permission of the authors and APA.*

nections or previous learning) will be conditioned to stimulus persons who are contiguous with these events. Such responses may cover a broad spectrum from autonomic to perceptual to overt physical to evaluative verbal. Overt responses mediated by a positive attitude, for example, may include a smile at the sight of a liked person, a complex pattern of motor responses classifiable as general "approach," and almost any specific act which may have been learned in the presence of that particular stimulus person.

Most research in the area of interpersonal attraction has relied almost exclusively on verbal self-report behavior such as sociometric choices or responses to rating and ranking scales as the source of inferences regarding attitudes toward persons. Cook and Selltiz (1964) have noted this deficiency with respect to the measurement of attitudes in general. It is clearly desirable to make inferences about interpersonal attitudes from a large variety of measures which sample the broad class of behaviors which people can be expected to manifest in the presence of liked and disliked others. The objectice of the present paper is to report and evaluate the findings from three studies in each of which a verbal report measure of liking (rating scale or sociometric test) is shown to be positively related to indirect, oblique, or unobtrusive measures which do not require self-disclosure of attitudes but which were predicted, on the basis of conceptual considerations, to be valid reflectors of interpersonal attraction.

TREASURE HUNT AND LOOKING BOX

Nunally, Duchnowski, and Parker (1965) reported the use of two novel techniques in an experiment in which nonsense syllables were differentially associated with reward (gain of two pennies), no reward, or punishment (loss of one penny). Following this association, second-grade children were tested with these stimuli in two ways. In a Treasure Hunt game, the subjects were presented with 21 identical white boxes; on top of each there was printed a nonsense syllable and the subjects were asked to find the box that had 25¢ hidden under it. Those boxes which had on them the syllable which had been previously associated with reward were looked under more frequently than the other boxes. The subjects were also tested on a Looking Box which made visible for .4 second a stimulus slide behind a window, when the subject pressed the appropriate button. The children had a choice of viewing any of three different nonsense syllables (each of which appeared in two windows) by activating the light behind any one at a time. When the light went off, another button push was required if the subject wished to view the same stimulus again. It was found that the make-believe word (nonsense syllable) which had been previously associated with reward was viewed longer than the others. Nunally

and his associates have used these techniques in subsequent research and in one study (Nunnally, Duchnowski, & Knott, 1967) found positive effects 5 weeks after the conditioning sessions even though the subjects had no experience with the experimenter or materials at any time during the delay period.

The first two investigations to be reported here make use of the Looking Box and Treasure Hunt, somewhat modified and adapted for use as measures of liking by children for one another. Both of these techniques seemed highly relevant to the study of interpersonal attraction since our theoretical analysis assumes that a liked person evokes an anticipatory goal response which should mediate approach behavior and that a disliked person evokes anticipatory pain or frustration which should mediate avoidance behavior. Since approach and avoidance seem to be reflected, in different ways, by responses to the Looking Box, Treasure Hunt, and a simple Liking Scale it was expected that significant positive relations would be obtained among these measures when the same sample of children was tested on each to determine their degree of attraction to their peers.

STUDY 1

METHOD

Subjects. Twenty children served as subjects. Enrolled in summer classes in creative dramatics, the children had been meeting with a male teacher three times a week for several weeks before the investigation was begun. One group of younger children (Group Y) contained seven girls and four boys ranging in age from 6 to 12 years; the second group (O) consisted of older children, six girls and three boys, between 13 and 16 years of age.

Procedure. Each member of both

groups (Y and O) was photographed individually (draped with a black cloth below the neck) by a professional photographer. A 35 mm. color slide and a $2\frac{1}{2} \times 3\frac{1}{2}$ inch black and white print were prepared for each. Fourteen children were present in Group Y and 10 in Group O on the day the photographs were taken, that is, three more and one more in Groups Y and O, respectively, than were present for subsequent portions of the study when measures of interpersonal attraction were obtained.

One week later, the three measures described below were administered in a counterbalanced order across subjects. Each subject was sent, individually, by the teacher into the experimental room where both the experimenter and an assistant were present. The experimenter gave all the instructions while the assistant recorded verbal responses. Neither the experimenter nor the assistant had any prior knowledge of sociometric relations within the groups, thus minimizing the possibility of experimenter bias influencing the results.

1. Liking Scale: This scale is composed of 15 steps, represented graphically in a descending order, from maximum to minimum liking. There are no numbers or other symbols marking the steps. Each subject was given a booklet containing a separate scale for each member of his particular class, excluding himself, and instructed to rate every class member by putting "an X on the step that shows how much you like him (or her)." It was carefully explained that each step represented a different degree of liking so that the larger the step marked, the greater the liking, and the smaller the step marked, the less the liking. Scores could range from 15, maximum liking, to 1, minimum liking. No verbal responses were required on this paper-and-pencil measure, and the subject's written responses were not seen by the experimenter.

2. Looking Box: Each subject was shown a commerical slide viewer (Pana-

vue electric) mounted on a wooden base on which there also was a button to activate the light of the viewer. A Hunter timer was connected to the viewer to regulate the amount of time the light stayed on after each button press (.3 second). A counter automatically recorded the number of times the button was pressed. Only the viewer and button were visible to the subject.

The subjects were instructed as follows: "...If you press the button a light will go on and you will be able to see a picture of someone you know. The light will stay on for only a short time and then go out, like this." The experimenter demonstrated the viewer and each subject worked it, with a slide of himself to view. "Now I am going to show you pictures of...children in your drama class...you may look at every picture as many times as you want."

The order of presenting slides of class members was random and differed for each subject. Group Y children viewed 13 slides; the slide of one boy in Group O could not be used because of poor processing so he had 9 slides to view while other Group O subjects had 8. The scores obtained from the Looking Box were the number of times the subject pressed the button to view the slide of each different classmate.

3. Treasure Hunt: Each subject was presented with a group of randomly arranged $3\frac{1}{4} \times 4$ inch cardboard boxes, each one covered with a black and white photograph of a different class member, excluding himself. The subjects in Group Y were shown 14 stimulus boxes while those in Group O were shown 8, except for one subject who was shown 9.

Each child was told that 25¢ was hidden under one of the boxes, that he could keep the money if he found it, and that he could make five choices, one at a time. The order and name of classmate-boxes chosen was recorded for each subject. No money was actually hidden under any box, but after all choices were made the experimenter assured the subject that he would be given a quarter later.

After all the data were collected, the experimenter returned to the two groups, thanked the children for their cooperation and gave each a quarter and his own photograph to keep.

RESULTS

To test the hypothesis of a positive relation between Liking Scale ratings and number of times a slide picture was viewed in the Looking Box, each rating made by each subject was first categorized as: high—a rating of 15–11; moderate—a rating of 10–6; or low—a rating of 5–1. For each subject the mean number of times he had viewed the slides of class members whom he had rated high, moderately, and low on the Liking Scale was separately calculated. (Data on three subjects could not be included because they had been given incomplete instructions for the Looking Box.)

Although the liking ratings made by subjects of their classmates extended across the entire range of 15–1, some subjects made more restricted ratings. Thus, 17 subjects rated some peers in the high category, 14 subjects rated some peers in the moderate category, but only 6 subjects rated some peers in the low category. The mean ($\overline{M}$) number of times high-, moderate-, and low-rated classmates, respectively, were viewed in the Looking Box was 4.05, 3.48, and 3.67. A Wilcoxen matched-pairs signed-ranks test indicated that the difference between the number of times moderate- and low-rated classmates, combined, were viewed ($\overline{M} = 3.43$) by those subjects who had rated some classmates high and others moderate and/or low was highly significant ($T = 13$, $n = 14$, $p < .005$, one-tailed), as was also the difference between the number of

views of high-rated and low-rated classmates ($T = 8$, $n = 13$, $p < .005$, one-tailed). No reliable difference was found between number of views of low-rated peers and either moderate- or high-rated ones, but only a small number of subjects rated any of their classmates in the low category. Of the six high minus low differences, five are in the expected direction.

Treasure Hunt data were related to Liking Scale ratings in the following ways: First, for each subject the mean liking rating of the classmates he chose first and second (by choosing boxes with their photographs on them) was compared with the mean rating of the classmates he chose fourth and fifth. Means of these means are 12.71 and 10.95, respectively, indicating that the earlier Treasure Hunt choices tended to be for more highly liked classmates than the later choices. A Wilcoxen matched-pairs signed-ranks test of the difference scores showed them to be reliable, in the predicted direction ($T = 36$, $n = 18$, $p < .025$, one-tailed). In addition, mean liking ratings of classmates chosen on the Treasure Hunt were compared with mean liking ratings of other classmates. Since subjects in Groups Y and O differed in the number of stimulus boxes presented to them (13 and 8, respectively), the mean liking rating of all five choices made by Y subjects was compared with the mean liking rating of his remaining eight nonchosen classmates while for Group O subjects the mean rating of the first three Treasure Hunt choices were compared with that of the remaining five classmates. In this way the proportion of chosen classmates which is compared with other classmates is the same for all subjects (.38 or .37). Greater liking was expected and found for chosen ($\overline{M}_c = 11.84$) than for other classmates ($\overline{M}_o = 10.64$) and a Wilcoxen analysis indicated that the difference is reliable ($T = 34.5$, $n = 20$, $p < .005$, one-tailed).

STUDY 2

Because the number of subjects in Study 1 was small, a second investigation with a larger sample, from a different and independent population, was undertaken to replicate the first.

METHOD

Subjects. Forty-eight boys (8–14 years old) were studied while they attended a YMCA summer camp. The boys lived in eight same-age groups for a 2 week period; cabin size varied from five to seven, excluding counselors.

Procedure. On the day after the beginning of the camp session, photographs of all campers were taken by a professional photographer under standard conditions in a mobile research trailer parked on the camp grounds. Except for the fact that the boys were photographed in their own shirts (and not draped) the same photographing procedure was followed as in Study 1.

On 2 consecutive days just prior to the end of the camp session the experimenter administered, to each subject separately, the following measures: (*a*) a booklet containing a 15-step Liking Scale for each boy in his cabin; (*b*) the Looking Box slide viewer with one color slide for each cabinmate, presented sequentially in a predetermined random order which differed for each subject; and (*c*) the Treasure Hunt game with one black and white photocovered box for each cabinmate, all shown at the same time in a randomly arranged pattern. The subjects were instructed to find the box that covered a dime (instead of a quarter) and were asked to make two Treasure Hunt choices (instead of five); with these two exceptions the instructions and materials used in association with the measures were identical to those described previously for Study 1 and therefore need not be repeated.

The subjects were sent to the research trailer by the counselors in order of availability, and all testing was done there by the experimenter. The Liking Scale booklet was administered last to each subject, but the order of Treasure Hunt and Looking Box presentation was counterbalanced. After all the testing had been completed the experimenter gave the counselors candy bars and photographs to distribute to the boys.

RESULTS

The Liking Scale ratings were categorized, as in Study 1, as high (15–11), moderate (10–6), or low (5–1) and the mean number of times that each subject viewed his highly, moderately, and low liked cabinmates, respectively, was calculated. Of the total sample of 48 boys, only 1 rated no cabinmate in the high category while 7 subjects rated all cabinmates in that category. Thirty-four subjects rated some cabinmates in the moderately liked range, and 22 subjects made use of low liked ratings.

To test the relation between Liking Scale ratings and Looking Box behavior, difference scores were calculated for each subject, where the relevant data were available, as follows: mean number of views in the Looking Box of high-rated cabinmates minus mean number of views of moderate- and low-rated cabinmates, combined; high- minus moderate-rated cabinmates; high- minus low-rated; and moderate- minus low-rated. The relevant scores, summarized in Table 1, were evaluated by t tests for correlated measures. The mean number of views of high-rated peers was found to be significantly greater, as predicted, than the mean number of views of moderate- and low-rated peers, combined, and significantly greater than the number of views of low-rated peers and moderate-rated peers considered separately. Only the difference between views

TABLE 1

MEAN NUMBER OF TIMES THAT
DIFFERENTIALLY LIKED PEERS WERE
VIEWED IN THE LOOKING BOX BY
SUBJECTS IN STUDY 2

Peers	$\overline{M}$	s	n
High	6.75	5.1	47
Moderate and Low	5.96	4.7	41
Moderate	6.05	4.5	34
Low	4.15	4.5	22

Differences[a]	M_d	df	t	p[b]
High—moderate and low	1.47	39	2.49	$<.01$
High—moderate	1.13	32	1.95	$<.05$
High—low	1.94	20	2.20	$<.025$
Moderate—low	1.18	14	1.39	$<.10>.05$

[a] For each subject, a difference score could only be obtained if he had rated his cabinmates in more than one liking category.
[b] One-tailed.

of moderately and low liked peers was not reliable.

Each subject made two Treasure Hunt choices out of a possible 4–6 boxes presented to him (depending upon the number of boys in his cabin). The mean liking ratings of both choices ($\overline{M}_c$ = 11.47) were compared with the liking ratings of other, nonchosen boys ($\overline{M}_o$ = 10.57). The hypothesis of higher ratings for the former than the latter was evaluated by a t test for correlated measures and obtained some support ($\overline{M}_d$ = .90, t = .167, df = 47, $p < .10 > .05$, one-tailed); the obtained t is just short of the .05 level.

Because of the special nature of the subject sample used in the present study, the relationship between Treasure Hunt choices and Liking Scale ratings was examined in another way as well as in the manner just described. The boys had been living within eight small groups, 24 hours a day, for almost 2 weeks prior to testing. During this time they had numerous

opportunities for making peer choices in selecting ball game captains, hike leaders, etc., and it seemed probable that such choices could generalize to the Treasure Hunt situation where choice behavior was also required. Since there is good reason to believe that general popularity within one's group is related positively to the probability of being "chosen" for leadership in activities, it would follow then that a boy's general popularity or status within his group would also be a determiner of whether or not his photo covered box was chosen in the Treasure Hunt by his cabinmates. The Liking Scale data could provide an index of group status by obtaining for each boy the mean rating given to him by his cabinmates. It was expected, if our reasoning was correct, that boys whose photo-boxes were chosen in the Treasure Hunt by 50% or more of their peers would have a higher group status, as reflected by greater mean liking ratings received from their cabinmates, than those boys chosen on the Treasure Hunt by less than 50% of their peers. Table 2 presents the relevant data for each cabin. It can be seen that seven of the differences are in the anticipated direction, while there is one case of zero difference; these are significant findings (Sign Test, p = .008, one-tailed).

The preceding analysis makes use of group or cabin data. We can also focus on the boys individually. A Median Test applied to the individual scores shows that those boys who received mean liking ratings which were above the median were more frequently chosen on the Treasure Hunt by 50% or more of their own cabinmates than were the boys who received average liking ratings below the median (χ^2 = 3.46, df = 1, $p < .05$, one-tailed).

Since all subjects in this study made the same number of Treasure Hunt choices (two), it was more feasible here than in Study 1 to evaluate directly the

TABLE 2

RELATION BETWEEN MEAN RATING
RECEIVED ON LIKING SCALE AND
PERCENTAGE CHOSEN BY PEERS
ON THE TREASURE HUNT

Cabins	*Mean liking ratings of boys*	
	Chosen 50% or more on the Treasure Hunt	*Chosen less than 50% on the Treasure Hunt*
F1	10.9 (3)[a]	9.9 (3)
F2	13.4 (2)	10.3 (5)
I1	10.9 (4)	5.5 (1)
I2	12.0 (1)	11.0 (5)
P1	10.7 (4)	8.8 (1)
P2	13.4 (1)	10.0 (5)
P3	11.8 (2)	11.6 (4)
P4	11.7 (3)	11.7 (4)

[a] The numbers in parentheses indicate how many boys in each cabin are represented in each of the two-choice categories.

relationship between such choices and frequency of views in the Looking Box. The expectation that these two measures would be positively related was supported by the results of a *t* test for correlated measures ($M_d = .80$, $df = 47$, $t = 1.90$, $p < .05$, one-tailed); those boys whose picture-boxes were thought to hide 10¢ (in the Treasure Hunt) were viewed longer in the Looking Box ($\overline{M} = 6.95$) than boys whose boxes were not picked ($\overline{M} = 6.15$).

STUDY 3

RECOGNITION AND DRAWING TASKS

In this study two additional oblique measures were investigated: a Recognition Task which uses a tachistoscopic-like procedure; and a Drawing Task. It was predicted that behavior of first-grade children on both tasks, the recognition of classmates from slides exposed for a very brief duration and the drawing of classmates, would reflect differences in attraction toward these classmates, as measured by a

Sociometric Test. Prior to the administration of the Recognition and Drawing tasks, each subject was asked to choose two boys and two girls in his or her class whom he or she liked a great deal, disliked, and regarded neutrally. This simple self-report measure of interpersonal attraction was used in order to obtain from each subject the same number of like, neutral, and dislike affective responses to his peers.

Investigations by some of the "new look" researchers in perception (cf. Postman & Schneider, 1951) suggested that the value of a stimulus could influence aspects of the perceptual response made to it. Much of the early work has since been subjected to careful criticism on methodological grounds (cf. Natsoulas, 1965) but the proposition that perceptual responses may be functional in nature has by no means been discarded. Among recent investigations, Park and Smith (1966), for example, have reported that recognition time for value-related words, all of infrequent usage, correlated positively with the values of the subjects, and that this was especially so for those subjects characterized as "innerdirected." Johnson, Thomson, and Frincke (1960) tachistoscopically presented lists of words that were matched in frequency but varied in "goodness," as previously determined by semantic differential scale ratings, and found that the "good" words were reported at significantly lower thresholds than the matched "bad" ones.

We would expect that stimuli such as liked persons which have been conditioned to a variety of approach responses, should be more salient than neutral persons, and that these, under certain circumstances, should be more salient than disliked persons, although prediction for the latter is difficult. Evidence for perceptual "vigilance" (e.g., Bootzin & Stephens, 1967) suggests that negatively evaluated stimuli are high in salience whereas evidence for perceptual "defense" (e.g., Bootzin & Natsoulas, 1965) suggests the opposite. Our general expectation that some form of avoidance behavior is typically evoked by disliked persons provides no logically clear basis for prediction since greater salience of such stimuli should, under some conditions, increase the probability that effective overt avoidance responses can be made, whereas inaccurate or slow recognition of a negatively evaluated stimulus is itself interpretable as an avoidance response. Under the conditions of this investigation, the specific hypothesis tested was that slides of liked peers would be recognized with fewest errors and that neutral and disliked peers would be recognized with moderate and most errors, respectively, across four different brief exposure times.

The use of a drawing task as an index of liking was suggested by the reported relation between size of children's drawings and assumed affect toward the subject drawn. Solley and Haigh (1957) found a tendency for Santa Claus to be drawn larger before Christmas than after. This phenomenon was subsequently verified by Sechrest and Wallace (1964) who had some children draw Santa, others a man, and others a house, on three separate occasions. Santa was found to be largest (in height) during the Christmas season whereas the drawing of men and houses increased in size after Christmas.

It might also be expected that drawings of a symbol arousing negative affect would reflect avoidance tendencies in smallness of size drawn. Relevant to such a hypothesis are findings by Craddick (1962) regarding children's drawings of witches. Those drawn on Halloween were found to be significantly smaller than those drawn before and after Halloween, and the witches drawn prior to Halloween were smaller than those drawn after.

Another line of relevant evidence has come from research on the Draw-A-Person and House-Tree-Person (H-T-P) tests

where subjects are asked to draw an abstract or generalized Person and inferences are made regarding personality characteristics of the drawer. Swenson (1968) has summarized a fair amount of data which tends to support some positive relation between size of drawings and self-esteem. It seems reasonable, then, to expect that when instructed to draw a particular person, esteem for that person should also influence drawing size.

To test the general expectation that interpersonal attraction is detectable from children's drawings of one another, each child in our sample was asked to draw one same-sex classmate in each of three interpersonal attraction categories—like, neutral, and dislike; and these drawings were then compared. Since children do actually differ in height, it was felt that the drawings made by subjects of each other might well reflect these real differences as well as affect. In support of such a possibility are data reported by McHugh (1963). Puerto Rican children in a New York sample drew significantly shorter Persons (on the H-T-P test) than a matched group of white children, but did not draw smaller Houses or Trees and there was no size difference between the Person drawings of a Negro and white group. Since Puerto Ricans are generally shorter in stature than the general population, a plausible explanation of these fiindings may be that their Person drawings simply reflected this reality. Instead of total height, then, it was decided to focus on size of head in relation to total body.

The degree of detail of each drawing was also measured as a second possible index of attitude toward the classmate drawn. Since it is assumed here that a liked stimulus will be most salient and evoke the most approach responses relative to a neutral or disliked one, and that a disliked stimulus functions as a cue for avoidance behavior, it follows that a child should devote the most attention to, and hence produce the most detailed drawing of, a liked peer, and should devote the least attention to, and produce the least detailed drawing of, a disliked peer.

The specific hypotheses tested were that the drawings of liked classmates would differ from those of neutral classmates and that these would differ from drawings of disliked classmates in the order from most to least, on two measures: head size relative to total size of figure, and degree of detail. We were also interested in determining whether independent judges, utilizing subjective and global cues, could reliably differentiate among the drawings and choose, above chance, those of liked and disliked peers.

METHOD

Subjects. Twelve boys and 11 girls (6–8 years old) from the same first-grade class served as subjects. The investigation was carried out during early spring so that many months of prior close contact among the children was assured.

Procedure. Following a brief introduction of one of the investigators (Experimenter 1) by the teacher, the children were photographed by a professional photographer, one at a time, in a mobile research unit parked on the school grounds. A $2\frac{1}{2} \times 3\frac{1}{2}$ inch black and white print and a 35 mm. color slide were made for each child.

1. Sociometric data and drawings: One week later, a second investigator (Experimenter 2) was introduced to the class and the teacher sent one child at a time, in an order of her own choosing, to the research trailer where Experimenter 2 instructed the child as follows:

I want you to think about how much you like or don't like each boy and girl in your class. Now, first tell me the two boys [or girls—same sex was requested first] that you *like the best*

and that you *enjoy being with* the most...And, now tell me the two boys [or girls] that you *do not like* and that you *prefer not to play with.*

The order of asking for liked and disliked classmates was counterbalanced across subjects, but in all cases the final question was, "Now, then, which two boys (or girls) do you sort of feel half-and-half about; you *don't like them very much but you don't dislike them?*"[1]

Each subject was then given a new pencil and instructed in the Drawing Task, being assured that the drawings would not be graded or displayed. "I just want you to show me what you think the...(children) you decide to draw look like." Each subject was asked to draw one of the same-sex classmates that "you said you liked very much," one that "you do not like at all," and one that you "don't dislike but don't like very much either." The order of these drawings was varied so that two boys and two girls (randomly selected) were instructed in each of the following orders: like-neutral-dislike; neutral-like-dislike; dislike-like neutral; dislike-neutral-like; neutral-dislike-like; like dislike-neutral. The subjects were allowed 2 minutes per drawing; if after $1\frac{1}{2}$ minutes a child had not yet drawn a body, he was urged to do so.

Before being sent back to the classroom, each subject was thanked for his help, complimented on his drawings, and told that he could keep his pencil, which had "University of Kentucky" printed on it, as a souvenir. He was also asked to "promise not to tell any of the children in your class what you did here...I don't want any child to know what he or she will be asked to do until the right time...."

2. Recognition Task: Approximately 1 week later, Experimenter 1

[1] Two girls who had been absent for the picture-taking session were excluded as sociometric choices although they were part of the subject group. Any subject who named one of these two girls was asked to make another choice.

and another investigator, Experimenter 3, returned to carry out the final procedure. For each subject, six slides were presented two times each for .01, .02, .03, and .04 seconds duration (48 trials in all). The six different slides included one of a liked, neutral, and disliked same-sex peer, and one of a liked, neutral, and disliked opposite-sex peer. (These peers were, in every case, not the same as those whom subjects had been previously asked to draw.) Although the actual slides differed per subject, the same predetermined random order was used in slide presentation to vary duration time and attractiveness of the stimuli. Neither Experimenter 1, nor Experimenter 3 knew the affect value of any slides for any subject. On prearranged form the slides were identified only by number.

The subjects were called to the research trailer, one at a time, in a predetermined order which was random except for sex alternation, and given appropriate instructions. The apparatus consisted of a Pana-vue slide viewer. After a slide was inserted by Experimenter 1, the subject pressed the button on the viewer which illuminated the slide for the exposure time which Experimenter 1 had set for that particular slide. For this phase of the experiment Experimenter 1 acted as an assistant, inserting slides and setting the exposure timing mechanism, while Experimenter 3 instructed each subject and recorded his responses. The subject was told to look into the viewer and then select, from a master sheet of photographs, the child whose face he had seen. The master sheet contained randomly arranged black and white photos of every child in the class who been previously photographed. This procedure, of having the subject point to one face among a group of possible faces, was utilized in order to minimize verbal response bias. At a later date Experimenter 1 returned to the first-grade class with a candy bar and a photograph for each child.

RESULTS

Recognition Task. Because most of the slides were accurately recognized the exposure time variable was ignored in analyzing the data; errors were examined only in terms of whether they were associated with the subject's attitude toward the person pictured in the slide. The total number of errors made by the 11 girls in each of the three interpersonal attraction categories, like, neutral, and dislike, was seven, five, and one, respectively; and the number of errors made by the 11 boys[2] was two for liked peers, five for neutral peers, and seven for disliked peers. An error for a particular silde was counted only once, even if that same slide was missed again at a difierent exposure time, but since each subject was presented with the slides of two different peers in each attraction category, each subject could have made a maximum of two errors in each category, or the boys and girls, considered separately, could have made 22 possible errors in each category.

The errors made by the boys are in the predicted direction while those made by the girls are in the reverse direction. A critical ratio (CR) for correlated proportions indicates that the difference between proportion of errors in the liked and disliked categories is significant (two-tailed tests) for both boys (CR = 1.92, p = .05) and girls (CR = 2.25, p = .02). Critical ratios comparing boys and girls on the proportion of errors made on slides of liked peers (CR = 1.92, p = .05) and the proportion of errors made on slides of disliked peers (CR = 2.25, p = .02) show both of these differences to be statistically reliable (two-tailed). The number of errors made on neutral peer slides was the same for boys and girls and, in

[2] Responses obtained from a twelfth boy were invalidated by a procedural error.

each case, intermediate between the liked and disliked categories.

Drawings. Each of the three drawings made by every subject was measured with a centimeter ruler for total length and head length, and the percentage of head to total was calculated. Total length was defined by the vertical line, perpendicular to the bottom edge of the paper, running from the topmost of the head to the bottommost point of the lowest foot; the head was measured from the top point to the chin. These measurements were made by an assistant who was naive with respect to the hypothesis being tested and did not know which of the drawings were of liked, neutral, or disliked peers.

A 2×2 analysis of variance for repeated measures was preformed on the percentage of head relative to total scores[3] to evaluate the effect of sex of drawer and attitude toward the subject of the drawing (the liking variable). This analysis is summarized in Tables 3 and 4. Both variables proved significant, but not their interaction.

The mean percentage of head relative to total scores are given in Table 3

[3] To equalize the number of boys and girls, the n of the latter group was increased from 11 to 12 by utilizing the girls' means on liked, neutral, and disliked peer drawings, respectively, as the additional score in these categories.

TABLE 3

MEAN OF PERCENTAGE OF HEAD RELATIVE TO TOTAL
SCORES FOR DRAWINGS OF LIKED, NEUTRAL, AND DISLIKED PEERS

Subjects	Peers drawn					
	Liked		Neutral		Disliked	
	M	s	M	s	M	s
Boys	30.8	10.6	23.0	10.5	28.9	11.1
Girls	39.5	6.9	35.0	9.6	31.7	5.2
Combined	35.1	9.8	29.0	11.6	30.3	8.6

TABLE 4

SUMMARY OF ANALYSIS OF VARIANCE FOR
PERCENTAGE OF HEAD RELATIVE TO TOTAL SCORES

Source	df	MS	F
Between groups			
Sex (A)	1	1.175.1	6.59*
Error (subjects within groups)	22	178.3	
Within groups			
Liking (B)	2	247.4	6.40**
A $\times$ B	2	98.0	2.53
Error (B $\times$ subjects within groups)	44	38.7	

* $p < .05$.
** $p < .01$.

and it can be seen that the mean scores for girls are greater than those for boys, regardless of affect toward the peer drawn, and the variability among the girls is lower than that among the boys. Two-tailed tests of the significance of the sex differences showed them to be reliable for drawings of liked peers ($t = 2.35$, $p < .05$) and of neutral peers ($t = 2.93$, $p < .01$). With respect to the liking variable, the mean score (sexes combined) is greatest for drawings of liked peers, as predicted. Using a t test for correlated scores, it was found that the difference between the scores for drawings of liked and neutral peer is significant ($M_d = 6.08$, $df = 23$, $t = 3.20$, $p < .005$, one-tailed), as is also the difference between the scores for drawings of liked and disliked peers ($M_d = 4.83$, $df = 23$, $t = 3.26$, $p < .005$, one-tailed). The scores for neutral and disliked peer drawings do not differ reliably.

Six adult judges (three of each sex), working independently and without knowledge of which drawings were of liked, neutral, or disliked peers, were asked to rank each set of drawings made by the same subject with respect to degree of detail: most, intermediate, and least. The judges were instructed to attend only to the figure drawn and not to extraneous portions of the drawing (e.g., ball or books in figure's hands, grass, etc.). That drawing within each set of three which was chosen by most of the judges for a given detail category received that score $1 =$ greatest detail; $2 =$ intermediate detail; $3 =$ least detail. Agreement among judges was 81.8% with respect to judgments of least detail, 78.3% for most detail, and 67.4% for intermediate detail.

The hypothesis of a positive relation between degree of detail of drawings and interpersonal attraction toward the peer drawn was tested by means of a Friedman χ^2_r analysis which indicated a significant relationship in the predicted direc-tion ($\chi^2_r = 6.87$, $df = 2$, $p < .05$). The mean detail score for each of the three interpersonal attraction categories was as follows: liked peers, $M = 1.56$; neutral peers, $M = 2.13$; and disliked peers $M = 2.30$. Sign Tests for each pair of interpersonal attraction categories confirmed the hypotheses that drawings of liked peers were greater in detail, as judged, than drawings of disliked peers (6 negative signs out of 23 comparisons, $p = .017$) and also greater in detail than drawings of neutral peers (7 negative signs, $p = .047$). The difference in detail rank scores between neutral and disliked peer drawings was not reliable (10 negative signs).

To determine whether the drawings, when examined globally, could be reliably differentiated by observers with regard to the drawer's attitude or affect toward his three subjects, nine judges were instructed, independently, to view each set of three drawings, placed side by side, in the order in which they were drawn, and to select, first, the drawing of the most liked, and then the drawing of the least liked, peer. Judges include a 5½- and an 8-year-old girl, three graduate students in psychology, the teacher of the subject sample, a part-time minister, a secretary, and one of the investigators who had not administered the Drawing Task. The accuracy of the judgments was calculated for each judge, separately, for liked and disliked peer drawings. The mean percentage of accuracy for drawings in each category ($M = 44.4$ for liked peer drawings, and $M = 46.4$ for disliked peer drawings) was compared with chance accuracy (33.3%) and found to differ reliably in each case ($t = 3.58$, and $t = 3.97$ for liked and disliked peer drawings, respectively; $p < .01$, two-tailed).

By recording the frequency with which different drawings had been accurately judged it was apparent that the drawer's attitude toward his or her subject was clearly recognized in some drawings by most of the judges while other drawings were not accurately judged by any of the judges. In other words, the distinctiveness or affective clarity of the drawings differed, probably reflecting individual differences among the children in artistic skill as well as differences in the strength or magnitude of their liking and disliking for the peers they drew. An example of a set of drawings shown in the order in which they were drawn is given in Figure 1. The liked peer drawing was correctly recognized by all of the nine judges, while the disliked peer drawing was correctly chosen by seven judges.

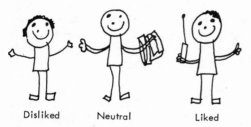

Disliked   Neutral   Liked

Figure 1. Artist's copies of drawings by Boy 9 of three different same-sex classmates: a disliked, neutrally regarded, and liked boy, respectively.

DISCUSSION

The results from Studies 1, 2, and 3, considered together, indicate that there is a positive relation between interpersonal attraction as measured by either a self-report paper-and-pencil rating scale or sociometric questions and other independent behavior samples which were expected, on theoretical grounds, to reflect attitudes toward persons.

With respect to one sample of behavior, the number of times children looked at color slides of each other (in the Looking Box), it was found that peers who were most liked were viewed significantly

more often than those who were less liked. That we should want to see highly liked persons more than lesser liked ones is a common-sense expectation, but it also clearly specifies one type of measurable approach behavior which a positive attitude can be said to evoke.

In apparent contradiction, both of our results and common sense, are data recently reported by Harrison (1968). He found that the adult male subjects looked *less* at liked stimuli than at disliked ones, as measured by the length of time they chose to expose a slide, using a remote control projector. One problem in interpreting Harrison's significant negative correlation between affect ratings and his measure of "exploration" (looking) is that the subjects who viewed the stimuli were not the same as those who had rated them (on either a good-bad or a liking scale) and there exists, therefore, the possibility that Harrison "ran afoul of individual differences" as has been suggested by Maddi (1968); the subjects who looked longest at certain stimuli might have expressed a preference for them, if they had been asked. It is also possible that predictions of approach behavior toward liked stimuli are simpler to make for children and that other variables add greater complexity to such predictions for adults.

Our second sample of behavior, choice of Photo-covered boxes in the Treasure Hunt, gets close to reflecting the anticipatory-goal concept which is central to our interpretation of interpersonal attraction. The children in Studies 1 and 2 chose boxes under which they hoped to find money and their choices were related to the degree to which they liked the persons whose photos were on the boxes. In Study 1 it was found that their first two choices, out of five, were for peers who were liked reliably more than their last two choices. In addition, the children whose picture-covered boxes were chosen were found to differ from the other children in (*a*) having received higher ratings on the Liking Scale from the same peers who chose them (both studies), (*b*) being more popular in their respective small groups (Study 2), and (*c*) being viewed more frequently in the Looking Box (Study 2).

In Study 3 since only a very small number of errors was made in recognizing classmates on tachistoscopically presented slides, it is probable that this technique is a poor potential index of interpersonal attraction for highly familiar persons. Nevertheless, the boys did behave as predicted and were reliably less accurate on disliked than on liked faces while the girls behaved in an opposite manner. Perhaps some persons learn to be more "vigilant" and others to be more "defensive" in their perceptual responses to anxiety-evoking (disliked) stimuli, and those individual differences may be sex related, at least in children.

It seems reasonable to conclude that our fourth behavior sample, obtained from the Drawing Task, proved to be a valid indicator of interpersonal attraction in light of the findings that (*a*) drawings of liked peers were reliably more detailed than those of disliked and of neutral peers, and (*b*) drawings of liked peers were significantly different from those of both neutral and disliked ones in the size of the figure's head relative to its total height.

The data obtained are consistent and as predicted (except for the behavior of the girls on the Recognition Test), support the view that a variety of behavioral indexes of interpersonal attitudes can be found. Such indexes may include verbal, perceptual, and motor behavior which is directly related to the object of the attitude. Mehrabian (1968), for example, has reported that variables such as body orientation and degree of relaxation, as well as eye contact with, and distance from, an imagined person all reliably indicate the degree of liking for that person by a communicator-subject. Other indexes of interpersonal attraction may potentially be derived from differential performance on tasks in the presence of the object of the attitude (Lott & Lott, 1966), or differential performance when the object of the attitude is presented contingent upon a particular response (Lott & Lott, 1969), or from the ease with which persons learn new associations to other people (Lott, Lott, & Walsh, 1970).

Discovery of a wide range of indicators of interpersonal attitudes should improve our ability to predict what people will do, along a variety of dimensions, when they are in the presence of other people to whom they are differentially attracted.

REFERENCES

BOOTZIN, R. R., & NATSOULAS, T. Evidence for perceptual defense uncontaminated by response bias. *Journal of Personality and Social Psychology*, 1965, **1**, 461–468.

BOOTZIN, R. R., & STEPHENS, M. W. Individual differences and perceptual defense in the absence of response bias. *Journal of Personality and Social Psychology*, 1967, **6**, 408–412.

COOK, S., & SELLTIZ, C. A multiple-indicator approach to attitude measurement. *Psychological Bulletin*, 1964, **62**, 36–55.

CRADDICK, R. A. Size of witch drawings as a function of time before, on, and after Halloween. *American Psychologist*, 1962, **17**, 307. (Abstract)

HARRISON, A. A. Response competition, frequency, exploratory behavior, and liking. *Journal of Personality and Social Psychology*, 1968, **9**, 363–368.

JOHNSON, R. C., THOMSON, C. W., & FRINCKE,

G. Word values, word frequency, and visual duration thresholds. *Psychological Review*, 1960, **67**, 332–342.

LOTT, A. J., & LOTT, B. E. Group cohesiveness and individual learning. *Journal of Educational Psychology*, 1966, **57**, 61–73.

LOTT, A. J., & LOTT, B. E. A learning theory approach to interpersonal attitudes. In A. G. GREENWALD, T. C. BROCK, & T. M. OSTROM (Eds.), *Psychological foundations of attitudes*. New York: Academic Press, 1968.

LOTT, A. J., & LOTT, B. E. Liked and disliked persons as reinforcing stimuli. *Journal of Personality and Social Psychology*, 1969, **11**, 129–137.

LOTT, A. J., LOTT, B. E., & WALSH, M. L. The learning of paired-associates relevant to differentially liked persons. Unpublished manuscript, University of Rhode Island, 1970.

MADDI, S. R. Meaning, novelty and affect: Comments on Zajonc's paper. *Journal of Personality and Social Psychology Monograph Supplement*, 1968, **9**, (6, pt. 2).

MCHUGH, A. H-T-P proportion and perspective in Negro, Puerto Rican, and white children. *Journal of Clinical Psychology*, 1963, **19**, 312–314.

MEHRABIAN, A. Relationship of attitude to seated posture, orientation, and distance. *Journal of Personality and Social Psychology*, 1968, **10**, 26–30.

NATSOULAS, T. Converging operations for perceptual defense. *Psychological Bulletin*, 1965, **64**, 393–401.

NUNNALLY, J. C., DUCHNOWSKI, A. J., &

KNOTT, P. D. Association of neutral objects with rewards: Effects of massed versus distributed practice, delay of testing, age and sex. *Journal of Experimental Child Psychology*, 1967, **5**, 152–163.

NUNNALLY, J. C., DUCHNOWSKI, A. J., & PARKER, R. K. Association of neutral objects with rewards: Effect on verbal evaluation, reward expectancy, and selective attention. *Journal of Personality and Social Psychology*, 1965, **1**, 270–274.

PARK, J. N., & SMITH, A. J. Recognition thresholds for value-related words: Differences between inner-directed and outer-directed subjects. *Journal of Personality and Social Psychology*, 1966, **3**, 248-252.

POSTMAN, L., & SCHNEIDER, B. H. Person values, visual recognition, and recall. *Psychological Review*, 1951, **58**, 271–284.

SECHREST, L., & WALLACE, J. Figure drawing and naturally occurring events: Elimination of the expansive euphoria hypothesis. *Journal of Educational Psychology*, 1964, **55**, 42–44.

SOLLEY, C. M. & HAIGH, G. A. A note to Santa Claus. *Topeka Research Papers, The Menninger Foundation*, 1957, **18**, 4–5. Cited by E. J. WEBB, D. T. CAMPBELL, R. D. SCHWARZ, & L. Sechrest, *Unobtrusive measures: Nonreactive research in the social sciences*. Chicago, Rand McNally, 1966.

SWENSON, C. H. Empirical evaluations of human figure drawings: 1957–1966. *Psychological Bulletin*, 1968, **70**, 20–44.

TECHNIQUES FOR ESTIMATING
THE SOURCE AND DIRECTION
OF CAUSAL INFLUENCE IN PANEL DATA

A. H. Yee / N. L. Gage

Contemporary scientists seem uncertain as to the value of causal analysis, especially in the social sciences. Explicit discussions of causality rarely occur. But, as Nagel (1965) observed, "though the *term* may be absent, the *idea* for which it stands continues to have wide currency," as "when scientists distinguish in various inquiries between spurious and genuine correlations [p. 12]." Simon (1957) also noted the common reference to causality in scientific writing, despite its "generally unsavory epistemological status [p. 11]."

In the natural sciences causal connections may be perceived in the tangible or visible mechanisms underlying the connections. Natural scientists also have the advantage of freedom to control and manipulate the matter they investigate: they can burn, catalyze, hybridize, electrolyze, break apart, boil, vivisect, bombard, and subject to acid tests almost as they please. Lacking such freedom, social scientists must place greater reliance upon

From: Psychological Bulletin, *1968, 70, 115–26. Copyright © 1968 by the American Psychological Association, and reproduced by permission of the authors and APA.*

statistical treatments than upon direct manipulation.

Recent statements by social psychologists indicate increasing concern with causal relationships. For example, Gerard and Miller (1967) noted in their review that "The study of the determinants and consequences of mutual attraction is a focus for a good deal of research in social psychology [p. 294]." Terms implying causality—such as, determine, influence, produce, affect, effect, modify, and attract —occur frequently in the literature. Occasionally, a direct reference to causality may be found; for example, Andrews (1967) studied the business organization as the "causal link" between a nation's achievement concern and its economic development. Causal connections must be exploited, of course, when social-psychological research findings are used in efforts to improve individuals and society, as in the programs of the "Great Society" and investigations into the causes of civil disorders. Greater precision in connecting theory and methods has led to more explicit use of causal inference in the social sciences (Lerner, 1965).

In recent years sociologists (e.g., Blalock, 1964), political scientists (e.g., Alker, 1966), and psychologists (e.g., Runkel, 1961), among others, have given increased attention to statistical methods for investigating causal relationships. Faris (1964) noted that

> the research equipment of sociology contains a rich and rapidly growing body of techniques for the extraction of causal generalizations from the data ...most important...is the fund of statistical methods, which can uncover regularities in masses of data too bewildering in their complexity to give up their secrets to any kind of personal skill or intuition.... These statistical, and related formal logical methods, employed in connection with modern high-speed computers, promise exponential progress in scientific knowledge of human and social behavior [p. 23].

Similarly, McGuire (1967) recommended that courses in experimental design and statistics for social psychologists "give more attention to techniques that allow us to tease out causal directions among covariants in situations where we do not have the resources to manipulate one of the factors [p. 134]."

One category of techniques for causal analysis consists of those that can be applied to panel data, that is, data collected on the same two or more variables on the same individuals at two or more points in time. This paper reviews two techniques of this kind—the 16-fold table (Lazarsfeld, 1948) and Campbell's cross-lagged panel correlation technique (Campbell & Stanley, 1963)—presents two new ones, and applies all four to the same data on relationships between teachers' and pupils' attitudes.

CAUSAL RELATIONSHIPS IN SOCIAL INTERACTION

Social psychology is largely the study of social interaction, in which the action of one person is a response to that of a second person, whose next response is in turn influenced by that of the first. "The actions of each are at once a *result* of and a *cause* of the actions of the other [Krech, Crutchfield, & Ballachey, 1962, p. 4]." Thus, influence flows in both directions as interacting individuals mutually determine the nature and outcome of the interpersonal behavior event.

In this framework, the "warmth" of a teacher toward his class may be regarded as at once a cause and an effect of the liking of the pupils for their teacher. The following questions can then be raised: Does teacher warmth tend to make the pupils like their teacher better? Or does teacher warmth make the pupils *less* favorably disposed toward their teacher? Or does the influence actually flow in the opposite direction, so that pupils' liking of their teacher increases teacher warmth? Or, finally, does the pupils' favorable attitude toward their teacher *decrease* teacher warmth?

These are four possible combinations of the source and direction of influence between persons in social interaction. These possibilities can characterize any human relationship. For example, Bell (1968) questioned the assumption that influence always flows from parent to child and presented evidence that children's characteristics influence parent behavior. The methods considered in this paper make possible the testing of alternative hypotheses concerning the source and direction of influence between characteristics and behaviors of interacting persons in any relationship. The methods are also useful in determining the relative strength of two influences *within* a set of persons, as the illustrative data for Lazarsfeld's (1948) method, discussed in a following section, indicate. Finally, the methods may be considered applicable to variables of any kind—economic, political, demographic, etc.—where the source and direction of causal influence are to be estimated.

Given paired measurements of two variables that may be causally related, one can compute correlations. With repeated measures, or panel data, one can compute test-retest and same-occasion correlations. These correlations may suggest the operation of causal influence in some direction when (*a*) the correlations between the variables increase (or decrease!) over time; and (*b*) there is marked stability in one variable and marked instability in the other. But, suggestive as such results may be, inferences of causal direction from such correlational results alone are suspect; other independent variables may be influencing the relationship. Suppose it is assumed, however, that no other independent variable is as potent as the two interacting variables in producing what Zeisel (1957) has designated as "true" correlations "which reflect a direct causal connection [p. 205]." Then the four previous questions may be raised: Does one variable affect the other more than it is affected by the other? Or less? Does an increase in the value of one variable increase the value of the other? Or decrease it?

THE DATA ON TEACHER-PUPIL RELATIONSHIPS

These questions can be illustrated with data from a recent study (Yee, 1966) of teachers' attitudes toward pupils (T) and pupils' attitudes toward their teacher (P). Here it is possible that T is determining P, or that P is determining T. In many studies of teacher-pupil interaction (e.g., Della Piana & Gage, 1955; Flanders, 1965, p. 65; Ryans, 1963, p. 432; Withall & Lewis, 1963), it has been suggested that the direction of influence is an open question.

In Yee's study, teachers' attitudes toward children and teacher-pupil rela-

tionships were measured with the Minnesota Teacher Attitude Inventory (MTAI); pupils' attitudes toward their teacher were measured with the 100-item "About My Teacher" inventory developed by Beck (1964). Pretests of these attitudes were made as early in the school year as administrators would allow, mostly during the second week of school. Posttests were made about 5 months later, after considerable interaction between teachers and pupils. Thus, the posttest measures represented teachers' and pupils' interpersonal attitudes that had evolved from initial attitudes. Corrected split-half and Horst (1949) coefficients in the high .80's indicated substantial reliability of the teachers' scores and pupils' class means, respectively.

Results were obtained not only for the total group but also for various subgroups based on classifications of teachers by years of teaching experience and of pupils by social class background. In addition to total scores, subscores based on factor analyses of the teacher and pupil attitude measures were analyzed. Hence, 720 correlations between T and P for all classifications were obtained. This report, however, deals only with results for (*a*) the total group of 212 teacher-class pairs and the two subgroups based on whether the modal pupils' social class background was lower class or middle class, and (*b*) total MTAI and "About My Teacher" scores.

First, Lazarsfeld's 16-fold table technique is described in terms of the intrapersonal opinion data to which he applied it. Then Campbell's cross-lagged panel correlation technique is described, applied to the authors' own data, and referred to problems with that technique noted by Campbell and also by the authors. Finally, two methods developed by the authors—the frequency-of-shift-across-median technique and the frequency-of-change-inproduct-moment technique—are described. In each section, the merits of the various techniques are examined.

LAZARSFELD'S 16-FOLD TABLE TECHNIQUE

The 16-fold table technique was described in two writings (Lazarsfeld, 1948; Lipset, Lazarsfeld, Barton, & Linz, 1954). Unfortunately, the published treatment of 1954 omitted and glossed over crucial features which may be found in the earlier mimeographed paper. In 1948 Lazarsfeld wrote:

> Now let us consider for a moment what we mean by saying that the attitude A has an "effect" on, or is the "cause" of the attitude B. We mean two things: First of all, the attitude A will tend to *generate* the attitude B; that is, if a person has the attitude A but not the attitude B, he will tend to acquire the attitude B: the attitude pattern $A\bar{B}$ (where $\bar{B}$ denotes the lack of B, or non-B) will tend to change to AB, and conversely, the pattern $\bar{A}B$ will tend to change to $\bar{A}\bar{B}$; secondly, the attitude A will tend to *preserve* the attitude B; that is, there will be fewer changes from AB to $A\bar{B}$ than we would expect from chance variations in the attitude B, that is, the attitude pattern AB will tend to be stable, and conversely, the attitude pattern $\bar{A}\bar{B}$ will also tend to be stable [p. 4].

In this passage, Lazarsfeld described four possibilities—two that do not change, $AB \rightarrow AB$, $\bar{A}\bar{B} \rightarrow \bar{A}\bar{B}$, and two that change in the "congruent" direction, that is, that raise the correlation between the attitudes, so that $A\bar{B} \rightarrow AB$, $\bar{A}B \rightarrow \bar{A}\bar{B}$. But, given A as cause and B as effect, there are two additional possibilities, $AB \rightarrow \bar{A}B$ and $AB \rightarrow A\bar{B}$, which represent possible change in the "incongruent" direction, that is, change that lowers the correlation be-

tween attitudes; these possibilities are not mentioned. Let us employ Lazarsfeld's own analogy to illustrate these possible causal relationships; in this analogy, A = consumption of vitamins and B = good health. One can find logical grounds for asserting that vitamin consumption while enjoying good health (AB) can change incongruently to the situation when vitamins may not be consumed but good health continues ($\bar{A}B$). Also, the AB situation can change incongruently to the situation where vitamin consumption continues but good health does not ($A\bar{B}$), especially when the wrong kind of vitamins or too many vitamins are consumed.

Although his illustration could be misleading, his method (Lazarsfeld, 1948) did not overlook the possibilities of incongruent influence. Lazarsfeld wanted to see which variable, party allegiance or attitude toward Willkie, was "cause" and which was "effect" in the 1940 presidential campaign. The two variables correlated highly at the time of the first interview ($r = .53$) and even higher at the time of the second ($r = .67$); data for the study are summarized in Table 1.

In Table 1, we see that Lazarsfeld took account of what he called "divergent" cases, namely, those where $(++)$ → $(+-)$ or $(-+)$, and those where $(--)$ → $(+-)$ or $(-+)$, which we have termed incongruent cases. Nevertheless, Lipset et al. (1954) concentrated only on the response patterns of people who "harmonized" their attitudes between the two interviews, that is, those where $(+-)$ → $(++)$ or $(--)$ and those where $(-+)$ → $(++)$ or $(--)$. In our terminology, these would be instances of congruent intrapersonal influence. Having only the 1954 description of the technique before him, a reader could easily be misled to consider only cases of congruent change.

In his 1948 paper, Lazarsfeld described a method of analyzing his data as

TABLE 1

CONCURRENT CHANGE IN VOTE INTENTION
AND PERSONAL LIKING FOR WILLKIE

Interview		Second interview				Total
		$++$	$+-$	$-+$	$--$	
First interview	Republican $(+)$ for Willkie $(+)$	129	3	1	2	135
	Republican $(+)$ against Willkie $(-)$	11	23	0	1	35
	Democrat $(-)$ for Willkie $(+)$	1	0	12	11	24
	Democrat $(-)$ against Willkie $(-)$	1	1	2	68	72
	Total	142	27	15	82	266

Note.—From Lipset et al. (1954, p. 1161). All entries represent the first and second sets of responses from the same Ss; e. g. 3 in Row 1. Column 2 represents the same Ss who were Republican $(+)$ for Willkie $(+)$ in the first interview but Republican $(+)$ against Willkie $(-)$ in the second interview

follows: "A good measure of the relative strength of the two attitudes, then, will be the number of adjustments toward 'vote intention' beyond the expected chance value, plus the excess beyond the expected chance value of losses of adjustment away from 'Willkie opinion' [p. 6]." He offered the following index for the relative strength of two variables:

$$I_{A,B} = \frac{8\left(\dfrac{\Delta_H}{N_H} + \dfrac{\Delta_V}{N_V}\right)}{N}$$

Where, as restated by us, with more concise notation:

$I_{A,B}$ is an index for the relative strength of two variables A and B, in causal relationship

$$\Delta_H = N_{(-+\rightarrow --)}N_{(+-\rightarrow ++)} - N_{(-+\rightarrow ++)}N_{(+-\rightarrow --)},$$

or net change toward congruence, where the first variable is the cause

$$N_H = N_{(-+\rightarrow --)} + N_{(+-\rightarrow ++)} + N_{(-+\rightarrow ++)} + N_{(+-\rightarrow --)},$$

or the sum of the four Ns in the Δ_H elements

$$\Delta_V = -[N_{(--\rightarrow +-)}N_{(++\rightarrow -+)} - N_{(--\rightarrow -+)}N_{(++\rightarrow +-)}],$$

or negative amount of net change

toward incongruence where the second variable is the cause

$$N_V = N_{(--\rightarrow +-)} + N_{(++\rightarrow -+)} + N_{(--\rightarrow -+)} + N_{(++\rightarrow +-)},$$

or the sum of the four Ns in the Δ_V elements,

N = total cases in study.

As Lazarsfeld (1948) explained this method:

In the ideal case, $\dfrac{\Delta_H}{N_H}$ and $\dfrac{\Delta_V}{N_V}$ will have the same sign: they will both be positive if the first variable (in the present example "vote intention") is stronger, and both negative if the second variable (in the present example "Willkie opinion") is stronger. Their relative magnitude will depend on the comparative frequency of adjustment and maladjustment cases, that is, on whether the correlation between the two variables has been increasing or decreasing in the interval between the two interviews [pp. 6–7].

Unfortunately, the 1954 publication merely stated that "The details of this index will be omitted here; suffice it to say that the index takes into account the stability of each variable separately and that the more change in one variable is influenced by change in another, the larger the index will be [Lipset et al., 1954, p. 1161]." Lazarsfeld's method takes into account both "adjustment," or congruent, cases (Δ_H), and "nonadjustment," or incongruent, cases (Δ_V).

In an appendix by William L. Robinson, Lazarsfeld (1948, p. vi) presented a significance test which requires computation of the variance of $\frac{\Delta}{N}$ and the mean deviation of $I_{A,B}$. Chi-square appears to offer greater power and to be simpler to compute and interpret. Applying chi-square tests to Lazarsfeld's data in Table 1 shows that party allegiance caused "Willkie opinion" to change; that is,

$$27 > 4$$

or

$$N_{(++\to+-)} + N_{(+-\to++)} + N_{(-+\to--)}$$
$$+ N_{(--\to-+)} > N_{(++\to-+)} + N_{(+-\to--)}$$
$$+ N_{(-+\to++)} + N_{(--\to+-)}$$
$$(\chi^2 = 15.6,\ p < .0001)$$

Furthermore, party allegiance caused "Willkie opinion" to change toward congruity; that is,

$$22 > 2$$

or

$$N_{(+-\to++)} + N_{(-+\to--)}$$
$$> N_{(+-\to--)} + N_{(-+\to++)}$$
$$(\chi^2 = 15.04,\ p < .0001)$$

Finally, party allegiance did not cause "Willkie opinion" to change significantly toward incongruity; that is,

$$5 > 2$$

$$N_{(++\to+-)} + N_{(--\to-+)}$$
$$> N_{(++\to-+)} + N_{(--\to+-)}$$
$$(\chi^2 = .57,\ p,\ \text{nonsignificant})$$

Despite its ingenuity, the 16-fold table technique has limitations. First, it is applicable only to dichotomous vari-

ables. Second, it has no readily understood metric, such as the value of r. And, as Campbell (1963) has pointed out, "regression becomes a plausible rival hypothesis when the item marginals are extreme and differ for the two variables [p. 241]."

CAMPBELL'S CROSS-LAGGED PANEL CORRELATION TECHNIQUE

In an attempt to extend Lazarsfeld's reasoning to continuous data, Campbell (Campbell & Stanley, 1963) offered the "cross-lagged panel correlation technique." The method was later discussed in greater detail by Campbell (1963) and has been noted by Blalock (1964, pp. 191–192), Pelz and Andrews (1964), and McGuire (1967).

Campbell (1963) argued that cross-lagged series can differentiate between opposing interpretations of the causal relationship between two variables:

Where two data series correlate,... the direction of causation may be equivocal.... In such a situation, $r_{C_nE_{n+1}}$ should be greater than $r_{C_{n+1}E_n}$, where C stands for cause, E for effect. These cross-lagged series correlations can frequently differentiate the relative plausibilities of competing causal interpretations. When both variables are on both sides of the comparison, i.e., when relative correlation magnitude is used rather than the absolute level of $r_{c_nE_n}$, secular trends of long-term cycles are controlled.... Our criterion becomes $r_{C_1E_2} > r_{C_2E_1}$ [pp. 235–236].

Campbell cited the following illustrative question: "Does lack of parental love cause children to be behavior problems, or does a difficult child cause parents to love less [p. 236]?" In Yee's (1966) data, the comparable question is: Do unsympathetic and unfavorable attitudes of the teacher toward pupils cause her pupils to develop a dislike for their teacher, or do hostile, aggressive pupils cause the teacher to develop unfavorable and unsympathetic attitudes toward pupils?

Using the cross-lagged technique, one would infer that pupils' attitudes P tend to influence teachers' attitudes T if $r_{P_1 T_2} >$ $r_{T_1 P_2}$. One would infer that teachers' attitudes influence pupil attitude if $r_{T_1 P_2} >$ $r_{T_2 P_1}$. But these two inferences are not the only possible ones. The first finding could result not only from greater pupil influence toward raising the correlation between teachers' and pupils' attitudes (which we term influence toward *congruity*), but also from greater teacher influence toward *incongruity* (i.e., toward lowering the correlation between teachers' and pupils' attitudes). In that event, teachers' influence may be greater than pupils' but in an incongruent direction. But it is impossible to ascertain this possibility from the cross-lagged r's because the latter confound, or prevent us from distinguishing between, the source and direction of influence of the two correlated variables.

This unexpected problem in the use of the cross-lagged technique was also found independently by Rozelle (1965), who noted that there were *four* competing hypotheses, namely, A increases B, B increases A, A decreases B, and B decreases A. Later, Rozelle and Campbell (1966) concluded that "The apparent power of the technique is now seen as much less than in previous estimates, even though under some conditions the confounded pair can be separately examined [p. 12]."

FREQUENCY-OF-SHIFT-ACROSS-MEDIAN (FSM) TECHNIQUE

Prior to our study of Lazarsfeld's 16-fold table technique, we developed one of our own that turned out to be highly similar, except that it entailed trichotomizing rather than dichotomizing each variable. The trichotomies consist of scores (*a*) above the median, (*b*) at the median, and (*c*) below the median. The matrix shown in Figure 1 provides for all possible types of shifts in paired trichotomous measures from pre- to posttest. This matrix forms the basis for what we termed the frequency-of-shift-across-median technique. In applying this technique, we determined the frequencies of teacher-class pairs that shifted between first and second testing in the various ways shown in Figure 1. Such shifts could be interpreted as (*a*) raising or lowering (i.e., shifting toward congruity or incongruity, respectively) the correlation between teachers' and pupils' attitudes, and (*b*) indicating whether the teacher or the pupils exerted the influence toward change. Table 2 presents interpretations of the 81 possible shifts between pre- and posttest.

As is shown in Table 2, the source of influence operating in each of the 81 resolutions was judged to be the teacher (T) or the pupils (P) on the basis of which participant in social interaction changed less in relation to the pre- and posttest medians. For example, if the teacher remained stable and pupils changed from below-the-pupils'-median to above-the-pupils'-median, then teachers' influence would be considered the cause of pupils' change. Cells in which it could not be determined whether teachers' or pupils' influence was operating were considered "uncertain"; such a case would be one where both teachers and pupils remained in the H–H cell on both testing occasions.

Table 2 also indicates whether the teachers' and pupils' attitudes shift toward congruent (C) or incongruent (I) states. If a cell showed teachers and pupils moving to or remaining in resolutions where their attitudes were similar (both above or both below the median), then

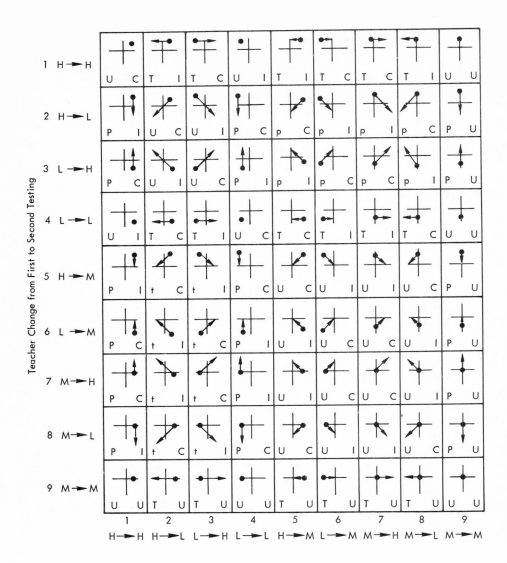

Pupil Change from First to Second Testing

Figure 1. Possible resolutions and nature of influence in the relationship of teachers' and pupils' attitudes. (Arrows both in the margins and in the cells denote direction of change in relationship to the medians of teachers' and pupils' measures: lack of arrow denotes no change. H = above median; L = below median; M = on median; T = teacher is dominant influence; P = pupils are dominant influence; U = uncertain influence; t = teacher causes pupils to change more than pupils cause teacher to change; p = pupils cause teacher to change more than teacher causes pupils to change; C = continuation in or change toward state of congruity; and I = continuation in or change toward state of incongruity. Whether cells in Row 9 and Column 9 are states of congruity or incongruity cannot be determined.)

TABLE 2

NATURE OF INFLUENCE IN 81 POSSIBLE RESOLUTIONS
IN THE CAUSE-EFFECT RELATIONSHIP OF TEACHERS'
AND PUPILS' ATTITUDES

Category type	Nature of influence	Cells[a]
TC	Teacher influence to increase correlation (Teacher stays high, pupils move higher. Teacher stays low, pupils move lower.)	1.3, 1.6, 1.7, 4.2, 4.5 4.8, 5.2, 6.3, 7.3, 8.2
TI	Teacher influence to lower correlation (Teacher stays high, pupils move lower. Teacher stays low, pupils move higher.)	1.2, 1.5, 1.8, 4.3, 4.6 4.7, 5.3, 6.2, 7.2, 8.3
PC	Pupil influence to increase correlation (Pupils stay high, teacher moves higher. Pupils stay low, teacher moves lower.)	2.4, 2.5, 2.8, 3.1, 3.6 3.7, 5.4, 6.1, 7.1, 8.4
PI	Pupil influence to lower correlation (Pupils stay high, teacher moves lower. Pupils stay low, teacher moves higher.)	2.1, 2.6, 2.7, 3.4, 3.5 3.8, 5.1, 6.4, 7.4, 8.1
UC	Uncertain influence, no change from pretest to posttest; teacher and pupils continue in state of congruity. Uncertain influence, teacher and pupils change in same direction, i.e., staying in state of congruity.	1.1, 4.4 2.2, 3.3, 5.5, 5.8, 6.6 6.7, 7.6, 7.7, 8.5, 8.8
UI	Uncertain influence, no change from pretest to posttest; teacher and pupils continue in state of incongruity. Uncertain influence, teacher and pupils change in opposite directions, i.e., staying in state of incongruity.	1.4, 4.1 2.3, 3.2, 5.6, 5.7, 6.5 6.8, 7.5, 7.8, 8.6, 8.7
TU	Uncertain teacher influence causing pupils to change.	9.2, 9.3, 9.5, 9.6, 9.7 9.8
PU	Uncertain pupil influence causing teacher to change.	2.9, 3.9, 5.9, 6.9, 7.9 8.9
UU	Uncertain influence, no change from pretest to posttest; teacher and pupils continue in uncertain state.	1.9, 4.9, 9.1, 9.4, 9.9

[a] Cell designations from Figure 1: first numbers represent teachers' raw and second numbers represent pupils' column.

that cell was considered "congruent." If a cell showed teachers' and pupils' attitudes moving to or remaining in resolutions where their attitudes were dissimilar (one above and the other below the median), then that cell was considered "incongruent." Whether some teacher-class pairs, such as those falling exactly on pre- and posttest medians (Row 9 and Column 9), shifted in congruent or incongruent directions could not be determined; these were judged "uncertain."

To summarize, the 9 × 9 table of 81 possible resolutions is based on the relationships of the teachers' and pupils' pre- and posttest attitudes to their medians, and two logical interpretations are made for each resolution: (*a*) whether it is caused by the teacher, the pupils, or an uncertain influence, and (*b*) whether it leads to a state of congruity, incongruity, or an uncertain attitude adjustment. Frequencies in each cell of the 9 × 9 table are tabulated and then summarized in the 3 × 3 schema shown in Table 3.

TABLE 3

SCHEMA FOR SUMMARIZING
FREQUENCIES IN TABLE 2

Source of influence	*Direction of influence*		
	Congruity	*Incongruity*	*Uncertain*
Teacher	TC	TI	TU
Pupil	PC	PI	PU
Uncertain	UC	UI	UU

The following hypotheses refer to the frequencies of teacher-class pairs reflecting the various sources and directions of influence indicated in Table 3.

H_1: Teacher-class pairs showing teacher influence toward either congruity or incongruity are more frequent than those showing pupil influence toward either congruity or incongruity. That is,

Teacher Influence (TC + TI + TU)

> Pupil Influence (PC + PI + PU)

H_2: Teacher-class pairs showing teacher influence toward congruity are more frequent than those showing pupil influence toward congruity. That is,

Teacher Influence toward Congruity (TC)
> Pupil Influence toward Congruity (PC)

H_3: Teacher-class pairs showing teacher influence toward incongruity are more frequent than those showing pupil influence toward incongruity. That is,

Teacher Influence toward Incongruity

(TI) > Pupil Influence toward
Incongruity (PI)

These hypotheses can be tested with chi-square, adjusted with Yates' correction for continuity, one-tailed with $df = 1$ (Guilford, 1965, pp. 228–230, 237–239).

FREQUENCY-OF-CHANGE-IN-PRODUCT-MOMENT (FCP) TECHNIQUE

In depending on shifts in relation to the medians, the FSM technique requires disregarding the many cases (about 60% in the present study) that do not change in relation to the medians from pre- to posttest. The frequency-of-change-in-product-moment (FCP) technique was developed in part to overcome this problem. It entails putting every teacher-class unit into one of the four categories of influence—TC, TI, PC, or PI—by the following procedure:

1. Convert the raw scores for teachers' and pupils' pre- and posttest attitudes to standard scores on the basis of their respective means and standard deviations. That is, determine $z = (x - \bar{x})/s$ for every score.

2. For each class, ascertain whether the cross-product of its posttest z scores is more positive or negative than the cross-product of its pretest z scores. If the cross-product of posttest z's, $z_{T_2}z_{P_2}$, is algebraically greater than $z_{T_1}z_{P_1}$, the direction of change is considered to become congruent; that is, the interaction between the teacher and her class makes the overall correlation more positive. If the cross-product of posttest z's is algebraically lower than that of pretest z's, the direction of change is considered to be incongruent; that is, the interaction between the teacher and her class makes the overall correlation more negative. This manner of assessing direction of influence is, of course,

TABLE 4

Summary of Results from the Three Techniques

Teacher-class group	r's						Frequency-of-shift-across-median frequencies[a]						Chi-squares[b]			Frequency-of-change in-product-moment frequencies				Chi-squares		
	T_1T_2	P_1P_2	T_1P_1	T_2P_2	T_1P_2	T_2P_1	TC	TI	PC	PI	UC	UI	H_1	H_2	H_3	TC	TI	PC	PI	H_1	H_2	H_3
Total $n = 212$	.79	.69	.19	.17	.10	.20	29	22	27	20	66	48	.09	.02	.02	56	65	45	46	3.97*	.99	2.92*
Lower class $n = 110$	.76	.62	.23	.21	.08	.25	12	16	8	5	40	29	4.78*	.45	4.76*	33	38	21	18	8.74*	2.24	6.45*
Middle class $n = 102$	.80	.71	.04	.05	.02	.06	8	14	12	6	29	33	.23	.45	2.45	28	25	24	25	.09	.17	.02

a No cases found for TU, PU, or UU.
b H_1: (TC + TI) > (PC + PI); H_2: TC > PC; H_3: TI > PI.
* $p < .05$.

441

based on the defining formula for the product-moment correlation coefficient:

$$r = \frac{\sum z_x z_y}{N - 1}$$

In short,

If $z_{T_1} z_{P_1} < z_{T_2} z_{P_2}$, classify as an instance of congruent change.

If $z_{T_1} z_{P_1} > z_{T_2} z_{P_2}$, classify as an instance of incongruent change.

3. For each class, examine the cross-lagged z products, $z_{T_1} z_{P_2}$, and $z_{P_1} z_{T_2}$. When direction of change is congruent, the variable whose pre-measure is part of the more positive product is considered to be the source of the influence. When direction of influence is incongruent, the variable whose premeasure is part of the more negative product is considered to be the source of the influence. That is,

If change is toward congruency, and if $z_{T_1} z_{P_2} > z_{T_2} z_{P_1}$, then T is source of influence;

if $z_{T_1} z_{P_2} < z_{T_2} z_{P_1}$, then P is source of influence.

If change is toward incongruency, and

if $z_{T_1} z_{P_2} > z_{T_2} z_{P_1}$, then P is source of influence;

if $z_{T_1} z_{P_2} < z_{T_2} z_{P_1}$, then T is source of influence.

RESULTS

Table 4 presents the results obtained with the cross-lagged, FSM, and FCP techniques. Findings with the 16-fold table technique will be discussed with results from the FSM technique.

RESULTS WITH THE CROSS-LAGGED PANEL CORRELATION TECHNIQUE

All three pairs of cross-lagged r's indicated greater pupil influence than teacher influence; that is, $r_{P_1 T_2} > r_{T_1 P_2}$. The greatest difference between cross-lagged r's occur-

red in the subgroup with lower-class pupils. Although none of the differences was statistically significant, according to the formula developed by Olkin (1967), the predominant source of causal influence, judged on the basis of the cross-lagged technique, was the pupils.

But the question now arises: Did pupil attitude influence teacher attitude in the congruent direction? Or did teacher attitude influence pupil attitude in the incongruent direction?

According to Campbell's earlier view (1963, pp. 239–240), if r's between teachers' and pupils' second measures ($r_{T_2 P_2}$) are higher than those between the first measures ($r_{T_1 P_1}$), then it may be inferred that there is some causal connection of unspecified direction. Thus, a partial answer may be found in the following same-occasion correlations: for the total sample, $r_{T_1 P_1} = .19$, $r_{T_2 P_2} = .17$; for the lower-class subsample, $r_{T_1 P_1} = .23$, $r_{T_2 P_2} = .21$; and for the middle-class subsample, $r_{T_1 P_1} = .04$, $r_{T_2 P_2} = .05$. Thus, the same-occasion r's did not increase from pre- to posttest. Hence, the possibility arises that pupil influence causing congruent teacher change is weaker than the alternative of teacher influence causing incongruent pupil change.

We are assuming from past evidence that the interaction of teachers and pupils in hundreds of classroom encounters significantly influences their attitudes. Such interaction can either raise or lower the correlation between teachers' and pupils' attitude measures. And the results of applying the cross-lagged technique are inadequate to portray such possibilities.

RESULTS WITH THE FREQUENCY-OF-SHIFT-ACROSS-MEDIAN TECHNIQUE

In Table 4, we see that the test of H_1 with the FSM technique yielded significant results favoring teacher influence in the lower-class subsample ($\chi^2 = 4.78$, $p <$

.02). The difference between the results on H_1 for the lower-class and middle-class subsamples is striking. For the lower-class pupils, the frequencies for (TC + TI) and (PC + PI) are 28 and 13, respectively; for the middle-class pupils, they are 22 and 18.

The results for H_2 and H_3 show that the teachers' significant influence on lower-class pupils is in the direction of incongruence; that is, for H_3, TI > PI, or 16 > 5 ($\chi^2 = 4.76$, $p < .02$). When it is recalled that the largest difference between cross-lagged r's shown in Table 4 was that for the lower-class subgroup, where $r_{P_1T_2} > r_{T_1P_2}$, or .25 > .08, it is evident that the FSM results indicate the *source* as well as the *direction* of influence for those teacher-class pairs that shift position in relation to the median attitude.

The FSM technique is very similar to Lazarsfeld's 16-fold table technique. If one compares the 16-fold table (Table 1) with the 81-cell table of the FSM method (Figure 1), it can be seen that the 16 cells in the upper-left corner of Figure 1 resemble those of the 16-fold table. Since most of the FSM frequencies were found in these 16 cells and few were tabulated in the other 65 cells in Figure 1, results of the two techniques should be equivalent.

RESULTS WITH THE 16-FOLD TABLE TECHNIQUE

When the 16-fold table technique is applied to the illustrative problem

Δ_C, or change toward congruity
$$= N_aN_b - N_cN_d$$
Where,

N_a = number of classes where teachers exert congruent influence, or TC, and pupils shift from + to −
N_b = number of classes where teachers exert congruent influence, or TC, and pupils shift from − to +
N_c = number of classes where pupils

exert congruent influence, or PC, and teachers shift from + to −
N_d = number of classes where pupils exert congruent influence, or PC, and teachers shift from − to +

Δ_I or change toward incongruity
$$= - [N_eN_f - N_gN_h]$$
Where,

N_e = number of classes where pupils exert incongruent influence, or PI, and teachers shift from + to −
N_f = number of classes where pupils exert incongruent influence, or PI, and teachers shift from − to +
N_g = number of classes where teachers exert incongruent influence, or TI, and pupils shift from + to −
N_h = number of classes where teachers exert incongruent influence, or TI, and pupils shift from − to +

In the subgroup with lower-class pupils, the frequencies are:

$N_a = 6, N_b = 6, N_c = 4, N_d = 4, N_e = 2,$
$$N_f = 3, N_g = 9, N_h = 7$$
$\Delta_C = (6)(6) - (4)(4) = 20$
$\Delta_I = - [(2)(3) - (9)(7)] = 57$

Both Δ_C and Δ_I show teachers' influence to be stronger, especially in Δ_I. This finding accords with the FSM and FCP results given in Table 4.

RESULTS FROM THE FREQUENCY-OF-CHANGE-IN-PRODUCT-MOMENT TECHNIQUE

Frequencies from the FCP technique for all three hypotheses, as shown in Table 4, indicate that teacher influence occurred more often than pupil influence. Significant chi-square results support H_1 and H_3 for the total group and the lower-class subgroup, but not for the middle-class group. The results for the middle-class subgroup are consistent with those obtained by the cross-lagged method, inasmuch as the near-zero r's for this subgroup could have resulted from the finding that influences of opposite direction and source were approximately equal in frequency. Also consistent are the FSM results showing statistically insignificant differences between competing frequencies.

Although the H_2 results for the total group and lower-class subgroup are not significant, the frequencies for TC are greater than those for PC. The significant H_1 results for the lower-class subgroup ($\chi^2 = 8.74$, $p < .001$) reflect the combined effect of greater teacher-congruent frequencies in H_2 and the strikingly greater teacher-incongruent frequencies in H_3 (TI = 38, PI = 18, $\chi^2 = 6.45$, $p < .01$). But all the results for the middle-class subgroup are nonsignificant. Similar results were obtained from the FSM technique, and both sets of results are consistent with those obtained with the cross-lagged technique for the lower-class subgroup. Significant H_1 and H_3 results for the total sample reflect the combination of both subgroups' frequencies. Refer to Yee (1968) for greater discussion of FCP results.

DISCUSSION

First, some interpretation of incongruent teacher influence of the kind revealed in these data should be attempted. Such influence means that teachers with relatively high initial MTAI scores tended to make their pupils have less favorable attitudes later in the school year, and vice versa. Perhaps high MTAI-scoring teachers tried to substitute "warmth" for instructional effectiveness, and their pupils eventually resented their ineffectiveness, while the opposite trends occurred in the classes of low MTAI-scoring teachers. But, of course, additional data on other variables would be needed to test this interpretation.

At any rate, the results obtained with the cross-lagged technique support the contention of Rozelle and Campbell (1966) that analyses of causal influence in panel data must consider incongruent as well as congruent outcomes. While results with the cross-lagged panel correlation technique are equivocal, the 16-fold table, FSM, and FCP techniques appear to be consistent in the objective estimates of source and direction of influence which they yield.

The FSM technique resembles the 16-fold table technique, for the majority of frequencies found by both methods in the illustrative problem were tabulated and interpreted similarly. By providing for the consideration of more types of shift, however, the FSM technique offers the potential advantage of handling a wider range of outcomes than is possible with the 16-fold table technique. The FSM method relies upon those cases that shift relative to the arbitrary criterion of the median; its results indicate causal source and direction for the cases that shift most.

The FCP method, in using all cases, has an advantage over the FSM method; in being applicable to continuous data, it has an advantage over both the FSM and 16-fold table methods; and in revealing both source and direction of influence it has an advantage over the cross-lagged panel correlation method. Analyses of other panel data, in which measures of two correlated variables are obtained on two or more occasions, should be made to explore the utility of the FCP method in testing causal hypotheses. Pending further experience with and analysis of this technique, the authors recommend its use in preference to the others.

REFERENCES

ALKER, H. R., JR. Causal inference and political analysis. In J. BERNEL (Ed.), *Mathematical applications in political science, II.* Dallas, Texas: The Arnold Foundation, Southern Methodist University, 1966.

ANDREWS, J. D. W. The achievement motive and advancement in two types of organizations. *Journal of Personality and Social Psychology*, 1967, **6**, 163–168.

BECK, W. H. Pupils' perceptions of teacher merit: A factor analysis of five hypothesized dimensions. Unpublished doctoral dissertation, Stanford University, 1964.

BELL, R. Q. A reinterpretation of the direction of effects in studies of socialization. *Psychological Review*, 1968, **75**, 81–95.

BLALOCK, H. M., JR. *Causal inferences in nonexperimental research.* Chapel Hill: University of North Carolina Press, 1964.

CAMPBELL, D. T. From description to experimentation: Interpreting trends as quasi-experiments. In C. W. HARRIS (Ed.), *Problems in measuring change.* Madison: Univrsity of Wisconsin Press, 1963.

CAMPBELL, D. T., & STANLEY, J. C. Experimental and quasi-experimental designs for research on teaching. In N. L. GAGE (Ed.), *Handbook of research on teaching.* Chicago: Rand McNally, 1963. (Also published as a separate: *Experimental and quasi-experimental designs for research.* Chicago: Rand McNally, 1966.)

DELLA PIANA, G. M., & GAGE, N. L. Pupils' values and the validity of the Minnesota Teacher Attitude Inventory. *Journal of Educational Psychology*, 1955, **45**, 167–178.

FARIS, R. E. L. The discipline of sociology. In R. E. L. FARIS (Ed.), *Handbook of modern sociology.* Chicago: Rand McNally, 1964.

FLANDERS, N. A. *Teacher influence, pupil attitudes, and achievement.* Document No.

OE-25040, 1965, Washington, D. C.: United States Government Printing Office.

GERARD, H. B., & MILLER, N. Group dynamics. *Annual review of psychology*, 1967, **18**, 287–332.

GUILFOLD, J. P. *Fundamental statistics in psychology and education.* (4th ed.) New York: McGraw-Hill, 1965.

HORST, P. A generalized expression of the reliability of measures. *Psychometrika*, 1949, **14**, 21–32.

KRECH, D., CRUTCHFIELD, R. S., & BALLLACHEY, E. L. *Individual in society.* New York: McGraw-Hill, 1962.

LAZARSFELD, P. F. Mutual effects of statistical variables. New York: Columbia University, Bureau of Applied Social Research, 1948. (Mimeo)

LERNER, D. (Ed.) *Cause and effect.* New York: Free Press, 1965.

LIPSET, S. M., LAZARSFELD, P. F., BARTON, A. H., & LINZ, J. The psychology of voting: An analysis of political behavior. In G. LINDZEY (Ed.), *Handbook of social psychology.* Vol. 2. Cambridge, Mass.: Addison-Wesley, 1954.

McGUIRE, W. J. Some impending reorientations in social psychology: Some thoughts provoked by Kenneth Ring. *Journal of Experimental Social Psychology*, 1967, **3**, 124–139.

NAGEL, E. Types of causal explanation in science. In D. LERNER (Ed.), *Cause and effect.* New York: Free Press, 1965.

OLKIN, I. Correlations revisited. In J. C. STANLEY (Ed.), *Improving experimental design and statistical analysis.* Chicago: Rand McNally, 1967.

PELZ, D. C., & ANDREWS, F. M. Detecting causal priorities in panel study data. *American Sociological Review*, 1964, **29**, 836–848.

ROZELLE, R. M. An exploration of two quasi-experimental designs: The cross-lagged panel correlation and the multiple time series. Unpublished master's thesis, Northwestern University, 1965.

Rozelle, R. M., & Campbell, D. T. More plausible rival hypotheses in the cross-lagged panel correlation technique. Evanston: Northwestern University, Department of Psychology, 1966. (Mimeo)

Runkel, P. J. Appendix Q: An index of influence by one individual on another for multiple-item, nonhomogeneous instruments. In J. T. Hastings, P. J. Runkel, & D. E. Damrin, *Effects on use of tests by teachers trained in a summer institute.* Vol. 2 Cooperative Research Project No. 702, 1961, University of Illinois, Urbana, United States Department of Health, Education and Welfare, Office of Education.

Ryans, D. G. Assessment of teacher behav-ior and instruction. *Review of Educational Research*, 1963, **33**, 415–441.

Simon, H. A *Models of man: Social and rational.* New York: Wiley, 1957.

Withall, J., & Lewis, W. W. Social interaction in the classroom. In N. L. Gage (Ed.), *Handbook of research on teaching.* Chicago: Rand McNally, 1963.

Yee, A. H. *Factors involved in determining the relationship between teachers' and pupils' attitudes.* Cooperative Research Project No. 5–8346, 1966, University of Texas, Contract OE-6-10-077, United States Department of Health, Education and Welfare, Office of Education.

Yee, A. H. The source and direction of causal influence in teacher-pupil relationships. *Journal of Educational Psychology*, 1968, **59**, 275–282.

Zeisel, H. *Say it with figures.* (Rev. ed.) New York: Harper, 1957.

CONTEMPORARY TRENDS
IN THE ANALYSIS OF
LEADERSHIP PROCESSES

Edwin P. Hollander / James W. Julian

The history of leadership research is a fitful one. Certainly as much, and perhaps more than other social phenomena, conceptions and inquiry about leadership have shifted about. The psychological study of leadership in this century began with a primary focus on the personality characteristics which made a person a leader. But the yield from this approach was fairly meager and often confused, as Stogdill (1948) and Mann (1959) among others documented in their surveys of this literature. In the 1930s, Kurt Lewin and his co-workers (Lewin, Lippitt, & White, 1939) turned attention to the "social climates" created by several styles of leadership, that is, authoritarian, democratic, or laissez-faire. Together with developments in the sociometric study of leader-follower relations (e.g., Jennings, 1943), this work marked a significant break with the past.

From: Psychological Bulletin, *1969,* 71, *387–97. Copyright* © *by the American Psychological Association, and reproduced by permission of the authors and APA.*

Two residues left by Lewin's approach fed importantly into later efforts, even with the limited nature of the original study. One was the concern with "leader style," which still persists, especially in the work on administrative or managerial leadership (see, e.g., McGregor, 1960, 1966; Preston & Heintz, 1949). The other was the movement toward a view of the differential contexts of leadership, ultimately evolving into the situational approach which took firm hold of the field by the 1950s (cf. Gouldner, 1950).

For the most part, the situational movement was spurred by the growing recognition that there were specialized demands made upon leadership, depending upon the nature of the group task and other aspects of the situation. Clearly, a deficiency in the older approach was its acceptance of "leader" as a relatively homogeneous role, independent of the variations in leader-follower relationships across situations. The disordered state in which the trait approach left the study of leadership was amply revealed by Stogdill in his 1948 survey, which marked a point of departure for the developing situational emphasis. The publication in 1949 of Hemphill's *Situational Factors in Leadership* contributed a further push in this direction.

The main focus of the situational approach was the study of leaders in different settings, defined especially in terms of different group tasks and group structure. Mainly, though not entirely, through laboratory experimentation, such matters as the continuity in leadership across situations with variable tasks was studied (e.g., Carter, Haythorn, Meirowitz, & Lanzetta, 1951; Carter & Nixon, 1949; Gibb, 1947). The findings of this research substantially supported the contention that who became a leader depended in some degree upon the nature of the task. With this movement, however, there came a corresponding deemphasis on the personality characteristics of leaders or other group members. Though a number of studies systematically placed people in groups on the basis of their scores on certain personality dimensions (e.g., Berkowitz, 1956; Haythorn, Couch, Haefner, Langham, & Carter, 1956; Scodel & Mussen, 1953; Shaw, 1955), more typically laboratory experimentation tended to disregard personality variables. In McGrath and Altman's (1966) review of small-group research for example, they reported that of some 250 studies reviewed, only 16 employed such measures as variables of study. Thus, in little more than a decade, the pendulum swung very much away from the leader as the star attraction.

Within the present era, characterized by a greater sensitivity to the social processes of interaction and exchange, it becomes clearer that the two research emphases represented by the trait and situational approaches afforded a far too glib view of reality. Indeed, in a true sense, neither approach ever represented its own philosophical underpinning very well, and each resulted in a caricature. The purpose here is to attempt a rectification of the distortion that these traditions represented, and to point up the increasing signs of movement toward a fuller analysis of leadership as a social influence process, and not as a fixed state of being.

AN OVERVIEW

By way of beginning, it seems useful to make a number of observations to serve as overview. First, several general points which grow out of current research and thought on leadership are established. Thereafter, some of the directions in which these developments appear to be heading are indicated, as well as those areas which require further attention.

One overriding impression conveyed by surveying the literature of the 1960s, in contrast to the preceding two decades, is the redirection of interest in leadership toward processes such as power and authority relationships (e.g., Blau, 1964; Emerson, 1962; Janda, 1960; Raven, 1965). The tendency now is to attach far greater significance to the interrelationship between the leader, the followers, and the situation (see, e.g., Fielder, 1964, 1965, 1967; Hollander, 1964; Hollander & Julian, 1968; Steiner, 1964). In consequence, the problem of studying leadership and understanding these relationships is recognized as a more formidable one than was earlier supposed (cf. Cartwright & Zander, 1968). Several of the particulars which signalize this changing emphasis may be summarized under four points, as follows:

1. An early element of confusion in the study of *leadership* was the failure to distinguish it as a process from the *leader* as a person who occupies a central role in that process. Leadership constitutes an

influence relationship between two, or usually more, persons who depend upon one another for the attainment of certain mutual goals within a group situation. This situation not only involves the task but also comprises the group's size, structure, resources, and history, among other variables.

2. This relationship between leader and led is built *over time,* and involves an exchange or *transaction* between leaders and followers in which the leader both gives something and gets something. The leader provides a *resource* in terms of adequate role behavior directed toward the group's goal attainment, and in return receives greater influence associated with status, recognition, and esteem. These contribute to his "legitimacy" in making influence assertions, and in having them accepted.

3. There are differential tasks or functions attached to being a leader. While the image of the leader frequently follows Hemphill's (1961) view of one who "initiates structure," the leader is expected to function too as a mediator within the group, as a group spokesman outside it, and very often also as the decision maker who sets goals and priorities. Personality characteristics which may fit a person to be a leader are determined by the perceptions held by followers, in the sense of the particular role expectancies and satisfactions, rather than by the traits measured via personality scale scores.

4. Despite the persisting view that leadership traits do not generalize across situations, leader effectiveness can and should be studied as it bears on the group's achievement of desired outputs (see Katz & Kahn, 1966). An approach to the study of leader effectiveness as a feature of the group's success, in system terms, offers a clear alternative to the older concern with what the leader did do or did not do.

A richer, more interactive conception of leadership processes would entertain these considerations as points of departure for further study. Some evidence for a trend toward this development is considered in what follows.

WHITHER THE "SITUATIONAL APPROACH"?

What was the essential thrust of the situational approach, after all? Mainly, it was to recognize that the qualities of the leader were variously elicited, valued, and reacted to as a function of differential group settings and their demands. Hemphill (1949a) capped the point in saying "there are no absolute leaders, since successful leadership must always take into account the specific requirements imposed by the nature of the group which is to be led, requirements as diverse in nature and degree as are the organizations in which persons band together [p. 225]."

Though leadership events were seen as outcomes of a relationship that implicates the leader, the led, and their shared situation, studies conducted within the situational approach, usually left the *process* of leadership unattended. Much of the time, leaders were viewed in positional terms, with an emphasis on the outcome of their influence assertions. Comparatively little attention was directed to followers, especially in terms of the phenomenon of emergent leadership (cf. Hollander, 1961). With a few exceptions, such as the work of McGregor (see 1966) and others (e.g., Slater & Bennis, 1964), the leader's maintenance of his position was emphasized at the expense of understanding the attainment of it through a process of influence.

But even more importantly, the situational view made it appear that the leader and the situation were quite separate. Though they may be separable for analytic purposes, they also impinge on one another in the perceptions of followers. Thus, the leader, from the follower's vantage point, is an element in the situation, and one who shapes it as well. As an active agent of influence he communicates to other group members by his words and his actions, implying demands which are reacted to in turn. In exercising influence, therefore, the leader may set the stage and create expectations regarding what he should do and what he will do. Rather than standing apart from the leader, the situation perceived to exist may be his creation.

It is now possible to see that the trait and situational approaches merely emphasize parts of a process which are by no means separable. One kind of melding of the trait and situational approaches, for example, is found in the work of Fiedler. His essential point, sustained by an extensive program of research (see 1958, 1964, 1965, 1967), is that the leader's effectiveness in the group depends upon the structural properties of the group and the situation, including interpersonal perceptions of both leader and led. He finds, for example, that the willingness of group members to be influenced by the leader is conditioned by leader characteristics, but that the quality and direction of this influence is contingent on the group relations and task structure (1967). This work will be discussed further in due course.

Another kind of evidence about the importance to group performance of the leader's construction of the situation is seen in recent research on conflict. Using a role-playing test situation involving four-person groups, Maier and Hoffman (1965) found that conflict is turned to productive or nonproductive ends, depending on the attitude of the discussion leader. Where the leader perceived conflict in terms of "problem subordinates," the quality of the decision reached in these discussion groups was distinctly inferior to that reached under circumstances in which the discussion leader perceived disagreements as the source for ideas and innovation. In those circumstances, innovative solutions increased markedly.

A leader, therefore, sets the basis for relationship within the group, and thereby can affect outcomes. As Hemphill (1961) suggested, the leader initiates structure. But more than just structure in a concrete sense, he affects the process which occurs within that structure. Along with other neglected aspects of process in the study of leadership is the goal-setting activity of the leader. Its importance appears considerable, though few studies give it attention. In one of these, involving discussion groups, Burke (1966) found that the leader's failure to provide goal orientations within the group led to antagonism, tension, and absenteeism. This effect was most acute when there was clear agreement within the group regarding who was to act as the leader. Though such expectations about the leader undoubtedly are pervasive in groups studied in research on leadership, they are noted only infrequently.

LEGITIMACY AND SOCIAL EXCHANGE IN LEADERSHIP

Among the more substantial features of the leader's role is his perceived legitimacy —how he attains it and sustains it. One way to understand the process by which the leader's role is legitimated is to view it as an exchange of rewards operating to signalize the acceptance of his position and influence.

In social exchange terms, the person in the role of leader who fulfills expectations and achieves group goals provides rewards for others which are reciprocated in the form of status, esteem, and heightened influence. Because leadership embodies a two-way influence relationship, recipients of influence assertions may respond by asserting influence in return, that is, by making demands on the leader. The very sustenance of the relationship depends upon some yielding to influence on both sides. As Homans (1961) put it, "Influence over others is purchased at the price of allowing one's self to be influenced by others [p. 286]." To be influential, authority depends upon esteem, he said. By granting esteem itself, or symbolic manifestations of it, one may in turn activate leadership, in terms of a person taking on the leader role.

The elicitation of leader behavior is now a demonstrable phenomenon in various experimental settings. In one definitive study conducted by Pepinsky, Hemphill, and Shevitz (1958), subjects who were low in leader activity were led to behave far more actively in that role by the group's evident support for their assertions. Alternatively, other subjects known to be high on leader activity earlier were affected in precisely the opposite way by the group's evident disagreement with their statements. In simplest terms, an exchange occurs between the group and the target person. The group provides reinforcement which in turn elicits favored behaviors. In other terms, the reinforcement of a person's influence assertions substantiates his position of authority.

Other, more recent, work suggested that even the use of lights as reinforcers exerts a significant effect on the target person's proportion of taking time as well as his perceived leadership status (Bavelas, Hastorf, Gross, & Kite, 1965; Zdep & Oakes, 1967). Thus, the lights not only produced a heightening of leader acts, but also created the impression of greater influence with the implication of legitimacy as well.

In a similar vein, Rudraswamy (1964) conducted a study in which some subjects within a group were led to believe they had higher status. Not only did they attempt significantly more leadership acts than others in their group, but they even outdistanced those subjects who were given more relevant information about the task itself.

It is also clear that agreement about who should lead has the effect in groups of increasing the probability of leader acts (e.g., Banta & Nelson, 1964). Relatedly, in a study of five-man groups involving changed as against unchanged leadership, Pryer, Flint, and Bass (1962) found that group effectiveness was enhanced by early agreement on who should lead.

When a basis is provided for legitimately making influence assertions, it is usually found that individuals will tend to act as leaders. This, of course, does not deny the existence of individual differences in the propensity for acting, once these conditions prevail. In a recent study by Gordon and Medland (1965), they found that positive peer ratings on leadership in army squads was consistently related to a measure of "aspiration to lead." Similarly, research findings on discussion groups (e.g., Riecken, 1958) indicated that the more vocal members obtain greater reinforcement, and hence experience the extension of legitimacy.

The "idiosyncrasy credit" concept (Hollander, 1958) suggests that a person's potential to be influential arises out of the positive dispositions others hold toward him. In simplest terms, competence in helping the group achieve its goals, and early conformity to its normative expectations for members, provide the potential for acting as a leader and being perceived as such. Then, assertions of influence which were not tolerated before are more likely to be acceptable. This concept applies in an especially important way to leadership succession, since it affords the basis for understanding how a new leader becomes legitimized in the perceptions of his peers. Further work on succession phenomena appears, in general, to be another area of fruitful study. There are many intriguing issues here, such as the question of the relative importance in legitimacy of factors such as "knowledge" and "office," in Max Weber's terms, which deserve further consideration (see, e.g., Evan & Zelditch, 1961).

THE PERCEPTION OF LEADERSHIP FUNCTIONS WITHIN GROUP STRUCTURE

A major deficiency in the older trait approach was its conception of "traits" within the framework of classic personality typologies. Personality measures were applied to leaders, often in profusion, without reference either to the varying nature of leadership roles or the functions they were to fulfill. As Mann's (1959) review revealed, such measures indeed do yield inconsistent relationships among leaders, variously defined. To take a common instance, dominance and extroversion are sometimes related positively to status as the leader, but mainly are neither related positively nor negatively to this status. On the other hand, Stogdill (1948) reported that such characteristics as "originality," "initiative," and "adaptability" have a low but positive relationship with leader status.

Granting that some essentially personality-type variables are more often found among those designated as leaders than among those designated as nonleaders, there can be no dismissing the widespread failure to treat the characteristics of the leader as they are perceived—and, what is more, as they are perceived as *relevant*—by other group members within a given setting. As Hunt (1965) and

Secord and Backman (1961) pointed out, traits are viewed relative to the interpersonal context in which they occur. In short, followers hold expectations regarding what the leader ought to be doing here and now, and not absolutely.

One probable source for the disparate findings concerning qualities of the leader is the existence of differential expectations concerning the functions the leader is to perform. In simplest terms, there are various leadership roles. Without nearly exhausting the roster, it helps to realize that the leader in various time-space-settings may be a task director, mediator, or spokesman, as well as a decision maker who, as Bavelas (1960) put it, "reduces uncertainty."

Whether in the laboratory or the field, studies of the perceptions of the leader's functions often have depended upon a sociometric approach (cf. Hollander, 1954). Thus, Clifford and Cohen (1964) used a sociometric device to study leadership roles in a summer camp, with 79 boys and girls, ranging in age from 8 to 13 years. Over a period of 4 weeks, they had nine elections by secret ballot asking the youngsters to indicate how the others would fit into various roles, including such things as planner, banquet chairman, swimming captain, and so forth. Their results indicated that the perceived attributes of campers were tied variously to their election for different leader roles. In line with the earlier point about the interpersonal context of leader traits, these researchers say, "the problem should be rephrased in terms of personality variables required in a leader role in a specific situation, which is in turn a function of the follower's perceptions [p. 64]."

Apart from personality traits, one prevailing expectation which does yield consistent findings across situations is that the leader's competence in a major group activity should be high. Dubno (1965), for example, reported that groups are more satisfied when leaders are demonstrably competent in a central function and do most of the work associated with that function. This is seen, too, in an experiment with five-man discussion groups, from which Marak (1964) found that the rewards associated with the leader's ability on a task led to greater perceived as well as actual influence. In general, the greater influence of a leader perceived to be more competent was verified experimentally by Dittes and Kelley (1956) and by Hollander (1960), among others.

Another leader attribute which evidently determines the responsiveness of followers is his perceived motivation regarding the group and its task. This was seen in Rosen, Levinger, and Lippitt's (1961) finding that helpfulness was rated as the most important characteristic leading to high influence potential among adolescent boys. In a more recent study of the role dimensions of leader-follower relations, Julian and Hollander (1966) found that, aside from the significance of task competence, the leader's "interest in group members" and "interest in group activity" were significantly related to group members' willingness to have a leader continue in that position. This accords with the finding of a field study by Nelson (1964) among 72 men who spent 12 months together in the Antarctic. While those men most liked as leaders had characteristics highly similar to those who were most liked as followers, Nelson reported that perceived motivation was the major factor which distinguished the two. Hollander (1958) considered this as one critical factor determining the leader's ability to retain status, even though nonconforming. In Nelson's study, the highly liked leaders were seen significantly more to be motivated highly toward the group in line with his hypothesis that, "a critical expectation held of the leader, if he is

to maintain esteem, is that he display strong motivation to belong to the group [p. 165]."

A study by Kirkhart (1963) investigated group leadership among Negro college students as a function of their identification with their minority group. In terms of follower expectations, he found that those selected most frequently by their peers for leadership roles, in both the "internal system" and the "external system" activities of the group, scored higher on a questionnaire expressing Negro identification. This quality of being an exemplar of salient group characteristics was noted long ago by Brown (1936) as a feature of leadership. Its relationship to processes of identification with the leader is discussed shortly.

SOURCE AND NATURE OF LEADER AUTHORITY

The structural properties of groups affect the processes which occur within them. In leadership, the source of the leader's authority constitutes a significant element of structure. Yet, experimentation on leadership has given little attention to this variable, apart from some promising earlier work by Carter et al. (1951) with appointed and emergent leaders, and the previously mentioned work by Lewin and his associates on the style of the leader and its consequences to the group's social climate (Lewin et al., 1939; Preston & Heintz, 1949). More recently, Cohen and Bennis (1961) demonstrated that where groups could elect their leaders, the continuity of leadership was better maintained than where their leaders were appointed. In research on the productivity of groups, Goldman and Fraas (1965) found that differences occurred among four conditions of leader selection, including election and appointment.

With four-man discussion groups, Julian, Hollander, and Regula (1969) employed a multifactor design to study three variables: the source of a leader's authority, in either election or appointment; his competence, in terms of perceived capability on the task; and his subsequent task success. Their main dependent measure was the members' acceptance of the leader as a spokesman for the group. The findings of this experiment indicated that the latter two variables were significantly related to this acceptance, but that these relationships were differentially affected by whether the leader was appointed or elected. The shape of the three-way interaction suggested that election, rather than making the leader more secure, made him more vulnerable to censure if he were either initially perceived to be incompetent or subsequently failed to secure a successful outcome as spokesman for the group. While this finding alone does not sustain a generalization that the appointed leader necessarily is more firmly entrenched, it does support the conclusion that the leader's source of authority is perceived and reacted to as a relevant element in the leadership process.

Other work on a differentiation of the leader's role, through the social structure, was conducted by Anderson and Fiedler (1964). In their experiment with four-man discussion groups, half the groups had leaders who were told to serve as a "chairman" in a participatory way, and the other groups had leaders who were told to serve as an "officer in charge" in a supervisory way. They found that the nature of the leadership process was affected markedly by this distinction, thus paralleling the main findings of Preston and Heintz (1949). In general, the more participatory leaders were significantly more influential and made more of a contribution to the group's performance. But, more to the point, the relationship between leader attributes, such as intelligence and group performance, was significant for certain tasks under the participatory condition, though not for any of the tasks under the supervisory condition. The conclusion that Anderson and Fiedler reached, therefore, is that the characteristics of a leader, including intelligence and other personality attributes, become more salient and more highly relevant to group achievement under conditions of participation by the leader, as against circumstances where a highly formal role structure prevails.

EFFECTIVENESS OF THE LEADER

By now it is clear that an entire interpersonal system is implicated in answering the question of the leader's effectiveness. The leader is not effective merely by being influential, without regard to the processes at work and the ends achieved. Stressing this point, Selznick (1957) said that, "far more than the capacity to mobilize personal support...(or) the maintenance of equilibrium through the routine solution of everyday problems," the leader's function is "to define the ends of group existence, to design an enterprise distinctively adapted to these ends, and to see that the design becomes a living reality [p. 37]."

As Katz and Kahn (1966) observed, any group operates with a set of resources to produce certain outputs. Within this system, an interchange of inputs for outputs occurs, and this is facilitated by leadership functions which, among other things, direct the enterprise. The leader's contribution and its consequences vary with system demands, in terms of what Selznick referred to as "distinctive competence." Taken by itself, therefore, the typical conception of leadership as one person directing others can be misleading, as already indicated. Though the leader provides a valued resource, the group's resources are not the leader's alone. Together, such resources provide the basis for functions fulfilled in the successful attainment of group goals, or, in other terms, group outputs.

Given the fact that a group must work within the set of available resources, its effectiveness is gauged in several ways. Stogdill (1959), for one, distinguished these in terms of the group's performance, integration, and member satisfaction as group outputs of a leadership process involving the use of the group's resources. Thus, the leader and his characteristics constitute a set of resources contributing to the effective utilization of other resources. A person who occupies the central role of leader has the task of contributing to this enterprise, within the circumstances broadly confronting the group.

One prominent exemplification of the system's demands and constraints on the leader's effectiveness is seen in Fiedler's "contingency model" (1964, 1965, 1967). He predicted varying levels of effectiveness for different *combinations* of leader and situational characteristics. Thus, depending upon the leader's orientation toward his co-workers, in the context of three situational variables—the quality of leader-member liking, the degree of task structure, and the position power of the leader—he finds distinct variations in this effectiveness.

In a recent test of his model, Fiedler (1966) conducted an experiment to compare the performance of 96 three-man groups that were culturally and linguistically homogeneous or heterogeneous. Some operated under powerful and others under weak leadership positions on three types of tasks varying in structure and requirements for verbal interaction. Despite the communication difficulties and different backgrounds heterogeneous groups performed about as well on the nonverbal

task as did homogeneous groups. Groups with petty officers as leaders (powerful) did about as well as the groups with recruits as leaders (weak). The main finding of the experiment was support for the hypothesis from the contingency model that the specific leadership orientation required for effectiveness is contingent on the favorableness of the group-task situation. Partial support for this hypothesis came also from a study by Shaw and Blum (1966) in which they manipulated some of the same variables with five-person groups, and with three tasks selected to vary along a dimension reflecting different levels of favorability for the leader. Their results indicated that the directive leader was more effective than the nondirective leader only when the group-task situation was highly favorable for the leader, but not otherwise.

IDENTIFICATION WITH THE LEADER

For any leader, the factors of favorability and effectiveness depend upon the perceptions of followers. Their identification with him implicates significant psychological ties which may affect materially his ability to be influential. Yet the study of identification is passé in leadership research. Though there is a recurring theme in the literature of social science, harking back to Weber (see 1947), about the so-called "charismatic leader," this quality has a history of imprecise usage; furthermore, its tie with identification processes is by no means clear. Putting the study of the sources and consequences of identification with the leader on a stronger footing seems overdue and entirely feasible.

Several lines of work in social psychology appear to converge on identification processes. The distinction made by Kelman (1961) regarding identification, internalization, and compliance, for example, has obvious relevance to the relationship between the leader and his followers. This typology might be applied to the further investigation of leadership processes. The work of Sears (1960) and of Bandura and Walters (1963), concerning the identification of children with adult models, also has implications for such study.

One point which is clear, though the dynamics require far more attention, is that the followers' identification with their leader can provide them with social reality, in the sense of a shared outlook. An illustration of this is seen in work on the social psychology of political leadership by Hollander (see 1963). In two phases, separated by an interval of 8 years, he studied Republicans in 1954 who had voted for President Eisenhower in 1952 and who would or would not vote for him again in 1954; and then in 1962, he studied Democrats who had voted for President Kennedy in 1960 and who would or would not vote for him again in 1962. He found that continuing loyalty to the President of one's party, among these respondents, was significantly associated with their views on issues and conditions and with their votes for the party in a midterm congressional-senatorial election. The defectors showed a significant shift in the precise opposite direction, both in their attitudes and in their voting behavior. In both periods, the ideology of loyalists was highly consistent with the leader's position. In the economic realm, for example, even where actual well-being varied considerably among loyalists, this identification with the President yielded highly similar attitudes regarding the favorability of the economic picture facing the nation.

With appropriate concern for rectifying the balance, there may be virtue in reopening for study Freud's (1922) contention that the leader of a group represents a common "ego ideal" in whom members share an identification and an ideology. Laboratory experimentation on groups offers little basis for studying such identification in light of the ephemeral, ad hoc basis for the creation of such groups. In fact, a disproportionate amount of our current knowledge about leadership in social psychology comes from experiments which are methodologically sophisticated but bear only a pale resemblance to the leadership enterprise that engages people in persisting relationships.

There also is the problem of accommodating the notion of identification within prevailing conceptions of leader-follower transactions and social exchange. But that is not an insurmountable difficulty with an expansion of the reward concept to include, for instance, the value of social reality. In any case, as investigators move increasingly from the laboratory to studies in more naturalistic settings, one of the significant qualities that may make a difference in leadership functioning is precisely this prospect for identification.

SOME CONCLUSIONS AND IMPLICATIONS

The present selective review and discussion touches upon a range of potential issues for the further study of leadership. The discussion is by no means exhaustive in providing details beyond noting suggestive developments. It is evident, however, that a new set of conceptions about leadership is beginning to emerge after a period of relative quiescence.

In providing a bridge to future research here, these newer, general ideas are underscored in a suggestive way. The methodologies they demand represent a challenge to imaginative skill, especially toward greater refinements in the conduct of field experiments and field studies which provide a look at the broader system of leadership relationships. Then, too, there is a need to consider the two-way nature of the influence process, with greater attention paid to the expectations of followers within the system. As reiterated here, the key to an understanding of leadership rests in seeing it as an influence process, involving an implicit exchange relationship over time.

No less important as a general point is the need for a greater recognition of the system represented by the group and its enterprise. This recognition provides a vehicle by which to surmount the misleading dichotomy of the leader and the situation which so long has prevailed. By adopting a systems approach, the leader, the led, and the situation defined broadly, are seen as interdependent inputs variously engaged toward the production of desired outputs.

Some release is needed from the highly static, positional view of leadership if we are to analyze its processes. A focus on leadership maintenance has weighted the balance against a more thorough probe of emerging leadership and succession phenomena. Investigators should be more aware of their choice and the differential implications, as between emerging and ongoing leadership. In this regard, the significance of the legitimacy of leadership, its sources, and effects requires greater attention in future investigations.

In studying the effectiveness of the leader, more emphasis should be placed on the outcomes for the total system, including the fulfillment of expectations held by followers. The long-standing overconcern with outcome, often stated only in terms of the leader's ability to influence, should yield to a richer conception of relationships geared to mutual goals. Not irrelevantly, the perception of the leader held by followers, including their identification with him, needs closer scrutiny. In this way,

one may approach a recognition of stylistic elements allowing given persons to be effective leaders.

Finally, it seems plain that research on task-oriented groups must attend more to the organizational frameworks within which these groups are imbedded. Whether these frameworks are industrial, educational, governmental, or whatever, they are implicated in such crucial matters as goal-setting, legitimacy of authority, and leader succession. Though not always explicit, it is the organizational context which recruits and engages members in particular kinds of tasks, role relationships, and the rewards of participation. This context deserves more explicitness in attempts at understanding leadership processes.

REFERENCES

ANDERSON, L. R., & FIEDLER, F. E. The effect of participatory and supervisory leadership on group creativity. *Journal of Applied Psychology*, 1964, **48**, 227–236.

BANDURA, A., & WALTERS, R. H. *Social learning and personality development.* New York: Holt, Rinehart & Winston, 1963.

BANTA, T. J., & NELSON, C. Experimental analysis of resource location in problem-solving groups. *Sociometry*, 1964 **27**, 488–501.

BAVELAS, A. Leadership: Man and function. *Administrative Science Quarterly*, 1960, **4**, 491–498.

BAVELAS, A., HASTORF, A. H., GROSS, A. E., & KITE, W. R. Experiments on the alteration of group structure. *Journal of Experimental Social Psychology*, 1965, **1**, 55–70.

BERKOWITZ, L. Personality and group position. *Sociometry*, 1956, **19**, 210–222.

BLAU, P. *Exchange and power in social life.* New York: Wiley, 1964.

BROWN, J. F. *Psychology and the social order.* New York: McGraw-Hill, 1936.

BURKE, P. J. Authority relations and descriptive behavior in small discussion groups. *Sociometry,* 1966, **29,** 237–250.

CARTER, L. F., HAYTHORN, W., MEIROWITZ, B., & LANZETTA, J. The relation of categorizations and ratings in the observation of group behavior. *Human Relations,* 1951, **4,** 239–253.

CARTER, L. F., & NIXON, M. An investigation of the relationship between four criteria of leadership ability for three different tasks. *Journal of Psychology,* 1949, **27,** 245–261.

CARTWRIGHT, D. C., & ZANDER, A. (Eds.) *Group dynamics: Research and theory.* (3rd ed.) New York: Harper & Row, 1968.

CLIEFORD, C., & COHEN, T. S. The relationship between leadership and personality attributes perceived by followers. *Journal of Social Psychology,* 1964, **64,** 57–64.

COHEN, A. M., & BENNIS, W. G. Continuity of leadership in communication networks. *Human Relations,* 1961, **14,** 351–367.

DITTES, J. E., & KELLEY, H. H. Effects of different conditions of acceptance upon conformity to group norms. *Journal of Abnormal and Social Psychology,* 1956, **53,** 100–107.

DUBNO, P. Leadership, group effectiveness, and speed of decision. *Journal of Social Psychology,* 1965, **65,** 351–360.

EMERSON, R. M. Power-dependence relations. *American Sociological Review,* 1962, **27,** 31–41.

EVAN, W. M., & ZELDITCH, M. A laboratory experiment on bureaucratic authority. *American Sociological Review,* 1961, **26,** 883–893.

FIEDLER, F. E. *Leader attitudes and group effectiveness.* Urbana: University of Illinois Press, 1958.

FIEDLER, F. E. A contingency model of leadership effectiveness. In L. BERKOWITZ (Ed.), *Advances in experimental social psychology.* Vol. 1. New York: Academic Press, 1964.

FIEDLER, F. E. The contingency model: A theory of leadership effectiveness. In H. PROSHANSKY & B. SEIDENBERG (Eds.), *Basic studies in social psychology.* New York: Holt, Rinehart & Winston, 1965.

FIEDLER, F. E. The effect of leadership and cultural heterogeneity on group performance: A test of a contingency model. *Journal of Experimental Social Psychology,* 1966, **2,** 237–264.

FIEDLER, F. E. *A theory of leadership effectiveness.* New York: McGraw-Hill, 1967.

FREUD, S. *Group psychology and the analysis of the ego.* London & Vienna: International Psychoanalytic Press, 1922.

GIBB, C. A. The principles and traits of leadership. *Journal of Abnormal and Social Psychology,* 1947, **42,** 267–284.

GOLDMAN, M., & FRAAS, L. A. The effects of leader selection on group performance. *Sociometry,* 1965, **28,** 82–88.

GORDON, L. V. & MEDLAND, F. F. Leadership aspiration and leadership ability. *Psychological Reports,* 1965, **17,** 388–390.

GOULDNER, A. W. (Ed.) *Studies in leadership.* New York: Harper, 1950.

HAYTHORN, W., COUCH, A., HAEFNER, D., LANGHAM, P., & CARTER, L. F. The effects of varying combinations of authoritarian and equalitarian leaders and followers. *Journal of Abnormal and Social Psychology,* 1956, **53,** 210–219.

HEMPHILL, J. K. The leader and his group. *Education Research Bulletin,* 1949, **28,** 225–229, 245–246. (a)

HEMPHILL, J. K. *Situational factors in leadership.* Columbus: Ohio State University, Bureau of Educational Research, 1949. (b)

HEMPHILL, J. K. Why people attempt to lead. In L. PETRULLO & B. M. BASS (Eds.), *Leadership and interpersonal behavior.* New York: Holt, Rinehart & Winston, 1961.

HOLLANDER, E. P. Authoritarianism and leadership choice in a military setting. *Journal of Abnormal and Social Psychology,* 1954, **49**, 365–370.

HOLLANDER, E. P. Conformity, status, and idiosyncrasy credit. *Psychological Review,* 1958, **65**, 117–127.

HOLLANDER, E. P. Competence and conformity in the acceptance of influence. *Journal of Abnormal and Social Psychology,* 1960, **61**, 365–369.

HOLLANDER, E. P. Emergent leadership and social influence. In L. PETRULLO & B. M. BASS (Eds.), *Leadership and interpersonal behavior.* New York: Holt, Rinehart & Winston, 1961.

HOLLANDER, E. P. The "pull" of international issues in the 1962 election. In S. B. WITHEY (Chm.), Voter attitudes and the war-peace issue. Symposium presented at the American Psychological Association, Philadelphia, August 1963.

HOLLANDER, E. P. *Leaders, groups, and influence.* New York: Oxford University Press, 1964.

HOLLANDER, E. P., & JULIAN, J. W. Leadership. In E. F. BORGATTA & W. W. LAMBERT (Eds.), *Handbook of personality theory and research.* Chicago: Rand McNally, 1968.

HOMANS, G. C. *Social behavior: Its elementary forms.* New York: Harcourt, Brace & World, 1961.

HUNT, J. McV. Traditional personality theory in the light of recent evidence. *American Scientist,* 1965, **53**, 80–96.

JANDA, K. F. Towards the explication of the concept of leadership in terms of the concept of power. *Human Relations,* 1960, **13**, 345–363.

JENNINGS, H. H. *Leadership and isolation.* New York: Longmans, 1943.

JULIAN, J. W., & HOLLANDER, E. P. A study of some role dimensions of leader-follower relations. Technical Report No. 3, April 1966, State University of New York at Buffalo, Department of Psychology, Contract 4679, Office of Naval Research.

JULIAN, J. W., HOLLANDER, E. P. & REGULA, C. R. Endorsement of the group spokesman as a function of his source of authority, competence, and success. *Journal of Personality and Social Psychology,* 1969, **11**, 42–49.

KATZ, D., & KAHN, R. *The social psychology of organizations.* New York: Wiley, 1966.

KELMAN, H. C. Processes of opinion change. *Public Opinion Quarterly,* 1961, **25**, 57–78.

KIRKHART, R. O. Minority group identification and group leadership. *Journal of Psychology,* 1963, **59**, 111–117.

LEWIN, K., LIPPITT, R., & WHITE, R. K. Patterns of aggressive behavior in experimentally created "social climates." *Journal of Social Psychology,* 1939, **10**, 271–299.

MAIER, N. R., & HOFFMAN, L. R. Acceptance and quality of solutions as related to leader's attitudes toward disagreement in group problem solving. *Journal of Applied Behavioral Science,* 1965, **1**, 373–386.

MANN, R. D. A review of the relationships between personality and performance in small groups. *Psychological Bulletin,* 1959, **56**, 241–270.

MARAK, G. E. The evolution of leadership structure. *Sociometry,* 1964, **27**, 174–182.

McGRATH, J. E., & ALTMAN, I. *Small group research: A critique and synthesis of the field.* New York: Holt, Rinehart & Winston, 1966.

McGREGER, D. *The human side of enterprise.* New York: McGraw-Hill, 1960.

McGREGOR, D. *Leadership and motivation.* (Essays edited by W. G. BENNIS & E. H. SCHEIN), Cambridge, Mass.: M.I.T. Press, 1966.

NELSON, P. D. Similarities and differences among leaders and followers. *Journal of Social Psychology,* 1964, **63,** 161–167.

PEPINSKY, P. N., HEMPHILL, J. K. & SHEVITZ, R. N. Attempts to lead, group productivity, and morale under conditions of acceptance and rejection. *Journal of Abnormal and Social Psychology,* 1958, **57,** 47–54.

PRESTON, M. G., & HEINTZ, R. K. Effects of participatory versus supervisory leadership on group judgment. *Journal of Abnormal and Social Psychology,* 1949, **44,** 345–355.

PRYER, M. W., FLINT, A. W., & BASS, B. M. Group effectiveness and consistency of leadership. *Sociometry,* 1962, **25,** 391–397.

RAVEN, B. Social influence and power. In I. D. STEINER & M. FISHBEIN (Eds)., *Current studies in social psychology.* New York: Holt, Rinehart & Winston, 1965.

RIECKEN, H. W. The effect of talkativeness on ability to influence group solutions to problems. *Sociometry,* 1958, **21,** 309–321.

ROSEN, S., LEVINGER, G., & LIPPITT, R. Perceived sources of social power. *Journal of Abnormal and Social Psycholoy,* 1961, **62,** 439–441.

RUDRASWAMY, V. An investigation of the relationship between perceptions of status and leadership attempts. *Journal of the Indian Academy of Applied Psychology,* 1964, **1,** 12–19.

SCODELL, A., & MUSSEN, P. Social perception of authoritarians and nonauthoritarians. *Journal of Abnormal and Social Psychology,* 1953, **48,** 181–184.

SEARS, R. R. The 1958 summer research project on identification. *Journal of Nursery Education,* 1960, **16,** (2).

SECORD, P. F., & BACKMAN, C. W. Personality theory and the problem of stability and change in individual behavior: An interpersonal approach. *Psychological Review,* 1961, **68,** 21–33.

SELZNICK, P. *Leadership in administration.* Evanston: Row, Peterson, 1957.

SHAW, M. E. A Comparison of two types of leadership in various communication nets. *Journal of Abnormal and Social Psychology,* 1955, **50,** 127–134.

SHAW, M. E., & BLUM, J. M. Effects of leadership style upon group performance as a function of task structure. *Journal of Personality and Social Psychology,* 1966, **3,** 238–242.

SLATER, P. E., & BENNIS, W. G. Democracy is inevitable. *Harvard Business Review,* 1964, **42**(2), 51–59.

STEINER, I. Group dynamics. *Anual review of psychology,* 1964, **15,** 421–446.

STOGDILL, R. M. Personal factors associated with leadership: A survey of the literature. *Journal of Psychology,* 1948, **25,** 35–71.

STOGDILL, R. M. *Individual behavior and group achievement.* New York: Oxford University Press, 1959.

WEBER, M. *The theory of social and economic organization.* (Trans, and ed. by T. PARSONS & A. M. HENDERSON.) New York: Oxford University Press, 1947.

ZDEP, S. M., & OAKES, W. I. Reinforcement of leadership behavior in group discussion. *Journal of Experimental Social Psychology,* 1967, **3,** 310–320.

Index

Date Due

MAR - 7 76			
GB	PRINTED	IN U. S. A.	